FREEDOM

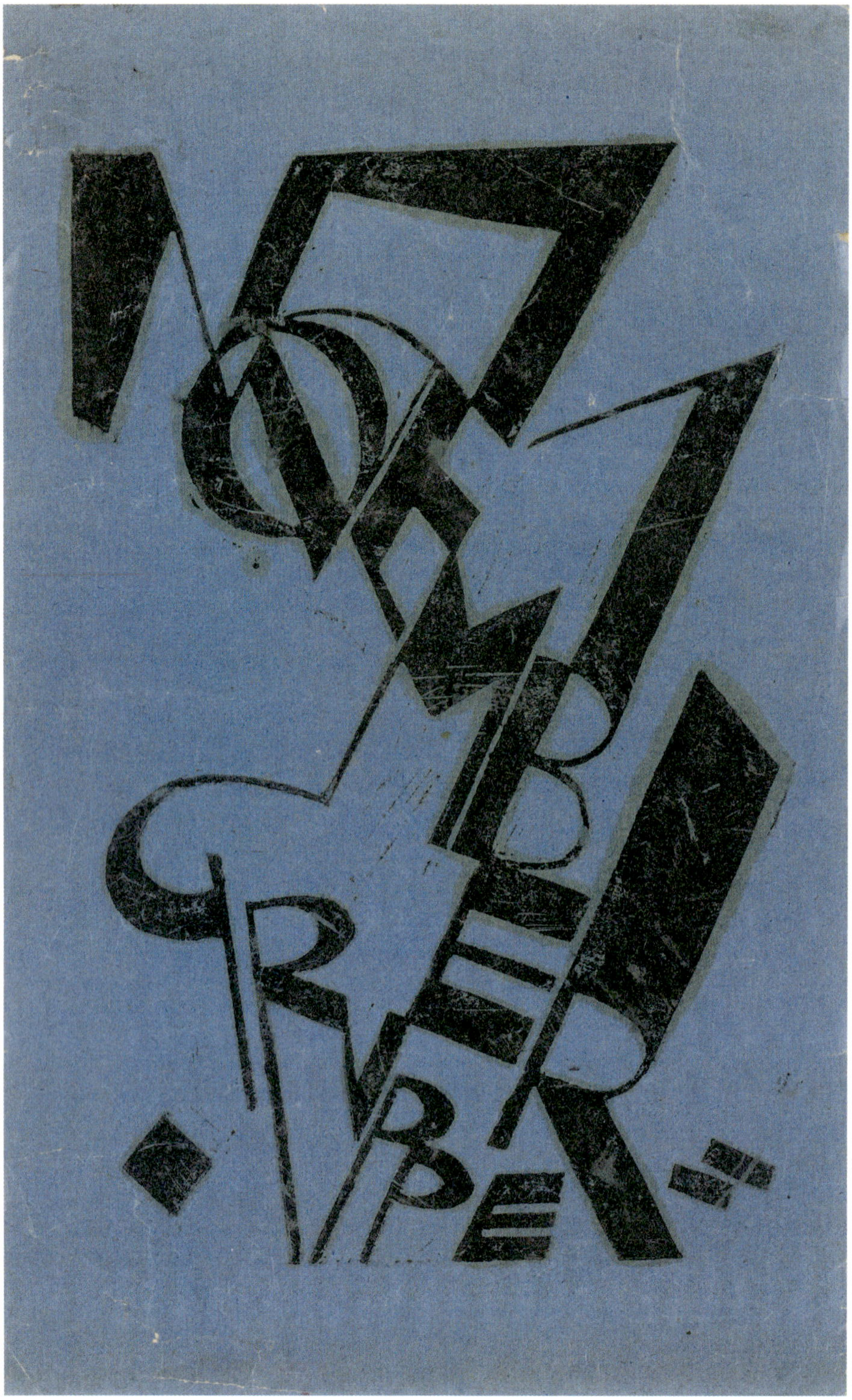

01

MORIZ MELZER

Novembergruppe (typographic design), c. 1922

India ink on blue high-gloss paper, 35.5 × 21.5 cm
Berlinische Galerie

BG

FREEDOM

THE ART OF THE NOVEMBERGRUPPE 1918–1935

Edited by Thomas Köhler,
Ralf Burmeister and Janina Nentwig

PRESTEL
Munich · London · New York

The patron of the exhibition is
Michael Müller, Governing Mayor of Berlin.

The exhibition and catalogue were kindly funded by

This exhibition is taking place within the themed winter
100 Years of Revolution — Berlin 1918–19

THOMAS KÖHLER

FREEDOM

The Art of the Novembergruppe from 1918 to 1935

> "The miracle was that, with few exceptions, everyone felt part of one community, morally committed to believing in the good in people and to creating the best of all possible worlds."[1] (Will Grohmann)

In January 1919 the Novembergruppe office launched a membership drive, sending out an appeal to which it attached a list of "Novembergruppe Guidelines". Item IV reads:

"We demand influence and participation:

1. *in all architectural tasks as a matter of public concern,*
   urban design — settlement planning — public buildings for administration, industry and welfare — private construction — conservation of monuments — removal of pompous buildings with no artistic value
2. *in reforming the art schools and their teaching,*
   an end to state paternalism — selection of teachers by the artists' associations and students — an end to scholarships — co-ordination of the schools for architecture, sculpture, painting and decorative art — provision of places to work and experiment
3. *in transforming the museums,*
   an end to the one-sided approach to collecting — abolition of scholarly overload — conversion into people's art venues — into unprejudiced emissaries of timeless laws
4. *in allocating exhibition rooms,*
   abolition of prerogatives and capitalist influences
5. *in art legislation.*
   social equality for artists as workers of the mind — protection of artistic copyright tax exemption for works of art (free export and import)"[2]

Anyone reading the Novembergruppe guidelines without knowing when they were written will be struck by just how topical these demands are now. The demise of the Empire and its repressive structures, the euphoria of starting afresh in the Weimar Republic, triggered a tide of innovation, an unbridled enthusiasm and a militancy that are hard to imagine today. Many of the items on this list still have their justification. The first demand for the "removal of pompous buildings with no artistic value" takes on a curious piquancy in view of the reconstruction of the Berlin Palace. One hundred years after the revolution of 1918, a republic is re-erecting a building once torn down as a symbol of feudal, undemocratic rule. Similarly, the dreary reality of present-day urban planning testifies to the visionary quality of those demands by the "Novembrists" and their deep desire to inspire society as a whole with their will to shape the environment. Furthermore, the second reform mentioned in the "Guidelines", the revamp of art schools and art teaching, could hardly be more in tune with present-day issues in cultural education. The educational philosophy prevalent under the Kaiser, where school students were treated as passive recipients, had already been criticized in the late nineteenth century by Alfred Lichtwark, an art teacher and director of the Kunsthalle in Hamburg. Lichtwark was unhappy with the inadequate social and aesthetic education fed to his contemporaries and insisted that art should not be elitist but part and parcel of everyone's lives. In the Novembergruppe, it was above all the painters Georg Tappert, Bernhard Hasler and Otto Möller who campaigned for changes in the way art was taught and took up Lichtwark's ideas. Thanks to their efforts, training for art teachers underwent significant modifications in the 1920s. The Novembergruppe also took issue with institutional presentation and collection practices: the Kaiser had personally influenced the exhibition and purchasing policies of public museums. The Novembergruppe wanted the exhibition institutes to open up their content, communication and research. Museums should become "people's art venues", places for dialogue and reflection, and no longer just for pomp. The association had distinct views, moreover, on the allocation of exhibition space, was resolutely opposed to the commercial exploitation of artists and specifically included taxation in its position paper.

That the Berlinische Galerie can now devote an exhibition to the Novembergruppe is due to the happy circumstance that Janina Nentwig, a former trainee curator at our museum, was able to undertake a research project funded by the Gerda Henkel Stiftung. It was only logical that she should team up with Ralf Burmeister, the head of our Artists' Archives, to produce a blueprint for this exhibition and catalogue marking the centenary of the group's foundation. I cordially thank Ralf Burmeister and Janina Nentwig for this feat of scholarship and curatorship. They were assisted in this by trainee curators Nuno de Brito Rocha and Juschka Marie von Rüden.

Our registrar Anne Seyda and museum archivist Philip Gorki contributed in significant ways to carrying out the project. They deserve warm thanks for their commitment.

Our exhibition architect David Saik, a partner of this museum for many years, has devised a magnificent spatial solution for such an abundant display of material.

The technical department at the Berlinische Galerie responded with great aplomb to the challenges of this project, working with our conservators to ensure the safe and extremely professional handling of the exhibits.

Our well-stretched resources have been wisely deployed by our prudent director of administration Birgitta Müller-Brandeck and our head of finance Susanne Teuber.

Ulrike Andres and her communication and education team have taken care not only to keep the media informed by excellent means but also to devise a state-of-the-art insight programme.

The catalogue, which no doubt will have a future as a standard work, brings together a number of knowledgeable articles. I am warmly grateful to the authors for their contributions. Lilla Hinrichs and Anna Sartorius of e o t . essays on typography have taken the design in hand once again, combining illustrations and text in a highly aesthetic form.

Although we have many works by Novembergruppe artists here in the Berlinische Galerie collection, loans were naturally indispensable for our exhibition.

Above all I wish to thank Udo Kittelmann, director of the Nationalgalerie Berlin, and his colleagues for the large number of works that we have been able to acquire on loan from the high-calibre holdings of the Staatliche Museen. We realize that we cannot take such generosity for granted and hope that we can draw on this trust and cooperation in future projects.

Financing this exhibition venture was a bold undertaking, as the Berlinische Galerie does not have its own exhibition budget and every project has to be implemented with third-party funds. Lotto Stiftung Berlin was able to provide a modest sum, and so we were all the more delighted to receive support from the Ernst von Siemens Art Foundation [*Ernst von Siemens Kunststiftung*] and the Capital Cultural Fund [*Hauptstadtkulturfonds*]. I would specifically like to thank Mr Martin Hoernes, general secretary of the Ernst von Siemens Kunststiftung, as well as the jury of the Capital Cultural Fund.

The exhibition is embedded within the themed winter "100 Years of Revolution — Berlin 1918–19". My cordial thanks for this go to Moritz van Dülmen, CEO of Kulturprojekte Berlin, for his unconventional backing. He has included our show in the full programme and allowed us to piggy-back on communications about the themed winter.

We wish our visitors a stimulating discovery
of this so very important association of artists!

1 Will Grohmann, "Zehn Jahre Novembergruppe", in: *Zehn Jahre Novembergruppe*, special issue of *Kunst der Zeit. Zeitschrift für Kunst und Literatur*, vol. 3, 1928, nos. 1–3, pp. 1–9, here 1.

2 See the illustration on p. 227 of this catalogue, also in Kliemann 1969, p. 57.

With thanks to ...

We cordially thank all those who supported this exhibition with their donations, notably: Waldtraut Braun, Deutsche Kreditbank AG, HAHN Bestattungen GmbH und Co KG, Berlin, Gisela Knobloch, Dr Gunhild Kühn, Edeltraud Traugott-Minski, Thomas Minski, Irmgard Sprung.

We are particularly grateful to the Nationalgalerie, Staatliche Museen zu Berlin, and specifically to Dr Joachim Jäger, Udo Kittelmann and Dr Dieter Scholz, for loaning an abundant quantity of works.

We extend our thanks to every individual and institution both public and private and to our colleagues for all their expert support:

- Akademie der Künste, Berlin: Catherine Amé, Dr Eva-Maria Barkhofen, Werner Heegewaldt, Juliane Kreissl, Dr Anke Matelowski
- Bauhaus-Archiv, Berlin: Sibylle Hoiman, Dr Annemarie Jaeggi
- Bauhaus-Universität Weimar, Sammlung für Architektur, Ingenieurbau, Kunst und Design: Dr Christiane Wolf
- Hendrik A. Berinson, Galerie Berinson, Berlin
- Stefan Frey, Bern
- Germanisches Nationalmuseum, Nuremberg: Dr Yasmin Doosry, Prof. G. Ulrich Grossmann
- Harald Gnade, Berlin
- Prof. Nils Grosch, University of Salzburg
- Hamburger Kunsthalle: Prof. Christoph Martin Vogtherr
- Gerda Henkel Stiftung, Düsseldorf
- Dr Markus Krause, Grisebach GmbH, Berlin
- Dr Anna-Carola Krausse, Berlin
- Kulturstiftung Sachsen-Anhalt Kunstmuseum Moritzburg Halle (Saale): Thomas Bauer-Friedrich, Anke Dornbach
- Kunsthalle Mannheim: Dr Inge Herold, Dr Ulrike Lorenz
- Kurt und Ernst Schwitters Stiftung, Hanover: Dr Isabel Schulz
- Lehmbruck Museum, Duisburg: Dr Söke Dinkla
- Lindenau-Museum, Altenburg: Dr Roland Krischke, Dr des. Benjamin Rux
- Julia Moldenhawer, Potsdam
- Museum Kurhaus Kleve – Ewald Mataré-Sammlung, Kleve: Prof. Harald Kunde, Valentina Vlašić
- Museum Ludwig, Cologne: Dr Yilmaz Dziewior, Dr Julia Friedrich
- Nachlass César Klein, Dr Matthias Esche
- Khalil and Misha Norland, United Kingdom
- Prof. Olaf Peters, Martin Luther University, Halle-Wittenberg
- Sammlung Karl H. Knauf, Berlin
- Sammlung Stuckenberg der Niedersächsischen Sparkassenstiftung at the Städtische Galerie, Delmenhorst
- Sprengel Museum, Hanover: Dr Reinhard Spieler
- Staatliche Museen zu Berlin, Kunstbibliothek: Dr Joachim Brand Kupferstichkabinett: Dr Holm Bevers, Dr Andreas Schalhorn, Dr Christina Thomson Zentralarchiv: Dr Petra Winter
- Staatsgalerie Stuttgart: Prof. Christiane Lange
- Städtische Galerie, Delmenhorst: Dr Annett Reckert
- Stiftung Deutsches Historisches Museum, Berlin: Prof. Raphael Gross, Andrea von Hegel
- Stiftung Stadtmuseum Berlin: Annette Bossmann, Karin Dömsky, Paul Spies, Andreas Teltow
- Technische Universität Berlin, Architekturmuseum: Dr Hans-Dieter Nägelke, Franziska Schilling, Claudia Zachariae
- Wolfgang Wittrock, Berlin

and to all who loaned exhibits but prefer to remain anonymous.

RALF BURMEISTER / JANINA NENTWIG

"FREEDOM FOR EVERY PULSE"

An Introduction

"If we could finally get used to not treating works of art like something for museums but look at them instead as people should when observing human tensions, the Novembergruppe's exhibition would no longer be such a singular event in these climes."
(Lothar Brieger, 1925)[1]

1918/2018: One hundred years after the November Revolution that spawned Germany's first parliamentary democracy, the contribution made by artists to this historical awakening has been all but forgotten. What role did they play in the social transformation, and how did they seek to shape the new society actively through their art? These questions are addressed by the first comprehensive retrospective about the best-known unknown association of artists in the Weimar Republic — the Novembergruppe.

"We stand on the fertile soil of the revolution. Our motto is: *Liberty, Equality, Fraternity!*" declared the first few lines in a manifesto drafted by the Novembergruppe just after its foundation in the heady days of insurgency.[2] The association owed its name to the epochal events of that November, while its slogan was borrowed from the French Revolution, invoked as a historical godmother to watch over the political upheaval in Germany. The objective defined by the creative forces in Berlin who joined this "association of radical fine artists" was the "closest possible mingling of the people and art"[3] — and they threw their weight behind this task, most prominently by mounting numerous exhibitions. Although the group guidelines drawn up in early January 1919 did not call for reforms to the social fabric as a whole, the association did lay claim to a voice in a thorough democratization of the arts in all fields of public life, aimed primarily at overcoming traditional structures and privileges initiated under the Kaisers. However, the Novembergruppe was not consistent in its pursuit of these cultural policy demands, especially as reforming the arts in the fledgling republic remained firmly in the hands of civil servants and politicians. The practical activities undertaken by the association were intended to unfold without party-political affiliations, and throughout its existence it refused to be exploited for such ends.

Its maxim from the outset, however, was to promote and relay any expressions of radical art, in all their broad variety, which reflected "freedom for every pulse",[4] and this was the creed that defined its democratic stance and steadfast commitment to renewal. Art — these confident "revolutionaries of the mind" firmly believed — was the matrix for a future world where a cleansed human community could co-exist in peace and in a productive society undivided by class. The revolution in artistic form would — so the philosophy — culminate directly in changes to the social order, and the Novembergruppe offered an umbrella to the stylistically heterogeneous avant-gardes of the post-war years — from Late Expressionism and Dada via Constructivism and New Objectivity to *Neues Bauen*, New Music and Absolute Film.

Eberhard Roters, the founding director of the Berlinische Galerie, was ahead of his time in recognizing the role played by the Novembergruppe in establishing what is now regarded as Classical Modernism and also in boosting the cultural credentials of this city. In the slender 20-page catalogue published by our museum — still without a roof of its own — to accompany the very first display from its collection at the Academy of Arts in 1975, the Novembergruppe is mentioned as the pinnacle of multi- and interdisciplinary artistic output in the early 1920s. The collection already included works by members of the association, including RUDOLF BELLING, ERNST FRITSCH, RAOUL HAUSMANN, HANNAH HÖCH, WALTER KAMPMANN, ISSAI KULVIANSKI, MORIZ MELZER, HEINRICH RICHTER-BERLIN and ARTHUR SEGAL.[5] Moreover, the Architecture Collection at the Berlinische Galerie held material on work by Novembergruppe activists HUGO HÄRING, WASSILI and HANS LUCKHARDT, HANS SCHAROUN, and BRUNO and MAX TAUT. When the museum acquired the literary estate of Hannah Höch in 1979, a unique corpus in both its size and its quality, it was enriched by a trove of documents shedding light on the association's activities and internal disputes (fig. 01). The literary estate of RAOUL HAUSMANN, which includes the papers predating his emigration in 1933, acquired in 1991, and the literary estate OTTO MÖLLER, obtained by the Artists' Archives at the Berlinische Galerie in 1999 in the form of a generous gift (fig. 02), likewise harbour important documents by and on the Novembergruppe. The history of reception surrounding the association is also ripe for the archives, as testified by the records and manuscripts underlying the first monographic account of the Novembergruppe in 1969, kindly handed over the museum in 1999 by its researcher and author Helga Kliemann (fig. 03). All in all, here was a wide-ranging collection of source material about the group which also contained material — in object biographies, for example — on associated works held in the Berlinische Galerie collection, and in its substance it is probably

01

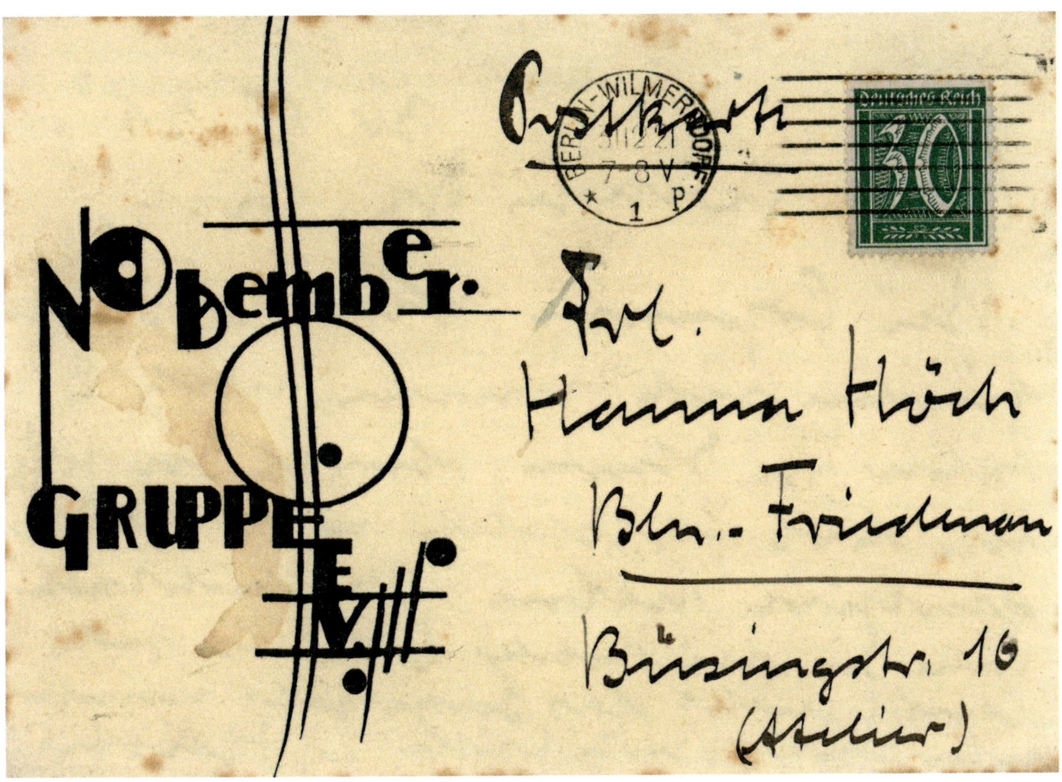

01 Hans Siebert von Heister to Hannah Höch, post card with the Novembergruppe's emblem, 30 December 1921
Berlinische Galerie

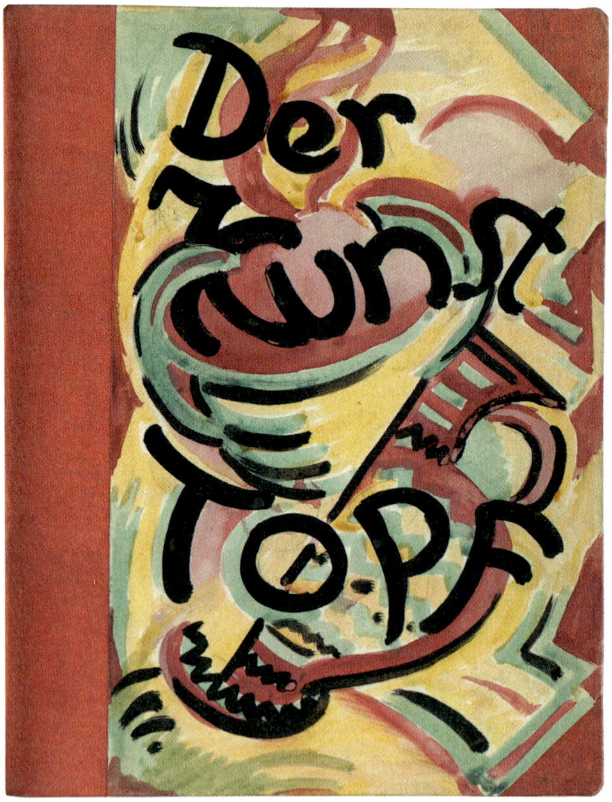

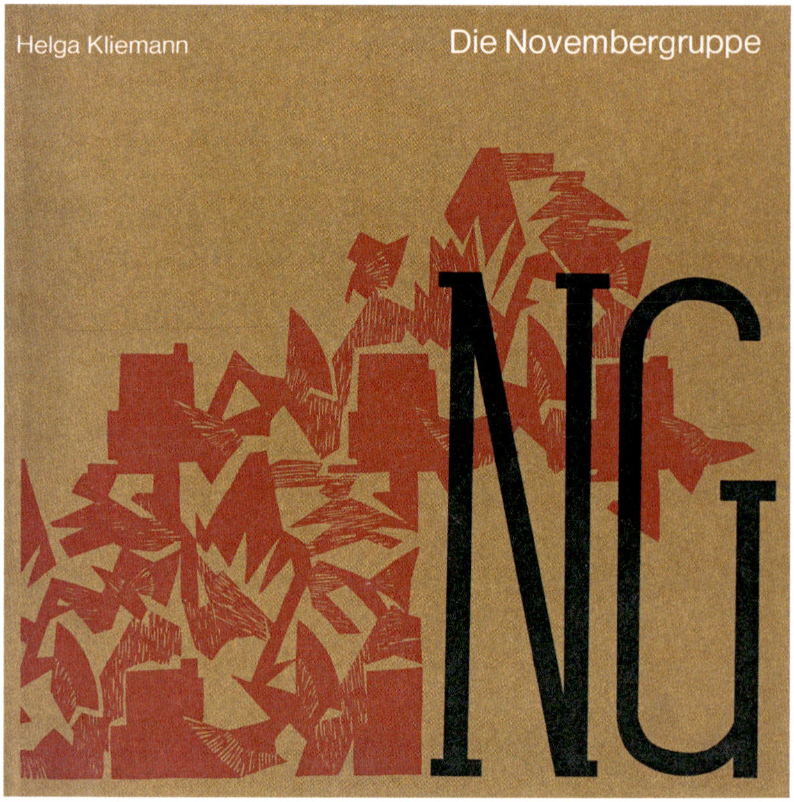

02 [OTTO MÖLLER] Binder design for the Novembergruppe's periodical *Der Kunsttopf*, vol. 1, 1920 Berlinische Galerie

03 Helga Kliemann, *Die Novembergruppe*, 1969

unmatched by any other corpus within the German museum and archive community. This collection essentially called upon scholars to revisit the Novembergruppe, sparking a research project lasting several years with funding from the Gerda Henkel Stiftung. The output from that project provided the groundwork for the genesis of this exhibition.

Novembergruppe, Restating the Accounts

Anyone exploring the art of the Weimar Republic will inevitably stumble across the Novembergruppe. There is hardly any prominent artist who was not a member at some point or at least a guest at an exhibition or an evening of music and literature organized by the association. By the same token, there were many artists in its ranks who still await well-deserved rediscovery. In this catalogue, members and associates of the Novembergruppe have been highlighted typographically by the use of capital letters. More than 480 artists have so far been identified as contributing to a Novembergruppe show.[6] If we study the biographies of the protagonists, we will find that they always emphasize their involvement in the group as an important chapter in their life and pay tribute to its formative role, especially in the art landscape of Berlin. And yet while references in the specialist literature are numerous, there have been few works of scholarship devoted explicitly to the Novembergruppe. In her seminal monograph, so far the only one, on the history and activities of the association, Helga Kliemann began in the Introduction by expressing a hope that her study would encourage further research.[7] She lamented the many gaps in the material at her disposal, partly because not all the facts had been recorded on paper in the turbulence of foundation and partly because so many sources had been destroyed in the Second World War. (Indeed, it has still not been possible to identify a comprehensive set of Novembergruppe files.[8]) Moreover, when Kliemann was pursuing her search in the late 1960s she had limited access to posthumous papers and archives due to the political situation in a divided Germany. Her principal sources were historical publications by the Novembergruppe, in particular the jubilee volume published in 1928 on the occasion of its tenth anniversary. On the other hand, the author was still able to meet or correspond with some former members in person, and these memories were incorporated into her well-founded portrayal, something noted by reviewers at the time as a particular accomplishment.[8] Music and film studies have stood out since then for delving more deeply into aspects of the Novembergruppe that concern these specialized domains.[10] In art history too, the Novembergruppe has repeatedly been the subject of essays in catalogues to accompany themed exhibitions and personal retrospectives. Unlike in the other disciplines, however, the facts, appraisals and hypotheses presented here rarely went beyond the insights of Helga Kliemann.[11] Her assessment still dominates the way art historians view the Novembergruppe: as an association which set out as a community of kindred spirits with political ambitions and radical artistic ideals and evolved into an alliance of convenience with the primary purpose of facilitating joint exhibitions without applying rigorous criteria to the quality of the art. This verdict has been adopted by many writers, as has the overtone of disappointment in Kliemann's conclusion that the Novembergruppe — contrary to its programmatic name and formulated objectives — was unable to make a real political impact.[12] This echoes a reproach expressed by left-leaning artists around **RAOUL HAUSMANN** in an open letter published in the magazine *Der Gegner* way back in 1921 and which prompted them to leave the association. Nazi art policy, on the other hand, identified the precise opposite in the "anti-nationalist art" of the Novembergruppe: Wolfgang Willrich, whose defamatory treatise *Purging the Temple of Art*, published in 1937, provided covering fire for the exhibition Degenerate Art, was particularly vituperative about the Novembergruppe, handing it a share in the blame for the "origin and advance of the red contamination of art".[13]

In assessments of the Novembergruppe to date, only Elizabeth Prelinger (1977) and Eberhard Roters (1995) have depicted its alleged abandonment of political objectives in an affirmative light, albeit with different slants. Prelinger saw the focus on art production as 'core business' as a triumph for artistic freedom and as a refusal to allow (specifically communist) politics to co-opt art. Crucially for her, this was ultimately about democratizing the arts, not least in the historical context of constructing a new political system after the abolition of monarchy.[14] Roters, on the other hand, felt that the Novembergruppe had been following a pragmatic strategy which made sense in commercial terms, especially given the situation faced by artists during the period of high inflation. Although the Novembergruppe was not a professional lobby that could shield their economic interests, as a forum for multiple styles it did offer artists an important business platform in the form of exhibitions and events.[15]

These differences in emphasis are symptomatic of the different social and political settings in which the authors themselves were operating. Kliemann, swayed by the activism of the 1968 generation, was dismayed by what appeared to be a betrayal of political ideals, whereas Prelinger, writing in the United States during the Cold War of the 1970s, stressed the virtues of a free, democratic culture. Against the backdrop of a booming West German economy in the 1980s, Roters attributed a pragmatic stance to a Novembergruppe guided by commercial concerns and seeking to reconcile "enthusiasm and fried potatoes".[16] What all three positions have in common is their conclusion that the association's activities marked a retreat from socio-political commitment.

A hundred years after its foundation, our verdict on the Novembergruppe acquires a different flavour, because the most striking feature from today's perspective is the astonishing openness of this liberal association as a powerful force for integration. It may not have achieved the "closest possible mingling of the people and art"[17] as it initially set out to do, but it certainly established a relationship between the people and art founded on an enlightening dialogue, as closer scrutiny of its shows will confirm. It was of eminent importance in cultivating the art landscape in Berlin and in the form-busting revolutionization of the arts. At the annual presentations that took place from 1919 until 1932 (with the exception of 1925) as a separate section of the Great Berlin Art Exhibition, it provided a widely acclaimed platform for the avant-garde phenomena of the day. In 1920, 1921, 1925, 1929 and 1931 it also staged exhibitions of its own at various venues. Furthermore, an exhibition that toured southern and eastern Germany in the spring and summer of 1920 testifies to a sense of mission beyond regional borders, and even abroad the Novembergruppe demonstrated a notable presence. Thanks to excellent networking with artists in other countries the association exhibited in Rome in 1920, in Amsterdam in 1921 and in Moscow in 1924. It also regularly invited the participation of international artists, among them MARC CHAGALL, GEORGES BRAQUE, EL LISSITZKY, THEO VAN DOESBURG and PIET MONDRIAN.

Doubtless the artists' commitment to social change cannot be measured with the yardstick of politics. Seen through that lens, its artistic activities must come across as indecisive and some of the works as denials of social reality. And yet in its own way the Novembergruppe helped to undermine prevailing cultural and artistic codes and to offer alternative ways of seeing the world, not least by demonstrating options for change and transformation. Inspired by the idea that the formal idiom of Modernism and an aesthetic approach to generating new categories of beauty must be the motor behind major social change,[18] the Novembergruppe, as a vehement champion of the avant-garde, played a decisive role in popularizing radically new artistic statements in the years between the two world wars. Its focus on the revolution in art turns out to be a strength and its pluralism to be a meaningful socio-political factor.

The Exhibition

The exhibition *Freedom: The Art of the Novembergruppe 1918–1935* is the first tribute devoted entirely to the association by a museum.[19] The presentation shadows its history in chronological order, linking the evolution of the association to the artistic output made available to a broad audience through its exhibitions, musical soirées and film screenings. In keeping with the historical model, a conscious decision was made not to categorize rigorously according to artistic isms. Almost all the exhibits, numbering about 120, are known to have been displayed by the Novembergruppe or reproduced in its publications.

The first section is entitled "Liberating Energies of the New Art", citing Adolf Behne's foreword to a special issue of the magazine *Menschen* devoted to the Novembergruppe in 1919.[20] The "new art" to which this title refers was primarily a stylistic amalgam of Cubism, Futurism and Expressionism, and this dominated exhibitions by the group until 1921. These styles had already emerged before 1914, but because of the "liberating energies" they manifested they were now read as an appropriate expression of current revolutionary upheavals. A new social order called for a new idiom, and this was inconceivable without discarding the "old" ways: the academic conventions, Naturalism and even Impressionism. Sloughing off this old skin would give rise to a new kind of person, cleansed by art in an almost religious sense, with energy and visions to tackle the construction of a new, fairer, peaceful society — an aspiration that finds visual expression in compositions of cosmic spheres or kaleidoscopic refractions. In 1919 and 1920 the press tended to associate the art of the Novembergruppe with the new system or parliamentary democracy and the wave of political reforms unleashed by the young republic, but above all reviewers saw the art as an unbridled response to transformations in society. Public reactions extended as far as physical assaults on exhibits — an indication of the unsettling impact of those early Novembergruppe shows.

In 1921 the association was plunged into a fundamental crisis, and this is portrayed in the second section. The exhibition in 1920 had featured numerous works — some inspired by Dada, others by Verism — which had incurred the displeasure not only of the general public and the critics, but also of the political chain of command. The following year the organizers of the Great Berlin Art Exhibition were under pressure from government quarters not to admit works of this kind, even though assurances had been received by the participating associations of artists that there was to be no jury. In order not to jeopardize its overall show, the Novembergruppe removed two brothel scenes by RUDOLF SCHLICHTER and OTTO DIX from its section, although provocative works like GEORG SCHOLZ's *Industrial Farmers* (cat. 42, p. 95) remained among the exhibits. This concession triggered accusations among members that the association was tolerating censorship and betraying its revolutionary aims, and a group of artists thereupon announced their resignation. However, the Novembergruppe emerged all the stronger from this crisis. The responses to its exhibitions grew increasingly positive, and they were broadened to include avant-garde styles from other countries: from 1922 Russian and East European artists regularly took part in the shows, some of them exiles from post-revolutionary Russia who had made their homes in Berlin. By remaining open to experiment, the association enabled EL LISSITZKY, for example, to exhibit his legendary *Proun Room* for the first time (cat. 55, p. 119). In 1923 and 1925 *De Stijl* artists brought along their non-figurative works. Like the Russian Constructivists, they exerted a powerful influence on the subsequent course of art in Germany. Juxtaposing their works with those of German protagonists flags up overlaps between the various purely abstract movements. We present these in the third section alongside works of New Objectivity, a style the Novembergruppe was similarly quick to publicize and promote as an innovative form of figurative art.

In the mid-1920s the input from architects became a major focus for the association after LUDWIG MIES VAN DER ROHE took over the chair in 1924. The fourth section therefore presents models, buildings and designs from members engaged in the building profession, all of them displaying features of *Neues Bauen*. The Novembergruppe set its stamp on public debate about this functional, no-frills architecture in significant ways. By exhibiting their progressive ideas on new forms of living and working, architects were able to present their answers to urban restructuring in a fast-changing society for the consideration of a wider audience.

Despite the remarkable diversity of Novembergruppe displays, critics in the latter half of the 1920s, a time when avant-garde movements were universally losing momentum, observed that the creative powers of the artists it represented were on the wane. The fifth section, "Belated Revolution", illustrates how the association responded to this criticism and how it came up with strategies to define its own history when celebrating its tenth anniversary in 1928–29. Whereas it had hitherto insisted that it sought a "revolution in art" and had no desire to engage with politics, it now highlighted its origins in the revolutionary turmoil and the impetus emanating from that backdrop. By mustering all its forces for the jubilee exhibition in 1929 and placing works of social criticism centre stage, the association seemed to be conjuring up its own artistic and social forces in an attempt to ward off its fading significance. However, in a period of relative political stability and greater tolerance for Modernist art, its contribution had an air of obsolescence. In October 1929, three weeks after the anniversary exhibition closed, the Wall Street Crash unleashed the world economic crisis that has gone down in history as the Great Depression, further eroding all that had been achieved.

The last section of the exhibition recounts the demise of the Novembergruppe. From 1930 the association was visibly crumbling. Only four artists took part in the final performance at the Great Berlin Art Exhibition in 1932. Inward-looking detachment speaks increasingly from the works, symptomatic of a general sense of resignation. Precarious times did not generate a fresh injection of political energy, and the circumstances that precipitated an end to the Weimar Republic were not echoed in motifs or manifestos from the artists. There is no evidence of any activity by the association after 1933. Nazi propaganda whipped up sentiment against the "red Novembergruppe" as a spearhead of "cultural bolshevism". In 1935 it was, at its own expense, struck off the register of associations in the city of Berlin. Many former members were discredited as "degenerate" and their works were removed from public collections. The group did not re-form after the Second World War, and its substantial contribution to establishing the avant-gardes fell into oblivion. Today we are ready to rediscover the Novembergruppe, not only for its art but as a driving force for freedom. Its desire to champion diversity and to promote tolerance and openness towards the new has become urgently relevant again in the face of the global political climate in an age 'cleansed' of utopias.

1 Lothar Brieger, "Berliner Kunstsommer", quoted in Berlinische Galerie 1995, 2. Abt., 25.54, p. 242.

2 Novembrist manifesto (draft), quoted in: *Zehn Jahre Novembergruppe*, special issue of *Kunst der Zeit. Zeitschrift für Kunst und Literatur*, vol. 3, 1928, nos. 1–3, p. 16.

3 Novembergruppe, circular, 13 December 1918, in: ibid., p. 12.

4 "The dishonesty of conventions is fought by today's artists until final destruction. New art bears a pledge. Its motive force heralds the anarchist freedom that will evolve into the ultimate eternal order. The new artist banishes hypocritical self-denial, demolishes all infertile pathos. Crushes deceitful tranquillity. Knows the rolling circle of life, tears apart the delusion of realities. He acknowledges the futility of intents. Proclaims the freedom of all pulses. Human life to the full." BWR [Bruno W. Reimann], "Zur Kunst", in: *Der Kunsttopf*, vol. 1, 1920, no. 1, pp. 6f.

5 See Berlinische Galerie 1975, unpaginated.

6 In the 1990s Armin Schulz, a former researcher at the Berlinische Galerie, compiled an initial systematic list of Novembergruppe members associated with the museum's collection for in-house purposes. It was the basis for the present, much expanded compilation. Who was active when in the Novembergruppe and with how many works can be found at www.berlinischegalerie.de/sammlung/kuenstlerinnen-archive. We are grateful to Armin Schulz for his meticulous spadework.

7 The publication appeared as the third of four volumes in the series *Bildende Kunst in Berlin*, published by the artists' association *Deutsche Gesellschaft für Bildende Kunst*, which disbanded that same year (1969) and was replaced by new organizations in the form of the grass-roots *Neue Gesellschaft für Bildende Kunst* (ngbk) and the *Neuer Berliner Kunstverein* (NBK).

8 Searches in Russian archives for Novembergruppe documents were equally unfruitful.

9 See Pehnt 1970.

10 See *inter alia* the essays in Grosch 2018, as well as Grosch 1999 and Wilmesmeier 1994.

11 The first exhibition to acknowledge the Novembergruppe after the Second World War was *Berlin, Ort der Freiheit für die Kunst* (Nationalgalerie 1960), but apart from numerous pictorial reproductions there were merely short quotations from contemporary reviews on the Novembergruppe. The following essays and catalogues take their cue from Kliemann: *Die Novembergruppe. Tendenzen der zwanziger Jahre* (Kunstamt Wedding 1977), here the Introduction (Pfefferkorn 1977); *Künstler der Novembergruppe* (Nierendorf 1985) with an Introduction by Florian Karsch. A compilation of source material, *Kunstmetropole Berlin 1918–1933,* was published in East Berlin in 1987; it expands on Kliemann, but the editors Bärbel Schrader and Jürgen Schebera do not deviate from her appraisal (Schrader and Schebera 1987, pp. 35–48). The comprehensive catalogue put together on the Novembergruppe by the gallery Bodo Niemann in 1993 contains three essays by Armin Schulz, Anita Beloubek-Hammer and Annette Ludwig which quote some new sources, but this material also simply supports Kliemann's propositions. Similarly, Freya Mühlhaupt (2007) and most recently Isabel Wünsche (2017) essentially endorse Kliemann's assessment.

12 See *inter alia* Joan Weinstein, whose study *The End of Expressionism: Art and the November Revolution in Germany, 1918–19* compares the Novembergruppe with the *Arbeitsrat für Kunst* and whose assessment also echoes that of Kliemann, although without observing the association's development after 1920 (Weinstein 1990, pp. 89–92, 95f.).

13 Wolfgang Willrich, *Säuberung des deutschen Kunsttempels. Eine kunstpolitische Kampfschrift zur Gesundung deutscher Kunst im Geiste nordischer Art,* Munich 1937, pp. 40–90, here p. 52, and pp. 168f. with an index of 179 names of Novembergruppe members.

14 Prelinger 1977.

15 Roters 1995. Eberhard Roters follows a similar argument in early articles on the Novembergruppe, including in the catalogue for the 43rd Ruhrfesttage *Freiheit, Gleichheit, Brüderlichkeit. Künstlergruppen in Deutschland 1918–1923* [*Liberty, Equality, Fraternity: Artist Groups in Germany 1918–1923*] (Roters 1989).

16 Roters 1995, p. 93, ref. in note 7.

17 Ref. in note 2.

18 For a fundamental account see Murphy 1999, esp. Ch. 2 on the revolution and the Expressionist avant-garde, pp. 49–73; Shapiro 1976, esp. Ch. 7 with a pan-European overview of the links between art and revolution from 1918 to 1921, pp. 173–200.

19 In 2015 the Bröhan-Museum Berlin included the association in its exhibition *Turn of an Era – From the Berlin Secession to the November Group,* without focussing broadly or in detail on the history or work of the Novembergruppe (Hoffmann 2015).

20 Adolf Behne, [Introduction], in: *Menschen. Buchfolge Neuer Kunst,* special issue *Novembergruppe. Graphik und Plastik von Mitgliedern der Novembergruppe Berlin,* vol. 2, 1919, issue 14 (nos. 81–86), pp. 1–2.

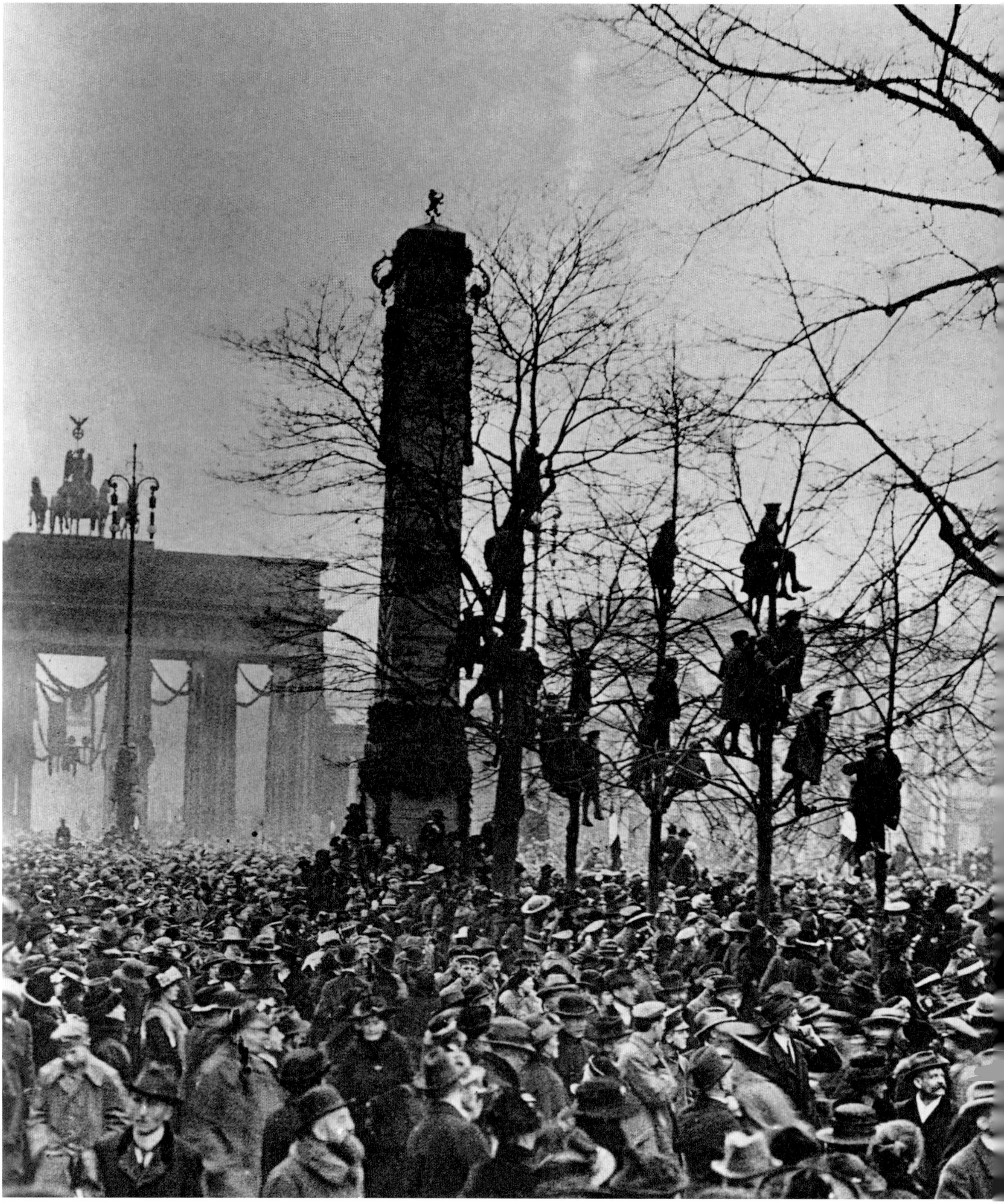

NG
PROLOGUE

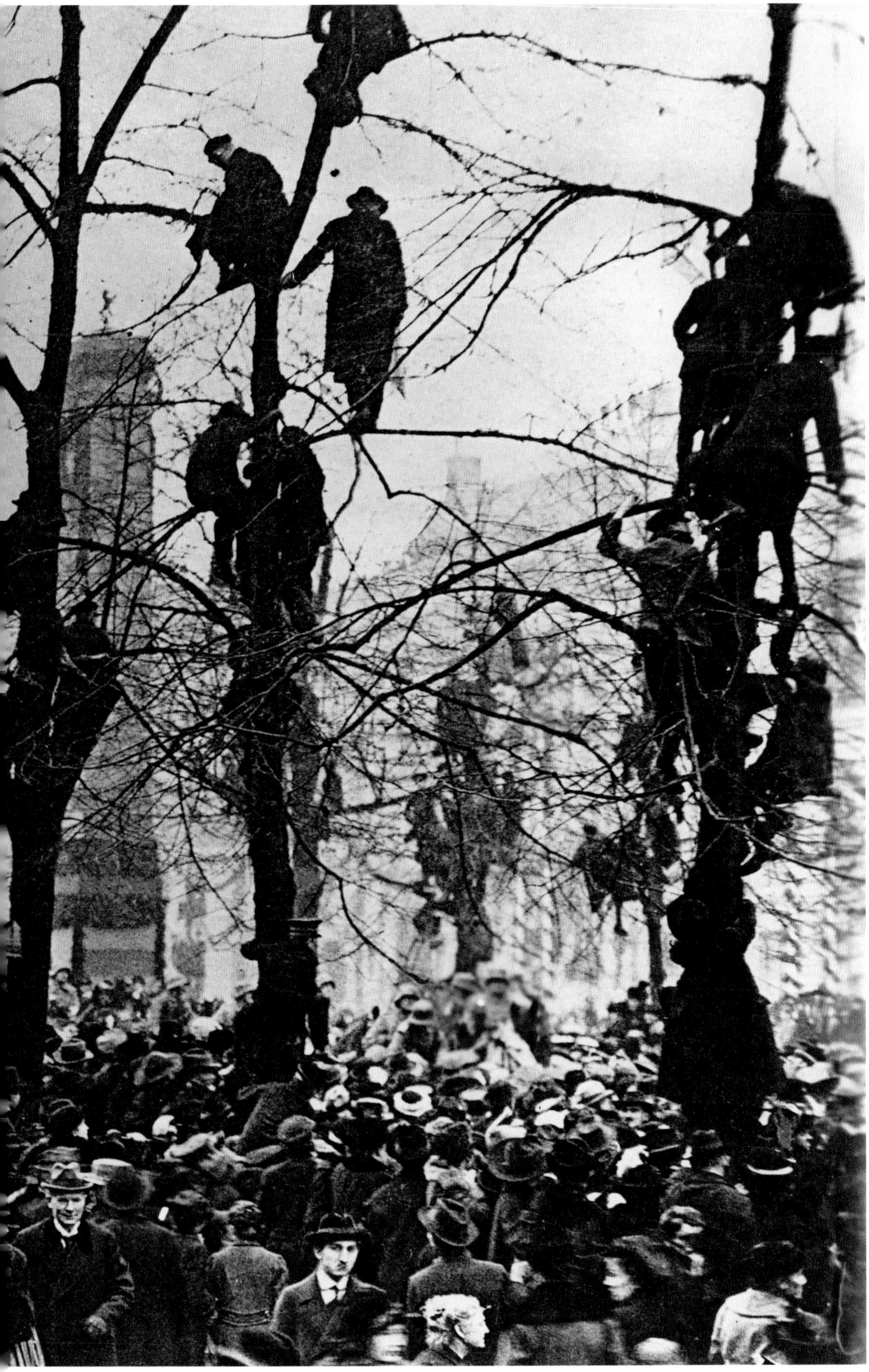

Willy Römer, Untitled (troops returning: Berliners climb trees outside the Adlon hotel on Unter den Linden for a better view), 10 December 1918
Berlinische Galerie

RALF BURMEISTER / JANINA NENTWIG

"THE KAISER HAS ABDICATED!" BERLIN, 1918–19

On 9 November 1918 the midday editions and special bulletins finally proclaimed what many had long been expecting: "The Kaiser has abdicated!". In war-weary Germany, revolution had been smouldering for days, with hunger and other deprivations rife after two million lives were lost in the First World War. At the end of October, when sailors in Wilhelmshaven and Kiel refused to put out to sea for a "last battle" against the British fleet, mutiny spread like wildfire across the country. In the big cities, town halls were taken over by workers' and soldiers' councils, similar to the soviets born of the Russian revolution. On the morning of 9 November, the revolution reached Berlin, and long columns of soldiers and striking workers marched on the government district. Of his own accord and against the will of Wilhelm II, Max von Baden, the Chancellor of the Reich, announced that the Emperor was stepping down and passed his reigns of office to Friedrich Ebert, chairman of the Majority SPD, the moderate rump of the divided Social Democratic Party. At two o'clock in the afternoon the Social Democrat Philipp Scheidemann proclaimed a "German republic", which was to be constituted by a freely elected national assembly. A mere two hours later Karl Liebknecht, the leader of the Spartacus League, declared a "free socialist republic" that would be governed by a system of elected councils similar to the model in post-revolutionary Russia.

Amid this open-ended upheaval, people working in the arts were eager to have a voice of their own in creating this new system. The end of the monarchy offered a one-off opportunity to campaign for radical political, social and, of course, cultural change and — in the perception of these artists caught up in the whirl of history — to shape the country's future. Many believed that the revolution in art unleashed by pre-war isms — Futurism, Cubism, Expressionism — had heralded and ultimately paved the way for this revolution in society. Now they felt their time had come to play a leading role in state structures and public life.[1] The very next day, 10 November, saw the formation of a *Rat geistiger Arbeiter* — a council to represent "workers of the mind". It demanded the right to participate in political decisions as well as "personal freedom and social justice".[2] Some fine artists and architects evidently felt, however, that this overarching alliance dominated by writers and intellectuals would not speak sufficiently for them, because before long two more organisations had sprung up: the *Arbeitsrat für Kunst* and the Novembergruppe. Their members were painters, sculptors and architects hoping to exert their own influence on future arts policy.[3]

Before December was out, some activists in the *Arbeitsrat für Kunst* and the Novembergruppe began working for the *Werbedienst*, the publicity operation supporting the German socialist republic.[4] Originally set up as a propaganda unit for the Berlin Workers' and Soldiers' Council, this institution was soon realigned behind the Council of People's Deputies, the transition government over which

Ebert now presided. The *Werbedienst* commissioned mostly Expressionist artists to produce posters and leaflets for the elections to a constituent national assembly and to appeal for prudence and calm among the populace. Posters with the latter purpose, in particular, reflected a dilemma facing the Council of People's Deputies: asserting public order while preserving a "revolutionary attitude".[5] Slogans to accompany the visuals by **HEINRICH RICHTER-BERLIN**, **HEINZ FUCHS** and other designers were, for example, "No food without coal" or "Strikes destroy us, working feeds us", which put the political message across loud and clear (cat. 07, 08, p. 26-27). The message was blatantly at odds, however, with the formal idiom of lively fragmentation and motifs drawn from mass demonstrations, most of them revolutionary in tone. The political uncertainty and dynamism were thus foregrounded rather more patently than the people responsible probably wished. With their designs for the *Werbedienst*, bearing its emblem of a flaming torch, artists such as **CÉSAR KLEIN** and **MAX PECHSTEIN** were siding with moderate left-wing forces, notably the Majority SPD (MSPD), which advocated a parliamentary democracy. Meanwhile, segments of the Independent SPD (USPD), along with the Communist Party of Germany (KPD) founded on 1 January 1919, campaigned for a soviet-style republic, and the Spartacist Uprising sought to achieve this by force. This mass revolt was quashed by government troops and anti-republican *Freikorps* paramilitaries, culminating in the murder of Karl Liebknecht and Rosa Luxemburg on 15 January 1919.

A national constitution was adopted in July 1919, but the fledgling Weimar Republic remained vulnerable. In March 1920, sections of the armed forces led by General Walther von Lüttwitz and the politician Wolfgang Kapp, a member of the German National People's Party (DNVP) still loyal to the monarchy, tried to topple the democratically elected government. The coup failed, not least because civil servants in ministries refused to take orders from Kapp as a self-appointed chancellor of the Reich. At the same time, 12 million workers joined the biggest general strike in German history, forcing the right-wing extremists into retreat. The putsch attempt only lasted four days and in Berlin there were not many skirmishes on the streets. The Expressionist artist Else Hertzer nevertheless depicted the situation as a dynamic nocturnal street scene (cat. 02, p. 22): a car full of people with a red flag, symbolising the revolution of 1918–19, rushes to the defence of the republic.

1 See among others Hoffmann 2010, Weinstein 1990, Friedel 1993, Guenther 1989. On groups of artists as a Modernist phenomenon see Wilhelmi 1996–2006. Volume 1 on Germany, Austria and Switzerland contains a list of the groups formed in Germany between 1918 and 1921 (Wilhelmi 1996, pp. 374f.).

2 For an introduction see Weipert 2015, pp. 319–328.

3 On the relationship between the *Arbeitsrat für Kunst* and the Novembergruppe see the essay by Nentwig in this catalogue, pp. 140f. The notes there suggest further literature on the *Arbeitsrat*.

4 For a detailed account of the *Werbedienst* see Vogel 2008.

5 Ibid., p. 22.

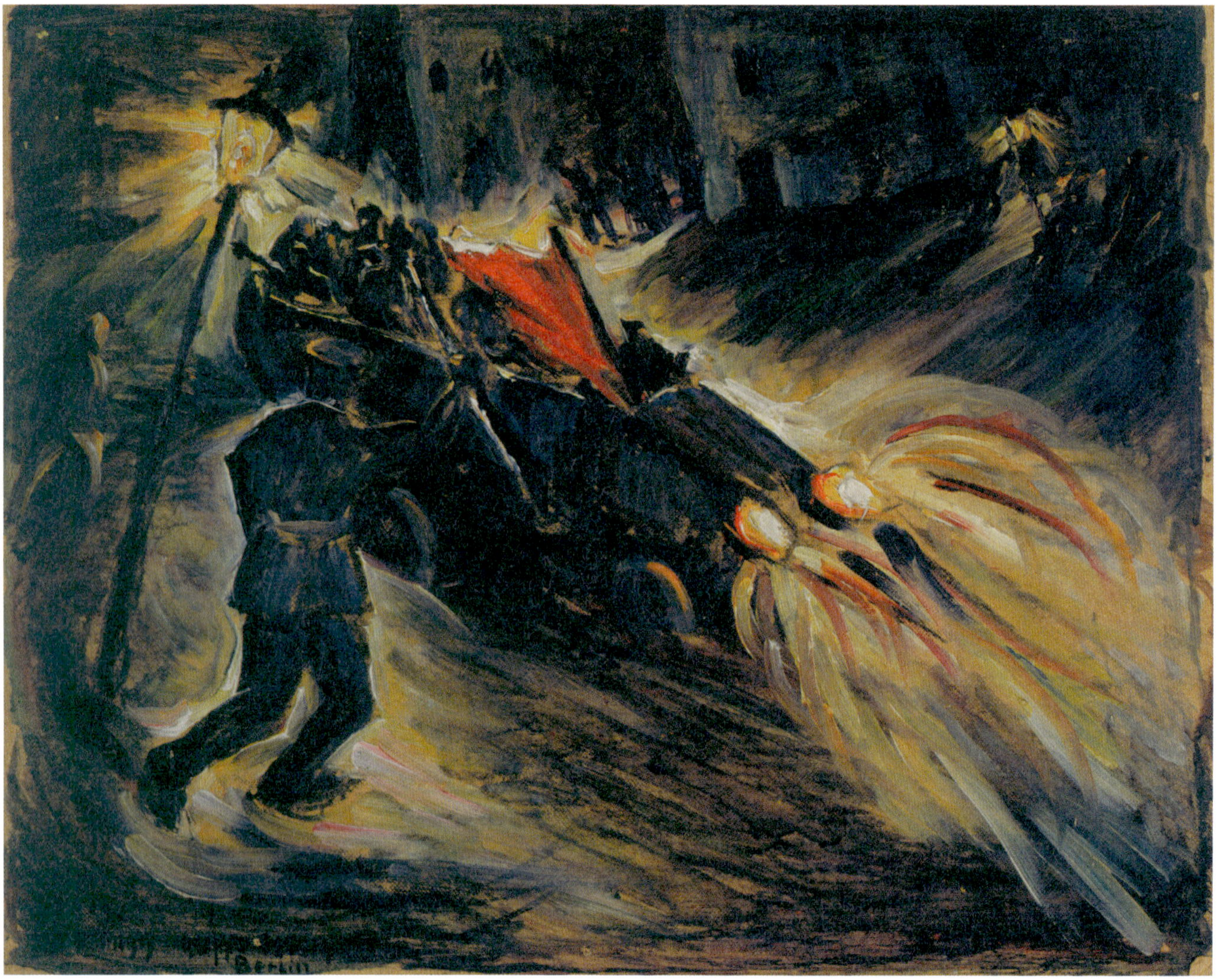

02

ELSE HERTZER

Kapp-Putsch, c. 1920

Oil on paperboard, 32 × 39.5 cm
Berlinische Galerie

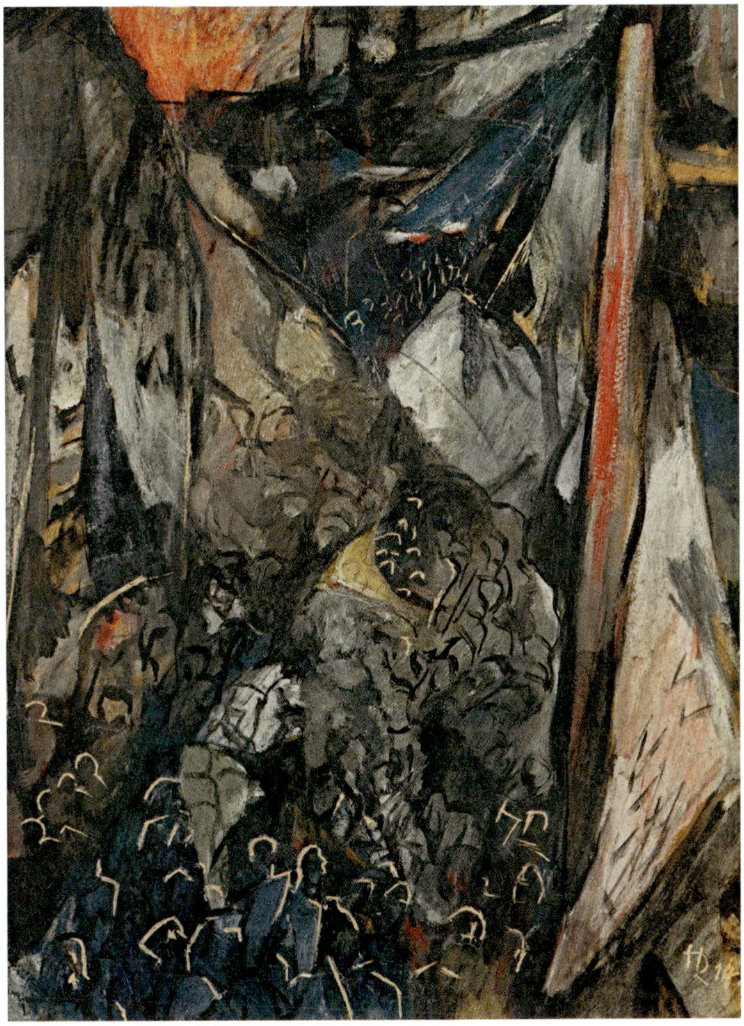

03

HANS RICHTER
Revolution, 1914 [?]

Oil on paperboard, 63.5 × 48 cm
Berlinische Galerie

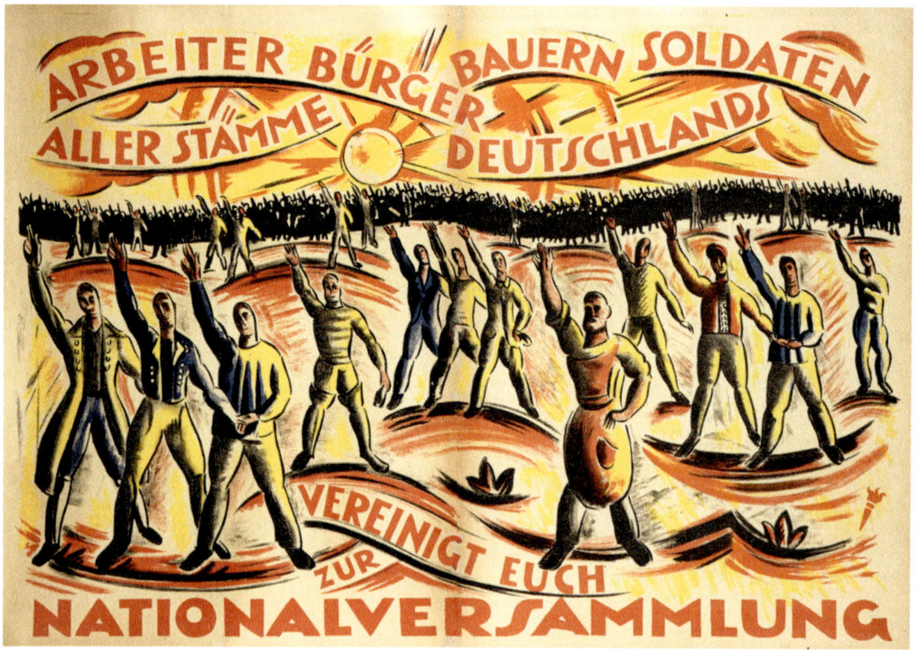

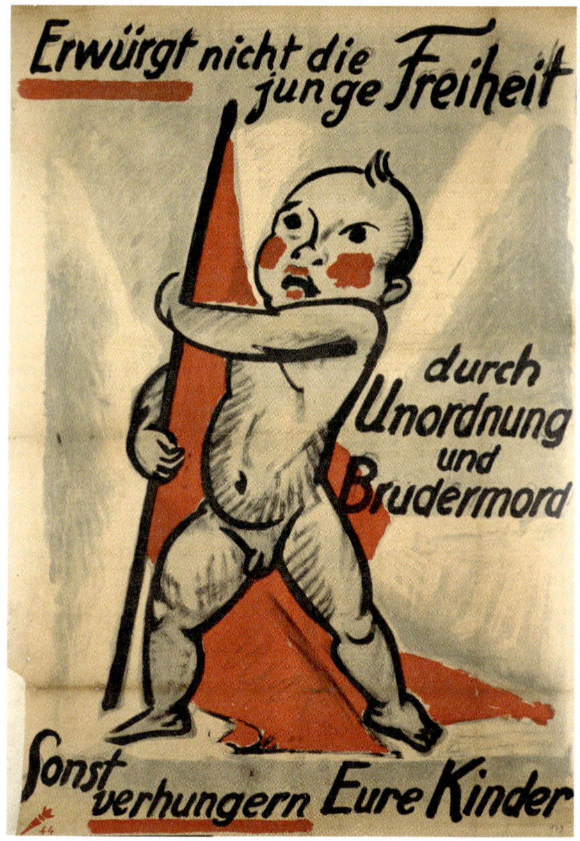

04
CÉSAR KLEIN
Call to vote for the National Assembly, 1919

Lithograph, 68 × 99.5 cm
Stiftung Deutsches Historisches Museum, Berlin

Poster for the *Werbedienst der deutschen sozialistischen Republik*

05
MAX PECHSTEIN
A call for law and order, 1919

Lithograph, 100 × 67.3 cm
Stiftung Deutsches Historisches Museum, Berlin

Poster for the *Werbedienst der deutschen sozialistischen Republik*

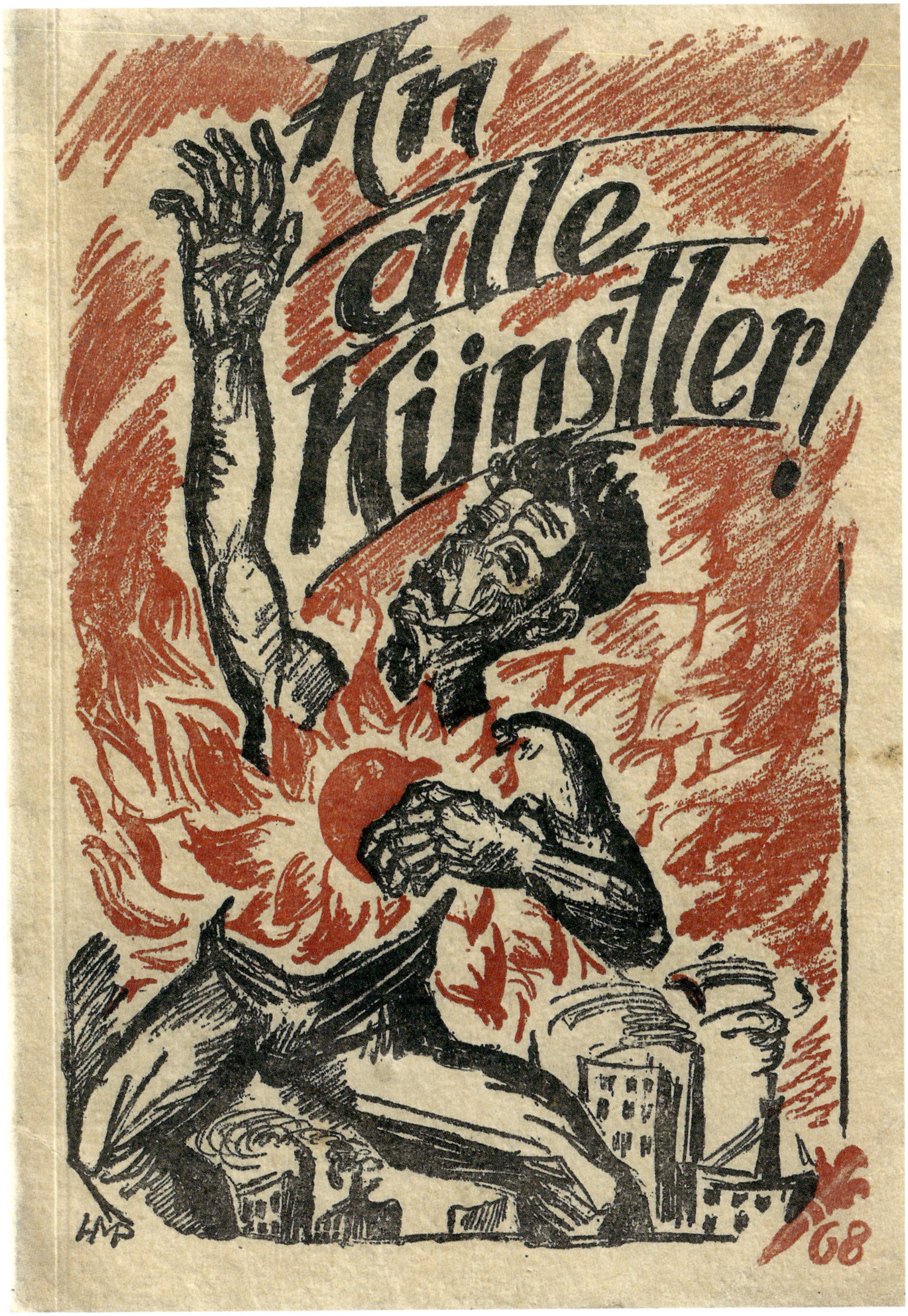

06
MAX PECHSTEIN
To All Artists!

Cover illustration. Brochure published by the *Werbedienst der deutschen sozialistischen Republik*, Berlin 1919

Berlinische Galerie

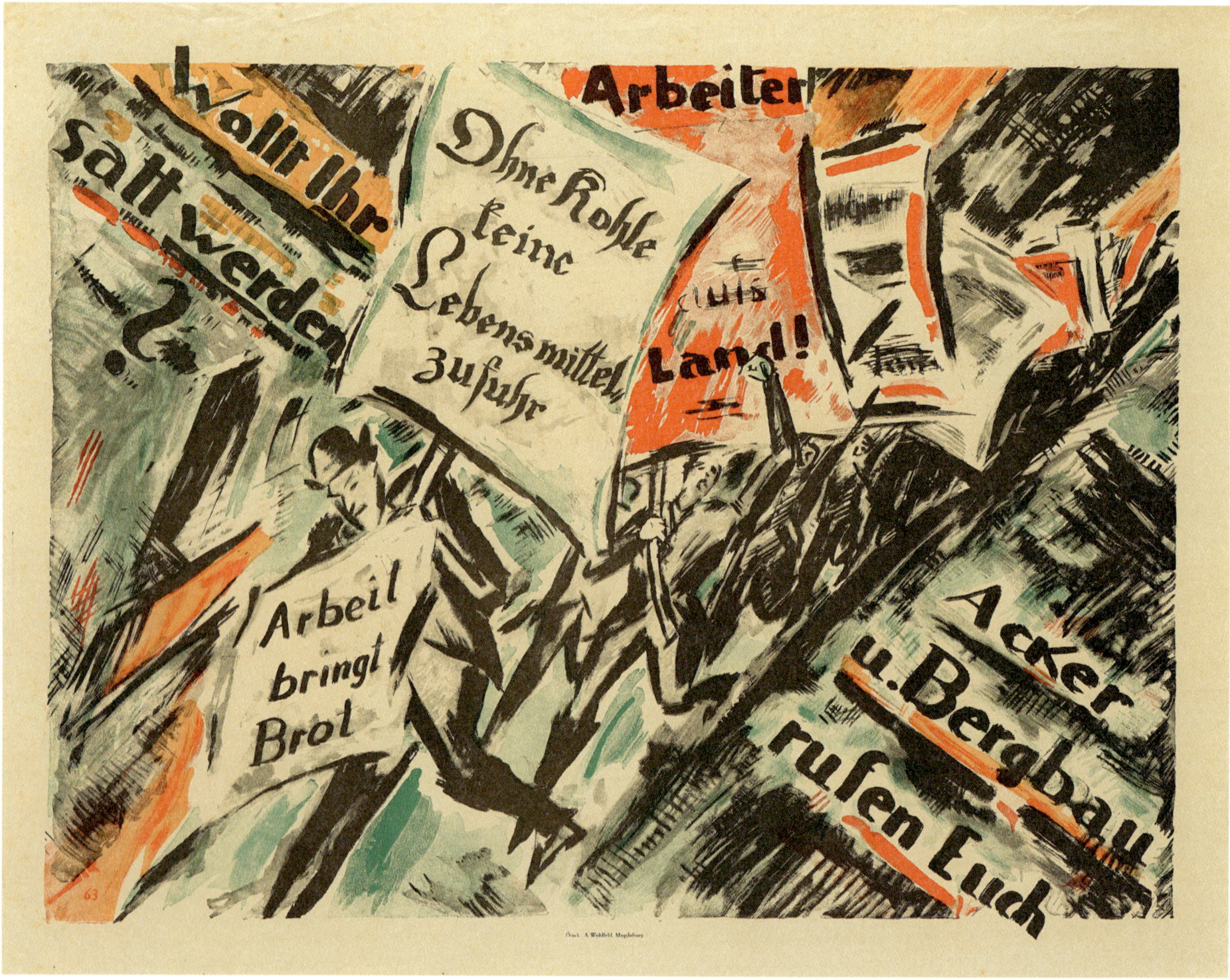

07
HEINZ FUCHS
Call to work on the land and in mining, 1919

Lithograph, 76 × 84 cm
Stiftung Deutsches Historisches Museum, Berlin

Poster for the *Werbedienst der deutschen sozialistischen Republik*

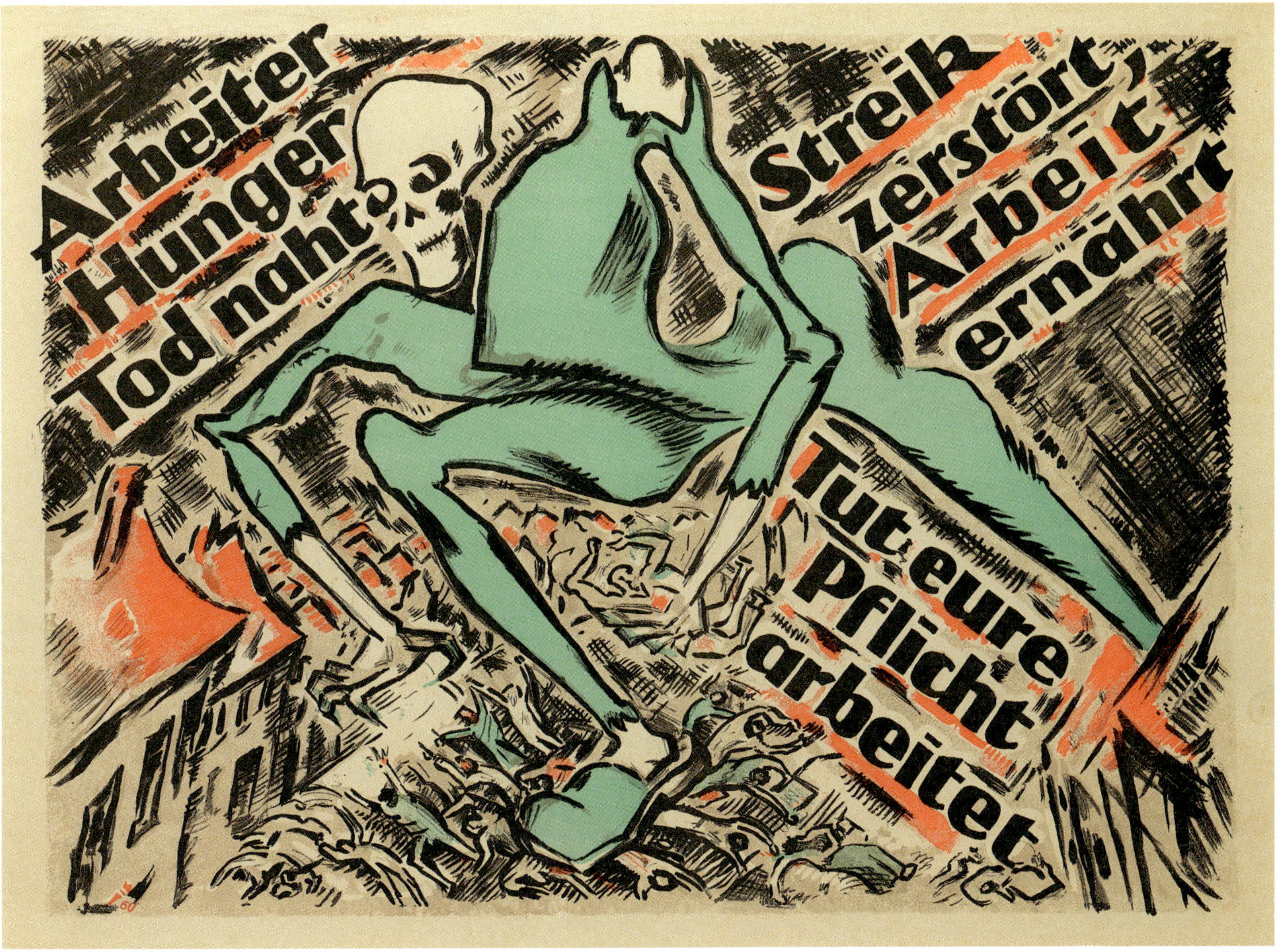

08

HEINZ FUCHS

Call to work and not strike, 1919

Lithograph, 73.7 × 103.9 cm
Stiftung Deutsches Historisches Museum, Berlin

Poster for the *Werbedienst der deutschen sozialistischen Republik*

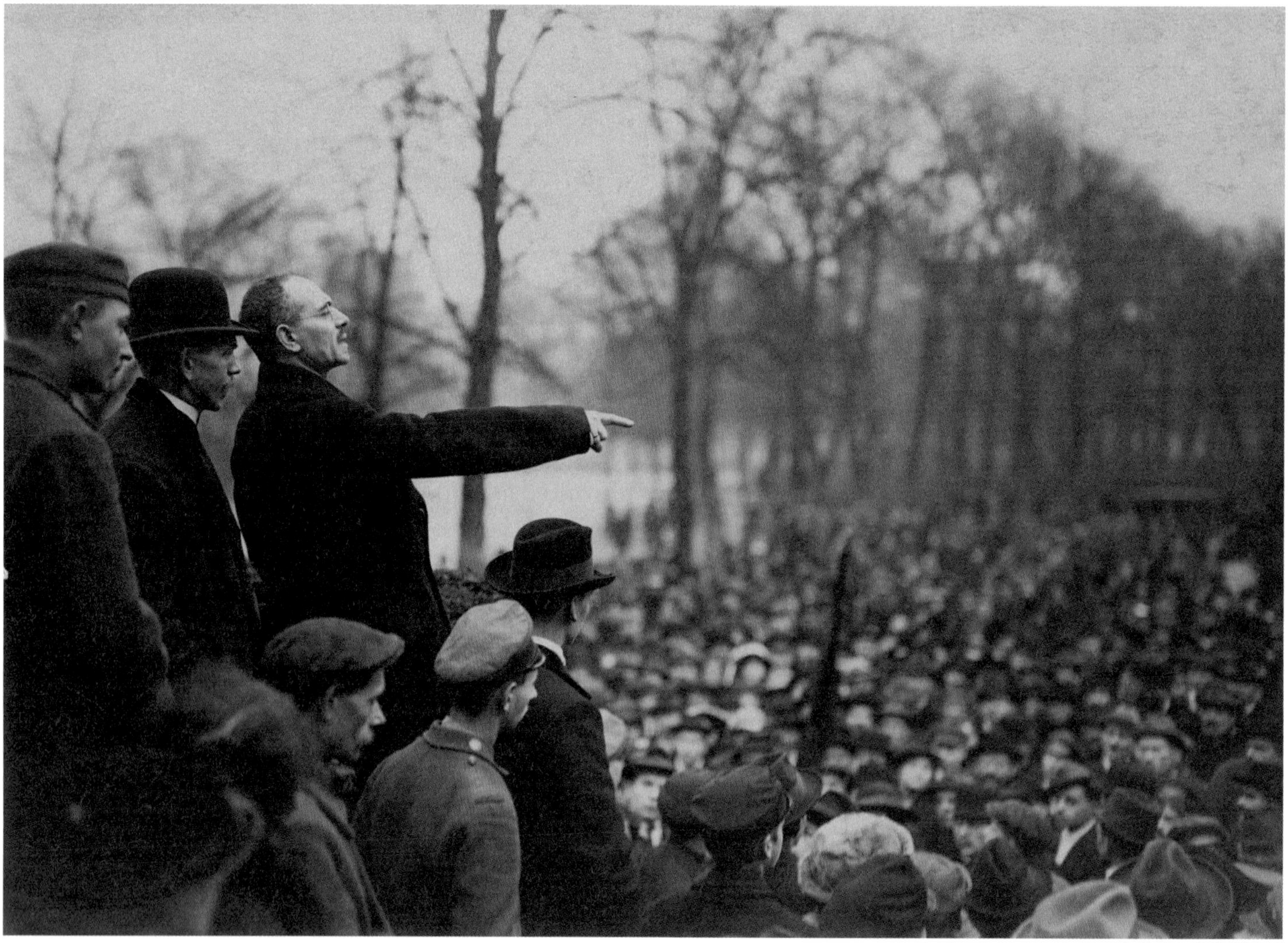

09

ROBERT SENNECKE

Karl Liebknecht speaks in Tiergarten, December 1918

Gelatin silver print, 17 × 23.2 cm
Berlinische Galerie

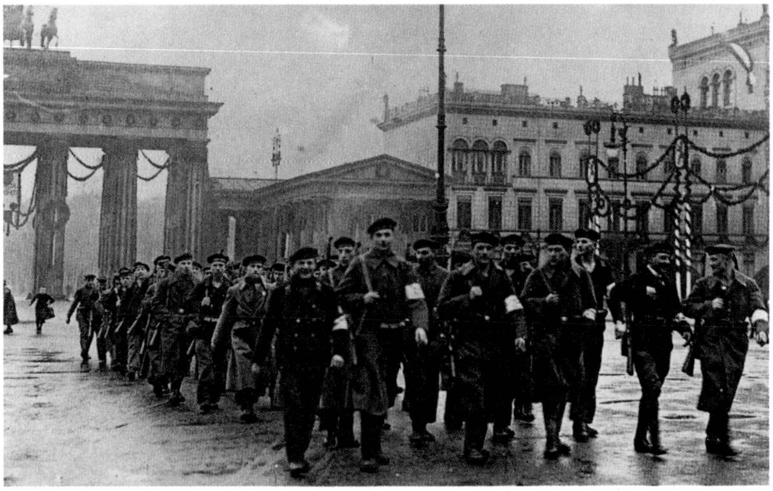

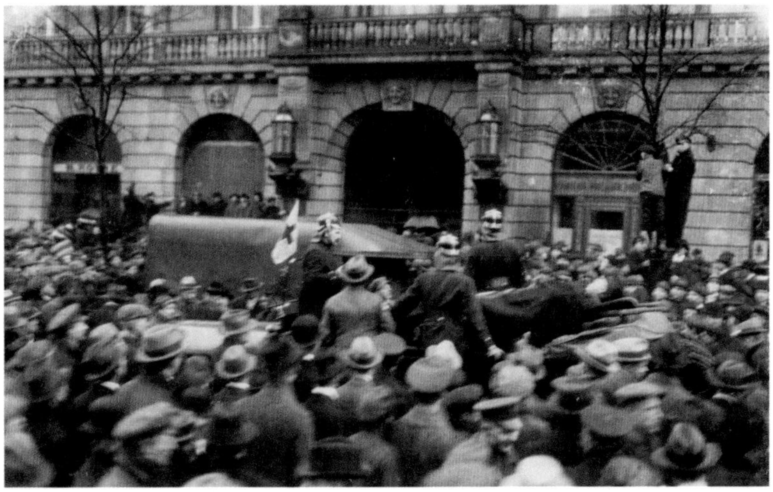

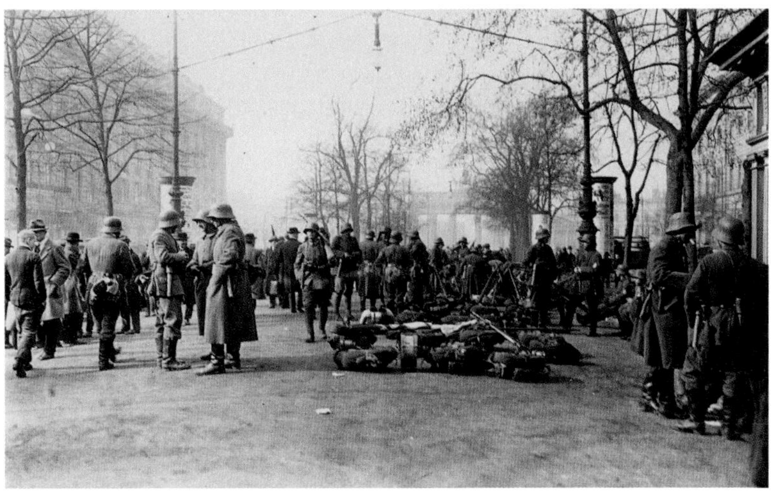

10
WILLY RÖMER
Untitled (outside Hotel Adlon, People's Navy division enters Berlin), November 1918

Gelatin silver print, 10.6 × 16.3 cm
Berlinische Galerie

11
WILLY RÖMER
Untitled (people wounded in shooting at Brandenburg Gate tended in Hotel Adlon), 1919

Gelatin silver print, 11.7 × 17.2 cm
Berlinische Galerie

12
WILLY RÖMER
Untitled (Kapp-Putsch, 7 am on Unter den Linden), 13 March 1920

Gelatin silver print, 11.6 × 17.2 cm
Berlinische Galerie

KRISTINA KRATZ-KESSEMEIER

PAVING THE WAY FOR FREE MODERNISM

The Novembergruppe's Role in Shaping Art Policy During the Weimar Republic

Founded in November 1918 in revolutionary Berlin, immediately after the end of the war, the Kaiser's abdication and the proclamation of the republic, the Novembergruppe pursued a clear arts policy from the outset: the new republic should acknowledge the latest developments in modern art and the state should adopt a progressive approach to funding the arts in clear contrast to the one-sidedly conservative policies of the German Empire.

The Novembergruppe summed up its political demands in January 1919 when, like its close ally, the *Arbeitsrat für Kunst*,[1] it presented a manifesto calling for "influence and involvement" "in all architectural tasks as a matter of public interest", in "reforming the art colleges and their teaching", "transforming the museums", "allocating exhibition space" and "legislating for the arts".[2] A crucial principle was that state authorities should stop paternalizing artists and establish two-way lines of communication instead. At the same time, by demanding that art colleges should reflect practice and that there should be a "harmonization of colleges for architecture, sculpture, painting and decorative art" and for museums a "transformation into places for people's art, into unprejudiced conveyors of timeless laws",[3] the manifesto referenced ardent reform debates which had been going on since around 1900.

In this way, the Novembergruppe drew on currents of reform in the Imperial era and placed this new art policy squarely on the agenda of the embryonic republic. But did the association really manage to help define the contours of art policy in the Weimar Republic in the following years? This essay is a first attempt at closer scrutiny of the role played by the Novembergruppe as the Weimar Republic introduced increasingly modern policies for the arts.

One thing is certain: in 1918 the Novembergruppe was already charting this change of course. Its demands were aimed at the supreme authority in this field in both Berlin and the country as a whole: the Prussian Ministry of Culture, which had been taken over by the revolutionary government on 12 November 1918. On the very day that the new minister Konrad Haenisch, a Social Democrat, took office, he was approached by progressive representatives of the arts. Herwarth Walden, manager of the gallery Der Sturm, an important source of Novembergruppe membership, wrote: "We do not seek a dictatorship of Expressionism or anything of that kind, but we do want our efforts to be granted the same rights and to receive the same state support and assistance as all the other currents in art."[4] RUDOLF BAUER, a co-founder of the Novembergruppe, urged Haenisch to allow "a broader circle to benefit" from the "revolutionizing progress accomplished by higher laws" which had "for some time also taken hold in art". To this end, "the time has come to establish, in a purely artistic sense, a number of new chairs and craft ateliers in the art academies, such as do not yet exist, with the aid of qualified people. Consideration should also be given to expanding the museums and exhibition affairs from this perspective."[5] The *Arbeitsrat für Kunst* similarly dispatched a delegation to the ministry — with WALTER GROPIUS and BRUNO TAUT, who were later also active in the Novembergruppe.[6]

Haenisch was open to these ideas. He would, he replied, "of course also endeavour to give the freest scope to the art movement you represent", but he could "not commit exclusively to Expressionism".[7] Freedom of art was the new maxim. The new name of the "Ministry of Science, Art and Education" signalled a willingness for reform and a new role for art.[8] To BAUER, Haenisch held out the prospect that "once things have settled down somewhat I will gladly and gratefully take up the offer for your circle to be involved".[9] On public policy grounds, however, he left the old civil servants in their posts at the ministry and in the academies and museums. This caused some displeasure among the revolutionary artists.[10] Novembergruppe member RUDOLF BELLING was prompted to argue for creating an entirely new culture ministry which would more rigorously "reflect our thinking".[11]

In late 1918 the SPD newspaper *Vorwärts* published more of the demands being made of the state by artists, including members of the Novembergruppe.[12] Then in February 1919 the *Werbedienst*, the publicity unit set up by Germany's socialist republic, went onto the offensive with a brochure entitled *To All Artists!* (cat. 06, p. 25), juxtaposing the Novembergruppe with the ministry itself and reprinting a piece that Haenisch had written for the press which it called the "art manifesto of the Prussian government".[13] The illustrations for the brochure were prints by Novembergruppe pioneers MAX PECHSTEIN, GEORG TAPPERT, CÉSAR KLEIN, MORIZ MELZER and HEINRICH RICHTER-BERLIN and also by LYONEL FEININGER. The emotional, religious symbolism and innovative style lent expression to the idea of a new dawn for society underpinned by the arts.[14] TAPPERT'S print (fig. 02) was symbolically placed next to Haenisch's article. This put the case for a liberal policy of arts funding and was similar in content to an appeal by PECHSTEIN also contained in the publication.[15] PECHSTEIN wanted art college reforms to engage with the crafts and with life, and he wanted artists to use the new freedoms by participating in museums for the living, an ideal force of art for the people, "including the genesis of a unified art era for our time", which would require the republic's trust.[16] The Minister of Culture promised to "open the way for all 'styles' and — more importantly — all personalities, including those who have hitherto been forced into the shadows". And, he insisted: "In the field of the fine arts we shall work towards uniting all groups, first of all the artist community in Berlin, in the organization of joint exhibitions."[17]

Sure enough, in July 1919 the ministry under Haenisch, now structured more assertively around its own art department and an unaffiliated liberal under-secretary in the person of Carl Heinrich Becker, took a decisive step towards cooperation between the republic and the Novembergruppe: in a demonstrative policy gesture the big state-funded exhibition, the Great Berlin Art Exhibition [*Grosse Berliner Kunstausstellung*], in the Glass Palace [*Glaspalast*] near Lehrter Bahnhof in Berlin — one of the venues once reserved for art conforming to the Kaiser's tastes and since 1892 *the* venue for presenting officially approved art to a mass audience — was not only removed from the control of the conservative art academy,

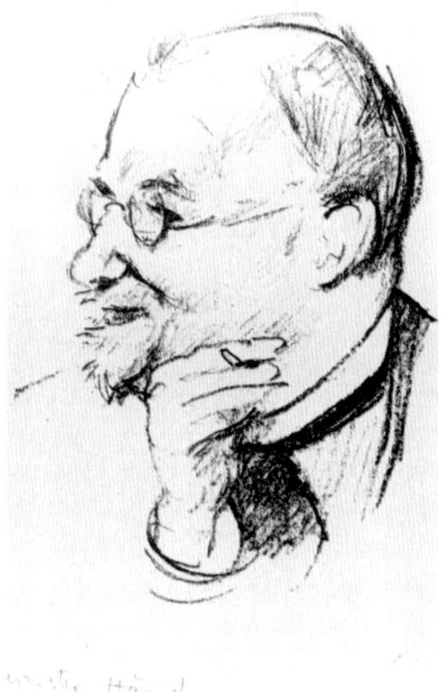

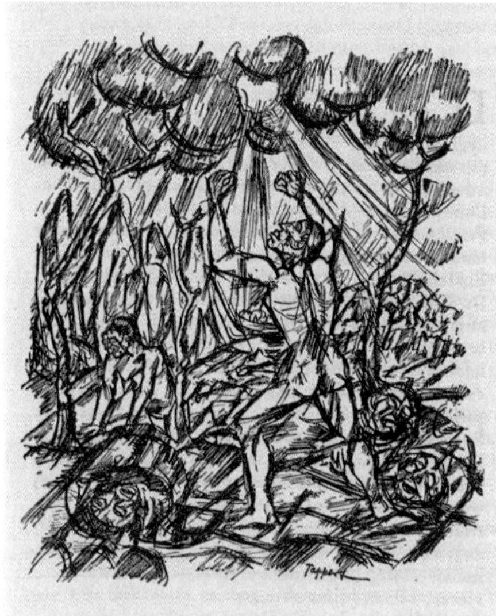

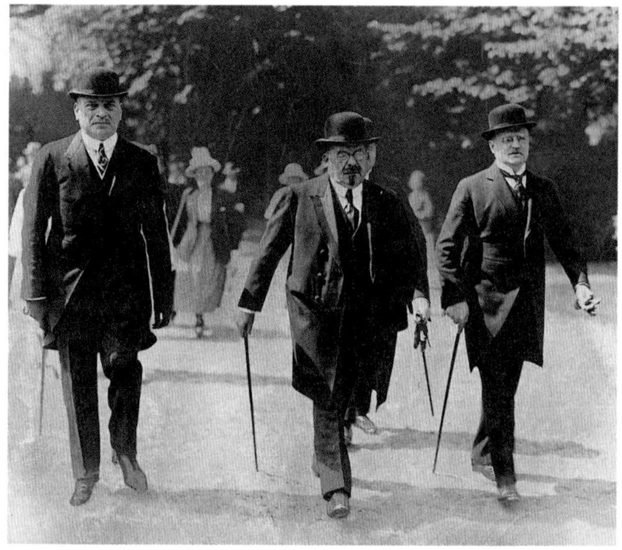

01 EMIL ORLIK
Konrad Haenisch at the Deutsches Theater, 1919

02 GEORG TAPPERT
Print from the brochure *To All Artists!*, 1919

03 Wilhelm Waetzoldt, President Friedrich Ebert and Otto Meissner, Head of the President's Office, on their way to open the Great Berlin Art Exhibition, 21 June 1921

but emblematically opened to modernism by incorporating a section specifically for the Novembergruppe. The Novembergruppe thus became a flagship for this more open-minded arts policy. It was not alone: the *Verein Berliner Künstler* (the professional association of artists in Berlin) and the Berlin Secession and Freie Secession were also represented at the "Glass Palace". Friedrich Ebert, President of the Reich, opened the exhibition amid a flurry of interest. The republic had launched a clear signal. The culture ministry was offering the Novembergruppe a platform and an opportunity to sell work. The latest in modern art was thereby integrated into the public art market and the group was free to appoint its own exhibition committee.[18]

Barely two weeks later the ministry confirmed how serious it was about acknowledging modern art when, on 4 August 1919, a "Gallery of the Living" opened in the *Kronprinzenpalais* as a satellite of the Nationalgalerie. It was the first time that Expressionists, among them PECHSTEIN and FEININGER, were shown at the museum. Artists of different styles had been invited to sit on the purchasing committee. The museum was designed by the director of the Nationalgalerie, Ludwig Justi, who interpreted Expressionism as a form of national expression. The ministry's main objective was to throw open the gallery to the diversity of modern art since Impressionism.[19]

The stylistic openness of the Novembergruppe sat extremely well with the new pluralist intentions of Haenisch's ministry. In 1920 it was again given a prominent billing in the *Glaspalast*. The cover page of the catalogue sported not only the title of the event but also the full significance of the venue: *Art Exhibition Berlin 1920 in the Landesausstellung Building made available to the Verein Berliner Künstler and the Novembergruppe by the Ministry of Science, Art and Education.*[20]

The fact that the Ministry of Science, Art and Education chose such a full-on approach to involving the Novembergruppe must also be seen in the context of contemporary discourse about forging close links between art and the republic — as advocated, for example, in an exposé published by the public information service, "The Spirit of the New National Community".[21] The ministry and the Novembergruppe were profoundly influenced by these ideas, rooted in the reform philosophy developed before 1918 by a liberal arts and crafts movement which sought to infuse all areas of life with its innovative aesthetic. After the war was lost, these ideas acquired additional relevance in conjunction with calls for a democratic education system and a new sense of national identity to be cultivated through art. The ministry attached fundamental social significance to consciousness raising through the enjoyment of art and to the free development of contemporary creativity.[22] The Novembergruppe proclaimed: "We regard it as our principal duty to dedicate our best energies to the moral construction of this young, free Germany."[23] Promoting modern art was thus intertwined with the new republican vision of a cultural community.

From 1920, therefore, the republic became even more robust in promoting its arts policy. For the first time, and until 1933, art historians sympathetic to modern art provided the underlay for the state's commitment to the arts. While Edwin Redslob, known for his affinity for Expressionism and the *Werkbund*, exercised the newly created national office of Guardian of the Arts,[24] Wilhelm Waetzoldt (fig. 03), a professor of art history from Halle, injected the latest thinking into the politics of the Prussian culture ministry. He had just published his book "German Painting since 1870", which—inspired by the *Brücke* aesthetic—had already identified a "new common point of orientation", a "new disciplined style".[25] The doors were now wide open for integrating further innovative stylistic positions.

On the other hand, sections of the Novembergruppe now questioned the whole principle of cooperating with the state. Building on a left-wing critique which had been gaining force since 1919, and which also took issue with the exhibitions in the *Glaspalast*,[26] eleven members wrote an open letter in early 1921 distancing themselves from the association's strategy, which they described as bourgeois, aestheticizing, focussed on commercial success and fame, and far too accommodating towards the government.[27] These artists included OTTO DIX, MAX DUNGERT, GEORGE GROSZ, RAOUL HAUSMANN, HANNAH HÖCH, RUDOLF SCHLICHTER and GEORG SCHOLZ. One alternative to the Novembergruppe was Dada, while the *Arbeitsrat für Kunst* disbanded altogether.[28] Ultimately, however, this dissenting voice merely prompted the Novembergruppe to state its position more clearly: the association firmly believed "that the pursuit of radical political aims was a matter for every individual, that the group as an association had merely to pursue radical artistic aims."[29]

Certainly, in the years that followed, the Novembergruppe's approach to the Great Berlin Art Exhibition—where it continued until 1932, with the exception of 1925, to show in its own rooms but within the official framework—was primarily to present new styles in art. In 1920 state secretary Carl Heinrich Becker had already linked the event to the genesis of a modernism fit for the day by declaring at the inauguration that the "aim was to establish firm formal principles supported by a clear sense of style reflecting our present lives".[30] From this point on the Novembergruppe showed the most recent art, put together initially by the founders along with RUDOLF BELLING or OSWALD HERZOG, and from 1923 by LUDWIG MIES VAN DER ROHE, PETER FOERSTER, ARTHUR SEGAL or MAX DUNGERT, across a huge spectrum from Cubo-Futuro-Expressionism via Abstract and Constructivist art to New Objectivity, and from 1922 the latest in architectural design.[31] Showcasing this experimental field was initially controversial, but the critical response grew increasingly positive,[32] and it played an active role in the ideal of paving the way for an innovative aesthetic worthy of the republic.

Nevertheless, the Novembergruppe's art was often provocative, and this put the new state maxim of artistic freedom to the test. Already in 1920, the "non-art" it presented at the *Glaspalast* had triggered attacks on Haenisch's ministry, which was accused of misunderstanding the "disgusting manifestations of present-day artistic degeneration" as the "dawn of a new, great art constructed entirely by its own internal laws".[33] While Ludwig Justi at the Nationalgalerie felt the Novembergruppe did not yet meet the standard for exhibition abroad,[34] there was a sharpening awareness that the professional promotion of modern art should hinge decisively on expert assessments of artistic quality. When works by GEORG SCHOLZ (cat. 48, p. 101) on show with the Novembergruppe at the *Glaspalast* were confiscated in 1922, Waetzoldt submitted his own report arguing that they should be released.[35] In 1924 Novembergruppe exhibits provoked hefty questions about the boundaries of art, even for Waetzoldt. At the urging of the culture ministry judicial review panels composed of specialists were finally established.[36] Here again, the Novembergruppe contributed to staking out the leeway for modern art. On the panel in Berlin, the association was represented by HEINRICH RICHTER-BERLIN.[37]

By now the Novembergruppe shows were assets in republic art policy, above all as places where all classes could come to discover modern art.[38] Press coverage was a clear reflection of the challenging art which met the viewer here.[39] The Novembergruppe exhibition guides, designed to explain these artistic statements to a broad readership,[40] catered to the ministry's interest in new communication formats, which also bore fruit at the *Kronprinzenpalais*.[41] The aim of facilitating open-minded encounters, especially with often inscrutable modern art, was closely linked to the idea of encouraging differentiated personal development and ultimately of cultivating responsible citizenship.[42]

The ministry's art policy at the time was deeply influenced by the concept of independent "seeing". This was evident firstly in the art teaching provided by schools, where there was also some common ground with the Novembergruppe,[43] and secondly in museums, where individual seeing, geared to the educational methods of the museum reformer Alfred Lichtwark[44] and in cooperation with Ludwig Justi, was the creed of a new museum policy with clear, aesthetic staging and communication, a departure — for which the Novembergruppe had also campaigned — from older, elitist models of museum management. While the ministry began in 1924 to stimulate aesthetic perceptions free of preconceived notions through progressive museum design in the field on non-European art,[45] Novembergruppe exhibitions promoted a similarly intensive reception of modern art not yet displayed by museums. The catalogue for the show at the *Glaspalast* in 1924 makes clear references to the Novembergruppe's involvement in this new culture of seeing[46] and to experiments in art optics by MORIZ MELZER (cat. 26, p. 66) and ARTHUR SEGAL (cat. 39, p. 79).[47]

Parallel to this, education for artists provided common terrain for the Novembergruppe and the ministry. Working with well-known art college reformers like PETER BEHRENS and WALTER GROPIUS, members of the Novembergruppe, the ministry set out in mid-1919 to reform the Prussian art academies, drawing on ideas from the Werkbund and Bauhaus.[48] Hoping to extend the broad impact into everyday life, Prussia's art advisor Wilhelm Waetzoldt spoke out for training free artists, decorative artists and architects together with an emphasis on craft techniques. At the same time, he emphasized individual creativity, which would be promoted with great freedom in ateliers run by masters and would turn out the "pacemakers" of a contemporary style.[49] Novembergruppe exhibitions provided artistic backing for these reform efforts by integrating architecture and the applied arts but also, for example, by showing RUDOLF BELLING'S sculpture *Triad* (fig. 04, cat. 111, p. 215) as a symbol of unity between the arts.[50] Meanwhile, in 1924, the ministry overcame massive conservative resistance to found the United State Schools of Free and Applied Arts in Berlin. The academies in Breslau, Düsseldorf, Kassel and Königsberg became increasingly innovative.[51] Members of the Novembergruppe played an active part in this progressive policy: HANS POELZIG became a driver of reforms when he set up his own atelier at the *Akademie der Künste* in Berlin in 1920.[52] CÉSAR KLEIN, who had

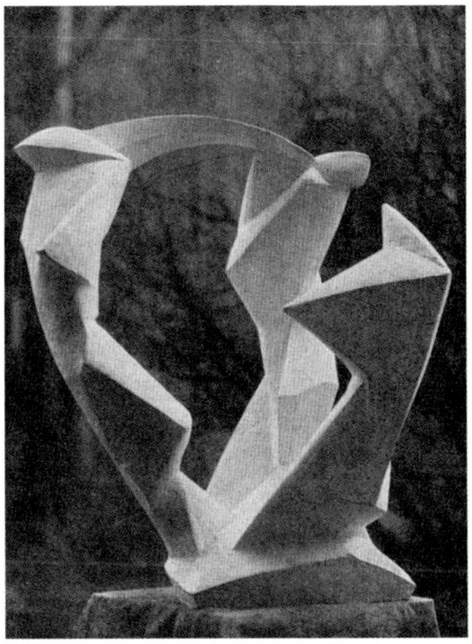

04

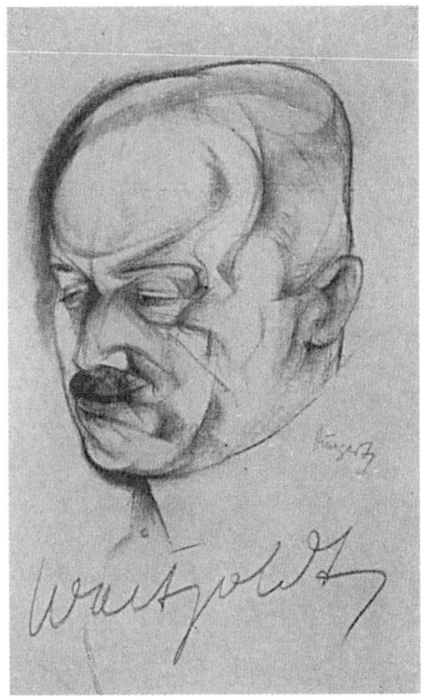

05

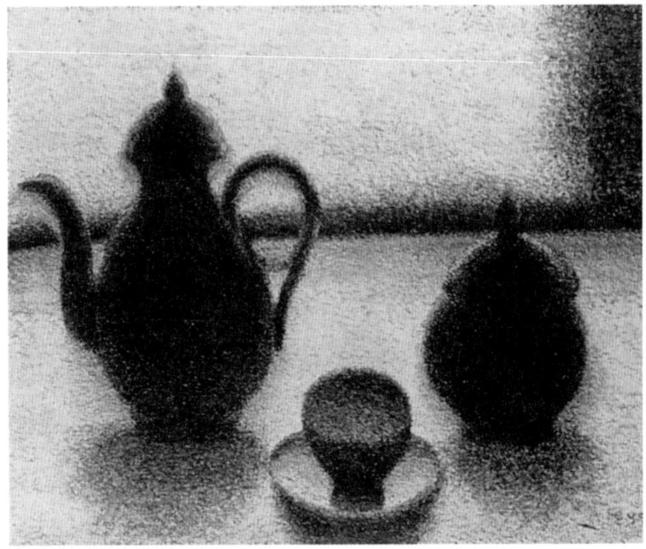

06

04 RUDOLF BELLING
Triad, 1920
Art Exhibition Berlin 1920, Novembergruppe section, no. 1096 (plaster version)

05 MAX DUNGERT
Portrait of Wilhelm Waetzoldt, date of origin and whereabouts unknown

06 ARTHUR SEGAL
Prismatic Still Life, 1925, destroyed
Purchased by the Ministry of Culture in 1925 during the Novembergruppe exhibition of that year at the Berlin Secession, no. 81

been teaching since 1919 at the school attached to the *Kunstgewerbemuseum*, the museum of decorative arts in Berlin, championed the creation of a new art college for the city and worked from 1924 at the United Schools.[53] Carlo Mense was appointed professor in Breslau from 1925, JOHANNES MOLZAHN from 1928 and OSKAR SCHLEMMER from 1929.[54]

In 1925 Carl Heinrich Becker took over as minister, remaining in the post until 1930. During this period more and more Novembergruppe activists became established figures in the confidently modern arts policies of the consolidating republic, where the disparate strands in New Objectivity and *Neues Bauen* [New Architecture] seemed to fulfil the 'yearning for style'. Becker threw his weight behind this trend with some trenchant ideas on educating the New Person.[55] Through the freedom it offered, the Novembergruppe had helped to smooth the aesthetic paths towards this goal.[56] In 1925 it exhibited at the Berlin Secession, highlighting its own role: as an "organization of artistic and creative forces in Germany" it was able "today to champion successfully, with ever growing activity, nascent phenomena in all fields of the arts. To contribute decisively to resolving artistic and cultural questions and problems". The aim was "an art that springs from life, is an expression of our time".[57] The fact that MAX DUNGERT published a portrait of Waetzoldt (fig. 05) at the time[58] seems to confirm the interplay between the association and the state's new policies for the arts.

The Novembergruppe advanced another step inside the state art establishement when it was invited to participate in ministerial purchasing policies from 1925. In June 1925, under MIES VAN DER ROHE, it had joined with the *Kartell der Vereinigten Verbände bildender Künstler Berlins*, a confederation of professional artists' associations in Berlin, to call explicitly for such purchases in the light of improved budgets.[59] The ministry thereupon initially acquired seven works at the Novembergruppe show in 1925: AUGUST WILHELM DRESSLER (*Engaged* [*Die Verlobten*]), MAX DUNGERT (*Picture 25.I* [*Bild 25.I*]), BERNHARD KLEIN (*The Old Captain* [*Der alte Kapitän*]), RUDOLF MÖLLER (a watercolour), ARTHUR SEGAL (*Prismatic Still Life* [*Prismatisches Stilleben*]; fig. 06), FRANZ STOCK (*Farm* [*Bauernhof*]) and KARL VÖLKER (*Picture of Industry* [*Industriebild*]; fig. 07).[60] Group exhibitions at the *Glaspalast* were followed in 1926 by ten ministerial purchases[61] and in 1927 by another four: PETER FOERSTER (*Italian Landscape I* [*Italienische Landschaft I*]), ERNST FRITSCH (*Tiergarten*), EWALD MATARÉ (wooden sculpture *Bull* [*Stier*]) and another by BERNHARD KLEIN (*Elbe Shore* [*Elbstrand*]; cat. 78, p. 138).[62] In 1929, at

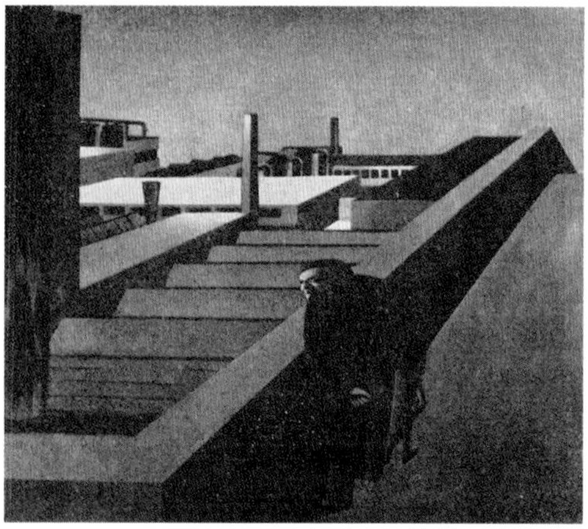

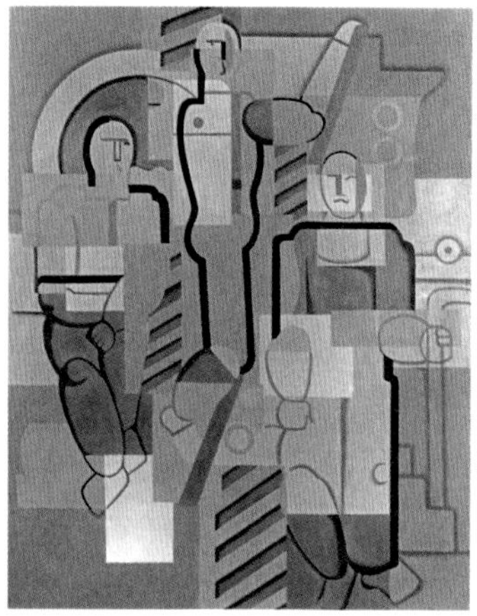

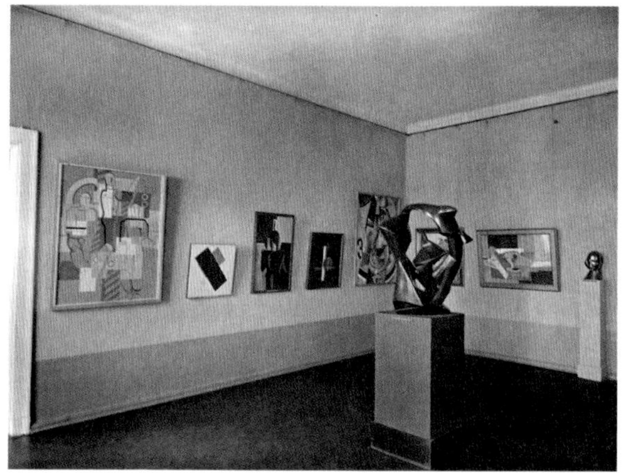

07 08 09

07 KARL VÖLKER
Picture of Industry, 1925, whereabouts unknown
Purchased by the Ministry of Culture in 1925 during the Novembergruppe exhibition of that year at the Berlin Secession, no. 91 or 91a

08 WILLI BAUMEISTER
Three Assembly Workers, 1927, whereabouts unknown
Purchased by the Ministry of Culture in 1929–30 in conjunction with the Jury-Free Art Show 1929, exhibition Ten Years of the Novembergruppe, not in the catalogue

09 Exhibition room in the Kronprinzenpalais, 1930–31, with Willi Baumeister's *Three Assembly Workers*, Oskar Schlemmer's *Concentric Group*, Jean Metzinger's *The Boat* or *En Canot* and Rudolf Belling's *Triad*

the Novembergruppe's tenth-anniversary show, the ministry bought works by WILLI BAUMEISTER (*Three Assembly Workers [Drei Monteure]*; fig. 08), CHRISTOF DREXEL (*Flower Woman [Blumenfrau]*) and JEAN METZINGER (*The Boat/En Canot [Im Boot]*).[63] After the association's attention was drawn to this possibility in 1925,[64] the ministry continued purchasing works shown by Novembergruppe artists at other exhibitions until 1931, and from 1930 there were also direct acquisitions—from JANKEL ADLER (*Chassid*), OTTO DIX (*Portrait of Theodor Däubler [Bildnis Theodor Däubler]*), DRESSLER (*By the River Havel [An der Havel]*), LYONEL FEININGER (*Beach Hotel [Strandhotel]*, *Cutter Class [Kutterklasse]*), FRITSCH (among others *Still Life [Stilleben]*), GEORGE GROSZ (*Bengali Night [Bengalische Nacht]*, *Street in Pointe Rouge [Straße in Pointe Rouge]*, *Houses in Gardens [Häuser in Gärten]*), WASSILY KANDINSKY (*Calmed [Ruhe]*), MATARÉ (among others the bronze *Bull*, watercolours), MORIZ MELZER (*Stormy Journey [Sturmfahrt]*), JOACHIM RINGELNATZ (*11 pm [11 Uhr nachts]*), EMY ROEDER, OSKAR SCHLEMMER (*Concentric Group [Konzentrische Gruppe]*), RUDOLF SCHLICHTER (*Portrait of Gilbeaux [Bildnis Gilbeaux]*) and GEORG SCHRIMPF (*Girl at the Window [Mädchen am Fenster]*).[65]

Some of these works went on display at the ministry itself but most were sent to the *Kronprinzenpalais*, where they joined other striking specimens of the republic's art policy.[66] Here in the state gallery on Unter den Linden, BELLING'S *Triad* could be seen around 1930 alongside works by MATARÉ, BAUMEISTER, SCHLEMMER and METZINGER (figs. 09 and 10). Meanwhile the prominent role played by the Novembergruppe in the official exhibition programme was slowly on the wane. When it appeared at the *Glaspalast* from 1927 onwards it did so as part of the *Kartell der Vereinigten Verbände bildender Künstler Berlins*, which enjoyed ministerial backing as a confederation.[67] The time had come for "the artistic struggle in a community of colleagues",[68] and as a result the Novembergruppe took back stage as an independent association.[69] From 1928 other formats were the focus of state exhibition policy, such as the nationwide *Deutsche Kunst Düsseldorf* 1928 or Paul Westheim's "talent shows".[70] A new generation was taking up position, while the Novembergruppe, already "a piece of art history",[71] continued to set its stamp on the modern republic in academies and museums, but also in shaping the lived environment.[72]

Once more the ministry demonstratively involved prominent Novembergruppe artists in its art policy at the start of the 1930s when, from 1930 to 1932 under the last Prussian Minister of Culture, the social democrat Adolf Grimme, the republic responded to the rise of National Socialism with some confident displays of its modern ethos. In early 1930 the *Kartell*, including MORIZ MELZER for the Novembergruppe, called for the new public exhibition site in the Tiergarten, which had been under discussion since 1926, to be implemented at long last,[73] and in August 1930

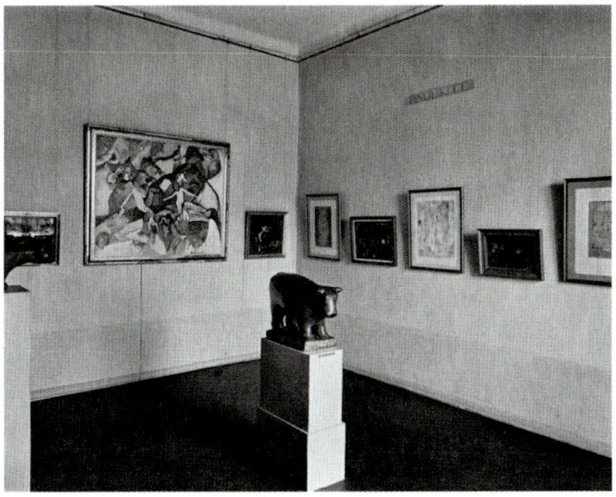

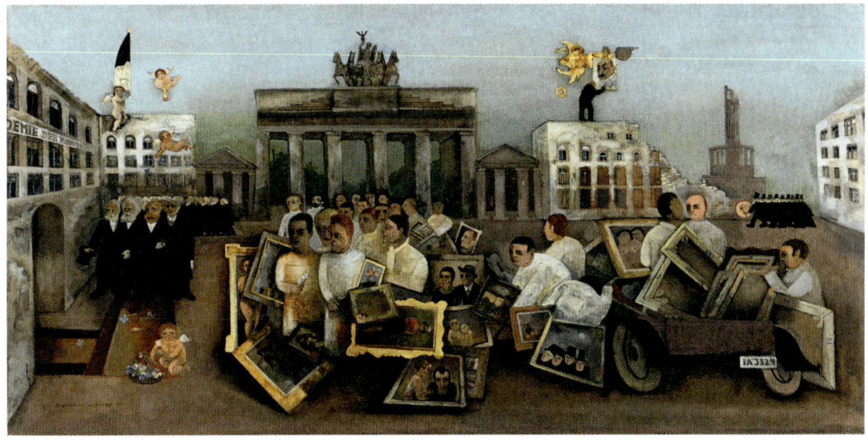

10 Exhibition room in the Kronprinzenpalais with Ewald Mataré's *Bull*, c. 1930

11 **FELIX NUSSBAUM**
The Folly Square, 1931
Berlinische Galerie

Grimme accordingly endorsed a new building by MIES VAN DER ROHE,[74] responding to ideas first put forward by the Novembergruppe in 1922. The republic's international image owed much by now to Novembergruppe activists such as LUDWIG MIES VAN DER ROHE, OTTO DIX, PAUL KLEE and MAX PECHSTEIN.[75]

On 11 August 1931, a symbolic choice as it was Constitution Day, the ministry made another bold statement on behalf of modern art by appointing 13 progressives to join the Berlin academy, hitherto paralysed by conservative forces. They included RUDOLF BELLING, OTTO DIX, ERICH MENDELSOHN, BRUNO TAUT and MIES VAN DER ROHE from the Novembergruppe.[76] That same year GEORG MUCHE was called to the academy in Breslau and PAUL KLEE to the academy in Düsseldorf, and in 1932 EWALD MATARÉ followed him to Düsseldorf.[77] Felix Nussbaum's painting *The Folly Square* [*Der tolle Platz*] of 1931 (fig. 11) illustrates how, amid an awareness that the republic was under threat, modern art gained entrance to the academy with students following on the heels of their mentors.[78] This was the generation born between 1875 and 1895, raised in the days of Imperial art policy, who from 1918 had, through the Novembergruppe, paved the way for a freer modern spirit, and who continued to participate actively in the republic's progressive art policy until the bitter end.

However, in the years of economic crisis the art debate acquired increasingly ideological tones. Adolf Grimme and the republican modernists around the Novembergruppe were fighting a losing battle. The Nazis wasted no time in denouncing Weimar's art policy and the Novembergruppe. Many of the works purchased from the association since 1925 were seized as "degenerate",[79] and some went on display in 1937 in the exhibition *Degenerate Art* [*Entartete Kunst*].[80] Thus the Nazi dictatorship put an end to the development towards an open, liberal art policy in which the Novembergruppe had played its part. Not until after 1945 would Germany return to this path of broad liberty and once again treat modernism not as a party-political affair but as a matter of art.

1 See Kliemann 1969, p. 14; Steneberg 1987; Nentwig 2018.

2 Guidelines, January 1919, quoted in: Will Grohmann (ed.), *Zehn Jahre Novembergruppe*, special issue *Kunst der Zeit. Zeitschrift für Kunst und Literatur*, year 3, 1928, nos. 1–3, pp. 11f.

3 Ibid.

4 Letter from Herwarth Walden to Konrad Haenisch, 12 November 1918, Bundesarchiv Berlin, 90 HA 4, no. 452, f. 8.

5 Letter from Rudolf Bauer to Konrad Haenisch, 12 November 1918, ibid., f. 9f.

6 See Kratz-Kessemeier 2008, pp. 29f., 41f. and 45.

7 Letter from Konrad Haenisch to Herwarth Walden, 13 November 1918, Bundesarchiv Berlin, 90 HA 4, no. 452, f. 15.

8 See also Belling, in: Grohmann 1928, ref. in note 2, p. 15.

9 Letter from Konrad Haenisch to Rudolf Bauer, 13 November 1918, Bundesarchiv Berlin, 90 HA 4, no. 452, f. 29.

10 For a fundamental discussion of the art policies of the Prussian Ministry of Culture from 1918 to 1932 see Kratz-Kessemeier 2008, here pp. 21–125.

11 Belling, in: Grohmann 1928, ref. in note 2, p. 15.

12 "Der freie Volksstaat und die Kunst" [including contributions by Fritz Stuckenberg, Bruno Taut and Peter Behrens], in: *Vorwärts*, vol. 35, no. 354, 25 December 1918.

13 *An alle Künstler!*, Werbedienst der deutschen sozialistischen Republik, no. 68, Berlin 1919; see Vogel 2008, especially pp. 79–84, 129 and 192–200; Kratz-Kessemeier 2008, pp. 35–38.

14 See Vogel 2008, pp. 196–200.

15 See ibid., pp. 192–194.

16 Max Pechstein, "Was wir wollen", in: *An alle Künstler!*, ref. in note 13, pp. 18–22, here 19 and 22.

17 Konrad Haenisch, "Das Kunstprogramm der preußischen Regierung", in: *An alle Künstler!*, ref. in note 13, pp. 37f.

18 See Kratz-Kessemeier 2008, pp. 146–163; *Kunstausstellung Berlin 1919 im Landesausstellungsgebäude* (exhib. cat., 24 July – 30 September 1919), Berlin 1919, p. 3; Nentwig 2018.

19 See Kratz-Kessemeier 2008, pp. 126–146; Kratz-Kessemeier 2011, pp. 33–35; Baumann 2016, here pp. 37–51.

20 *Kunstausstellung Berlin 1920 im Landesausstellungsgebäude, das vom Ministerium für Wissenschaft, Kunst und Volksbildung dem Verein Berliner Künstler und der Novembergruppe zur Verfügung gestellt ist* (exhib. cat., 21 May – September 1920), Berlin 1920.

21 Zentrale für Heimatdienst (ed.), *Der Geist der neuen Volksgemeinschaft. Eine Denkschrift für das deutsche Volk*, Berlin 1919.

22 See Kratz-Kessemeier 2008, pp. 164–193 and 219–229.

23 Manifest, undated, quoted in: Grohmann 1928, ref. in note 2, p.16.

24 On Redslob's role in art policy in general and specifically for the Novembergruppe see Belling 1955; Kratz-Kessemeier 2010.

25 Wilhelm Waetzoldt, *Deutsche Malerei seit 1870*, Wissenschaft und Bildung, 144, 2nd ed., Leipzig 1919, p. 102.

26 See e.g. Franz Schulz, "Kunst, Bürger, Staat", in: *Das Forum*, vol. 4/2, no. 9, June 1920, pp. 655–660.

27 "Offener Brief an die Novembergruppe", in: *Der Gegner*, vol. 2, 1920–21, no. 8–9, pp. 297ff., quoted in: Kliemann 1969, pp. 61–64.

28 See Nentwig 2018.

29 Novembergruppe, "Erwiderung", in: *Der Gegner*, vol. 3, no. 1, 21 March 1922, p. 30, quoted in: Kliemann 1969, p. 64; see also Belling 1955, p. 169; exhib. cat. Galerie Bodo Niemann 1993, p. 8.

30 *Vossische Zeitung*, evening edition, 21 May 1920, Geheimes Staatsarchiv Preußischer Kulturbesitz, Berlin, HA I Rep. 92 Nl. C. H. Becker, no. 7359.

31 See Nentwig 2015a, p. 179; Hoffmann 2015a, pp. 233 and 240.

32 See "Presse" in Kliemann 1969, pp. 84–89; Grohmann 1928, ref. in note 2, pp. 17, 19–21, 29, 31, 58, 81 and 88.

33 Otto Koester, "Berliner Kunstskandal", in: *Weltbühne*, vol. 16/2, no. 32, 5 August 1920, pp. 165–168, here 167. The objects of wrath were collages by Yefim Golyshev and Edmund Kinzinger, ref. note 20, pp. 72 and 75.

34 See letter from Justi to the Kultusministerium, 6 April 1921, Staatliche Museen zu Berlin, Zentralarchiv, I/NG 602; also Bundesarchiv Berlin, R 32, no. 69, f. 51f.

35 This was about *Der sentimentale Matrose* and *Entwurf zu einer patriotischen Wanderbühne*, see Kratz-Kessemeier 2008, pp. 288f.; *Grosse Berliner Kunstausstellung 1922 im Landesausstellungsgebäude am Lehrter Bahnhof* (exhib. cat., 20 May – 17 September 1922), Berlin 1922, p. 65; Grohmann 1928, pp. 40–42; Hoffmann 2015a, pp. 234f.

36 For context see Belling 1955, p. 169; Kratz-Kessemeier 2008, pp. 154–156 and 284–295; Kratz-Kessemeier 2010, pp. 237f.

37 See Mitgliederliste Gesamtkunstausschuss Berlin, 17 February 1927, Archiv der Akademie der Künste, Berlin, PrAdK 2.1/051, f. 33.

38 See Nentwig 2015a, p. 198.

39 See Kliemann 1969, pp. 84–89; Grohmann 1928, ref. in note 2, pp. 17, 20f., 29, 31 and 58; Kratz-Kessemeier 2008, pp. 150–153.

40 See Kliemann 1969, pp. 27f. and 71–74.

41 See Ludwig Justi, *Neue Kunst. Ein Führer zu den Gemälden der sogenannten Expressionisten in der National-Galerie* (Amtliche Veröffentlichungen der National-Galerie), Berlin 1921.

42 See Kratz-Kessemeier 2008, pp. 194–205 and 434–445; Kratz-Kessemeier 2013.

43 See Kliemann 1969, pp. 44, 81f. and 130f.

44 See also the dedication in: Waetzoldt 1919, ref. in note 25.

45 See Kratz-Kessemeier 2008, pp. 401–433.

46 See the quotations on art reception in: *Grosse Berliner Kunstausstellung 1924 im Landesausstellungsgebäude am Lehrter Bahnhof* (exhib. cat., 31 May – 1 September 1924), Berlin 1924, pp. 4–6.

47 See: ref. in note 2, pp. 42–44; Kliemann 1969, p. 41; Foerster 1996, pp. 26–28, 37f. and 62.

48 See Kratz-Kessemeier 2008, pp. 80–82, 106–123, 219 and 302–313.

49 Wilhelm Waetzoldt, *Gedanken zur Kunstschulreform*, Leipzig 1921, p. 29.

50 On this see also Kliemann 1969, pp. 18–21.

51 See Kratz-Kessemeier 2008, pp. 313–333.

52 See ibid., pp. 109f., 310, 320, 342, 355 and 358f.

53 See "Entschließung des Lehrerkollegiums der bisherigen Unterrichtsanstalt des Kunstgewerbemuseums an das Kultusministerium", 27 May 1924, in: *Mitteilungen des Deutschen Werkbunds*, vol. 1924–25, no. 3, 28 June 1924, pp. 2f.; exhib. cat. Akademie der Künste 1996, pp. 439f. and 442f.

54 Heinrich Campendonk had also been a professor in Düsseldorf since 1926.

55 See Kratz-Kessemeier 2008, pp. 269–278 and 445–458; Kratz-Kessemeier 2015, pp. 225–231.

56 See also Hoffmann 2015a, p. 240.

57 *Ausstellung der Novembergruppe in den Räumen der Berliner Secession in Berlin. Juni 1925. Malerei, Plastik, Architektur* (exhib. cat., June 1925), Archiv der deutschen Kunst, vol. 5, 1925, no. 3, Berlin 1925, pp. 4f.

58 Max Dungert, *20 Köpfe*, with a foreword by Otto Brattskoven, Berlin 1925, p. 11; see exhib. cat. Galerie Bodo Niemann 1993, p. 8.

59 See the letter from the *Kartell der Künstlerverbände* to the Kultusministerium, 15 June 1925, and the letter from Carl Heinrich Becker to the *Kartell der Künstlerverbände*, 28 August 1925, Geheimes Staatsarchiv Preußischer Kulturbesitz, Berlin, HA I Rep. 169 D, Abt. XI, A, no. 1, adh. 2, f. 11–14.

60 See Staatliche Museen zu Berlin, Zentralarchiv, I/NG 468, f. 742 and 767f.; I/NG 469, f. 8, 48f. and 125; Kratz-Kessemeier 2008, pp. 500–508, 677f., 686, 692 and 700–702; *Ausstellung der Novembergruppe in den Räumen der Berliner Secession in Berlin*, ref. in note 57, pp. 6–8; exhib. cat. Galerie Bodo Niemann 1993, pp. 15 and 35; ref. in note 2, p. 22.

61 See the letter from the Kultusministerium to Ludwig Justi, 22 June 1926, Staatliche Museen zu Berlin, Zentralarchiv, I/NG 469, f. 125.

62 See Staatliche Museen zu Berlin, Zentralarchiv, I/NG 469, f. 8, 48f., 125, 382f., 454, 466 and 509; I/NG 470, f. 429, 438, 440 and 465f.; Kratz-Kessemeier 2008, pp. 508–516, 679, 686 and 691; *Grosse Berliner Kunstausstellung 1927. Veranstaltet vom Kartell der Vereinigten Verbände Bildender Künstler Berlins e. V. im Landesausstellungsgebäude* (exhib. cat., 7 May–30 September 1927), Berlin 1927 (Veröffentlichungen des Kunstarchivs; no. 41–42), pp. 15, 18, 43, 59 and 97; Grohmann 1928, ref. in note 2, p. 58.

63 See Staatliche Museen zu Berlin, Zentralarchiv, I/NG 470, f. 670f., 690f., 696, 701 and 704f.; I/NG 471, f. 26; Kratz-Kessemeier 2008, pp. 673, 678 and 692. The work *Bavarian Landscape* [*Bayerische Landschaft*] by Ines Wetzel was gifted to the state.

64 See letter from the Nationalgalerie to Wetzel, 4 November 1925, in: Staatliche Museen zu Berlin, Zentralarchiv, I/NG 928.

65 See Kratz-Kessemeier 2008, pp. 511–515, 671f., 675, 677–681, 685, 691f., 696, 698 and 700. The ministry furthermore awarded prizes to August Wilhelm Dressler, Ernst Fritsch, Herbert Garbe, Walter Kampmann and Rudolf Schlichter and grants to Arthur Segal and Ewald Mataré; see ibid, pp. 662, 708, 710f. and 714; Staatliche Museen zu Berlin, Zentralarchiv, I/NG 525.

66 See Kratz-Kessemeier 2011, pp. 36–39.

67 See *Grosse Berliner Kunstausstellung 1927*, ref. in note 62, p. 9; letter from the ministry to the *Bund der Freien*, 21 November 1926, Archiv der Akademie der Künste, Berlin, PrAdK, 2.1/010, f. 188–190.

68 *Grosse Berliner Kunstausstellung 1927*, ref. in note 62, p. 8.

69 At the show in the *Glaspalast* in 1927 the artists' names were given without indicating their membership. In 1928 the simple abbreviation "NG" was added, see *Grosse Berliner Kunstausstellung 1927,* ref. in note 62; *Grosse Berliner Kunstausstellung 1928. Veranstaltet vom Kartell der Vereinigten Verbände bildender Künstler Berlins e. V. im Landesausstellungsgebäude* (exhib. cat., 9 May–end of July 1928), Berlin 1928.

70 See Kratz-Kessemeier 2008, pp. 536–546.

71 Ref. in note 2, p. 1.

72 See, for example, the advertisement for commissions to be awarded to artists in: *Grosse Berliner Kunstausstellung 1927,* ref. in note 62, p. 39.

73 See the artists' resolution of 20 January 1930 and the letter from the *Kartell der Künstlerverbände* to the Preußische Bau- und Finanzdirektion, 14 March 1930, Geheimes Staatsarchiv Preußischer Kulturbesitz, Berlin, HA I Rep. 151, no. 1047, f. 6 and 19f.

74 Letter from Adolf Grimme to the Prussian Ministry of Finance, 15 August 1930, Geheimes Staatsarchiv Preußischer Kulturbesitz, Berlin, HA I Rep. 151, no. 1047, f. 24f.; see Kratz-Kessemeier 2008, pp. 520f., 546–549 and 606.

75 See Kratz-Kessemeier 2008, pp. 521 and 580–582. The ministry made several purchases from Pechstein, who was no longer active in the association after 1919, see ibid., pp. 511–513 and 695; on Pechstein's special role see Kliemann 1969, pp. 15f.; Saehrendt 2005, pp. 20– 22; Grosskopf 2015, p. 112.

76 See Belling 1955, p. 170; Kratz-Kessemeier 2008, pp. 358–363.

77 See Kratz-Kessemeier 2008, pp. 328f. There were plans to include Grosz, Dix, Feininger, Mies van der Rohe, Mendelsohn and Max Taut in new appointments at the United State Schools; see exhib. cat. Akademie der Künste 1996, pp. 439f.

78 On the painting featuring Klee see exhib. cat. Akademie der Künste 1996, pp. 434f.; *Das Kunstblatt*, vol. 15, 1931, pp. 159 and 277.

79 Including the works by Adler, Baumeister, Dix, Dressler (*Engaged*), Drexel, Dungert, Feininger, Fritsch (*Tiergarten*), Kandinsky, Metzinger, Rudolf Möller, Ringelnatz, Schlemmer, Segal and Völker, as well as Wetzel's gift and Belling's *Triad*; see database on works confiscated during the "Degenerate Art" campaign, Forschungsstelle "Entartete Kunst", Freie Universität Berlin, EK catalogue nos. 12100, 12102, 12103, 12109, 12119, 12120, 12307, 14137, 14144, 15029, 15804, 16056, 16067, 16073, 16176, 16201 and 16228.

80 Including the purchases of Baumeister, Belling, Drexel, Kandinsky, Metzinger, Schlemmer and Völker; see Barron 1992, pp. 22, 56, 60, 68, 70, 76, 106, 111, 202, 210f., 231, 264, 268, 300, 339 and 354; exhib. cat. Galerie Bodo Niemann 1993, p. 15.

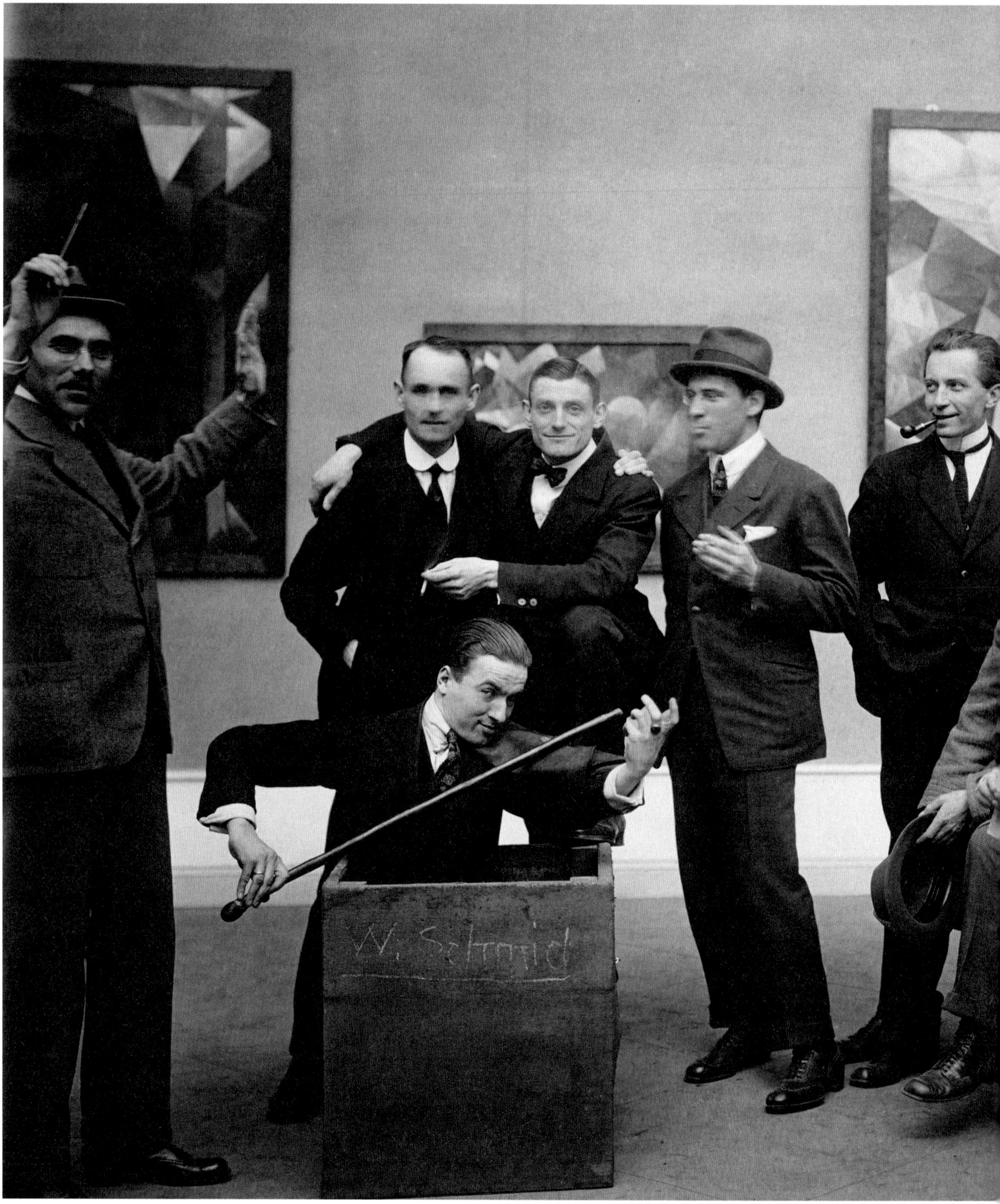
W. Schmid

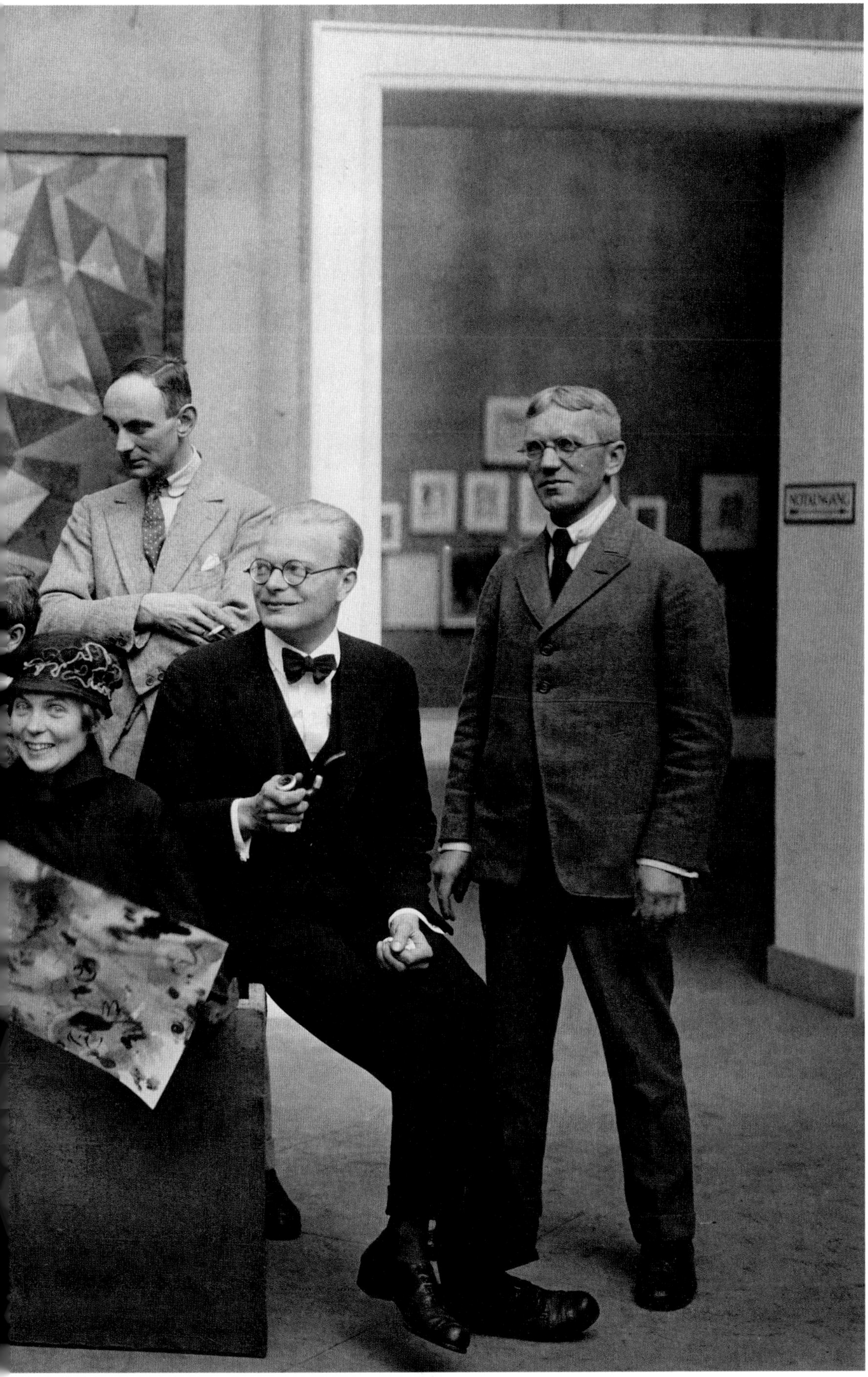

NG
1918–1922

Art Exhibition Berlin 1920, Novembergruppe members in a room in their section
From left to right (standing) César Klein, unknown, Rudolf Belling, Heinrich Richter-Berlin, unknown, Heinz Fuchs, Moriz Melzer, seated Wilhelm Schmid, unknown, Emy Roeder, Herbert Garbe
Stiftung Stadtmuseum, Berlin

JANINA NENTWIG

"LIBERATING ENERGIES OF THE NEW ART"

The Early Novembergruppe Years from 1918 to 1920

Amid the revolutionary turmoil of 1918–19 painters, sculptors and architects in Berlin founded the Novembergruppe as an association of "radical fine artists".[1] HEINRICH RICHTER-BERLIN, a member from the outset, recalls those turbulent times: "When the revolution was a few days old, a lot of people always gathered on Potsdamer Platz at midday to catch up with the latest news. Crossing the square, I bumped into Max Pechstein. He had a plan. He thought there should be a new start. I was to round up my crowd (Tappert, Klein, Melzer) and he would bring *Brücke*. He already had a name: *Novembergruppe*! At that moment a truck drove past piled with rifles and the sailors sitting on top were yelling: 'Citizens, comrades, the Potsdam garrison is marching here to break up the revolution. Take arms, resist!' The sculptor Leschnitzer and the printmaker Leni had been standing ten metres away from us. When I looked round, they were just vanishing into the underground station. Max Pechstein thought it would be best to do the same. I shared his opinion entirely. That was the moment the Novembergruppe was born!"[2]

No matter how much truth there is in this anecdote, it epitomizes the future approach of the creatives who were about to organize in the Novembergruppe.[3] Even if the name of the association, redolent of the 'November Revolution', suggests otherwise, its members did not fight shoulder to shoulder with soldiers and workers for the dawn of a new era, but sought by artistic means to engage with the historic transformation and encourage its progress. They saw their place in the studio rather than on the street. Like countless artists of their day, the founders of the Novembergruppe firmly believed, in the wake of the collapse of the German monarchy, that they could contribute to building the young republic. Many of them, including the above-mentioned HEINRICH RICHTER-BERLIN, MAX PECHSTEIN, GEORG TAPPERT, MORIZ MELZER, CÉSAR KLEIN and GEORG LESCHNITZER, already knew each other from the New Secession, the Expressionist association of artists which had disbanded during the First World War. The group around TAPPERT, who like PECHSTEIN was a driving force behind the formation of the Novembergruppe,[4] had been deeply politicized by the war and were working on the undogmatic left-wing magazine *Die Aktion* set up by the professing pacifist Franz Pfempfert.[5]

Relations between most avant-garde artists and the working class were, however, quite cool. TAPPERT, for example, expressed his outrage in a letter to Pfempfert after attending a revolutionary meeting: "The proletarian misguidedly believes that all new art is a product of bourgeois society and now expects like a dictator to prescribe to the artist the paths along which the new (now naturally socialist) art shall proceed. [...] We want to shape what is to come with our own form of expression, not have it imposed on us by some party bigwig or the masses. [...] We need no dogma machine, but vivid sensibility, a new humanity."[6]

The last sentence in particular heralds the philosophy which the Novembergruppe was to uphold throughout its existence: art should not be subjugated to the purposes and constraints of party politics or to other people's wishes and conceits. The freedom of the artistic imagination was the foundation of freedom for all — and the artists had a quite elitist awareness of the messianic role this conferred on them. It was not for artists to adjust to the new social relations, but for people to pursue 'renewal' with the aid of art. These ideas had above all evolved in the entourage of Expressionism before the First World War, nourished by a variety of sources: nineteenth-century philosophers, above all Friedrich Nietzsche and Arthur Schopenhauer, the anti-rational vitalism of Henri Bergson, even gnostic and mystic teachings such as theosophy and anthroposophy. The common ground for these diverse schools of thought was the idea that art could save modern humanity from the alienation caused by a world perceived as materialistic. As a substitute for religion, it was an effective means of overcoming the dualistic divide between subject and object, body and soul, and achieving a new oneness between individual, world and cosmos. The aim was to capture internal and external reality through the emotions; and the neutralization of reason, which in the eyes of many artists had unleashed the cruel mechanisms of war, bore the potential to penetrate transcendental truths. Art was thus a tool for achieving all-embracing insight and the working class should have as much access to it as anyone else.[7]

Although TAPPERT refers in his letter of 20 November 1918 to the need to facilitate this goal by creating a resolute association of artists, he does not mention any specific plan for doing so. The Novembergruppe must have formed within the next few days, for on 28 November 1918 the painter CURT STOERMER in Worpswede declared his membership of the new association.[8] Its first offices were at no. 113, Potsdamer Strasse in Villa II.[9] The address was familiar to the art community because it belonged to the famous Galerie Gurlitt, and even if the group's letterhead makes no mention of the former royal art dealer, artists would have been acutely aware of the tenancy arrangement.[10] The founding members CÉSAR KLEIN, RUDOLF BELLING and MAX PECHSTEIN had close ties with the gallery, which had been promoting Expressionism for a long time. The three artists had been working since 1917 on the interior decoration for Villa I, recently acquired on the same site by Wolfgang Gurlitt,[11] and so the address was no doubt also a practical choice. Far away in his artists' colony in northern Germany, STOERMER expressed some alarm at this proximity to the mercantile class, urging the artists in Berlin: "Socialism must be your absolute bedrock, [...]. Be not Expressionists of art, but Expressionists of humanity. Cubists, down with the capitalist art form. Into the human surge, shatter into shards, abandon yourselves".[12] When this steadfast class warrior[13] composed these lines, he probably did not realize that on that same day, 28 November 1918, Kaiser Wilhelm II in Dutch exile was signing his deed of abdication, laying the monarchy in Germany to rest. In the newly emerging political vacuum, the reform of society with the aid of art seemed possible and necessary. But how was the transformation to take place? While TAPPERT had no desire to join hips with the people, STOERMER championed the opposite view, and so tensions, arguments and discord within the Novembergruppe were bound to come about. In the very first recorded meeting (fig. 01) on 3 December 1918, it was noted that everyone in attendance regarded the association as necessary, but there was no agreement about its purpose and objectives.[14] Even the term 'socialism', which the artists used as frequently and randomly as the word 'radical', provided no orientation, as it was applied generically to all left-wing demands for breaking with the old system. The spectrum ranged from moderate social democrats in the Majority SPD to communists. In the winter of 1918–19, which political ideas would prevail was a completely open question.[15]

"Revolutionaries of the mind"

It appeared all the more urgent to emphasize the important role of art in the revolution and to claim its central place in the future social order. The first known official statement by the Novembergruppe, a circular dated 13 December 1918, bore the traces of recent political events: "The future of art and the gravity of the present hour force us revolutionaries of the mind (Expressionists, Cubists, Futurists) to unite and close ranks. We therefore urge all fine artists who have broken out of the old forms of art to declare membership of the 'Novembergruppe'. The elaboration and implementation of a broadly defined programme, applied with our stewards in the various centres of art, will bring us the closest possible mingling of the people and art."[16]

What items this "broadly defined programme" would include and how this "closest possible mingling of the people and art" would be organized was explained a few days later. The policy guidelines circulated in early January 1919 (p. 227, fig. 03) do not call for broad social reforms but for an influence and role in public affairs of cultural relevance, notably the award of building contracts and exhibition space, the reform of art colleges and museums and any legislation for the arts. These professional demands were ultimately aimed at placing artistic activities on a more democratic footing and dismantling traditional privileges, such as those enjoyed by Prussia's venerable art academy — the *Preussische Akademie der Künste* — in curating official exhibitions in the Empire. One member, OTTO FREUNDLICH, felt that the Novembergruppe guidelines did not go far enough, as they encouraged a transition of the old structures rather than the creation of new organizational and social paradigms. He urged the association, not unlike STOERMER, to pursue the "renunciation of all capitalist, *arriviste* and power-hungry affectations". Artists had a mission, as "teachers of a new perspective on the world", to help build an international community of communist inspiration.[17]

Admittedly, the Novembergruppe was not alone, following the Kaiser's abdication, in placing an initial focus on the professional concerns of its members. Almost identical demands were formulated by the *Arbeitsrat für Kunst*, a "works council for art", likewise founded in November 1918, which had ties with the Novembergruppe via many dual memberships. While the Arbeitsrat constantly reiterated its calls and even presented its case to the Ministry of Culture,[18] the Novembergruppe only published its political desiderata once and did not follow the matter up. Ultimately the efforts of the Arbeitsrat also came to nothing. The reform of cultural life in the young republic remained firmly in the hands of civil servants and politicians.[19]

Nevertheless, those who took charge after the monarchy had been toppled did seek contact with the avant-garde and sought to infuse social change with a new aesthetic. The *Werbedienst der deutschen sozialistischen Republik,* established to carry out an information and education campaign in Germany's socialist republic, was answerable to the transition government, the Council of People's

Deputies, and it commissioned primarily Expressionist artists to design posters, leaflets and brochures, printed in some cases by the millions and bearing the flaming torch logo.[20] Some members of the Novembergruppe likewise supplied designs for the *Werbedienst*, which was headed from January 1919 by the writer Paul Zech. Publications he approved include numerous appeals to the creative community, seeking their commitment to the new state. The best-known booklet is programmatically titled *To All Artists!* (cat. 06, p. 25) and contains some illustrations by members of the Novembergruppe, including a cover page by MAX PECHSTEIN. For this reason, the brochure has often been attributed to the Novembergruppe, although the flaming torch and the publication number on the bottom right of the cover clearly identify it as a *Werbedienst* product and the texts inside do not even mention the association. PECHSTEIN'S cover illustration epitomizes the way many artists saw themselves during that period. It depicts a muscular man with a naked torso grasping at a burning heart, his gaze and his right hand reaching for the sky. In this personification of the artist, PECHSTEIN combines a figure reminiscent of Hercules sturdily mastering future challenges with the Christian symbol of the sacred heart of Jesus, which in traditional iconography stands for Christ's burning devotion to humanity. The artist is stylized as a mighty redeemer of the masses, also evoked by PECHSTEIN in his article "What We Want".[21]

By working for the *Werbedienst* the participating artists were throwing in their lot with moderate left-wing forces who opposed the soviet-style republic—a model championed by, among others, the Communist Party around Rosa Luxemburg and Karl Liebknecht, for which leading members of the Arbeitsrat für Kunst like BRUNO TAUT and Adolf Behne had some sympathy.[22] Did MAX PECHSTEIN, HEINRICH RICHTER-BERLIN, CÉSAR KLEIN and HEINZ FUCHS believe that the "closest possible mingling" of their art and the broad masses stood a better chance in a parliamentary democracy? Certainly, their personal commitment on behalf of the *Werbedienst* should not be confused with a specific political alignment within the Novembergruppe as a whole. The group fiercely resisted monopolization by any kind of party politics,[23] even if their activities were political and were perceived as such—a paradox reflected, for example, in their first exhibitions in 1919 and 1920.

"Madhouse" and "Hall of Fun": the First Novembergruppe Exhibition

From the outset, exhibitions were the most important and effective medium for the Novembergruppe to implement its declared aim of bringing together art and society. The group's very first circular announced an ambitious project: "Renewed contact with like minds of the world is our duty. For many years creative instinct has united us as brothers. As a first sign of our convergence we plan an exhibition together. It is to be shown in all the major cities in Germany and later Europe."[24] Just over a month after the truce was signed in Compiègne, these vague plans must have come across to contemporaries as utopian. At negotiating tables and on the streets, all the talk was about reparations and who was to blame for the war, and these "revolutionaries of the mind"[25] were citing not only Expressionism, regarded as a German phenomenon, but also, quite explicitly, Cubism and Futurism as crown witnesses to appear at the proposed exhibition. These styles were intimately associated with France and Italy, which had fought on the other side of the trenches to Germany and its allies. Europe was broken, and the Novembergruppe was countering this with its vision of a peaceful, cross-border

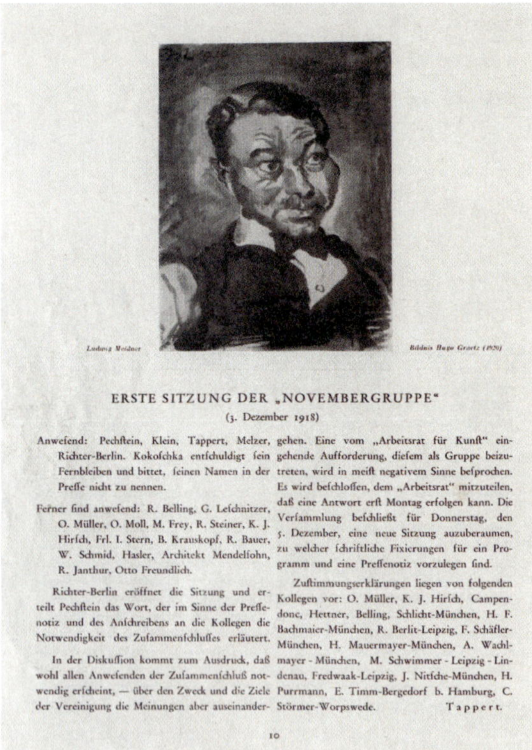

Ludwig Meidner — Bildnis Hugo Graetz (1920)

ERSTE SITZUNG DER „NOVEMBERGRUPPE“

(3. Dezember 1918)

Anweſend: Pechſtein, Klein, Tappert, Melzer, Richter-Berlin. Kokoſchka entſchuldigt ſein Fernbleiben und bittet, ſeinen Namen in der Preſſe nicht zu nennen.

Ferner ſind anweſend: R. Belling, G. Leſchnitzer, O. Müller, O. Moll, M. Frey, R. Steiner, K. J. Hirſch, Frl. I. Stern, B. Krauskopf, R. Bauer, W. Schmid, Hasler, Architekt Mendelſohn, R. Janthur, Otto Freundlich.

Richter-Berlin eröffnet die Sitzung und erteilt Pechſtein das Wort, der im Sinne der Preſſenotiz und des Anſchreibens an die Kollegen die Notwendigkeit des Zuſammenſchluſſes erläutert.

In der Diskuſſion kommt zum Ausdruck, daß wohl allen Anweſenden der Zuſammenſchluß notwendig erſcheint, — über den Zweck und die Ziele der Vereinigung die Meinungen aber auseinandergehen. Eine vom „Arbeitsrat für Kunſt“ eingehende Aufforderung, dieſem als Gruppe beizutreten, wird in meiſt negativem Sinne beſprochen. Es wird beſchloſſen, dem „Arbeitsrat“ mitzuteilen, daß eine Antwort erſt Montag erfolgen kann. Die Verſammlung beſchließt für Donnerstag, den 5. Dezember, eine neue Sitzung auszuberaumen, zu welcher ſchriftliche Fixierungen für ein Programm und eine Preſſenotiz vorzulegen ſind.

Zuſtimmungserklärungen liegen von folgenden Kollegen vor: O. Müller, K. J. Hirſch, Campendonc, Hettner, Belling, Schlicht-München, H. F. Bachmaier-München, R. Berlit-Leipzig, F. Schäfler-München, H. Mauermayer-München, A. Wachlmayer-München, M. Schwimmer-Leipzig-Lindenau, Fredwaak-Leipzig, J. Nitſche-München, H. Purrmann, E. Timm-Bergedorf b. Hamburg, C. Störmer-Worpswede.

Tappert.

10

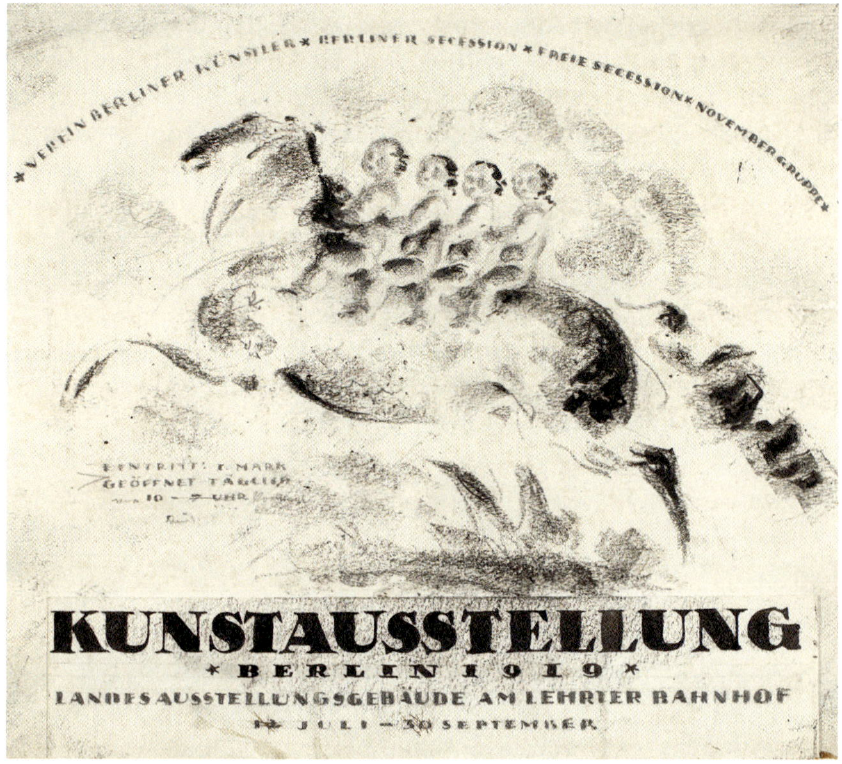

01 Minutes of the first meeting of the Novembergruppe on 3 December 1918, reprinted in *Ten Years of the Novembergruppe*, 1928
The illustration is a portrait (now lost) by Ludwig Meidner of the art dealer Hugo Graetz, who was secretary to the association from 1925.

02 PAUL SCHEURICH
Poster for the Art Exhibition Berlin 1919
Stiftung Stadtmuseum, Berlin

community of artists and reviving the international thrust of the avant-garde,[26] already visualized before the war in a stylized amalgam of these movements at the gallery Der Sturm. The future of art and of a new society lay in overcoming "backwardness and reaction", which the Novemberists sought to fight "boldly and unreservedly", as their draft manifesto made clear: "We regard it as our particular duty to collect all valuable gifts in the artistic field and make them available for the public benefit of all. We are neither a party nor a class of our own, but people, people who tirelessly perform hard work in the places allocated them by nature, which like any other work, if it is to benefit the nation as a whole, must meet the general public interest and requires the appreciation and acknowledgement of the greater community."[27]

For the Novembergruppe, the preferred vehicle for acquiring this acknowledgement was an exhibition, even if the European dimension of the venture did not initially seem feasible. In *Werkstatt der Kunst*, a bulletin for fine artists, the group announced in April 1919 that in the coming summer it intended to show "a selection of work by radical painters, sculptors and printmakers in Berlin and artists' associations in Germany with similar principles".[28] The short news item did not mention a venue for this exhibition in Berlin, but the group was still thinking in big terms. Apart from the latest contemporary art, there would be a retrospective section to indicate how modern art was evolving and even space for African and Oceanic artefacts. These would not be arranged according to "ethnographic aspects" but "for the first time to artistic factors"[29] — an incredibly modern-day approach, even from today's perspective.

The first public display by the "radical fine artists" was unable to keep this pledge, although it did attract a lot of publicity. It was incorporated into the annual regional art show, the Art Exhibition Berlin 1919, which was held at the exhibition hall near Lehrter Bahnhof and was intended to replace the traditional *Grosse Berliner Kunstausstellung*. Inspired by the *Salon de Paris* as a place where art could be both exhibited and sold, the Great Berlin Art Exhibition took over the functions of the former academy shows. For many decades it had represented official taste and state art policy, showcasing the kind of works that enjoyed public patronage. Under the Kaiser, the event had been managed by the *Preussische Akademie der Künste* and the conservative artists' association, the *Verein Berliner Künstler*. Under the rigorous eye of the jury, modern art was largely excluded. The first post-war event was to light a beacon for democratic renewal. The academy was no longer involved, and the Secession, the Freie Secession and the Novembergruppe exhibited alongside the old association.[30] The two Secessions had already taken part in the Great Berlin Art Exhibition in 1917 and 1918, when it was relocated to Düsseldorf due to the war and, at a safe distance from the capital, opened its doors to the avant-garde. The only complete newcomer in 1919, "at the behest of the new Government"[31], was the Novembergruppe, which attracted particular attention as a flagship of the desire for reform and the new dawn in politics. The design for the exhibition poster and catalogue cover (fig. 02), however, is not strikingly innovative: the four participating associations are personified by four naked, innocent children, lined up in cosy concord on the back of a 'high' horse symbolizing the state show, an anodyne metaphor intended to illustrate the change in exhibition content and structure.

The Novembergruppe had solid, by all means pragmatic reasons for taking part in this annual state-backed event (which was to revert to the name Great Berlin Art Exhibition from 1921). For one thing, it ensured maximum public visibility, because unlike shows at the usual avant-garde galleries it attracted not only connoisseurs, but a broad section of the population — hundreds of thousands, it would seem, at its peak.[32] Regularly opened by the President of the Reich, the "GroBeKa" was given coverage not only in the art journals, but also in the national daily newspapers. For another, the works on display were available for sale: for younger artists, many of whom had not yet settled into a relationship with a gallery, this was of existential importance and made participating an attractive proposition.

Each association was responsible for the rooms it had been allocated, without a jury exerting any influence. The *Verein Berliner Künstler* exhibited on one side of the pavilion and the modern associations on the other. The exhibition committee for the Novembergruppe included RUDOLF BELLING, BERNHARD HASLER, OSWALD HERZOG, CÉSAR KLEIN, LUDWIG MEIDNER, MORIZ MELZER, MAX PECHSTEIN, HEINRICH RICHTER-BERLIN and GEORG TAPPERT.[33] The group presented over 170 works by nearly 80 artists — impressive statistics for an association that was not yet a year old.[34] Groups of artists from all over Germany answered the call from the Novembergruppe to join as local branches[35] and take part in the 1919 edition, including the Karlsruhe group Rih and the Stuttgart group Üecht.[36] The fact that the Novembergruppe was open to so many contributors can be interpreted in the spirit of its demand for greater egalitarian involvement in public art. The aim of reviving international contacts was not achieved until the following years, but this first exhibition did include MARC CHAGALL with his large-format painting *Homage to Apollinaire* (fig. 03) and five watercolours.[37]

Compared with the other sections of the Art Exhibition Berlin 1919, it was the rooms of the Novembergruppe (fig. 04) that attracted the most attention, although of an entirely negative kind. The abundant press reports about the exhibition revolved in the main around the same criticisms: an accusation that the works were of mediocre quality paired with a decisive rejection of the formal idiom employed. Even the liberal *Berliner Tageblatt* saw the works on display as an un-

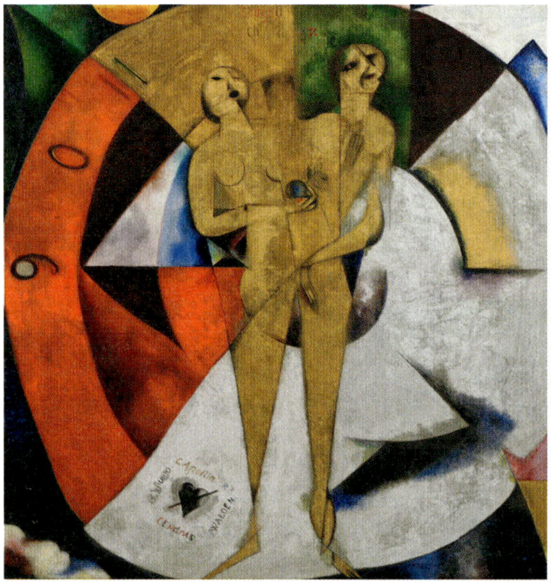

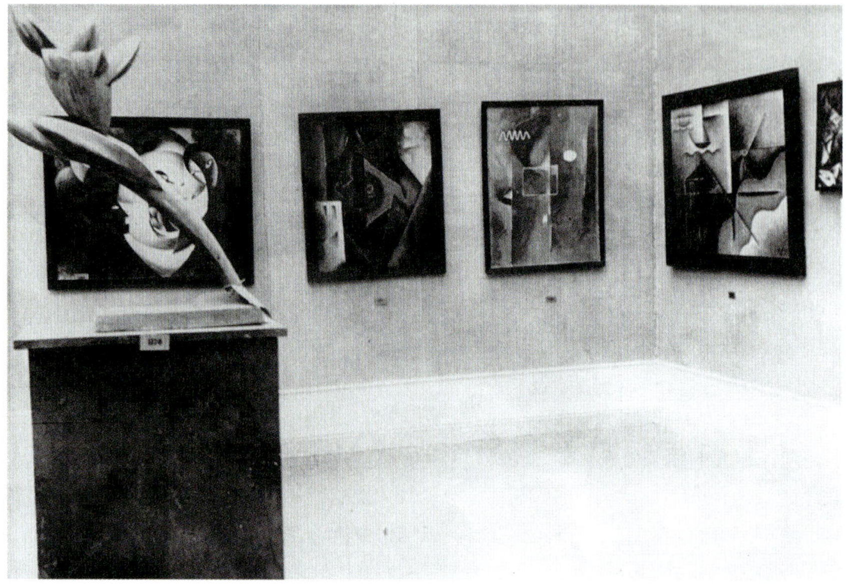

03 **MARC CHAGALL**
Homage to Apollinaire, 1913
Van Abbemuseum, Eindhoven
Art Exhibition Berlin 1919, Novembergruppe section, no. 1121

04 Art Exhibition Berlin 1919, a room in the Novembergruppe section
In the foreground Oswald Herzog's sculpture *Furioso*, at the back on the left Georg Scholz's painting *The Happy Family*

bridled reflex in response to the recent revolution and called the rooms a "madhouse",[38] while left-wing newspapers lamented a lack of reference to political issues and an "unbearable intellectualism".[39] This flags up a contradiction, and it is revealing about the difficulties contemporaries experienced with the Novembergruppe. The style of its members was perceived as revolutionary, and yet the religious or transcendental orientation of most of the works had little to do with revolutionary events at the time. As the works by MARC CHAGALL and GEORG TAPPERT (cat. 15, p. 57) on show in 1919 illustrate, many artists were more concerned about the genesis of a new breed of humanity with cosmic or heavenly connotations. Their pictorial content was defined not by social struggle and revolution, but by liberation and a romanticized journey into a new age. Such motifs had already been in evidence before the First World War and were now infused with new significance nourished by recent history. In the light of these works, some of the other artists in the exhibition, such as ERICH HECKEL[40] and PECHSTEIN (fig. 05), formerly with *Brücke*, and sculptors of the older generation like BERNHARD HOETGER look like "arch-reactionaries",[41] even though HOETGER painted his sculpture of the dancer Sent M'ahesa, made in 1917, in ultramarine blue.[42]

The great majority of reviewers and visitors failed to grasp the implicit message of the Novembergruppe section with all its stylistic heterogeneity, which was that change and transformation through art offered emancipation from all those social chains and a shared new dawn. The *Berliner Volkszeitung* wrote of the "revolutionaries": "The kaleidoscopic paintings hang by the dozen. The walls scream with colours, tapeworms squirm, there are pictures here which are nothing but a conglomeration of lines, colours and indecipherability."[43] Visitors reacted with disapproval and incomprehension, treating the section at best as a "hall of fun".[44] The sculptors' works, in particular, were regarded as the "height of oddity"[45] and elicited an amused echo that was also caught by the press cartoonists (fig. 06). Journalists vied with each other over wittily deprecatory descriptions, referring to the works by FREUNDLICH as "rolled up snakes"[46] or even "twined intestine"[47] (fig. 07). One reviewer observing OSWALD HERZOG'S contribution reported: "Teenage girls creasing with laughter almost squeal as they poke each other in front of sculptures imitating a mountain of whipped cream which are actually supposed to portray 'rapture'"[48] (cat. 34, p. 75). A glimpse into the section occupied by the *Verein*

Berliner Künstler, where the female nude *Opus 60* by the established sculptor Arthur Lewin-Funke proved a sensation (fig. 08), helps to place the radical impact of the Novembergruppe's abstract exhibits in perspective and to explain negative public reactions to such unfamiliar and alien art. As the weeks went by, however, the behaviour of some visitors became downright iconoclastic. Items were physically attacked on several occasions, prompting LESCHNITZER to withdraw his sculptures from the show altogether. Newspapers even reported visitors attacking each other and damaging artworks in the process.[49] *BZ am Mittag* pinned the blame on a group of right-wing extremists, the Anti-Bolshevist League. An "emissary of this peculiar association" was regularly whipping up sentiment against the art of the Novembergruppe, recounted the high-circulation daily: "As soon as a fair number of listeners have gathered around him, he launches into a propaganda speech: They might be laughing now, but essentially such abominations and frivolities are a dreadfully serious problem. This is the 'art' that debases and dishonours our fatherland. The dissolute spirit that speaks from this art must be fought in every field. The nihilism that is sabotaging values once firmly held in art resulted in public life in the overthrow... In short, this is propaganda not only for Wilhelminian art and a Wilhelminian spirit, but also for a Wilhelminian regime."[50]

Paradoxically, after the attacks on Novembergruppe exhibits people rushed to defend the group recently subjected to such hefty criticism. The destruction of art resulted not from sound judgement but from poor education, commented Oskar Bie in the *Münchner Zeitung*. In his eyes, however, the reaction was hardly surprising, because up until now the avant-garde could only be seen in the galleries that promoted it, such as Kunstkabinett I. B. Neumann or Der Sturm. "But the people do not go to these places, only connoisseurs and buyers go there. A small cluster of collectors are recruited here, while the people are left out in the cold, wander through exhibitions in bewilderment, grow weary, become bored—where is the great teacher and leader who can bridge this abyss, join these cultures?"[51]

The hope of winning a mass audience over to the latest developments in art and converting them into 'new' men and women ended for the time being in bitter disappointment, but the Novembergruppe had evidently touched a nerve with its works. To mark its first anniversary, the group published a special issue of the journal *Menschen*, and Adolf Behne, one of the leading minds behind the Arbeitsrat für Kunst, penned the foreword. Shortly beforehand, the two associations had entered into "close cooperation"[52], although the Arbeitsrat advocated

05 MAX PECHSTEIN
Japanese Kimono (Purple Kimono), 1917, whereabouts unknown
Art Exhibition Berlin 1919, Novembergruppe section, no. 1230

06 CURT SCHULZ-STEGLITZ
Visitors to the Novembergruppe section at the Art Exhibition Berlin 1919 react to a fountain sculpture by Rudolf Belling
Press drawing in the newspaper *Volk und Zeit*, 1919

07 OTTO FREUNDLICH
Study of a Woman Reclining, c. 1917, whereabouts unknown
Art Exhibition Berlin 1919, Novembergruppe section, no. 1144

05
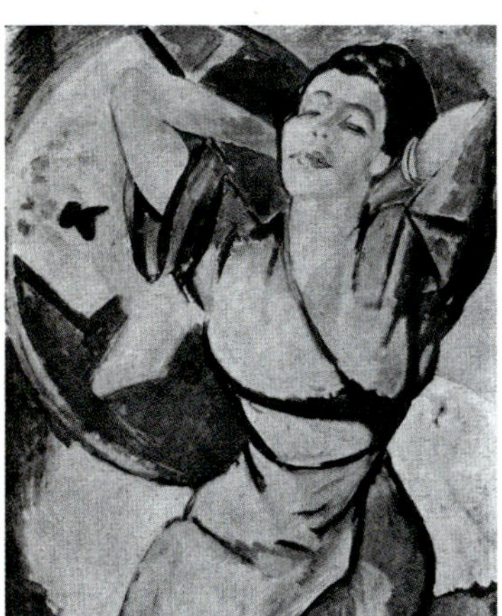

06
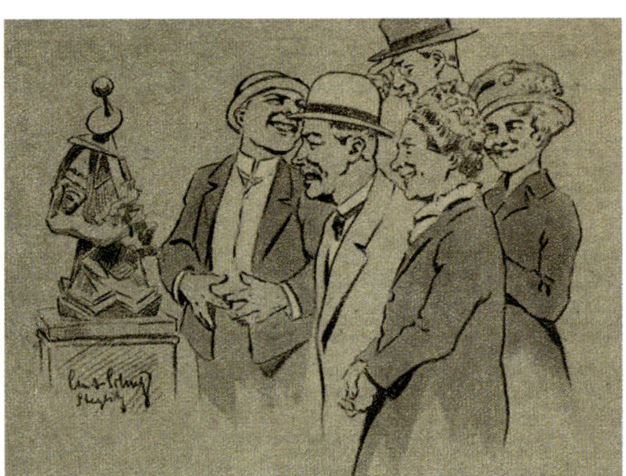

07
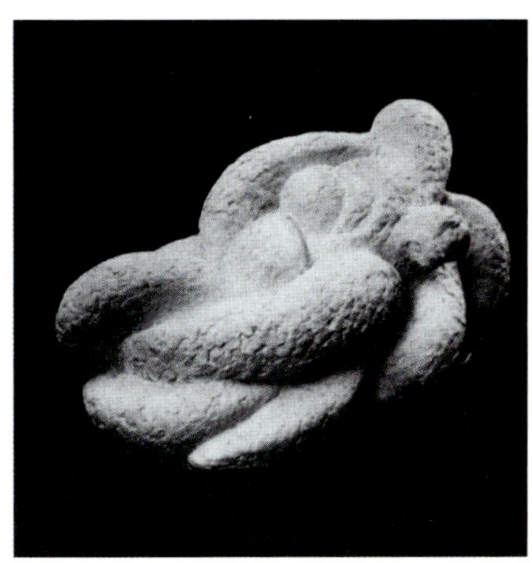

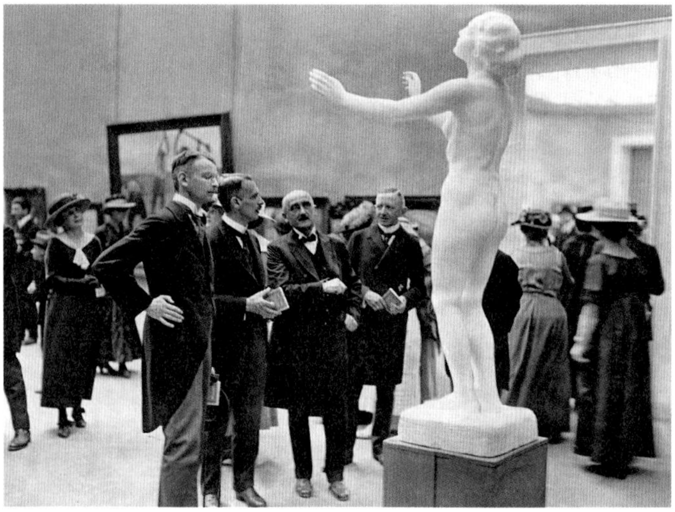

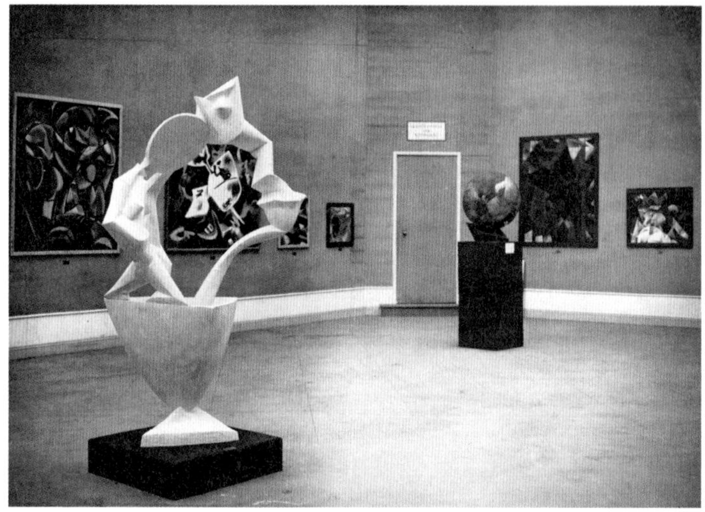

08 09

08 Art Exhibition Berlin 1919, a room in the *Verein Berliner Künstler* section, 1919, photo: Robert Sennecke
Exhibition director Max Schlichting (centre right) explains Arthur Lewin-Funcke's sculpture *Opus 60* to visitors.

09 Art Exhibition Berlin 1920, a room in the Novembergruppe section
In the foreground a *fountain sculpture*, in the background the *Monument to Fallen Soldiers from Berlin University* by Rudolf Belling

far more radical views than the Novembergruppe.[53] Hardly surprising, then, if the lines Behne composed for the Novembergruppe album appealed for a clearer commitment to socialism and revolution — and especially to the proletariat. It was vital, he argued, to prevent the avant-garde being taken over by commercial interests and a bourgeois understanding of art: "There are still art-loving citizens who find any correspondence between the two things — in short: Expressionism and world revolution — unappealing. [...] They can live with the liberating energies of the new art, but they certainly do not wish to see those interesting energies exert any impact beyond the picture frame. The effect should remain an aesthetic one confined to the *cognoscenti*."[54]

Behne wanted the Novembergruppe to pay more attention in future to injecting these "liberating energies" into society and to revolutionizing the exhibition format rather than working around its bourgeois nature. The first exhibition at the Glass Palace had not come up to expectations, but for Behne it had "demonstrated in no uncertain terms that the audience, which only here is a truly mass audience, takes an extremely strong interest in the new art. This first exhibition by the Novembergruppe has, through its material, already exerted a revolutionizing influence on great masses."[55]

"You should look at these things. You should make an effort."

The Novembergruppe only partially implemented Behne's recommendations. In January 1920 the Arbeitsrat für Kunst staged an exhibition on the premises of the proletarian youth association *Freie Jugend*, displaying drawings by children and workers together with works by Heinrich Zille, MARC CHAGALL and other fine artists.[56] The Novembergruppe, meanwhile, clung to the old exhibition formats and expanded its activities outside Berlin. In spring it set a travelling exhibition on the road through galleries and art clubs in southern and eastern Germany, and in autumn it exhibited watercolours in Rome.[57] Its principal project, despite the bad experience of the previous year, was to organize its own section again at the annual Art Exhibition Berlin, where the Secessions would not be in attendance due to a clash of timetables.[58] Consequently the *Verein Berliner Künstler* and the Novembergruppe were directly juxtaposed without the mediating presence of the Impressionist schools. The Novembergruppe section had grown to more than 400 exhibits. Prominent founding members such as LUDWIG MEIDNER and MAX

PECHSTEIN were no longer in evidence, but this time the association was able to include many more international guests. Apart from the French artists GEORGES BRAQUE, ALBERT GLEIZES and FERNAND LÉGER, who presumably submitted pre-war works, there were the Russians VLADIMIR GEORGIEVICH BEKHTEYEV, ALEXEI JAWLENSKY and VASSILY KANDINSKY, and the Italian Futurists NICOLA GALANTE and ENRICO PRAMPOLINI.[59] They supplied the genealogical trail for the "Cubo-Futuro-Expressionism"[60] which once again infused the exhibition. A particular show-stealer were the material images and collages by EDMUND DANIEL KINZINGER, OTTO DIX, JEFIM GOLYSCHEFF and CURT EHRHARDT, inspired by Dada.[61] BELLING'S spherical *Monument to the Fallen Soldiers of Berlin University* [*Denkmal für die Gefallenen der Berliner Universität*], in a gesture of absurd alienation, bore the names of Novembergruppe members and gave the opening day of the exhibition as their date of death. This was among the works that attracted the most attention and many shakes of the head[62] (fig. 09). Once again there were fisticuffs during the event,[63] and Paul Landau went so far as to call the exhibition a victory for Dadaism, which had now made its name as a style.[64] But there were also works by artists such as WILHELM SCHMID[65] and OTTO LANGE (figs. 10 and 11) which already revealed Veristic features soon to be associated with the *New Objectivity* [*Neue Sachlichkeit*]. Although these paintings were powerfully geared to a representational depiction of the world, the contrast with the works displayed by the *Verein Berliner Künstler* could hardly be more blatant, just as in the previous year: in the one section garish techniques with strident colours and shocking motifs centred on prostitution and madness, in the other idyllic ambiences like *The River Spree* [*Die Spree*] (fig. 12) by Max Fabian, a successful Berlin Impressionist.[66]

Like the year before, the Novembergruppe was perceived as a government protégé. In fact, the magazine *Kladderatsch* identified it as the new state art (fig. 13): beneath the heading "From the Art Exhibition Berlin 1920" the cartoonist Max Richter sketched a fictional oil painting attributed to the recent chancellor Hermann Müller, who had headed a transition government after Gustav Bauer's cabinet was replaced. Evidently taking his cue from works such as OTTO MÖLLER'S *Picture 8* (cat. 28, p. 69), on show in this section in 1920, Richter projected the chaotic dynamism of such compositions onto the situation in government. President Ebert's name can be made out in the middle of the drawing, and the policies are marked by confusions, befuddlement and an abundance of question-marks.[67]

In 1920, in response to the public perplexity of the previous year, the Novembergruppe produced its own exhibition guide. As a 'school of seeing', the Novembergruppe guides published in the years until 1924 adopted a style of language consciously aimed at a broad lay audience conceived as having a degree of education. This was a new approach to expressing the purpose and aims of the Novembergruppe in popularizing the avant-garde and disseminating its promise of salvation among the people. Although the introductions to these guides were very disparate, reflecting the personality of their various authors, and it is fair to wonder whether they achieved their function of warming the hearts of the masses for the art of the Novembergruppe,[68] at least the effort that was invested in these guides should be taken seriously. Unlike conventional museum guides of the period, such as those produced by Ludwig Justi for the Nationalgalerie,[69] the Novembergruppe kept the artworks mentioned in the texts anonymous. Thus, the individual artists step back behind the exhibited art as a whole, which Peter Leu, the author of the 1920 guide, claimed could function as a "blessing and enrichment of our life's spiritual resources".[70] Leu vehemently protested in the name of the Novembergruppe against attempts by third parties to impose control or influence. The artists in the association, wrote Leu, wished to "listen to the vibra-

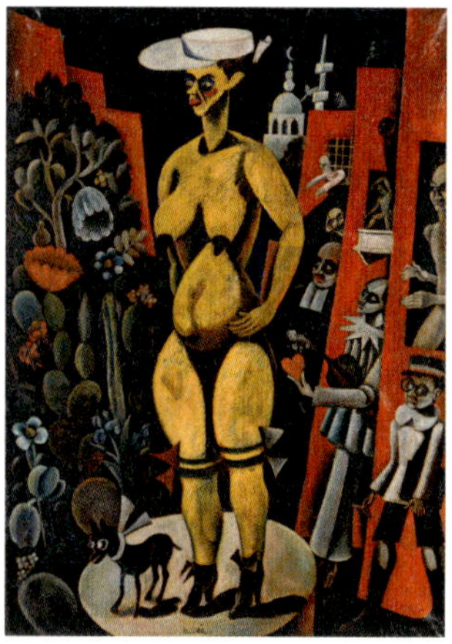

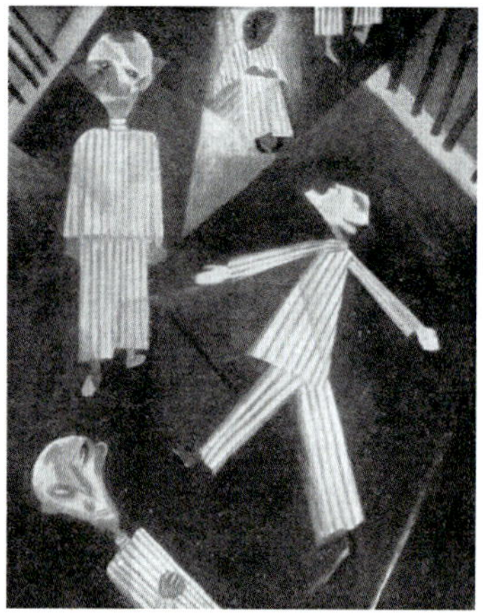

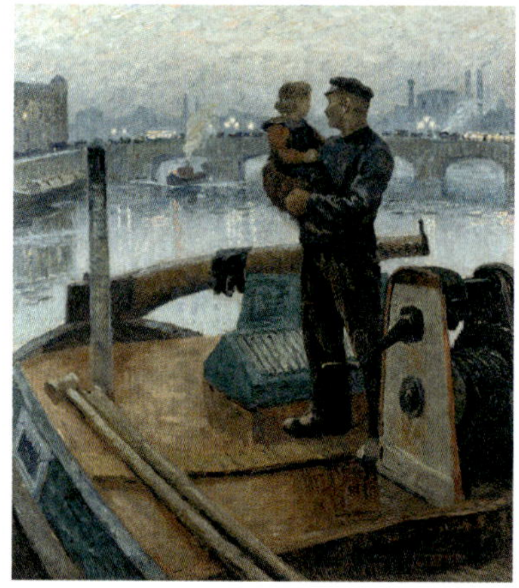

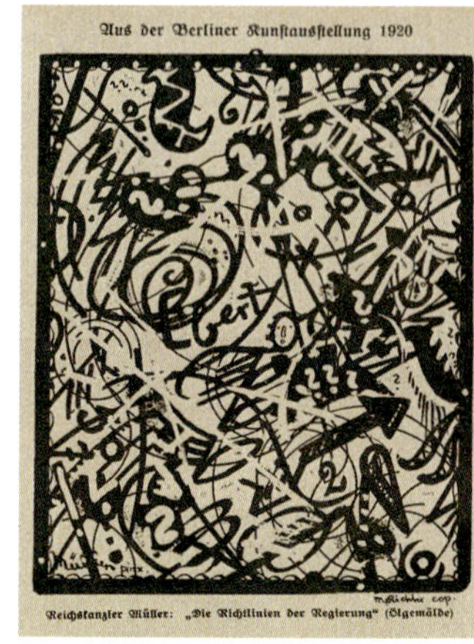

10 11 12 13

10 WILHELM SCHMID
Luna (Mona Luna), 1920
Argauer Kunsthaus, Aarau
Art Exhibition Berlin 1920, Novembergruppe section, no. 1443

11 OTTO LANGE
Lunatics in the Yard, c. 1920
whereabouts unknown
Art Exhibition Berlin 1920, Novembergruppe section, no. 1354

12 MAX FABIAN
The Spree I (or III), 1919
Stiftung Stadtmuseum, Berlin
Art Exhibition Berlin 1920, *Verein Berliner Künstler* section, no. 139 or 141

13 MAX RICHTER
From the Art Exhibition Berlin 1920
Caricature in the magazine *Kladderadatsch*

tions of their souls rather than the noise of the alleyways, search for the beauties and values in life within their own hearts, heed their inner stirrings and feelings rather than the turbulent screech of military and political manoeuvres".[71] That was why the group had not sworn allegiance to any particular 'movement', but might be said to represent the style of its age, which called for a new artistic and hence general world view: "And so this art means: subordination to the service of the greater community, *merging into the universal feeling of our time, service to life.* The form in which the artists wage the common cause is still unfamiliar to the crowd, aware that they are the instruments of creation, careless of applause, non-recognition, non-comprehension, in the sacred belief in their calling. They know that they will be victorious despite the battles."[72]

The blame for the rejection of the avant-garde, in Leu's opinion, lay with the art critics, who had failed to comply with their task of presenting and explaining, because the public had been miseducated into "preconceived, warped views": "Is it insolent to show you works conceived out of an honest will? Where have you learned to observe, to understand works of art, you who daily go about your bourgeois occupations?"[73] asks Leu, swaying between reproach and sympathy, of a readership addressed in the plural and thus, comparable to the community of artists, perceived as a collective, and he appeals to them with an admonishing imperative: "You should look at these things. You should make an effort."[74] The viewer should open up, benevolently and impartially, to the new and delight in being snatched away from their familiar everyday environment: "You will depart rich and happy!"[75] Although very few visitors left the exhibition with this uplifting sensation and the bulk of the reviews were just as scathing as the previous year, the feedback in the press had started to include some favourable tones, and this may in part have been due to reading Leu's text.[76] Even if the ice between the Novembergruppe and the general public had not yet been completely broken, the "liberating energies" of the new art were producing an initial impact by — for all the resistance — freeing the gaze for an aesthetic counter-world in which the artists were subverting the dominant cultural and artistic codes of their day. The group, officially entered in Berlin's register of associations in August,[77] saw out the year 1920 with a little show at the gallery Fraenkel & Co, almost unnoticed by the public compared to its earlier appearance in the halls at Lehrter Bahnhof.[78] The modest leaflet accompanying this presentation bore a confident motto for the coming years proclaiming that the association would continue along its chosen route as a committed facilitator and agent for the avant-garde in all its variations and genres: "The Novembergruppe is a coalition of radical artists / radical in discarding previous forms of expression / radical in applying new expressive techniques".[79]

1 Letter with policy guidelines and articles of association for the Novembergruppe, 18 December 1918/January 1919, Berlinische Galerie, Teilnachlass of Otto Möller, BG-OM 285.

2 Nierendorf 1974, p. 9.

3 See [Georg Tappert], provisional list of Novembergruppe members, [winter 1918–19], Berlin, Bauhaus-Archiv, Walter Gropius estate, GS 2/folder 9, 2.5 (p. 252 of this catalogue).

4 See Kliemann 1969, p. 11.

5 See Nentwig 2015a, pp. 172f.

6 Letter from Georg Tappert to Franz Pfempfert, 20 November 1918, quoted in Wietek 1980, pp. 48–50, here 49f. The event that triggered Tappert's reflections was probably a meeting in Spichernstrasse on 19 November 1918 where the workers flatly rejected the manifesto of the *Rat geistiger Arbeiter*. (See Weipert 2015, p. 325).

7 For an introduction to this theme see Beloubek-Hammer 2007, vol. 1, pp. 23–68.

8 Curt Stoermer to the Novembergruppe, 28 November 1918, quoted in *Zehn Jahre Novembergruppe*, special issue of *Kunst der Zeit. Zeitschrift für Kunst und Literatur*, vol. 3, 1928, nos. 1–3, p. 30. The first documented meeting of the association was held on 3 December 1918 (see ibid., p. 10). This date has often been wrongly equated in the literature with the date of foundation.

9 See the first letters, including the circular of 13 December 1918, in: ref. in note 8, p. 12; and the letter with policy guidelines and articles of association of 18 December 1918, ref. in note 1.

10 See *inter alia* the letter from Heinrich Campendonk to Walter Dexel, 16 December 1918, Museum Penzberg, Sammlung Campendonk, Letter 192.

11 Wolfgang Gurlitt had taken over Villa II along with the business from his father Fritz Gurlitt. On the modernization and conversion of the two Gurlitt villas, which were destroyed in the Second World War, see Gropp 2000, pp. 127–136. The Expressionist project was often reviewed and illustrated, see *inter alia* P.W. [Paul Westheim]: "Wohnung Wolfgang Gurlitt", in: *Das Kunstblatt*, vol. 5, 1921, pp. 373–378. Villa VI at Potsdamer Strasse 113 had belonged to the court painter and Academy chairman Anton von Werner, who died in 1915.

12 Ref. in note 8.

13 Stoermer played an active role in the soviet republic declared in Bremen, along with Heinrich Vogeler. See Hannemann 1993, p. 379, although this source gives the wrong year for his admission to the Novembergruppe, which Stoermer joined in 1918, not 1920.

14 Georg Tappert, "Erste Sitzung der 'Novembergruppe' (3. Dezember 1918)" [Minutes], in: ref. in note 8, p. 10.

15 See the essay by Burmeister and Nentwig in this catalogue, pp. 20f.

16 Circular dated 13 December 1918, quoted in: ref. in note 8, p. 12. The same wording also appeared as an "Appeal" in the advertising section of the December issue of *Die Schöne Rarität*, where Tappert was now a co-editor. See *Die Schöne Rarität*, vol. 2 (1918–19), p. 144.

17 Letter from Otto Freundlich to the Novembergruppe, 11 February 1919, quoted in: ref. in note 8, pp. 33f., here 34.

18 See Whyte 1981, p. 85; Kratz-Kessemeier 2008, pp. 29f. For further efforts to influence the Ministry see ibid. pp. 41f.

19 For a detailed account see Kratz-Kessemeier 2008.

20 For a history of the *Werbedienst* and its 81 known publications see Vogel 2008.

21 Max Pechstein, "Was wir wollen", in: Werbedienst der deutschen sozialistischen Republik (ed.), *An alle Künstler!* Berlin 1919, pp. 18–22.

22 See Whyte 1981, pp. 98f.

23 See *inter alia* Otto Möller: Draft response by the Novembergruppe to the open letter from the opposition in the magazine *Der Gegner*, Berlinische Galerie, Teilnachlass of Otto Möller, BG-OM 294.

24 Ref. in note 16.

25 Ibid.

26 See Wiese 1989.

27 Novembrist Manifesto (draft), quoted in: ref. in note 8, p. 16.

28 "Geplante Ausstellungen", in: *Werkstatt der Kunst*, vol. 18, 1918–19, no. 30, p. 204.

29 Ibid.

30 For more about how the Great Berlin Art Exhibition opened up to all styles, see the essay by Kratz-Kessemeier in this catalogue, pp. 30–33; also Kratz-Kessemeier 2008, pp. 146–163. On the art shown as the *Kunstausstellung Berlin* 1919 see Hoffmann 2015b.

31 *Kunstausstellung Berlin 1919 im Landesausstellungsgebäude* (exhib. cat., 24 July–30 September 1919), Berlin 1919, p. 3.

32 See Nungesser 1988, p. 90.

33 Ref. in note 31, p. 6. Meidner is listed in the first list of members of the Novembergruppe (p. 252 of this catalogue). In the catalogue to the *Kunstausstellung Berlin* of 1919 he is named as a member of the exhibition committee of the Novembergruppe and included with two works (nos. 1215 and 1216). However, the letter he sent Georg Tappert on 20 July 1919 suggests that he may not have actually showed them (see facsimile of the letter printed in the anniversary publication by the association, ref. in note 8, p. 29).

34 Not all the artists who showed in the Novembergruppe section were regular members. Membership was a fairly casual affair, and there was also a high rate of fluctuation. See the essay by Nentwig in this catalogue, pp. 250f.

35 Ref. in note 1.

36 Other local branches at the exhibition in 1919 were *Die Kugel* in Magdeburg, the *Expressionistische Arbeitsgemeinschaft* in Kiel, the *Hallische Künstlergruppe* in Halle and the Hamburg-based *Kräfte*. Officially this was the only year that local groups appeared with the

Novembergruppe. The lexicon *Dresslers Kunsthandbuch* of 1923 does, however, mention local groups continuing to exist as elements of the Novembergruppe structure (see the entry "Novembergruppe E.V.", in: Willy Oskar Dressler (ed.), *Dresslers Kunsthandbuch*, Berlin 1923, p. 206). Why links with these "local branches" in other German towns ultimately failed is as yet unclear. Probably the groups wanted to preserve their independence. Besides, many of them disbanded soon after foundation. See Kliemann 1969, p. 12; Ludwig 1993.

37 Ref. in note 31, nos. 1121 and 1122.

38 Fritz Stahl, "Kunstausstellung Berlin 1919", in: *Berliner Tageblatt*, 24 July 1919, no. 338.

39 Lisbeth Stern, "Große Ausstellung 1919", in: *Sozialistische Monatshefte*, 29 September 1919, pp. 937–939, here 939; see also Willy Pastor, "Kunstausstellung Berlin 1919", in: *Tägliche Rundschau*, 24 July 1919, newspaper cutting, Berlinische Galerie, Teilnachlass of Otto Möller, BG-OM 229.

40 Heckel showed four prints of landscapes and children with the Novembergruppe (ref. in note 31, nos. 1162–1165) and also exhibited in the *Freie Secession* section (no. 995 f.). After 1919 Heckel apparently never contacted the Novembergruppe again.

41 Ref. in note 38. See also Michael Charol, "Kunstausstellung Berlin 1919", in: *Der Kritiker*, vol. 1, 1919, no. 22, p. 6. Presumably this criticism partially explains why Pechstein parted company with the Novembergruppe soon afterwards. He only took part in its exhibitions at the Art Exhibition Berlin in 1919 (ref. in note 31, nos. 1229–1234).

42 *Kunstausstellung Berlin* 1919, no. 1175. The information about the colours is owed to Stahl, ref. in note 38.

43 Ernst Collin, "Die große Berliner Kunstausstellung im neuen Gewande", in: *Berliner Volkszeitung*, 25 July 1919, no. 339.

44 Hilde Drahn, "Kehraus in der Kunstausstellung!", in: *Volk und Zeit*, 28 September 1919, no. 14; see also E.W., "Steglitzer Künstler auf der Berliner Kunstausstellung", in: *Steglitzer Anzeiger*, 7 August 1919, newspaper cutting, Berlinische Galerie, Teilnachlass of Otto Möller, BG-OM 230.

45 Hans Schmidkunz, "Kunstausstellung Berlin 1919", in: *Die christliche Kunst*, vol. 16, 1919–20, pp. 37f. and 44–46 (supplement), here 46.

46 Ibid.

47 Ref. in note 43.

48 Drahn, ref. in note 44.

49 See *inter alia* Ludwig Reve, "Bilderstürmer im Glaspalast. Politische Agitation in der Kunstausstellung", in: *BZ am Mittag*, 5 September 1919, no. 201; *Berliner Lokalanzeiger*, 9 September 1919, unlabelled newspaper cutting, estate of César Klein.

50 Reve, ref. in note 49. Although the Anti-Bolshevist League immediately denied responsibility for what was happening in the Novembergruppe exhibition, *BZ am Mittag* had no doubts about the implausibility of this denial (see "Bilderstürmer im Glaspalast", in: *BZ am Mittag*, 6 September 1919).

51 Oskar Bie, "Kunst", in: *Münchner Zeitung*, 18 September 1919, newspaper cutting, Deutsches Kunstarchiv Nürnberg, estate of Georg Tappert, I, B-93 a; See also "Tätliche Kunstkritik", in: *Berliner Tageblatt*, 10 September 1919, no. 423.

52 Adolf Behne, [Introduction], in: *Menschen. Buchfolge Neuer Kunst*, special issue *Novembergruppe. Graphik und Plastik von Mitgliedern der Novembergruppe Berlin*, vol. 2, 1919, 14 (no. 81/86), pp. 1–2, here 2.

53 See Nentwig 2018.

54 Ref. in note 52, p. 1.

55 Ref. in note 52, p. 2.

56 See Akademie der Künste 1980, pp. 111f.

57 See the essay by Nentwig in this catalogue, p. 228.

58 See Kratz-Kessemeier 2008, 152. The *Freie Secession* put in one more appearance at the *Grosse Berliner Kunstausstellung* in 1921. The *Berliner Secession* returned from 1927.

59 *Kunstausstellung Berlin 1920 im Landesausstellungsgebäude* (exhib. cat., 21 May–September 1920), Berlin 1920, nos. 1094, 1109, 1159, 1170, 1245, 1262 and 1367.

60 Roters 1995, p. 77.

61 Ref. in note 59, nos. 1116–1117, 1133–1141, 1181 and 1263–1265. See the essay by Burmeister in this catalogue, p. 83.

62 See the descriptions in John Schikowski, "Die Berliner Kunstausstellung. 2. Die Jüngsten", in: *Vorwärts*, 10 June 1920; Anna Kappstein, "Wofür? Berliner Kunstbrief", in: *Schwäbischer Merkur*, 2 August 1920, newspaper cuttings, estate of César Klein.

63 Rz., "Glossen zur Berliner Kunstausstellung 1920", in: *Tilsiter* [handwritten addition] *Allgemeine Zeitung*, May 1920, newspaper cutting, Deutsches Kunstarchiv Nürnberg, estate of Georg Tappert, I, B-93 a.

64 Paul Landau, "Die Ausstellung der Novembergruppe. Vom Expressionismus zum Dadaismus", in: *Berliner Börsen-Zeitung*, 1 July 1920, no. 283.

65 The Swiss painter Wilhelm Schmid took part in at least 21 Novembergruppe exhibitions (See the table of all artists at all Novembergruppe exhibitions at www.berlinischegalerie.de). From September 2018 Potsdam Museum will be showing a comprehensive retrospective on this artist, accompanied by a catalogue.

66 On the life and work of Max Fabian see Bartmann 2000.

67 See also Gülker 2001, p. 207, who attributes the inspiration to pictures and woodcuts by Richter-Berlin.

68 See the essay by Andrea Gottdang in the proceedings of the symposium *Novembergruppe Berlin 1918–2018: Interdisciplinary Perspectives*, published by the Kurt-Weill-Gesellschaft in Dessau in autumn 2018.

69 For more about these guides see Steinkamp 2013, pp. 289f.

70 Peter Leu, *Führer durch die Abteilung der Novembergruppe. Kunstausstellung Berlin*. Berlin 1920, p. 7. Extracts from the text (without ellipses) are reprinted in Kliemann 1969, pp. 71f.

71 Leu, ref. in note 70, p. 8.

72 Ibid., p. 28.

73 Ibid., p. 29

74 Ibid.

75 Ibid., p. 31

76 See *inter alia* Paul Landau, "Kunstausstellung Berlin 1920", in: *Berliner Börsen-Zeitung*, 30 May 1920, no. 229.

77 See the entry on the *Novembergruppe* in *Dresslers Kunsthandbuch*, ref. in note 36.

78 This exhibition has hitherto been dated 1919 following Kliemann (1969, 26), although Matelowski (2017, 335f.) argues compellingly that this should be corrected to 1920.

79 *Erste Ausstellung der Novembergruppe. Gemälde, Plastiken. Bei Fraenkel & Co. (Josef Altmann), Buch- und Kunst-Antiquariat,* (leaflet for the exhibition, 4–30 November [1920]), Berlinische Galerie, Teilnachlass of Otto Möller, BG-OM 175, reproduced in parts in Kliemann 1969, p. 26, where it is wrongly dated 1919 (see Note 78).

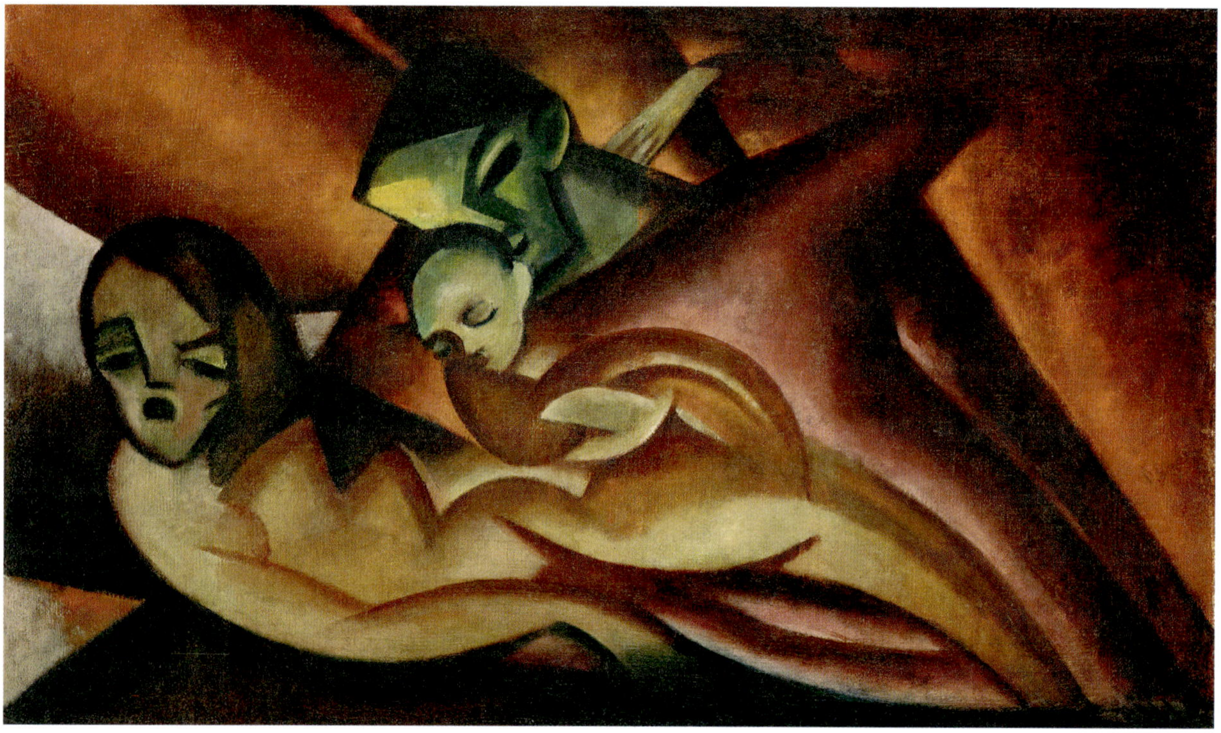

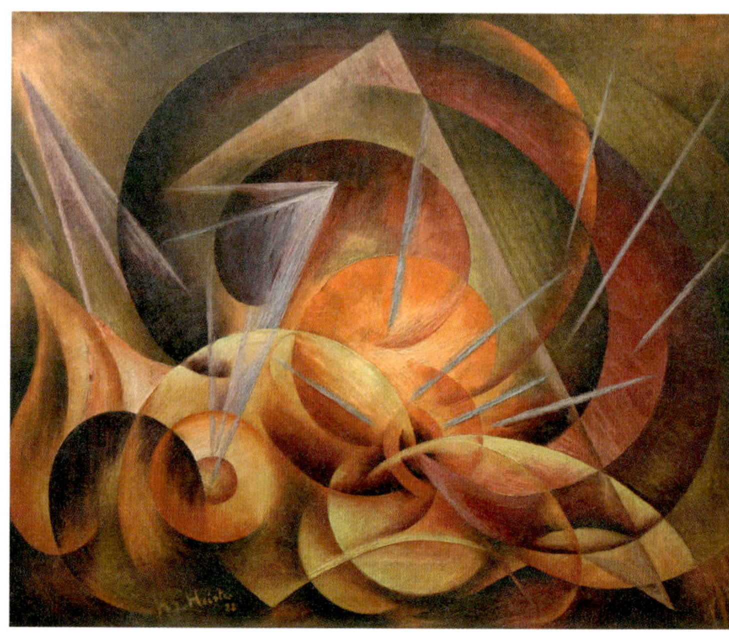

13
KARL VÖLKER
Birth, 1919

Oil on canvas, 77.5 × 129.5 cm, Kulturstiftung Sachsen-Anhalt, Kunstmuseum Moritzburg Halle (Saale)

Art Exhibition Berlin 1920, Novembergruppe section, no. 1491, repro. in the catalogue

14
HANS-SIEBERT VON HEISTER
The Peak, 1922

Oil on canvas, 53 × 63 cm
Loan from a private collection

Great Berlin Art Exhibition 1922, Novembergruppe section, no. 1274 (similar, now lost work of the same title)

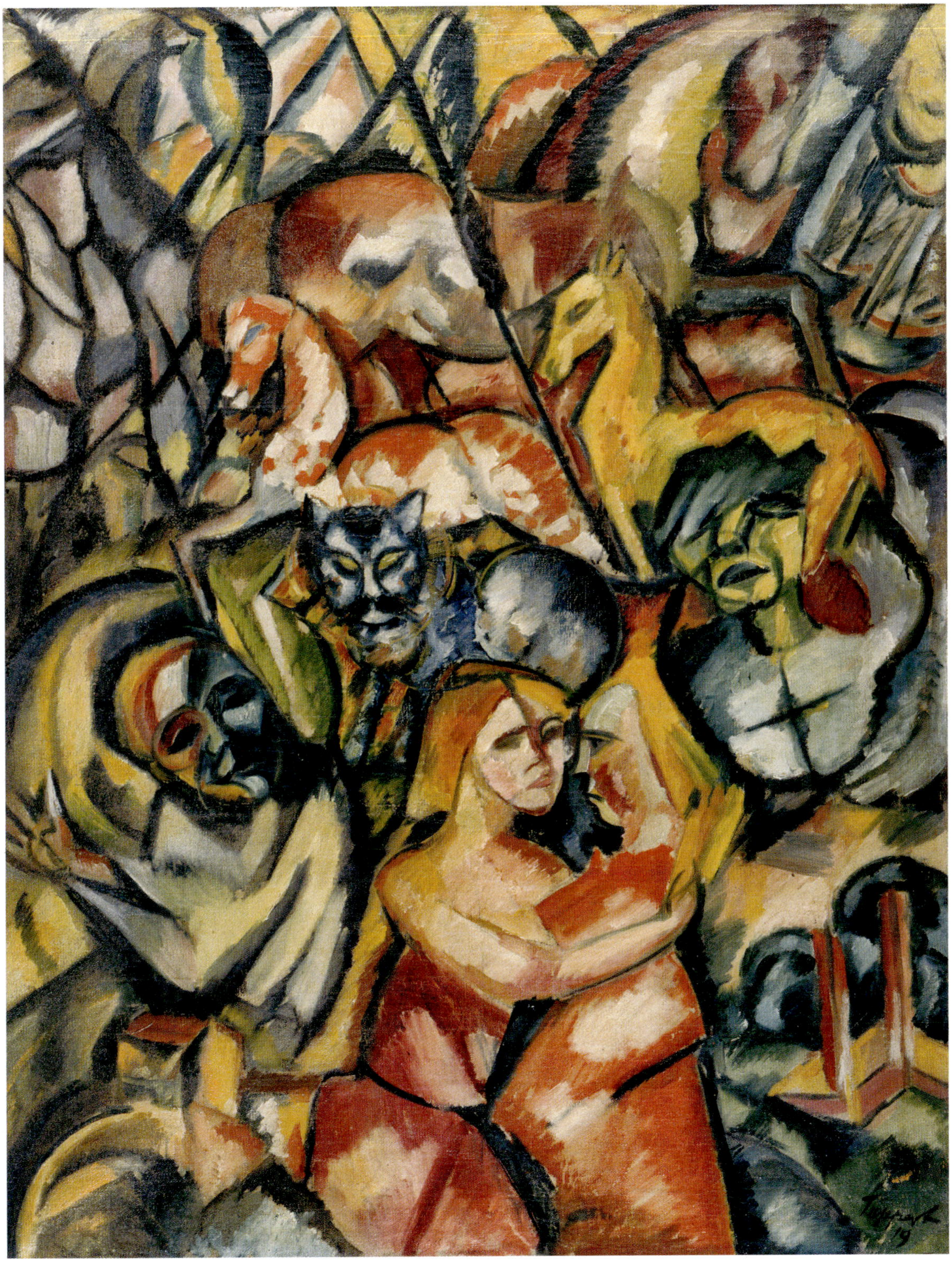

15

GEORG TAPPERT

Composition I, 1919

Oil on canvas, 124.5 × 94 cm
Germanisches Nationalmuseum, Nuremberg

Art Exhibition Berlin 1919, Novembergruppe section, no. 1269, repro. in *Zehn Jahre Novembergruppe* 1928, p. 49

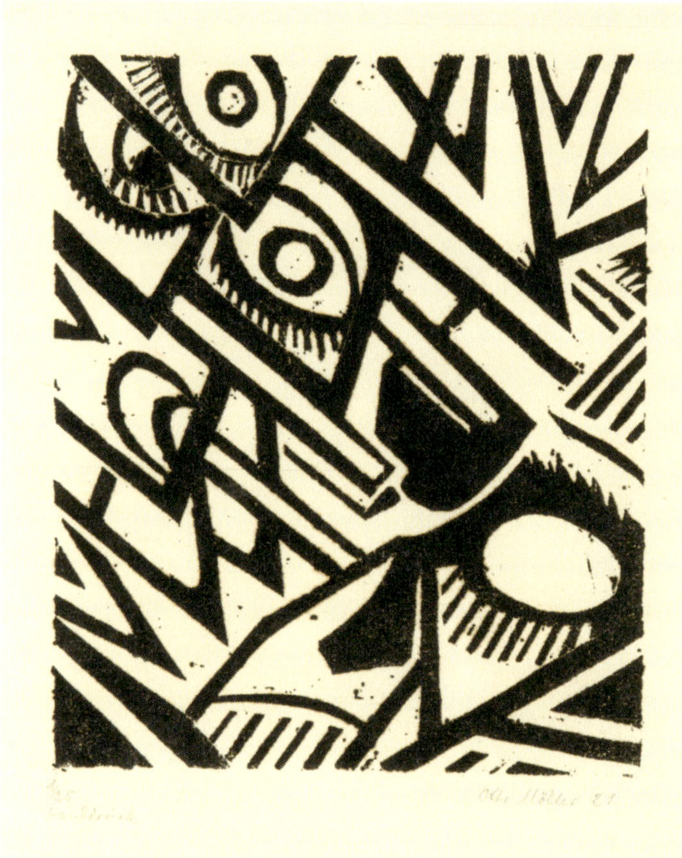

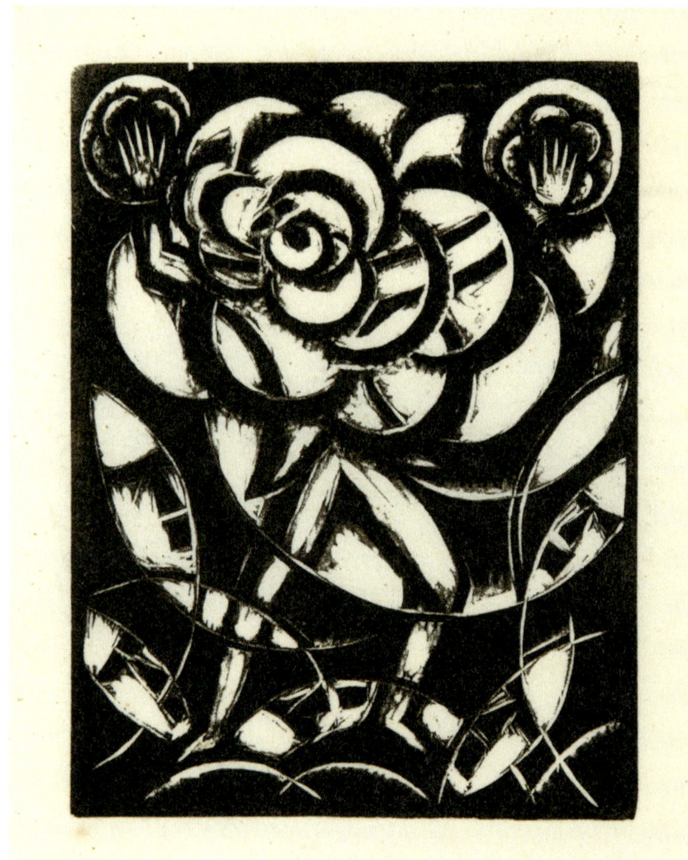

16
OTTO MÖLLER
A Dreadful Memory, sheet 6 in the portfolio of 10 woodcuts based on the short story "A Gentle Spirit" by F. M. Dostoyevsky, 1921

Woodcut, 16.8 × 13.9 cm
Berlinische Galerie

Repro. in *Der Kunsttopf*, 1920, no. 6, p. 103

17
OTTO MÖLLER
The Speaker, 1920/1950

Woodcut on Japan paper,
21.1 × 15.7 cm
Berlinische Galerie

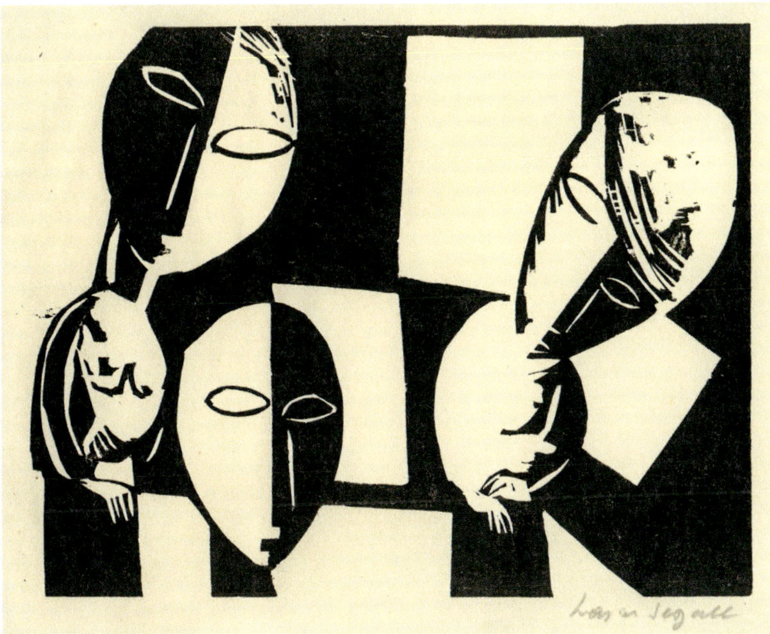

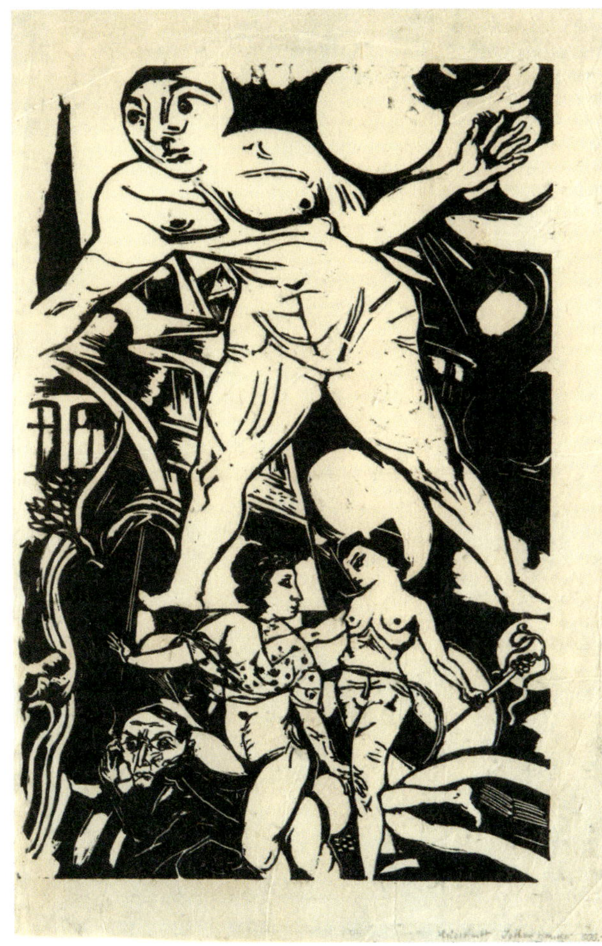

18
LASAR SEGALL
Untitled (Wandering Women), 1920–1925

Woodcut, 27 × 32.5 cm
Galerie Berinson, Berlin

Great Berlin Art Exhibition 1923, Novembergruppe section, no. 1360 (painted version), repro. in *Zehn Jahre Novembergruppe* 1928, p. 82

19
LOTHAR HOMEYER
Revolution (Youth and Age), 1920

Woodcut, 42 × 26.5 cm
Berlinische Galerie

Great Berlin Art Exhibition 1922, Novembergruppe section, no. 1288

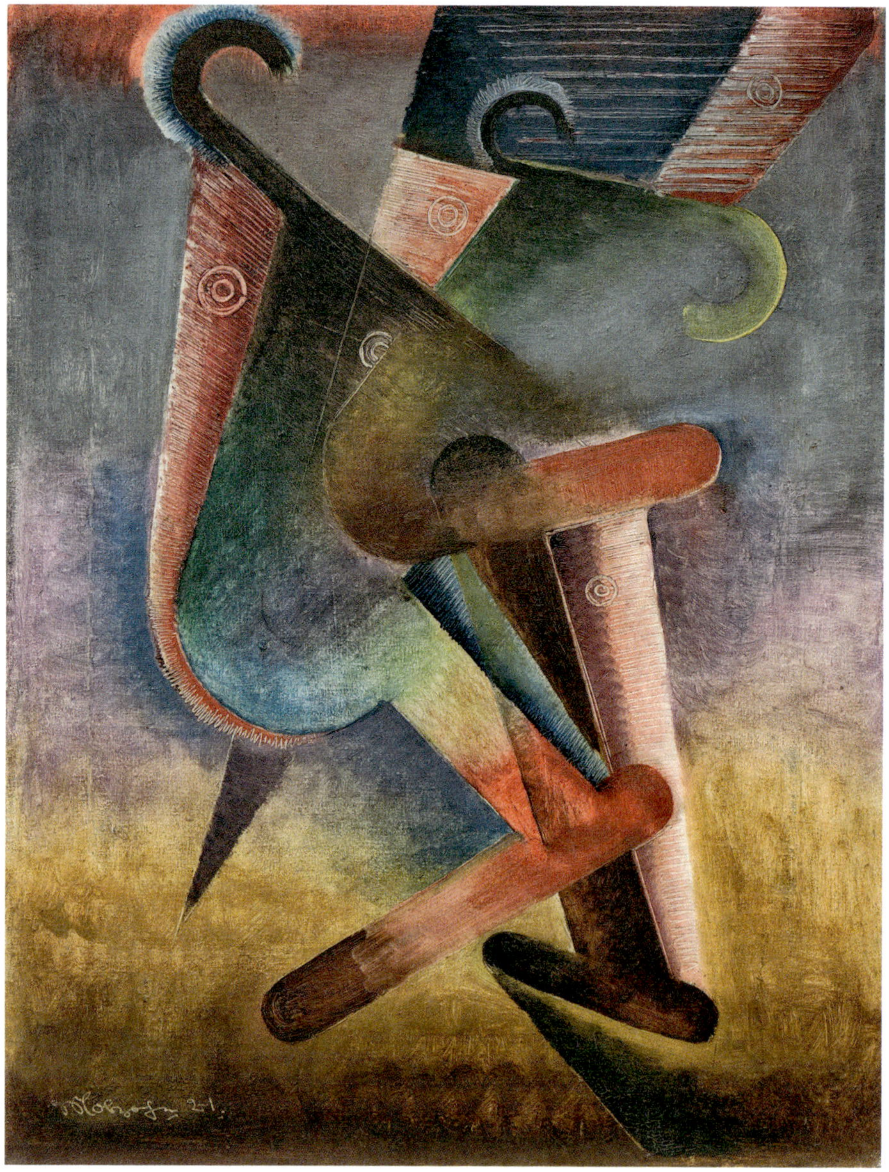

20

JOHANNES MOLZAHN

Primal Forms, 1921

Oil on canvas, 63 × 48.5 cm
Museum Wiesbaden

Great Berlin Art Exhibition 1921, Novembergruppe section, no. 1139, repro. in the catalogue

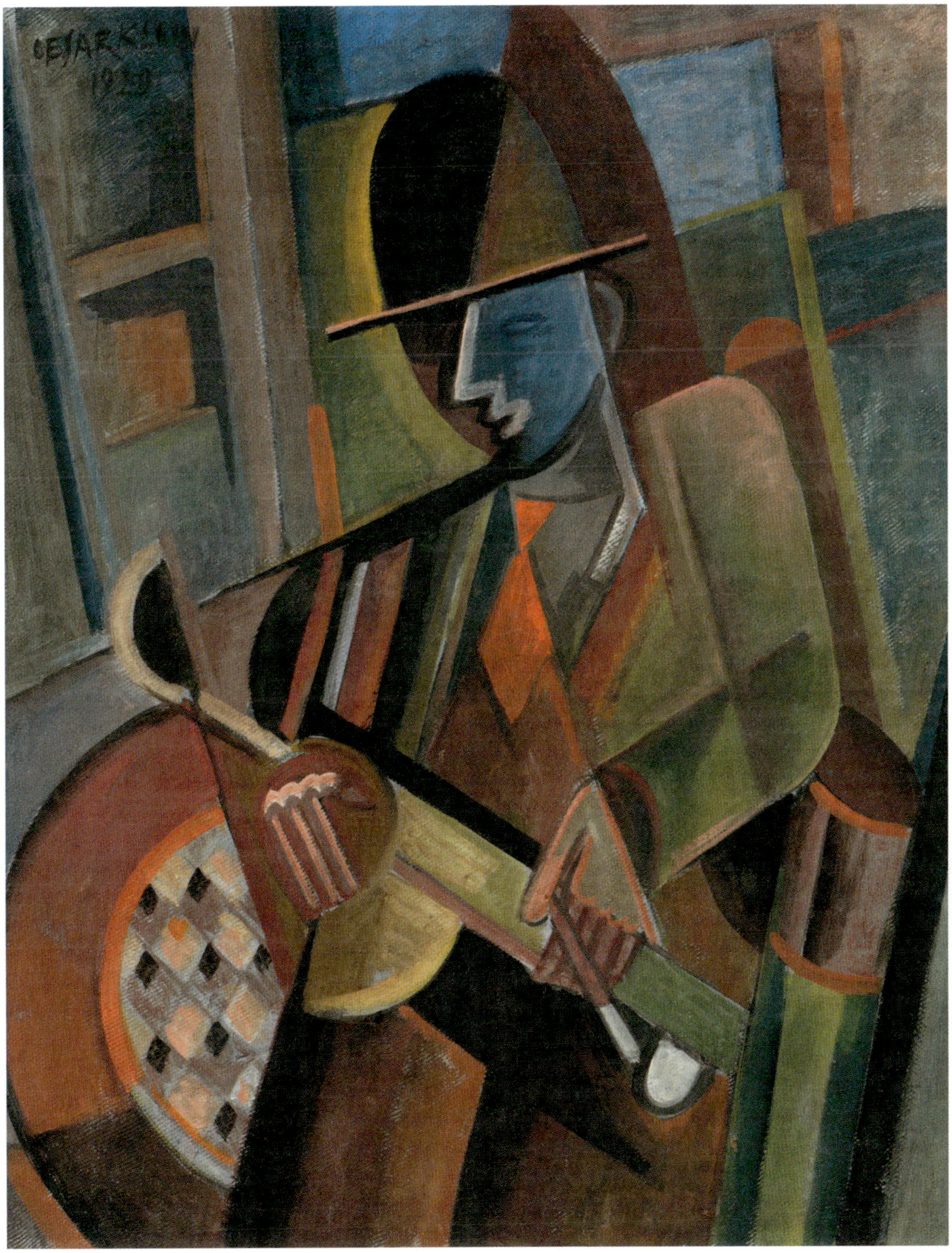

21

CÉSAR KLEIN

Man with Pipe, 1920

Oil on canvas, 114 × 88 cm
Berlinische Galerie

Art Exhibition Berlin 1920,
Novembergruppe section, no. 1272

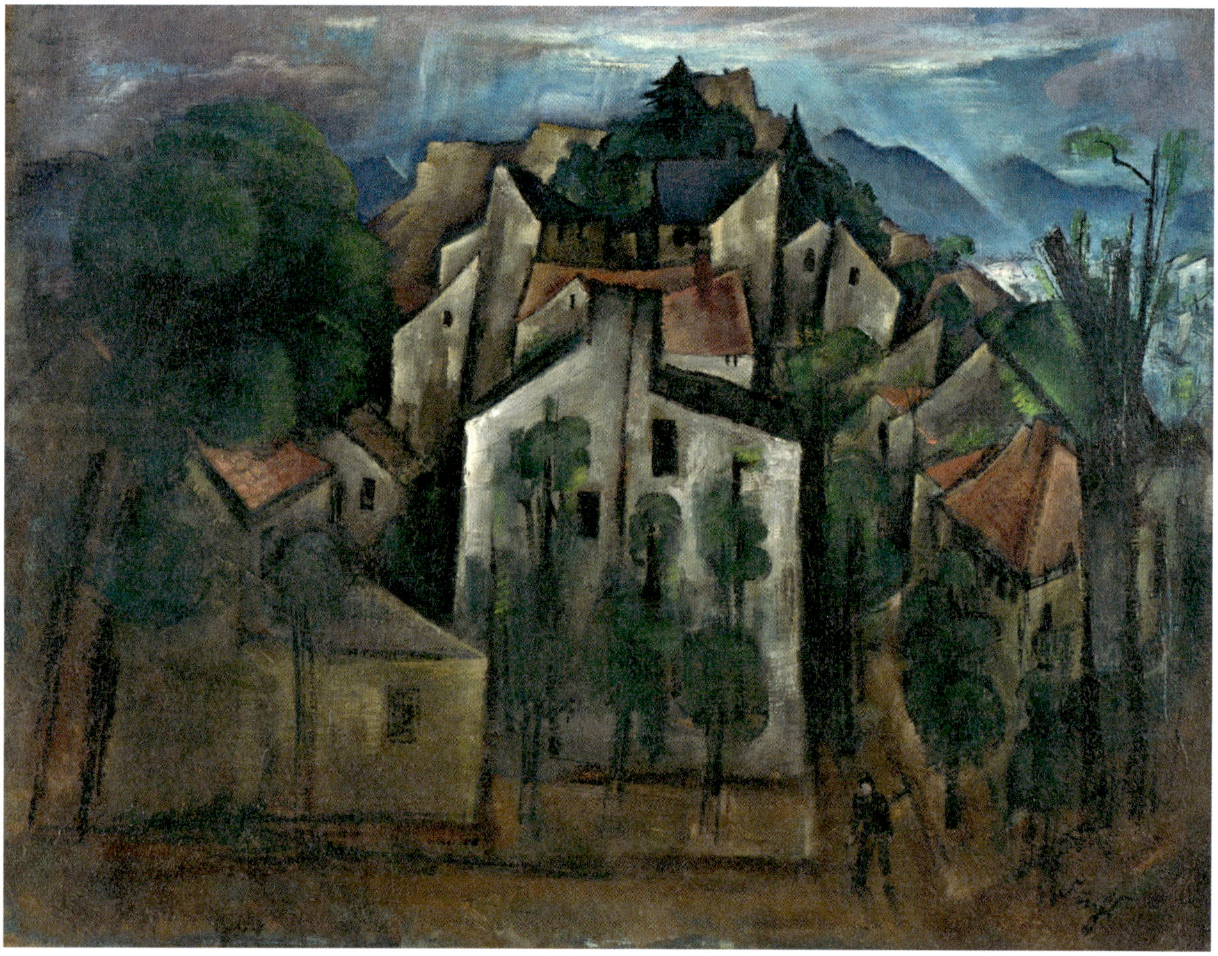

22

HEINZ FUCHS

Picture XV (Houses on a Hill), 1920–21

Oil on canvas, 68 × 87 cm
Berlinische Galerie

Great Berlin Art Exhibition 1921, Novembergruppe section, no. 1069, repro. in the catalogue

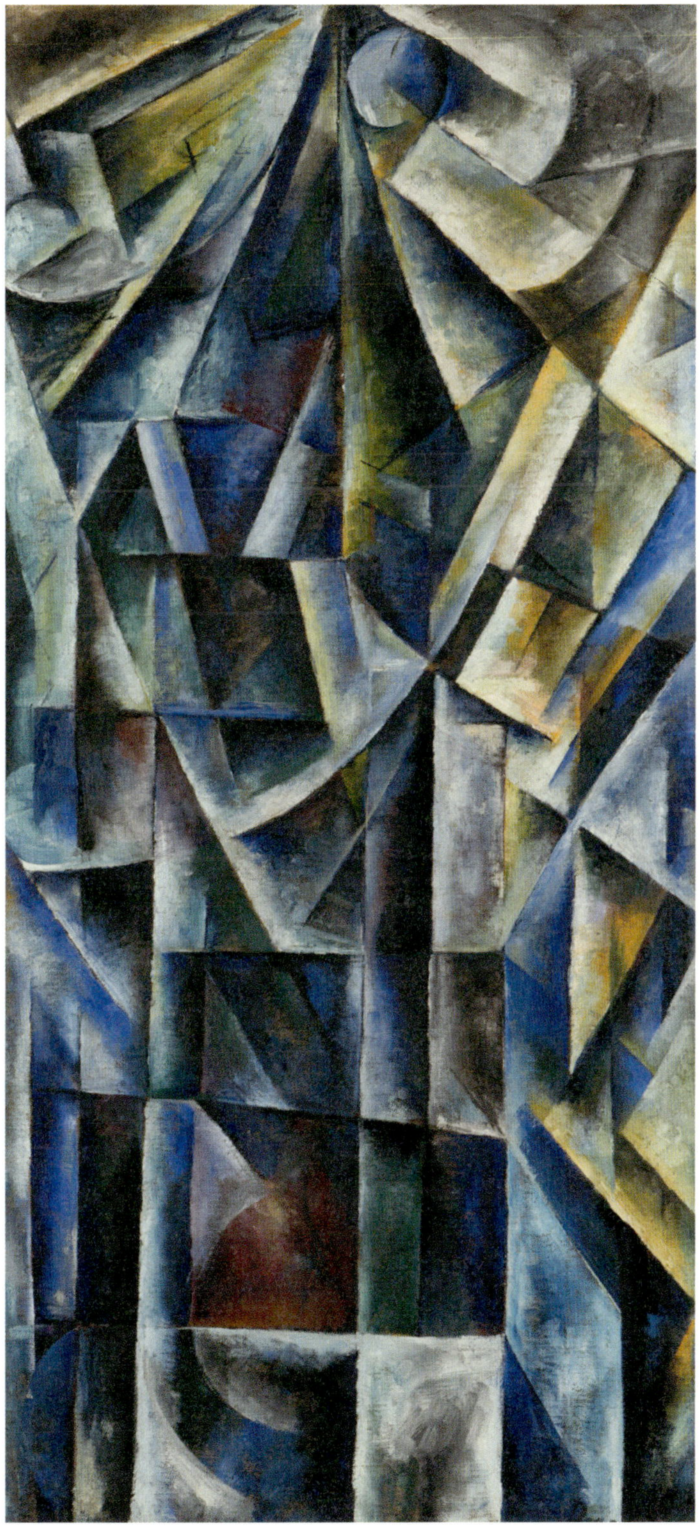

23
MAX DUNGERT
Tower, 1922

Oil on canvas, 162 × 76 cm
Berlinische Galerie

Great Berlin Art Exhibition 1922, Novembergruppe section, no. 1226, repro. in *Zehn Jahre Novembergruppe* 1928, p. 52

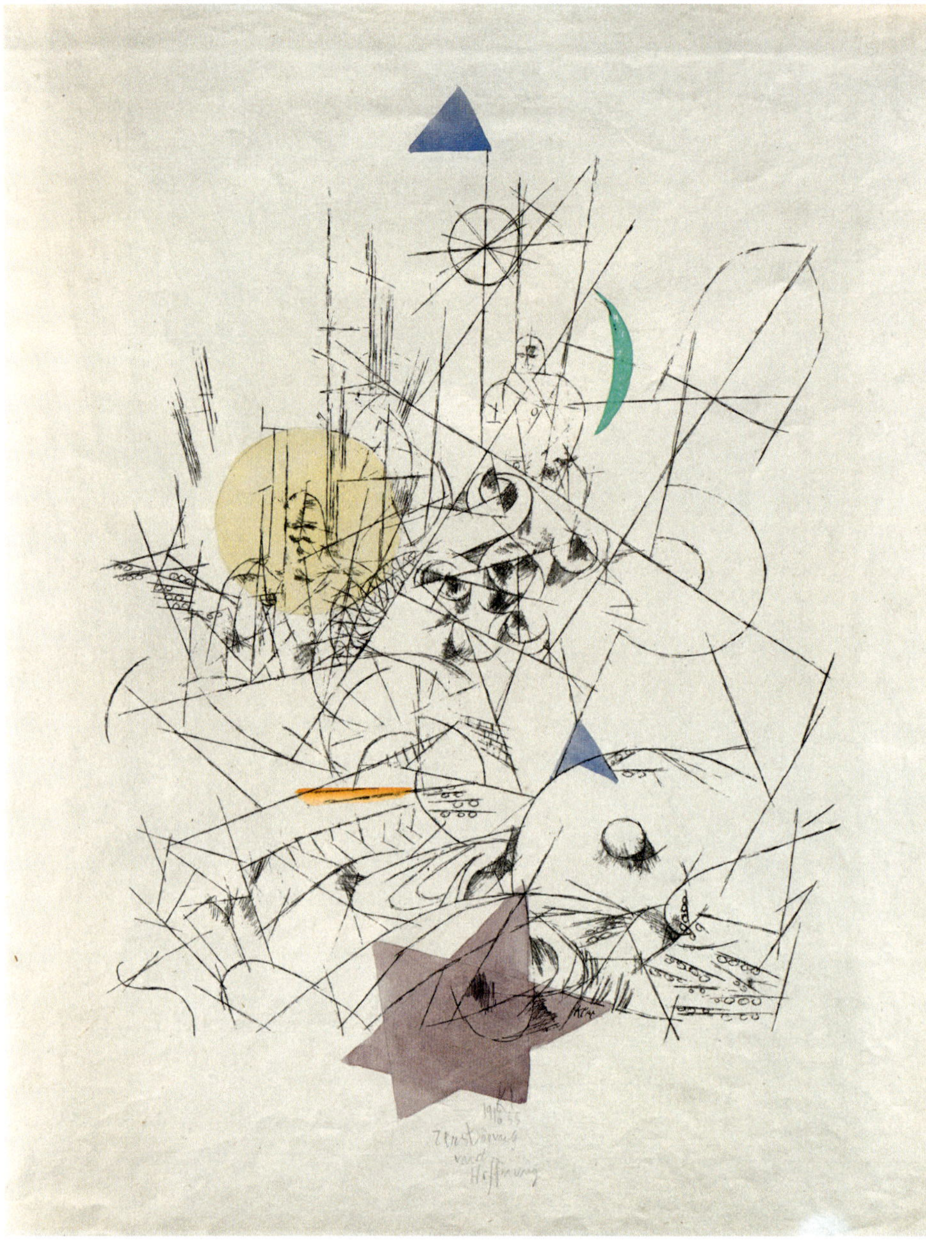

24

PAUL KLEE

Destruction and Hope (Ruins and Hope; Conquered Fort; Destroyed Fort), 1916

Lithograph, watercolour, 48 × 33 cm
Wolfgang Wittrock, Berlin

Art Exhibition Berlin 1919, Novembergruppe section, no. 1203

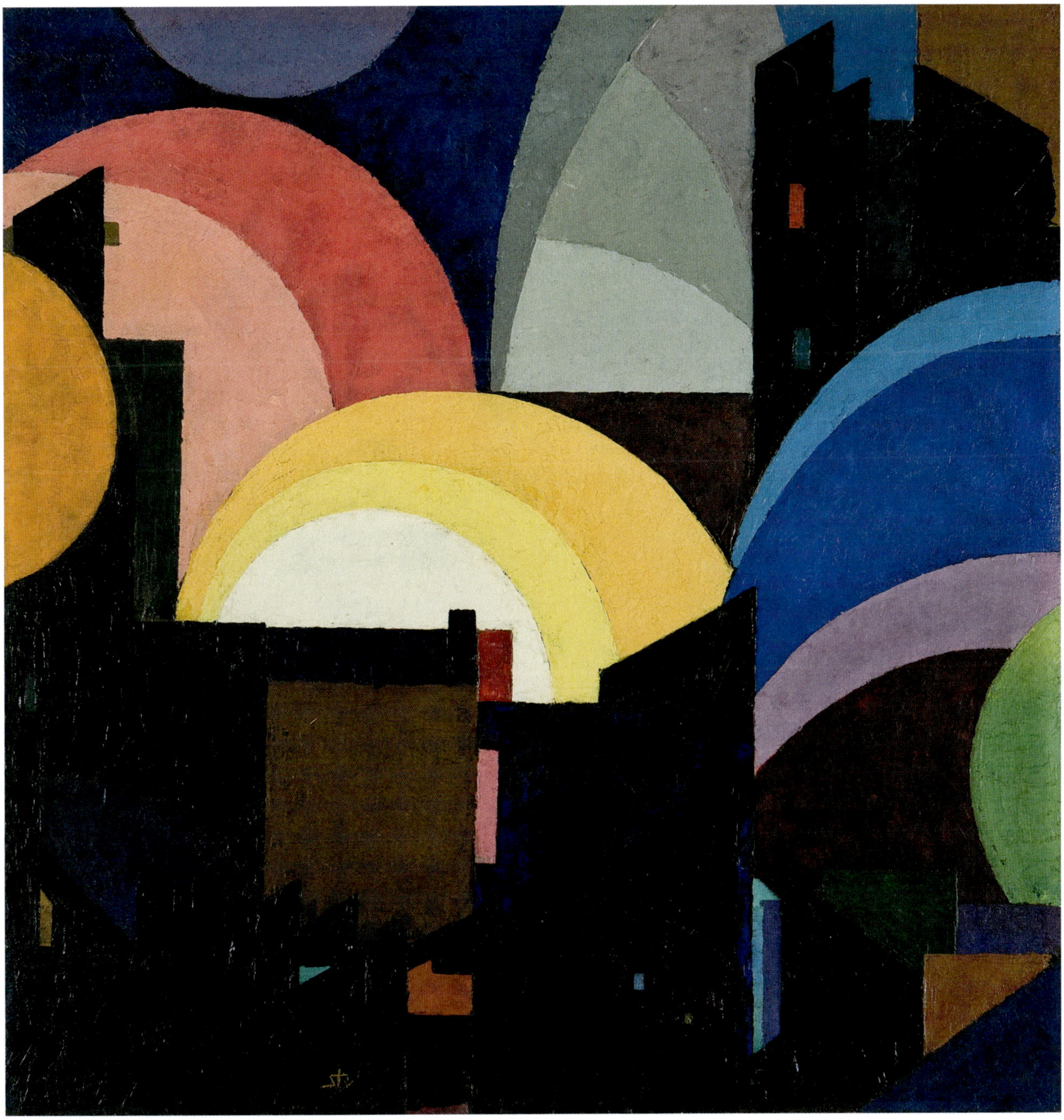

25

FRITZ STUCKENBERG

Sticky Air, c. 1919

Oil on canvas, 76 × 72 cm
Sammlung Stuckenberg der Niedersächsischen Sparkassenstiftung in der Städtischen Galerie Delmenhorst

Art Exhibition Berlin 1920, Novembergruppe section, no. 1471

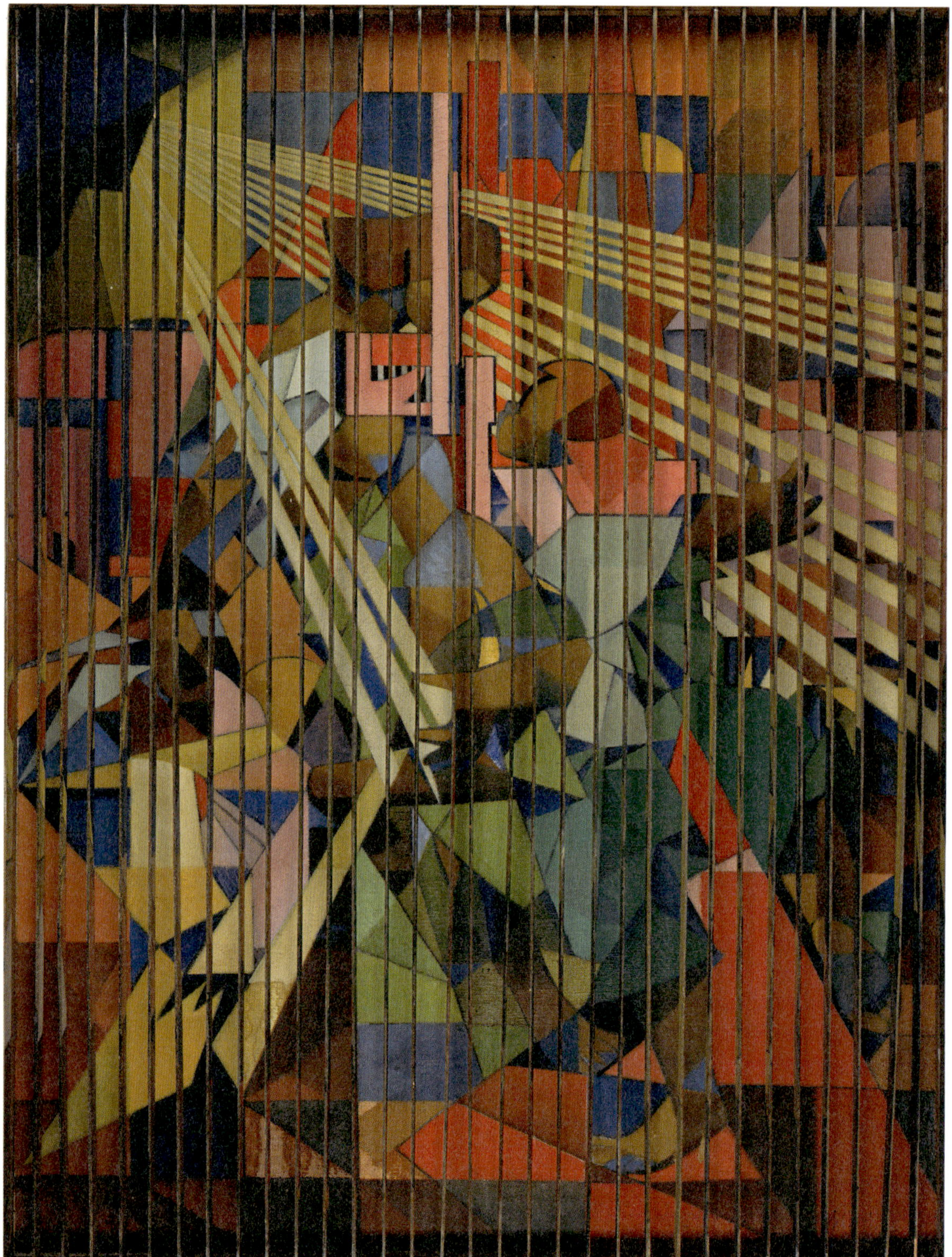

26

MORIZ MELZER

Blessing, 1917–1922

Oil on wood, with slats, 136 × 103 cm
Staatliche Museen zu Berlin, Nationalgalerie.

Great Berlin Art Exhibition 1922, Novembergruppe section, no. 1342; Jury-Free Art Show Berlin 1929, exhibition Ten Years of the Novembergruppe, no. 800, repro. in the catalogue

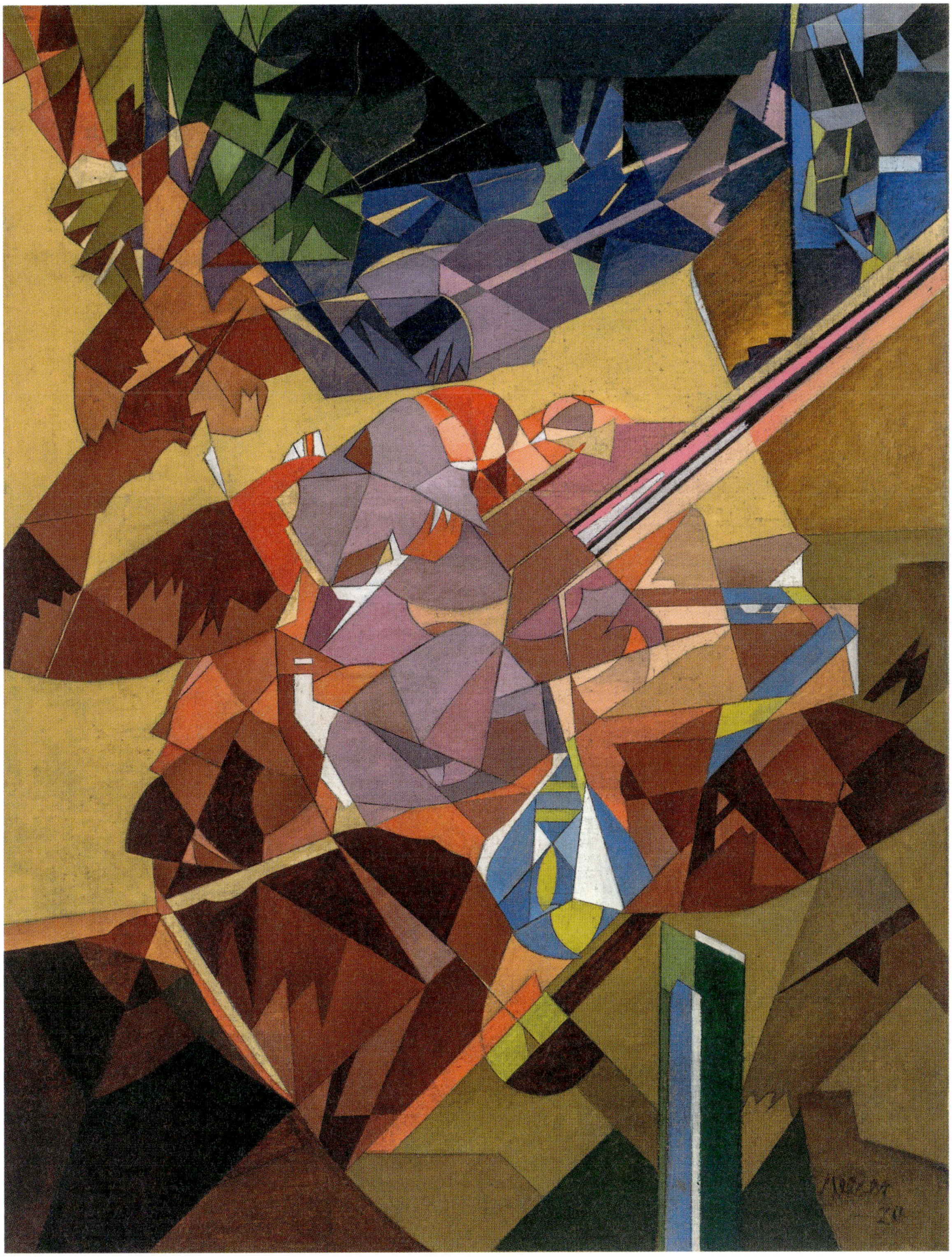

27

MORIZ MELZER

The Frog, c. 1920

Oil on canvas, 130.5 × 99.5 cm
Galerie Berinson, Berlin

Art Exhibition Berlin 1920, Novembergruppe section, no. 1313, repro. in the catalogue

OTTO MÖLLER
Street Noise, 1920

The Novembergruppe had not been in existence for long when it declared an ambition to influence "the future of art schools and their teaching".[1] Early activists such as GEORG TAPPERT, MORIZ MELZER, HEINZ FUCHS, RUDOLF AUSLEGER, CÉSAR and BERNHARD KLEIN and OTTO MÖLLER belonged to a working group on education formed within the association. "Teachers must themselves be artists", for art lessons had been leading pupils "away from art rather than towards it", Möller liked to say.[2] It was a common idea that art was key to the aesthetic formation and personality development of the broader population and no longer merely the middle classes.[3] Möller argued that this education meant turning "schools for learning into schools for experiences",[4] and he firmly believed that the seed of social renewal lay in art education.[5] His position as a college lecturer, where he taught trainee art teachers, enabled him to put his aims into practice for many years.[6]

Otto Möller attached major priority to awakening and fostering a perceptive faculty in children by teaching them to draw, a fundamental skill in art education, and empowering them to express themselves visually without the burden of tradition. "If the teaching of art is to achieve this aim," wrote Möller, "then it must not infect the child with an academic, 'classical' ideal innately alien to the people, or indeed any ready-made adult viewing habits, but must cultivate the original dispositions encountered in all children."[7]

The Weimar Republic was founded just as the movement to reform education, born in the late nineteenth century in response to industrial society and the functionalization of the individual, was at its height.[8] The only style in contemporary art taken seriously by the theoreticians of art education was Expressionism, while other styles were more or less ignored.[9] Expressionism was seen as a chance to formulate the inner workings of the soul, to articulate sensual impressions and to establish a new visual idiom. Those Expressionist artists in the Novembergruppe who also worked as teachers saw their work in art education as a form of social commitment and were given "effective support" by the group in seeking to play an active political role in this manner.[10]

Otto Möller, who exhibited with the association regularly until 1931, showed *Street Noise* [*Straßenlärm*] (cat. 28, p. 69) in the Novembergruppe section at the Berlin Art Exhibition in 1920 under its original title *Picture 8* [*Bild 8*].[11] The work translated the hard, angular, black-and-white idiom of his etchings and woodcuts into fluid oils on canvas. Möller's hints at a real urban landscape around the edges flout perspective and spatial technique. The centre dominates, however, with its intensely hued geometric shapes and cyphers. At the heart of the composition is an almost synesthetic graphic rendering of movement, speed and acoustic waves. *Street Noise* is Möller's attempt to capture the frantic bustle of the city visually in a kind of kaleidoscope.

NUNO DE BRITO ROCHA

1 Letter with policy guidelines and articles of association for the Novembergruppe, 18 December 1918/January 1919, *Berlinische Galerie*, Teilnachlass of Otto Möller, BG-OM 285.

2 Otto Möller, "Aufgaben des Zeichenunterrichts", in: [unknown source, 1919/1920], *Berlinische Galerie*, Teilnachlass of Otto Möller, BG-OM 83.

3 See Kerbs 1976, p. 54.

4 Ref. in note 2.

5 See Hamann 1997, p. 83.

6 From 1920 until 1940 Otto Möller taught educational methods and theory at Berlin's teacher training college, the *Zentralinstitut für Unterricht und Erziehung*, and from 1945 to 1955 he was a professor in the art education department of the art academy, the *Staatliche Hochschule für Bildende Künste*, headed first by Georg Tappert and then by Ernst Fritsch, both members of the Novembergruppe. During this period Möller published two books on teaching art to young children at school: *Wertung der Kinderzeichnung in der Grundschule* (1948) and *Die Kinderzeichnung im Unterricht* (1950).

7 Ref. in note 2.

8 See Hamann 1997, p. 8.

9 Ibid., p. 84.

10 Draft reply by the Novembergruppe to an open letter to the Novembergruppe published in the magazine *Der Gegner* in 1921, *Berlinische Galerie*, Teilnachlass of Otto Möller, BG-OM 294, 2.

11 The title *Street Noise* was first used in 1969 in a catalogue published by *Galerie Nierendorf*. See Thomas 1969.

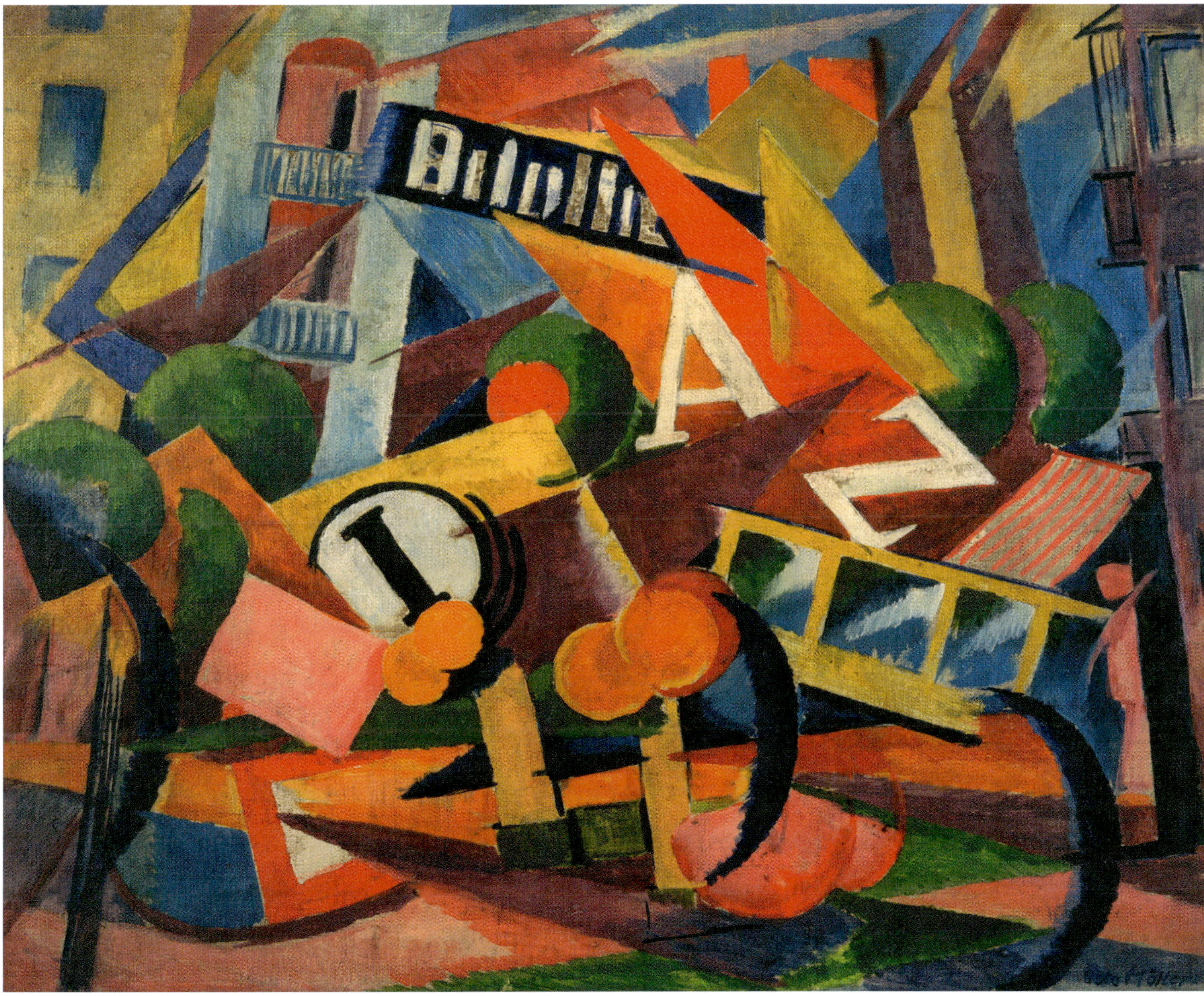

28

OTTO MÖLLER

Street Noise, 1920

Oil on canvas, 62.5 × 75.5 cm
Berlinische Galerie

Art Exhibition Berlin 1920, Novembergruppe section, no. 1324 (under the title *Picture 8*), repro. in the catalogue

BERNHARD KLEIN
The Cubic Box, 1920

To finance its many exhibitions and concerts, the Novembergruppe threw frequent parties — fancy-dress balls and artists' festivities — which soon became regular fixtures in Berlin's ball season.[1] The first event on 20 March 1920 came at a time of major political uncertainty. Only three days earlier, an attempted coup by German generals and a band of right-wing extremists had been put down in Berlin. The "Kapp-Putsch", named after the civil servant Wolfgang Kapp, left Germany tottering on the brink of civil war. Calm had hardly been restored in the capital when party-goers accepted an invitation from the Novembergruppe to dress up in crepe paper and colourful rags and come dancing. As the poster by BERNHARD KLEIN (cat. 29, p. 71) announced, "colours to paint the skin" were available

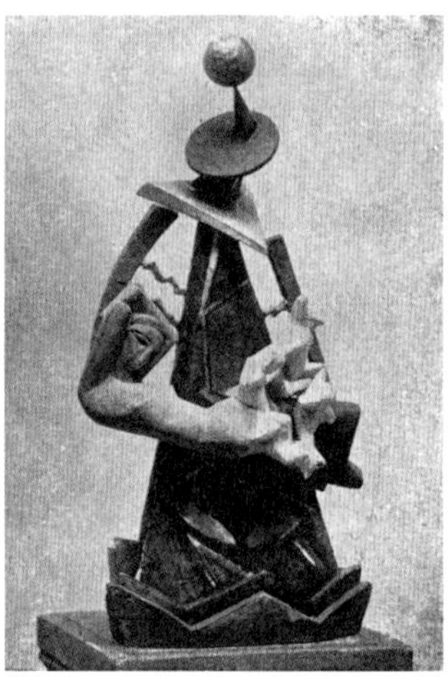

01 RUDOLF BELLING, Model of a fountain, 1918, destroyed, Art Exhibition Berlin 1919, Novembergruppe section, no. 1104

in the cloakroom of the *Gartensaal* at the Zoo. Highlights included a raffle and a "Dada cabaret".[2]

The theme, *The Cubic Box*, was not merely a tautology intended to elicit a giggle. There is a concealed hint here about the art of the *Novembergruppe*: "cubic" is only one syllable removed from Cubism, a style which, like Expressionism and Futurism, was dear to the hearts of many members, especially those in the entourage of Herwarth Walden's gallery Der Sturm. At the first group exhibition in summer 1919, housed in an independent section of the Art Berlin Exhibition, this "Cubo-

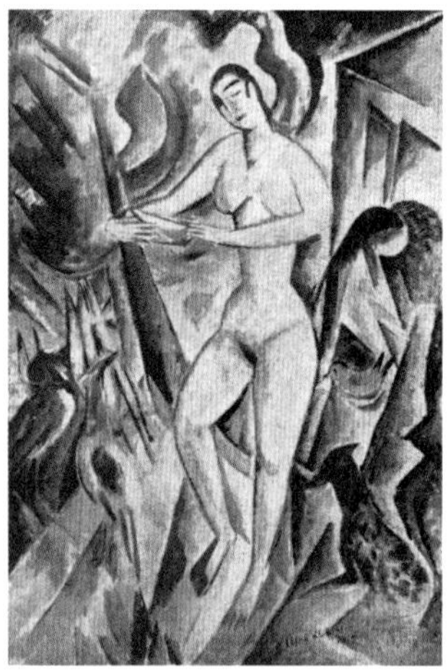

02 CÉSAR KLEIN, Woman with Animals, c. 1918, whereabout unknown, Art Exhibition Berlin 1919, Novembergruppe section, no. 1207

Futuro-Expressionism"[3] had been lampooned by the press. The rooms were described as a "madhouse" and the works as an uncontrolled reflex triggered by recent events. The general public voiced similar disapproval and incomprehension at the sight of the exhibits.[4] The 'cubic box' in Klein's sketch is full of references to this art exhibited a few months earlier by the Novembergruppe. The animals and the nude top left seem to be inspired by RUDOLF BELLING'S design for a fountain (fig. 01) and the painting *Woman with Animals* [*Frau mit Tieren*] by Bernhard's brother CÉSAR KLEIN (fig. 02), except that — in keeping with the festive nature of the occasion — they are far jollier and more animated than the originals. The same applies to the mischievous face in the middle, which is at once a piece of the box and the head of a diving figure — cheerfully paraphrasing works such as those by GEORG TAPPERT and HANS BRASS (fig. 03) in the 1919 exhibition. All these elements spill out of the 'cubic box' and combine with abstract components of buildings and landscapes to create a whirling, chaotic roundelay. This was the impression many reviewers had gained as they walked around the Novembergruppe show, and they had taken the association to task for its stylistic jumble. Klein's composition is a self-assured reply to this criticism: as a liberal forum for every variety of avant-garde creativity, the Novembergruppe celebrated artistic individuality

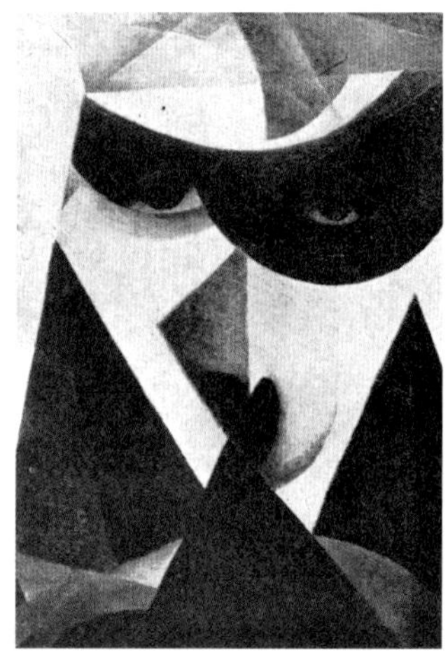

03 HANS BRASS, Painting 12, c. 1918, whereabouts unknown, Art Exhibition Berlin 1919, Novembergruppe section, no. 1119

and experimentation, and the asociation had no intention of shutting such programmatic diversity into a simple box.

JANINA NENTWIG

1 See Butting 1955, pp. 119f.; Kliemann 1969, pp. 30–35; Zepter 2012, pp. 212–217. An essay by Janina Nentwig about Novembergruppe festivities will appear in 2019 in the conference proceedings *Künstlerfeste* to be published by the *Kunsthistorisches Forum Irsee*.

2 It is unclear which (if any) members of Berlin's Club Dada were on stage and what was on the programme. Raoul Hausmann and Hannah Höch were certainly present (see Berlinische Galerie 1989, 13.10, p. 647). The "Dada cabaret" seems to have been a success, because another was put on for the next fancy-dress ball on 1 December 1920 (see the poster, also by Bernhard Klein, p. 229, fig. 08). On the relationship between Dada and the Novembergruppe, see the essay by Burmeister in this catalogue, pp. 80–91.

3 Roters 1995, p. 77.

4 See the essay by Nentwig in this catalogue, pp. 49f.

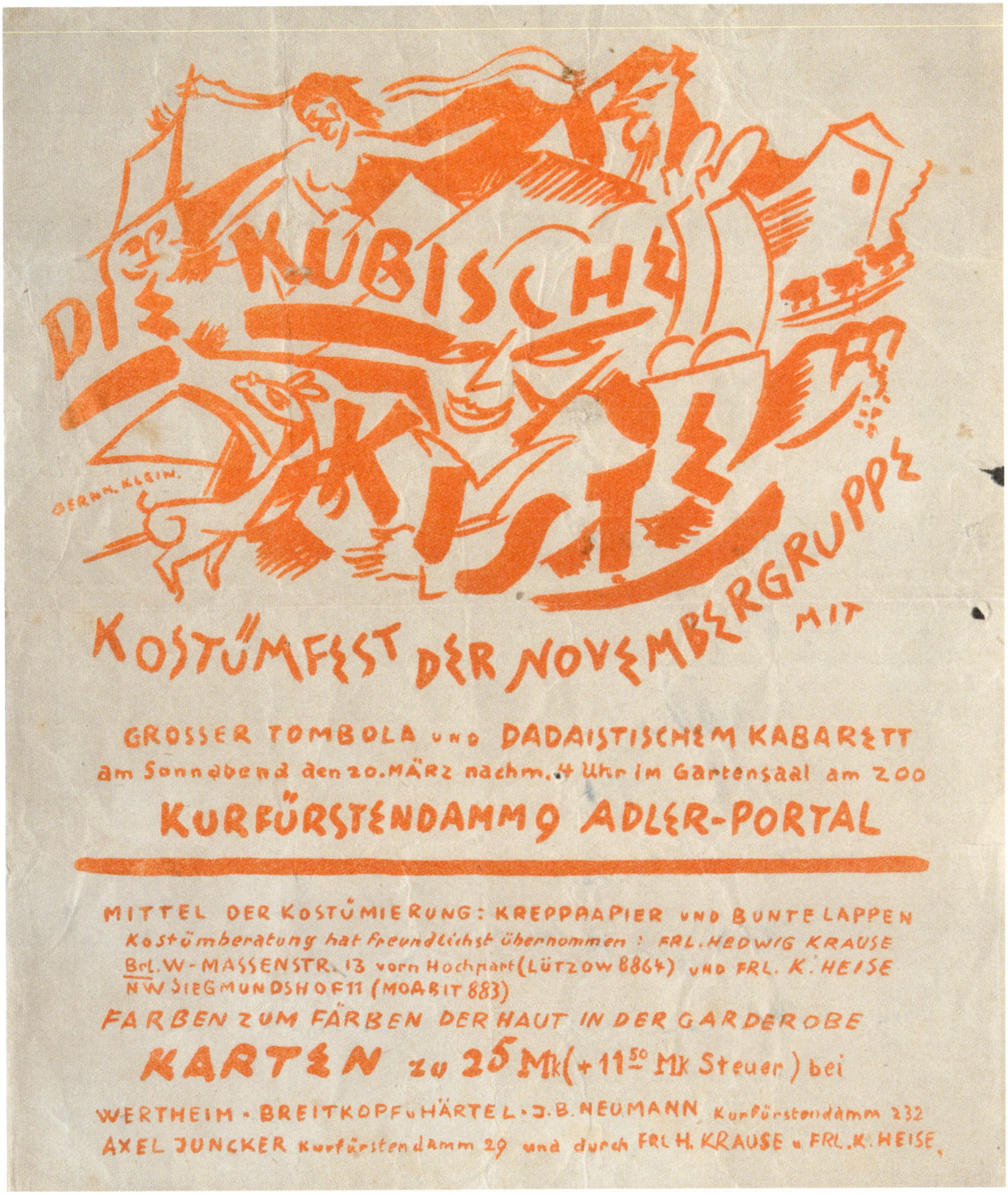

29

BERNHARD KLEIN

The Cubic Box, Novembergruppe Fancy-Dress Ball, 1920

Poster, 28.2 × 24.2 cm
Berlinische Galerie

OSWALD HERZOG
Enjoying, c. 1920

"To fill space with dynamic life, to endow it with the rhythmic forms of a living soul—that is the task of the new art."[1] This was the principle OSWALD HERZOG applied to his sculptures, according to an article he wrote for NG, the Novembergruppe's magazine, in 1921. As a major exponent of the avant-garde in Germany and a founding member of the Novembergruppe, Herzog contributed both as an artist and as a theoretician to discourse about post-war Expressionism. Art, he believed, was "absolute"[2], and he set out his reflections on the subject in a series of slightly esoteric, metaphysical writings on art theory,[3] inspired not only by the philosophy of Henri Bergson but also by his own thoughts on the rhythmic figures in motion sculpted by Alexander Archipenko.[4] The contacts he had fostered since 1912 with Herwarth Walden and his gallery Der Sturm also exposed him to the influence of Italian Futurists.

The 'absolute', in Herzog's view, was distilled from a process of abstraction driven by the tensions between opposites: "Rhythm draws its measure from the polarity of big and small, strong and weak, rest and motion. Between these poles lie all nature's abundant forms, and life flows with its manifold movements, rising and fading. Effect and counter-effect are the architects of the world."[5] Herzog made no attempt to replicate nature but sought ideas for the shapes he produced within its creative processes. Herzog expressed these by making the emotional world of humans his theme, exploring the motions of the soul and translating these into plastic form. *Enjoying* [*Genießen*] (cat. 30, p. 73), made in 1920, suggests a seated body in dancing pose that reaches into space, static yet bursting with tension. This antithesis is mirrored in the composition of the abstract figure: the artist combines angular, crystalline and fluid, organic forms into a rhythmic equilibrium, a motif that might also reflect a harmony of body and soul. The bronze *Fleeing* [*Entfliehen*] (fig. 01) dating from the same year is even more abstract with no hint of naturalistic depiction. The streamlined figure tapering

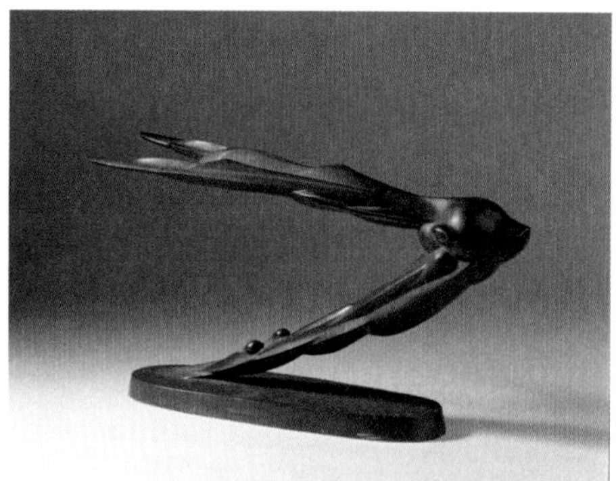

01 OSWALD HERZOG, Fleeing, 1920, private collection, Novembergruppe exhibition on the premises of the *Verein Berliner Künstler* 1931, no. 21

to a point at one end seems to be frozen in motion. It floats freely in space, with only its lower tip attached to the minimal base, reinforcing the dynamic feel. The openness to one side and compressed momentum on the other illustrate the polarity principle underlying the design.

Few of Herzog's sculptures survived the war, and those that did tend to be the

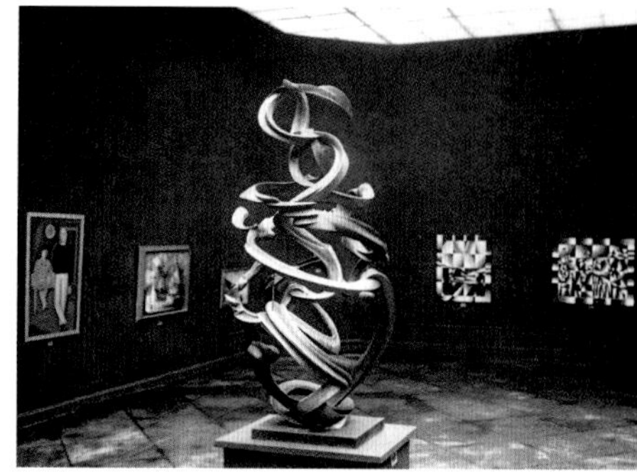

02 Great Berlin Art Exhibition 1924, Novembergruppe section, room 17, in the foreground Oswald Herzog's sculpture *Counterpoint*, hanging in the background are two works by Arthur Segal

smaller ones. Some of his lost monumental works were recorded in photographs during Novembergruppe exhibitions (fig. 02). Frequent media visibility meant that sculptures by Oswald Herzog, like the work of RUDOLF BELLING, crucially moulded the public image of the association.[6] Between 1919 and 1930 Herzog took part in at least 18 shows by the Novembergruppe, often serving on the exhibition committee, and published articles in several periodicals edited by the association.[7] In his essay on abstraction in the fine arts, which appeared in the first issue of *Der Kunsttopf*, Oswald Herzog aptly summarized his views on breathing motion into sculpture: "A work of art is an independent organic structure with its own inner life—its own will [...]. The will to form is the idea—the experience. The work of art must express this convincingly."[8]

JUSCHKA MARIE VON RÜDEN

1 Oswald Herzog, "Vom Ausdruck der Form", in: Hans Siebert von Heister, Raoul Hausmann (eds.), *NG. Veröffentlichung der Novembergruppe*, vol. 1, 1921, no. 1, pp. 32–34, here 34.

2 See Oswald Herzog, "Abstraktion der Bildenden Kunst", in: Novembergruppe (ed.), *Der Kunsttopf*, vol. 1, 1920, no. 1, pp. 22–25, here 24f.

3 The sculptor published several books on art theory, including: Oswald Herzog, *Die stilistische Entwicklung der Kunst: Einführung in das Wesen der Kunst*, Berlin 1912; *Sinfonie des Lebens*, Berlin 1921; *Zeit und Raum. Das Absolute in Kunst und Natur*, Berlin 1928.

4 See Beloubek-Hammer 2007, p. 395.

5 Oswald Herzog, *Sinfonie des Lebens*, Berlin 1921, p. 11.

6 I am grateful to Janina Nentwig for pointing out the media coverage of the Novembergruppe.

7 Refs. in notes 1 and 2 and Oswald Herzog, in: *Zehn Jahre Novembergruppe*, special issue *Kunst der Zeit. Zeitschrift für Kunst und Literatur*, vol. 3, 1928, nos. 1–3, p. 14.

8 Ref. in note 2, p. 25.

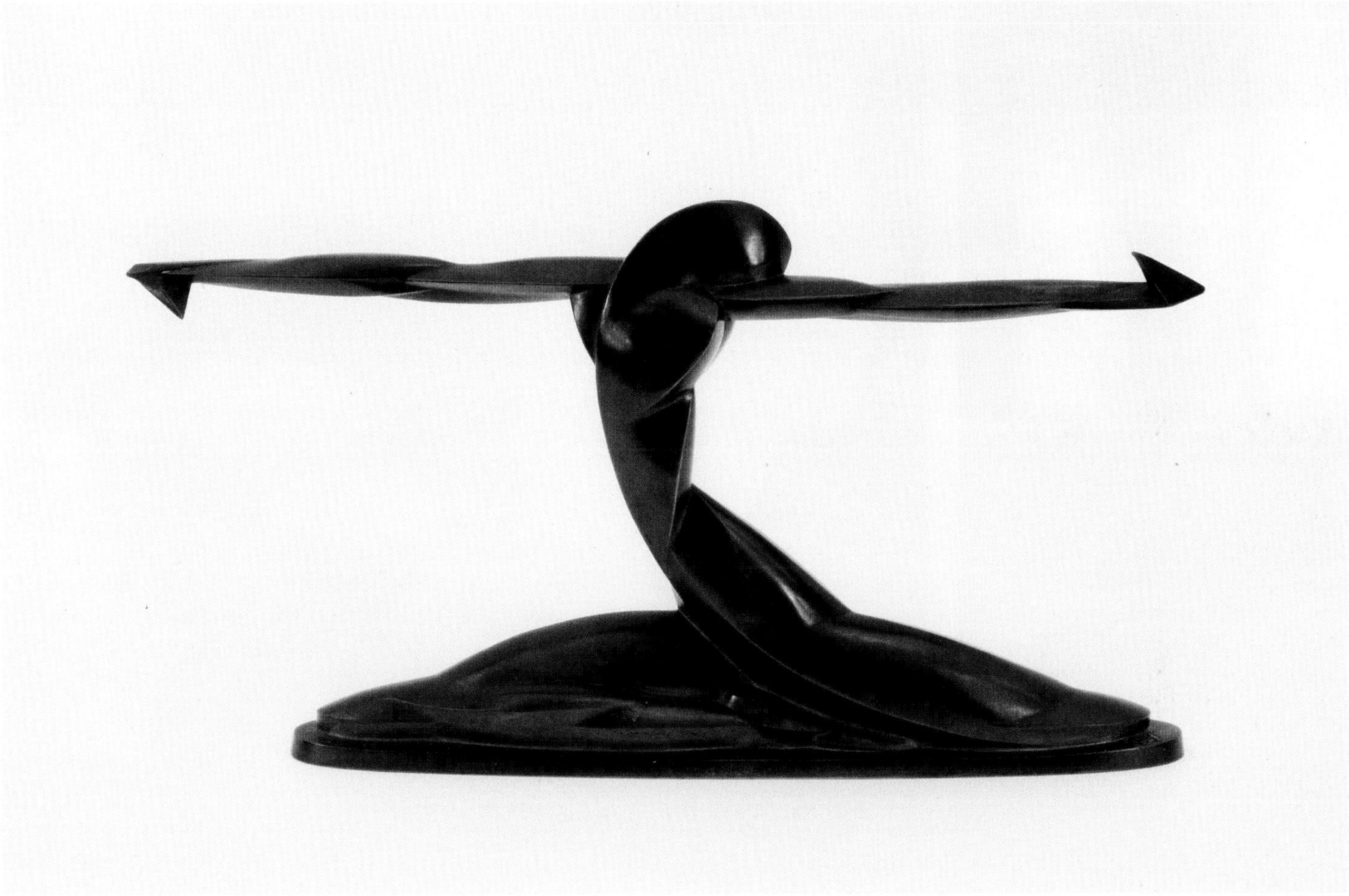

30

OSWALD HERZOG

Enjoying, c. 1920

Bronze, 20.5 × 38.5 × 7 cm
Berlinische Galerie

Art Exhibition Berlin 1920,
Novembergruppe section, no. 1218

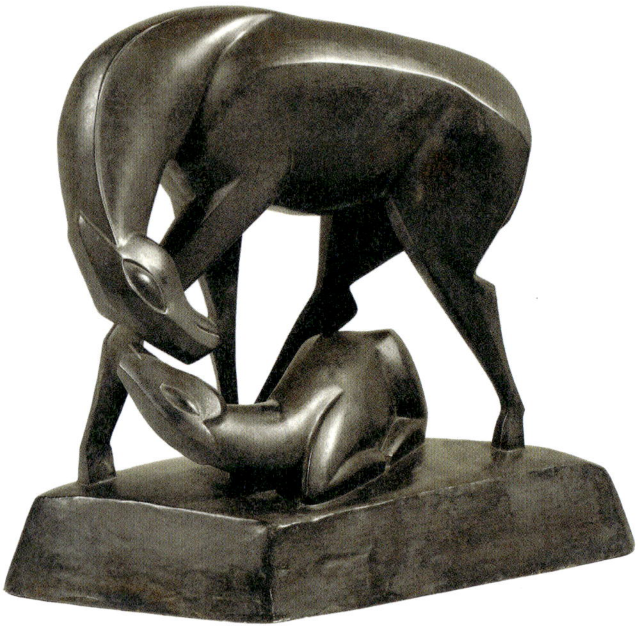

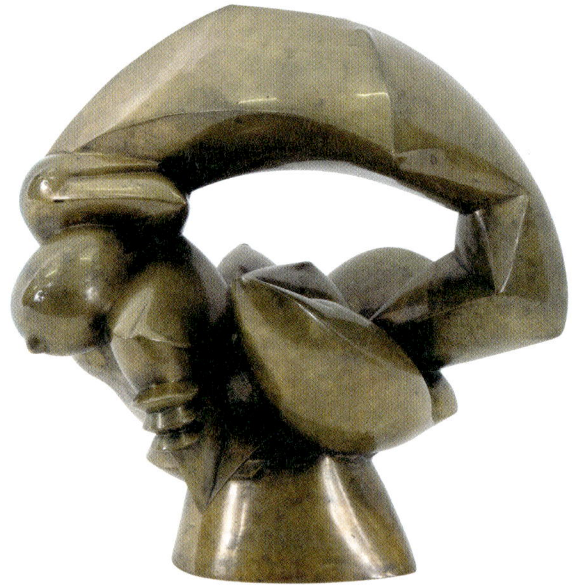

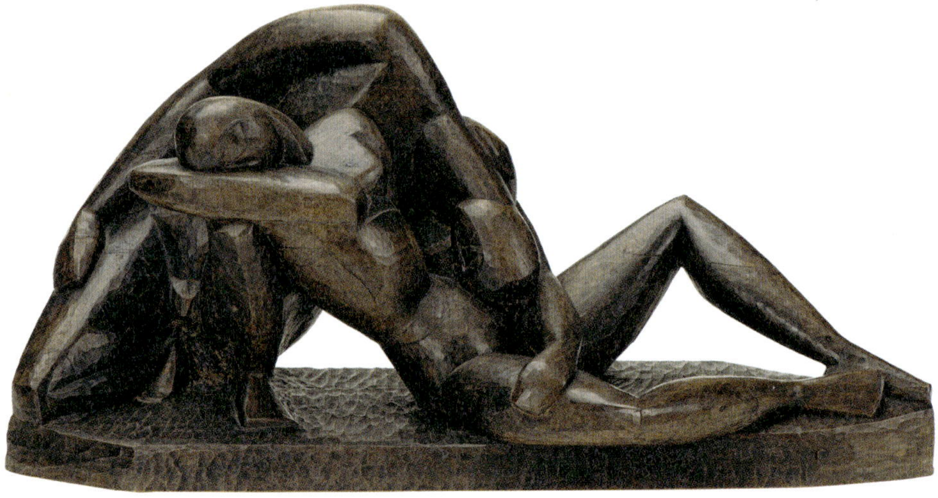

31
EMY ROEDER
Mare and Foal, 1919

Bronze, 31.5 × 35.5 × 20 cm
Staatliche Museen zu Berlin, Nationalgalerie

Art Exhibition Berlin 1920, Novembergruppe section, no. 1396

32
HERBERT GARBE
Lovers (Sleep), 1919

Limewood, 45 × 90 × 36.5 cm
Sprengel Museum Hannover

Repro. in the special issue of *Menschen* on the Novembergruppe, 1919, p. 40

33
RUDOLF BELLING
Eroticism, 1920

Bronze, 32 × 30 × 24 cm
Berlinische Galerie

Art Exhibition Berlin 1920, Novembergruppe section, no. 1097 (plaster version)

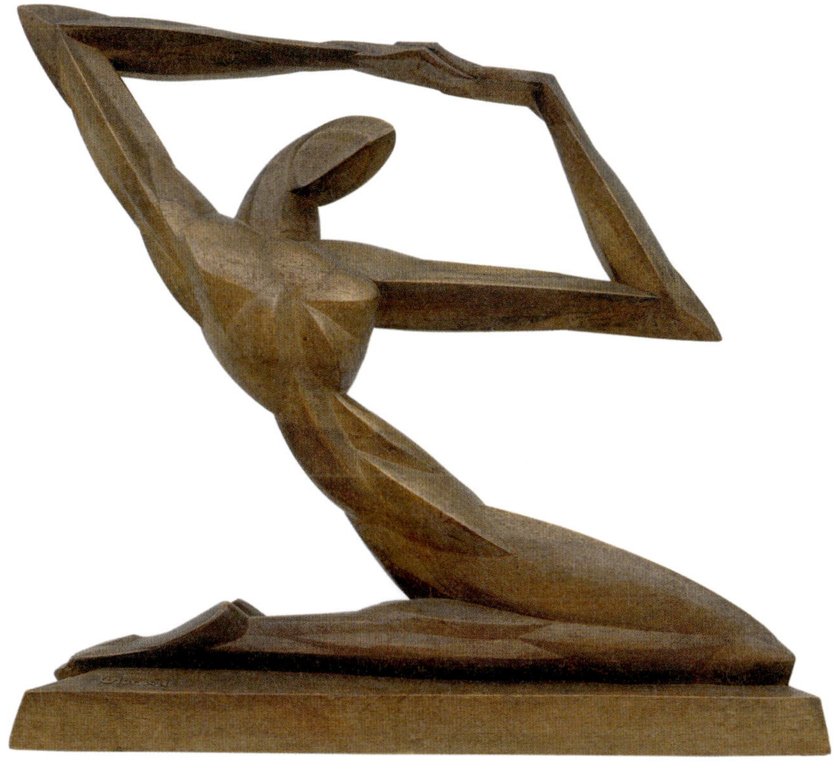

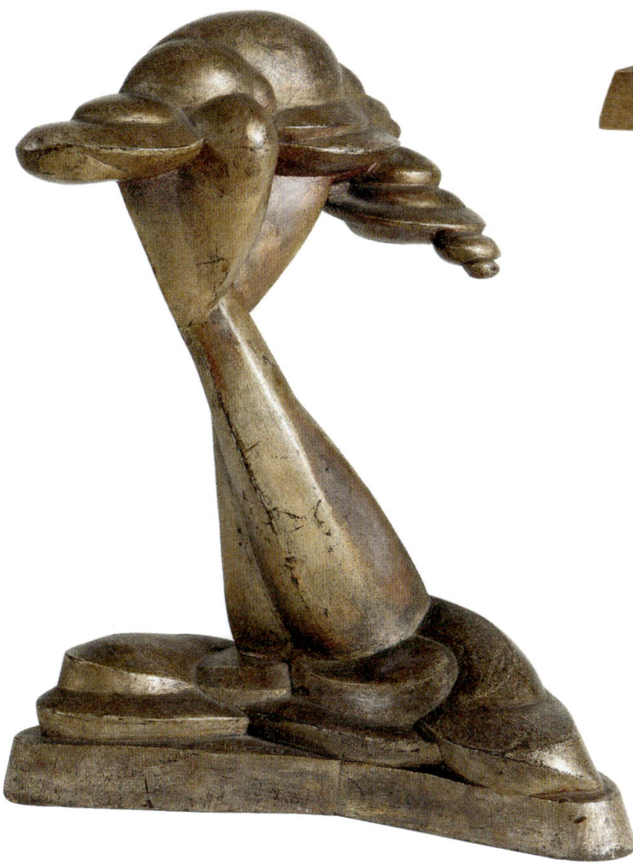

34
OSWALD HERZOG
Rapture, 1919

Wood, silver stain, 53 × 42 × 33 cm
Kunsthalle Mannheim, Mannheim

Art Exhibition Berlin 1919, Novembergruppe section, no. 1169 (plaster version); Novembergruppe exhibition at the *Verein Berliner Künstler,* 1931, no. 22 (wood), repro. in each catalogue

35
OSWALD HERZOG
Woman Kneeling, c. 1920

Wood, 48.5 × 49.5 × 15.5 cm
Staatliche Museen zu Berlin, Nationalgalerie

Art Exhibition Berlin 1920, Novembergruppe section, no. 1215 (with the title *Consecration*)

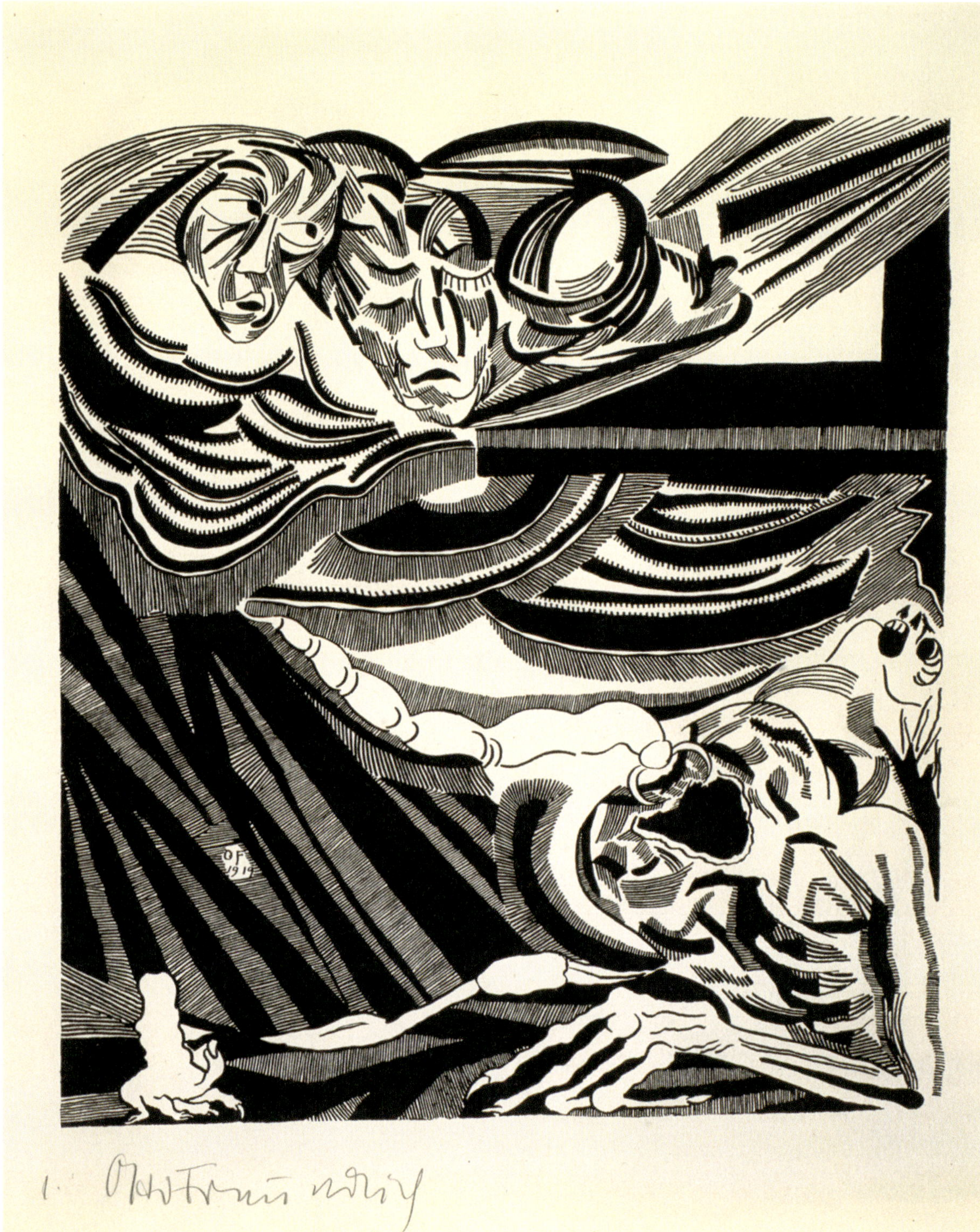

36
OTTO FREUNDLICH
The Marks, Sheet 1, 1920

Zincograph, brush overworking
6 prints, each 78 × 62 cm
Lindenau-Museum Altenburg

Great Berlin Art Exhibition 1921,
Novembergruppe section, no. 1068

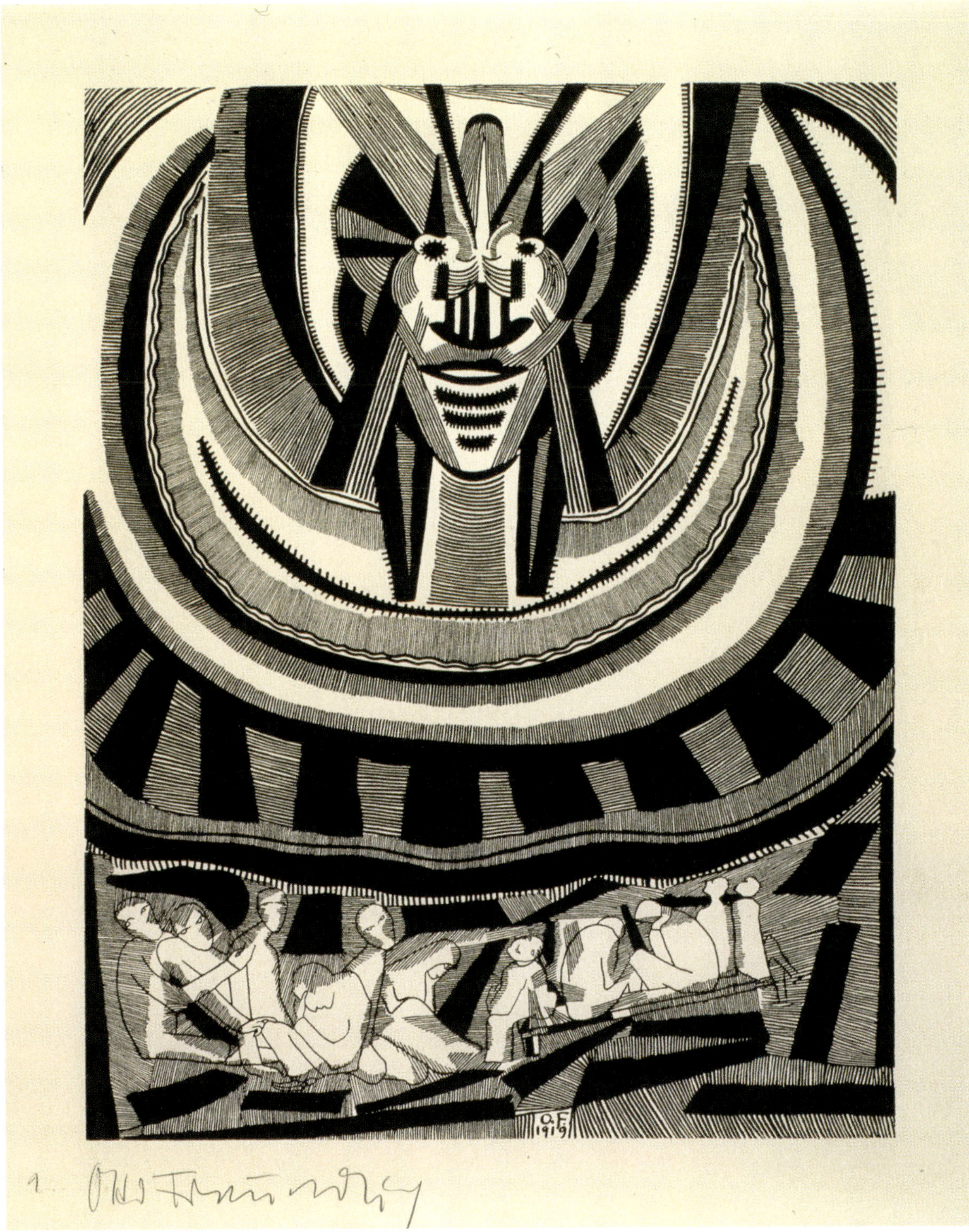

37

OTTO FREUNDLICH

The Marks, Sheet 2, 1920

Zincograph, brush overworking
6 prints, each 78 × 62 cm
Lindenau-Museum Altenburg

Great Berlin Art Exhibition 1921,
Novembergruppe section, no. 1068

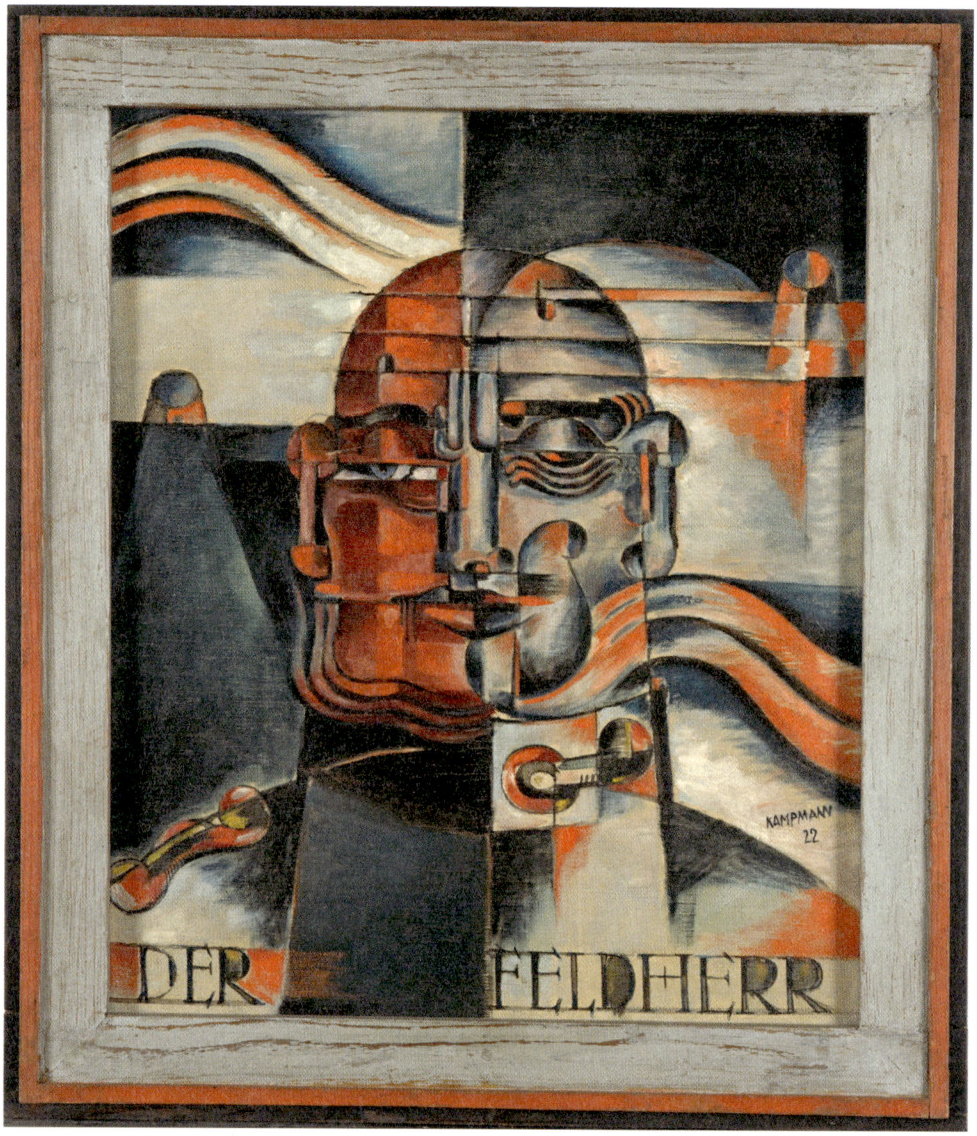

38
WALTER KAMPMANN
The Commander, 1922

Oil on canvas, 62 × 51 cm
Berlinische Galerie

Great Berlin Art Exhibition 1922,
Novembergruppe section, no. 1301

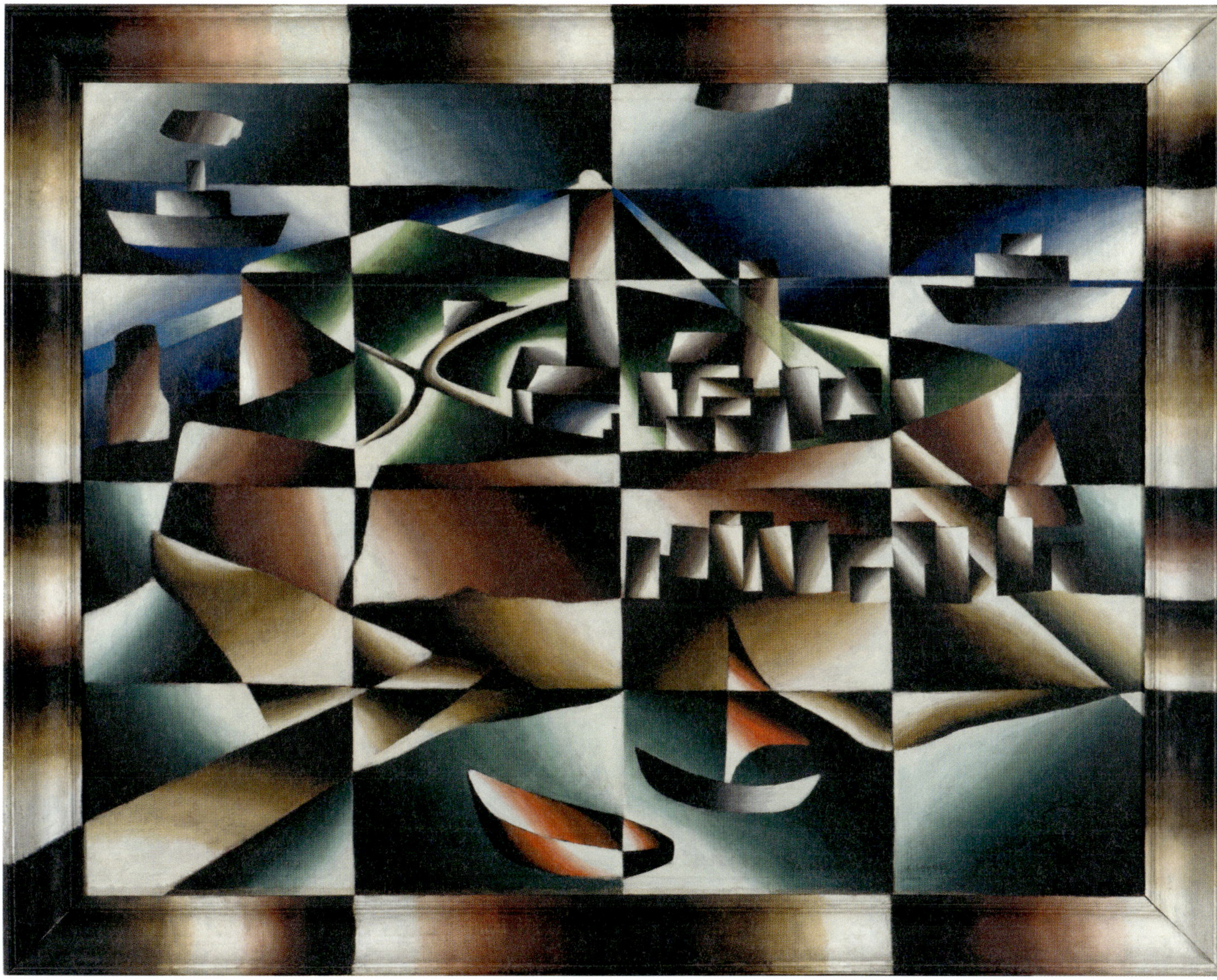

39

ARTHUR SEGAL

Heligoland, 1923

Oil on canvas, 101 × 130 cm
Berlinische Galerie

Segal exhibited two more Helgoland compositions in the Novembergruppe section at the Great Berlin Art Exhibition 1924 (nos. 990 and 991, now Gemeentemuseum Den Haag and Museum of Modern Art, New York).

RALF BURMEISTER

INCOMPATIBLY RADICAL

Dada and the Novembergruppe

"... One cannot be an artist and believe in history."
(Hugo Ball, *Flight out of Time*, on 22 March 1917)

Antipodes

1918 was the year when, after the battles from Ypres and Verdun to Gallipoli and Isonzo, the horrendous balance sheet of industrially waged slaughter unleashed by the First World War had accrued more than nine million dead soldiers around the world. 2.7 million victims returned to Germany from the front physically and mentally crippled,[1] many of them suffering from what the British called 'shell shock' and the Germans called 'war trembles'. They were a distressing everyday sight on the streets. At the beginning of the year, Club Dada was founded in Berlin.[2] On 12 April 1918 a star cast of Dadaists gave their first public performance in the capital of the Reich—in the building, in fact, normally used by the Berlin Secession, where they threw their original spectacular Dada Soirée in the middle of a Lovis Corinth retrospective to mark the artist's 60th birthday.[3]

Productive provocation, designed to blow open narrow bourgeois patterns of thought and perception, were a hallmark of Dada, and this occasion produced its own crowning glory when the electric lights were switched off, thereby preventing the audience from attacking the performers and saving the paintings on show from damage. 'Worldada' Richard Huelsenbeck, 'Propagandada' GEORGE GROSZ and 'Dadasoph' RAOUL HAUSMANN declaimed programmatic Dada scripts, lampooning familiar shibboleths. The conceptually admissible was undermined and the unheard of was heard. When Else Hartwiger, with her vivid rendering of F. T. Marinetti's Futurist verses "Transporting the Wounded" and "Bombardment", accompanied by a wooden gun and children's trumpet, prompted epileptic convulsions in a visiting soldier (this was a symptom of war trembles), the audience "had a fit", as HAUSMANN recalled (fig. 01).[4] The *Dada Manifesto* distributed in the hall by Richard Huelsenbeck as Club Dada's first publication expounds the mental underlay of the Dadaist furore in its opening paragraph: "Art depends for its production and direction on the time in which it lives, and artists are creatures of their era. The highest art will be that which presents in its conscious content the thousand-fold problems of the time, patently shaped by last week's explosions, always gathering up its limbs under yesterday's blow. The best and most outrageous artists will be those who by the hour pluck the shreds of their bodies from the confusion of life's cataracts, clinging grimly to the intellect of the time, bleeding from their hands and hearts."[5]

Those pivotal concepts "creatures", "explosions", "limbs", "shreds" and those tropes nourished by rage and theatricality are redolent of the existential trauma triggered by the First World War and etched into the cerebral gyri even of those who had escaped mutilation or stayed at home (fig. 02). One of Dada's principal aims was to ventilate the trauma in and through art rather than suppressing the experience. The Berlin Dadaists, in particular, adopted the stance of enlightened, progressive cynics, seeking through their art to facilitate the self-detoxification of a society where nationalism and militarism had engendered the collapse of civilization and triggered previously unimaginable scenes of war. This — so the aspiration — called for a radically new art, one that broke with the past, was utterly of its day and saw itself as "total rebellion against every habit, belief and prerogative".[6] The forms of expression created by Dada — the bruitist poem, the typographical, optophonetic sound poem, the assemblage and above all the collage as a way to promote insights into what was really going on in the world — are results of that socially committed aspiration to draw art closer to life.

The first Dada performance at the Berlin Secession gave rise to both laughter and anger in the audience, and one reason for the furore was that the *Dada Manifesto* called the antipodes of Dada by their name, and it pulled no polemical punches: "the German philistine" (aka the bourgeois)[7] and the Expressionists. The latter's art was nothing but "insipid abstraction"[8] by "idle mind(s)" whose "gestures of abstract pathos [...] presuppose an empty, comfortable and stagnant life".[9] Dada's antidote to this Expressionist 'soul propaganda' and aesthetic harmony was "the most primitive of relations with the reality around us"[10] and the explicit integration of all its contradictions. Lovis Corinth, who was not merely the birthday boy on display but also the chairman of the Berlin Secession and hence the host for that evening's appearance by the Dadaists, must have welcomed the anti-Expressionist tenor of the event more than anything else.[11] He was trying to give the Secession a contemporary makeover, wanted his association of artists to become more political and would later, in 1921, offer the room to 'Dadadix' OTTO DIX to exhibit his paintings *Barricade* [*Barrikade*], *Skat Players* [*Skatspieler*] and *Prager Strasse* [*Prager Straße*] (all 1920) as a Dada triptych because they depicted "life undiluted"[12]. In April 1918, however, on the night of the Dada soirée, DIX was still serving on the Western front.

And so the incompatibility between these different artistic positions was pinpointed early on: on the one hand Dada, a counter-bourgeois (anti-art) art movement that mocked the aesthetic ivory tower of *l'art pour l'art*, and on the other Expressionism, which the Dadaists saw as stuck in the same old apolitical navel contemplation that dated back to before the war. Over time this innate difference

01 Shell-shocked after 1918
film still

02 OTTO DIX
Wounded Man, Autumn 1916, Bapaume, 1924
Lindenau-Museum Altenburg

01
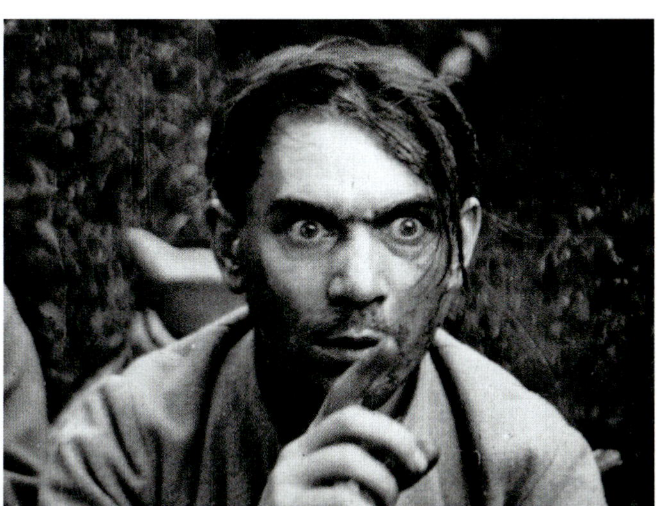

02
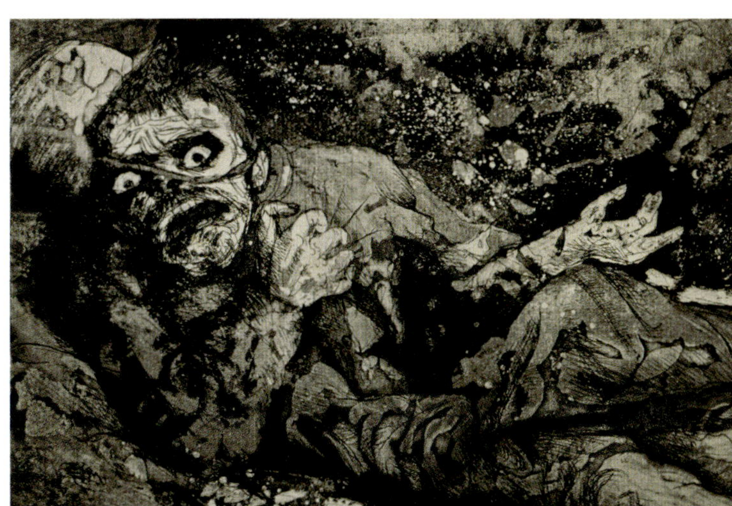

would prevent sustainable cohabitation under the roof of the Novembergruppe, given that the group's profile was heavily influenced not only by the Expressionists MAX PECHSTEIN, GEORG TAPPERT, MORIZ MELZER and CÉSAR KLEIN, who ranked among its founders, but also — especially between 1918 and 1920 — by artists attached to a Cubo-Futuro-Expressionist style, many of whom were recruited from the entourage of Herwarth Walden's gallery Der Sturm. There were differences, too, in the rules governing organizational accountability: the Novembergruppe was incorporated as an association with binding byelaws,[13] whereas Dada was a club "which one can join without assuming any liabilities", where "everyone presides" as long as they demonstrate a Dadaist "spirit",[14] shunning programmatic commitments in order to resist the governmental straitjacket and to pursue activities without exposure to the cultural policies of the corral.[15]

Rapprochement and Involvement

Nevertheless, the way the Novembergruppe defined itself, as set out in the leaflet to accompany an exhibition in November 1920 at Fraenkel & Co., a second-hand bookshop and art dealer in Berlin, sat very well with the aspirations of the Dadaists, and this motivated some of them to approach the association.[16] The Novembergruppe, says the printed text, was a "union of radical artists / radical in discarding old formats / radical in applying new tools of expression". 'Radical', however, is a broad concept open to individual interpretation.

At the legendary First International Dada Fair in August 1920[17] it became clear just how radical the Dadaists intended to be with the innovative use of materials in their products (they carefully avoided the term "art" due to its affirmative, bourgeois connotations) and how potentially provocative this was going to prove. With its 174 items from 28 exhibitors the Fair was the culmination and also the apotheosis of the international Dada movement. Notably it took place in the same building, at Lützowufer 13, as the Novembergruppe show by Fraenkel, except in the art dealership run by Dr. Otto Burchard from the same address. In the catalogue for the show, 'Progressdada' Wieland Herzfelde clearly enunciated the objectives which Dada associated with its "tools of expression": "Essentially any product is Dada if it is made without influence, unbothered by public authorities or value concepts, as long as what does the depicting is hostile to illusion, forged from the need to subvert and drive forward the present world, which is clearly dissolving, undergoing metamorphosis."[18] To the iconoclastic clarion call "Down with art", nailed like a poster to the wall, the *Dada Fair* jumbled together these "life art" products without discrimination, from big photographs, magazines, designs for advertisements, book covers and dolls to a cookery prize, all alongside oil paintings, watercolours, collages and assemblages, piled into a grotesque spatial experience which left visitors accordingly discombobulated (fig. 03).

This unique display, accurately described by the philosopher Odo Marquard as a "direct negative total artwork",[19] had nothing in common with tried-and-tested exhibitions of paintings and sculptures such as the Great Berlin Art Exhibition [*Grosse Berliner Kunstausstellung*] (p. 50, fig. 09). Nevertheless, the conventional framework provided there by the Novembergruppe did not prevent RAOUL HAUSMANN — who had organized the Dada Fair with GEORGE GROSZ and JOHN HEARTFIELD — or HANNAH HÖCH, the only woman among the Dadaists of Berlin, from sensing a kinship with the group as "revolutionaries of the spirit", or from joining the group early on and exhibiting with it.[20] OTTO DIX, YEFIM GOLYSHEV and GEORG SCHOLZ from Karlsruhe likewise seized this opportunity, using the Novembergruppe as a platform to present their creations to a wide audience. GOLYSHEV co-authored the manifesto *What is Dada and what does it want in Germany?* [*Was ist der Dadaismus und was will er in Deutschland?*][21] and together with HAUSMANN he had initiated Dada's first show at I. B. Neumann's Graphic Cabinet in April–Mai 1919, while SCHOLZ was represented at the *Dada Fair* with a Verism-inspired painting (now lost) with the telling title *Hindenburg Jelly: An aromatic birthday present for Field Marshal Hindenburg* [*Hindenburgsülze. Ein duftendes Geburtstags-Geschenk für den Feldmarschall Hindenburg*]. To understand which works Dada activists and supporters did and did not submit for the Novembergruppe exhibition in the Glass Palace at Lehrter Bahnhof, it helps to take a closer look at some examples.

The Ukrainian-born composer and painter YEFIM GOLYSHEV was a true saboteur of artistic boundaries who in 1919, according to HAUSMANN, became the first person to construct material collages from things not usually associated with art[22] and thereby flout traditional views about the aesthetic garments which it was considered seemly for art to wear. In 1920 he showed a work with the Novembergruppe entitled *My Self-Portrait* [*Mein Selbstporträt*][23] composed of "leftover bits of cigarette packets, matches and crusts of bread glued together *in natura*".[24] Critics read the work as "ultraviolet radicalism"[25] or simply a "joke"[26], but certainly a challenge and utterly devoid of artistic value. CURT EHRHARDT, not part of the Dada circle but open to Dada's invitation to process new materials, exhibited *The Coffee Mill* [*Die Kaffeemühle*] (cat. 40, p. 92) at the same Novembergruppe show within the Art Exhibition Berlin [*Berliner Kunstausstellung*][27] held from 21 May until the end of September 1920.[28] This was his title for a relief painting, colourfully Orphist and Cubist à la Robert Delaunay, with implants including the painted lid of a tin, a wooden comb, letters torn from newspapers, dyed feathers and thin strips of wood, defying both painterly illusion and pure abstraction as it explored the interaction between the painted picture space and the concrete existence of things. Moreover, the verbal associations triggered in the work—rhyming "mulierum", derived from the Latin word for woman and written with a brush, with "Du bist dumm" ("You are stupid") and juxtaposing these with an advertisement for "the trendy new spring-bell hairstyle"—satirize a conservative, middle-class image of women that urges the 'little lady' to doll herself up and get on with the housework rather than seek an emancipated role in the real world of employ-

03 Opening of the *First International Dada Fair*
Berlin, 1920
Left to right: Hannah Höch, Raoul Hausmann, Otto Burchard, Johannes Baader, Wieland and Margarete Herzfelde, Otto Schmalhausen, George Grosz and John Heartfield

04 OTTO DIX
The Sailor Fritz Müller from Pieschen, 1919
Galleria Civica d'Arte Moderna, Turin
Art Exhibition Berlin 1920, Novembergruppe section, no. 1116

03

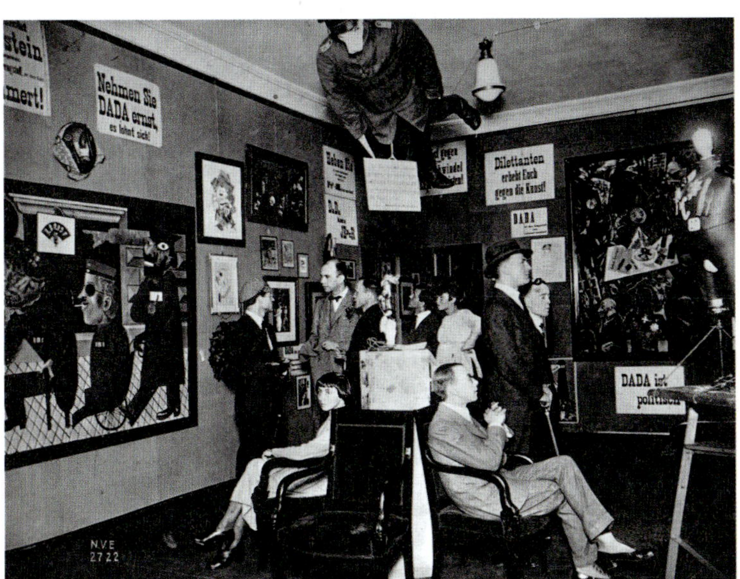

04

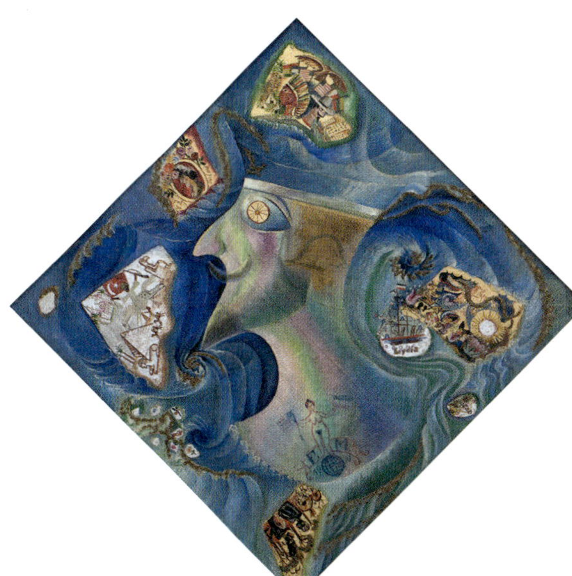

ment.[29] To top it all, EHRHARDT inserted the fragmentary word "MERZ", chosen by KURT SCHWITTERS in July 1919 as his art logo, over the middle of the picture. Evidently the self-taught CURT EHRHARDT agreed with SCHWITTERS about using "all imaginable materials for artistic purposes" to achieve direct expression "by shortening the path of intuition to the visualization of the art work".[30] Critical minds saw it, as in the case of GOLYSHEV, as mere *"Gschnas"*,[31] a Viennese term for pointless frippery.

OTTO DIX, a founding member in 1919 of the Dresden Secession, a group of artists who maintained close ties with the Novembergruppe for a while, also seized the chance to show three works to a broad audience in the capital city[32] (the attendance figures for the Great Berlin Art Exhibition apparently ran into six digits[33]). One of them, entitled *The Sailor Fritz Müller from Pieschen* [*Der Matrose Fritz Müller aus Pieschen*] (1919), is the portrait of a mariner born of the surf and the open waves (fig. 04). This anti-bourgeois male prototype fascinated DIX at the turn of the 1920s and he used the motif in more than 40 works.[34] Quite possibly this one, the first of DIX'S sailors, could have been motivated in part by the sailors' uprising in Kiel in early November 1918. However, this particular specimen is no revolutionary but the personification, verging on *kitsch*, of the longing for an exotic life of freedom, foreign climes and a girl in every port. The integrated elements of collage, little vignettes underlaid with gold and silver paint, already hint at the 'Dadadix' who, a few months later at the First International *Dada Fair,* would be displaying far more forthright works in terms of materials and motifs. One was a moving figure (now lost), an early participatory *objet d'art* inviting active intervention by the viewer (fig. 05). The superimposed, interconnected silhouettes, probably painted cardboard cut-outs, depicted a naked woman in suspenders, a moustachioed man dressed in a collar and bow-tie, and a grazing cow, and the visitor was asked to place them in the "right" positions. With this jumping-jack mechanism, DIX breathed tongue-in-cheek life into Dada's slogan "rise up, ye amateurs, against art". Another work now vanished without trace was *45% Employable! (The War Cripples)* [*45% Erwerbsfähig! (Die Kriegskrüppel)*] (1920).[35] In this painting, hung prominently in the main hall of the *Dada Fair,* OTTO DIX paraded war invalids in a grotesque procession of everyday existence. As a portrait of deformity, this is the antithesis to the male dream in *The Sailor Fritz Müller from Pieschen*. There are no wet fantasies here about the taste of the salty seas and the erotic encounters beyond. The men on the canvas have lost their vital functions. They populate the streets on crutches and in wheelchairs, with faces sewn together and artificial limbs, robbed of their masculine potency. This merciless spotlight on reality also exposes the militaristic mentalities still rife in the fledgling Weimar Republic and challenged by Dada. Whether or not it was a conscious decision on his part, the works OTTO DIX exhibited with the Novembergruppe were less provocative in their social content than these.

HANNAH HÖCH'S contributions to the group display at the regional exhibition in 1920 were almost anodyne. At the time, HÖCH and HAUSMANN were a couple and she had acquired the function of 'Dadasopher' in the feminine form. She showed four abstract watercolours and a wooden sculpture called *Birth* [*Geburt*] which later came into the possession of a friend, the Dutch architect Jan Buijs.[36] Although they were anti-academic in technique and drew on the Expressionist-Constructivist formal repertoire widespread among artists in the Novembergruppe, the watercolours, modestly entitled *Picture X* to *Picture XIII,*[37] bore not the remotest trace of Dada's effort to interrogate the existential condition of a newly emerging society by means of (anti-)art which radically questioned all traditional values (fig. 06). This was not where HANNAH HÖCH chose to exhibit the technique so germane

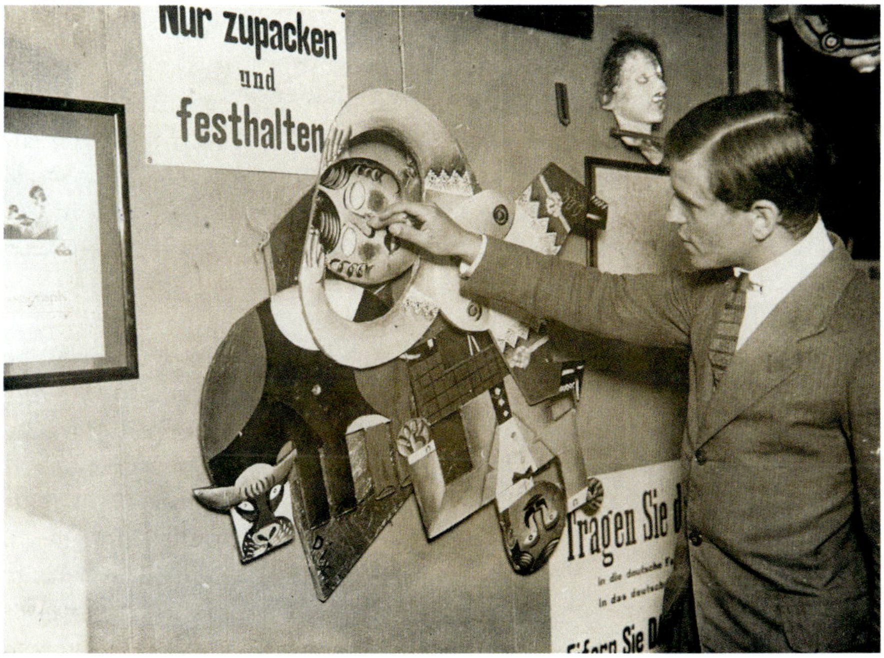

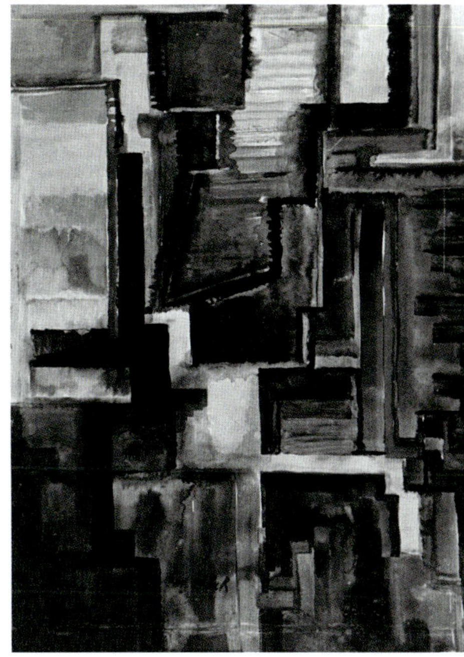

05 *Wieland Herzfelde by Otto Lasker-Dix's moving figure at the Dada Fair*, Berlin, 1920
Berlinische Galerie

06 HANNAH HÖCH
Picture 13: Red–Yellow, 1919
Art Exhibition Berlin 1920, Novembergruppe section, no. 1224
Berlinische Galerie, Hannah-Höch-Archiv

to this challenge, the photomontage or collage, where the contours of an egregious situation are exaggerated by sticking them together to make a distorted mirror.[38] Instead she took her magnificent critique of culture and society to the concurrent *Dada Fair*, demonstrating collage as a survival strategy and a critical tool in the form of *Cut with the Kitchen Knife Dada through Germany's Last Weimar Beer Belly Cultural Era* [*Schnitt mit dem Küchenmesser Dada durch die letzte Weimarer Bierbauchkulturepoche Deutschlands*] (1919–20) and her *Dada Review* [*Dada-Rundschau*] (1919) (fig. 07). Perhaps the artist suspected there would be trouble if President Friedrich Ebert, who opened the Art Exhibition Berlin in 1920 and took a tour of the halls to soak up the flavour, should chance upon *Dada Review*, in which HÖCH took the mickey out of politicians, the president among them. Ebert was prominently positioned in the centre of the collage, cut from the cover page of the *Berliner Illustrirte Zeitung* in August 1919, which revealed him in swimming trunks enjoying a summer break with his similarly clad defence minister Gustav Noske—an awkward motif prompting diatribes against the country's new leaders from both left-wing and reactionary quarters.[39] Even RAOUL HAUSMANN, who saw Dada as an instrument for undermining the conceptual pillars of the bourgeoisie and who believed that any Expressionist seeking to avoid the pitfalls of petty convention ought to be a Dadaist, contributed a painting when participating a little tardily, in 1921, in his first (and last) show with the Novembergruppe, rather than an assemblage like his iconic *Mechanical Head (The Spirit of Our Age)* [*Mechanischer Kopf (Der Geist unserer Zeit)*] (1919). This unknown exhibit, entitled *Head in Eccentric Movement* [*Kopf in exzentrischer Bewegung*] and executed by HAUSMANN in his "very personal Cubism"[40], was probably a pre-Dada portrait of his lover HANNAH HÖCH.[41] GEORGE GROSZ and 'Monteurdada' JOHN HEARTFIELD, who had already joined the Communist Party of Germany (KPD) in late 1918, positively refused to have anything to do with the Novembergruppe in its early years, and not until 1927 did they join the proceedings with works that were Dadaist in spirit.[42]

Nevertheless, apart from the examples already mentioned there were quite a few works among the almost 450 by 128 artists displayed by the Novembergruppe at the Art Exhibition Berlin of 1920 which so disturbed visitors and reviewers alike that the very presence of the association — perceived as a collective government protégé — elicited disapproval. Culture minister Konrad Haenisch was vociferously attacked for making this precious space in a public exhibition hall available to the "producers of burps and farts in frames"[43]. Otto Koester, in the left-wing weekly *Die Weltbühne,* was among those who echoed the condemnation of the Novembergruppe exhibits as "non-art". His polemic elaborates further: "Given the dreadful shortage of housing, it does not seem unreasonable to ask why the Prussian government should not have the public premises over which it can freely dispose done up as emergency homes for dozens of proletarian families, rather than using them to accommodate muck which, to make matters worse, cannot even be used in agriculture."[44] Haenisch responded by insisting that he was no "police thug" and would have nothing to do with "interventions by the authorities in artistic matters".[45] However, the warning shots from the press had hit their mark and a year later political officials threatened the Novembergruppe with exclusion if such undesirable works were submitted again.[46]

The Conflict and the Split

RAOUL HAUSMANN may have been tentative about placing his artistic output with the Novembergruppe, and he never repeated that one-off decision to exhibit, and yet he did show signs of a strategy for seeking and then expanding a role in the artist community.[47] He was well versed in the art of pamphleteering, enlisting the written word to win arguments and influence. In the fourth issue of the Novembergruppe magazine with the unfortunate name *Der Kunsttopf* ("the art pot") — which even contemporaries could not resist mocking, because many ingredients can be tossed into a saucepan and stewed over a low flame — he published an article which, wittingly or otherwise, failed to live up to the promise in the title: "Objective Thoughts on the Role of Dadaism".[48] His linguistic rage against the mercantile success of Expressionism, which served "as a means to reassure the bourgeois and stabilize his existence by distracting him from unpleasant contemporary events"[49], was too caustic not to antagonize a fair number of Novembergruppe members with his "objective" views, and yet HAUSMANN only honed his credentials as a result. It was a typical gesture of the Novembergruppe to carry the text in its leading periodical alongside replies by the sculptor GEORG LESCHNITZER and the architect and executive board member ALFRED GELLHORN. After all, the role of art in reshaping society was dear to all their hearts.[50] GELLHORN sought a consensual approach with his dictum "Synthesis, not antithesis!", appealing for quality and independence for "living art", which should set aside divisions about isms and disagreements about whether to target an audience of intellectuals or industrial workers: "Anyone aware of the necessity of his work will not be deterred by a lack of success and will attach little value to recognition. But you Dadaists are basically only interested in recognition and you judge art by artists wanting the same. Those who were truly creative, however, looked neither to the right nor to the left. A thought for the good. Now get on with your scuffling. Let's shake the place up!"[51]

RAOUL HAUSMANN was not (really) a man of compromise. In January 1921, in a text not published at the time, he described a revamp of *Der Kunsttopf* — both its content and some vital international framing — and put himself forward as the editor of such a journal. Here he entirely echoed the aims of the Novembergruppe — and of ALFRED GELLHORN — by opposing "dogma and doctrine". "*Der Kunst-*

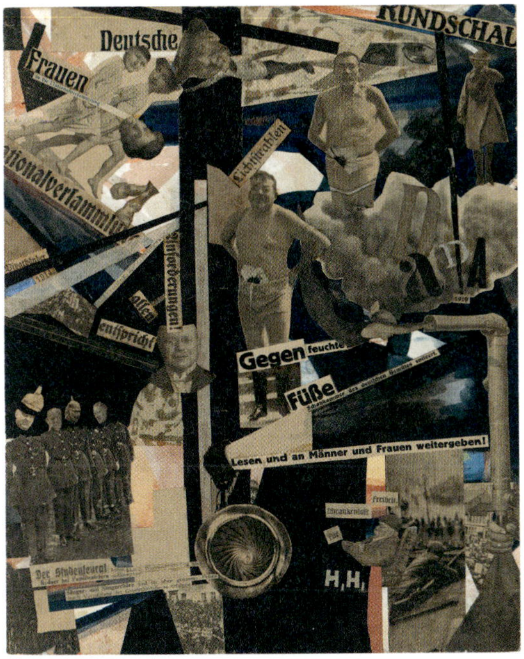

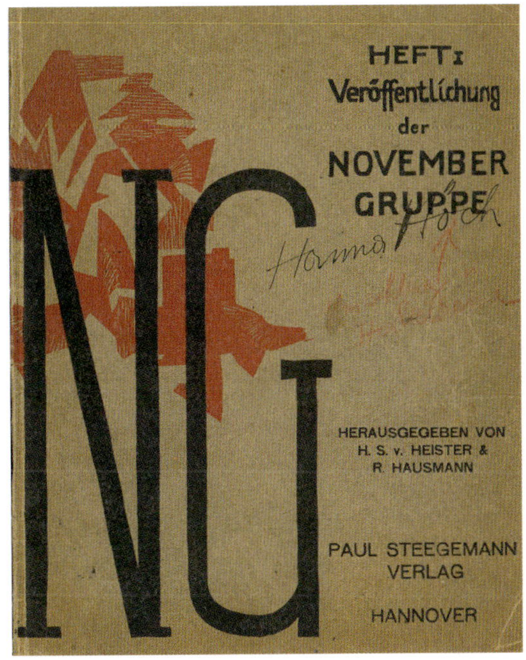

07 HANNAH HÖCH
Dada Review, 1919,
Berlinische Galerie

08 *NG. Publication of the Novembergruppe*, 1921, no. 1
cover design by Hannah Höch
Berlinische Galerie

07 08

topf," reasons HAUSMANN, "is the place to discuss the creative questions which critics and historians, as uncreative people, cannot talk about — the style of a work depends on its vibrant insights, not the extent to which it is modern in form, for only historians base their classifications on that. The art historians talk of style or movement, but art cannot be shoehorned into this concept even retrospectively, because in art there is no style, that is aesthetic formalism. [...] Art is driven by its time and drives its time, not as a question of fashion or civilization, but as a human affair." Consequently, *Der Kunsttopf* should "not portray current movements, but the development of a process of the mind" in order to reach out to a broad readership. The aim was "overcoming individualism and the emergence of a new sense of community" — in and through art.[52]

Both the tone and the direction of the thoughts RAOUL HAUSMANN set out here for the mouthpiece of the artists' association evidently garnered support. So much so that in May 1921, together with HANS SIEBERT VON HEISTER, he was already functioning as the editor of the "Novembergruppe publication". The realignment of *Der Kunsttopf* after just six issues had to be made visible. In pursuit of this new brand strategy the title was changed to *NG* and the old cover design by CÉSAR KLEIN was replaced by a typographical logo created by HANNAH HÖCH (fig. 08). As for pluralism of expression, however, the first — and, as it turned out, last — issue of *NG* was a limited accomplishment. HAUSMANN had gathered a horde of friends around him who shared his artistic and intellectual views, and he offered them a platform to publish articles.[53] He had succeeded in asserting his influence and playing a perceptible part in defining the Novembergruppe's intellectual course, and this also explains his co-option onto the association's exhibition committee for the Great Berlin Art Exhibition of 1921. He even wrote the guide to the Novembergruppe section, formulating it in an accessible language that was not usually his hallmark. One interesting feature is that he describes the works without reference to their artists, hence — as promised — helping to overcome individualism and to pursue a "socio-aesthetic collectivization of artistic aspirations".[54]

At the same time, due to his operational commitment on behalf of the Novembergruppe, HAUSMANN found himself in a pickle, and he was not alone in facing the

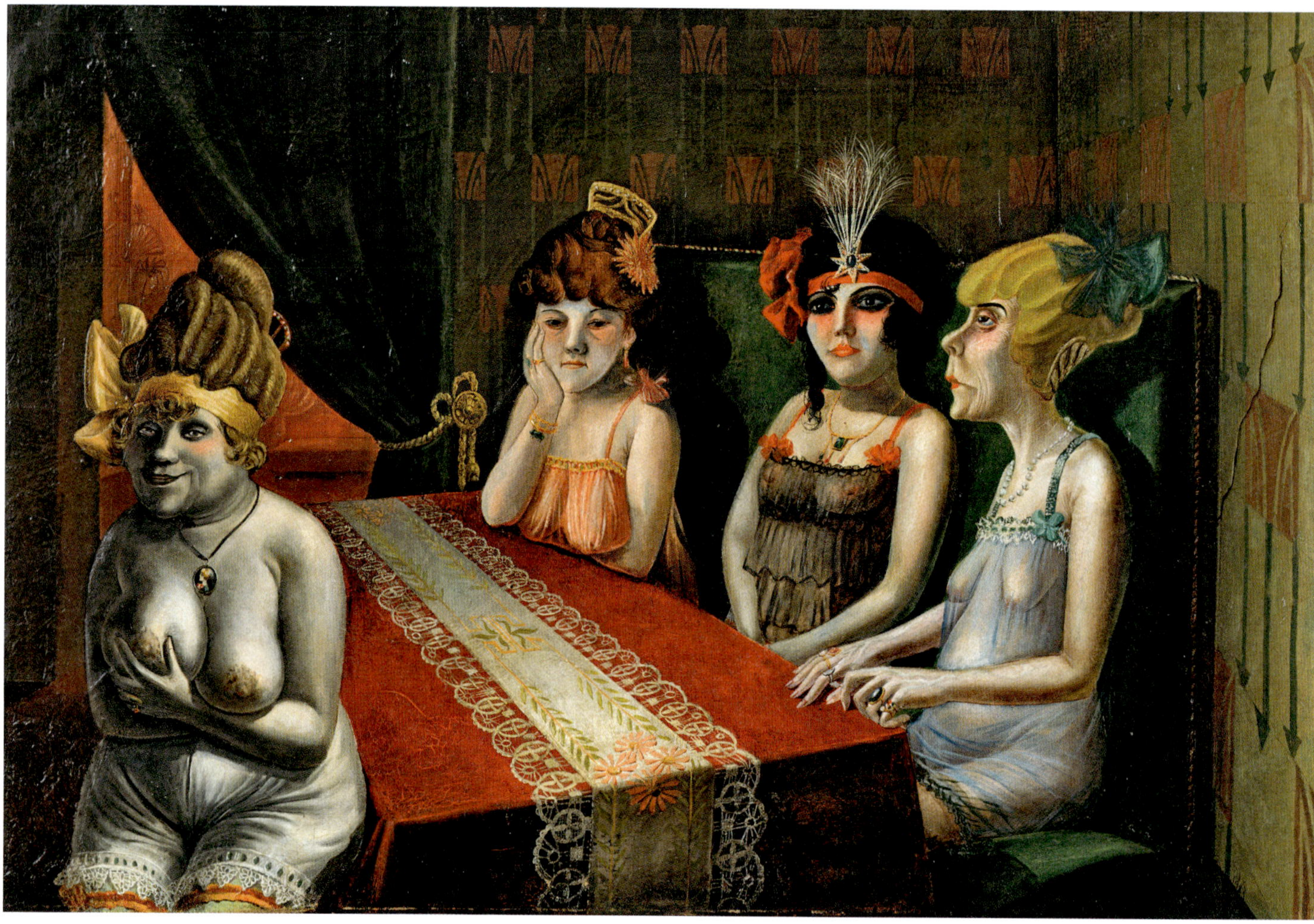

09

09 OTTO DIX
Salon I, 1921
Kunstmuseum Stuttgart

consequences. Although immune to accusations from reviewers that it was parading radicality as a fashion trend, the association certainly had acquired some sensitivity and was keen to avoid offensive content which might contribute to the contemporary debate on censorship or, even worse, trigger police intervention on the basis of §184, the statutory ban on pornography, because that would jeopardize its participation in the big art show.[55] Under pressure from Max Schlichting as chairman of the management committee for the Great Berlin Art Exhibition, the exhibition committee therefore removed two works at the pre-screening stage. They had been submitted, of all people, by RUDOLF SCHLICHTER and OTTO DIX, both with links to Dada. SCHLICHTER'S *Love Life in Berlin W.* [*Liebesleben in Berlin W.*], now lost, may well—to judge from its title—have illustrated some slap and tickle from the red-light district, and it was deleted from the list of exhibits without a replacement. Meanwhile, the painting *Salon I* (1921) by OTTO DIX (fig. 09), a brothel scene in a Veristic vein, also fell prey to this self-censorship by the Novembergruppe. The decision elicited a sharp-tongued letter from DIX to HAUSMANN in early May 1921: "dear Raul tell the Nov. Gr. they are pitiful philistines and i pay these people my deepest contempt the work is not immoral but the brains of these upright troopers probably are who furthermore scornfully turn up their snouts at anything out of the provinces In the Dresden Secession which is doubtless very reactionary i could have exhibited this painting without a fuss It is an outrage to remove the best painting of all. Show the picture to lots of people and make the point that the Nov. Group cannot exhibit it I authorize you to sell it. I suggest and you can tell the Nov. gr. this that they should call themselves the Preliberal Group".[56] OTTO DIX was at least able to replace this entry with his painting *Suleika, the Tattooed Wonder* [*Suleika, das tätowierte Wunder*] (1920) (cat. 45, p. 99). Evidently this depiction of a bare-breasted, fully-tattooed woman from the cabinet of curiosities of a travelling fair was seen as exotic rather than indecent.[57] For RAOUL HAUSMANN, however, this kowtowing by the Novembergruppe was unpardonable, not least because he risked losing face himself.

On 20 June 1921, five weeks after the Great Berlin Art Exhibition opened, he used the magazine *Der Gegner*—published by Malik, an imprint with close links to Dada—to place an "Open Letter to the Novembergruppe" in which he recounted what had occurred and voiced his discontent, going on to list everything which, in his view, was wrong with the organization. The letter ended with his resignation and that of the other signatories, among them DIX and SCHLICHTER.[58] The "Novembergruppe opposition" accused the association of having an unrevolutionary mindset and lacking attitude. Other key criticisms were that art had been depoliticized and commercialized by a "cult of individuality", that the group was currying favour with the government, that its "celebrities"[59] were engaged in a bourgeois pursuit of cushy jobs and that by the same token there were now first- and second-class members. Focussing on an aesthetic revolution and renouncing the original objectives went hand in hand with betraying the proletarian revolution. The "Open Letter" ended in an appeal with a communist turn of phrase: "We call on those members who understand that art today is a protest against bourgeois somnambulance and against the perpetuation of exploitation and philistine individuality to join our opposition and help to bring about the much-needed clean-up of objectives. We know that we must be the expression of revolutionary forces, the instrument of the needs of our time and of the masses [...] and having recognized our task we mean to get down to business: working to build the new human community, the community of working people!"[60]

The response from the Novembergruppe, belatedly printed in 1922 and likewise in *Der Gegner*, was brief. The association had long believed and repeatedly stated "that the pursuit of radical political aims was a matter for every individual, that the group as an association had merely to pursue radical artistic aims".[61] The support given to individual members by the Novembergruppe in terms of revolutionary art was to be regarded as political.[62]

Dada and the Novembergruppe agreed to disagree: they were radically incompatible.

1 Data provided by the *Deutsches Historisches Museum*.

2 The morning edition of the *Vossische Zeitung* of 27 January 1918 reported it as the foundation of a "branch of the major international culture movement Dada".

3 Schwarz 1998, pp. 135ff.

4 According to Raoul Hausmann's account, in: Riha and Kämpf 1992, pp. 23–28.

5 *Dadaistisches Manifest*, quoted in: Riha and Schäfer 1994, pp. 91–94, here 91.

6 Quoted in Riha and Kämpf 1992, p. 7.

7 Raoul Hausmann, "Der deutsche Spießer ärgert sich" (December 1919), in: Erlhoff 1982, vol. 1, pp. 82–84.

8 *Dadaistisches Manifest*, quoted in Riha and Schäfer 1994, pp. 91–94, here 94.

9 Ibid., p. 91.

10 Ibid., p. 92.

11 Schwarz 1998, pp. 135ff.

12 Otto Dix, in: exhib. cat. Museum Villa Stuck 1985, p. 279.

13 The plan to register the association dated back to January 1919, although officially it did not happen until 25 August 1920. See Willy Oskar Dressler (ed.), *Dresslers Kunsthandbuch*, Berlin 1923, p. 206.

14 *Dadaistisches Manifest*, quoted in Riha and Schäfer 1994, pp. 91–94, here 93f.

15 On Dada's sardonic response to a revolutionary attitude that seeks reassurance in statutes like the Novembergruppe's articles of association see Nentwig 2015, p. 41.

16 Anke Matelowski has succeeded, backed by sources, in correcting the long-perpetuated error that the Novembergruppe's first independent exhibition was held in November

1919. The show actually took place a year later in 1920. See Matelowski 2017, pp. 335f.

17 On the *First International Dada Fair* see Adkins 1988 and Bergius 2000, pp. 233–414.

18 Wieland Herzfelde, "Zur Einführung", in: *Erste Internationale Dada-Messe*, John Heartfield, Wieland Herzfelde (eds), exhib. cat. Berlin 1920, p. 2.

19 Quoted in Bergius 2000, p. 241.

20 The exact arrangements for joining are unknown, and the source material extant offers no precise data about when members signed up or left. However, Hausmann and Höch published woodcuts in the very first issue of the Novembergruppe's journal *Der Kunsttopf* in July 1920, suggesting that they were members at the time.

21 Riha and Schäfer 1994, pp. 138–139.

22 See Riha and Kämpf 1992, p. 20.

23 Exhib. cat. *Kunstausstellung Berlin* 1920, no. 1181; this is a blanket entry: "50 watercolours".

24 Adolph Donath, "Kunstausstellungen. Berliner Sezession, Große Kunstausstellung Berlin, Franz Metzner", in: *Der Kunstwanderer*, vol. 1, 1919–20, 1st June issue, pp. 382–383, here 383. See also Otto Koester's description of the work under the heading "Berlin art scandal": "[...] protruding into the self-portrait and likewise fixed to the card is a slice of dry bread, evidently intended, with the aid of an affixed lump of soap (nose), a trouser button (eye), two rows of matchstick tips (teeth) and bits of a cigarette packet (hat), to evoke the profile of a human face". In: *Die Weltbühne*, vol. 16, no. 32, 5 August 1920, pp. 165f.

25 Willi Kurth, "Berliner Ausstellungen", in: *Die Kunst für alle*, year 35, 1919–20, nos. 21–22 (August 1920), pp. 401f.

26 Hans Schmidkunz, "Kunstausstellung Berlin 1920", in: *Die christliche Kunst*, vol. 17, 1920–21, pp. 24–29, here 25.

27 As the *Grosse Berliner Kunstausstellung* was temporarily known.

28 Ehrhardt took part in exhibitions from 1920 to 1922 and was in all likelihood a member of the Novembergruppe. See Arlt 2002, pp. 20–27.

29 The concept "associative thing composition" used by Ehrhardt also characterizes this work. See Arlt 2002, p. 26.

30 Kurt Schwitters, "Die Merzmalerei", in: *Der Sturm*, 10th vol., 1919, no. 4, p. 61 (reprinted in: Lach 1981, p. 37). Ehrhardt could not have foreseen that Merz would remain a one-man art movement embodied by Schwitters and that Curt Ehrhardt would sink almost into oblivion and be regarded today as an epigone of the Hanoverian.

31 Ref. in note 26.

32 Apart from *The Sailor Fritz Müller from Pieschen* these were the collage *Tram* and *Cats (dedicated to Theodor Däubler)*, ref. in note 23, nos. 1116–1118.

33 Nungesser 1983, p. 90.

34 Söll 2012, pp. 49f.

35 Formerly in the Stadtmuseum Dresden; confiscated as "degenerate art" and displayed in 1937 at the defamatory Nazi exhibition of that name in Munich as "painted sabotage of national defence"; the work is still lost.

36 Ref. in note 23, nos. 1221–1225.

37 In the artist's documentary estate there is a black and white photographic reproduction of *Picture 13: Red-Yellow* (1919) with Höch's handwriting on the back. This tells us that the work was shown both at the Novembergruppe exhibition in 1920 and previously at the first Dada exhibition in April–May 1919 in I. B. Neumann's Graphic Cabinet.

38 Hannah Höch joined the Novembergruppe in 1918 and exhibited regularly at its shows until 1931. In 1927 and 1929, however, while living in The Hague, Höch did not submit any works. Intriguingly, it was not until 1930, after returning from The Netherlands, that she finally contributed 15 works of collage and photomontage, the medium most intimately associated with her. Prior to this, at the Novembergruppe exhibition held at the Berlin Secession in June 1925, the artist had shown two paintings, *The Journalists* and *Roma* (both 1925), which transposed her collage principle into oils.

39 For a detailed interpretation of this collage see Bergius 1989.

40 Berlinische Galerie 1989, 6.36, p. 140.

41 This is born out in a note written by Höch retrospectively listing the works that she and Hausmann had shown at Novembergruppe exhibitions. See Berlinische Galerie 2001, vol. 2, Ud. 373, p. 458.

42 See the essay by Nentwig, pp. 198f. of this catalogue.

43 Otto Koester, "Berliner Kunstskandal", in: *Die Weltbühne*, vol. 16, no. 32, 5 August 1920, pp. 165–168, here 167.

44 Ibid.

45 Konrad Haenisch, in: *Die Weltbühne*, vol. 16, no. 35, 26 August 1920, p. 247. On culture minister Haenisch's commitment to absolute freedom in the arts as a token of progressive politics in post-revolutionary Prussia, see Kratz-Kessemeier 2008, pp. 152–163.

46 "Offener Brief an die Novembergruppe", in: *Der Gegner*, vol. 2, 1920–21, nos. 8–9, p. 299.

47 Nentwig 2015, pp. 49–52.

48 In: *Der Kunsttopf*, published by the Novembergruppe, year 1, October 1920, no. 4, pp. 62–68. (reprinted in: Erlhoff 1982, vol. 1, pp. 108–113).

49 Raoul Hausmann, "Objektive Betrachtung des Dadaismus", ibid., pp. 62–68, here 66.

50 Georg Leschnitzer, "Über die Tragik des heutigen Kunstschaffens" (ref. in note 48), pp. 68–75. Leschnitzner sees Dada primarily as a criticism of artistic and intellectual life, but argues in the same breath that critics take their criticism too seriously. He believes that modernism has nothing to offer the proletariat and champions a return to the crafts as an expression of popular art. I am grateful to Janina Nentwig for drawing my attention to this debate.

51 A(lfred) G(ellhorn), "Ein Wort zum Guten" (ref. in note 48), pp. 75–77.

52 Raoul Hausmann, "Der Kunsttopf", in: Berlinische Galerie 1995, vol. 2, 21.54, pp. 42f.

53 Hausmann published "Art and Time" ["Die Kunst und die Zeit"]; the philosopher Salomo Friedlaender, whose ideas on "creative indifference" were a major influence on Hausmann and Höch, submitted an epistemological text about his friend Ernst Marcus entitled "The Cosmic Brain" ["Das kosmische Gehirn"]; Hannah Höch contributed the grotesque "Journey to Italy" ["Italienreise"], while Otto Freundlich set out his views on combining social and natural totality in "Humans" ["Der Mensch"].

54 Roters 1995, p. 78.

55 On the conflict between the culture and justice ministries over censorship on grounds of morality, see Kratz-Kessemeier 2008, pp. 157–159.

56 Berlinische Galerie 1995, vol. 2, 21.26, p. 24.

57 According to the surviving correspondence, Dix submitted three works (see Berlinische Galerie 1995, vol. 2, 21.23, p. 22). However, the catalogue for the *Grosse Berliner Kunstausstellung* of 1921 only lists two: the painting *Salon* (no. 1052), which fell prey to censorship after the catalogue was printed, and *Alma* (no. 1167). Presumably the jury had to restore the status of *Suleika, the Tattooed Wonder* to enable it to stand in as a proxy.

58 "Offener Brief an die Novembergruppe", in: *Der Gegner*, vol. 2, 1920–21, nos. 8–9, pp. 297–301. The signatories included not only Dix, Hausmann and Schlichter but also Max Dungert, George Grosz, Hanna(h) Höch, Ernst Krantz, (Franz) Mutzenbecher, Thomas Ring, Georg Scholz and Willy Zierath.

59 Names mentioned here were Moriz Melzer, César Klein, Georg Tappert, Oswald Herzog, Hans Brass and Rudolf Belling.

60 Ref. in note 58, p. 301.

61 Novembergruppe, "Erwiderung", in: *Der Gegner*, vol. 3, no. 1, 21 March 1922, p. 30.

62 The reply was evidently composed by Otto Möller, who was on the working committee of the Novembergruppe. The typed manuscript, which was abridged for print, is among Otto Möller's posthumous papers held by the Berlinische Galerie (BG-OM 294). See Roters 1995, pp. 82f.

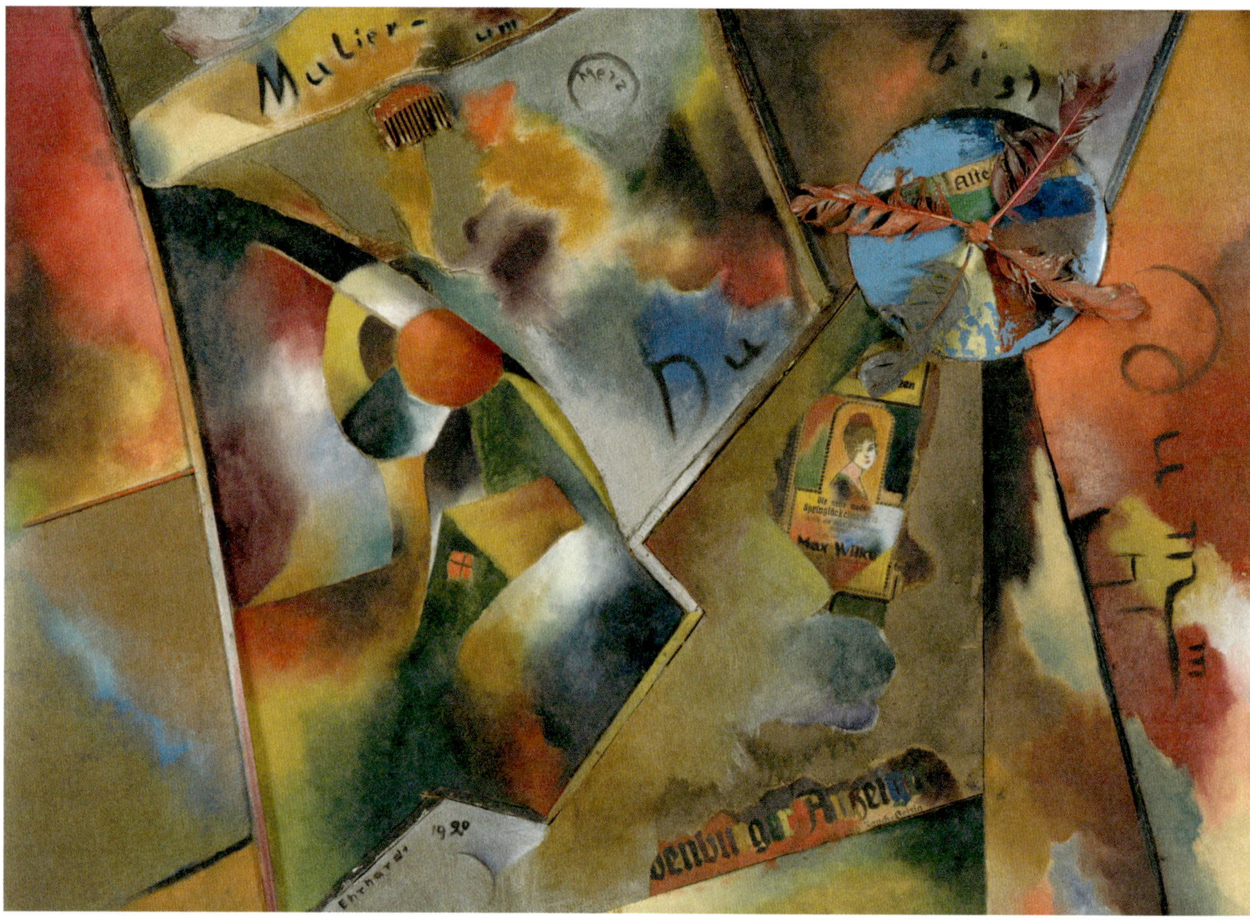

40
CURT EHRHARDT
The Coffee Grinder, 1920

Mixed media, collage, 70 × 93 cm
Berlinische Galerie

Art Exhibition Berlin 1920,
Novembergruppe section, no. 1138

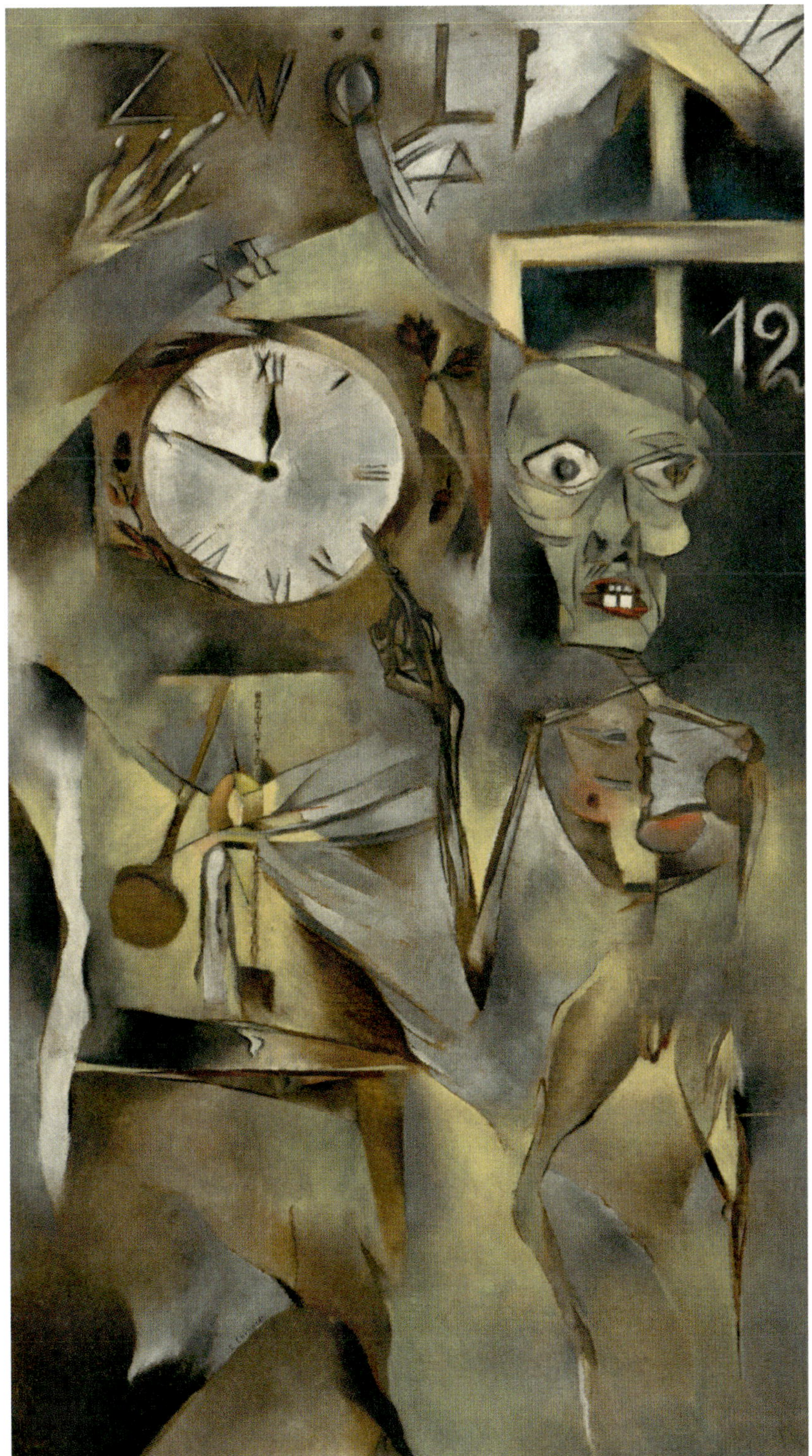

41

CURT EHRHARDT

At 12 Midnight, 1921

Oil on paperboard, 112 × 62.5 cm
Private collection Harald Gnade, Berlin

Great Berlin Art Exhibition 1922,
Novembergruppe section, no. 1231

GEORG SCHOLZ
Industrial Peasants, 1920

His socially critical paintings were "forthright pictorial sermons about life as it really is today"[1], wrote the art historian and essayist Hans Curjel about GEORG SCHOLZ. One of the best-known works by Scholz is *Industrial Peasants* [*Industriebauern*] (cat. 42, p. 95), exhibited with the Novembergruppe at the Great Berlin Art Exhibition in 1921. His contributions to the group exhibitions in 1919 and 1920 had been inspired by Futurism and Expressionism, but this time the card-carrying communist Scholz presented a new, grossly exaggerated form of objectivity later known as Verism.[2] Expressionism, claimed the artist when explaining this style shift in the group's magazine *NG*, was utterly apolitical and just boiled down to art for its own sake: "It is better to paint 'tendentious' works than *l'art pour l'art*!"[3]
Scholz put his opinion into practice with this depiction of a rapacious, bigoted farming family: the caricatured figures are repulsive and grotesquely distorted. The head of the household with his scarred face and swinish snout clutches a Bible to his chest, while, among the many elements of collage in this picture, real share certificates literally sprout from his skull. Scholz was inspired to adopt this device by the Berlin Dadaists: he had close personal links with them and they invited him to take part in the First International Dada Fair in the summer of 1920.[4] Past research has assumed that Scholz seized this opportunity for a first public airing, not only of his *Hindenburg Jelly* [*Hindenburgsülze*] (now lost), but also of *Industrial Peasants*, given that both works are listed in the Dada Fair catalogue.[5] A letter to the Novembergruppe on 12 November 1920 reveals, however, that the artist had been unable to dispatch *Industrial Peasants* to Berlin from Grötzingen in Baden. He therefore asked the Novembergruppe to reproduce the work in the monthly journal *Der Kunsttopf* instead,[6] a plan that was promptly carried out in December.[7]
In the spring of 1921, Scholz submitted the work for the Great Berlin Art Exhibition. He told the Novembergruppe that he looked forward to it having "some impact on the public", adding that it had "never been exhibited anywhere at all yet".[8] Scholz's hopes were not dashed. On the very first day, while Germany's president Friedrich Ebert was being shown around, *Industrial Peasants* caused quite a stir and several right-wing members of parliament indignantly left the venue.[9] Despite this protest, the work stayed where it was in the Novembergruppe section, unlike two paintings by the Verists OTTO DIX and RUDOLF SCHLICHTER, ousted under pressure from the management of the Great Berlin Art Exhibition. This act of censorship prompted a serious crisis within the Novembergruppe. Scholz was one of the signatories under the open letter in which RAOUL HAUSMANN and other members announced their resignation.[10] Scholz himself soon yielded to requests from the association to return, candidly admitting that he had no wish to miss out on the opportunities to exhibit.[11]

JANINA NENTWIG

1 Hans Curjel, "Zur Entwicklung des Malers Georg Scholz", in: *Das Kunstblatt*, vol. 7, 1923, pp. 257–264, here 260.
2 On the life and work of Georg Scholz see Sternfeld 2004, who considers this specific work on pp. 129–133.
3 Georg Scholz, "Brief an Hans Siebert von Heister, Grötzingen, 31. März 1921, mit einer Anmerkung von Hans Siebert von Heister", in: *NG. Veröffentlichung der Novembergruppe*, vol. 1, 1921, pp. 42–45, here 44.
4 See Sternfeld 2004, 127–129; Bergius 1989, p. 270.
5 *Erste Internationale Dada-Messe. Ausstellung und Verkauf dadaistischer Erzeugnisse* (exhib. cat. Berlin, Kunsthandlung Dr. Otto Burchard), Berlin 1920, nos. 92 and 93.
6 Letter from Georg Scholz to the *Novembergruppe*, 12 November 1920, Archives of the Staatsgalerie Stuttgart, estate of Will Grohmann.
7 *Der Kunsttopf*, vol. 1, 1920, no. 6, p. 109.
8 Letter from Georg Scholz to Hans Siebert von Heister, 20 March 1921, private collection.
9 See Sternfeld 2004, pp. 132f.
10 See the essay by Burmeister in this catalogue, p. 89.
11 See the letter from Georg Scholz to Willy Storck, director of the Kunsthalle in Karlsruhe, 15 June 1921, copy in the archives of Kunsthalle Karlsruhe, first quoted by Holsten 1990, pp. 61f.

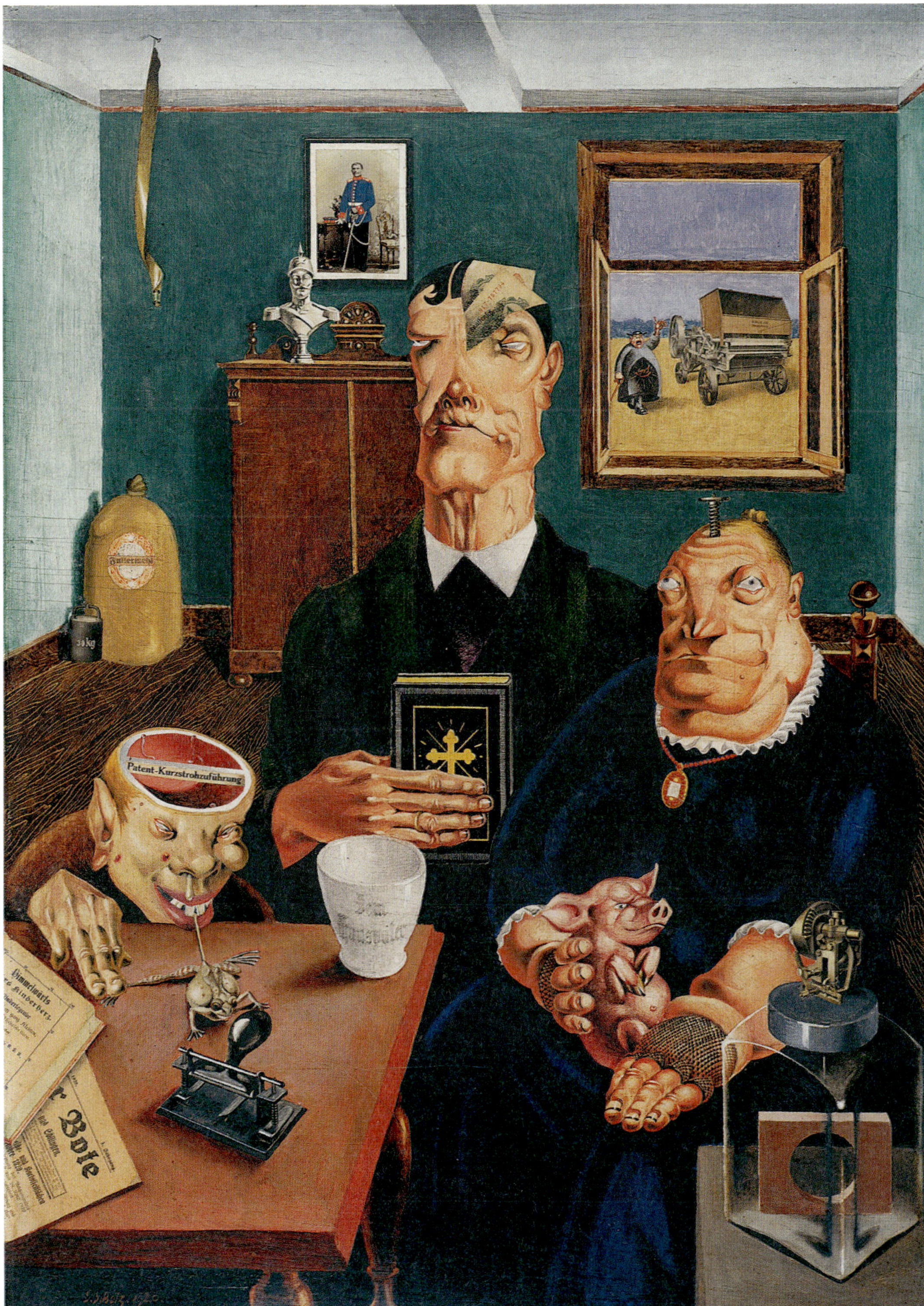

42

GEORG SCHOLZ

Industrial Farmers, 1920

Oil and collage over pencil on plywood, 98 × 70 cm,
Von der Heydt-Museum Wuppertal

Great Berlin Art Exhibition 1921, Novembergruppe section,
no. 1173; First International Art Exhibition Düsseldorf 1922, no. 329

KURT SCHWITTERS
Watercolour 5: He and She, 1919

There were not many encounters between KURT SCHWITTERS and the Novembergruppe. It is true that his name crops up in foundation year 1918 in the first list of members written out in the hand of GEORG TAPPERT (p. 252), and also that the following year he published six of his poems in a special issue of the journal *Menschen* dedicated to *Kräfte*, a group of artists who at that time constituted the Hamburg branch of the Berlin-based association.[1] However, Schwitters only exhibited with the Novembergruppe on two occasions, the first time at the show *Esposizione Espressionisti Novembergruppe* organized by ENRICO PRAMPOLINI in 1920 at the Casa d'Arte Italiana in Rome (p. 227, fig. 04), and then ten years later, when he was included in the Novembergruppe section in Berlin with a *Composition* [*Komposition*] and a *Merz Drawing* [*Merzzeichnung*].[2]

One of the two works Schwitters showed in Rome may have been the watercolour *He and She* [*Er und Sie*] (cat. 43, p. 97).[3] In 1919 he produced about 40 pencil-and-watercolour drawings, most of them in primary colours, in response to the art of that decade.[4] In this series, windmills, funnels, wheels, bottles, eyes and animals concoct a repertoire of recurring motifs, combined with numbers and words. With no concern for proportions, the collage-like parts on the paper resemble weightless objects in an undefined picture space. At first the elements seem unrelated, but Schwitters links them with arrows, lines and colour, setting up a dynamic rhythm between them that guides the viewer's gaze around the picture.

This confluence of disparate motifs, and in other works of disparate materials and media, coincided with the foundation of Schwitters's art movement, which he called "Merz" and embodied in person. Kurt Schwitters took an all-embracing view and wanted Merz to "create relationships, preferably between everything in the world",[5] thereby tearing down the boundaries between art and life, sense and nonsense. This artistic maxim is also reflected in his broad interpretation of drawing, which to Kurt Schwitters meant "that a thing can turn into another thing (for example a piece of string into a line)".[6] Schwitters formed this new understanding of material at the end of the First World War: "I felt free and had to trumpet my jubilation to the world. Out of parsimony I used whatever I could find, as we were an impoverished country. You can scream equally well with refuse, and that I did, by gluing and nailing it together."[7] Kurt Schwitters bore the revolutionary mood of his time in his heart and in Merz. He was an all-round artist with no regard for concepts of genre, working in an interdisciplinary manner with painting, drawing, sculpture, prints and collage and as a poet, typographer, impresario and communicator. The Novembergruppe likewise created a space in its exhibitions for every form of artistic expression. This was not the only common ground between Schwitters and the group in their attitude to the radically new.

NUNO DE BRITO ROCHA

1 The six poems are: "Erhabenheit" ("Grandeur"), "Weltfrühe" ("Young World"), "Weite" ("Expanse"), "Schicksal" ("Destiny"), "Graugrüne Gier" ("Grey-Green Greed") and "Die Welt" ("The World"), in: *Menschen. Buchfolge Neuer Kunst*, vol. 2, 1919, vol. VII, no. 54–61, pp. 55–58.

2 The catalogue for the Great Berlin Art Exhibition [*Grosse Berliner Kunstausstellung*] at Schloss Bellevue in 1930 lists two works by Kurt Schwitters: *Merzzeichnung*, 1928 (no. 336) and *Komposition*, 1929 (no. 337).

3 We are grateful to Dr Isabel Schulz at the Kurt und Ernst Schwitters Stiftung in Hanover for pointing this out.

4 After the war Kurt Schwitters met protagonists of Dada like Hans Arp, George Grosz, Raoul Hausmann and Hannah Höch "and was infected by their unconventional and liberating ideas which challenged the dominant aesthetic", Schulz 2011, p. 26.

5 Kurt Schwitters, quoted in Orchard 1998, p. 37.

6 Schulz 2011, p. 7.

7 Quoted in Orchard 1998, p. 36.

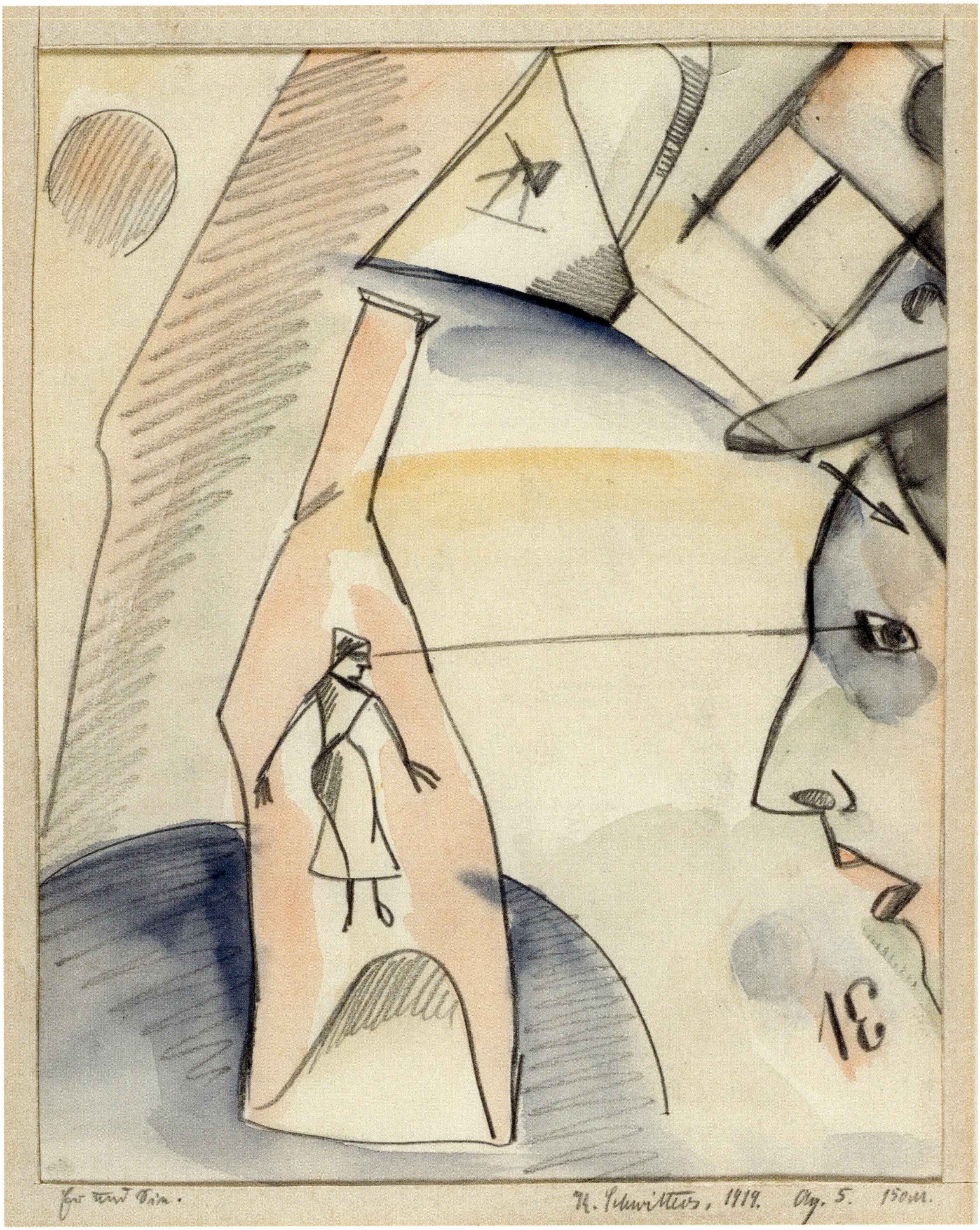

43

KURT SCHWITTERS

Watercolour 5: He and She, 1919

Watercolour and pencil on paper,
original passe-partout cut-out 23.1 × 18.6 cm,
original passe-partout 26.5 × 21.9 cm
Kurt und Ernst Schwitters Stiftung, Hannover

Possibly *Esposizione Espressionisti Novembergruppe*, Rome 1920, no. 40

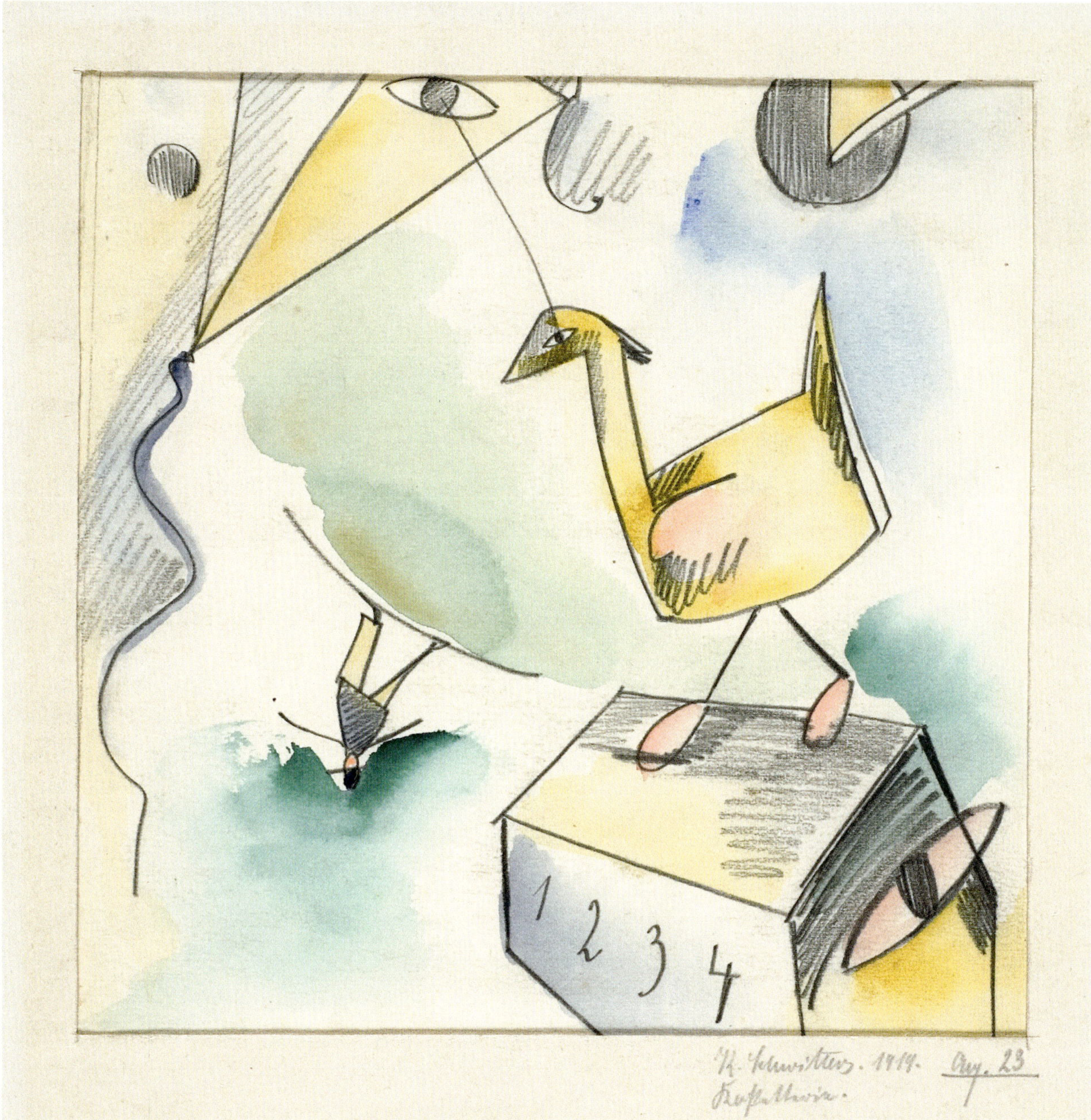

44

KURT SCHWITTERS

Watercolour 23: Coquetry, 1919

Watercolour and pencil on paper,
original passe-partout cut-out 18.6 × 18.6 cm,
original passe-partout 39.5 × 29.5 cm
Kurt und Ernst Schwitters Stiftung, Hannover

Possibly *Esposizione Espressionisti Novembergruppe*, Rome 1920, no. 40

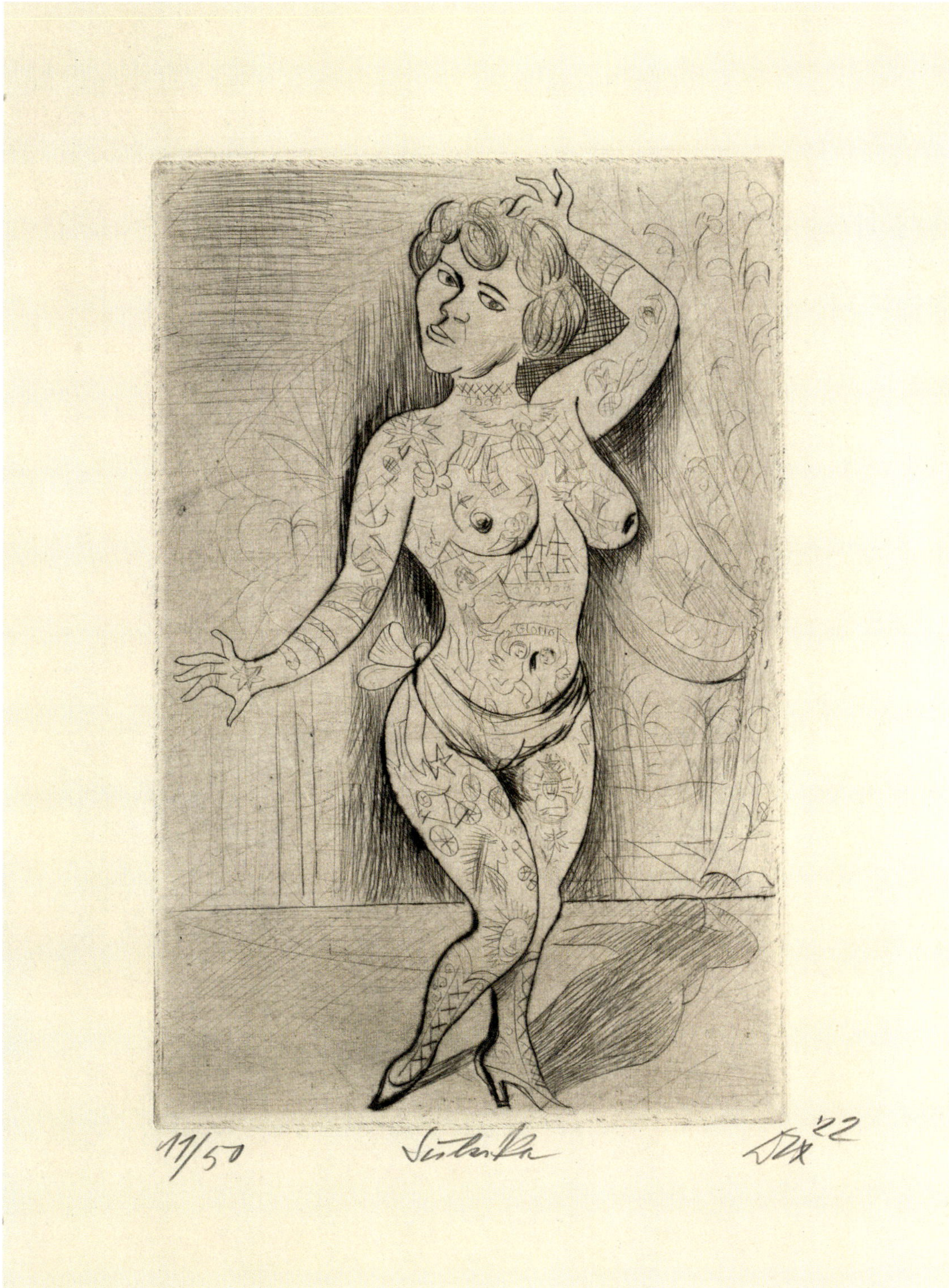

45

OTTO DIX

Suleika, the Tattooed Wonder (Maud Arizona) [from the "Circus" portfolio], 1922

Drypoint, 30 × 20 cm
Staatliche Museen zu Berlin, Kupferstichkabinett

Great Berlin Art Exhibition 1921, Novembergruppe section, ex-catalogue (painted version)

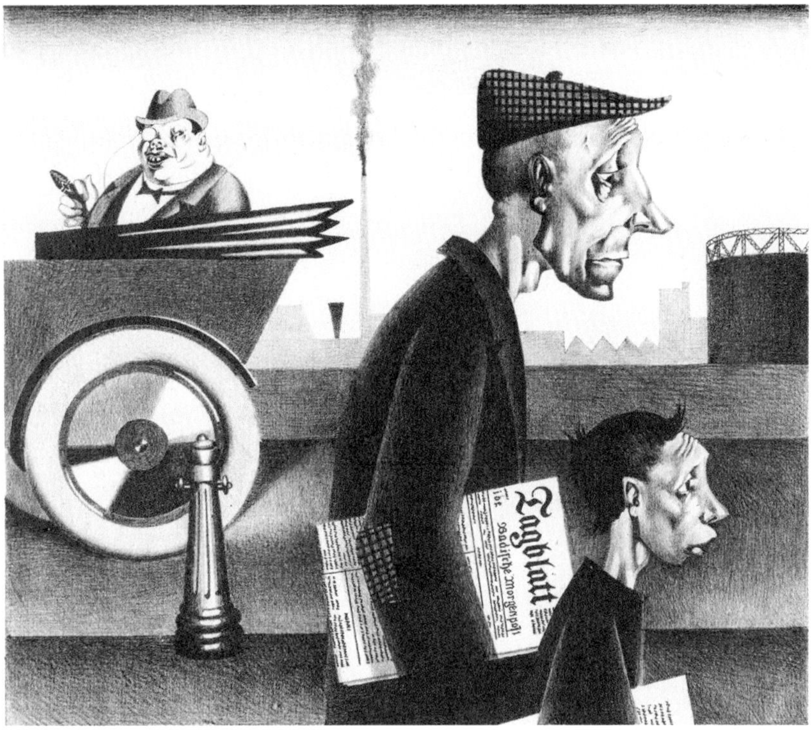

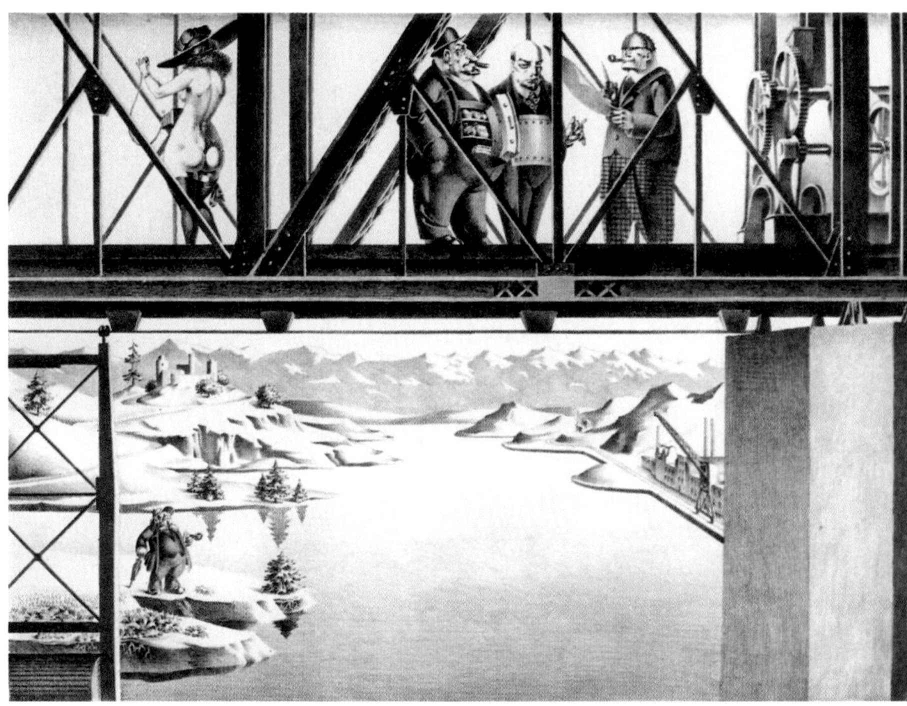

46
GEORG SCHOLZ
Newspaper Carriers, 1922

Lithograph, 20 × 22 cm
Collection Frank Brabant, Wiesbaden

Great Berlin Art Exhibition 1922, November-gruppe section, no. 1400; First International Art Exhibition Düsseldorf 1922, no. 333

47
GEORG SCHOLZ
The Lords of the World, 1922

Lithograph, 29.7 × 40 cm
Collection Frank Brabant, Wiesbaden

Great Berlin Art Exhibition 1922, November-gruppe section, no. 1398; First International Art Exhibition Düsseldorf 1922, no. 332

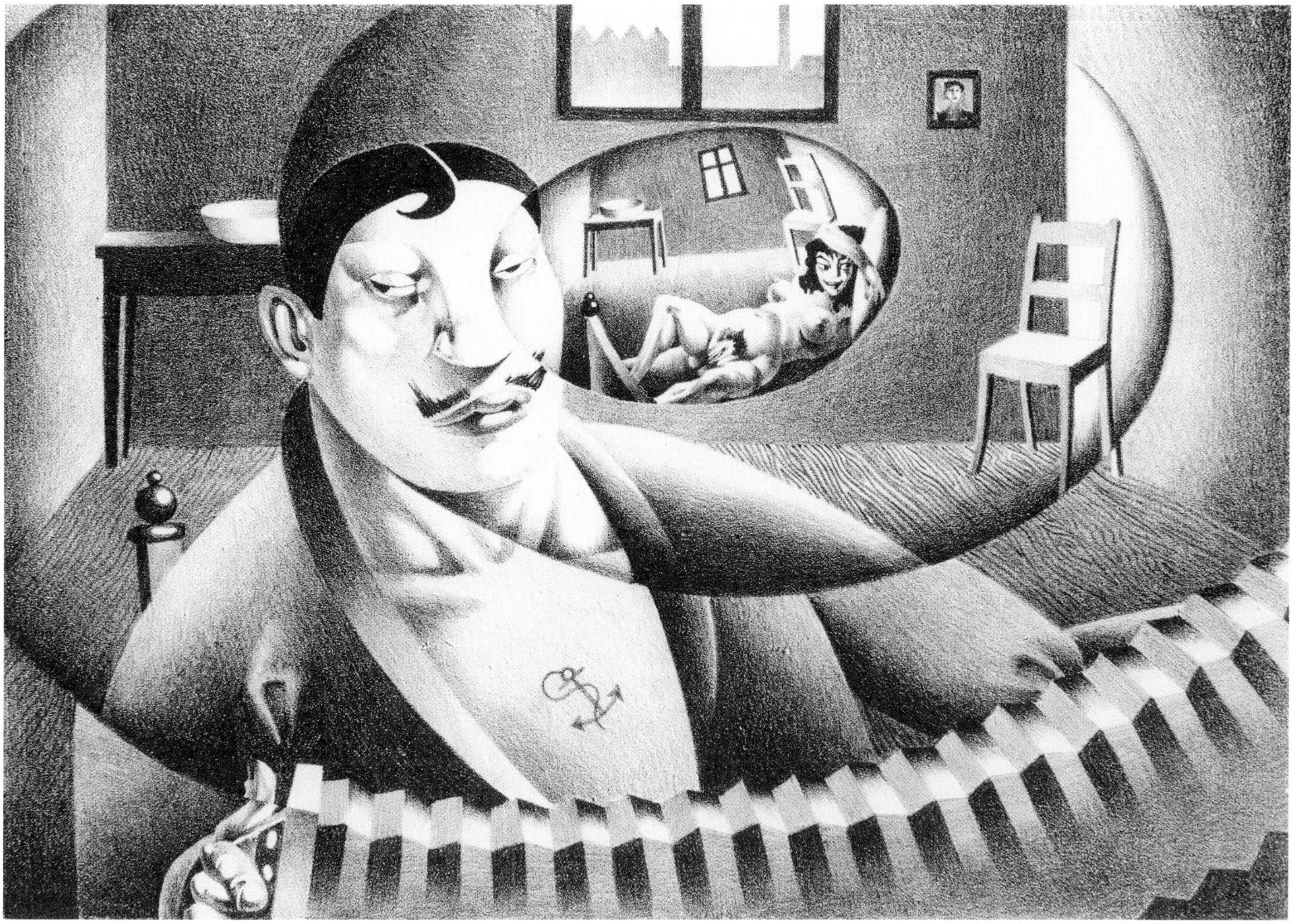

48

GEORG SCHOLZ

The Sentimental Sailor, 1922

Lithograph, 15.9 × 22.3 cm
Collection Frank Brabant, Wiesbaden

Great Berlin Art Exhibition 1922, Novembergruppe section, no. 1399; First International Art Exhibition Düsseldorf 1922, no. 331

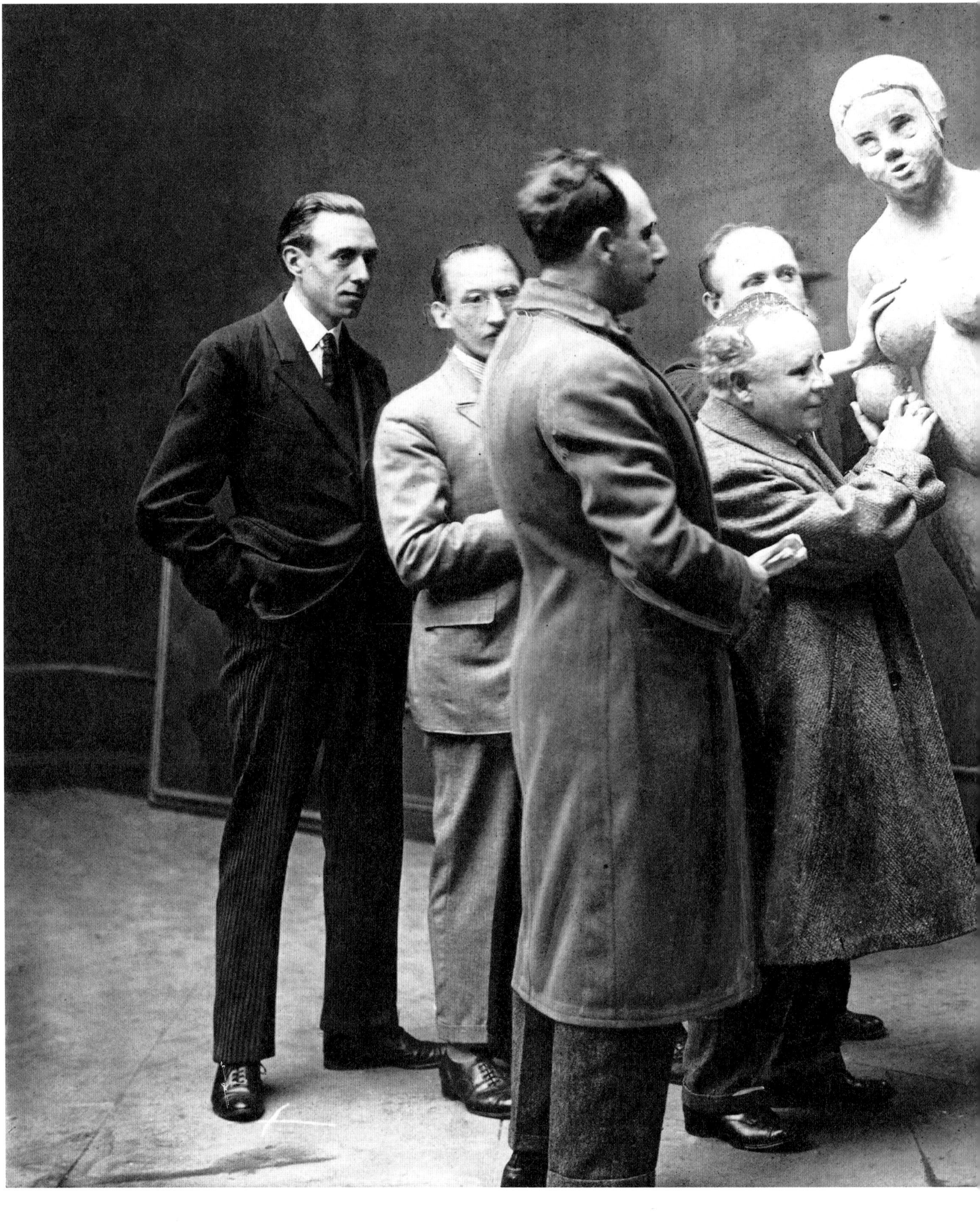

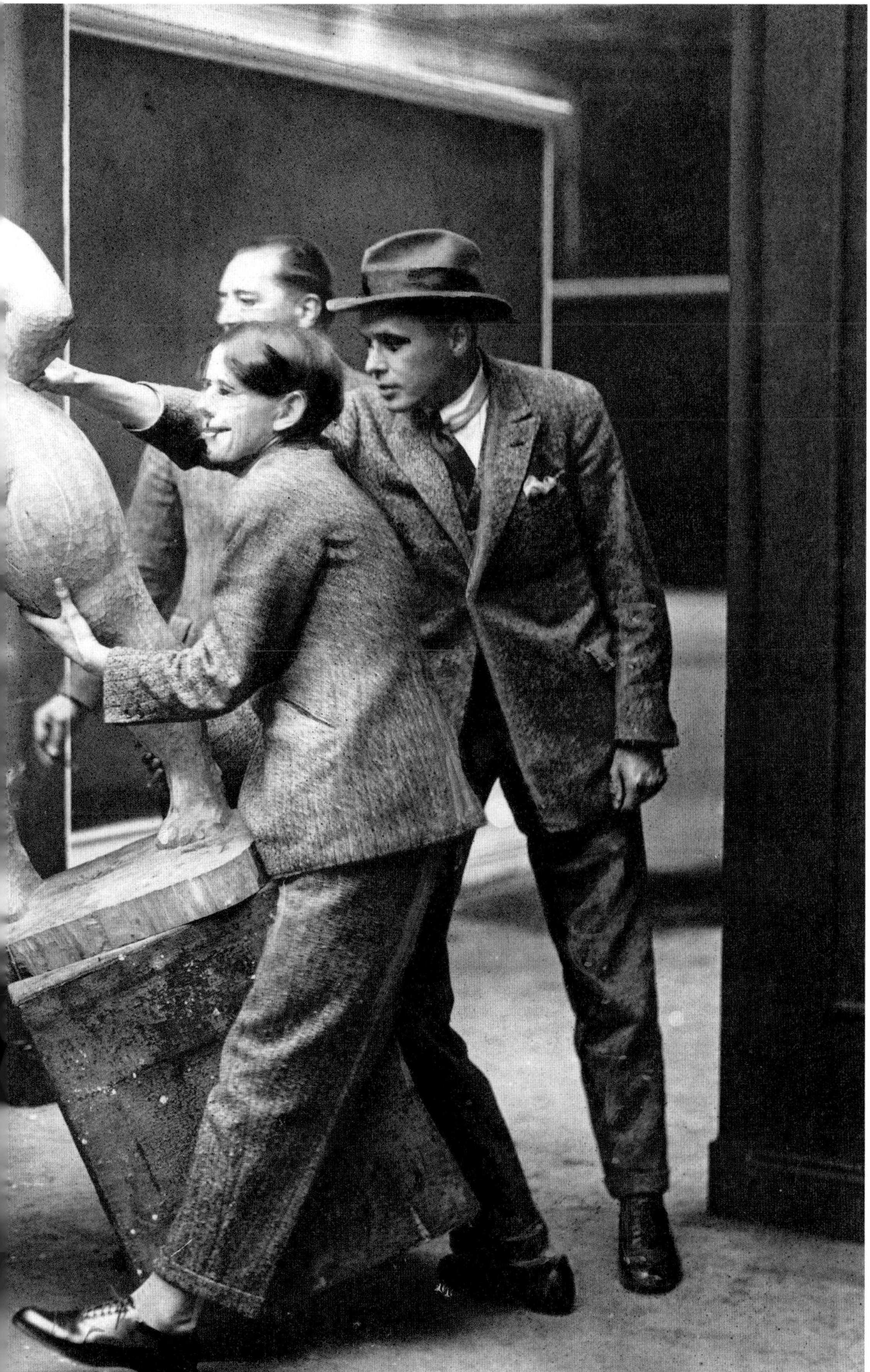

NG 1922–1928

Great Berlin Art Exhibition 1924, the Novembergruppe's exhibition committee with a nude sculpture by Christoph Voll
Left of the sculpture from left to right (back) Bernhard Klein, Peter Foerster, [Arthur Korn], (front) unknown, Arthur Segal, right of the sculpture (front) Max Dungert, (far back) Ludwig Mies van der Rohe, (right) Hans Siebert von Heister
Bundesarchiv

RALF BURMEISTER

CONSTRUCTIVITY AND OBJECTIVITY

Stylistic Pluralism in the Novembergruppe

Liberty, Equality — and Fraternity in Art?

What the Novembergruppe set out to achieve was political — in the broadest sense. The general direction was already clear in its foundation period in 1918–19, during the euphoria of historical upheaval, when it aspired to a role in shaping Germany's first democratic system and adopted the motto of the French Revolution — *"liberté, égalité, fraternité"* — as the basis for its own objectives. With and through art the group wanted to promote more international exchange to counter the national — and cultural — chauvinisms which had led to the disaster of the Great War.[1] As a community of radical artists, it refrained from party politics and refused to be exploited by political organizations. Initial demands about exerting an influence on cultural policy were soon dropped,[2] but the unshakable overriding principle from the moment the association was created until its demise was its commitment to developing and displaying a broad spectrum of artistic styles and techniques — and therein lay its democratic credentials. One hallmark of the post-war avant-gardes was the belief that art provided a matrix for building a better world where the 'New Person' would be able, with a cleansed soul and a lighter heart, to countenance an ideal future in peaceful social productivity undivided by class. In December 1918, only a few weeks after the hostilities had ended, the Novembergruppe published its *Appeal* [*Aufruf*] (fig. 02, p. 226), articulating the duty it saw to resume contact "with like-minded people of all countries", who had been united across borders "as brothers" prior to 1914 by "the creative instinct".[3] In May 1922 these ideas were picked up elsewhere: "Art needs connection between the people it inhabits. Setting aside all matters of state and without any ulterior political motive or selfish advantage, our slogan now must be: 'Artists of the world, unite!' Art must become international or it will perish."[4]

These lines are not taken from a manifesto published by the Novembergruppe, but from a document to which it put its signature along with other associations of artists: the Founding Declaration of the Union of International Progressive Artists, drawn up in March 1922 along with an invitation to attend a congress in Düsseldorf in May of the same year. The congress was hosted by an association of artists in the Rhine area called *Das Junge Rheinland*, and the attendance list shows members of the *Dresdner Sezession*, the *Hallesche Künstlergruppe*, the *Darmstädter Sezession*, the *Deutscher Werkbund* and, of course, the Novembergruppe, whose delegation consisted of HANS SIEBERT VON HEISTER, MORIZ MELZER, WILHELM SCHMID and RUDOLF BELLING.[5] Also present was 'Dadasopher' RAOUL HAUSMANN, whose temporary burst of commitment to the Novembergruppe had led in late

1921 to a stand-off and ultimately to a rift with the association.[6] He was accompanied by Stanislaw Kubicki, Stanislawowa and OTTO FREUNDLICH,[7] who all belonged to *Die Kommune*, a short-lived community of artists with communist leanings.[8] Der Sturm was represented by its guiding spirit Herwarth Walden. Artists attending the congress from other countries included the Italian Futurists Ruggero Vasari and ENRICO PRAMPOLINI, the go-between for the Novembergruppe's exhibition of prints in Rome two years previously (p. 227, fig. 04), delegations from France and Japan and assorted colleagues from Austria, Poland and Romania. The Constructivists were heavily represented, spearheaded by the Dutch *De Stijl* activists THEO VAN DOESBURG and CORNELIS VAN EESTEREN, with EL LISSITZKY (for Russia), WERNER GRAEFF (for Germany), HENRYK BERLEWI (for Poland), VIKING EGGELING (for Sweden), HANS RICHTER (for Romania!) and LÁSZLO PÉRI (for Hungary), all of whom had links with the Novembergruppe. IVAN PUNI, who was currently showing five works, including his seminal *Synthetic Musician* [*Synthetischer Musiker*] (cat. 50, p. 115), with the Novembergruppe at the Great Berlin Art Exhibition, was there with his wife, the painter XENIA BOGUSLAVSKAYA. So too was the art writer Will Grohmann, who in 1928 was to reflect on the association's history and impact for the tenth anniversary publication.[9] It was a congress of many voices, and this heterogeneity of artistic positions was to be synthesized under the notion of "progress" (rather than "radicalism"). A passionate yet futile undertaking.

Accounts of the three days at the Congress and of heated disputes about a joint manifesto are tinged by the personal stance of their narrators.[10] Differences over organizational strategy, and especially the commercial orientation of the association, led to a flamboyant walk-out by the Constructivists from *De Stijl*, EL LISSITZKY and the group around HANS RICHTER, OTTO FREUNDLICH and RAOUL HAUSMANN. The last named could not resist striking up the traditional Christmas ditty *"Oh Tannenbaum"* as he left.[11] Equally incompatible were the declarations and declamations on artistic questions. Progress in art meant progress in society, and the Constructivist faction defined a "progressive artist" as "one who rejects and resists the dominance of the subjective in art and does not build a work on lyrical caprice but on the principle of Neo-Plasticism by organizing resources systematically so as to achieve a universally understandable form of expression."[12] This set them apart from artists who articulated themselves in a Cubo-Futuro-Expressionist manner, including the Novembergruppe constituency. Once the Constructivists had withdrawn prematurely from the gathering, everything proceeded in an 'orderly' fashion, as Hermann Wederkopp reports: "After this the Congress got down to the positive business and people fled because there was no antagonism any more and it was as boring as if the hall had been full of civil servants. German organization was able to shine again".[13] A Union of International Progressive Artists had no future.[14]

The Socialism of Seeing

All the more noteworthy, then, that THEO VAN DOESBURG, the fundamentalist of the right angle, engaged with the Novembergruppe, along with the artists in his entourage, enabling them to show at the Great Berlin Art Exhibition — and perhaps even to sell a few works (although they took a dim view, in general, of commercial utility in art). VAN DOESBURG was a tremendous networker and evangelist for an "elemental art" of the kind also advocated by RAOUL HAUSMANN, HANS ARP, IVAN PUNI and LÁSZLÓ MOHOLY-NAGY, an art that should be subject neither to fashionable styles nor to individualism and "does not philosophize, being constructed entirely out of its

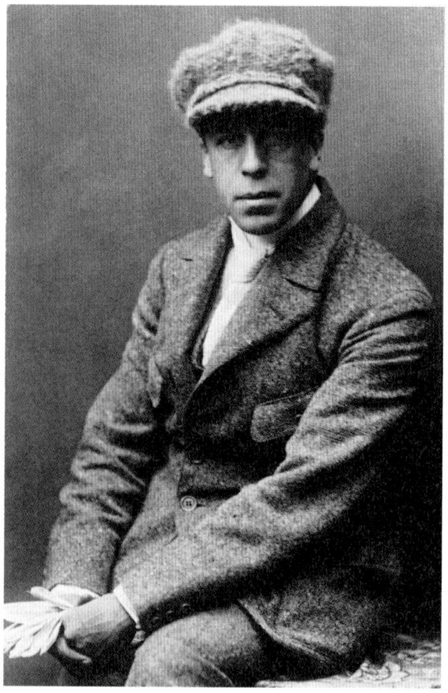

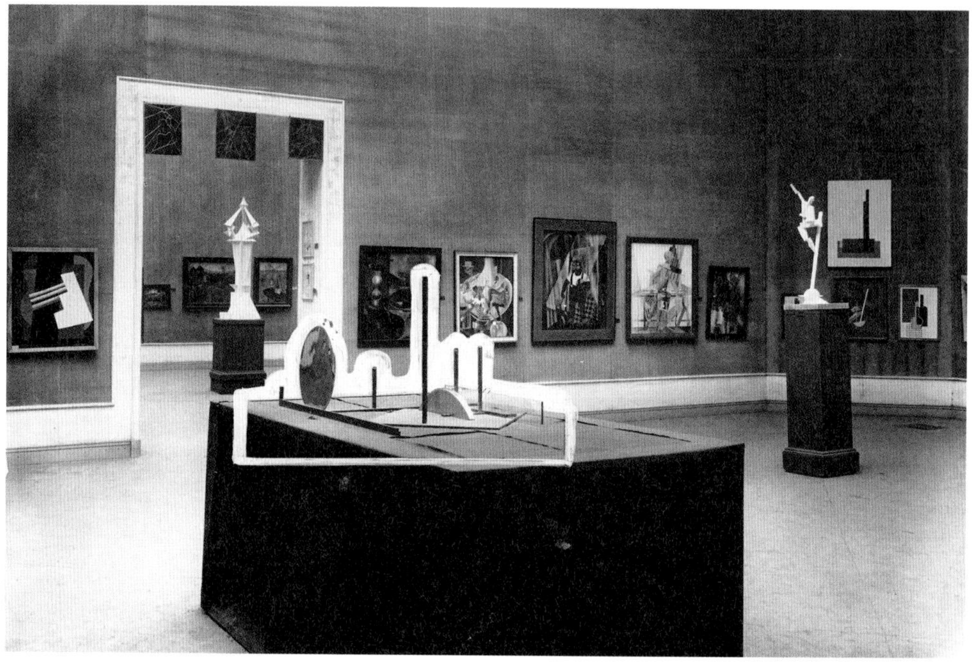

01 Theo van Doesburg in Weimar on 31 December 1920

02 A view of the Novembergruppe section, Great Berlin Art Exhibition 1923, Room 25, in the foreground a material construction by László Moholy-Nagy

own elements".[15] VAN DOESBURG (fig. 01) had already exhibited in Berlin in 1920, representing 'young Dutch art' at a show organized by *Die Kornscheuer* in the *Kronprinzenpalais*.[16] Visiting the metropolis on this occasion in December 1920, he had been introduced by the architecture critic and Dada fan Adolf Behne[17] not only to the experimental film-maker VIKING EGGELING but also to HANS RICHTER and RAOUL HAUSMANN, key figures in the Dada movement in Zürich and Berlin.[18] VAN DOESBURG, too, was a character of many facets on the stage of art. Under his pseudonym "I. K. Bonset"[19] the Constructivist was simultaneously active in Dada and, when the assembly on the Rhine failed to set up a Union of International Progressive Artists (not to his chagrin), he convened his own International Congress of Constructivists and Dadaists, held in Weimar on 25 and 26 September 1922.[20] This alliance between two groups with extremely different visual formulations was founded on a common denominator: they both disliked Expressionism. Both felt that the idea of artists who tapped deep into their individuality to create merely pandered to a bourgeois cult of genius and was a thing of the long-gone past. It had been replaced by the ideal of collective artistry, bringing together pioneers of a new culture of seeing and making. These artists, Hausmann maintained, were bold enough "to form a world-view by visual means" and "speak in an unknown language"[21] in their pursuit of a radically new social community: "The art of our time must be elemental, precise and all-embracing. It is the art of Constructivism. Constructivism is neither proletarian nor capitalist. Constructivism is just starting out, without a class, without a precursor. [...] Constructivism is pure content. It is independent of frame and plinth. It encompasses industry and architecture, objects and relationships. Constructivism is the socialism of seeing."[22] LÁSZLÓ MOHOLY-NAGY, the author of this creed, and THEO VAN DOESBURG were not at all of one mind on the issue of allowing socialist or communist politics to encroach into art.[23] The *Proletarian Art Manifesto* [*Manifest Proletkunst*] signed by VAN DOESBURG, KURT SCHWITTERS, HANS ARP, Tristan Tzara and the Hanover-based publisher Christof Spengemann, which appeared in April 1923, invokes the all-embracing impact of art, transcending discourse about class struggle: "Art is a function of the human mind with the purpose of delivering people from the chaos of life (tragedy). [...]

If, however, art were to serve solely the proletariat, quite apart from the fact that the proletariat has been infected by bourgeois taste, then this art would be limited, just as limited as specifically bourgeois art. Such art would not be universal, would not grow from a sense of global nationality, but from views restricted to individuals, societies, time and space. [...] The art we want, this art is neither proletarian nor bourgeois, for it unleashes forces powerful enough to influence all culture, rather than being influenced by social conditions. [...] What we are preparing for, by contrast, is the total work of art, which is superior to any poster, be it for champagne, Dada or communist dictatorship."[24]

From May 1923, only a month after this manifesto appeared, the proponents of Constructivist elemental art and design put in a substantial numerical appearance amid the almost 130 artists on show in the Novembergruppe section at the Great Berlin Art Exhibition, where they were greeted with acclaim by the press. The driving force behind this turn-out was presumably once again THEO VAN DOESBURG. He had recruited not only PIET MONDRIAN (cat. 58, p. 123),[25] co-founder of *De Stijl*, and the Dutch architects JACOBUS JOHANNES PIETER OUD, GERRIT RIETVELD and MART STAM,[26] likewise members of the group, as well as the painter and graphic designer VILMOS HUSZÁR and the painter, sculptor and typographer CÉSAR DOMELA-NIEUWENHUIS, but also WALTER DEXEL (cat. 57, p. 122) and Bauhaus students WERNER GRAEFF and KARL PETER RÖHL, who had set up a *De Stijl* group in Weimar.[27] This international Constructivist faction was reinforced by EL LISSITZKY, who installed his three-dimensional *Proun Room* at the show, enabling visitors to walk into and witness for themselves just what dynamic design based on a primitive square could achieve.[28] The Hungarian MOHOLY-NAGY, who had just taken over the metal workshop at the Bauhaus in spring 1923, had four works on display, including a material construction, now lost, made of plastic, glass, nickel, wood and steel, which unfolded the compositional structure of his non-figurative paintings into this three-dimensional space in concrete form (fig. 02).[29] THEO VAN DOESBURG himself presented five works, intended to demonstrate his artistic trajectory (p. 144, fig. 08).[30] The painting *The Card Players* [*De kaartspelers*] dating from 1916–17, with its direct reference to Paul Cézanne's *Les Joueurs de cartes* (1890–92), was an early indication of the repertoire of geometric shapes that would eventually determine VAN DOESBURG'S concrete painting, although this canvas is still a figuration and only partly abstract.[31] It was also the first time that he had exhibited his works *Peinture pure* (1920)[32] (figs. 03, 04) and *Composition XVIII in three parts* [*Compositie XVIII in drie delen*] (1920)[33] (fig. 05) outside the Netherlands, perfectly illustrating the 'ascetic', purely abstract formal idiom of 'Neo-Plasticism' [*Nieuwe Beelding*].

Only a year had passed since art critics, in particular Max Osborn and Curt Glaser, had been accusing EL LISSITZY'S *Proun* works (cat. 51-54, pp. 116-117) at the Great Berlin Art Exhibition 1922 of "schematism" and "mathematical mysticism" devoid of any plausible notion of quality,[34] but this time the reviews were generally kinder: "Theo van Doesburg manages very prettily to colourfully animate and cohesively compose his puzzle figures," acknowledged the *Berliner Börsen-Zeitung*.[35] Curt Glaser conceded that in the "painting of young Dutch artists" there was "evidently a feeling for colour and harmony" in the "proportion and configuration" of geometric shapes, but that their "aspiration to be rated as easel painting [was] certainly a mistake" and these artists would be better suited to "tackling colour schemes for interiors".[36] Given that Glaser was hereby endorsing the interdisciplinary principles of *De Stijl*, his criticism was not as cutting as it otherwise might have been. The architect and urban planner LUDWIG HILBERSEIMER, who had joined the Novembergruppe by 1925 at the latest, clearly grasped the crea-

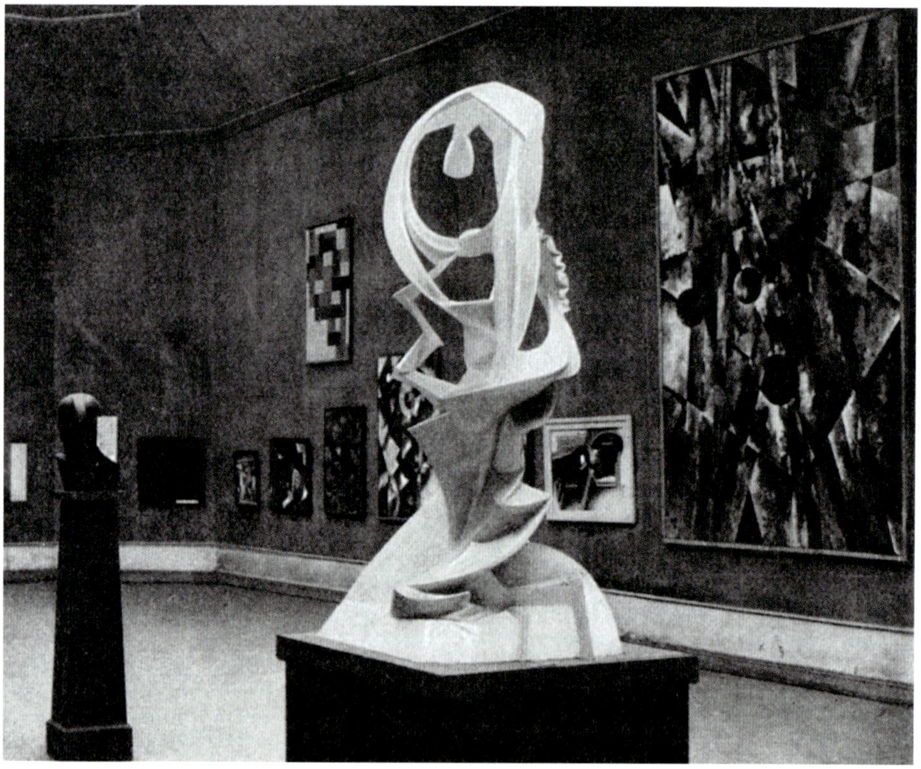

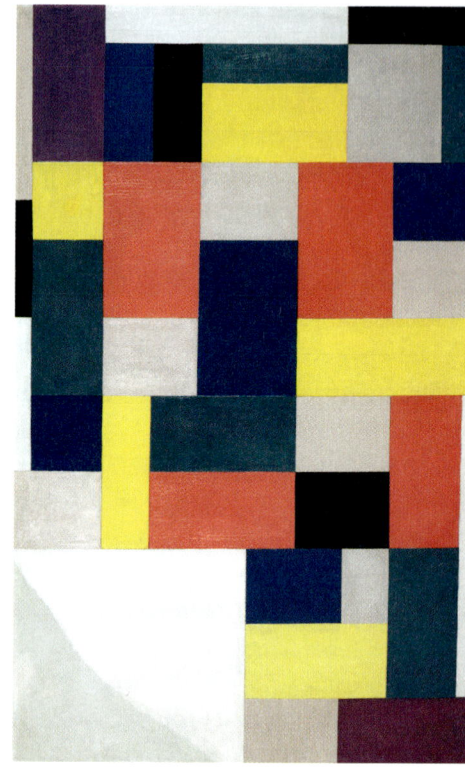

03 A view of the Novembergruppe section, Great Berlin Art Exhibition 1923, Room 27, high on the right wall van Doesburg's *Peinture pure*

04 THEO VAN DOESBURG
Peinture pure, 1920
Centre Pompidou, Paris
Great Berlin Art Exhibition 1923, Novembergruppe section, no. 1146

tive potential of this purely abstract art to reach out into other areas of life: "With great determination the Constructivists have set out down a new road. That of reality. Their constructions are still non-utilitarian, but reveal an unmistakable will to take possession of reality. The Constructivists have shifted from construction in painting to the construction of objects. To architecture in the broadest sense of the term. [...] Mathematical clarity, geometric rigour, organization fit for purpose, extreme economy and high-precision constructivity are not just technical, but eminently artistic problems. They are the essential core or our epoch. The constructive method draws every object into the sphere of design. Not copying into a still life but moulding as reality."[37] Will Grohmann was the most perceptive about the significance of these exhibits — and the art history of the future was to bear him out: "Artistic taste [...] was at its most threatening when it rebelled against the Abstracts and Constructivists. It is this wing of the Novembergruppe that has achieved much for the general good; it has succeeded in expanding not only the boundaries of creation but also those of reception."[38]

THEO VAN DOESBURG took part in only one more exhibition by the Novembergruppe. In 1925 he showed an axonometric composition from a joint project with CORNELIS VAN EESTEREN.[39] He nevertheless remained sympathetic to the association. In fact, responding to a request from his friend HANNAH HÖCH he tried in 1926 to organize a major group show by *De Stijl* artists and to link this, in line with the wishes of the Novembergruppe, to a cross-section of important, innovative French works for Berlin (figs. 06, 07).[40] His efforts turned out, however, to be based on a misunderstanding, as a chance meeting in Paris with the painter WILHELM SCHMID, who belonged to the Novembergruppe, revealed. HÖCH immediately forwarded to PETER FOERSTER the indignant letter she received from VAN DOESBURG in patchy German: "I have run around the whole week in Paris and never came home without a sweaty bum!!! until I met Mr Schmid, who claimed it was only about a few paintings by Metzinger, Léger, Picasso, Braque etc. You will understand how disappointed I was and how my energy suddenly converted into the opposite"[41]. This was not a selection that VAN DOESBURG would ever have made, and the special display of *De Stijl* artists, envisaged for a forthcoming Novembergruppe exhibition, did not bear fruit either.

Tensions

The Novembergruppe had a radical liberal attitude — even if this was perceived by some artists among its own ranks, like the Dadaists, as political indifference and even if its exhibition practice, which was open to all "radical" techniques — meaning those not fixed in tradition — garnered criticism in the illustrated magazines of the day. Being trapped between political and aesthetic fronts is never comfortable. The group primarily saw itself as a community of opinion whose principal concern was to facilitate the free development of art without regard for formal aesthetic constraints. In terms of the bandwidth of stylistic idioms, it was always programmatically undogmatic. This was a pluralist community, a place for multiple forms of artistic modernism to meet. The impetus was demonstrated every year by the hanging practice at the Great Berlin Art Exhibition. Wall by wall and frame by frame, compositions by Constructivists were juxtaposed with works of figurative painting that were nonetheless quite unlike academic realism. This latter trend gained pace from the early 1920s and Gustav Hartlaub coined a multifaceted and controversial term for it: "New Objectivity" ["Neue Sachlichkeit"]. Evolving parallel to non-figurative art and critically distinct from 'feely' Expressionism, this movement to represent the objective world was characterized by a broad stylistic variation. The common denominator was its sobriety — both in its protocol of depiction and in the attitude of the artists who, after the chaos of the First World War, sought assurance for their own identities by confronting the world of objects. Unlike the Constructivists, the painters of New Objectivity did not affiliate to a defined group and had no organized structure. But they found a roof in the Novembergruppe: HEINRICH MARIA DAVRINGHAUSEN, CONRAD FELIXMÜLLER, ERNST FRITSCH, HEINZ FUCHS, OTTO GRIEBEL, BERNHARD KLEIN, ISSAI KULVIANSKI, OTTO NAGEL, ANNELIESE

05

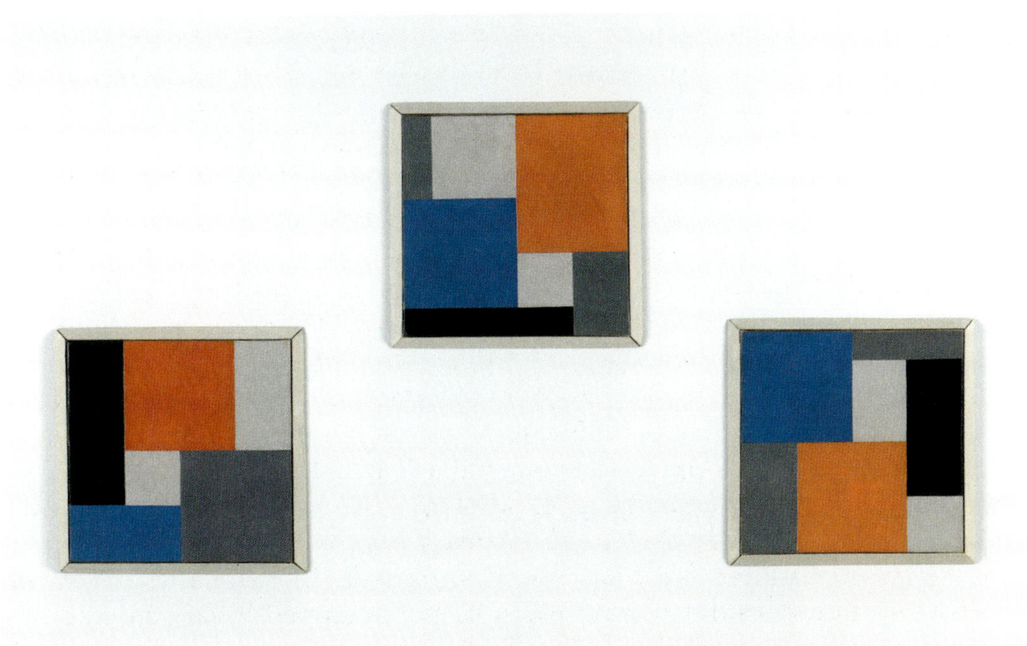

05 THEO VAN DOESBURG
Composition XVIII in Three Parts [*Compositie XVIII in drie delen*], 1920
Kröller-Müller Museum, Otterloo
Great Berlin Art Exhibition 1923, Novembergruppe section, no. 1147

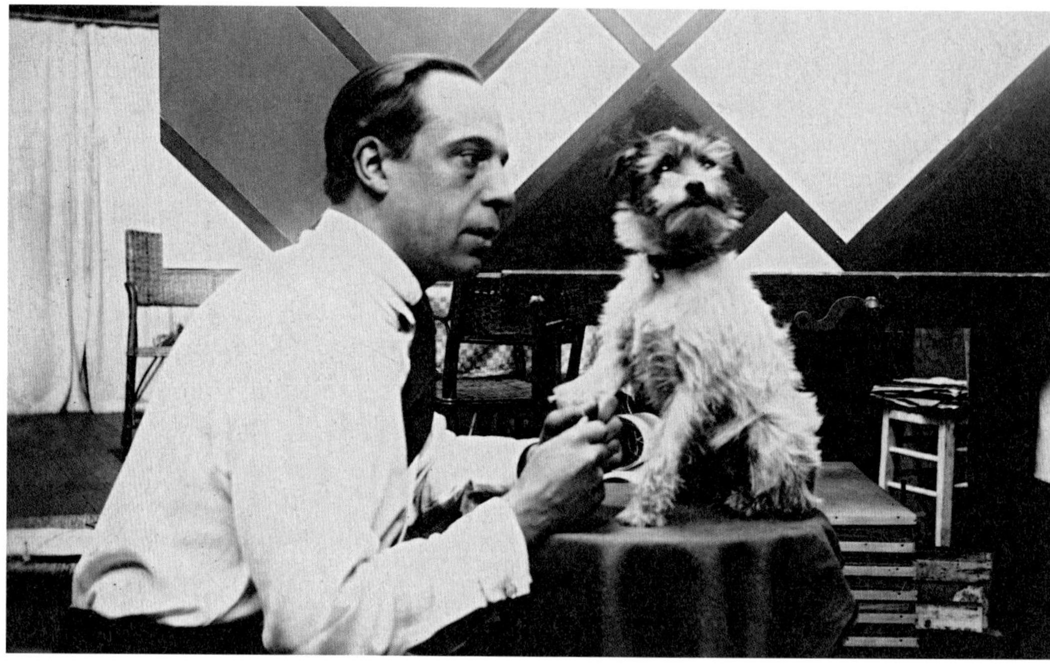

06 Theo van Doesburg with his dog Dada, Paris, 1926

06

RATKOWSKI, RUDOLF SCHLICHTER, GEORG SCHOLZ (fig. 08), RICHARD ZIEGLER and others were all granted visibility, however disparate their personal techniques.

This prompted Adolf Behne to lament an aesthetic sea change which, in his eyes, took place at the Great Berlin Art Exhibition in 1924 through the auspices of the Novembergruppe. He accused the association of using its stylistic pluralism in an effort to prove that it was not one-sidedly abstract and, as a consequence, mollycoddling the figurative painters — in Behne's words "neo-naturalist reactionaries" who produced "nothing but highly superfluous rehashes of blissful hobby-garden kitsch".[42] While conceding that "what is called abstract painting" could not "gratuitously continue", he insisted that it had performed a service by "guiding the problems of painting towards that elemental objectivity whence they must inevitably become pure problems of configuration". For Behne — and he may have had compositions by VAN DOESBURG in mind (p. 144, figs. 07, 08) — there was only one way forward for creative practice: "From picture to architecture (in the broadest sense) or back to illustration." The latter, however, was already abundantly supplied by those representing the *Verein Berliner Künstler* at the Great Berlin Art Exhibition, which meant there was no reason for the Novembergruppe to be showing these "retrogressives".[43]

Behne's sharp-tongued condemnation was aimed in particular at proponents of neo-classical Objectivity, including the exhibiting artists GEORG SCHRIMPF and ALEXANDER KANOLDT. The young woman squatting on the steps in SCHRIMPF'S *Resting on Steps* [*Hockende*] (1923) was typical of the people he painted at the time. The subdued palette reinforces the mournful mood and introspection of the figures, freezing them in a kind of counter-world to social reality (fig. 09). Although Schrimpf had helped to set up the Action Committee of Revolutionary Artists in Munich in 1919 and taken part in the soviet republic in that city, belonging briefly to the Communist Party of Germany, there is no longer any trace of his revolutionary left-wing roots in these silent trances. The fractured idyll presented by SCHRIMPF did not appeal to Adolf Behne, who felt far more affinity with the socially critical, veristic Objectivity of a GEORGE GROSZ (cat. 106, p. 211) or an OTTO DIX (p. 88, fig. 09) and who regarded GROSZ'S claim that he painted "out of protest" and "to convince the

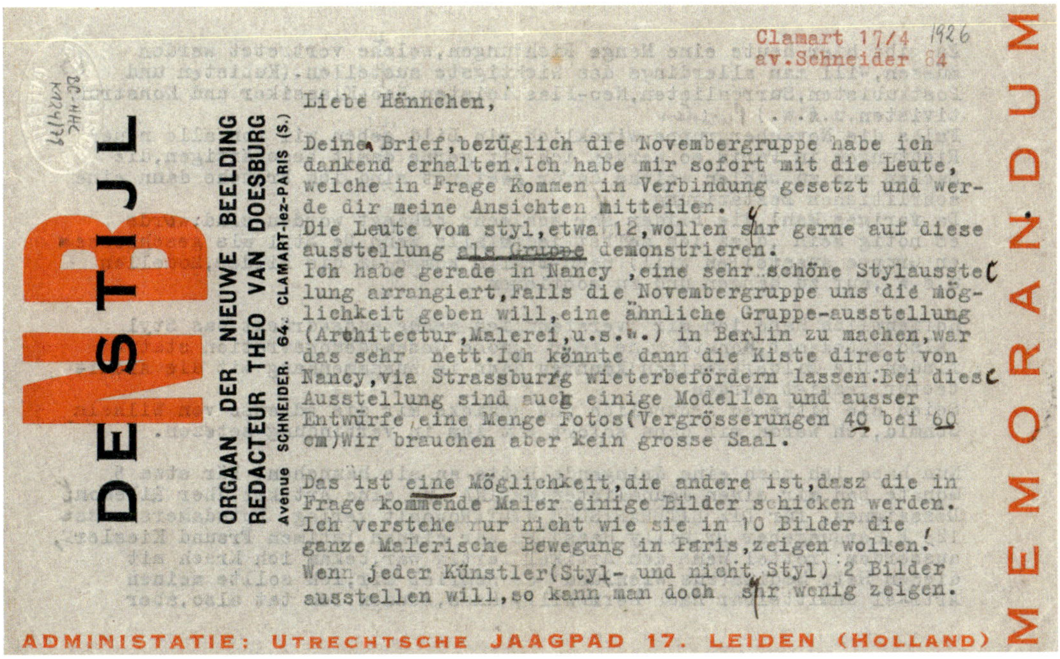

DE STIJL NB

ORGAAN DER NIEUWE BEELDING
REDACTEUR THEO VAN DOESBURG
Avenue SCHNEIDER. 64. CLAMART-lez-PARIS (S.)

Clamart 17/4 1926
av.Schneider 64

Liebe Hännchen,

Deinen Brief, bezüglich die Novembergruppe habe ich dankend erhalten. Ich habe mir sofort mit die Leute, welche in Frage Kommen in Verbindung gesetzt und werde dir meine Ansichten mitteilen.
Die Leute vom styl, etwa 12, wollen sehr gerne auf diese ausstellung als Gruppe demonstrieren.
Ich habe gerade in Nancy, eine sehr schöne Stylausstellung arrangiert, Falls die Novembergruppe uns die möglichkeit geben will, eine ähnliche Gruppe-ausstellung (Architectur, Malerei, u.s.w.) in Berlin zu machen, war das sehr nett. Ich könnte dann die Kiste direct von Nancy, via Strassburg wieterbefördern lassen. Bei diese Ausstellung sind auch einige Modellen und ausser Entwürfe, eine Menge Fotos (Vergrösserungen 40 bei 60 cm) Wir brauchen aber kein grosse Saal.

Das ist eine Möglichkeit, die andere ist, dasz die in Frage kommende Maler einige Bilder schicken werden. Ich verstehe nur nicht wie sie in 10 Bilder die ganze Malerische Bewegung in Paris, zeigen wollen!
Wenn jeder Künstler (Styl- und nicht Styl) 2 Bilder ausstellen will, so kann man doch sehr wenig zeigen.

ADMINISTATIE: UTRECHTSCHE JAAGPAD 17. LEIDEN (HOLLAND)

MEMORANDUM

07 Letter from Theo van Doesburg to Hannah Höch, Clamart, 17 April 1926

world that it is ugly, sick and dishonest"[44] as a legitimate conviction articulated in visual art. The critic was equally unimpressed by KANOLDT'S *Still Life II* [*Stillleben II*] (1924), executed with all the craft of the old masters, where the thingness of reality, a focus for many protagonists of New Objectivity, offers a counterpoint to a world in tumult (fig. 10).

Max Osborn, another resounding voice in art criticism, feared that the spread of figurative painting, even more visible at the Novembergruppe exhibition in 1925 on the premises of the Berlin Secession, signalled the arrival of "a sentimental return to Biedermeier", and he urged the association to reclaim the "achievements of the revolution", by which he meant the revolution in art.[45] The Novembergruppe remained caught up in the tension not only between opposing artistic strategies but also, naturally, between the diverging assessments they provoked. Paul Friedrich, who wrote reviews for the *Berliner Börsen-Zeitung*, welcomed the "will for representation", observing: "One side finds this sort too extreme, another finds the other too reactionary. They want an art that springs from life. Ultimately they all want that, or all believe they do. In my humble opinion that may be one of the essentials. But listen on: 'It is not the task of art to suggest moods, but to change our surroundings creatively, to shape them artistically.' That, please note, is not essentially the same thing. Why should poor art always have to be something more than art. Oh, how wonderful it would be if all art needed to be was art! [...] To me 'abstract' painting is *passé*".[46]

The conservative attitude articulated here was to escalate dramatically after 1933.

1 See "Manifest der Novembristen (Entwurf)", in: *Zehn Jahre Novembergruppe*, special issue of *Kunst der Zeit. Zeitschrift für Kunst und Literatur*, vol. 3, 1928, nos. 1–3, p. 16.

2 See the essay by Nentwig, p. 227 of this catalogue and Kratz-Kessemeier, pp. 30–39.

3 Circular of 13 December 1918, see ref. in note 1, p. 12; published as "Aufruf" in: *Die Schöne Rarität*, vol. 2 (1918/19), p. 144.

4 Founding Declaration of the Union of International Progressive Artists, 30 May 1922, quoted in Kunstsammlung Nordrhein-Westfalen 1992, p. 301.

5 On the Congress of the Union of International Progressive Artists see Müller 1992; a list of members is reprinted there on p. 18.

08 GEORG SCHOLZ
Seated Nude with Plaster Bust, 1927
Staatliche Kunsthalle, Karlsruhe
Reproduction in *Ten Years of the Novembergruppe* 1928, p. 41

09 GEORG SCHRIMPF
Resting on Steps, 1923
Private collection
Great Berlin Art Exhibition 1924, Novembergruppe section, no. 989

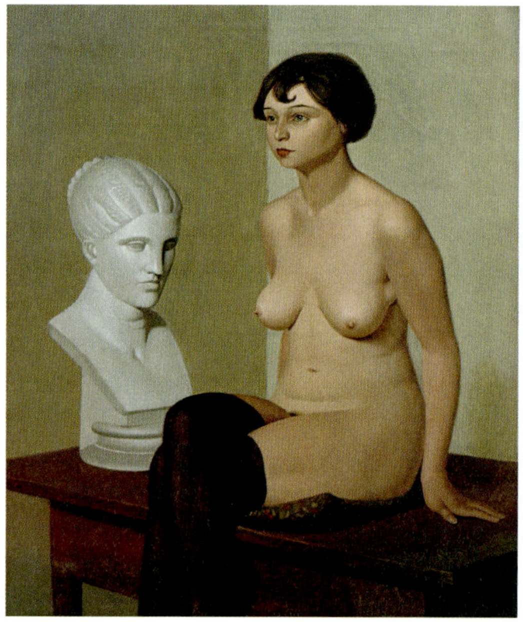

08

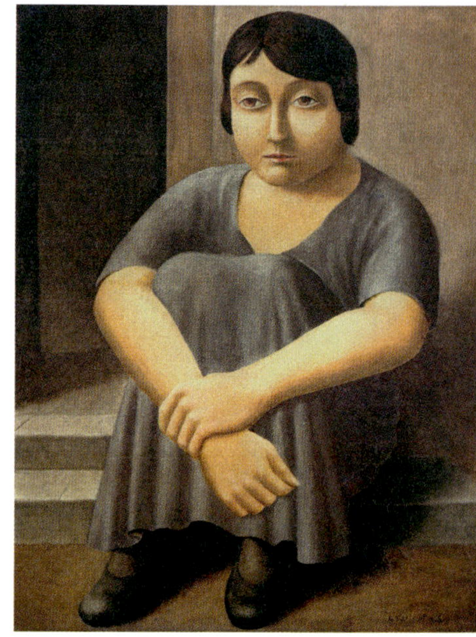

09

6 See the essay by Burmeister, pp. 86f. of this catalogue.

7 See Müller 1992, p. 22, note 12.

8 See Kliemann 1969, pp. 66–68.

9 See Will Grohmann, "Zehn Jahre Novembergruppe", ref. in note 1, pp. 1–9. Reprinted in Rudert 2012, pp. 26–30.

10 See Müller 1992, pp. 19f.

11 See Hermann von Wedderkop, "Internationale Liebe in Düsseldorf", in: *Die Weltbühne*, vol. 18/II, 20 July 1922, pp. 55–60, here 59.

12 Theo van Doesburg, El Lissitzky, Hans Richter, "Declaration of the International Faction of Constructivists", quoted in Kunstsammlung Nordrhein-Westfalen 1992, p. 304.

13 Ref. in note 11.

14 A chronology of events and a verdict on the failed initiative for a Congress were provided by van Doesburg in *De Stijl*, vol. 5, 1922, no. 4, pp. 49–64. See the German translation from Dutch in: Kunstsammlung Nordrhein-Westfalen 1992, pp. 300–303.

15 "Aufruf zur elementaren Kunst", in: *De Stijl*, vol. 4, no. 10, October 1921.

16 See catalogue section in: *Die Kornscheuer. Monatsschrift für die Gesamtinteressen der Kunst*, special issue *Holland*, vol. [1], December 1920.

17 "Dada shows the world 1920. Many will say: even 1920 isn't that awful. The fact is: man is a machine, culture is rags, education is conceit, mind is brutality, the average is stupidity and the military are lords of all." Adolf Behne, "Dada", in: *Die Freiheit*, 9 July 1920 (evening edition)

18 See Straaten 1983, p. 98.

19 Anagram of the Dutch "ik ben sot" (I am daft).

20 See Wendermann 2007.

21 Raoul Hausmann, "Die neue Kunst", in: *Die Aktion*, vol. 11, Berlin, 14 May 1921, pp. 281–285, quoted in: Erlhoff 1982, vol.1, p. 185.

22 László Moholy-Nagy, "Elementarismus", in: *MA (Today)*, 1922, quoted in Moholy-Nagy 1972, p. 31.

23 See Wendermann 2007, pp. 13–16.

24 "Manifest Proletkunst", in: *Merz 2. Nummer i*, Hanover, April 1923, p. 25.

25 Mondrian showed three works not in the catalogue; see Joosten 1998, nos. B 123, B 126, B 146.

26 On the Novembergruppe architects see the essay by Nentwig on pp. 140–151 of this catalogue.

27 *Grosse Berliner Kunstausstellung 1923 im Landesausstellungsgebäude am Lehrter Bahnhof* (exhib. cat., 19 May–17 September 1923), Berlin 1923, Novembergruppe section, nos. 1139–1143 (Dexel), 1198–1200 (Graeff), 1228 (Huszár), 1290–1291 (Domela-Nieuwenhuis), 1408 (Stam, Rietveld).

28 See the essay by Nentwig, p. 118 of this catalogue.

29 Ref. in note 27, nos. 1279–1282.

30 Ref. in note 27, nos. 1144–1148.

31 See Hoek 2000, WVZ-Nr. 513.

32 Listed in the catalogue to the Great Berlin Art Exhibition 1923, see ref. in note 27, no. 1146, as "Decomposition" ["Dekomposition"]; see Hoek 2000, WVZ-Nr. 652.

33 Listed in the catalogue to the Great Berlin Art Exhibition 1923, see ref. in note 27, no. 1147, as "Wall painting (in 3 parts)" ["Wandbild (in 3 Teilen)"]; see Hoek 2000, WVZ-Nr. 648.

34 Max Osborn, "Junge Kunst. Zur Großen Berliner Kunstausstellung", in: *Vossische Zeitung*, 14 June 1922, no. 277; See also Curt Glaser, "Große Berliner Kunstausstellung", in: *Berliner Börsen-Courier*, 21 May 1922, no. 237.

35 Paul Landau, "Große Berliner Kunstausstellung II.", in: *Berliner Börsen-Zeitung*, 15 June 1923, no. 273.

36 Curt Glaser, "Drei Räume in der Großen Berliner Kunstausstellung", in: *Berliner Börsen-Courier*, 5 August 1923, no. 363.

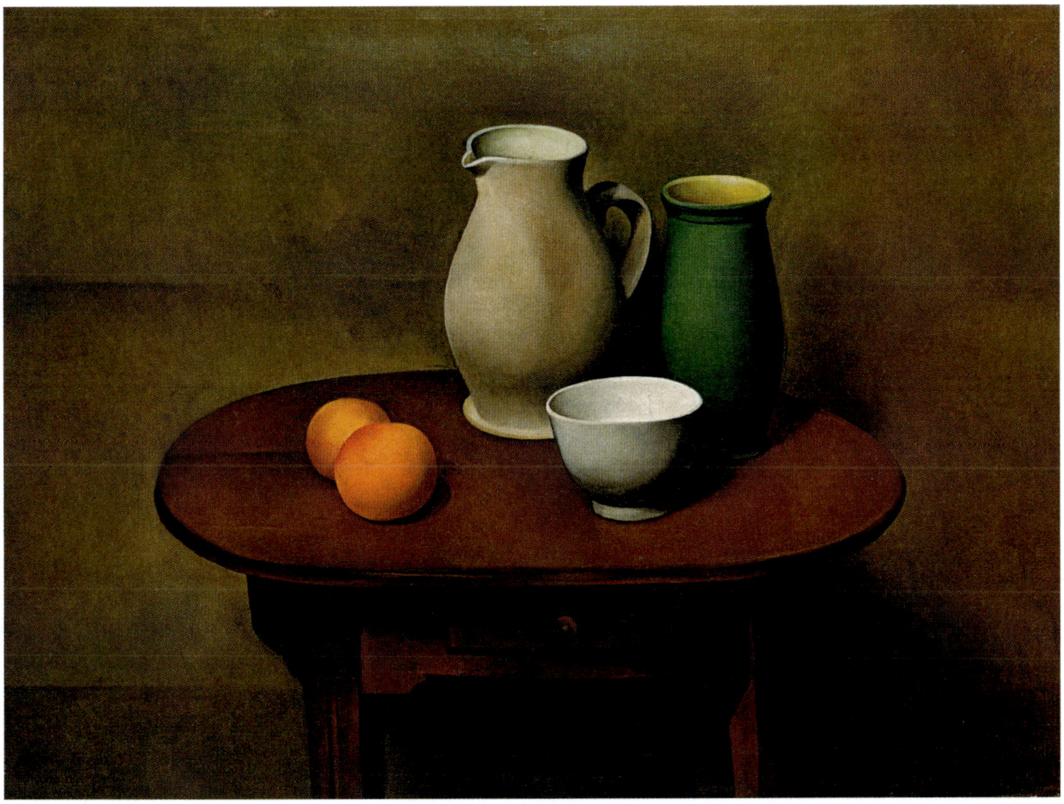

10 **ALEXANDER KANOLDT**
Still Life II, 1924
Osthaus Museum Hagen
Great Berlin Art Exhibition 1924, Novembergruppe section, no. 919

10

37 Ludwig Hilberseimer, "Anmerkungen zur Neuen Kunst" (1923), in: Grohmann 1928, pp. 55–57, here 56f.

38 Will Grohmann, "Zehn Jahre Novembergruppe", ref. in note 1, pp. 7f. Reprinted in Rudert 2012, p. 30.

39 *Ausstellung der Novembergruppe in den Räumen der Berliner Secession in Berlin. Juni 1925. Malerei, Plastik, Architektur*, Archiv der deutschen Kunst, vol. 5, no. 3, Berlin 1925, no. 98; see Hoek 2000, WVZ-Nr. 702.III und 702.IIw. I am grateful to Janina Nentwig for pointing this out and identifying the work.

40 See letter from Theo van Doesburg to Hannah Höch, 17 April [1926], in: Berlinische Galerie 1995, 2. Abt., 26.6, p. 254.

41 Letter from Theo van Doesburg to Hannah Höch, 1 May [1926], quoted in: Berlinische Galerie 1995, 2. Abt., 26.7, p. 256.

42 Adolf Behne, "Große Berliner Kunst-Ausstellung 1924", in: *Die Weltbühne — der Schaubühne*, vol. 20-2, 1924, pp. 66-68, here 66f.

43 Ibid.

44 George Grosz, "Verismus", in El Lissitzky, Hans Arp (eds.), *Die Kunstismen*, Munich and Leipzig 1925, p. XI.

45 Max Osborn, "Novembergruppe. Die Ausstellung in der Sezession", *Vossische Zeitung*, 24 June 1925, no. 295, evening edition.

46 Paul Friedrich, "Die Novembergruppe in der Sezession", in: *Berliner Börsen-Zeitung,* 31 May 1925, no. 251.

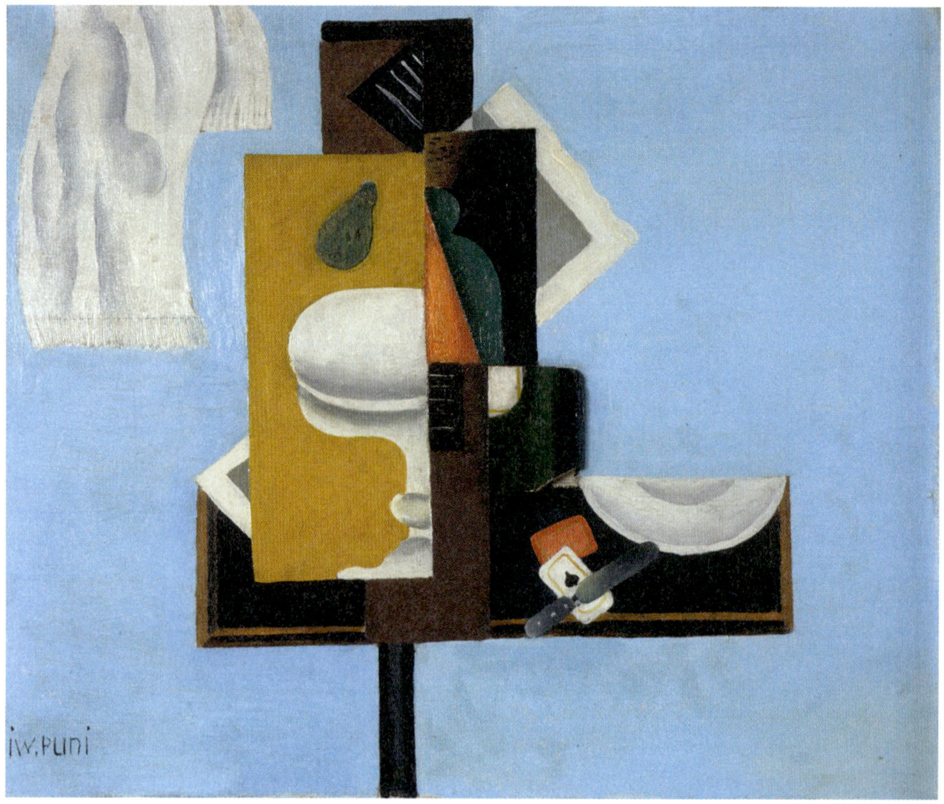

49

IWAN PUNI

Composition, Constructivist Still Life, 1920

Oil on canvas and ceramic collage, 54 × 63 cm
Berlinische Galerie

Great Berlin Art Exhibition 1923,
Novembergruppe section, no. 1308 or 1309

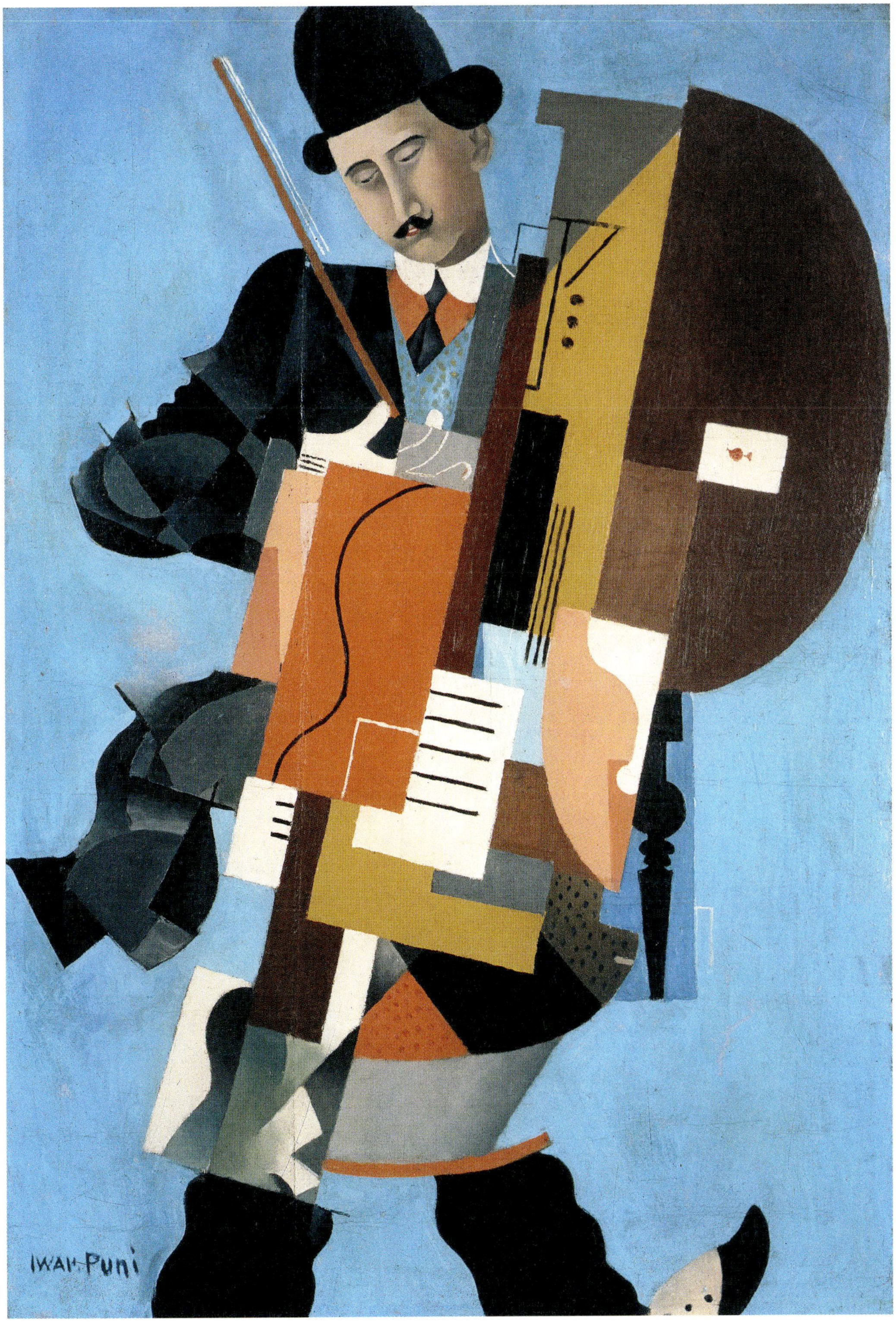

50

IWAN PUNI

Synthetic Musician, 1921

Oil on canvas, 145 × 98 cm
Berlinische Galerie

Great Berlin Art Exhibition 1922,
Novembergruppe section, no. 1376

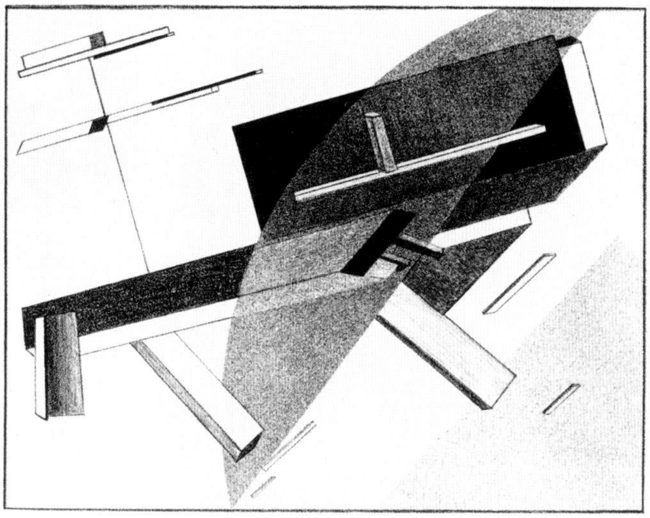

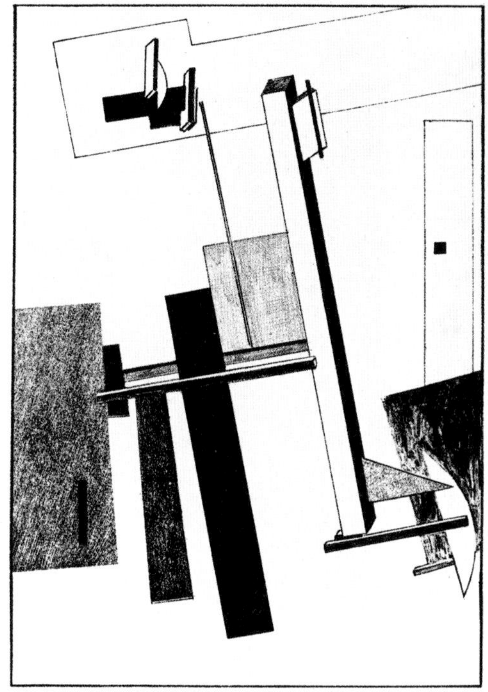

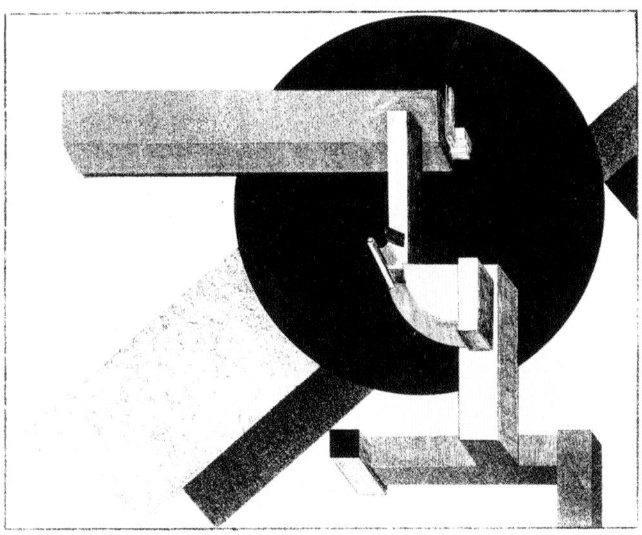

51
EL LISSITZKY
Proun 2 B (Proun portfolio) 1921

Lithograph, 34.2 × 45.5 cm
Staatliche Museen zu Berlin, Kupferstichkabinett

Great Berlin Art Exhibition 1922, November-gruppe section, no. 1325, repro. in the catalogue

52
EL LISSITZKY
Proun 1 D (Proun portfolio), 1921

Lithograph, 34 × 44.5 cm
Staatliche Museen zu Berlin, Kupferstichkabinett

Great Berlin Art Exhibition 1922,
Novembergruppe section, no. 1326

53
EL LISSITZKY
Proun 2 C (Proun portfolio), 1921

Lithograph, 45.2 × 35.5 cm
Staatliche Museen zu Berlin, Kupferstichkabinett

Great Berlin Art Exhibition 1922,
Novembergruppe section, no. 1327

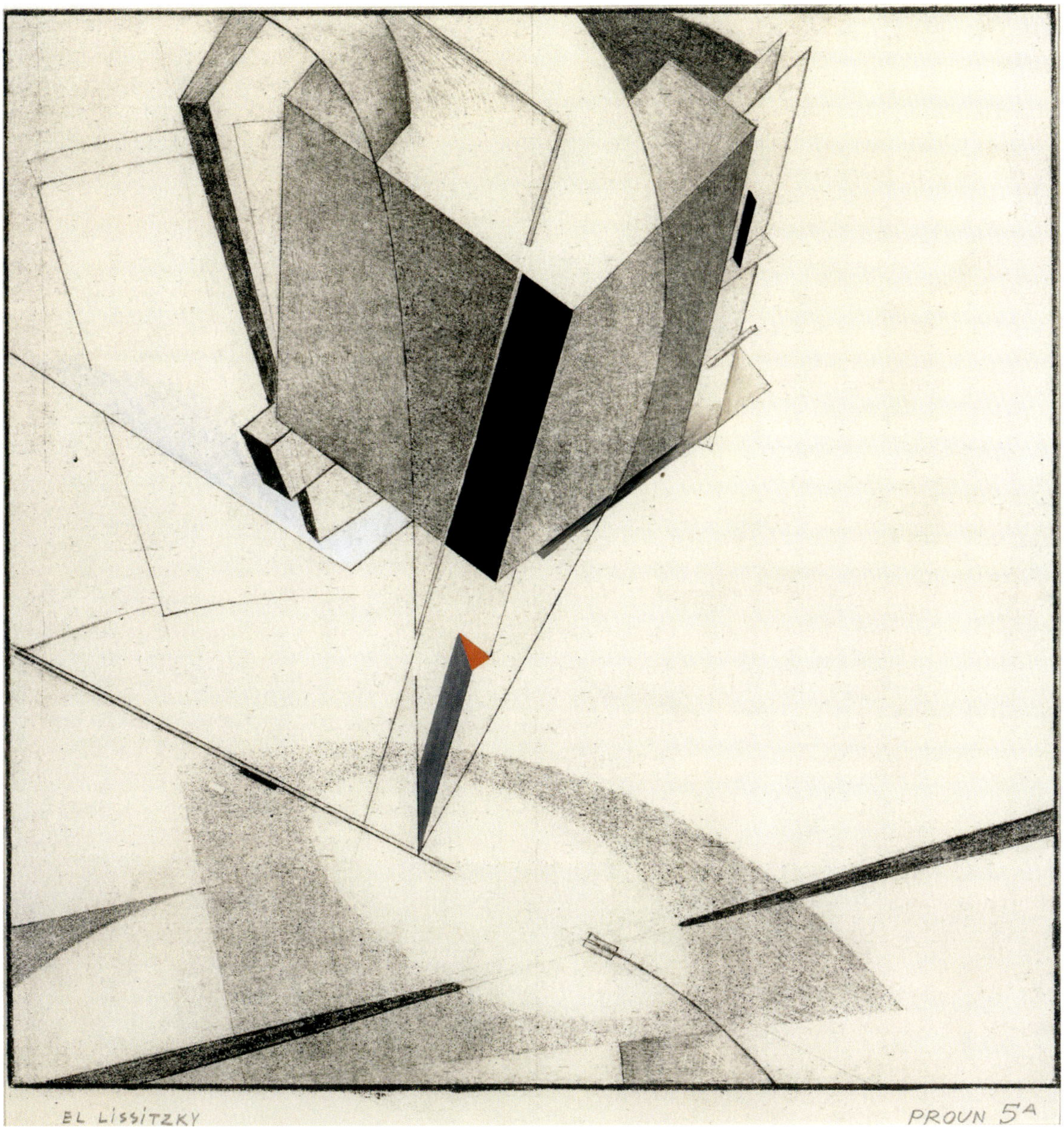

54

EL LISSITZKY

Proun 5 A (Proun portfolio), 1921

Lithograph, 29 × 26.7 cm
Staatliche Museen zu Berlin, Kupferstichkabinett

Great Berlin Art Exhibition 1922,
Novembergruppe section, no. 1328

EL LISSITZKY
Proun Room, 1923

"Proun" was EL LISSITZKY'S term for his abstract works, abbreviated from Russian words meaning "project for the affirmation of new art".[1] This was a mission he shared with Kasimir Malevich, the artist behind the iconic *Black Square*. Unlike his mentor, however, El Lissitzky was keen to make a political connection: he wanted his non-figurative visual idiom to play a defining role in the everyday life of revolutionary Russia.[2] In late 1921, at the age of 31, he left for Berlin, probably at the behest of the Soviet government, and quickly made contacts in the art community.[3] By the spring of 1922 he was already exhibiting with the Novembergruppe at the Great Berlin Art Exhibition, and among his exhibits were items from the *Proun Portfolio* (cat. 51–54, pp. 116–117) which he had begun in Russia. His compatriot IVAN PUNI (cat. 50, p. 115) also took part in the Novembergruppe section along with his wife KSENIA BOGUSLAVSKAYA. "God preserve us from the Prounists,"[4] wrote Max Osborn in the *Vossische Zeitung* in response to the Russian entries, singling out El Lissitzky as an example of empty schematism and design for its own sake.

Despite this negative criticism, echoed by many journalists, the Novembergruppe invited Russian Abstract artists to show in the following year too. 1923 likewise featured quite a few members of the Dutch movement *De Stijl*.[5] El Lissitzky, who had studied architecture, now had his first chance to translate his art into three dimensions. For the *Proun Room* [*Prounenraum*] (cat. 55, p. 119), regarded today as a seminal work of the 1920s, the group gave him one of the little cabinets immediately adjacent to their hall of architecture (fig. 01).[6] On display there, apart from examples of *Neues Bauen* in the form of photographs and drawings, were other abstract interior designs. ERICH BUCHHOLZ showed four pictures of his Berlin studio by the canal at Herkulesufer in Berlin (fig. 02), regarded as an important inspiration for the *Proun Room*, and also present were ideas for interior decoration from *De Stijl* members, with whom El Lissitzky fostered a vigorous exchange.[7] In contrast to the fairly static abstraction of these domestic and studio settings, El Lissitzky saw his installation as a dynamic exhibition, a "demonstration space" that sought to break through the boundaries formed by the walls.[8] Visitors entered a three-dimensional Proun work and were totally enveloped by its pure, rhythmically structured geometry. Here "design becomes logical reality"[9], observed the guide issued by the Novembergruppe in its crisp and cryptic fashion. Evidently El Lissitzky found that description too concise and simultaneously published his own text in the magazine *G*, elaborating in detail on the use of colour and relief and making his message clear: "Whether we 'paint' *walls* or hang pictures on a wall, both are equally wrong. The new space needs and wants no pictures — is not an image to be transposed onto surfaces. That explains why the picture painters are so hostile towards us: we are destroying the wall as a bed of rest for their pictures."[10] Ironically, visitors to the Great Berlin Art Exhibition passed the *Proun Room* on their way to the sales office to buy art for the walls at home.

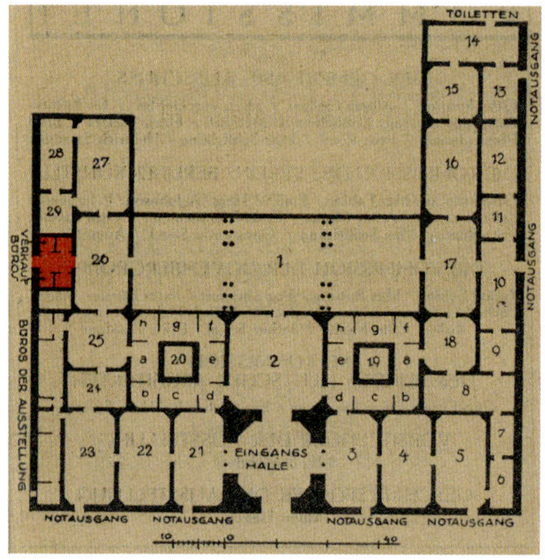

01 Floor plan of the Landesausstellungsgebäude at Lehrter Bahnhof, Great Berlin Art Exhibition 1923. El Lissitzky's *Proun Room* was in one of the cabinets marked in red.

JANINA NENTWIG

1 Translations in the literature vary. The word "proun" derives from pro-Unovis, and Unovis was the name of the group of artists founded by El Lissitzky together with Kazimir Malevich at the art school in Vitebsk. Unovis, in turn, was an acronym for "Champions of New Art".

2 Hemken 1990 is still valuable as an introduction.

3 See Forgács 2003, pp. 47 and 61–66.

4 Max Osborn, "Junge Kunst. Zur Großen Berliner Kunstausstellung", in: *Vossische Zeitung*, 14 June 1922, no. 277.

5 See the essay by Burmeister in this catalogue, pp. 105–109.

6 See *Führer durch die Abteilung der Novembergruppe. Kunstausstellung Berlin 1923*, Berlin 1923, unpag. [Notes on Room 26].

7 One of them, Vilmos Huszár, presented *Designs for interior colour schemes* which defy specific identification (see exhib. cat. *Grosse Berliner Kunstausstellung 1922, Abt. der Novembergruppe*, no. 1228). Forgács 2003 provides a detailed account of these and other influences.

8 See El Lissitzky, "Prounenraum Grosse Berliner Kunstausstellung 1923", in: *G. Zeitschrift für elementare Gestaltung*, vol. 1, 1923, no. 1, unpag.

9 Ref. in note 6.

10 Ref. in note 8.

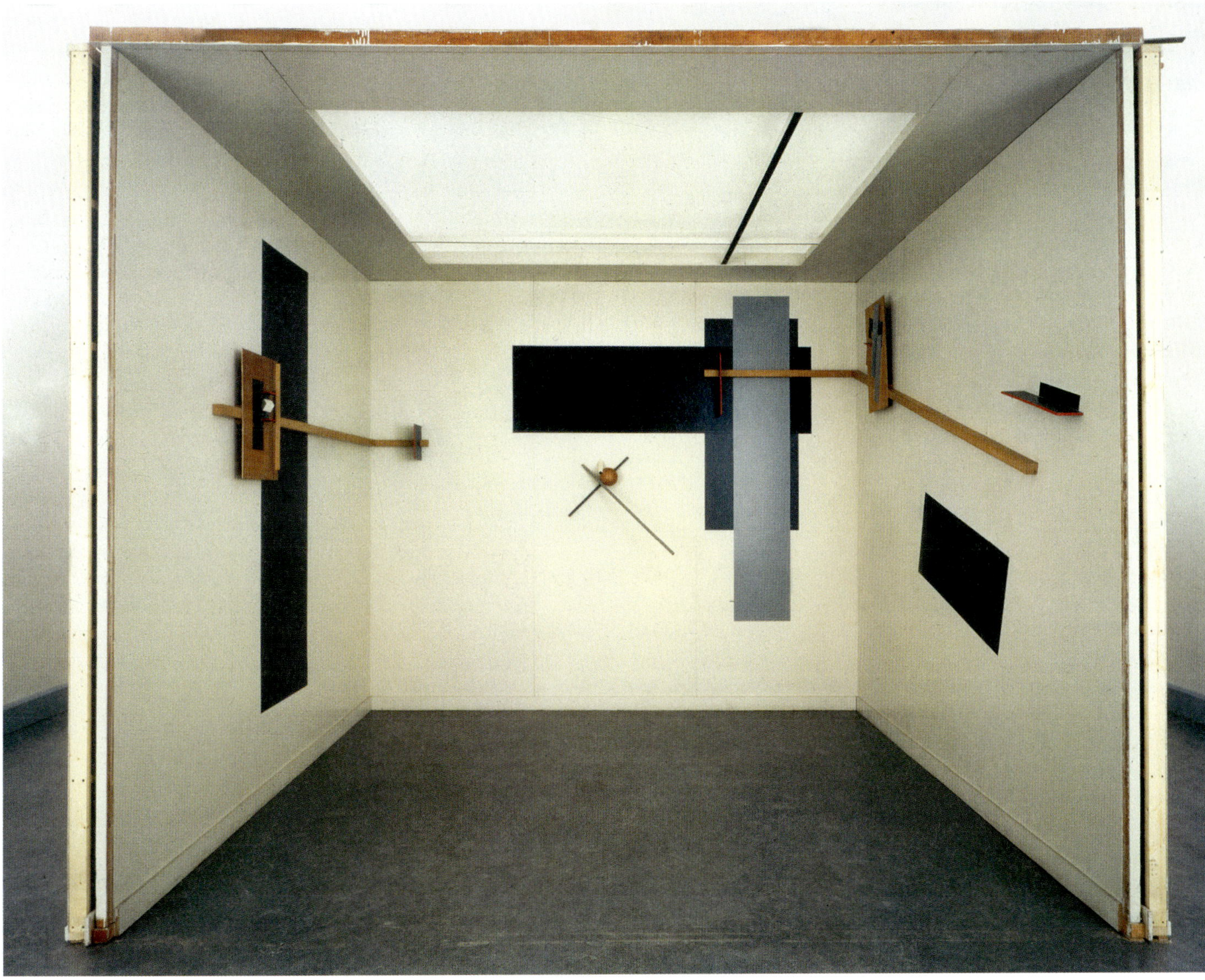

55

EL LISSITZKY

Proun Room for the Great Berlin Art Exhibition, 1923 (reconstruction 1965)

Wood, painted, glass, 310 × 365 × 365 cm
Berlinische Galerie

Great Berlin Art Exhibition 1923,
Novembergruppe section, no. 1253

WALTER DEXEL
Composition 1927 I, 1927

WALTER DEXEL'S artistic development—from Expressionist forms to bare-boned Constructivism—was closely linked to his work directing exhibitions for the art society in the town of Jena. Between 1916 and 1928 he presented the contemporary avant-garde—including the Novembergruppe in September 1920[1]—and was in touch with artists close to the gallery Der Sturm[2] and its founder Herwarth Walden, with teachers and students at the Bauhaus in Weimar and with THEO VAN DOESBURG of *De Stijl*. Doesburg came to Germany in 1921 and was a crucial influence on Dexel, whose paintings, often titled 'Composition', ceased to be figurative between 1922 and 1923. The variation and arranging of colours, shapes and surfaces revealed similarities to works by Doesburg and PIET MONDRIAN. Dexel's works, however, were not confined to straight lines, right angles and pure primary colours. The artist allowed himself a broader range of constructive composition, with intermediate colours, diagonals, curved motifs, and also letters and digits.

He acknowledged Doesburg for injecting "the whole world into our insularity, because a close exchange of ideas kept him in touch with everyone in the avant-garde".[3] The Novembergruppe likewise facilitated this kind of international exchange. That was how Walter Dexel encountered other Dutch artists and architects like JACOBUS JOHANNES PIETER OUD. In 1925, through the association, Oud showed a drawing for his project *Café de Unie* (fig. 01) in Rotterdam and met with praise from Dexel: it was the "first good example of the thorough mutual infusion of architecture and advertising".[4]

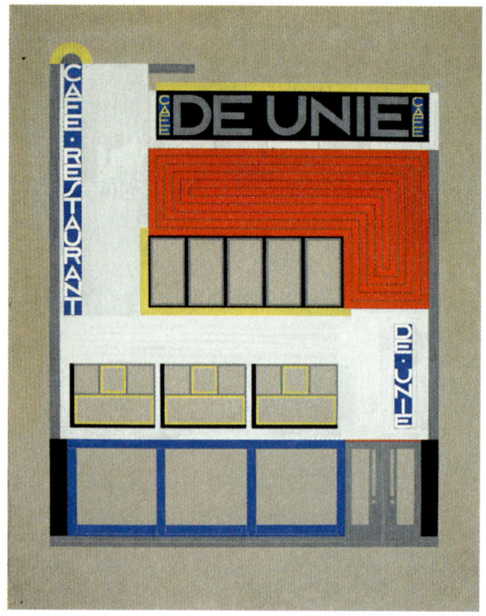

01 J. J. P. OUD, Design for De Unie Café, 1925, Collection Het Nieuwe Instituut

Dexel had gained his own first experience with this combination in 1924 when creating signs and illuminated columns in Jena. Two years later ADOLF MEYER invited him to Frankfurt, where he became an advisor to the city council and was able to carry on implementing his interdisciplinary ideas. Dexel's lamp advertising accounted for much of his production based on the applied arts, and like his paintings it was heavily influenced by Constructivist elementarism. Walter Dexel saw his own designs for advertising—but also business cards, invitations and posters—as "purely pragmatic formations [whose] colour and shape merely serve to reinforce the impact of the lettering"[5]. Dexel's lamp advertising might be seen as the sequel to his reverse glass paintings, which he similarly exhibited with the Novembergruppe.[6]

Dexel's ideas and output in the field of fine art were put to wide-ranging use: from painting via publicity design to lecturing in Magdeburg and Berlin, where he passed on his experience. In everything he did—set design, architecture, advertisements and paintings, teaching art and making prints—Dexel was always interdisciplinary. His ultimate purpose was to apply artistic design to the whole environment.

The painting *Composition 1927 I* [*Komposition 1927 I*] (cat. 56, p. 121), which Walter Dexel showed with the Novembergruppe the year it was made, had already appeared in 1925 as an element in a wall arrangement, and it features as part of the interior design sketched in *Study for Mrs von H.* [*Arbeitszimmer Frau von H.*] (fig. 02). The artist also designed furniture, "unadorned and built with simple forms", for the Hollander family. The room in question consisted of a low bed, black shelves up to the ceiling and the painting *Composition 1927 I*.[7] "'What is that supposed to be?' our visitors often asked when they saw Dexel's abstract paintings on our walls at home,"[8] recalls the daughter of the family.

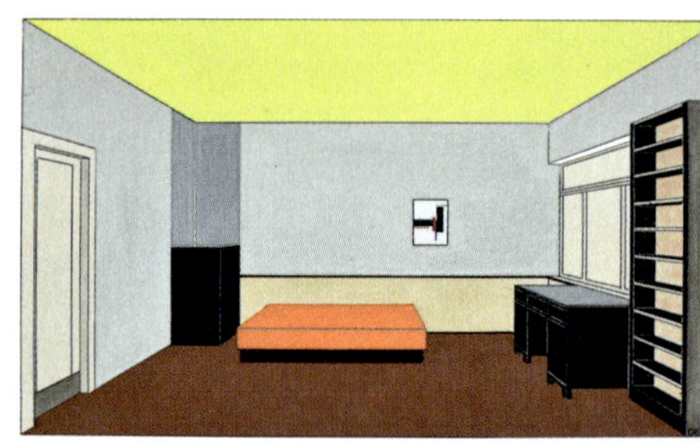

02 WALTER DEXEL, Mrs v. H.'s study, 1925, Stadtmuseum Jena

NUNO DE BRITO ROCHA

1 *Der Kunsttopf*, vol. 1, 1920, no. 2, p. 40.
2 Walter Dexel exhibited at *Der Sturm* in 1918, 1920 and 1925.
3 Quoted in Galerie Stolz 1990, pp. 83f.
4 Quoted in Fleischmann 1987, p. 95.
5 Güse 1979, p. 21.
6 Walter Dexel presented his reverse glass paintings in the Novembergruppe section at the Great Berlin Art Exhibition in the years 1923 (no. 1143), 1924 (no. 856) and 1926 (no. 1526).
7 See Brigitte Kranz, "Eine Freundschaft", in: Schmid 2002, p. 129.
8 Ibid.

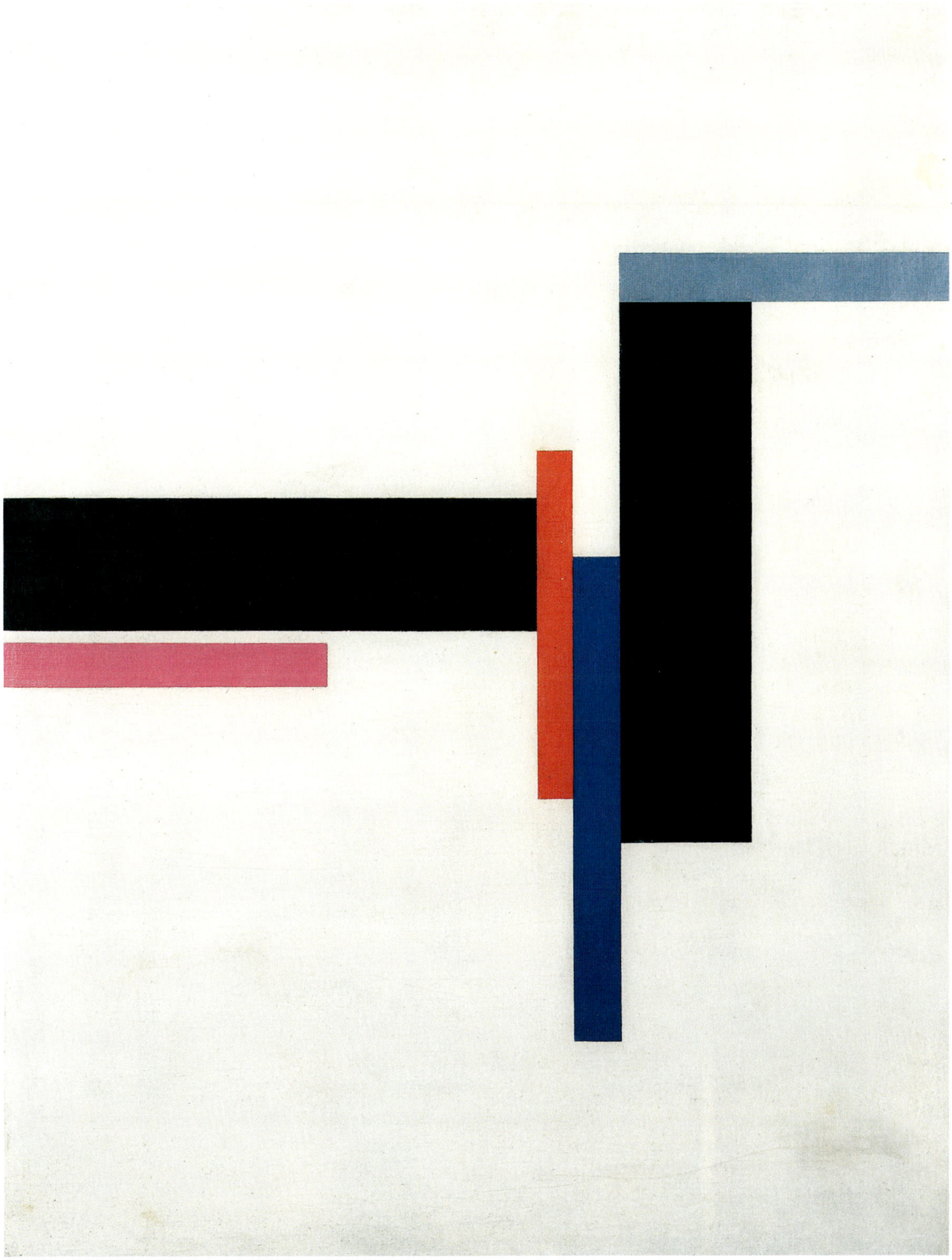

56

WALTER DEXEL

Composition 1927 I, 1927

Oil on canvas, 89 × 67 cm
Von der Heydt-Museum Wuppertal

Great Berlin Art Exhibition 1927,
Novembergruppe section, no. 83

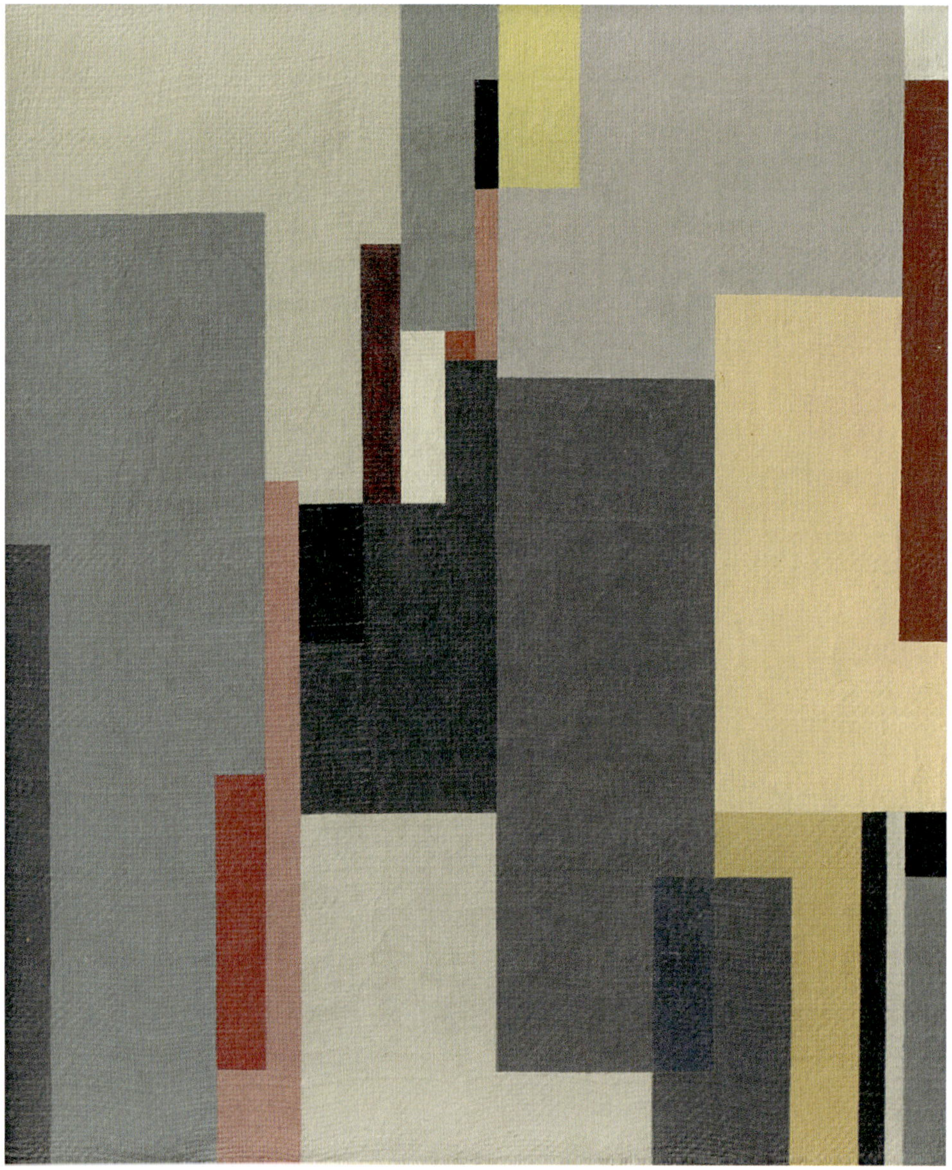

57

WALTER DEXEL

Composition 1923 IV, 1923

Oil on canvas, 48 × 39 cm
Private collection

Great Berlin Art Exhibition 1923, Novembergruppe section, no. 1140, repro. in the catalogue (as *Composition II*)

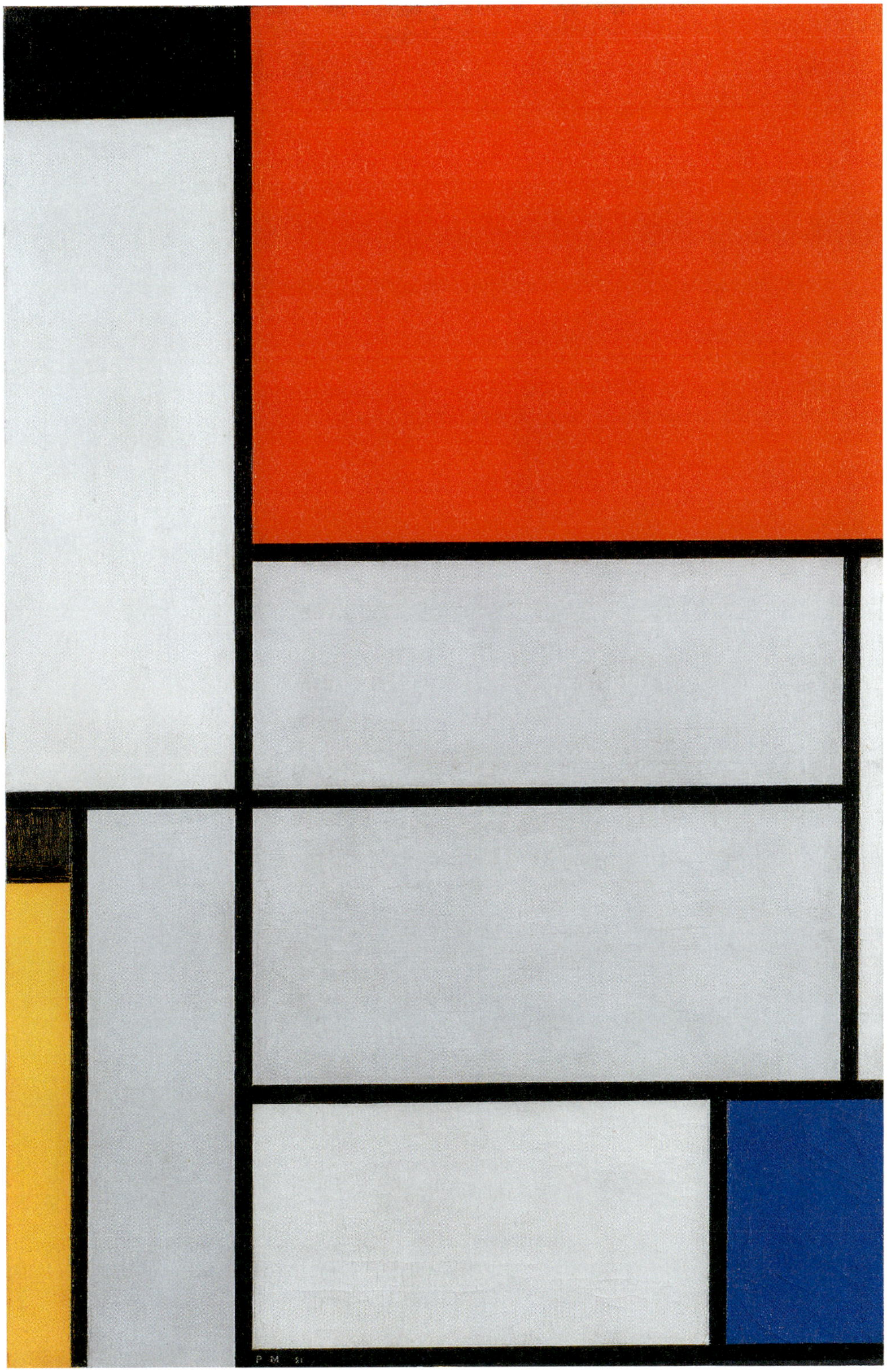

58

PIET MONDRIAN

Tableau I, 1921

Oil on canvas, 96.5 × 60.5 cm
Museum Ludwig, Köln

Great Berlin Art Exhibition 1923,
Novembergruppe section, ex-catalogue

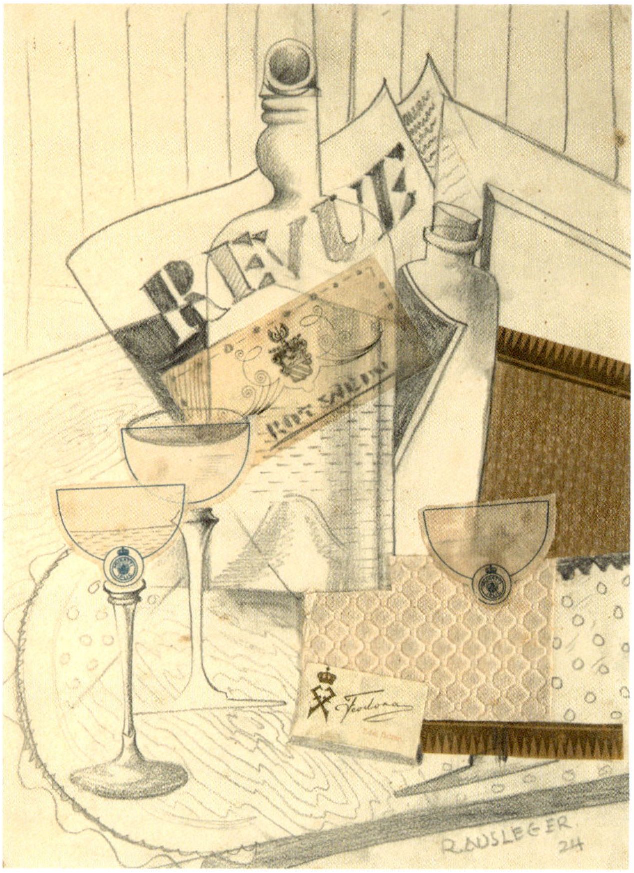

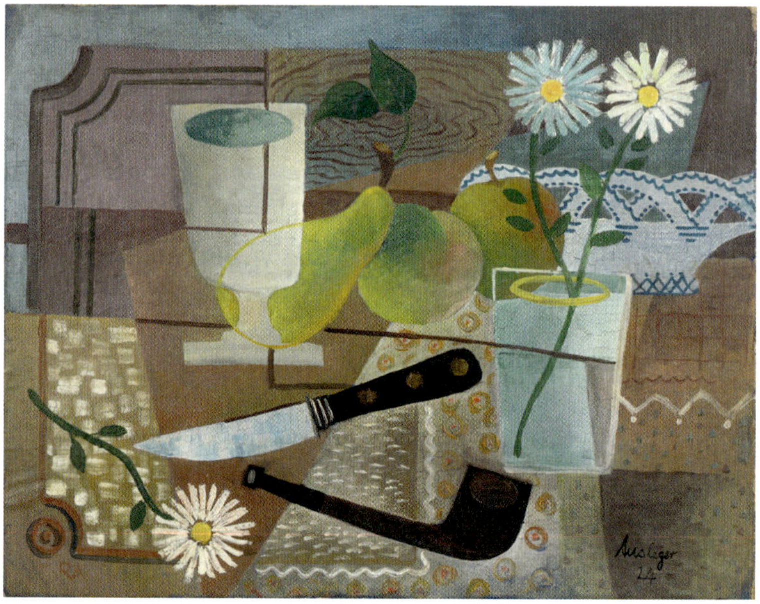

59
RUDOLF AUSLEGER
Untitled, 1924

Collage with pencil and printed, embossed wrapping papers on art paper
39.2 × 28.7 cm
Berlinische Galerie

60
RUDOLF AUSLEGER
Still Life with Pipe, 1924

Oil on paperboard, 30 × 38 cm
Berlinische Galerie

Ausleger showed numerous still lifes with the Novembergruppe between 1920 and 1931. None of the exhibited works have yet been identified.

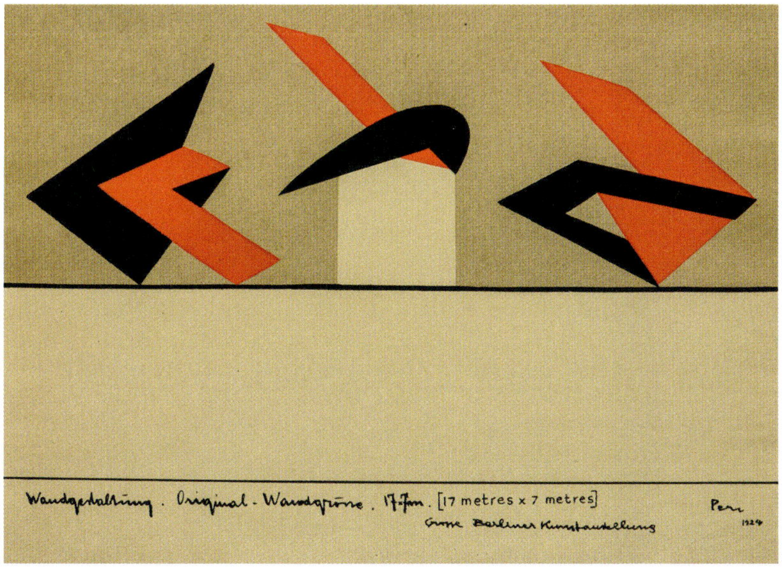

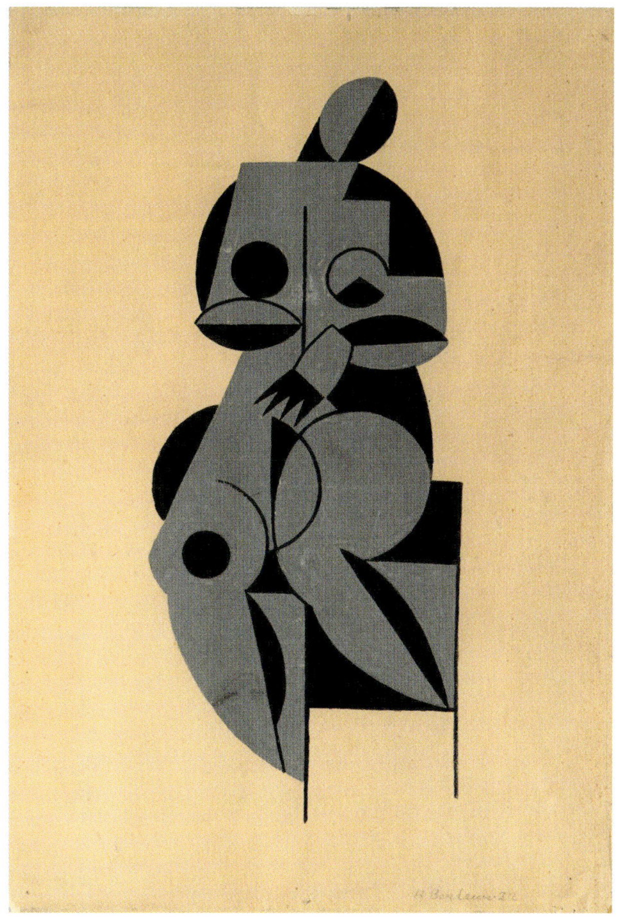

61

LÁSZLÓ PÉRI

Wall composition for the Great Berlin Art Exhibition (design), 1923–1924 / c. 1960

Silkscreen print from a linocut, 33.5 × 46.5 cm
Berlinische Galerie

Great Berlin Art Exhibition 1923, Novembergruppe section, no. 1303 (under the title *Spatial Constructions*); the date 1924 was added subsequently

62

HENRYK BERLEWI

Woman Seated, 1922

Gouache on art paper, 48.2 × 31.2 cm
Berlinische Galerie

At the Great Berlin Art Exhibition 1923 Berlewi showed works in the style of *Woman Seated* in the Novembergruppe section.

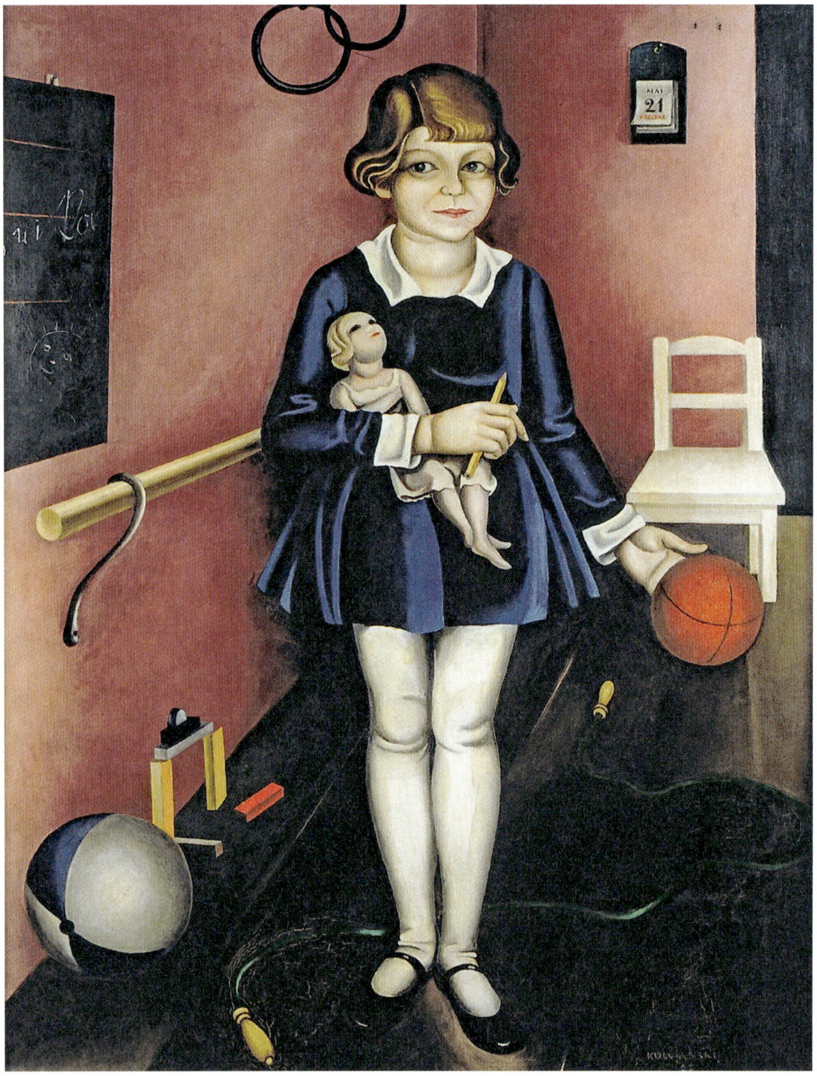

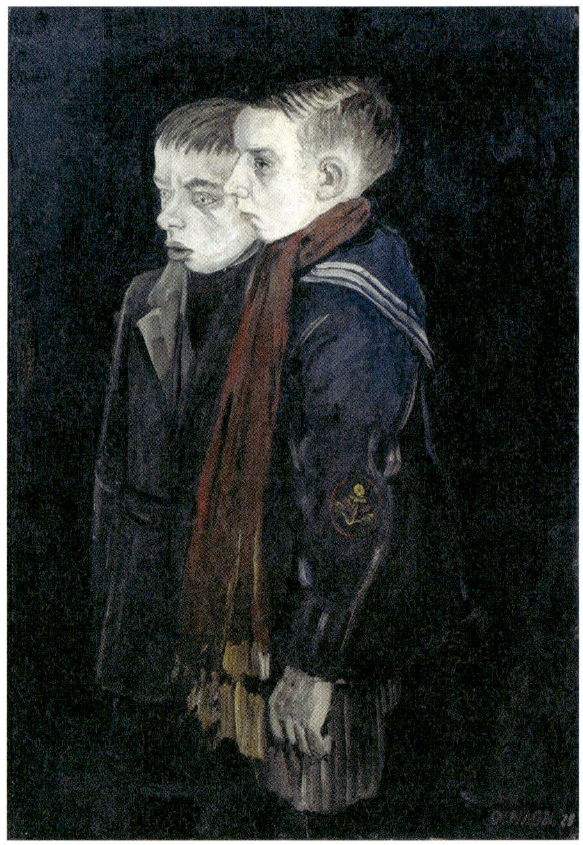

63
ISSAI KULVIANSKI
My Little Daughter Kiki, 1927

Oil on canvas, 127 × 96 cm
Berlinische Galerie

Great Berlin Art Exhibition 1927, Novembergruppe section, no. 278, repro. in the catalogue; Jury-Free Art Show Berlin 1929, exhibition Ten Years of the Novembergruppe, no. 664

64
OTTO NAGEL
Boys from Wedding, 1928

Oil on canvas, 91 × 62 cm
Staatliche Museen zu Berlin, Nationalgalerie

Great Berlin Art Exhibition 1928, Novembergruppe section, no. 691; Jury-Free Art Show Berlin 1929, exhibition Ten Years of the Novembergruppe, no. 870; Novembergruppe exhibition at the *Verein Berliner Künstler,* 1931, no. 49

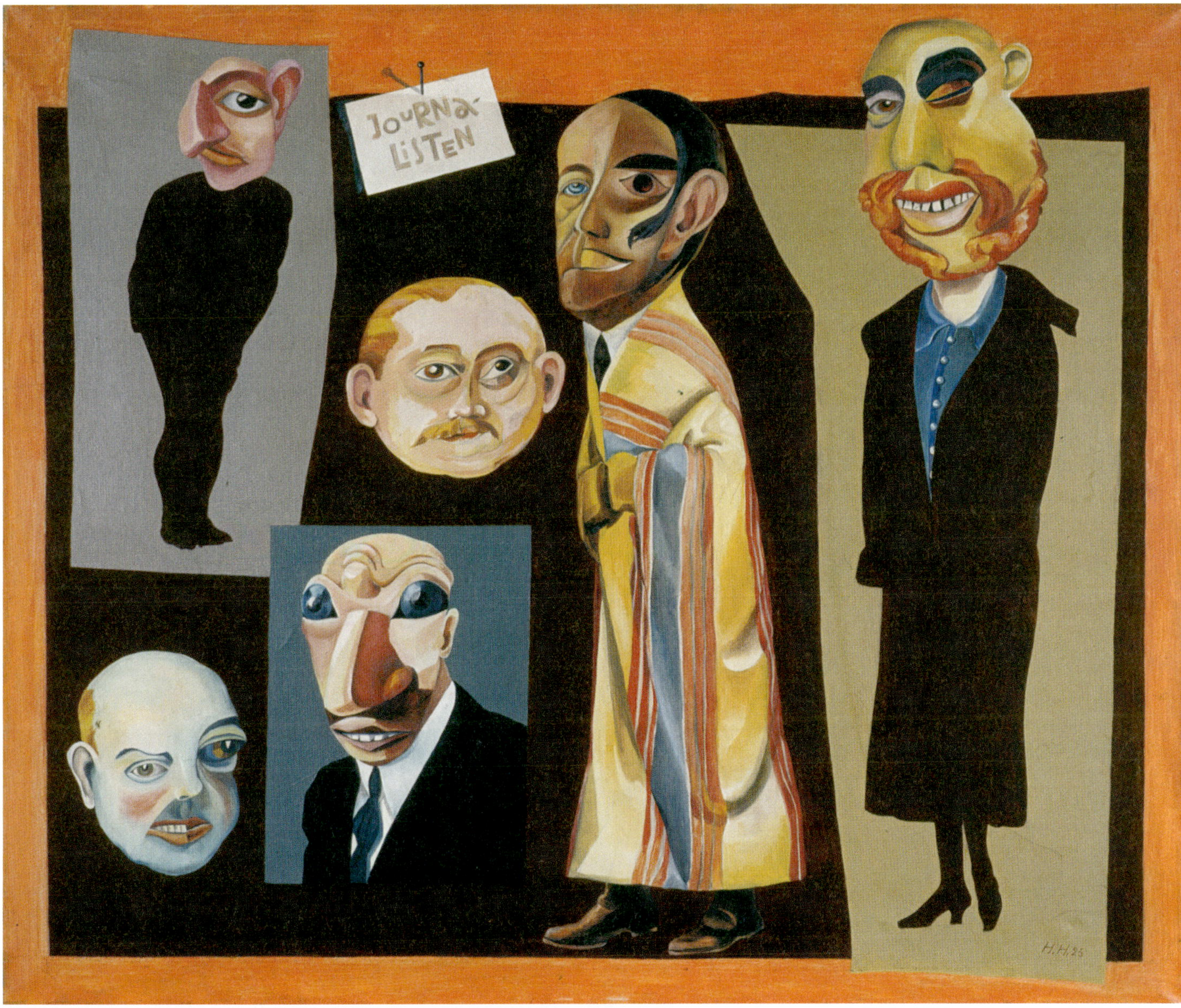

65
HANNAH HÖCH
The Journalists, 1925

Oil on canvas, 86 × 101 cm
Berlinische Galerie

Novembergruppe exhibition at the Berlin Secession, 1925, no. 41

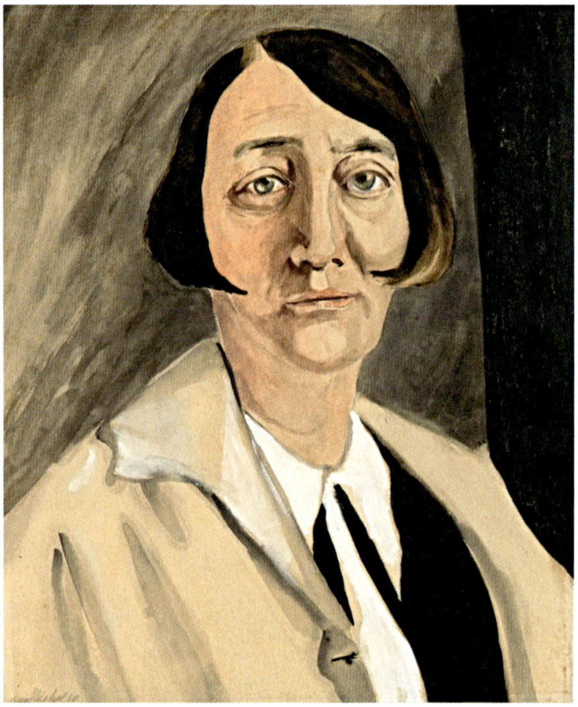

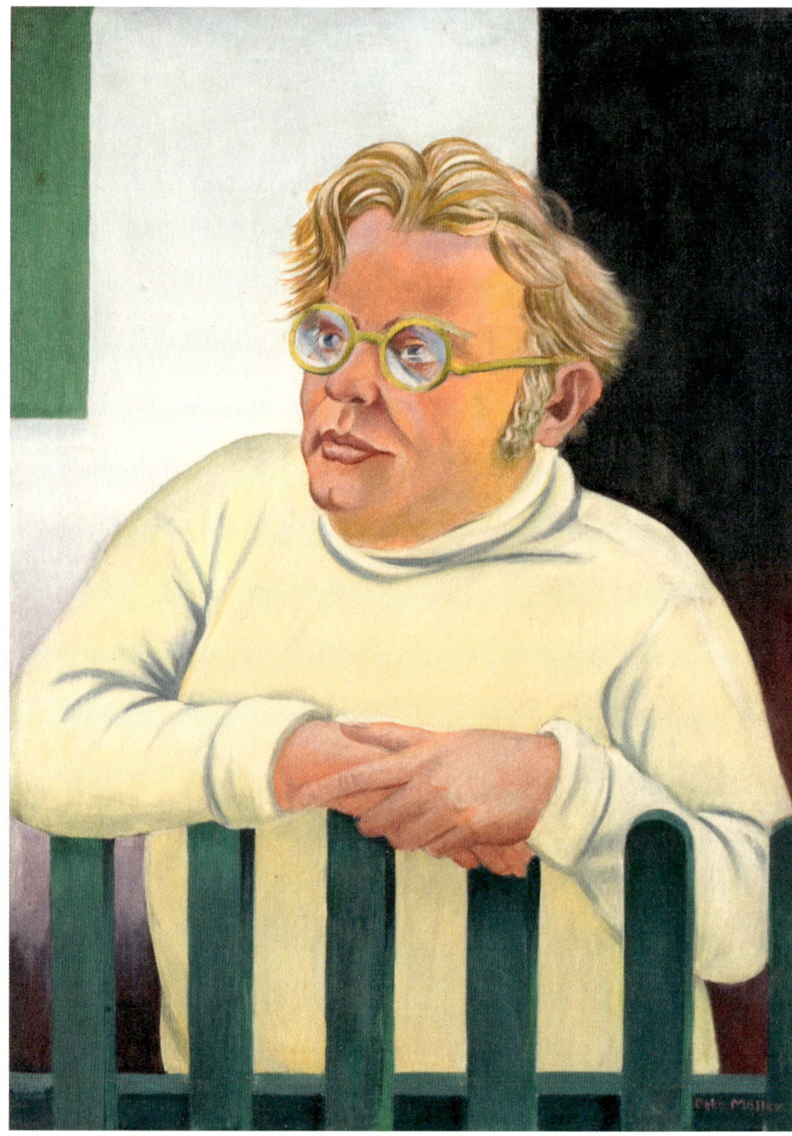

66
INES WETZEL
Self-Portrait, 1930

Watercolour, gouache and pencil
on art paper, 47 × 38.4 cm
Berlinische Galerie

67
OTTO MÖLLER
Portrait of Walter Kampmann, 1927

Oil on canvas, 94 × 67 cm
Berlinische Galerie

Great Berlin Art Exhibition 1927, Novembergruppe section, no. 335

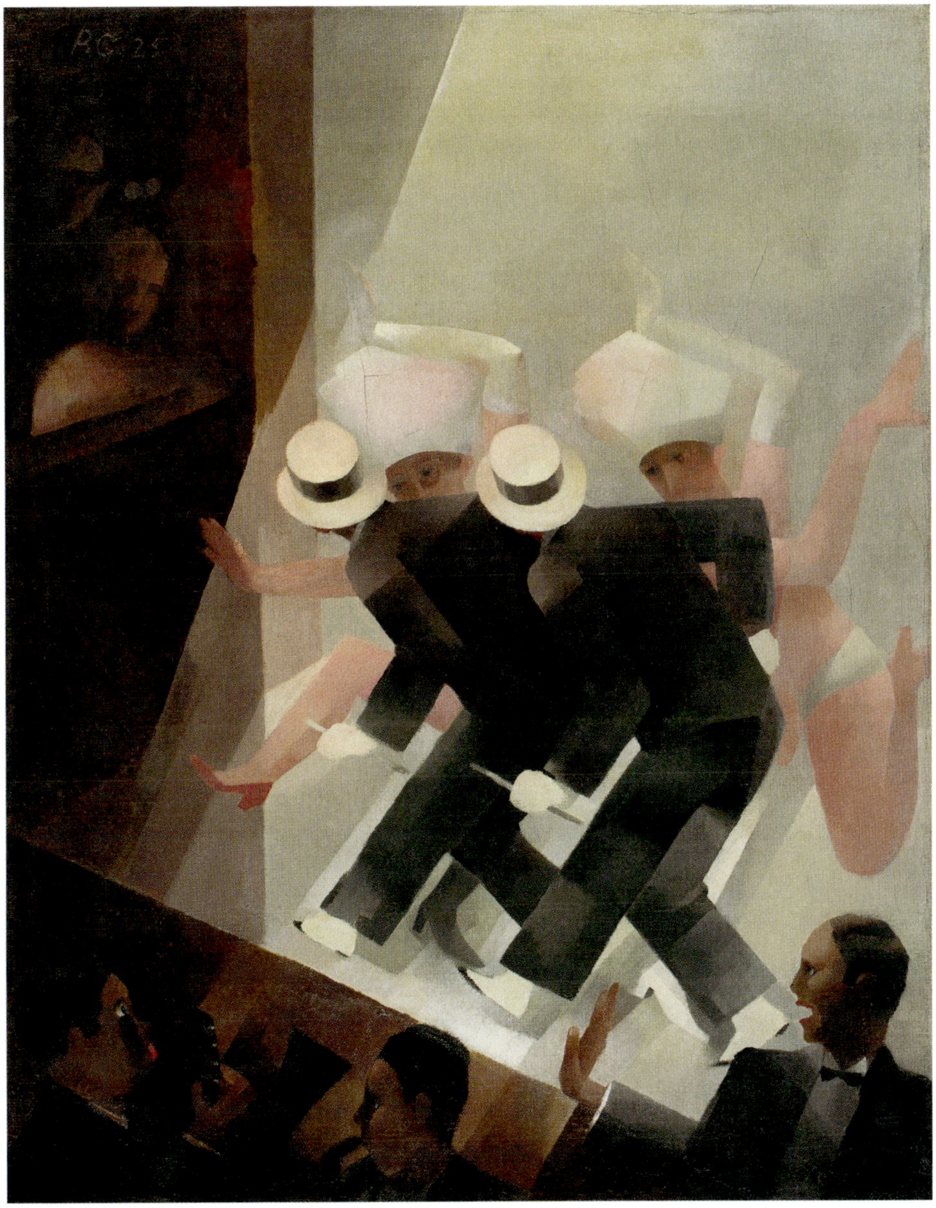

68
PAUL GRUNWALDT
Varieté, 1925

Oil on canvas, 59 × 46.5 cm
Stiftung Stadtmuseum Berlin

KARL VÖLKER
Concrete, c. 1924

"People and the militant struggle for them were my manifesto and that is still the case. Anyone who looks properly will find them everywhere in my work. My theme is and remains people."[1] (Karl Völker, 1961)
In 1918–19, when revolutionary élan gripped radical artists all over the country, the painter, printmaker and architect KARL VÖLKER joined with like-minded colleagues in Halle (Saale) to form the *Hallische Künstlergruppe*. Although he was already a member of the Novembergruppe, which had a nationwide reach, he believed there was a crucial need for a local organization to influence cultural affairs in the city. The two associations expressed equivalent demands on the new democratic system and had a common vision of an emancipated, politically effective alliance of artists who would, "in union with the intelligentsia, who are permeated by the same contemporary spirit, [bring] the state to a cultural flowering".[2]
For Karl Völker and other left-leaning members of the *Hallische Künstlergruppe*, art became a tool for championing the needs of the working class. After the First World War, Halle experienced major industrial expansion, triggering a growth in the urban population. At the same time, inflation was spiralling. This led to a dramatic worsening of the workers' plight. Left-wing radicalization, civic unrest, demonstrations and strikes ensued.[3] Karl Völker's prints captured the regional uprising in 1921, the brutal shootings of insurgents by paramilitaries and the deprivation of the early 1920s.

Völker's social and political commitment was also reflected in his support for Workers' International Relief, an organization closely allied to the Communist Party of Germany (KPD). His involvement in *Hunger*, a portfolio of lithographs published in 1924, including donations from renowned artists such as Käthe Kollwitz and GEORGE GROSZ, is a particular testimony to his solidarity with impoverished workers.[4]
Between 1923 and 1925 the artist produced woodcuts for the socialist newspapers *Das Wort* and *Klassenkampf*. In *Niedner's Class Justice* [*Niedners Klassenjustiz*] (fig. 01) Völker responded to the dispensation of justice by Alexander Niedner, a presiding judge at the Supreme Court with a reputation for being particularly harsh on communists but soft on offenders with far-right affiliations. The image is dominated by the judge's face, his duelling scars, his cap and robe and the legal code tucked under his arm. His robust frame resolutely displaces the stylized figures packed together behind him, amalgamated into an ornamental mass where individuality dissolves.[5] The artist transposed the aesthetic clarity and intensity of these woodcuts into a series of large-format paintings, his *Pictures of Industry* [*Industriebilder*], which feature workers in alienated industrial settings. In his painting *Concrete* [*Beton*] (cat. 69, p. 131) he dispensed altogether with human depictions. The monumental factory with forbidding, windowless walls is completely deserted. From a dark tunnel on the lower edge, rail tracks rise steeply into the depths of the empty space. The vanishing point in this bold perspective composition is hidden behind a black wall protruding into the picture from the left. This work of New Objectivity strikingly expresses Völker's fascination with an objectified, predominantly industrial landscape that confronts people with an unhospitable, even hostile habitat.[6] Völker's *Pictures of Industry* were shown at Novembergruppe exhibitions between 1925 and 1926 and praised in the socialist press: "Only a few works stand out from the general norm, such as the pictures by Karl Völker, Willi Baumeister, Ivan Puni and the sculptures by Rudolf Belling and Ewald Mataré."[7]

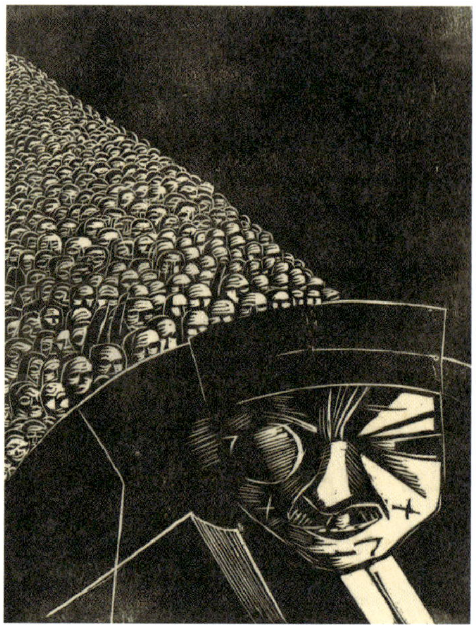

01 KARL VÖLKER, Niedner's Class Justice, 1924, Kulturstiftung Sachsen-Anhalt – Kunstmuseum Moritzburg Halle (Saale)

JUSCHKA MARIE VON RÜDEN

1 Quoted in Ullmann 1978, p. 3.
2 "Aus dem Manifest der Hallischen Künstlergruppe", in: *Zehn Jahre Novembergruppe*, special issue of *Kunst der Zeit. Zeitschrift für Kunst und Literatur*, vol. 3, 1928, nos. 1–3, p. 13; see also Wilhelmi 1996, p. 174.
3 See Meinel 2007, p. 112.
4 See Schulze 1974, p. 12.
5 See Meinel 2008, p. 85.
6 See Schulze 1974, pp. 20f. On notes 4 and 6: Karl Völker's work was known in the German Democratic Republic, where it was interpreted from a communist perspective. Although he supported socialist organizations, Völker never joined the KPD.
7 Ludwig Hilberseimer, "Novembergruppe", in: *Sozialistische Monatshefte*, no. 31, vol. 62, 1925, p. 518.

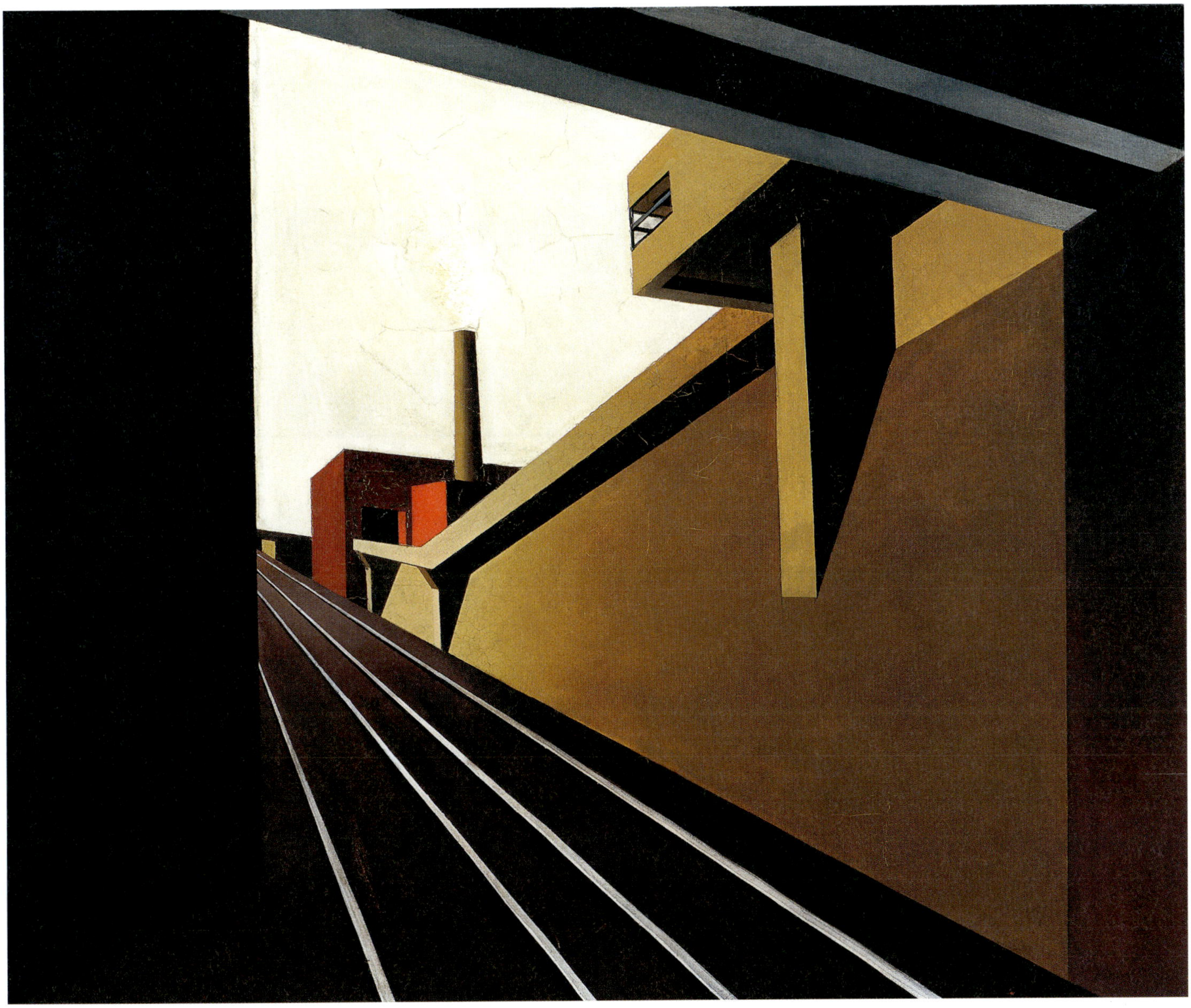

69

KARL VÖLKER

Concrete, c. 1924

Oil on canvas, 84.5 × 100 cm,
Kulturstiftung Sachsen-Anhalt,
Kunstmuseum Moritzburg Halle (Saale)

Possibly Novembergruppe exhibition at the
Berlin Secession, 1925, no. 91 or 91a

EWALD MATARÉ
Room in the Novembergruppe Section, Great Berlin Art Exhibition, 1928

In the summer of 1928, the sculptor EWALD MATARÉ wrote in his diary: "I currently have a collective exhibition of my work in wood in Berlin at the Great Berlin Art Exhibition, 20 pieces in all, and the little room, where I had them span a low [textile] ceiling, I then lined entirely with cork. It had long been my wish to clad out a space, and my things are very well suited to the rough, splendidly brown colour and the resultant unevenness. Besides, it was much acclaimed in the press, and my colleagues are granting me more consideration than I deserve."[1]

Previously the artist had only had a small personal show at Galerie Gurlitt, so this "collective exhibition" was a significant success in his career. What Mataré's few lines do not mention, however, is the Novembergruppe, the association that gave him this opportunity by integrating his work into the group presentation at the Great Berlin Art Exhibition. They provided Mataré with a whole room and gave him a free hand to implement its unusual décor. The sculptor designed a space that set off his bronze and smoothly polished wooden sculptures to maximum effect. According to an enthusiastic review in the *Berliner Volkszeitung*, he not only used cork oak panelling for the walls, but blue tiles on which to stand his works, "these visions of animal bodies which, in definitive form, reveal the ineffable beauty of the beast while dispensing with all detail".[2]

The fascinating play on contrasts—warm and cool, rough and smooth—is even evident in a black-and-white photograph, preserved in the estate, depicting an excerpt of the setting (cat. 70, p. 133). A group portrait (pp. 192-193) taken in this room and reproduced in the print media demonstrates the significance attached by the Novembergruppe to Mataré's work and this *mise-en-scène*.[3] It shows the artist with HUGO GRAETZ, group secretary at the time, flanked by the hanging committee.

The Novembergruppe frequently highlighted the œuvre of a particular member in a special display, normally during group exhibitions. Mataré was the first sculptor to be honoured with an 'exhibition within an exhibition' of this kind. The artist was highly critical of the dominance of painters in the association, and this might be why his diary fails to mention the Novembergruppe as the patron of his art. In 1923, presumably soon after joining, he wrote: "Yesterday visited architect Mies van der Rohe, with whom I talked about many an artistic matter, he belongs as I do to the 'November Group', but hopes like me to prise this association of artists away from the eternal monotony of its aestheticism and to see more people active in the group whose work really does restore material to its place, because all this picture painting has entirely lost its value and its justification nowadays."[4]

The Novembergruppe proved resistant to such influence, but Mataré nevertheless remained a faithful member. Between 1923 and 1931 he took part in eight of its exhibitions, where he presented the larger part of his sculptural output from that period.

JANINA NENTWIG

1 Ewald Mataré, diary entry of 12 June 1928, quoted in Mataré and Schilling 1997, p. 152. The catalogue for the Great Berlin Art Exhibition in 1928 lists 17 works by Mataré (nos. 1555–1571). To these we should add at least one relief (Schilling 1987, no. 18) incorporated by Mataré into the wall cladding, which can be detected on the left margin of a photograph depicting the room in question (pp. 192–193). (I am grateful to Maja Kufferath for pointing this out.) On the artist's life and work until 1933, see *inter alia* Museum Kurhaus Kleve 2015.

2 Ernst Collin, "Die Riesen-Kunstschau im Landes-Ausstellungsgebäude", in: *Berliner Volkszeitung*, 10 May 1928, no. 219.

3 "Bilder der diesjährigen Großen Berliner Kunstausstellung. Zum Vortrag von Hans S. v. Heister in der Funk-Stunde, Berlin, am 13. Mai", in: *Der Deutsche Rundfunk*, vol 6, 1928, p. 1305.

4 Ewald Mataré, diary entry of 20 October 1923, quoted in Mataré and Schilling 1997, p. 74.

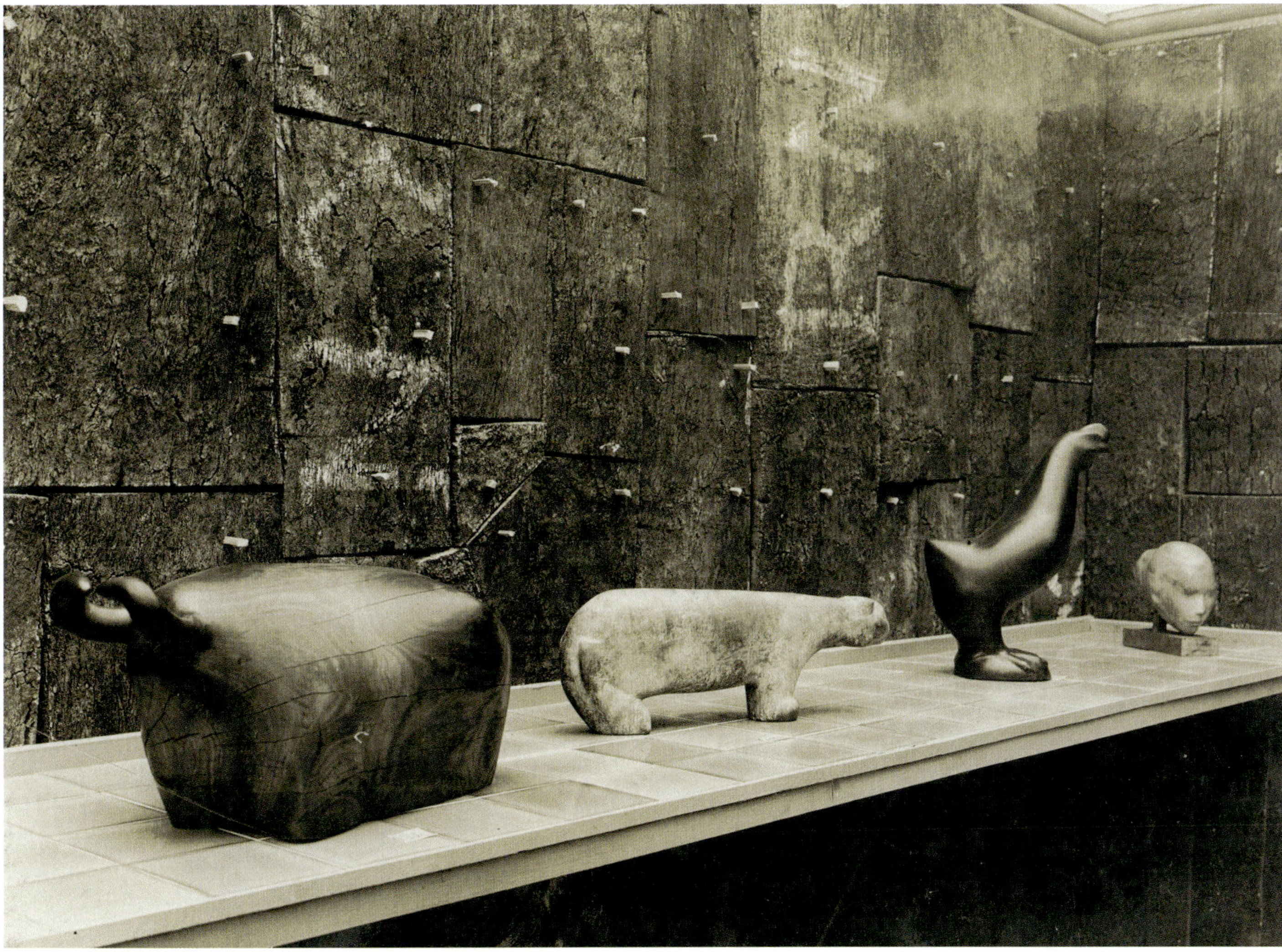

70

EWALD MATARÉ

Historical view of the Mataré Room at the Great Berlin Art Exhibition, 1928

Gelatin silver print (vintage print), 16.5 × 12 cm
Museum Kurhaus Kleve – Ewald Mataré-Sammlung, Kleve / Permanent loan from the Ewald Mataré estate

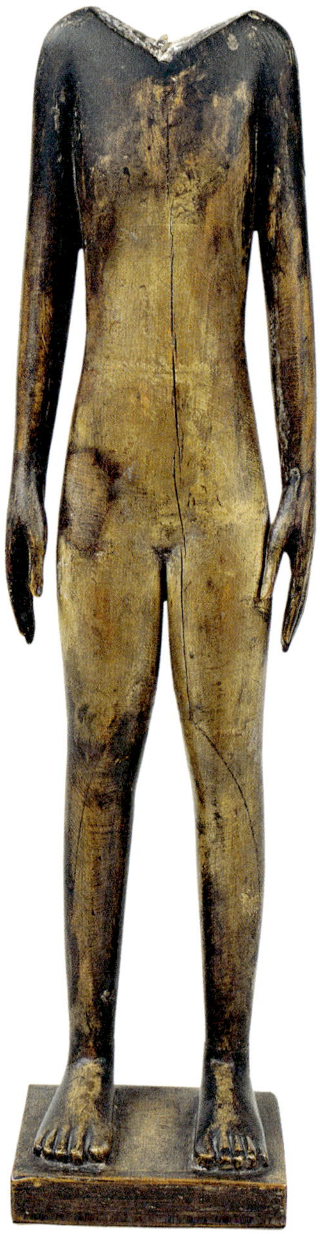

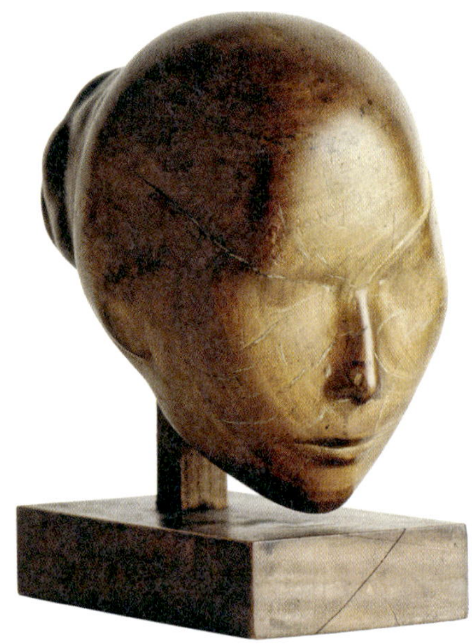

71
EWALD MATARÉ
Female torso "Woman Standing", 1924–1925

Walnut wood, originally gilded, 55 × 14.3 × 11.8 cm
Lehmbruck Museum, Duisburg

Great Berlin Art Exhibition 1928, Novembergruppe section, no. 1558 under the title *Girl's Torso*

72
EWALD MATARÉ
Female Head (Portrait of Hanna H.), 1922

Birchwood, 24 × 14.3 × 20.9 cm

Museum Kurhaus Kleve – Ewald Mataré-Sammlung, Kleve / Permanent loan from the Ewald Mataré estate

Great Berlin Art Exhibition 1928, Novembergruppe section, no. 1560 under the title *Girl's Head*

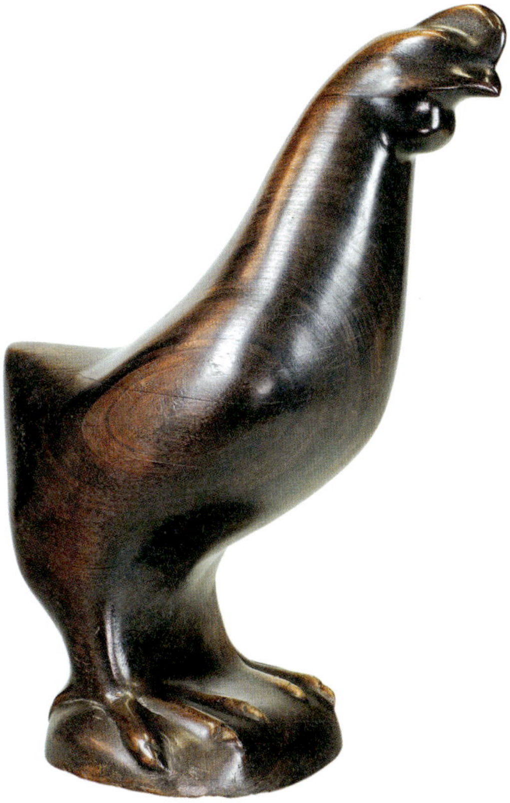

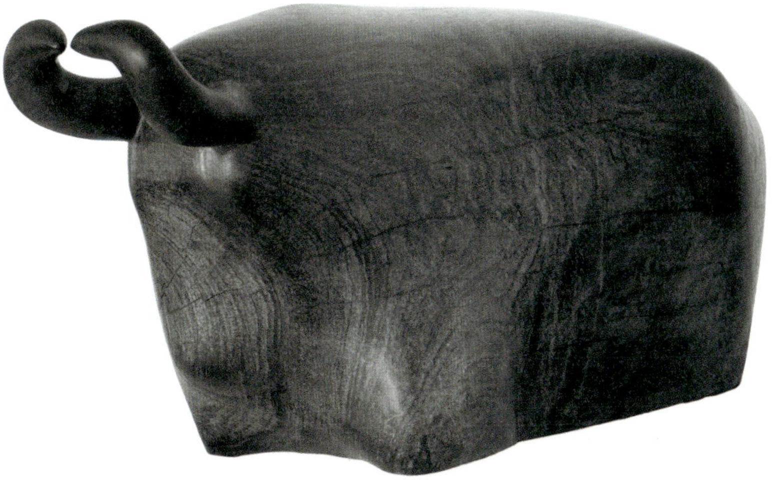

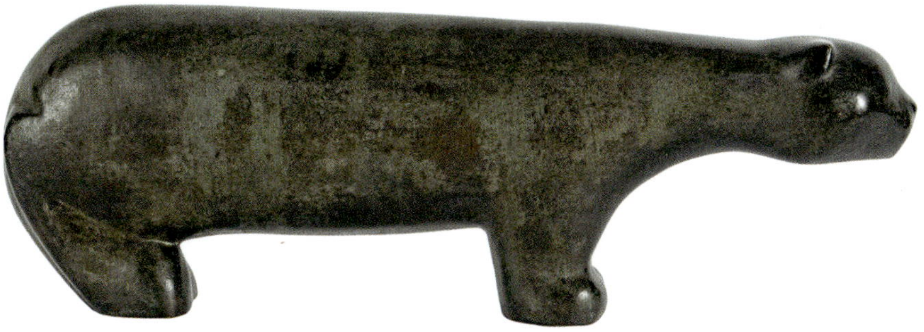

73
EWALD MATARÉ
Hen, 1925

Wood, 48 × 36 × 19 cm
Collection Karl H. Knauf, Berlin

Great Berlin Art Exhibition 1928, Novembergruppe section, no. 1562

74
EWALD MATARÉ
Cat, 1928

Bronze, 20 × 58 × 9.3 cm
Private collection

Great Berlin Art Exhibition 1928, Novembergruppe section, no. 1565

75
EWALD MATARÉ
Bull Lying, 1927

Cocobolo wood, 27 × 59 × 30.5 cm
Hamburger Kunsthalle

Great Berlin Art Exhibition 1928, Novembergruppe section, no. 1568

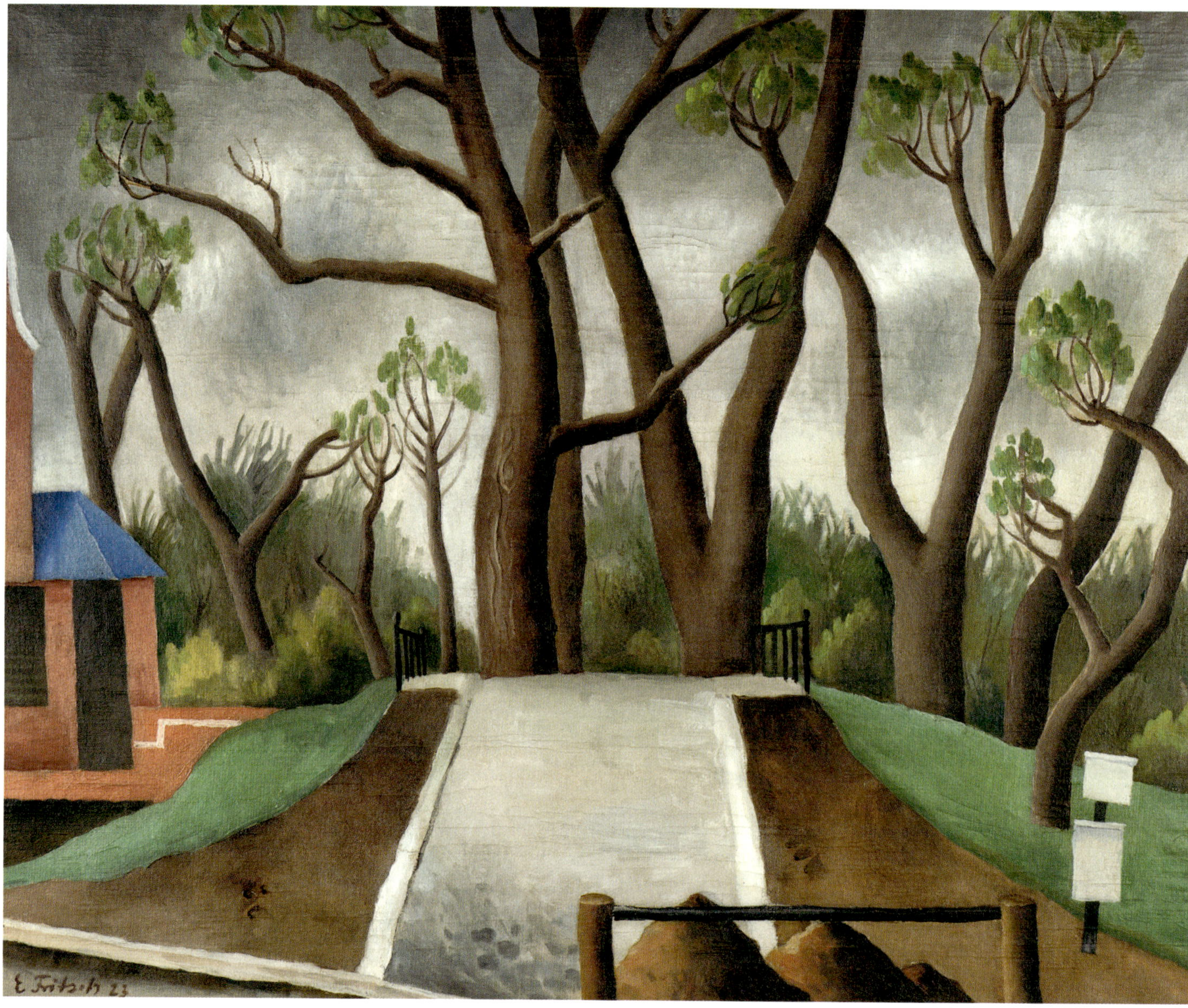

76

ERNST FRITSCH

Tiergarten Bridge, 1923

Oil on canvas, 74 × 89 cm
Berlinische Galerie

Great Berlin Art Exhibition 1923, Novembergruppe section, no. 1172, repro. in *Zehn Jahre Novembergruppe* 1928, p. 19

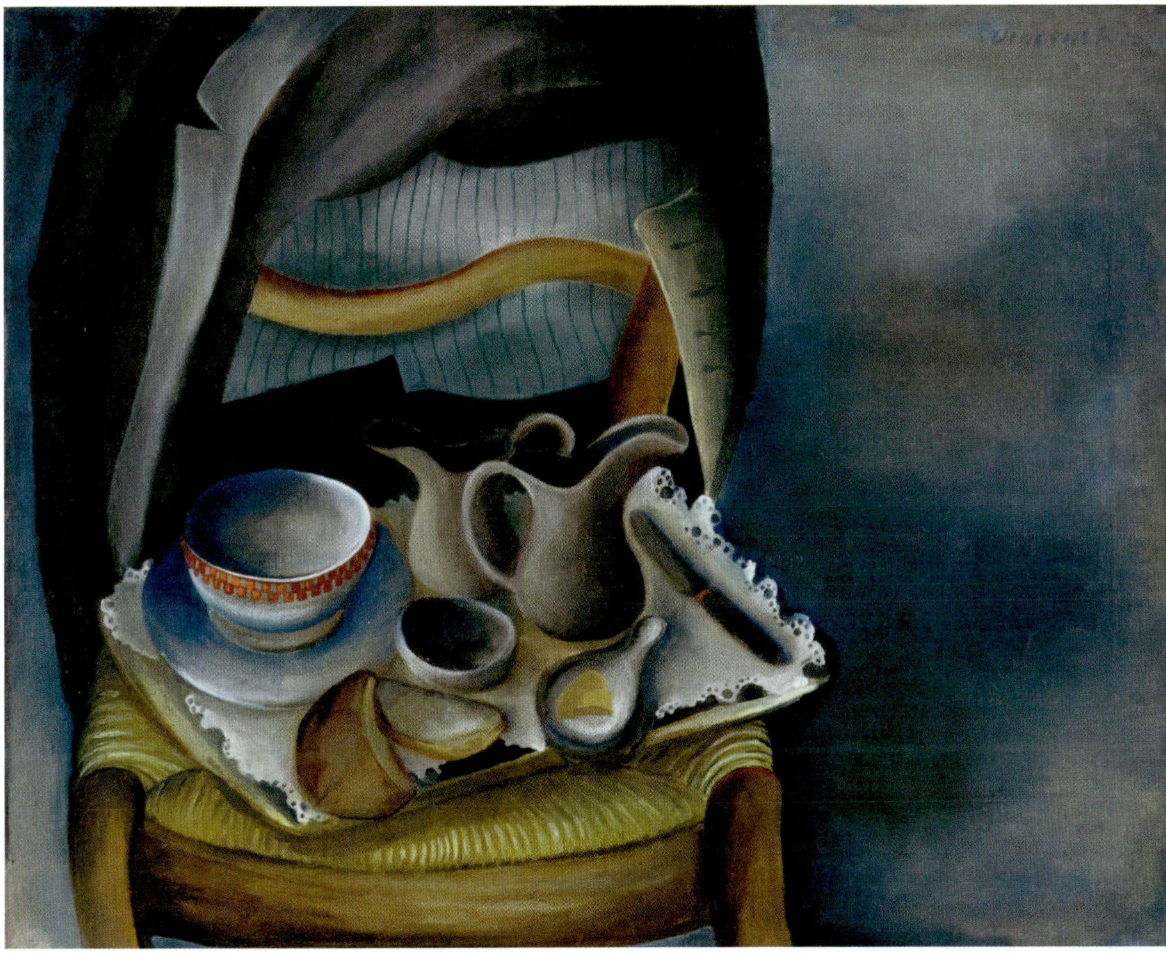

77
VINCENT WEBER
The Lodger's Breakfast, 1925

Oil on canvas, 64 × 78 cm
Berlinische Galerie

Great Berlin Art Exhibition 1928,
Novembergruppe section, no. 1073

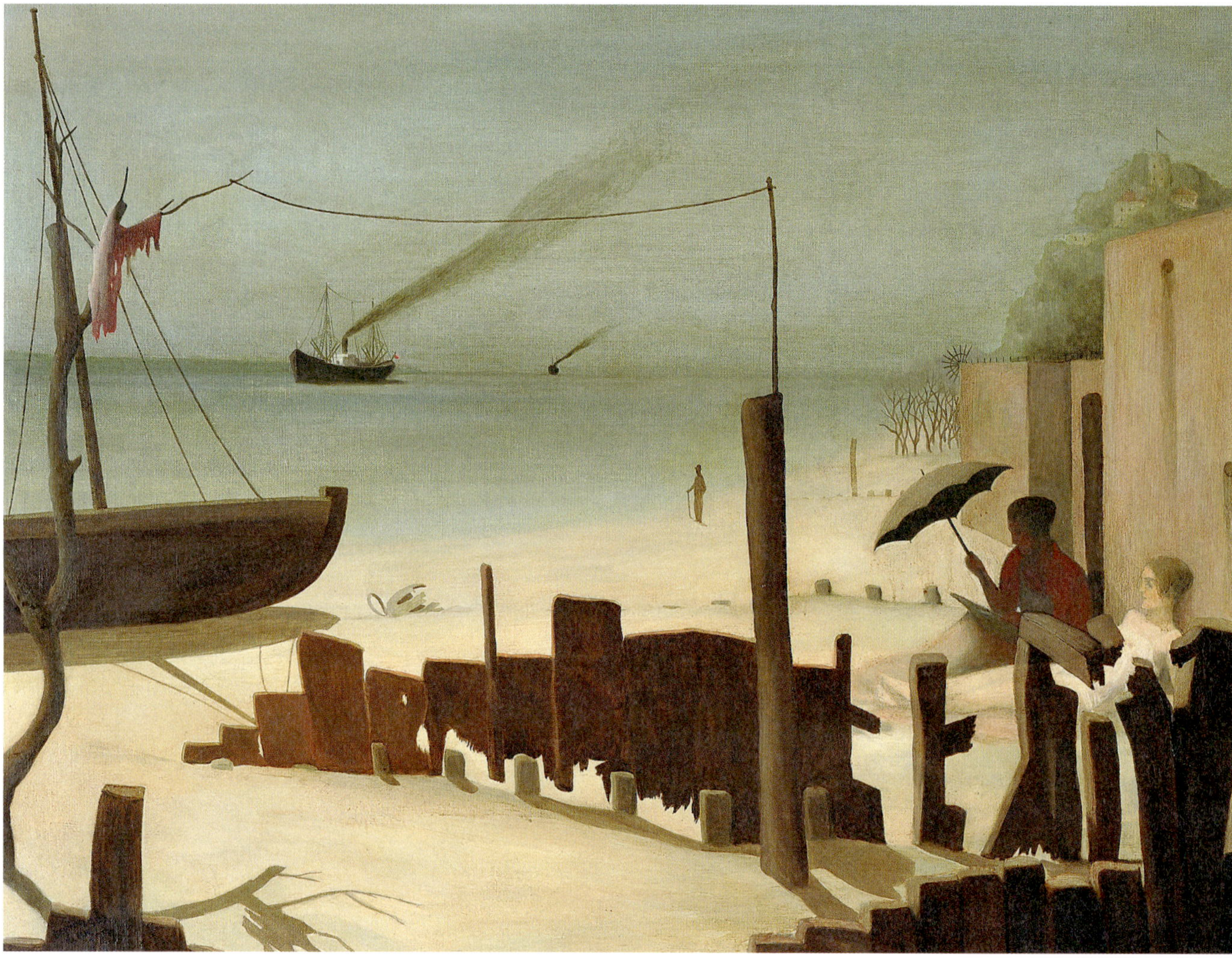

78

BERNHARD KLEIN

Elbe Shore (II), 1927

Oil on canvas, 70 × 91 cm
Staatliche Museen zu Berlin, Nationalgalerie

Great Berlin Art Exhibition 1927, Novembergruppe section, no. 247, repro. in the catalogue

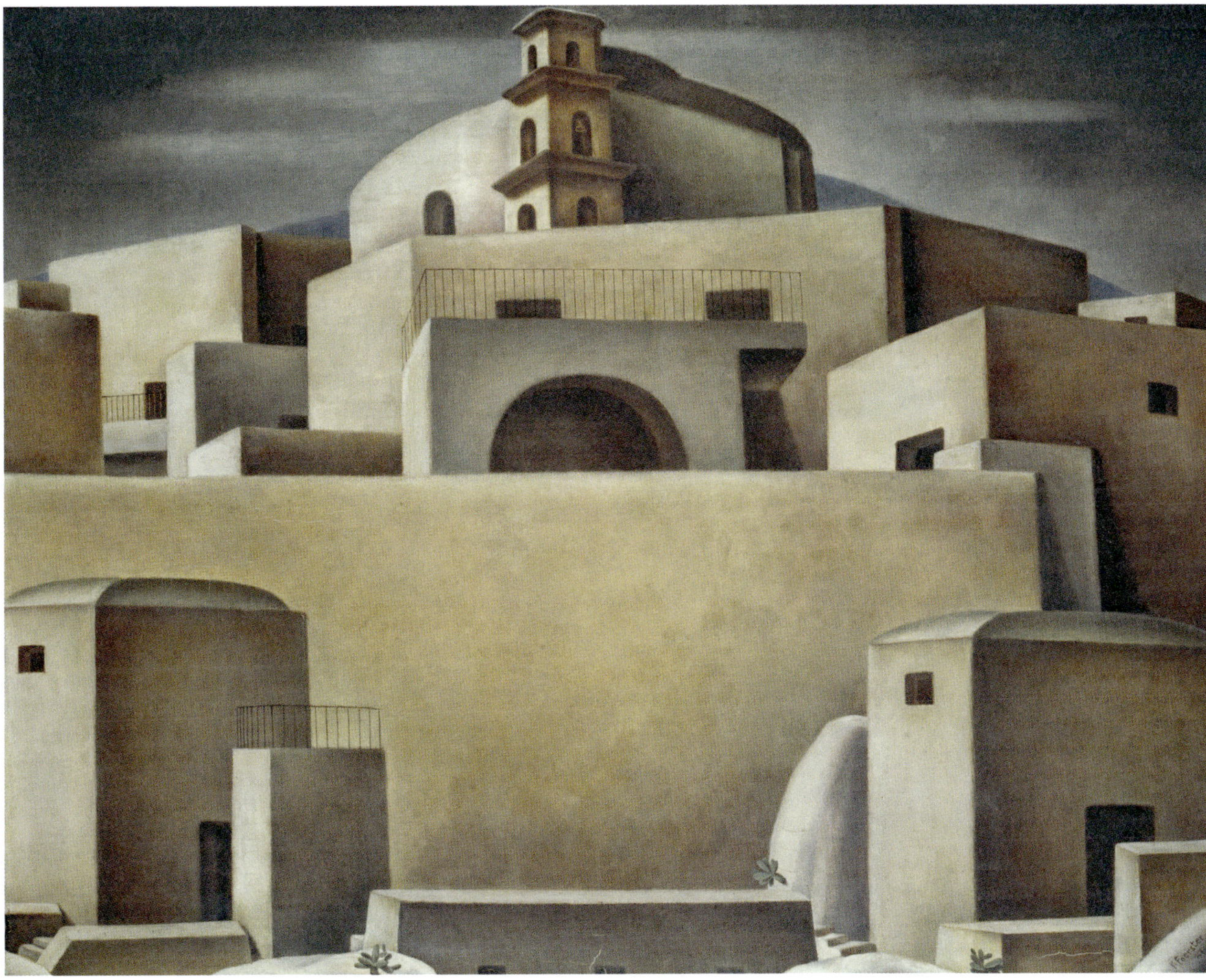

79

PETER FOERSTER

Italian Landscape II, 1927

Oil on wood, 50 × 61 cm
Staatliche Museen zu Berlin, Nationalgalerie

Great Berlin Art Exhibition 1927, Novembergruppe section, no. 124, repro. in catalogue

JANINA NENTWIG

"A STRONG WILL FOR NEW ARCHITECTURE"

The Novembergruppe and the Art of Building

An impressive array of architects feature in the register of Novembergruppe members: PETER BEHRENS, MARCEL BREUER, FRED FORBÁT, ALFRED GELLHORN, WALTER GROPIUS, HUGO HÄRING, LUDWIG HILBERSEIMER, ARTHUR KORN, HEINRICH KOSINA, CARL KRAYL, HANS KREBS, HANS and WASSILI LUCKHARDT, ERICH MENDELSOHN, LUDWIG MIES VAN DER ROHE, J. J. P. OUD, HANS POELZIG, HANS SOEDER, MART STAM, BRUNO and MAX TAUT, HEINRICH TESSENOW.[1] All of them championed the International Style which, in the Weimar Republic, was known as "*Neues Bauen*"— the "new way of building". By 1921 at the latest, they had turned their backs on Historicism, Jugendstil and Expressionism in favour of a clear, rational idiom and functional design, and they set their stamp on Novembergruppe exhibitions, especially in the period from 1923 to 1926. OTTO BARTNING, ADOLF RADING, NAUM GABO, EL LISSITZKY, VILMOS HUSZÁR, CORNELIS VAN EESTEREN and many other architects from Germany and abroad put in guest appearances, complementing the display of formal and technical innovation in construction at this public forum staged annually by the Novembergruppe. And yet the association is rarely mentioned, and at best peripherally,[2] in literature about modern architecture between the two world wars. The research has focussed instead on other German organizations: the *Arbeitsrat für Kunst*, the *Gläserne Kette* [*Crystal Chain*], *Der Ring* and above all the Bauhaus.[3] Many of the people who took part in these were simultaneously members of the Novembergruppe, but how does the latter fit in here? What role did architecture play in the association before most architects abandoned it in early 1927? What were the reasons for their exodus? And how did the group respond? After all, it explicitly defined itself as multidisciplinary and was loath to dispense with architecture as a major force in the construction of a new society.

"We Shall Combat Error in Every Guise"

Among the founders of the Novembergruppe there was only one architect amid the many painters and sculptors, and that was ERICH MENDELSOHN.[4] As a member of the "central working committee", he was a signatory to the letter in January 1919 which set out guidelines for the future work of the fledgling association. In this document the group demanded "influence and participation" in shaping public life in the arts. At the top of the list they called for the right to be consulted "*on all architectural tasks as a matter of public concern,* urban design — settlement planning — public buildings for administration, industry and welfare — private construction — conservation of monuments — removal of pompous buildings with no artistic value".[5] These wide-ranging and radical ambitions are similar, as are the other four items on the list, to the ideas published in various newspapers and magazines a few weeks earlier, in December 1918, by the recently founded *Arbeitsrat für Kunst*.[6] The overlap is not particularly surprising: numerous dual memberships were in themselves enough to ensure affinities. Apart from MENDELSOHN, several founders of the Novembergruppe were simultaneously active in this "works council for art", including the painters GEORG TAPPERT, MAX PECHSTEIN, CÉSAR KLEIN, MORIZ MELZER and HEINRICH RICHTER-BERLIN and the sculptor RUDOLF BELLING. In the latter, however, architects around BRUNO TAUT, WALTER GROPIUS and Adolf Behne were a major presence, and for them architecture played a leading role as the *mater artium*. "Art and people must form a unity. Art must no longer be for the enjoyment of the few, but for the life and happiness of the masses. Bringing the arts together under the wings of great architecture is the goal,"[7] declares the mission statement of the *Arbeitsrat für Kunst*. The first two sentences doubtless met with the unconditional approval of the Novembergruppe, for they too wished to see the "closest possible mingling of the people and art".[8] Most, however, did not subscribe to such an absolute dominance of architecture over the other arts. A merger with the *Arbeitsrat* was initially rejected, but in November 1919 a decision was finally taken to seal a closer partnership.[9] Given the lack of other sources, it has been difficult to establish what practical forms this took. We do know that the first exhibitions organized by the Novembergruppe only featured architecture in a handful of Expressionist designs by KRAYL, SCHAROUN, GELLHORN (fig. 01) and POELZIG, as well as some architectural fantasies by the Italian Futurist ENRICO PRAMPOLINI.[10] Meanwhile, in 1919 and 1920, the *Arbeitsrat für Kunst* staged two seminal shows devoted to architecture. The titles were in themselves manifestos: *Exhibition for Unknown Architects* and *Neues Bauen*, although the latter term was not yet associated with the functional forms now regarded as the movement's defining aesthetic. At both events, the *Arbeitsrat* proclaimed either a crystalline, fractured or an organic, rounded type of Expressionism, inspired less by the specific needs of construction than by an all-embracing utopia of the kind being discussed by the correspondents in the association known as the *Gläserne Kette*.[11] Evidently the Novembergruppe, which was open to every genre and art, did offer architecture a significant place in its scheme. One indication of that is an essay published by ALFRED GELLHORN[12] and other artists in the group journal *Der Kunsttopf* under the title "Die Richtung" ("The Way Forward"). GELLHORN fully echoed the ideas advocated by the *Arbeitsrat für Kunst* and the *Gläserne Kette*, writing: "Not only the form, but the tasks must be reborn. We shall combat error in every guise: not harmonious beauty, but authenticity of expression. Not purpose as goal, but expression of supreme meaning. [...] Not a question of style or school."[13]

"Much Life and Future"

Not until 1922 did architecture play a bigger role in the annual exhibitions of the Novembergruppe, which in turn were independent sections of the Great Berlin Art Exhibition. The *Arbeitsrat für Kunst* had been disbanded in May 1921 due to financial difficulties and disagreements over policy.[14] Designs by those architects who now joined the Novembergruppe reveal a shift away from radical utopias. When the LUCKHARDT brothers, POELZIG and MIES VAN DER ROHE submitted examples of their work to the 1922 exhibition, they were not inspired by visions like BRUNO TAUT's recent dream of a superstructure over the Alps, but by high-rise buildings

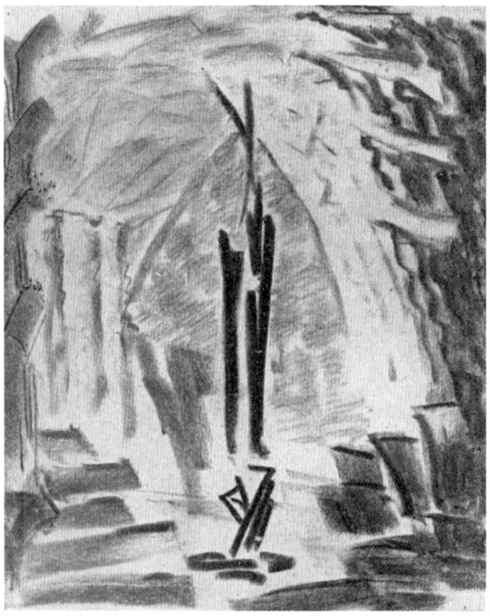

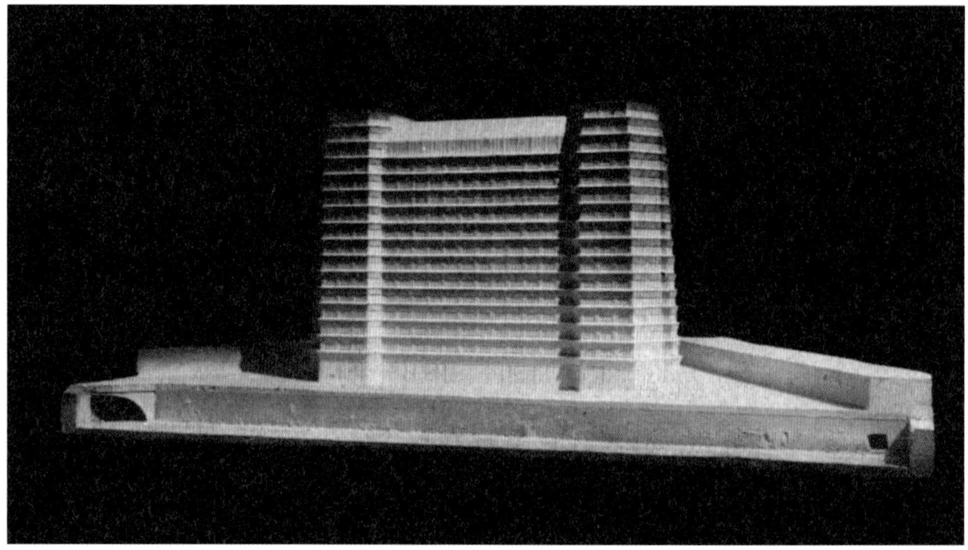

01 ALFRED GELLHORN
A Space, c. 1919
whereabouts unknown
probably Art Exhibition Berlin 1920, Novembergruppe section, no. 1167

02 HANS and WASSILI LUCKHARDT
Tower for Friedrichstrasse, Berlin, 1921, whereabouts unknown
Great Berlin Art Exhibition 1922, Novembergruppe section, no. 1335

as a technical challenge and symbol of a new era. The LUCKHARDTS (fig. 02) and POELZIG (cat. 94, p. 160) showed the designs they had entered into a competition of ideas, widely debated at the time, for a tower structure next to Friedrichstrasse station.[15] MIES VAN DER ROHE also displayed designs for this project in the Novembergruppe section. His proposal, anonymously coded "Honeycomb", had not been considered during the jury stage of the competition, probably because it did not comply with the brief,[16] or perhaps he had not submitted it in the first place.[17] Now, for the exhibition of "radical artists", he produced a monumental charcoal drawing (fig. 03) with a low-angle view of the building.[18] He also used the Novembergruppe show to demonstrate a model (cat. 101, p. 165) of a glass skyscraper, a further development of the design for Friedrichstrasse.[19] The critics were extremely positive about all the projects on display, which by now entirely reflected the *Neues Bauen* ethos.[20] The models and drawings went on show in different rooms surrounded by fine art. This scatter approach is surprising, given that all the submissions were devoted to the same theme: a vision for Berlin's first "skyscraper".[21]

In the years that followed, the architects' contributions were a highlight of Novembergruppe exhibitions. In 1923 the event attracted nearly 20 architects. They were given their own space, hung with photographs of actual buildings designed by Dutch colleagues, among them *De Stijl* member GERRIT RIETVELD and the chief architect of Rotterdam J. J. P. OUD, who had also belonged to the *De Stijl* group until 1921.[22] The room for the architects was one of the biggest available to the association. This separate presentation, which Max Osborn described in the highly regarded newspaper *Vossische Zeitung* as "outstanding"[23], was a powerful performance for *Neues Bauen*. An exhibition was something the movement had not yet experienced in Germany.[24] "There is much life and future in these building designs, which show our architecture to be on a new road towards goals as yet uncharted,"[25] concluded another daily, the *Berliner Börsen-Zeitung*. The LUCKHARDT brothers were present again, this time with a tower design for the *Chicago Tribune*, a competition which had also attracted entries from MAX TAUT and HANS SCHAROUN.[26] TAUT was one of the few architects in inflation-ridden Germany with an almost complete major project to his name, and he brought along a model and two photographs of his offices for the General Confederation of German Trade Unions (ADGB) (fig. 04). This corner building in Berlin was one of the first larger buildings to be completed after the Great War, and there are still touches of Expressionism in the façade on Inselstrasse, notably the sharp angles that distinguish the conference hall and another of the windows. The rigorous modernity of the rest of the structure nevertheless made it an exemplar of *Neues Bauen*.[27] This trade union building by TAUT, like the projects implemented in the Netherlands, acquired an important publicity function at the exhibition, championing an adoption of modern architecture that seemed highly unlikely in the Germany of 1923. Inflation was in full swing, and neither private nor public clients were awarding building contracts of any notable magnitude. For younger architects in particular, this posed a threat to professional survival. MIES VAN DER ROHE, for example, had still had no opportunity since the war to put his recent ideas into practice. It was through the Novembergruppe in 1923 that he first exhibited his projects based on reinforced concrete.[28] Visitors were no doubt impressed by the sheer size of one drawing, a design for an office block (fig. 05), which measured almost 1.40 by 2.90 metres and visually dwarfed the other items in the room. The exhibition guide published by the Novembergruppe explained why this construction principle was so innovative: because there was no need for supporting walls around the outside, a structure could be built by layering mass against non-mass, and this permitted large areas of glazing. For the interested lay reader, the text also summarized the general aims and features of *Neues Bauen*: "The essence is the inner structure, the inner design, which subordinates the outward formation to economic utility. Simple, strong, ascending lines and moving load do not encumber the outer appearance with issues of arrangement and style where inner form establishes the basic law of the building. [...] The material, used in the past like heavy armour as an encasement and unifying the façade with its intrinsic weight-bearing capacity, now assumes a greater practical task with thrifty efficiency, which is to create a simple, strong, inner structure to support the building and submit to human purpose."[29]

But purpose was not the only formative factor in the new architecture. It is widely claimed that the abstract art of the *De Stijl* movement in the Netherlands and the East European avant-garde also exerted a powerful influence, but this has rarely been borne out by evidence of direct references. Avant-garde journals were not the only places where architects could study the works of international Constructivists; Novembergruppe exhibitions were an ideal place to do this too. In 1923, for example, THEO VAN DOESBURG, PIET MONDRIAN, LÁSZLÓ MOHOLY-NAGY and EL LISSITZKY were prominently displayed in the association's section of the Great Berlin Art Exhibition.[30] The formal aesthetic correspondences between architecture and painting were not lost on contemporaries, although architecture was felt to be the stronger medium.[31] Just how fruitful the encounters between painters and

03 LUDWIG MIES VAN DER ROHE
Friedrichstrasse Skyscraper Project, Berlin, 1922
The Museum of Modern Art, New York
Great Berlin Art Exhibition 1922, Novembergruppe section, no. 1386 or 1387

04 MAX TAUT
Offices for the General Confederation of German Trade Unions, Berlin, 1921–1923
Great Berlin Art Exhibition 1923, Novembergruppe section, no. 1370: a model and two photographs of this project

05 LUDWIG MIES VAN DER ROHE
Concrete Office Building Project, 1923
The Museum of Modern Art, New York
Great Berlin Art Exhibition 1923, Novembergruppe section, no. 1270

03
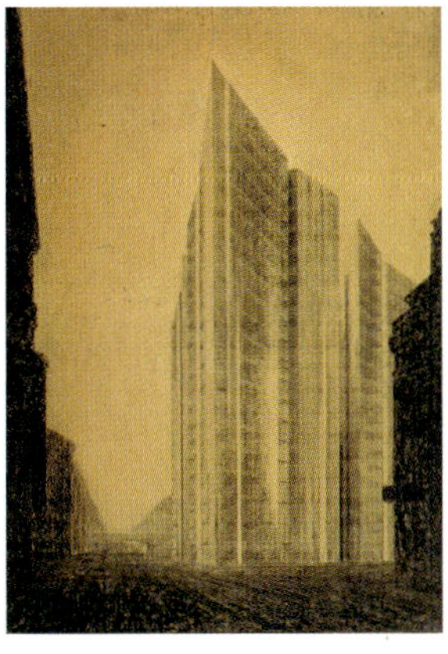
04
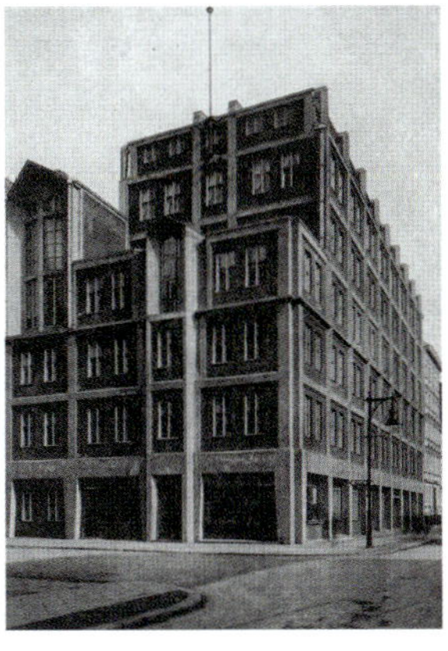
05
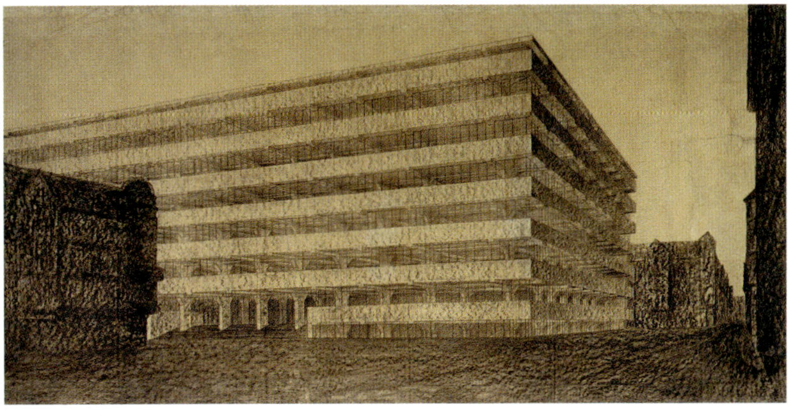

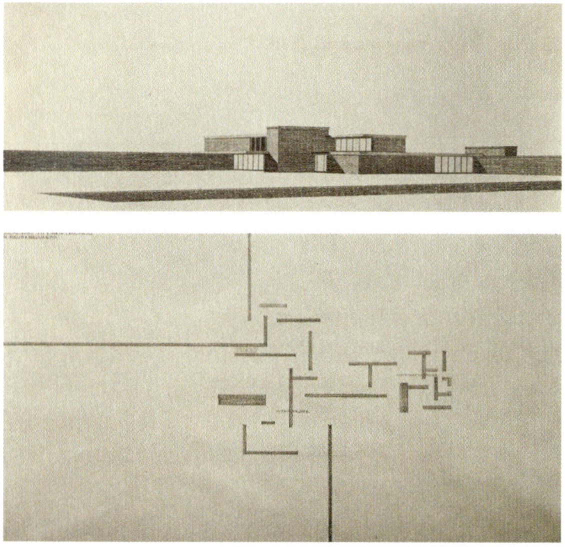

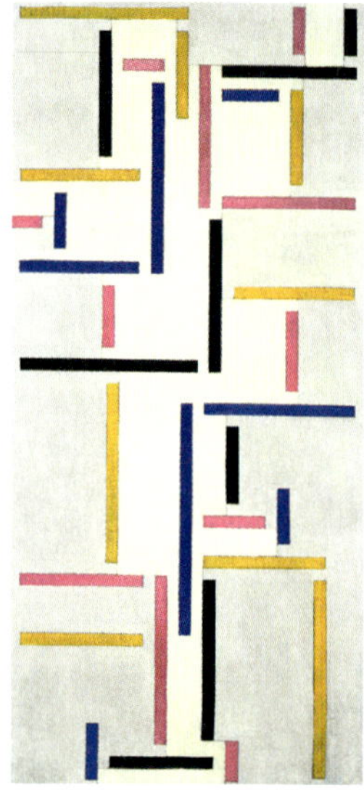

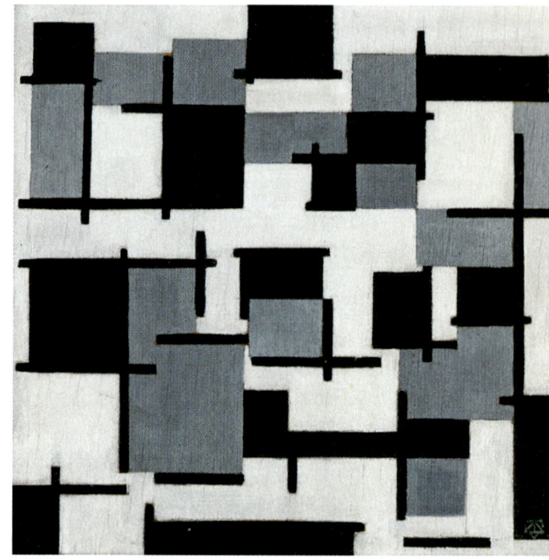

06 07 08

06 LUDWIG MIES VAN DER ROHE
Study for a brick country house (original plans lost)
Photograph of a perspective view and floor plan
Städtische Kunsthalle Mannheim
Great Berlin Art Exhibition 1924, Novembergruppe section, probably no. 963

07 THEO VAN DOESBURG
Rhythm of a Russian Dance, 1918
The Museum of Modern Art, New York

08 THEO VAN DOESBURG
Composition XIII, 1918
Stedelijk Museum, Amsterdam
Great Berlin Art Exhibition 1923, Novembergruppe section, no. 1148

architects in the Novembergruppe sometimes were is demonstrated by MIES VAN DER ROHE's Brick Country House (fig. 06), which he exhibited with the group a year later.[32] Scholars have often observed that MIES's flowing concept of space, fully elaborated here for the first time, was influenced by EL LISSITZKY's lively, rhythmical *Proun Room* (cat. 55, p. 119).[33] What is rarely mentioned, however, is that the *Proun Room* was on display in the Novembergruppe section in 1923,[34] and so were HANS RICHTER's sketches illustrating motion as a basis for a film—an exhibit entitled *Primary Momentum of a Film* [*Hauptmoment eines Films*]. Richter's abstract films have been investigated more recently as a source of inspiration for MIES VAN DER ROHE.[35] Ever since the catalogue in 1936 where Alfred J. Barr, the founding director of the Museum of Modern Art in New York, juxtaposed the Brick Country House with a painting in his collection, THEO VAN DOESBURG's *Rhythm of a Russian Dance* (fig. 07), the formal similarity between the floor plan of the building and the Dutchman's work has been a commonplace,[36] but nobody seems to have ascertained whether the architect had actually seen the canvas.[37] There is conclusive evidence, however, that MIES VAN DER ROHE saw the original paintings shown by VAN DOESBURG with the Novembergruppe in 1923, including *Composition XIII* (fig. 08). The link between this work and MIES VAN DER ROHE's architecture is far more evident: in the work by VAN DOESBURG horizontal and vertical lines touch and cross, just as the walls do in the floor plan. By contrast, in the New York painting the coloured bars seem to bounce apart and maintain a floating balance.[38] MIES VAN DER ROHE knew *Composition XIII* very well, just as he knew the exhibits by EL LISSITZKY and RICHTER on display in the Novembergruppe section in 1923. As a member of the exhibition committee,[39] the architect was probably personally involved in hanging or installing these pieces, and so the inspiration can safely be considered to have been direct.

Architecture as the "Mother of all Arts"

By early 1924 the architects had officially taken the helm at the Novembergruppe: MIES VAN DER ROHE was elected to the chair, enabling him to steer the course for the association as a whole.[40] GELLHORN, KORN and WASSILI LUCKHARDT now boosted the architectural presence on the working committee.[41] Under their aegis, the architects pulled off a significant coup: once again, a room would be reserved for their buildings and designs in the group's section of the Great Berlin Art Exhibition in 1924. The space itself was an immediate annex to an exhibition about the history of construction that Leo Nachtlicht had organized on behalf of the Association of German Architects in the central hall of the *Landesausstellungsgebäude.*[42] Many reviewers assumed that the architecture on show with the Novembergruppe was simply the modern section of Nachtlicht's exhibition, even though it had been conceived independently as part of the Novembergruppe event.[43] Thus the association came to be identified with the latest trends in the field, upstaging Nachtlicht's historical narrative, which was rooted in baroque designs, in the eyes of more progressively-minded critics.[44] Particularly eye-catching were the buildings that responded to contemporary traffic scenarios. The LUCKHARDT brothers included a design for large-scale indoor parking (cat. 96, p. 162), Gellhorn and MARTIN KNAUTHE exhibited a petrol-filling station they had conceived with BELLING (cat. 99, p. 163), while KOSINA displayed his model for an *Air Port* (fig. 09) on the Tempelhofer Feld. These, of course, were visionary solutions, and none of them had any prospects of implementation. The guide produced by the Novembergruppe bemoaned the persistent dearth of commissions for architects, which currency reform had so far done nothing to improve, at least not for advocates of an innovative, functional idiom: "One looks with envy and shame at the opportunities for development back then, when things were so much tighter due to the hardships of war and starvation. *The tasks would be there for us!* Unprecedented new ones, derived from the leaps and bounds in economic life. And unprecedented new opportunities to solve them too with soaring technology. [...] One need only consider the models and depictions in this room, how from the smallest pavilion to the giant complex a strong and honest *conviction,* without the trimmings of a façade conventionally segmented according to superficial aesthetic concepts, out of the fundamental elements of construction, from within, *unites adequacy to purpose with a will to design.* And then compare this with what the average national, provincial and local authority plonks down."[45]

GELLHORN expressed the same view in the magazine *Der Deutsche Rundfunk*, commenting on the Novembergruppe's display of architecture: "In our low-construction times one still sees little new architecture emerge alongside all the prolific bungling, possibly even because of it, yet in the work of 16 modern architects from all over Germany there is an abundance of serious achievement, visibly heralding a new style."[46] Another critic noted: "Again and again one senses the leading force of architecture as the mother of the arts. In this field lies the historical mission of the Novembergruppe."[47]

The introduction of a tax on the ownership of existing buildings and the end of inflation from 1924 made construction financially viable again and triggered a recovery in the building sector,[48] giving modern architects a chance to prove their mettle in the years that followed. As a result, the architecture section of the Novembergruppe was able to boast more and more completed projects, including numerous villas, factories and office blocks, but also residential estates in response to the persistent housing shortage. *Neues Bauen* ranged between stylistic extremes: rectilinear, flat-roofed cubes, like the terraced houses on Schorlemerallee designed by the LUCKHARDT brothers (fig. 10), and organic forms such as the Garkau farm in Scharbeutz built by HUGO HÄRING (cat. 88, p. 157).[49] Also on the rise were collaborative projects like GELLHORN's Haus Ebstein in Zehlendorf, where the sculptor OSWALD HERZOG and the painter MAX DUNGERT contributed to the interior decoration.[50] The latest international trends in building were again exhibited by the Novembergruppe in 1925 with a group of Prague-based architects including

JAROSLAV FRAGNER,[51] exhibits by EL LISSITZKY (fig. 11), LÁSZLÓ PÉRI and J. J. P. OUD, and collaborative designs by CORNELIS VAN EESTEREN and THEO VAN DOESBURG. 1926 again featured many Dutch guests, who received particular coverage.[52] Daily newspapers and art and construction journals alike were almost unanimous in praising the architecture shown by the Novembergruppe, preferring it to the fine artists who belonged to the association, regarded by journalists as far less creative than their colleagues.[53] Curt Glaser's appraisal of the Novembergruppe exhibition in 1925, held this time not with the Great Berlin Art Exhibtion but on Secession premises, echoed the general gist: "If one is to divine the ground-breaking factor in the youngest of the artists' associations, which carries on its banner the name of the revolutionary month, then it is the outstanding participation of the architects in their exhibitions. The long-familiar clarion call 'Away from easel painting!' is practised at this show in a double sense, negative in the poverty of painterly accomplishment, positive in engaging a strong will for new architecture."[54]

Verdicts like this no doubt caused the painters in the Novembergruppe to turn on the architects in exasperation. Within the association, arguments broke out about whether the conventional panel painting would have any role at all to play in this new architecture, with its long glass façades replacing the solid walls that were the ancestral home of paintings, and an intrinsic aesthetic that had no need of 'decoration'.[55] But this was not the only cause of the oft-cited tension between architects and fine artists.[56] Encouraged by MIES VAN DER ROHE, the architects became increasingly independent, describing the Novembergruppe as an association "to which Germany's modern architects belong"[57] without wasting a word on their colleagues in the fine arts, music and literature. In the run-up to the group exhibition in 1926, the chairman confidently spoke in invitations to foreign architects of a purely architectural display, despite the fact that all the genres had been included in the planning and organization.[58] On his initiative, the architects began to hold separate meetings[59] and in spring 1926 they took part in a housing exhibition in Gera.[60] Alongside their activities in the Novembergruppe, Mies van der Rohe and other members of the profession also founded an association of their own, the *Zehner-Ring* (Ring of Ten), which expanded in 1926 and became simply *Der Ring*.[61]

Despite these obviously divisive tendencies, 26 architects (even more than the catalogue stated) went on display in the Novembergruppe section of the Great Berlin Art Exhibition in 1926.[62] The magazine *Bauwelt* devoted a whole sequence of illustrations to the Novembergruppe[63] and, with great faith in the future, predicted that modern architecture would soon enter the social mainstream: "Now we are being offered new forms. Alien? Yes. But hostile? There is no reason why. Even the most backward-looking person today cannot help being more modern than the day before yesterday's revolutionary. Whether we like it or not, once the need to express our own time artistically has been clearly felt, expressing it becomes a historical necessity. It has to happen. So we must place ourselves within the new forms and gradually find a yardstick."[64]

A Split in the Novembergruppe?

In early 1927, the rift between the architects and the other members of the Novembergruppe finally occurred. The news of an alleged split even made it onto the pages of the newspaper *Hamburger Correspondent*, which reported on 29 January: "The differences which have been dogging the November Group since the autumn of last year have now resulted in about half the members leaving. All the architects in the group have gone except for Gellhorn: among the names are Peter Behrens, Gropius, Häring, Hilberseimer, Kosina, Mies van der Rohe, Hans and Wassily Luckhardt, Pölzig [*sic*], Bruno and Max Taut, Tessenow. The painters and sculptors who have left include Belling, Förster, Grunwald, Fuchs, Staegemann, as well as Feininger and Schlemmer from the Bauhaus in Dessau and the musicians Butting and Jarnach. It appears that those who departed are now contemplating a new group."[65]

The Novembergruppe reacted swiftly and published a placatory press release, quoted, among others, by the *Berliner Börsen-Zeitung*: "The formation of the '*Ring*' made it a technical matter of course that the architects incorporated with it would leave the Group. Of 68 fine artists, only four Berliners and three from elsewhere have gone, of twelve musicians only two. It can hardly be called a split. The Novembergruppe will continue to work in the interests of the new forces surging forward in all fields of the arts, without being deterred by consideration for memberships of associations."[66]

In the ensuing period, *Der Ring* advanced to become the leading association for modern architects, and in 1927 and 1928 it participated in the Great Berlin Art Exhibition alongside the Novembergruppe. There was growing visibility for *Neues Bauen* in Germany, whether in built form or in exhibitions and books. In 1927, for example, the Werkbund included the much-fêted *Weissenhofsiedlung*, an estate in Stuttgart, in its housing exhibition *Die Wohnung*, after which the display panels travelled on to many other German towns. LUDWIG HILBERSEIMER published a book about this new international movement in architecture called *Internationale neue Baukunst*, with photographs of the key projects. That same year the Bauhaus set up a class in architecture, and *Neues Bauen* featured with increasing prominence on university curricula and in construction magazines. Its clear, functional forms were now associated with the image of the young republic as a free society. Towards the end of the decade, town councils with a social democratic majority, in particular, began awarding projects for housing estates and community buildings to architects who championed the new style, and in many cases they even adopted the total art work philosophy by purchasing the associated standardized furniture (*"Typenmöbel"*) for the interiors.[67] In 1928 international exchange acquired an institutionalized format in the *Congrès Internationaux d'Architecture Moderne* (CIAM), which involved many former Novembergruppe members such as GROPIUS and HÄRING. The exodus of architects meant that the Novembergruppe could not contribute to the debate—resolutely spearheaded by the Bauhaus and reflected in a spate of articles across the media in the latter

09 HEINRICH KOSINA
Model of Tempelhof Airport, Berlin, 1924, whereabouts unknown
Great Berlin Art Exhibition 1924, Novembergruppe section, no. 940

10 HANS AND WASSILI LUCKHARDT
Experimental housing estate on Schorlemerallee, Dahlem (Berlin), 1924–25
Novembergruppe exhibition at the *Berlin Secession* 1925, no. 113

11 EL LISSITZKY
The "Wolkenbügel" (Cloud Iron), 1925, whereabouts unknown
Novembergruppe exhibition at the *Berlin Secession* 1925, no. 111b

09

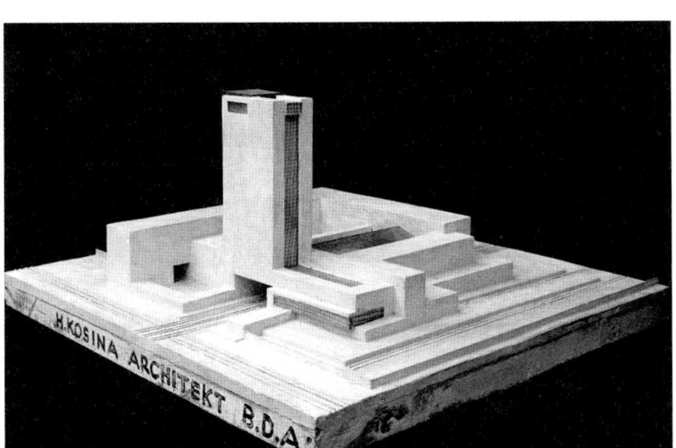

10

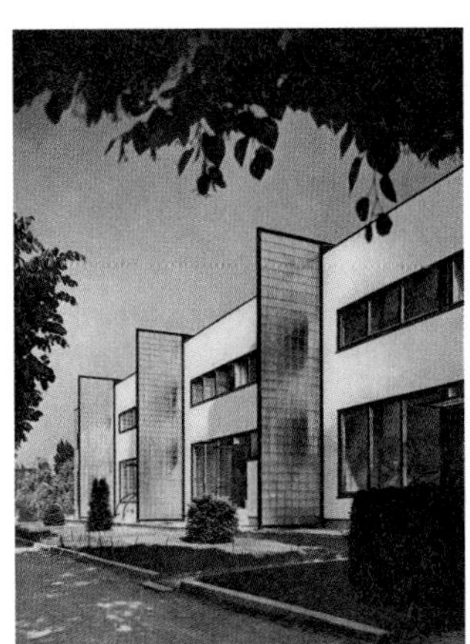

11

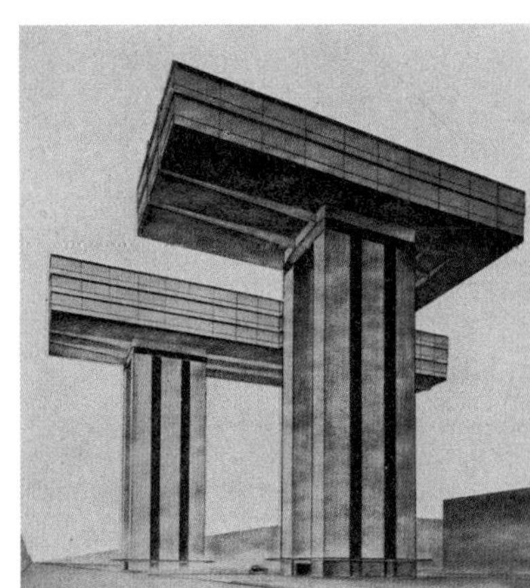

half of the 1920s—about the educational influence that this new architecture could exert on the 'New Person'.[68] Although almost all the architects who left the Novembergruppe contributed to the book and exhibition marking its tenth anniversary[69]—MIES VAN DER ROHE, for instance, showed photographs of his pavilion for the *International Exposition* in Barcelona (cat. 103, p. 167)[70]—they did not renew their membership. In 1931 the Novembergruppe undertook a final attempt to attract young architects and bring them together in an exhibition, but after a public call for participation all traces of the plan vanish.[71] Whether it could actually have been staged in the middle of the world economic crisis is, in any case, disputable.

The architects' association with the Novembergruppe had been fruitful in many respects, but it came to a sobering end. It is beyond doubt, however, that the association deserves credit for popularizing modern architecture and playing a central role in the architectural history of the Weimar Republic as a historical link between the *Arbeitsrat für Kunst* and *Der Ring*. Without the Novembergruppe and its section at the Great Berlin Art Exhibition, most of the German architects who now belong to the canon of *Neues Bauen* would have had no opportunity, in the precarious economic conditions of the early Weimar Republic, to present their ideas to a broad audience on this scale. Will Grohmann already observed in 1928 that, through the Novembergruppe exhibitions, "all modern architects gained access to the masses. Architecture was not yet fashionable in 1919 in the way it is today, few were building, but many had good designs and models".[72] Positive reviews in national dailies established a reputation for the Novembergruppe architects beyond the specialist publications at a time when inflation made practical implementation impossible. From this springboard, they were able to revive their careers from the mid-1920s and produce real buildings at last. They no longer needed the Novembergruppe or its exhibitions.

1 See the existing lists of members in this catalogue, pp. 252–255.

2 The only publication to name the Novembergruppe explicitly, even in the title, is the conference proceedings *Architecture 1918–1928: From the Novembergruppe to the C. I. A. M.* (Columbia University 1963). References to the Novembergruppe in the contributions, however, are peripheral.

3 Studies on specific aspects of *Neues Bauen* in Germany, whether construction projects, towns, regions or architects, have acquired a considerable magnitude in recent years. For an introductory overview, the best source remains Huse 1985. Huse includes not only the sober, objective features which can discernibly be traced back to around 1900, but also the diverse Expressionist architecture from 1918 with its predominantly utopian projects, seen as a result of the revolution and a period of socio-political transformation (Huse 1985, esp. pp. 9–25).

4 See the Minutes of the first meeting on 3 December 1918, reproduced in: *Zehn Jahre Novembergruppe*, a special issue of *Kunst der Zeit. Zeitschrift für Kunst und Literatur*, vol. 3, 1928, nos. 1–3, p. 10; [Georg Tappert], provisional list of Novembergruppe members, handwritten [1918–19], Bauhaus-Archiv Berlin, estate of Walter Gropius, GS 2/Mappe 9, 2.5, in this catalogue p. 252.

5 Letter with policy guidelines and articles of association for the Novembergruppe, 18 December 1918/January 1919, Berlinische Galerie, Teilnachlass of Otto Möller, BG-OM 285.

6 We have no exact date for the foundation of either the Novembergruppe or the *Arbeitsrat für Kunst*. See the essay by Nentwig in this catalogue, p. 43, and Whyte 1981, p. 82. On the *Arbeitsrat für Kunst* see also Steneberg 1987; Akademie der Künste 1980.

7 Reproduction of the leaflet "Ein neues künstlerisches Programm" in: Akademie der Künste 1980, p. 87; see also the subsequent leaflet, pp. 88f., here 88.

8 Novembergruppe circular of 13 December 1918, in: ref. in note 4, p. 12. The same wording was published as an "Appeal" in: *Die Schöne Rarität*, vol. 2, 1918–19, p. 144.

9 See the essay by Nentwig in this catalogue, pp. 227f.

10 Apart from the catalogues for the *Berliner Kunstausstellungen* in 1919 and 1920 and for the *Grosse Berliner Kunstausstellung* of 1921, see *inter alia* Hans Schmidkunz, "Kunstausstellung Berlin 1920", in: *Die christliche Kunst*, vol. 17, 1920–21, pp. 24–29 (supplement); also the guide *Führer durch die Abteilung der Novembergruppe. Kunstausstellung Berlin 1921*, Berlin 1921, p. 12. The *Bund Deutscher Architekten* (League of German Architects) also had a section at the *Grosse Berliner Kunstausstellung* in 1921 (nos. 1207–1334), where Krayl and the Luckhardt

brothers showed that year (nos. 1253, 1267 and 1268).

11 On the exhibitions by the *Arbeitsrat für Kunst* see Prange 2000.

12 By 1920 at the latest Gellhorn was a member of the Novembergruppe and served on its executive board. See the letter from Fritz Stuckenberg to Walter Dexel, 10 March 1920, in: Wandschneider and Götte 1993, p. 209, and the letter from Alfred Gellhorn to the *Expressionistische Arbeitsgemeinschaft Kiel*, 17 May 1920, Schleswig-Holsteinische Landesbibliothek Kiel, estate of Richard Blunck, Cb 104: 56.06.

13 Alfred Gellhorn et al., "Die Richtung", in: *Der Kunsttopf*, vol. 1, 1920, no. 3, pp. 47–54, here 48.

14 See Akademie der Künste 1980, pp. 109 and 114.

15 See Bauhaus-Archiv 1988. For how this competition fitted into the broader debate about skyscraper designs for Berlin, see Leutloff 2011.

16 See Bauhaus-Archiv 1988, pp. 8–16, esp. 8f. and 106.

17 See Weber 2013, pp. 14f.; Marx and Weber 2003.

18 On this drawing and the other photo-based views see the recent work by Sudhalter 2017.

19 On the genesis of this design see Weber 2013, pp. 17f. and the commentary by Rocha, p. 164 of this catalogue.

20 See *inter alia* Paul Landau, "Eröffnung der großen Berliner Kunstausstellung", in: *Berliner Börsen-Zeitung*, 20 May 1922, no. 234; H.B.H. [Herbert Behrens-Hangeler], "Berliner Kunstsommer. Akademie—Sezession—Grobeka—Kandinsky", in: *Volkswacht*, 1 June 1922, no. 126.

21 Whether it was a deliberate aesthetic choice by the exhibition committee, on which Poelzig and Wassili Luckhardt sat, or whether it was due to the relatively small number of architecture exhibits remains an open question.

22 See exhib. cat. *Grosse Berliner Kunstausstellung 1923 im Landesausstellungsgebäude am Lehrter Bahnhof* (19. Mai–17. September 1923), Berlin 1923, no. 1408. It has not yet been possible to establish which buildings were in the photographs.

23 Max Osborn, "Große Berliner Kunstausstellung", in: *Vossische Zeitung*, 19 May 1923, no. 235. Similarly positive reviews include Willi Wolfradt, "Große Berliner Kunstausstellung", in: *Cicerone*, vol. 15, 1923, pp. 522f.

24 The *Grosse Bauhaus-Ausstellung* in Weimar in 1923, with a section on international architecture, has hitherto been regarded as "the first collection point" (Winkler 2009, p. 262) for *Neues Bauen* in the post-war years (on this exhibition see ibid., pp. 275–283). However, the room devoted to Novembergruppe architects at the Great Berlin Art Exhibition from 19 May until 17 September 1923 pre-dates the show organized by Gropius, which opened on 15 August 1923. Apart from Gropius and Adolf Meyer, who joined the Novembergruppe the following year, the Weimar show included Mies van der Rohe and Max Taut, among others. In some cases, drawings from the same projects were shown at both venues. Examples of the Dutch avant-garde led by Oud, which Gropius had been able to observe at the Novembergruppe event, were likewise on display in Weimar. Unlike the Novembergruppe show, the Bauhaus featured exhibits from France, Czechoslovakia, Denmark and the United States.

25 Paul Landau: "Große Berliner Kunstausstellung II", in: *Berliner Börsen-Zeitung*, 15 June 1923, no. 273.

26 For an introduction to this competition see Bruognolo 1988.

27 See Menting 2003, pp. 74–82 and 257–260. The ceiling of the meeting hall was painted by Franz Mutzenbecher, acquainted with Taut from the Novembergruppe as well as the *Arbeitsrat für Kunst*. The architect and painter worked together on several occasions, once on the interior for the music shop Heinrichshofen in Magdeburg (cat. 84, 85, p. 154). A photograph of the showroom was also shown in the Novembergruppe section in 1923; see: ref. in note 22, no. 1373.

28 Researchers disagree about which projects Mies exhibited in the Novembergruppe section in 1923 (see Weber 2013, pp. 19–22). There is definitive evidence for the *Concrete Office Building* [*Bürohaus in Eisenbeton*], as it was reproduced in the catalogue for the *Grosse Berliner Kunstausstellung*. On this design see Dietrich Neumann, [catalogue essay], in: Riley and Bergdoll 2002, p. 186.

29 *Führer durch die Abteilung der Novembergruppe. Kunstausstellung Berlin 1923*, Berlin 1923, unpag. [Notes on Room 26].

30 See the essay by Burmeister, pp. 107f. of this catalogue.

31 Ref. in note 25.

32 See Tegethoff 1981, p. 37, note 6 and 40.

33 See the essay by Nentwig, p. 118 of this catalogue.

34 An exception is Schulze 1986, p. 115.

35 See, among others, Mertins 2002, notably pp. 125–128. On Mies as a champion of abstract film see Robbers 2013.

36 For a critical view see Mertins 2002, p. 124 and note 67.

37 It is not clear whether van Doesburg brought the painting, completed in June 1918 and almost 140 centimetres high, with him to Berlin in 1920, and whether it was shown in Germany in 1923–24 (see Hoek 2000, no. 593, pp. 234f.).

38 Early thoughts on a formal analysis of the similarities and differences between van Doesburg's art and Mies van der Rohe's floor plans in relation to *Rhythm of a Russian Dance* can be found in Tegethoff 1981, p. 51.

39 Ref. in note 22, p. 4.

40 Kliemann (1969, p. 119) gives 1923 as the start of Mies's chairmanship, a date he confirmed to the author upon enquiry (Ludwig Mies van der Rohe: Fragebogen zu Verbindung mit der Novembergruppe, 8 November 1967, Berlinische Galerie, BG-Ar 13/99, 144). The documents on the Novembergruppe in Mies van der Rohe's posthumous papers at the Washington Library of Congress (MSS32847, Correspondence, Box 2, File

Novembergruppe) suggest, however, that he only took over this function from Moriz Melzer in 1924. Behne, in his review of the Great Berlin Art Exhibition in 1924, explicitly mentions Mies as the new chairman (see Adolf Behne, "Große Berliner Kunst-Ausstellung 1924", in: *Die Weltbühne*, vol. 20, 1924, vol. 2, pp. 66–68).

41 See *Ausstellung der Novembergruppe in den Räumen der Berliner Secession in Berlin. Juni 1925. Malerei, Plastik, Architektur,* Berlin (Archiv der deutschen Kunst, vol. 5, 1925, no. 3), unpag.; *Handbuch des Kunstmarktes. Kunstadressbuch für das Deutsche Reich, Danzig und Deutsch-Österreich,* Berlin 1926, p. 260.

42 Some architects showed at both exhibitions. Whereas Bartning presented current projects in both venues (see *Grosse Berliner Kunstausstellung* 1924, no. 13 and 842-844), Behrens exhibited older projects in Nachtlicht's presentation and his latest designs in the Novembergruppe section (nos. 14–18 and 850–851). Kosina (nos. 84 and 940), Tessenow (nos. 178 and 1000) and Poelzig (nos. 135 and 975–976) adopted the same principle. The latter used the historical exhibition for his unrealized *Festspielhaus* in Salzburg, which he had shown with the Novembergruppe in 1921 (see *Führer durch die Abteilung der Novembergruppe. Kunstausstellung Berlin 1921,* Berlin 1921, p. 12).

43 See, among others, Walter Curt Behrendt, "Die Architektur auf der Großen Berliner Kunstausstellung 1924", in: *Kunst und Künstler*, vol. 22, 1924, pp. 347–352; Wilhelm Spaet, "Neue Wege in der Kunst. Ausstellung in der Akademie.—Die 'Große Berliner'", in: *Schlesische Volkszeitung*, 22 June 1924 (first published in: *Reichspost*, Vienna, 15 June 1924, no. 164).

44 See, among others, Curt Glaser, "Große Berliner Kunstausstellung", in: *Berliner Börsen-Courier*, 7 June 1924, no. 265; Ludwig Hilberseimer, "Berlin: Große Ausstellung 1924", in: *Sozialistische Monatshefte*, 30 September 1924, p. 600; Behne 1924, ref. in note 40.

45 *Führer der Novembergruppe* [durch die Abteilung auf der Großen Berliner Kunstausstellung 1924], Berlin 1924, unpag. [Notes on Room 20].

46 Alfred Gellhorn, "Eröffnung der Großen Berliner Kunstausstellung", in: *Der Deutsche Rundfunk*, vol. 2, 1924, pp. 1191f., here 1192.

47 G., "Sommerausstellung der Novembergruppe", in: *Die christliche Kunst*, vol. 21, 1924–25, p. 89 (supplement).

48 See, among others, Akademie der Künste 1990, p. 143.

49 See the commentary by Rocha, p. 156 of this catalogue.

50 On joint projects by Novembergruppe members see Kliemann 1969, pp. 43f. The idea of the total art work was not pursued by everyone in the Novembergruppe. Joint projects were usually the result of a personal commitment (see also Bußmann 2004, p. 39).

51 It was probably Gropius, a member of the Novembergruppe from 1924, who established the contact. He had invited some of the Czech architects on show, including Fragner, to exhibit at the Bauhaus in 1923 (see Winkler 2009, p. 280).

52 See, among others, "Zwei holländische Arbeiten. Auf der großen Berliner Kunstausstellung", in: *Bauwelt*, vol. 17 1926, special issue on the *Grosse Berliner Kunstausstellung*, art supplement, no. 20, pp. 13–16.

53 See, among others, Max Osborn, "Novembergruppe. Die Ausstellung in der Sezession", in: *Vossische Zeitung*, 24 June 1925, no. 295; Oskar Bie, "November im Sommer", in: *Stuttgarter Neues Tageblatt*, 15 June 195, no. 271; Paul Westheim, "Ausstellungen", in: *Kunstblatt*, vol. 9, 1925, pp. 217f.; Paul Fechter, "Die Große Berliner Kunstausstellung", in: *Deutsche Allgemeine Zeitung*, 21 May 1926, no. 233; Curt Glaser, "Große Berliner Kunstausstellung", in: *Berliner Börsen-Courier*, 22 May 1926, no. 233; Ludwig Hilberseimer, "Novembergruppe", in: *Sozialistische Monatshefte*, 20 September 1926, p. 666; Will Grohmann, "Ausstellungen", in: *Kunstblatt*, vol. 10, 1926, pp. 283f.

54 Curt Glaser, "Malerei und Baukunst. Zur Ausstellung der Novembergruppe", in: *Berliner Börsen-Courier*, 23 June 1925, no. 288.

55 See Alfred Gellhorn, "Zum Thema 'Bildende Kunst im neuen Hause'", in: ref. in note 4, pp. 66f.; Kliemann 1969, p. 43; letter from Martin Kessel to Helga Kliemann, 14 May 1968, Berlinische Galerie, BG-Ar 13/99,220, reproduced in Kliemann 1969, pp. 74f., here 75, and the undated essay by Arthur Segal, active from 1923 until 1925 in the working group and exhibition committee of the Novembergruppe, "Die Einstellung der modernen Architektur zur Malerei", [1925–26], Leo Baeck Institute, New York, Arthur Segal Collection, AR 7105.

56 See *inter alia* the letter from Arthur Segal to [Max Dungert], 22 November 1925, Landesarchiv Berlin, F Rep. 241, Acc. 841, no. 10, and later memories of some of the parties to the conflict in Butting 1955, p. 153; Kliemann 1969, pp. 74f.

57 Letter from Ludwig Mies van der Rohe as chairman of the Novembergruppe to Willem Marinus Dudok, 19 May 1925, Library of Congress, Washington D.C., Ludwig Mies van der Rohe Papers, MSS32847.

58 See the letters from Ludwig Mies van der Rohe as chairman of the Novembergruppe to Willem Marinus Dudok, 19 May 1925, and to Jacobus Johannes Pieter Oud, 19 May 1925, Library of Congress, Washington D.C., Ludwig Mies van der Rohe Papers, MSS32847.

59 See, among others, the letters from Max Butting and Alfred Gellhorn to Ludwig Mies van der Rohe, 10 October 1925, and Alfred Gellhorn to Ludwig Mies van der Rohe, 2 November 1925, Library of Congress, Washington D.C., Ludwig Mies van der Rohe Papers, MSS32847.

60 See ref. in note 4, p. 85; Rüdiger 1999, p. 70.

61 Different versions are told about the constitution of the *Zehner-Ring* in 1923 or 1924. There were actually nine, not ten, original members: apart from Mies van der Rohe they were Häring, Bartning, Behrens, Mendelsohn, Poelzig, Bruno and Max Taut as well as Walter Schilbach, who had no connections with the Novembergruppe. In 1926 the group, now known as *Der Ring,* expanded to 27 architects. For summaries see *inter alia* Menting 2003, p. 86, and Göckede 2008 with a proposal for a network theory analysis of this important association.

62 See exhib. cat. *Grosse Berliner Kunstausstellung 1926 im Landesausstellungsgebäude am Lehrter Bahnhof. Farbige Raumkunst* (22. Mai – 31. August 1926), Berlin 1926, nos. 1520f., 1531f., 1537, 1545–1547, 1551–1553, 1567–1572, 1578, 1583, 1597–1602, 1623, 1626f.; "Ausstellung 'Baukunst'. Aussteller im Rahmen der Novembergruppe", in: *Bauwelt*, vol. 17, 1926, special issue on the *Grosse Berliner Kunstausstellung*, nos. 20, p. 473.

63 "Die Baukunst auf der großen Berliner Kunstausstellung. Eine Auswahl aus der Ausstellung der Novembergruppe", in: *Bauwelt*, op. cit., pp. 9–12.

64 "Die neue Baukunst in der großen Berliner Kunstausstellung. Zur Kunstbeilage in diesem Heft", in: *Bauwelt*, op. cit., p. 475.

65 "Spaltung der Novembergruppe", in: *Hamburger Correspondent*, 29 January 1927, no. 47.

66 "Aus der Novembergruppe", in: *Berliner Börsen-Zeitung*, 6 February 1927, no. 61. The same wording appeared in: *Vossische Zeitung*, 5 February 1927, no. 61.

67 Apart from the *Weissenhofsiedlung*, another outstanding example of such housing estates is the *Dammerstocksiedlung* in Karlsruhe, built in 1929. For an introduction to the construction of estates and housing in the Weimar Republic see Huse 1985, pp. 64–102.

68 See Poppelreuther 2003.

69 For a detailed account of the anniversary see the essay by Nentwig in this catalogue, pp. 195–202.

70 The exhibition was an autonomous part of the *Juryfeie Kunstschau* in 1929. The catalogue merely sums up all the architects' exhibits as "architectures". The evidence that Mies showed photographs of his Barcelona pavilion is in a review of the exhibition by Curt Glaser, "Juryfreie Kunstschau", in: *Kunst und Künstler*, vol. 28, 1929, pp. 75f., here 75.

71 See "Mitteilungen", in: *Zentralblatt der Bauverwaltung*, vol. 51, 1931, no. 24, p. 35.

72 Will Grohmann, "Zehn Jahre Novembergruppe", in: Novembergruppe 1928, pp. 1–9, here 8f.

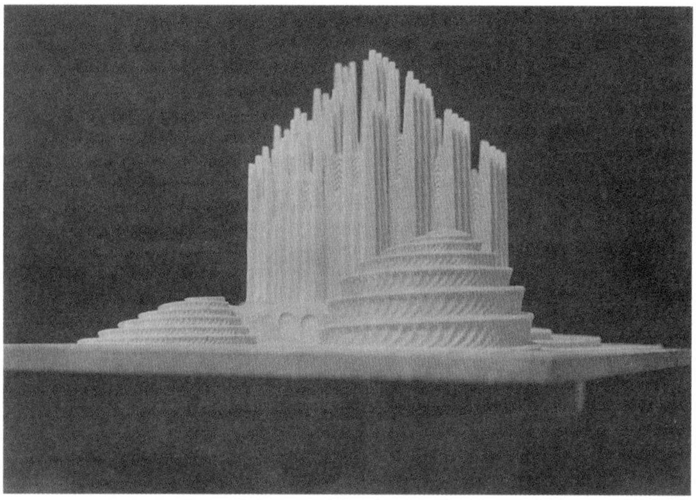

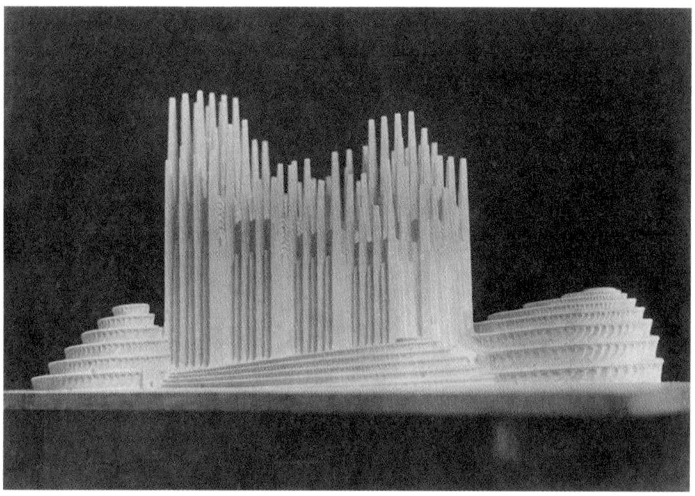

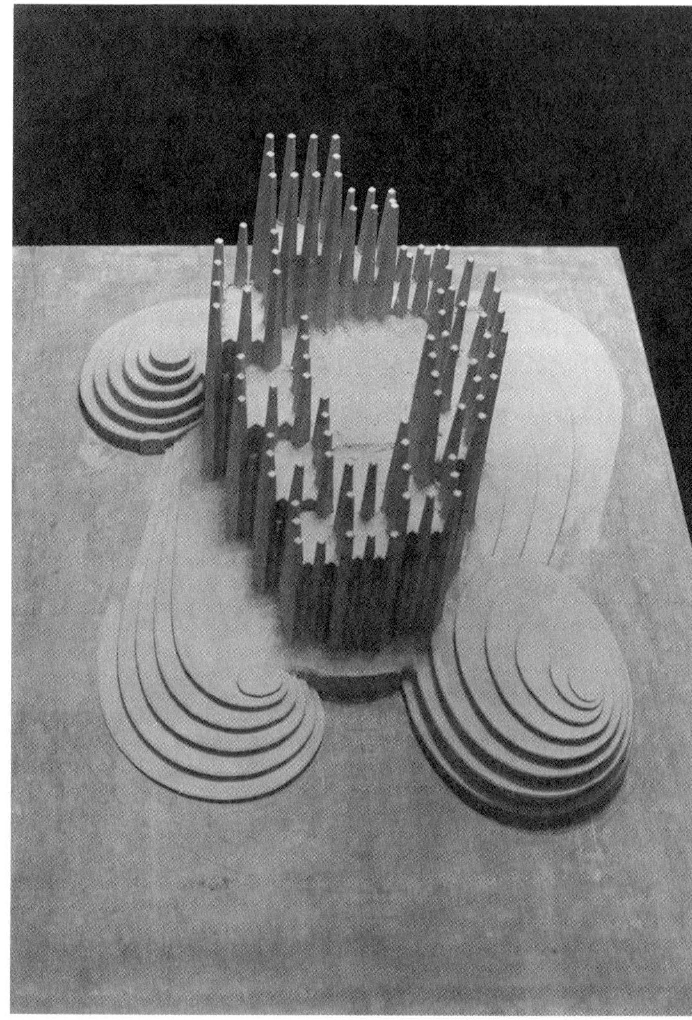

80–82
HANS AND WASSILI LUCKHARDT
House of Music and Festivals, 1919

Three photographs of the lost model,
13 × 18.2 cm / 13 × 18.3 cm / 18.3 × 13.2 cm
Akademie der Künste, Berlin

Repro. of model in *Zehn Jahre Novembergruppe* 1928, p. 84

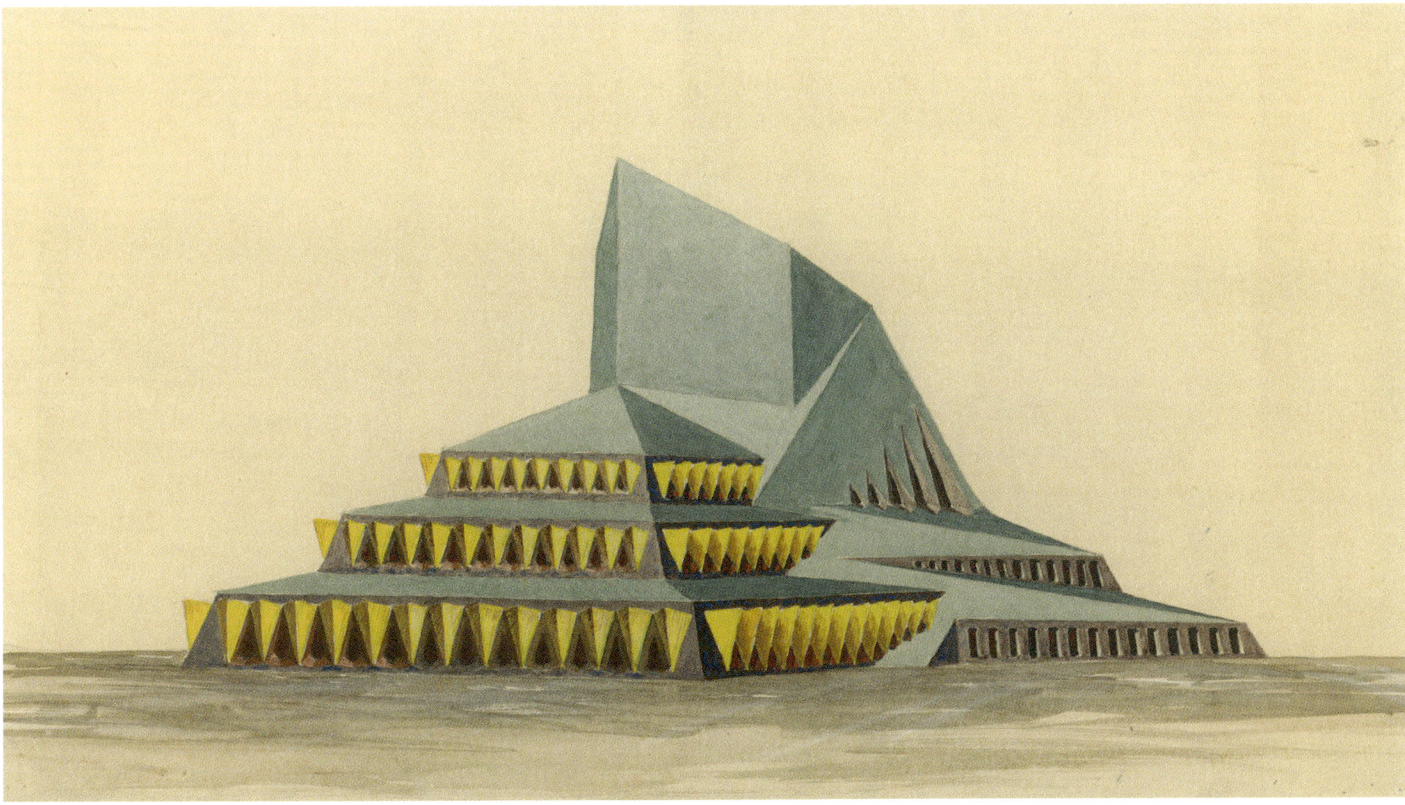

83

WASSILI LUCKHARDT

People's theatre, before 1921

Watercolour on paper, 43.5 × 76.5 cm
Akademie der Künste, Berlin

Repro. of the photo of a model in *Zehn Jahre Novembergruppe* 1928, p. 84

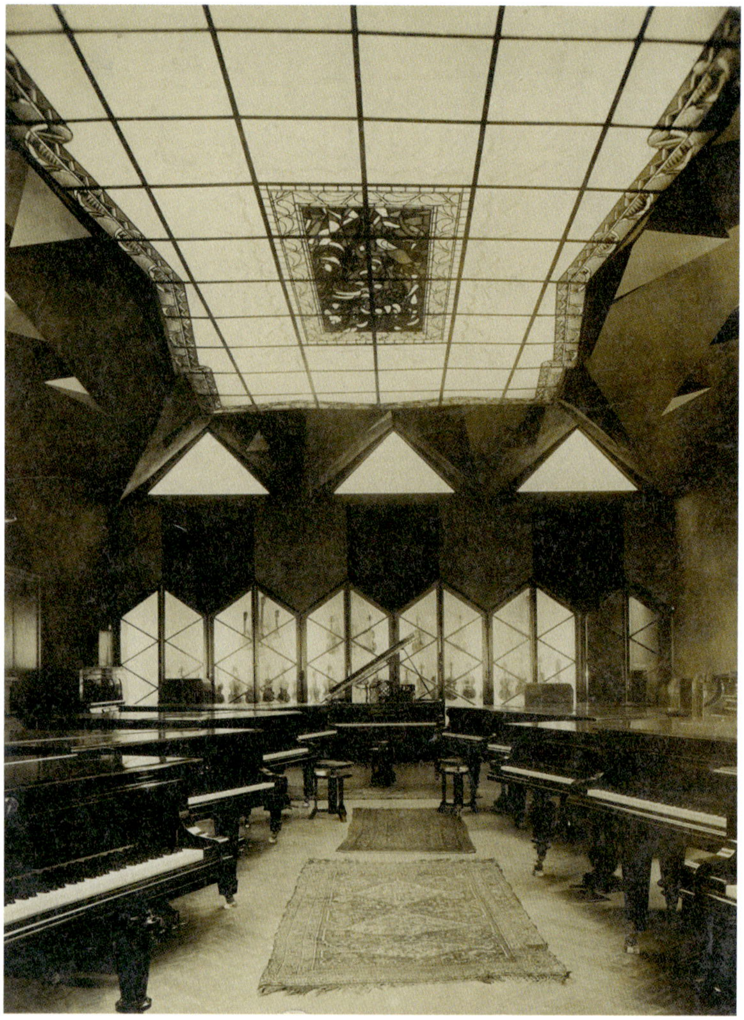

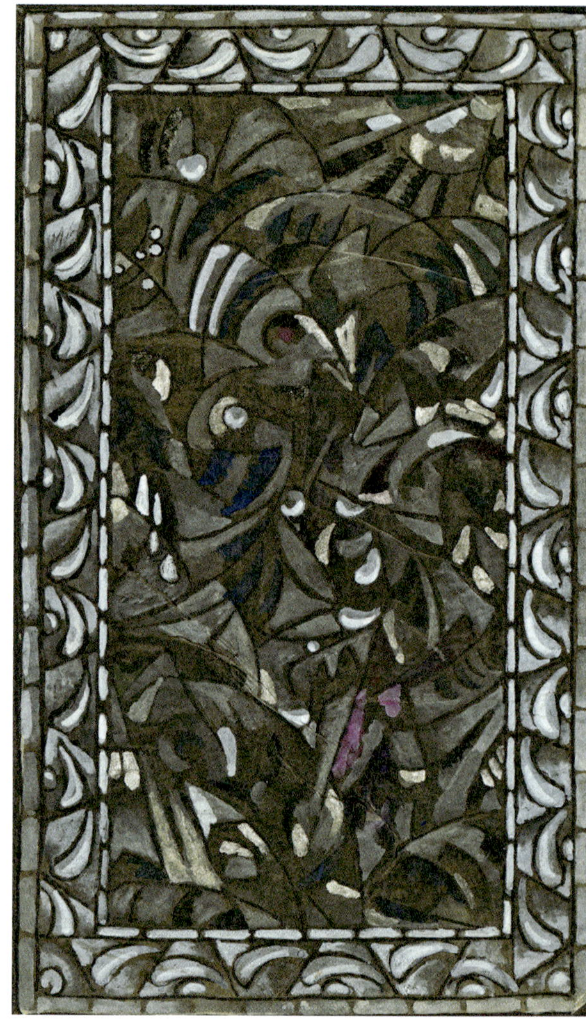

84
MAX TAUT
Display space for the music specialists Heinrichshofen in Magdeburg, glass ceiling by Franz Mutzenbecher, 1921–1922

Photograph, 18 × 24 cm
Akademie der Künste, Berlin

Great Berlin Art Exhibition 1923, Novembergruppe section, no. 1373 (a photograph of the display space)

85
FRANZ MUTZENBECHER
Drawing for a glass window, undated

Gouache on paperboard, 19.5 × 11.3 cm on 26 × 17.7 cm
Akademie der Künste, Berlin

Art Exhibition Berlin 1920, no. 1342, repro. in the catalogue, more repros. in *Der Kunsttopf*, vol 1, 1920, no. 6, p. 105 and *Zehn Jahre Novembergruppe* 1928, p. 91

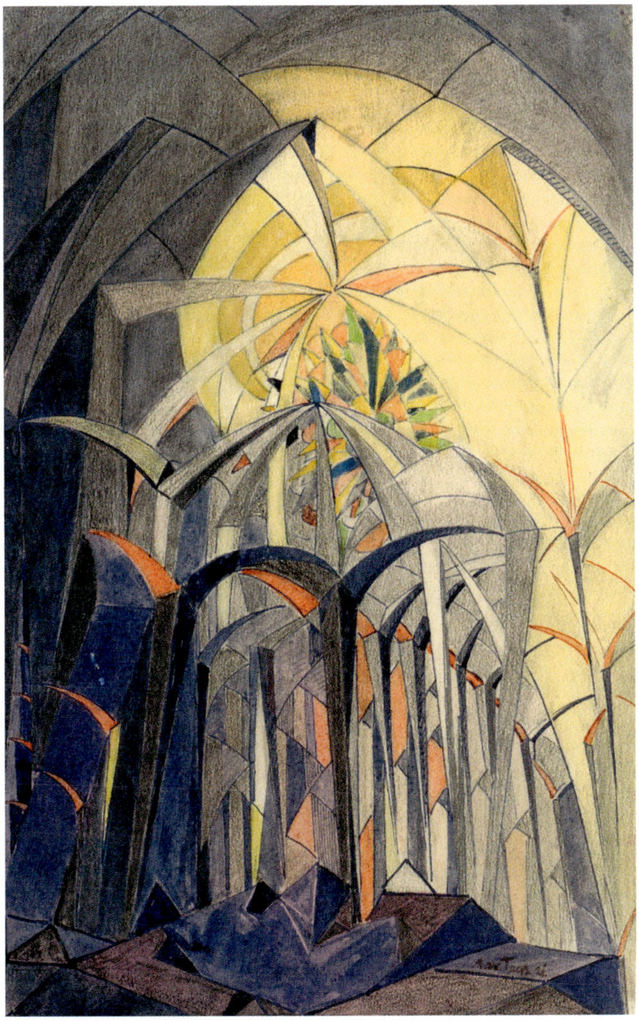

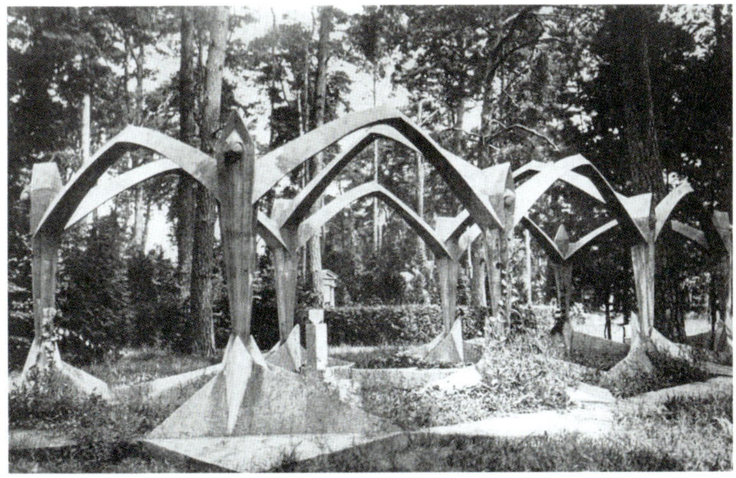

86
MAX TAUT
House of Blossoms, 1921

Colour drawing, mixed technique, 36 × 22 cm
Akademie der Künste, Berlin

87
MAX TAUT [WITH RUDOLF BELLING]
Wissinger family grave, Stahnsdorf near Berlin, 1921–1922

Photograph, 18 × 24 cm
Akademie der Künste, Berlin

Great Berlin Art Exhibition 1923, Novembergruppe section, no. 1371 (a model and two photographs)

HUGO HÄRING
Gut Garkau, 1924

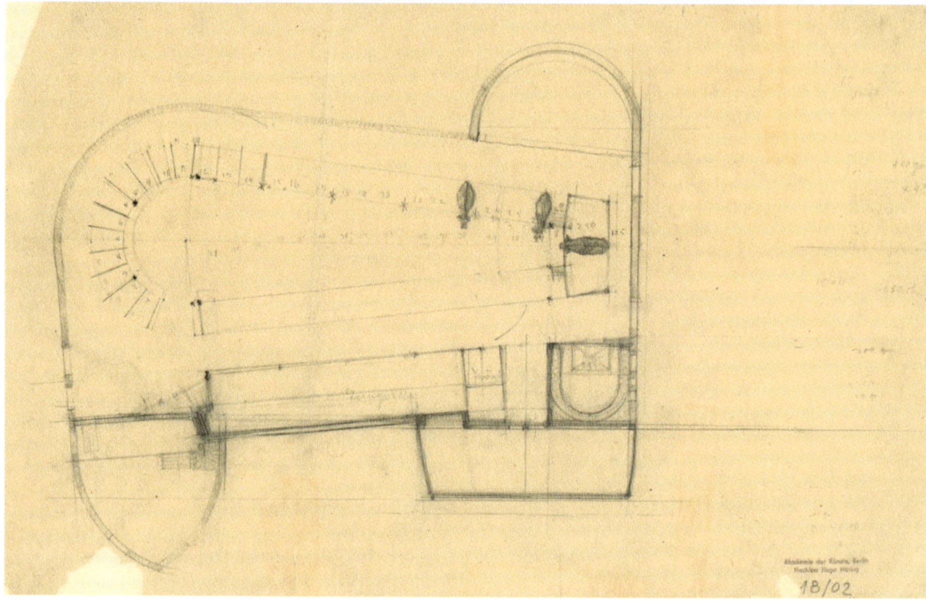

01 HUGO HÄRING, Floorplan of the cow shed, 1922, Akademie der Künste, Berlin, Hugo-Häring-Archives

When asked by HUGO HÄRING about the simplest strategy for feeding cows, Otto Birtner, who had commissioned the architect to design his farm, answered: "You throw a big pile of hay in the middle, and the cows stand around in a circle and eat."[1] This profane but pithy response inspired Häring's best-known blueprint, *Gut Garkau*, which exemplifies his ideas about organic architecture. The pear-shaped feeding zone derived from a circle is both a reference to the natural movement of cows and an effective spatial design in terms of agricultural use (fig. 01).

Häring epitomizes architecture created in response to a given topography and reflecting the specific tasks it is intended to meet.[2] For this architect, discovering the form was part of the design process: first you identify the functions and the site conditions, then you conceive a form that arises from nature.[3] To him, the building in itself was a living organism blending, not competing with the landscape. Purely geometric building that failed to respect the 'inner essence' of the natural conditions was, in Häring's opinion, "imposed form" and "coercive design".[4]

Residential buildings, bridges and canals all serve a purpose, just as everyday utensils do.[5] In Häring's view, functional buildings should come across as a matter of course, as if they have been designed by life itself, rather than displaying the signature of an individual artist or architect.[6] The buildings generated by *Neues Bauen*, argued Häring, were subject to the ideals of artistic expression and thus slaves to their time and prevailing tastes, creating an impression of transience. In his view, predefining a structure by applying right angles and straight lines is alien to the development of organic life, because a building only acquires its internal arrangement, expansiveness and housing quality when it has been liberated from geometry.[7]

It was presumably thanks to his connection with LUDWIG MIES VAN DER ROHE, who was the executive secretary of the Novembergruppe from 1924 and shared a studio in Berlin with Hugo Häring from 1921, that the architect presented his drawings and perspectives for Gut Garkau at the Great Berlin Art Exhibition in 1924 and 1925. To the north of Lübeck and west of the lake known as the Grosser Pönitzer See, Häring built the barn, cow byre and sheds for the farm, but not the complex as a whole. His designs illustrate the relationship between the various sections, each with its own formal idiom, and the proposed ensemble with no free-standing buildings (cat. 88, p. 157). The cow byre terminates the open yard to the north-west; the sheds stretch in an almost vertical line westwards from the yard, and the barn stands opposite. The selection and finishing of the materials are determined by regional traditions: dark red brick for the masonry, wooden cladding painted green for the upper section of the building, and steel-reinforced concrete painted white where the load-bearing system is visible. The ventilation, lighting and fodder distribution are resolved by tilted roofs and window strips.

Hugo Häring was the only proponent of organic building in the Novembergruppe, which distinguished him from all the other architects. His aim for Gut Garkau — and every other building he designed — was "to be an organ of home, life and work".[8]

NUNO DE BRITO ROCHA

1 Schirren and Claus 2001, p. 362.
2 Ibid., p. 363.
3 Ibid., p. 50.
4 See Hoffmann 1982, p. 12.
5 In his article *"ways to form" ["wege zur form"]* published in *Die Form* in 1925, Häring talks about the architect's expectations of functional forms and expressive forms in a building. This discussion provides the basis for a complementary antithesis between organics and geometry.
6 See Joedicke 1982, pp. 6f.
7 See Schirren and Claus 2001, p. 362.
8 Quoted in Joedicke 1982, p. 79.

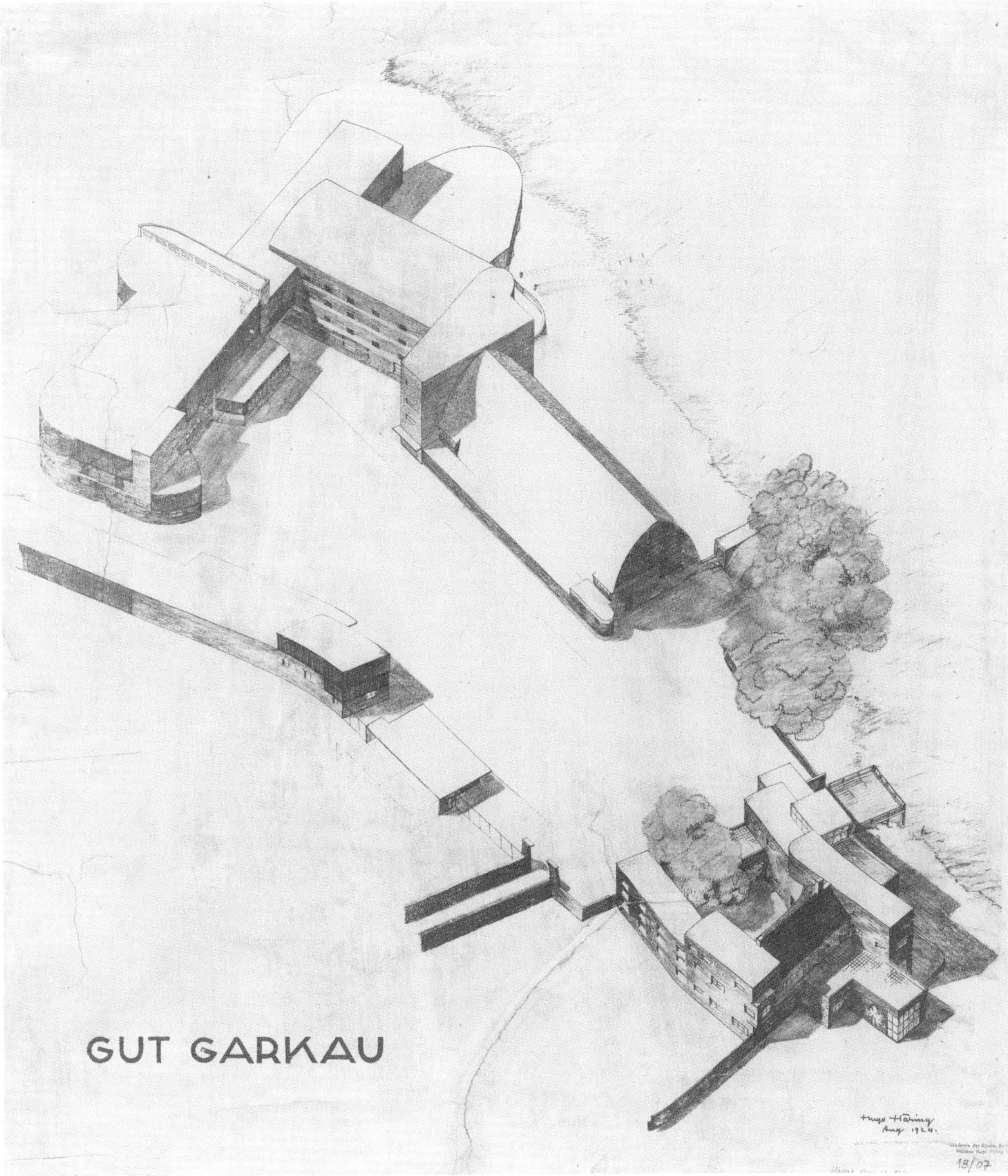

88

HUGO HÄRING

Gut Garkau, Scharbeutz (Ostholstein), August 1924

Blueprint, 89.4 × 76.8 cm
Akademie der Künste, Berlin

Great Berlin Art Exhibition 1924, Novembergruppe section, no. 900 (drawing of the farm buildings)

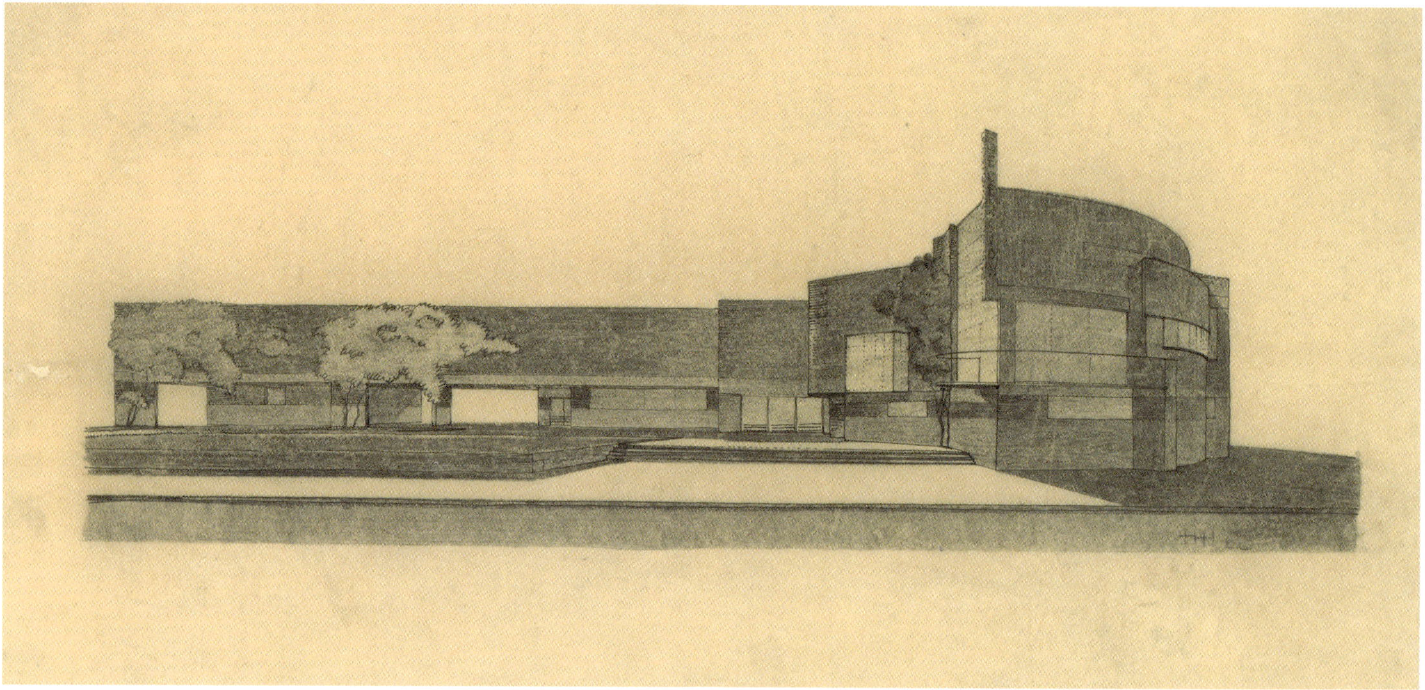

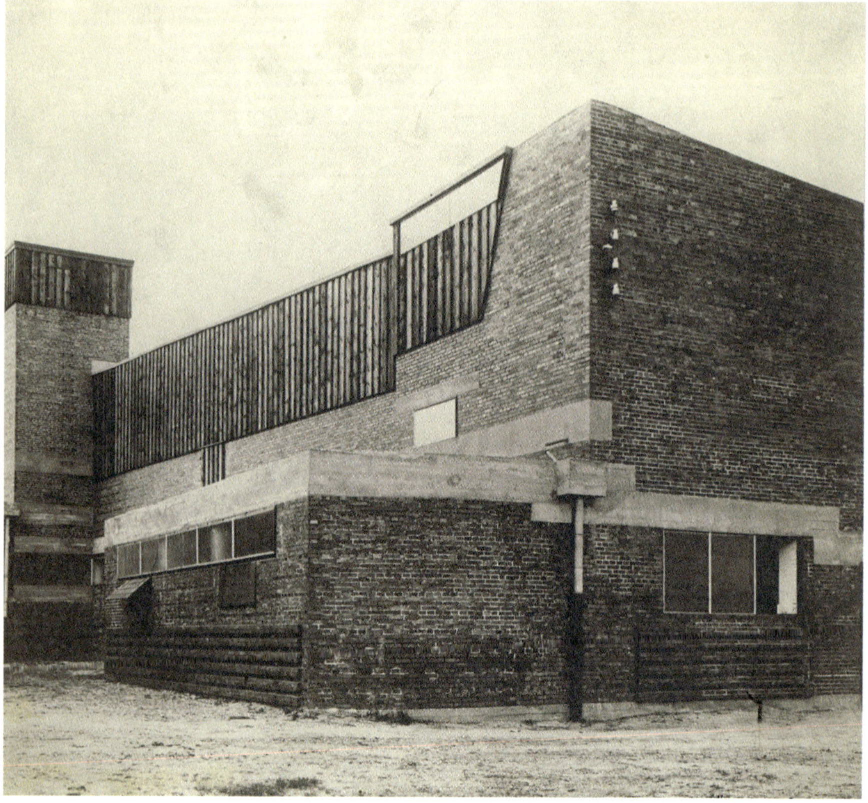

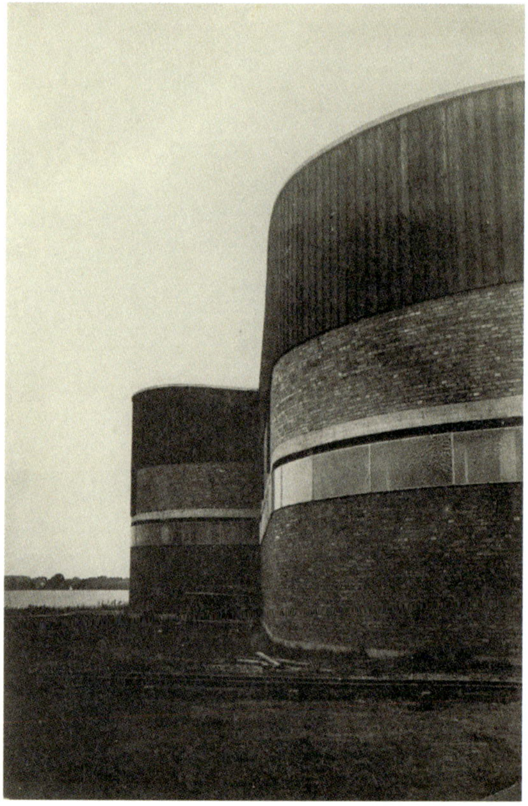

89
HUGO HÄRING
Exhibition pavilion for the Berlin Secession, Savignyplatz, Berlin-Charlottenburg, (not realized), November 1925

India ink on tracing paper, 47.3 × 55 cm
Akademie der Künste, Berlin

Great Berlin Art Exhibition 1926, Novembergruppe section, no. 1545

90
HUGO HÄRING
Gut Garkau, cattle shed, Scharbeutz (Ostholstein), 1922–1926

Photograph, 25.5 × 27.2 cm
Akademie der Künste, Berlin

90
HUGO HÄRING
Gut Garkau, cattle shed, Scharbeutz (Ostholstein), 1922–1926

Photograph, 31.7 × 21.5 cm
Akademie der Künste, Berlin

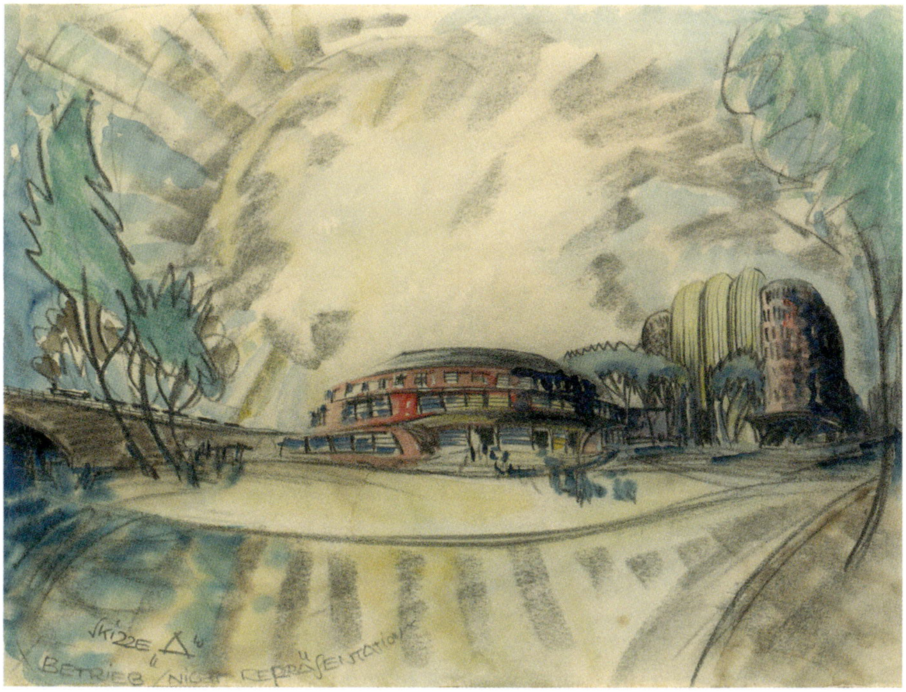

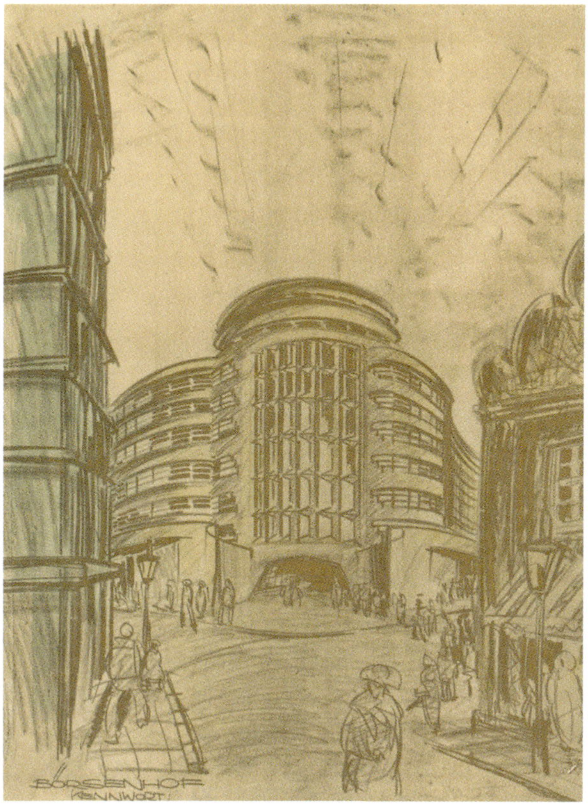

92
HANS SCHAROUN
Competition entry entitled "Operation, not representation" showing the station square, street An der Weide and post office, Bremen, 1922

Watercolour on paper, 50 × 66 cm, Akademie der Künste, Berlin

Great Berlin Art Exhibition 1923, Novembergruppe section, no. 1337

93
HANS SCHAROUN
"Börsenhof" with shops and offices, Königsberg [now Kaliningrad], competition, 1922

Blueprint [probably an iron gall ink copy] on paper with highlights in coloured pencil, 84.6 × 62.2 cm
Akademie der Künste, Berlin

Great Berlin Art Exhibition 1923,
Novembergruppe section, no. 1336

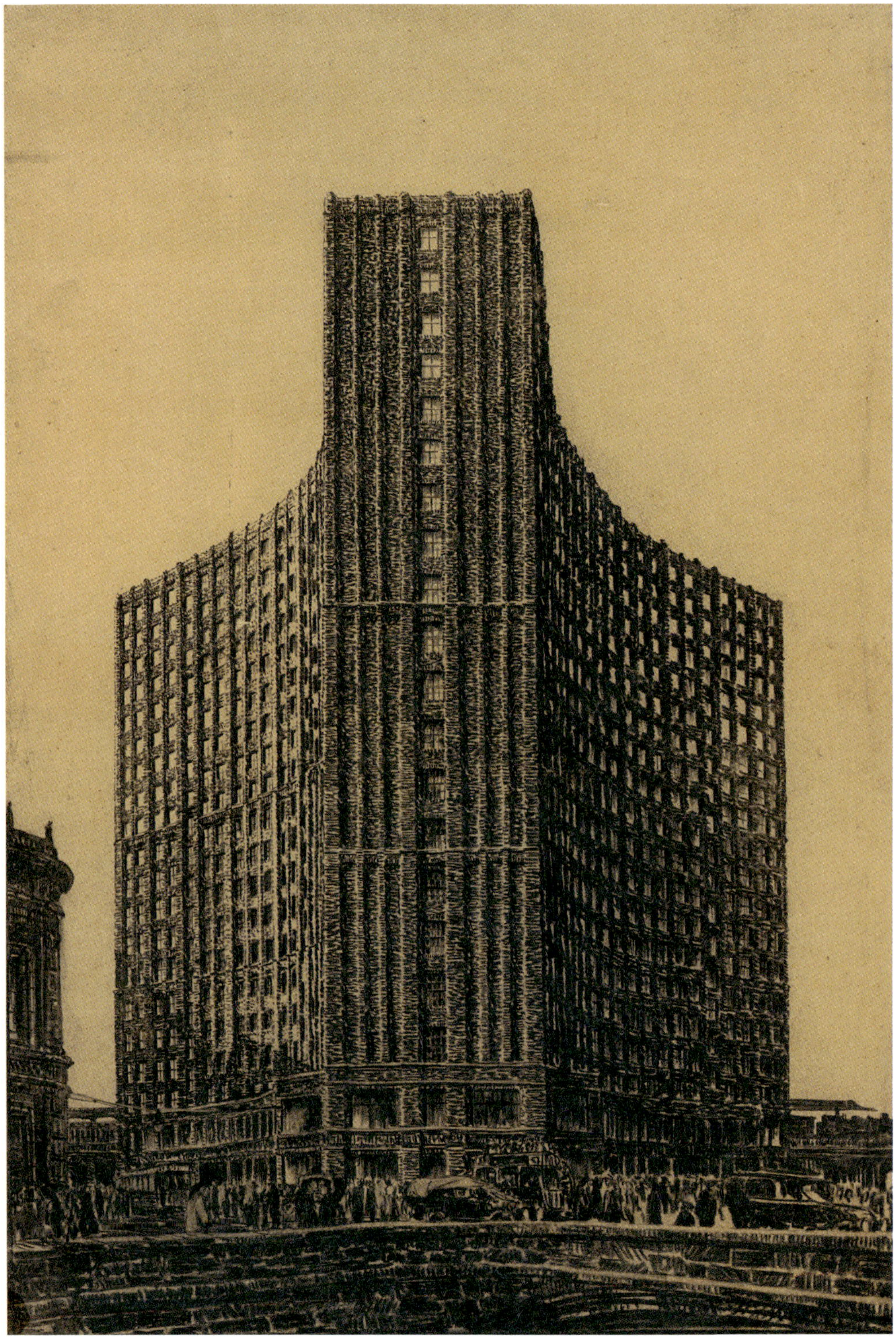

94

HANS POELZIG

Competition for "Turmhaus AG" high-rise building on Friedrichstrasse, Berlin, 1921

Charcoal on tracing paper, 109.9 × 77.5 cm
Architekturmuseum TU Berlin

Great Berlin Art Exhibition 1922, Novembergruppe section, no. 1371

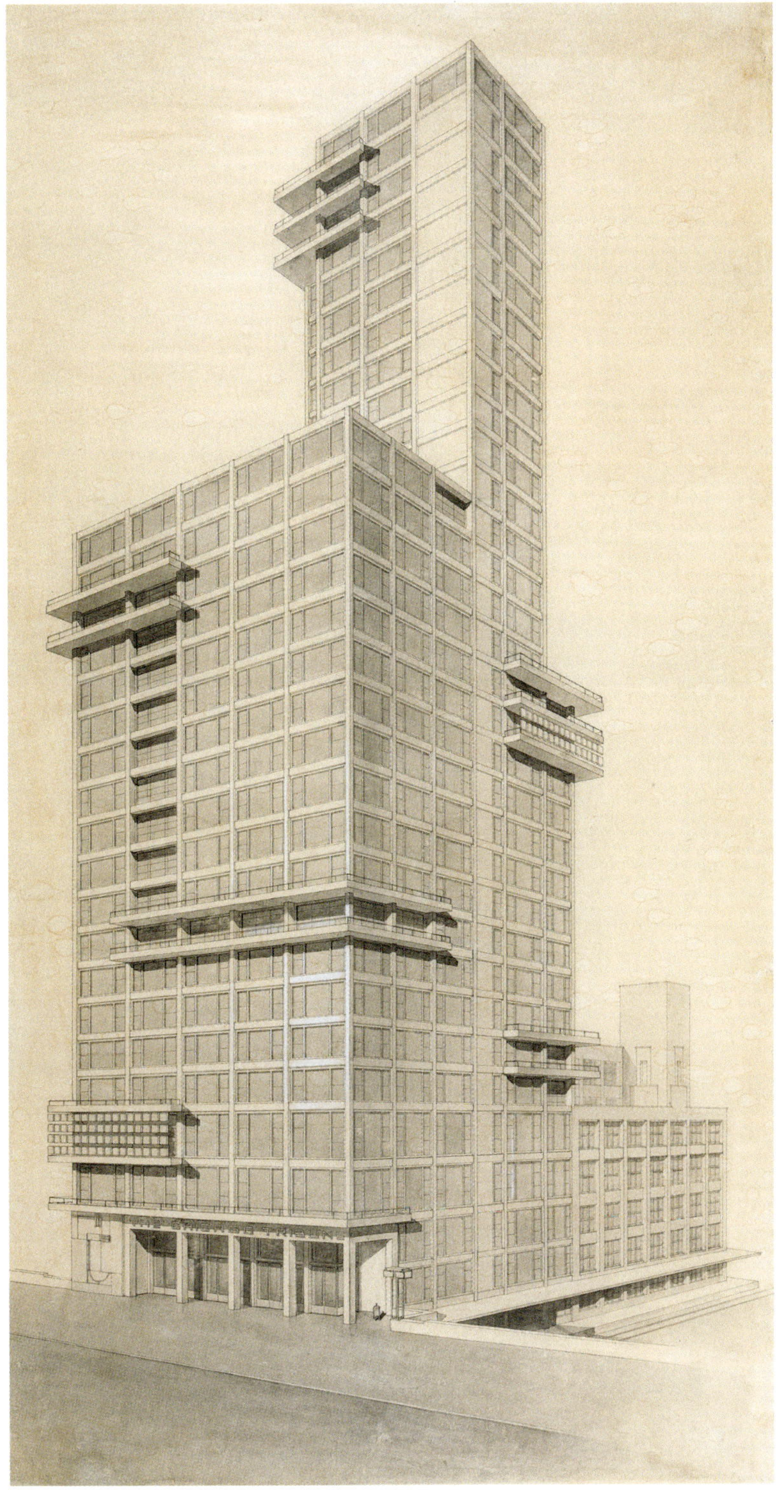

95

WALTER GROPIUS AND ADOLF MEYER

Tribune Tower, south-west perspective, competition entry for a Chicago Tribune office building, Chicago, 1922

India ink and wash on thin paper, 135 × 71.5 cm
Bauhaus-Archiv Berlin

Great Berlin Art Exhibition 1924, Novembergruppe section, no. 896, repro. in *Zehn Jahre Novembergruppe* 1928, p. 85

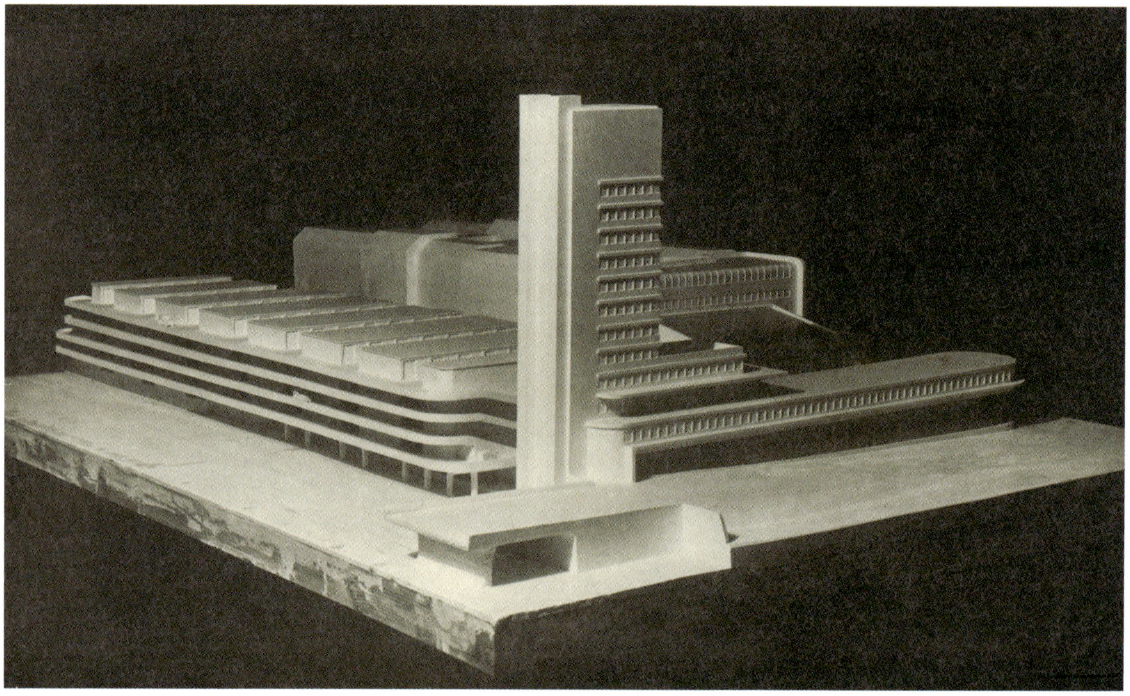

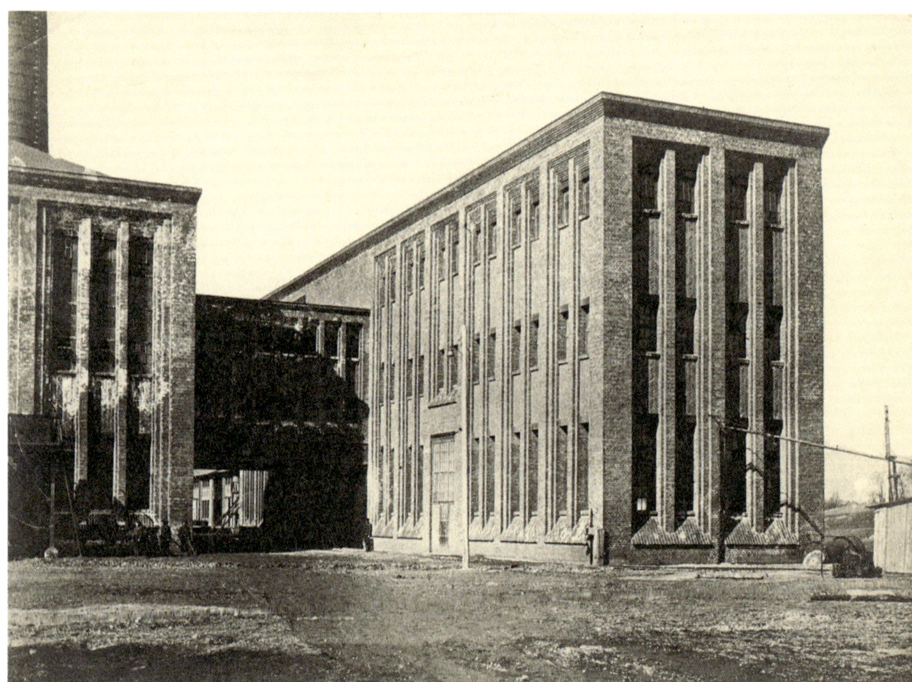

96
HANS AND WASSILI LUCKHARDT WITH ALFONS ANKER
Supergarage for 1000 motor cars, 1924

Photograph, 69.5 × 113 cm
Akademie der Künste, Berlin

Great Berlin Art Exhibition 1924, Novembergruppe section, no. 951

97
HANS POELZIG
Annagrube [ore mine]. Electrical substation, c. 1914

Gelatin silver print, 28.9 × 38.7 cm
Architekturmuseum TU Berlin

Repro. in the catalogue for the Novembergruppe exhibition at the Berlin Secession, 1925

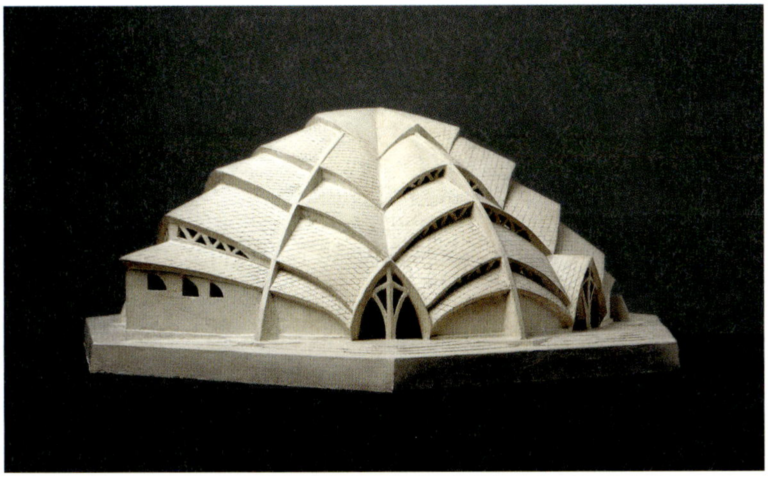

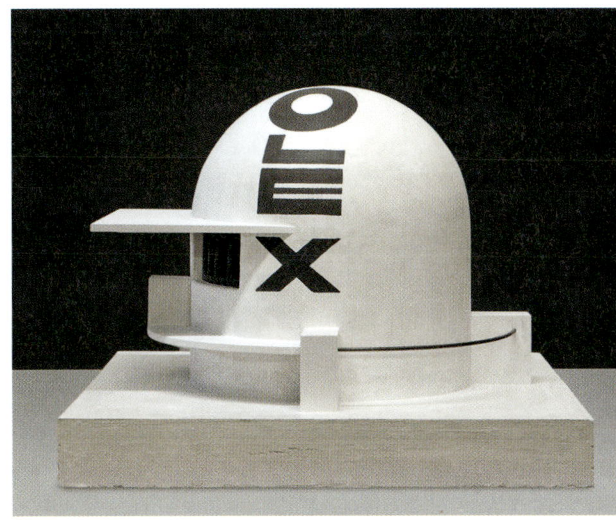

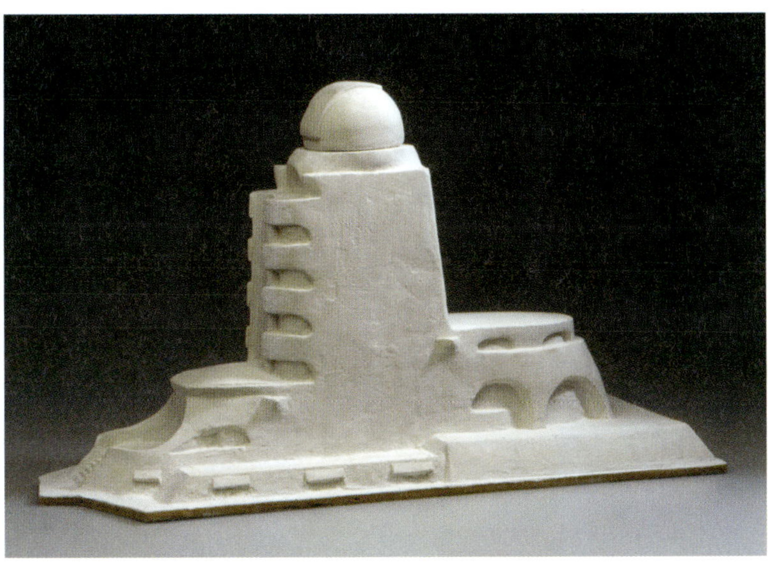

98
OTTO BARTNING
Star Church (design), 1921–1922, model after 1944

Plaster, wood, 42.5 × 80 × 79 cm
Berlinische Galerie

Great Berlin Art Exhibition 1924, Novembergruppe section, no. 842 (assisted by Oswald Herzog)

99
RUDOLF BELLING WITH ALFRED GELLHORN AND MARTIN KNAUTHE
Petrol station in Halle an der Saale (design),1923 (reconstruction 2017)

Plaster, 47.8 × 62 × 62 cm
Staatliche Museen zu Berlin, Nationalgalerie

Great Berlin Art Exhibition 1924, Novembergruppe section, no. 785 b

100
ERICH MENDELSOHN
Einstein Tower on Telegraphenberg, Potsdam (copy from model), after 1950

Plaster, wood, 36 × 25 × 60 cm
Berlinische Galerie

Repro. of the photo of the finished building in *Zehn Jahre Novembergruppe* 1928, p. 27

LUDWIG MIES VAN DER ROHE
Glass Skyscraper, 1922

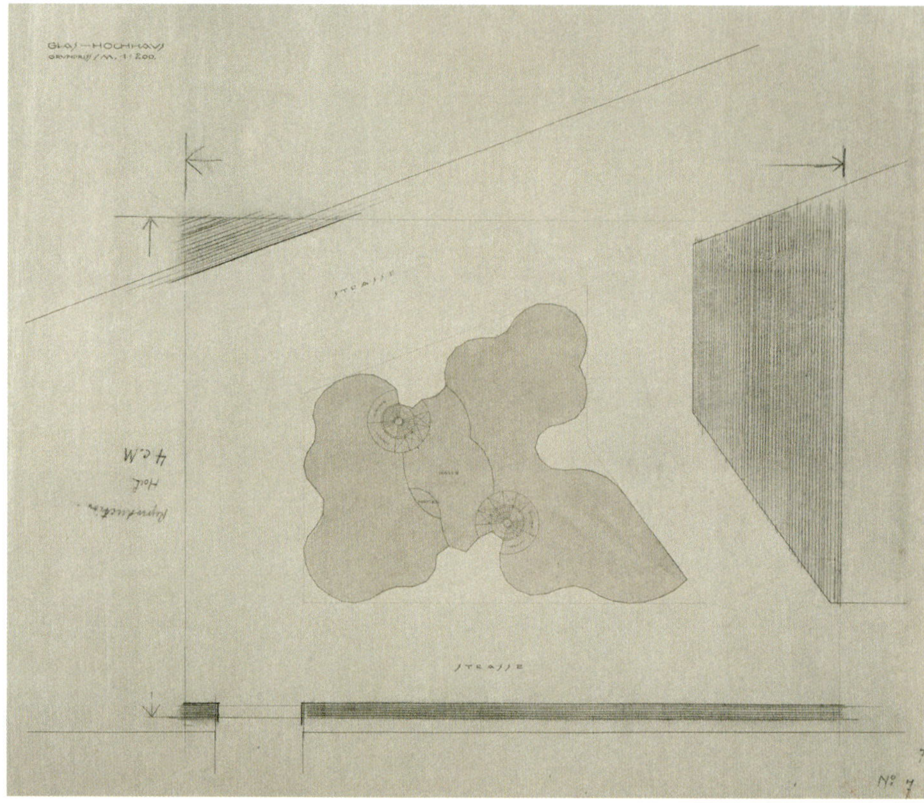

01 LUDWIG MIES VAN DER ROHE, Glass skyscraper project, 1922, The Museum of Modern Art, New York

"Skin-and-bones architecture"[1] was how LUDWIG MIES VAN DER ROHE termed the division of a building into its façade and its load-bearing structure, glass and steel respectively. This design for a Glass Skyscraper [*Glashochhaus*], first exhibited with the Novembergruppe in 1922 and published that year in the journal *Frühlicht* edited by BRUNO TAUT,[2] is a perfect example of this disconnection between the components of a building. Mies van der Rohe designed the Glass Skyscraper a year after submitting his "Honeycomb" to a competition for ideas for a tower block at Friedrichstrasse train station. The two designs, illustrated next to each other in Frühlicht, share both the construction technique—"skin and bones"—and the materials—glass and steel. For this reason, and because they originated at more or less the same time, they are often confused.

These two projects epitomize Mies van der Rohe's approach to *Neues Bauen* and signal a clean break with the architectural conventions of the time. He sought to dispense with all inherited forms and methods and instead to devise an appropriate solution to the immediate task in hand.[3] Using glass and steel allowed him to build higher, faster and more effectively. The idea that the form of a building is directly linked to its built function was advocated by Mies van der Rohe in the journal *G*, which he edited together with HANS RICHTER, EL LISSITZKY and THEO VAN DOESBURG. Here he articulated his rigorous rejection of formalism: he did not acknowledge any particular form, only structural problems; form was not his purpose, but the outcome of his work.[4] Producing, not reproducing, determined Mies van der Rohe's design process.[5]

True to this principle, he used his glass models to test structural forms. During the development process, the architect realized that he was less interested in the effects of light and shadow than in a abundant play of light reflexes.[6] In addition to this quality, the illumination of the interior space and the street impact of the built mass were decisive factors in the design of the structure's defining curves.[7] The photograph of the Glass Skyscraper highlights this impact: the model was shot from a low angle and integrated into a model of the surroundings made by OSWALD HERZOG (cat. 101, p. 165).

A top-down view picks out the curving glass façade of the tower as a polymorphous contour separating the inside from the outside without ever touching the load-bearing skeleton. Only where one of the polygons touches the plot boundary does the design display a sharp edge. Another three asymmetric curves complete the floor plan, identical for every storey (fig. 01). The stair and lift towers are the only fixed points. All other subdivisions of the floor plan are to be adapted to specific needs and executed in glass.[8] The inside and outside interweave visually because load-bearing walls have been radically eliminated. Only the filigree elements in the slender steel structure at the core of the building are visible.

Presented in the centre of Hall 24 at the Great Berlin Art Exhibition in 1922, Mies van der Rohe's Glass Skyscraper was the only architectural and three-dimensional item in the room. Within this staging, the glass contour of the building was diffused by the reflection of the light and "emerges suggestively more strongly in some places, more gently in others"[9]—just like the lines in the watercolours, as described in the guide, hanging in the same room of the Novembergruppe exhibition.

NUNO DE BRITO ROCHA

1 Hans Richter (ed.), *G. Zeitschrift für elementare Gestaltung*, year 1, 1923, no. 1.

2 Bruno Taut (ed.), *Frühlicht*, no. 4, 1922, pp. 212–214.

3 See Schulze 1985; Ludwig Mies van der Rohe, "Hochhäuser": ref. in note 2.

4 Hans Richter (ed.), *G. Zeitschrift für elementare Gestaltung*, year 1, 1923, no. 2, unpaginated.

5 See Neumeyer 1992, p. 13.

6 Ref. in note 3.

7 Ref. in note 3.

8 Ref. in mote 3, p. 214.

9 *Führer durch die Abteilung der Novembergruppe. Grosse Berliner Kunstausstellung* 1922, Berlin 1922, p. 9.

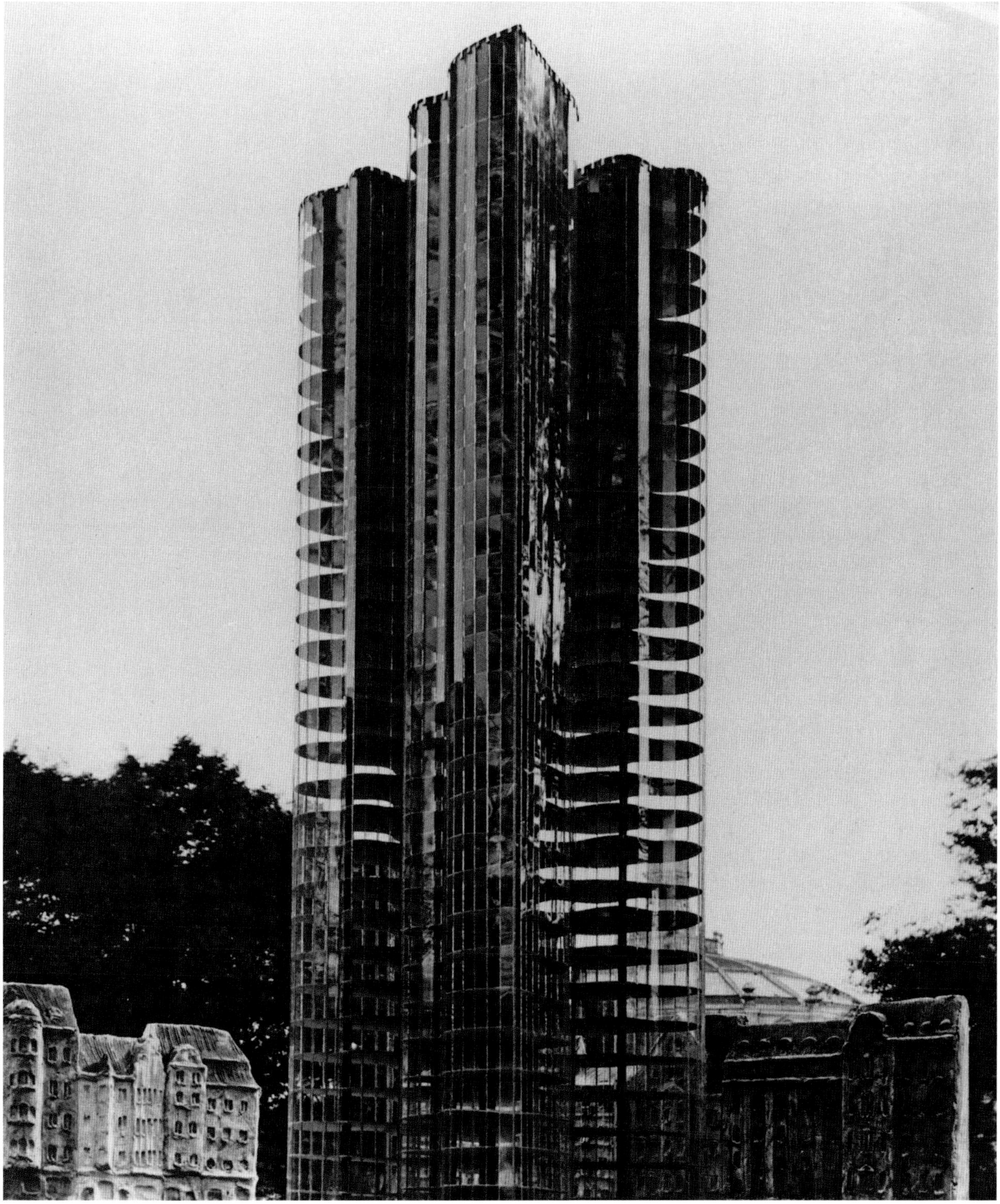

101
LUDWIG MIES VAN DER ROHE
Model of a glass skyscraper, 1922
(Photo: Curt Rehbein)

Gelatine silver paper (Reproduction from the Edward A. Duckel Collection, around 1987), 24 × 17.7 cm
Berlinische Galerie

Repro. of a similar photograph in *Zehn Jahre Novembergruppe* 1928, p. 26

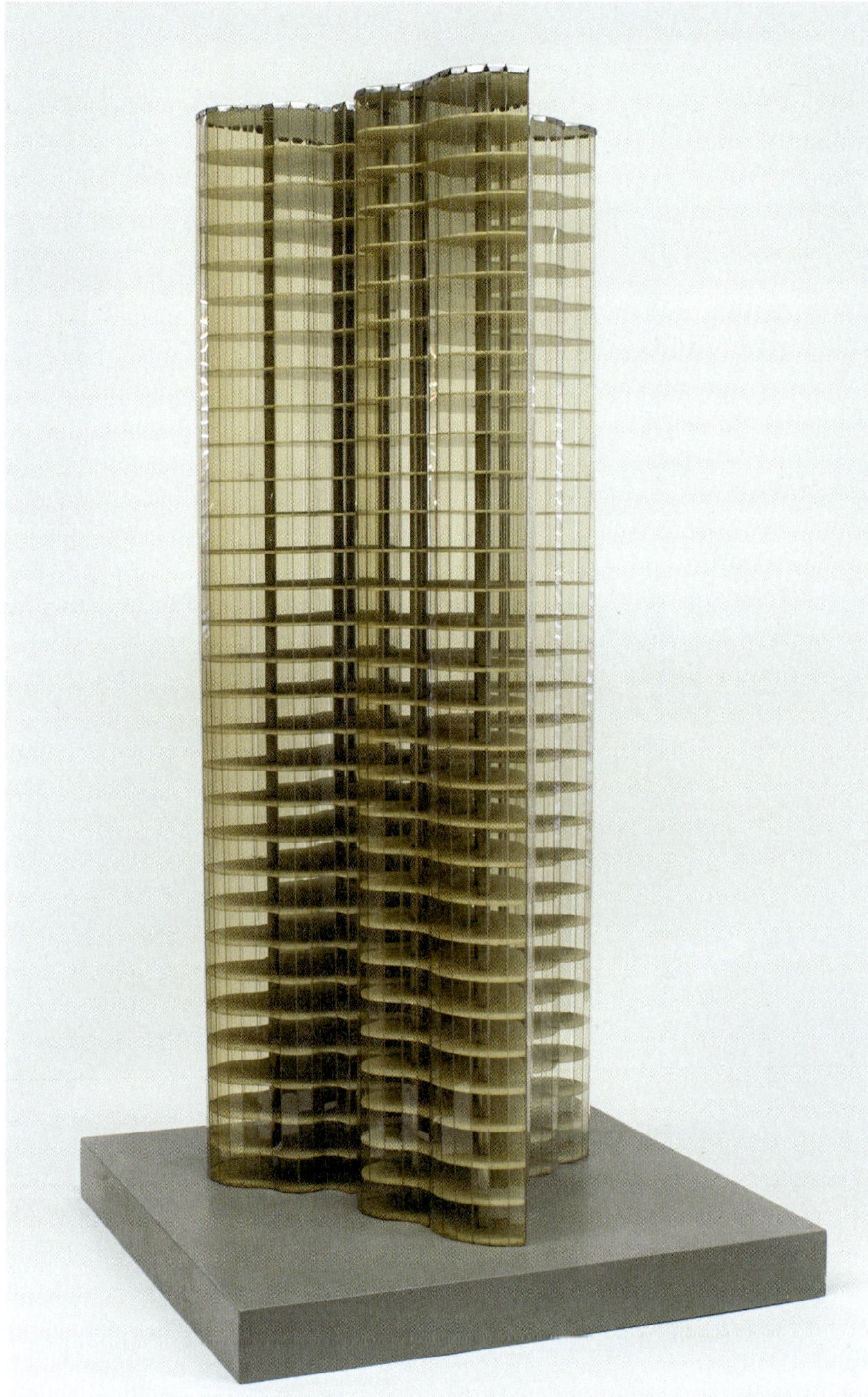

102

LUDWIG MIES VAN DER ROHE

Model of a glass skyscraper, 1922 (reconstruction 1986)

Wood, stained, plexiglass, metal, 94.2 × 50.2 × 100 cm
Bauhaus-Universität Weimar – Archiv der Moderne

Great Berlin Art Exhibition 1922, Novembergruppe section, no. 1385 (original model)

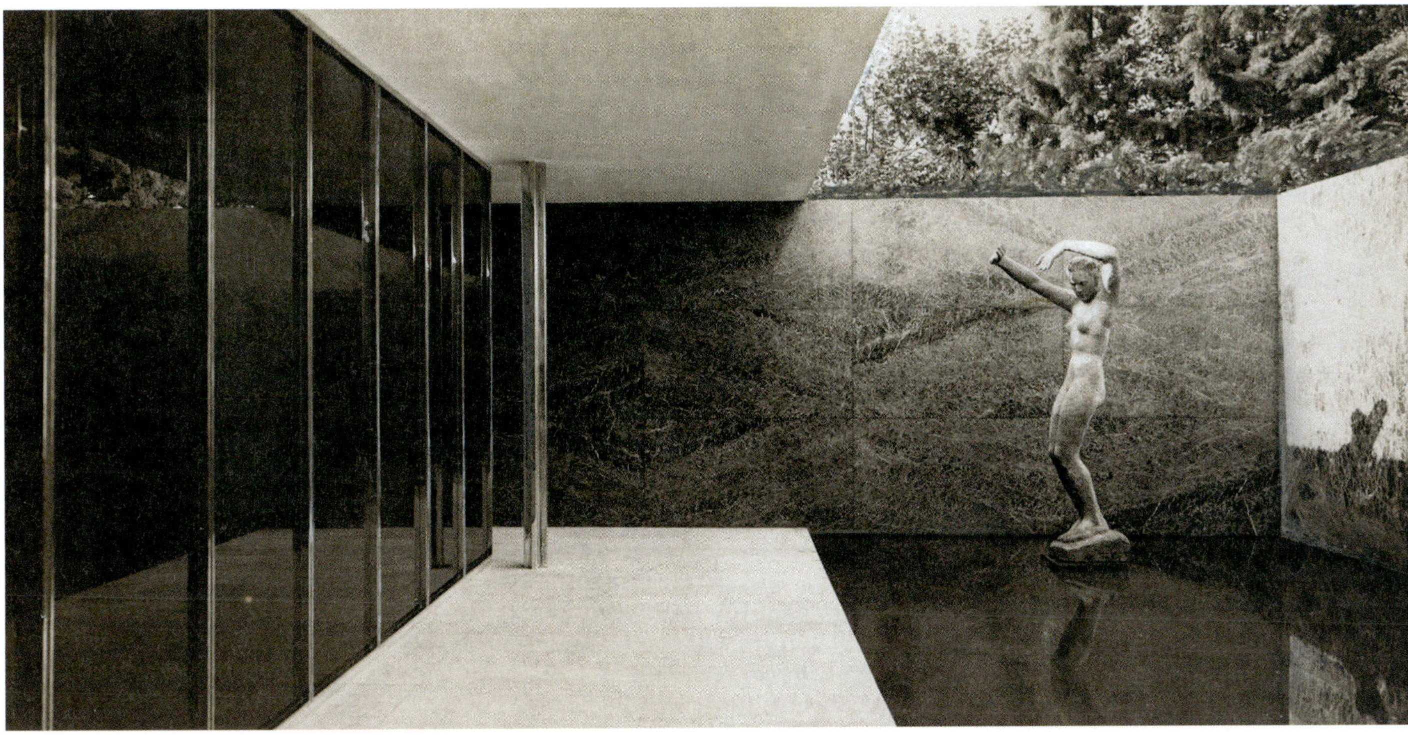

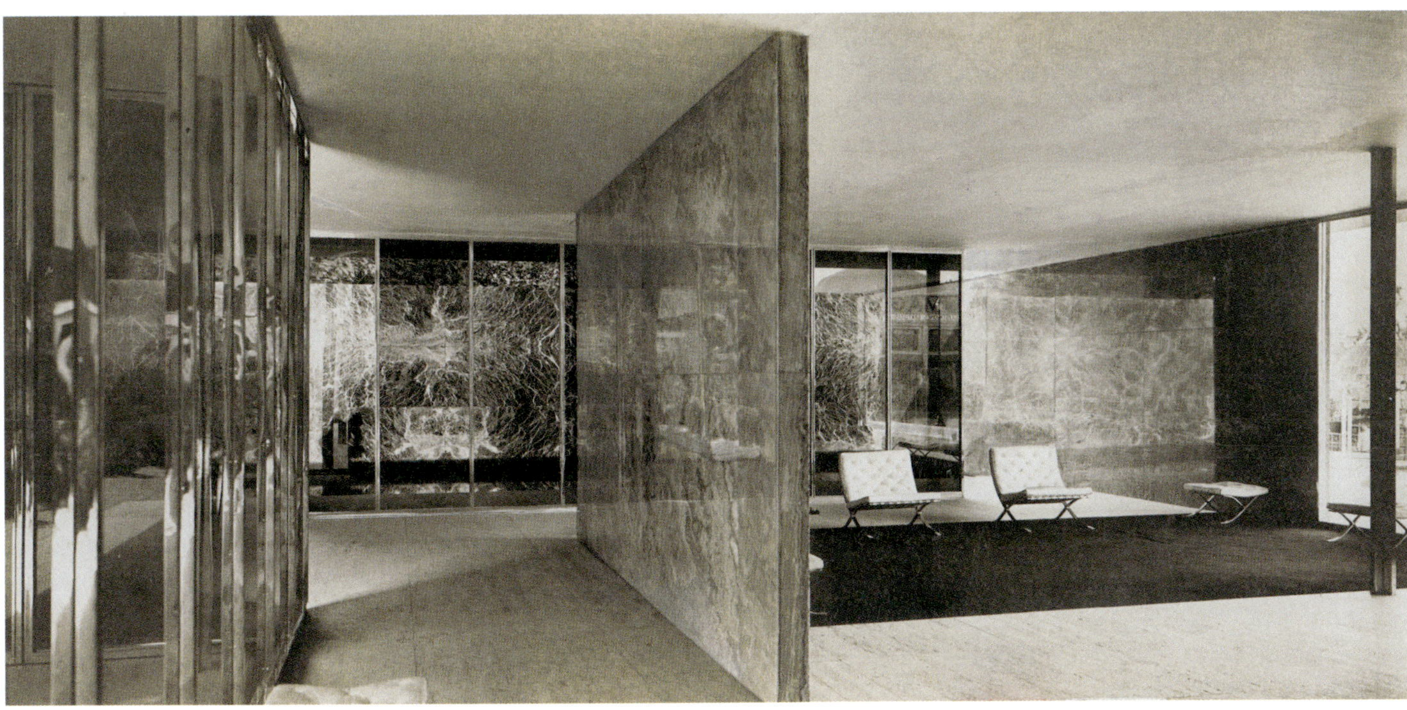

103

SASHA STONE

Pavilion by Mies van der Rohe to represent the German Reich at the Barcelona International Exposition, c. 1929

Two different views. Gelatin silver print, touched up in opaque white
11.2 × 22.5 cm. Berlinische Galerie

Jury-Free Art Show Berlin 1929, exhibition Ten Years of the Novembergruppe, no. 824 (according to press reports photographs of the pavilion)

ISABEL WÜNSCHE

THE NOVEMBER-GRUPPE WRITES ABSOLUTE FILM HISTORY

On 3 May 1925 the Novembergruppe, with the support of Universum Film AG (UFA), hosted a Sunday matinée in Berlin called *Absolute Film* [*Der absolute Film*]. On the programme were six moving image projects by French and German avant-garde artists: LUDWIG HIRSCHFELD-MACK'S *Colour Sonatina in Three Parts* [*Dreiteilige Farbensonatine*] from his *Reflected Colour Light Plays* [*Reflektorische Farbenspielen*], the abstract animations *Film is Rhythm* [*Film ist Rhythmus*] by HANS RICHTER, *Symphonie Diagonale* by VIKING EGGELING and *Opus II, III and IV* by WALTER RUTTMANN; and from France *Images mobiles — Ballet mécanique* by FERNAND LÉGER and DUDLEY MURPHY and *Entr'acte* by FRANCIS PICABIA and RENÉ CLAIR (fig. 07). UFA's 900-seat cinema on Kurfürstendamm was sold out, and so the event was repeated a week later. A third screening took place in Hanover on 22 May 1925 at the invitation of the *Kestner-Gesellschaft*.[1]

The UFA matinée is thought to have been the first public showing of abstract films in Germany and marks a watershed in experiments with absolute film, a genre that Rudolf Kurz in his 1926 book *Expressionismus und Film* defined as follows: "Story, plot, event are as rare in the absolute film as are conventional characters of any kind. The axiomatic exclusion of nature expels anything which might evoke the historical world. The elementary geometric shapes interact and within this composition the mind dramas unfold."[2]

VIKING EGGELING, HANS RICHTER and WALTER RUTTMANN were leading proponents of this new art form in Germany; all three were members of the Novembergruppe. Through the medium of film, they sought to combine the constituent elements of music and painting under a primacy of movement and time: the absolute film was to be "music for the eye" (EGGELING), "painting with time" (RUTTMANN) and "optical rhythm" (RICHTER). Their works deliberately dispense with the narrative structures adopted by plot-based cinema, which was influenced by literature and photography, and take their cue instead from the purely visual effects produced by the rhythmic movement of abstract shapes and colours.[3]

A Musical Projection of Coloured Light

The matinée opened with HIRSCHFELD-MACK'S presentation of his *Colour Sonatina in Three Parts*. In some ways it was the exception, as it was not strictly speaking an experimental abstract film, but a live colour-light performance produced by mechanical means. To a piano accompaniment, a team hidden behind a light box operated a series of projection lamps and various templates according to a specially written score (figs. 01).[4]

This polychromatic light display was composed of colourful squares, rectangles, triangles and circles travelling along separate pathways, multiplying and overlaying each other in diagonal cascades and in the process generating new shades of colour in the overlapping zones (figs. 02 and 03). The movement of the shapes and the alteration of the colours matched the music, which made it seem as though the polychromatic forms were dancing to the music and stopping whenever the music stopped. As the music grew louder or softer, so the colours became lighter or darker, and whenever the sound took on a greater complexity, the shapes increased in number.[5]

The original idea to experiment with coloured lights was born during an incident at the Bauhaus Lantern Festival in June 1922. An acetylene lamp had to be replaced during a performance of shadow play, in the process causing "a duplication of the shadows on the transparent paper".[6] LUDWIG HIRSCHFELD-MACK, one of the first generation of students at the Bauhaus in Weimar, put this observation to good use and soon had devised his own projection apparatus and polychromatic scripts: "a play of moving yellow, red, green and blue light fields with organically defined gradations" developing out of darkness into intense brightness alongside a synchronous musical sound track.[7]

HIRSCHFELD-MACK conceived his polychromatic plays as a way of taking the abstract paintings of his Bauhaus colleagues WASSILY KANDINSKY and PAUL KLEE a step further; the multiple projections transposed the implicit motion in abstract painting into real motion.[8] The invention of coloured light plays must also be seen as an inherent part of a reorientation at the Bauhaus with a shift away from the integration of arts and crafts and towards the connection of art with technology, as WALTER GROPIUS announced when opening the Bauhaus Exhibition in 1923.[9] LÁSZLÓ MOHOLY-NAGY, appointed by the Bauhaus in 1923, supported this trend. In his book *Malerei, Photographie, Film* [*Painting, Photography, Film*], published in the Bauhaus book series in 1925, he reproduced the score for the first three bars of the *Colour Sonatina in Three Parts (ultramarine-green)* and the notes by HIRSCHFELD-MACK, observing that its author had, in his opinion, been "the first to reveal the profusion of the most delicate transitions and unexpected variations of *coloured* planes in *motion*", creating a "movement of planes, prismatically controllable, which dissolves, conglomerates".[10] It was MOHOLY-NAGY who proposed marketing these polychromatic events as "Reflected Colour Displays".[11] In 1924 HIRSCHFELD-MACK began sounding out the potential for a practical application and commercial use of his polychromatic displays in theatres and advertising. This led him in 1925 to publish his own brochure about his "coloured light plays" entitled *Farbenlicht-Spiele: Wesen, Ziele, Kritiken*. The performances came to an end that same

01 A performance of Ludwig Hirschfeld-Mack's reflected coloured light plays, 1925

02 LUDWIG HIRSCHFELD-MACK *Coloured Light Plays (Sonatina II)*, reconstruction by Corinne Schweizer and Peter Böhm, 2000 *Absolute Film*, Novembergruppe matinée, 1925

03 LUDWIG HIRSCHFELD-MACK *Coloured Light Plays (Cross Play)*, reconstruction by Corinne Schweizer and Peter Böhm, 2000 *Absolute Film*, Novembergruppe matinée, 1925

01

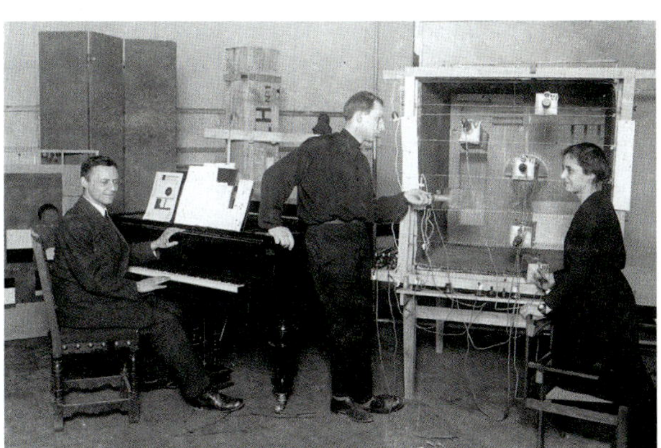

02

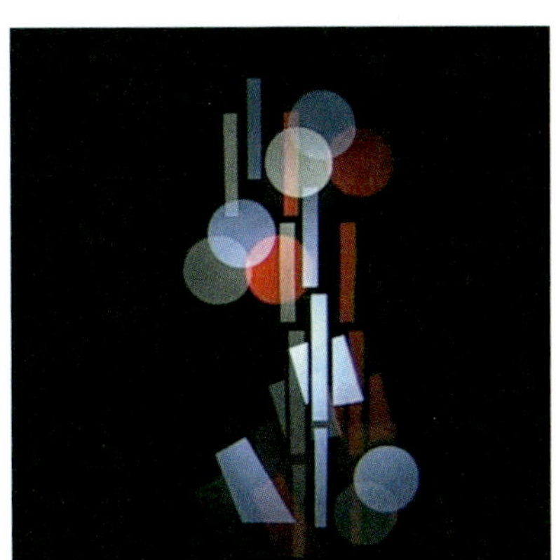

03

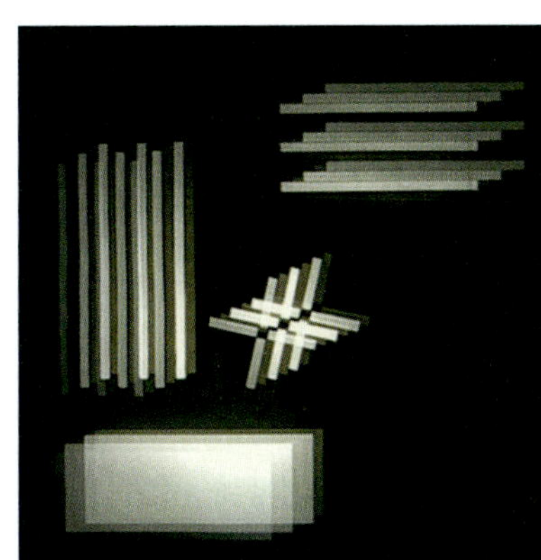

year, however, when the Bauhaus moved from Weimar to Dessau. The scripted light displays were not so very dissimilar in their effect and aesthetic from the abstract films screened at the matinée, because like the films they consisted of a continuous sequence of images. The only difference was the technical implementation: whereas the abstract films were produced on an animation stand and shown as a finished work, every performance of a coloured light play was unique and subject to a certain degree of randomness, given that the projection apparatus and dimmers were operated individually by hand.[12]

Painting with Time

The earliest examples of absolute film in Germany were WALTER RUTTMANN'S experimental shorts *Light-Play Opus I–IV* [*Lichtspiel Opus I–IV*]. RUTTMANN, who made his name with the montage *Berlin: Symphony of a Metropolis* [*Berlin—Die Sinfonie der Großstadt*] in 1927 and worked for UFA's advertising studio in the 1930s, approached film as a painter.[13] Speed, or rather "tempo", was to him a hallmark of the age. Attempts to depict movement in his paintings led him to adopt the medium of film, which he initially viewed solely in optical terms, as a form of moving images. To "lend artistic form to this entirely new way, sense of life", he talked of "painting with time": "An art for the eye, different from painting in that it plays out over time (like music) and that the artistic focus is not (as with a picture) to reduce a (real or formal) process to one moment, but precisely to develop the formal motif with time."[14]

In 1918 RUTTMANN produced his *Last Painting* [*Letztes Bild*] and turned to film. He built an animation desk that relied on a sequence of transparent, moving glass plates, had it patented and founded a company, Ruttmann-Film GmbH, based in Munich.[15] The public première of his twelve-minute *Light-Play Opus I* with a musical accompaniment by MAX BUTTING was held in Berlin on 27 April 1921. This was the first-ever public screening of an abstract film in Germany. RUTTMANN showed "an abstract play of shapes with circles and lines whose figures, fighting and uniting in harmony as they move, lured [him] towards ever new optical visions".[16] RUTTMANN carried on developing his cinematic ideas and perfecting his animation technique; in January 1922 *Opus II* was shown in Frankfurt am Main, 1924 brought *Opus III*, followed by *Opus IV* (1925). These three films were ultimately selected for the Novembergruppe matinée.

Opus II follows up on *Opus I*. It is an animation of amorphous, organic constructs and geometric shapes which expand, contract and are superimposed over other shapes; some sequences were tinted blue and red (fig. 04). *Opus III* is dominated by geometric shapes which rapidly blend into one another or are mutually overlaid; passages in red and blue alternate with sections in black and white. In *Opus IV* the interplay of rectangular shapes becomes a kinetic grid composition, black and white at first, then intensively blue and finally bright red (fig. 05). All in all, there is a shift away from the organic, softer animations in *Opus I* towards an increasingly geometric idiom and grid-like composition in *Opus IV*, just as there was a development towards Constructivism in the abstract painting of the 1920s.

RUTTMANN and his experiments soon attracted the attention of the cinema industry. In the 1920s he worked as an animator on commercial feature films, including Fritz Lang's *Die Nibelungen* (1924), Lotte Reininger's *The Adventures of Prince Achmed* [*Die Abenteuer des Prinzen Achmed*] (1924–1926) and the sequence *A Fantasy from Snowland and Tibet* [*Eine Phantasie aus dem Schneeland und Tibet*] for the film *Living Buddhas* [*Lebende Buddhas*] by Paul Wegener (1924). In addi-

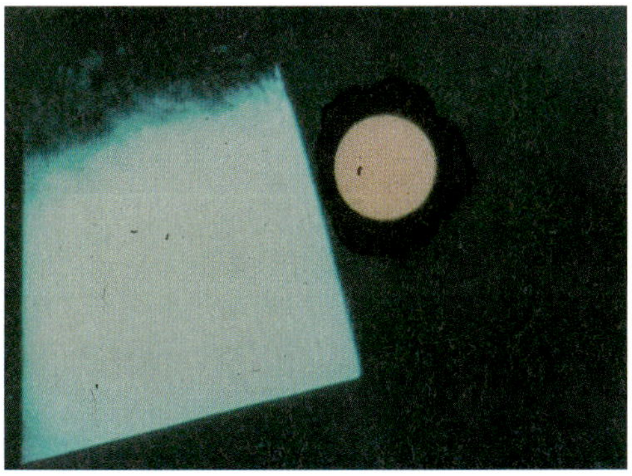

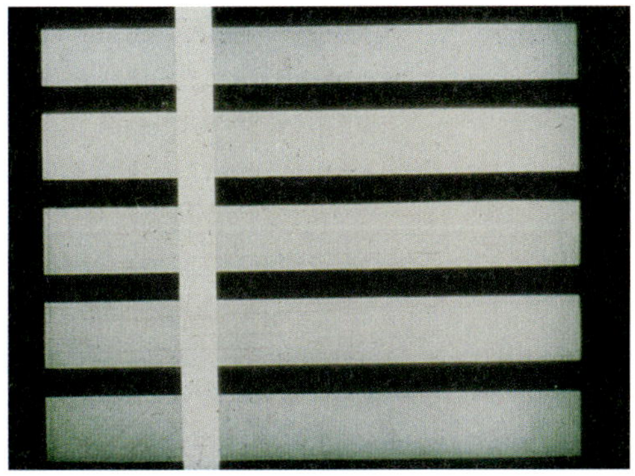

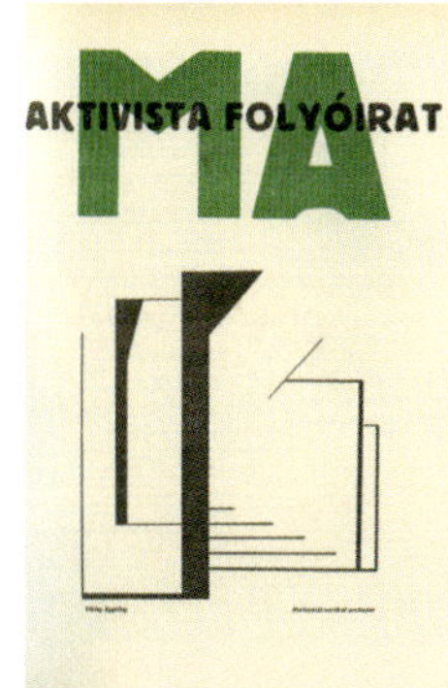

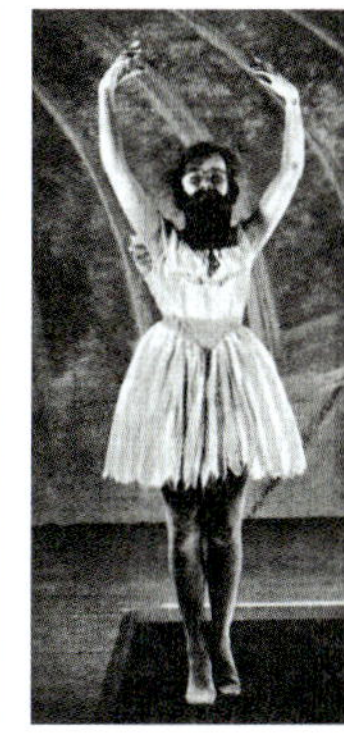

04 05 06 07

04 WALTER RUTTMANN
Opus I, 1922
Absolute Film, Novembergruppe matinée, 1925

05 WALTER RUTTMANN
Opus IV, 1925
Absolute Film, Novembergruppe matinée, 1925

06 VIKING EGGELING
Horizontal–Vertical Fair, cover of *MA* [*Today*], no. 8, August 1921

07 RENÉ CLAIR and FRANCIS PICABIA
Entr'acte, 1924
Absolute Film, Novembergruppe matinée, 1925

tion to this, he worked closely with Lore Leudesdorff to make twelve semi-abstract, multicolour advertising spots for Julius Pinschewer. RUTTMANN'S work had an enduring impact on later abstract film-makers, primarily via his influence on Oskar Fischinger, who had attended the first showing of *Light-Play Opus I* in 1921.[17] RUTTMANN himself declared in 1928 "art is no longer abstraction, but attitude"[18] and turned instead to talkies.

Music for the Eye

Like RUTTMANN, VIKING EGGELING and HANS RICHTER arrived at film from painting. The Swedish-born EGGELING had moved to Germany in 1897 and later lived in Italy, France and Switzerland. After the First World War he was active in the Dada movement in Zürich, where he met Hans Arp, Marcel Janco, Tristan Tzara and HANS RICHTER.[19] He and RICHTER came to Berlin in 1919 and joined the artistic avant-garde; both were members of the Novembergruppe. Soon afterwards they made their home on the Richter family estate at Klein Kölzig in Brandenburg, where they began experimenting with film.[20] It all began with EGGELING'S scrolls, rolls of paper up to 15 metres long containing pencil-drawn variations on graphic elements. One of these was *Horizontal–Vertical Fair* [*Horizontal-Vertikal-Messe*] (1919), a scroll with about 5000 separate drawings which was later turned into a ten-minute film. In 1920 the two men used EGGELING'S scrolls *Horizontal–Vertical Orchestra 1–3* when applying to UFA for support with their experiments.[21] A year later THEO VAN DOESBURG visited EGGELING and RICHTER in Klein Kölzig, and in May 1921 he published an article about their experiments with film in the magazine *De Stijl*.[22] That same year EGGELING published his programmatic essay *Theoretical Presentations of the Art of Movement* [*Elvi fejtegetések a mozgómuvészetröl*] in the Hungarian periodical *MA* [*Today*] (fig. 06). Explaining the illustrations, he writes: "The drawings reproduced here are key moments in processes conceived as motion. The works will be realized as film. The process itself: evolutions and revolutions composed as pure art (abstract shapes) rather like the musical events familiar to our ears."[23]

After a split with RICHTER in late 1921, EGGELING returned to Berlin, bought a hand-held camera and a projector, built an animation stand and carried on making his films. In 1923 he broke off the work on his unfinished project *Horizontal–Vertical Orchestra* and started instead on *Symphonie Diagonale*,[24] a black-and-white film composed from a handful of basic linear patterns. Over the course of the film these unfold and extend to reveal a sequence of extensions and variations. EGGELING'S templates consisted of figures he had cut out from paper or tin foil; while filming, he would cover them with black paper which was then gradually pulled away; he also cut figures into the paper.[25] He was assisted in this template animation by Erna Niemeyer, then a student at the Bauhaus in Weimar. On 5 November 1924 EGGELING showed his 149-metre-long silent film, which lasted a good seven minutes, for the first time at a private showing in Berlin. On 21 April 1925 the film was approved by the censor board, and on 3 May 1925 it was presented to the broader public at the matinée *Absolute Film*. EGGELING was unable to attend the screening of his only completed film, as he had been confined to hospital "for some months [...] at the Norbert-Krankenhaus in Schöneberg, Berlin", where he died on 19 May 1925.[26]

Like RUTTMANN, EGGELING wanted to produce 'painting in motion' and thus his own distinct genre of motion art. In the quest for a universal artistic language, he was guided by the rules of musical composition and the musical principle of counterpoint. The key elements in his silent films are movement and light. With the aid of *chiaroscuro*, changes of direction and a linear formal dynamic evolving out of curves, straight lines, harps and triangles, he sought to emphasize the temporal aspect and create an abstract formal idiom of universal validity.

Optical Rhythm

HANS RICHTER was introduced to experimental film by EGGELING; the two artists shared an interest in the pursuit of a genuine art of motion.[27] RICHTER, however, was less influenced by music. To him, film was "optical rhythm, presented by photo-technical means".[28] His artistic development was very much moulded by Dada; he had joined the Dadaists in Zürich in 1916. After the split with EGGELING at the end of 1921, RICHTER likewise returned to Berlin. He threw in his lot with the Dutch *De Stijl* group and the Constructivists, and from 1923 on, together with Werner Graeff and EL LISSITZKY and later LUDWIG MIES VAN DER ROHE and Friedrich Kiesler, he edited the journal *G: Material for Elementary Design* [*G: Material zur elementaren Gestaltung*].[29]

RICHTER'S first abstract film was *Rhythm 21* [*Rhythmus 21*], completed in Klein Kölzig in 1921, although he kept reworking it until 1923. On 6 July 1923 RICHTER gave *Rhythm 21* its first screening at the *Soirée du cœur à barbe* at the Théâtre Michel in Paris, and the work is still today regarded as a seminal film of the modernist era.[30] In this and the subsequent rhythm films, RICHTER used the play of light to articulate not only forms and space but also time by framing the animation of geometric shapes "in a consistent rhythm that pervades the whole image".[31]

Film is Rhythm was the programmatic title RICHTER chose in 1925 when he combined his abstract film experiments *Rhythm 21* and *Rhythm 23*. However, this abstract animation, the second item on the matinée programme, was in all likelihood not shown at the first screening of absolute films on 3 May 1925 as it was "not quite ready to present" and only featured on the bill at the repeat event on 10 May 1925.[32] The black-and-white film is made up of squares, rectangles and bars which "grow and vanish, leap or glide in well-articulated times and planned rhythms".[33] The film's impact is founded on contrasting alternations between light and dark, horizontal and vertical, big and small, fast and slow, reflecting RICHTER'S affinity with Constructivism. It resembles an animation of abstract paintings by THEO VAN DOESBURG, PIET MONDRIAN or Kazimir Malevich. Moreover, *Film is Rhythm* was the first film to use negative footage as a positive image.[34]

On the whole, contemporary cinema reviewers disliked the work. MOHOLY-NAGY described RICHTER'S film as an approach to visually implementing "a light-space-time continuum in the thesis of motion",[35] while Malevich responded to

RICHTER'S *Rhythm* films with an exposé for a collaborative Suprematist film called *Art and Problems of Architecture* [*Die Malerei und die Probleme der Architektur*]. The project was never completed.[36]

Rhythmic Play

Unlike the German films with their abstract composition and absolute rhythm, the French contributions focussed on parodies of various kinds and choreographies of everyday objects. They are fundamentally different from the German films because they "apply figurative and abstract forms but empty them of their normal significance and use them merely as expressions of their will to create art. With a gesture that is always amusing, they compel the natural object to appear as its own parody".[37] There were also fundamental differences in technique: whereas RICHTER, EGGELING and RUTTMANN produced their works on the animation stand, LÉGER and PICABIA mostly pieced theirs together from real-life footage.[38]

FERNAND LÉGER'S *Images mobiles—Ballet mécanique*, shot in France in 1924 with the American cameraman DUDLEY MURPHY, was first shown at the *International Exhibition of New Theatre Techniques* in Vienna in September 1924 and still ranks as a masterpiece of early experimental cinematic art.[39] The Dadaist film project was first initiated by MAN RAY and DUDLEY MURPHY, and it was Ezra Pound who later suggested that LÉGER could arrange the material (while MAN RAY withdrew from the project).[40] Although GEORGE ANTHEIL had composed music to accompany the work, it premiered as a silent film because the director and composer could not agree on how to resolve the problem of differing lengths.[41] For the matinée *Absolute Film* in May 1925, the work was entitled *Images Mobiles*.

The multi-faceted film reflects the influences and dissimilar styles of those who made it—MAN RAY in the close-ups of Kiki de Montparnasse, LÉGER in the composition and rhythm of the swing scene and the alienation of everyday objects, MURPHY in the technical sophistication of the kaleidoscopic elements. The film is a rapid sequence of different images: a Cubist, Chaplinesque character is followed by MURPHY'S wife Katherine on a garden swing; after her comes a swift alternation of everyday objects in motion, rotating mechanical parts and coloured shapes, interspersed with close-ups of made-up lips and eyes and a scenic snippet of a washerwoman climbing steps. The film combines animated geometries with photographic fragments of reality: "Dispensing with any form of plot, a rhythmic play of objects unfolds. Partial views of objects and people transmute as close-ups into symbolic wholes."[42] With the aid of lighting and motion, LÉGER alienated everyday objects to a state of abstraction.

The film was made without a script[43] and bears the hallmarks of *Léger's* response to the machine age after the catastrophe of the First World War, expressed in his "mechanical phase" when he sought to combine the abstraction of Constructivism with the anarchic absurdity of Dada to convey the dynamics of modern life. LÉGER was well networked within the European avant-garde, and he had already exhibited in Berlin with the Novembergruppe in 1920. EGGELING visited LÉGER in Paris in 1924, and HIRSCHFELD-MACK corresponded with him about his experiments with moving images in 1924–25. LÉGER'S montage of cinematic material with real-life footage influenced both RICHTER and RUTTMANN in the direction of their future film efforts. LEGÉR may have also been responsible for the inclusion of the last item on the UFA matinée, the film by RENÉ CLAIR.

Absurd Interlude

The French short *Entr'acte* by RENÉ CLAIR was premiered on 27 November 1924 as precisely that — an interlude during the break of a two-part ballet, *Relâche* by FRANCIS PICABIA, at the Théâtre des Champs-Élysées in Paris. Linking ballet and film was an innovation, an additional chapter in avant-garde efforts to combine painting, music, theatre and dance. The film itself, based on a storyboard by PICABIA consisting of eight bullet points (fig. 09), was produced thanks to a cross-genre collaboration between composer Eric Satie, painter FRANCIS PICABIA, solo dancer and choreographer Jean Börlin and director RENÉ CLAIR, who all appear in the film.[44]

The prologue shows PICABIA and Satie loading a canon in slow motion and then firing it at the audience in super-slow motion. This is followed by fast cuts and a series of unconnected images, as listed in the script, including two boxing gloves fighting, a game of chess between Duchamp and MAN RAY, a hunter taking aim at an ostrich egg that turns into a dove, and a ballerina who reveals herself to be a man with a beard (fig. 10). The film ends with a funeral procession, again in slow motion, as it follows along behind a camel-drawn hearse; the carriage careers out of control and the mourners rush along behind it in fast motion until it falls apart, leaving Börlin to rise from the coffin like a magician, waving his wand to make everything disappear.

Unlike the German contributions, *Entr'acte* and *Images mobiles* were not animations of abstract shapes, but sequences of unconnected visuals and scenes with moving images; CLAIR used a variety of special effects such as fast and slow motion, unusual camera angles and multiple exposures to create grotesques and surreal sequences. His cinematographic tricks met with huge enthusiasm, and the film was such a hit with the public that its director became a star of French cinema in the 1920s.[45]

The six moving image projects presented by the Novembergruppe at their matinée demonstrate the broad spectrum of experiments in abstract film in the early 1920s.[46] The artists shared a fascination for the speed and rhythms of modern life; they believed that the phenomenon of acceleration in the technical era called for a new art and were on a quest to come up with new, innovative formats for an authentic art of motion. In their film experiments, they sought to reflect the experience of accelerated reality by means of movement, rhythm and rapid alternations of place and time.

1 Wilmesmeier 1994. See also www.kunstwissenschaft.tu-berlin.de/fileadmin/i2/Forschung/Ufa_NG.pdf (accessed on 4 June 2018).

2 Rudolf Kurtz, *Expressionismus und Film*, Berlin 1926 (reprint Zürich 2007), p. 92.

3 Scheugl and Schmidt 1974, vol. 1, p. 29. See also Noll Brinckmann 1997, pp. 247–275.

4 Stasny 2000, pp. 94–112; see also www.kunstwissenschaft.tu-berlin.de/fileadmin/i2/Forschung/Hirschfeld-Mack.pdf (accessed on 4 June 2018).

5 Ibid., p. 99.

6 Hirschfeld-Mack, *Farbenlicht-Spiele. Wesen, Ziele, Kritiken*, Weimar 1925, p. 4.

7 Ibid.

8 Ibid., p. 2; see also Düchting 1996, pp. 49–55.

9 *Staatliches Bauhaus Weimar 1919–1923* (exhib. cat. Weimar, Bauhaus), Weimar 1923.

10 László Moholy-Nagy, *Malerei, Photographie, Film*, München 1925, p. 16. The score and notes are reproduced on pp. 72–73 and 75. In the English translation, *Painting, Photography, Film*, trans. by Janet Seligman, Cambridge MA, the quotation is on p. 21 and the explanations and score are on pp. 82–83.

11 Stasny 2000, pp. 97–98.

12 Hoormann 2003, p. 161.

13 Goergen 1989.

14 Walter Ruttmann, "Malerei mit Zeit" (ca. 1919–20), in: Kiening and Adolf 2012, p. 52.

15 www.difarchiv.deutsches-filminstitut.de/dt2tp0051.htm; cf. also www.kunstwissenschaft.tu-berlin.de/fileadmin/i2/Forschung/Ruttmann.pdf (accessed on 4 June 2018).

16 Ibid.

17 Moritz 1993, p. 8.

18 Walter Ruttmann, "Die 'absolute' Mode", in: *Film-Kurier*, no. 30,

Berlin, 3 February 1928, 1. Reprinted in: Kiening and Adolf 2012, p. 219.

19 O'Konor 1971.

20 Elder, Richter and Eggeling 2007, pp. 3–53.

21 Zglinicki 1956, p. 596.

22 Theo van Doesburg, "Abstracte Filmbeelding", in: *De Stijl*, vol. 4, no. 5, June 1921, pp. 71–75.

23 Viking Eggeling, "Elvi Fejtegetések a Mozgomüvészetröl", in: *MA [Today]*, vol. 6, no. 8, 1921, p. 105.

24 Elder, Richter and Eggeling 2007, p. 34.

25 www.kunstwissenschaft.tu-berlin.de/fileadmin/i2/Forschung/Eggeling.pdf (accessed on 4 June 2018).

26 Hein and Herzogenrath 1978, p. 46.

27 Together they wrote the manifesto *Universal Language [Universelle Sprache]*, sending it to influential figures and UFA. See Wolf 1989; see also www.kunstwissenschaft.tu-berlin.de/fileadmin/i2/Forschung/Eggeling.pdf (accessed on 4 June 2018).

28 Hans Richter, *G. Material zur elementaren Gestaltung*, nos. 5–6, April 1926; see www.kunstwissenschaft.tu-berlin.de/fileadmin/i2/Forschung/Richter.pdf (accessed on 4 June 2018).

29 Richter 1973; Hofmann 1989.

30 Bareither 2012.

31 Goergen 2003; see also www.berlinale.de/de/archiv/jahres¬archive/2014/02_programm_2014/02_Filmdatenblatt_2014_20148101.php (accessed on 4 June 2018).

32 Roland Schacht, "Absolute Filme", in: *Kölnische Zeitung*, 15 May 1925. See Wilmesmeier 1994, p. 22.

33 Hans Richter, see www.kunst¬wissenschaft.tu-berlin.de/fileadmin/i2/Forschung/Richter.pdf (accessed on 4 June 2018).

34 Scheugl and Schmidt 1974, vol. 2, p. 745.

35 Ref. in note 10.

36 Benson and Shatskikh 2013, pp. 52–68; Tupitsyn 2002.

37 Ref. in note 2.

38 Wilmesmeier 1994, p. 73.

39 Freeman 1987, pp. 28–45.

40 www.kunstwissenschaft.tu-berlin.de/fileadmin/i2/Forschung/Leger_Murphy.pdf (accessed on 4 June 2018).

41 Antheil's composition lasted about 30 minutes, but the film only about 16 minutes, as Léger allegedly deleted nude scenes. Antheil then turned his film score into a concert piece called *"Ballet Mécanique" (Ballet pour Instruments Mécaniques et Percussion)*. Horak 1995, pp. 129 and 135.

42 Zglinicki 1956, p. 601.

43 "C'est le premier film sans scenario," announced the opening credits, see www.cineclub¬decaen.com/realisat/leger/balletmecanique.htm (accessed on 4 June 2018).

44 Albersmeier 2004, pp. 215–234. See also www.kunst¬wissenschaft.tu-berlin.de/file¬admin/i2/Forschung/Entracte.pdf (accessed on 4 June 2018).

45 Cossart 1985; Billard 1998.

46 Turvey 2011.

ANDREAS ZEISING / SARA BEIMDIEKE

A MODERATE REVOLT

The Novembergruppe on Air in 1925 with "Young Writers and Composers"

"At last — after delaying for far too long, the broadcasting station in Berlin has decided to grant the young, vibrant art of our day space in its programme," crowed the radio magazine *Der Deutsche Rundfunk* in 1925.[1] The enthusiastic announcement heralded a live performance to be aired on 11 May 1925 under the title *An Evening with the Novembergruppe*. Between language courses, edifying lectures and chess challenges, the somewhat unadventurous Berliner Rundfunk would serve its listeners avant-garde fare of a kind they had never yet experienced (fig. 01).[2]

The soirée came at a time when radio, first rolled out in 1923, was expected not only by ministries and broadcasting corporations but also by the critical public to pursue the utopian mission of providing the 'broad masses' with 'intellectual elevation'.[3] If, in May 1925, the *Vossische Zeitung* referred to "radio as an educator", it was reflecting a mainstream consensus: "Yes, it is a school of the masses [...], a true public education institute, of which, as yet evolving, great things can come."[4] Regardless of the real needs of its listeners, who were in no sense consulted about the content of programmes, those responsible saw radio as a tool for introducing sections of the population who had not had much schooling to high-brow culture.

Their attitude to the artistic avant-garde, on the other hand, was ambivalent, although there were efforts to open radio up as a 'stage' for current art. After all, a medium seen as democratic should also provide a mouthpiece for the freedom for the arts enshrined in the constitution of the republic.[5] Initially, music programming relied on the classics and on light entertainment, but in 1924 more time was already made available for contemporary music, with dedicated slots created in the schedule.[6] Much time was also devoted to authors' readings, including 'new literature', when quite a few writers who were active on the political left also had their chance at the microphone.[7] All things considered, radio fulfilled the conditions for popularizing the avant-garde to an unprecedented degree. The Novembergruppe, which had been calling for popular education ever since its foundation, seemed an ideal partner for the task.

From the Song of the Blackbird to the Fall of Sin — the Lineup for the Novembergruppe's Evening on Air

For the Novembergruppe, organizing soirées with a mixed programme of music and other genres was nothing new.[8] Since 1922 the group had been admitting writers and composers to its ranks as well as visual artists.[9] Some of those soirées had been held in the smaller hall of Vox-Haus on Potsdamer Strasse. From 1923, this building had also accommodated the transmission studio for the *Funk-Stunde*, as the Berlin-based broadcaster was renamed in 1924, although it was not until May 1925 that one of these soirées was actually heard on the radio. Nils Grosch correctly observes that "a massive reorientation in the format of public performance"[10] began that evening when, instead of addressing a hand-picked circle of educated listeners as in the past, the Novembergruppe was exposed to the broadest of audiences: by that point in time, the station already had about 150,000 registered subscribers.

The credit for this particular event goes to the painter HANS SIEBERT VON HEISTER,[11] who was not only a co-founder and active member of the Novembergruppe but, as chance would have it, also editor-in-chief of the broadcasting magazine *Der Deutsche Rundfunk*. VON HEISTER, who earned a reputation as a critical journalist in the Weimar Republic, entered the field of radio journalism, like so many others, as a complete outsider, and alongside this work he continued to exhibit with the Novembergruppe.[12] Apparently unburdened by conflicts of interest, he used his prominent position to promote the group's activities among the listening public. From 1926, speaking at the microphone, he reported regularly to listeners from the Great Berlin Art Exhibition at Lehrter Bahnhof. The show was, after all, a flagship for Prussian art funding, and the Novembergruppe was a collective participant (fig. 02).[13]

All we know today about the radio schedule for the evening of 11 May 1925 has been derived from announcements in the press: during a live transmission from the Vox-Haus studio, "young writers and composers" would put together a 90-minute programme of music and recitations.[14] According to the original plan, the sculptor RUDOLF BELLING was going to open the proceedings with some observations on the "origin and task" of the Novembergruppe.[15] A retrospective report reveals, however, that his place was taken by the painter ARTHUR SEGAL,[16] who would later feature regularly on the radio.[17] We can only speculate about the reasons for this. Apparently, it was considered expedient for a fine artist to initiate the evening with a keynote address.

There were seven items on the bill for the soirée. After SEGAL'S introduction, musical and literary contributions alternated. The three composers whose music was heard that evening were not just leading proponents of contemporary music in Berlin; they had also been among the first musicians to join the Novembergruppe in 1922.

MAX BUTTING, who headed the music section, was perhaps the best person to represent his colleagues' creative response to the new medium of radio. In 1926 he was appointed to the cultural advisory board for the *Funk-Stunde*, which supervised programmes in the fields of art, science and education. The difficulty involved in proposing a proponent of New Music as a member of this body is well illustrated by the objections raised against his nomination by the management of the time, fearing "the one-sided musical perspective of Mr Butting, who in our assessment would exclusively seek to present only the hypermodern music that meets his own taste".[18] From 1928 BUTTING was, moreover, Professor of Radio Composition at the Rundfunkversuchsstelle, Berlin's experimental radio laboratory,[19] where he was able to reflect upon matters such as radio technology and the listening environment.[20]

BUTTING'S *Little Pieces for a String Quartet* [*Kleine Stücke für Streichquartett*] op. 26 were on the programme for the Novembergruppe evening. They were performed by the Havemann Quartet, whose first violin, GUSTAV HAVEMANN, also belonged to the association. The *Little Pieces* marked a major shift in BUTTING'S work, for he had recently resolved to enhance the clarity, simplicity and concision of his musical statement.[21] The instrumentation met a criterion for good radio music later defined by BUTTING, when he declared chamber music to be especially suited to the medium.[22] But clear sentence structure and phrasing as well as easily intelligible themes also became pivotal characteristics of works designed for radio in the ensuing years as composers sought to facilitate the musical experience for listeners at their wireless sets.[23]

BUTTING implemented the demands he himself had formulated by devoting each of his *Little Pieces* to a particular aspect of musical expression or compositional technique:[24] for the sedate No. 1 he built partly on rigorous imitation; No. 3, a march, gradually acquires density before a triple *fortissimo* fades into a *piano*, while No. 4 is a dreamy meditation in D minor and No. 8 surges forward on a wave of staccati and repeated notes. In granting the musicians freedom to choose the number and sequence of the ten short pieces, BUTTING both established a correlation with the Expressionist sabotage of cycles[25] and acknowledged the evolution of music designed specifically for radio: the suspicion that the attention span of wireless listeners might be shorter than that of a concert audience encouraged more modest formats, often combined in loose sequence into larger formations.[26]

The composer HEINZ TIESSEN, like BUTTING, set great store by radio, as it would enable a wider audience to participate in contemporary music. The "active involvement of the broadest sections of the people in musical programmes on the radio" was, he felt, an "ideal condition" worth striving for.[27] At the Evening with the Novembergruppe, TIESSEN personally performed his *Three Pieces for Piano* [*Drei Klavierstücke*] op. 31, which demonstrate his enthusiasm for the song of the blackbird. For many decades, TIESSEN systematically recorded blackbirds, culminating in 1953 in his book *Musik der Natur*. He resolutely wove the sounds, which he felt resembled modern music, into his compositions, scaling "triadic motifs" into "harmonic imperceptibility"[28] in a desire to generate new material independent of human creativity.[29]

After the in some ways sombre No. 1, the *Andante* which evolves slowly but is rich in contrasts, he picked one of the most complex blackbird songs he knew for No. 2,[30] letting its motifs define the entire movement. Like the natural call of a bird, No. 2 often leaves pauses after a phrase, and the score contains suggestions and dotted notes. No. 3 offers many variations, following on thematically from No. 2 with high-register sequences in the opening section reminiscent of birdsong or evoking a musical description of flight. The second part is basically songful with a tripping melody line, but TIESSEN also inserts extracts from popular music — sounds in keeping with the radio repertoire of those years.

Although TIESSEN'S op. 31 was not specifically written for radio, it does meet criteria that were defined at the time for broadcast compositions. His pieces supply the requisite consistency: in No. 2, for example, the ear can easily follow the blackbird song in the treble key. They have a balanced dynamic, a clear structure and recognizable motifs. The choice of the piano likewise confirms an awareness of how music is heard over the radio, for it was soon noticed that smaller ensembles ensured better transmission quality.[31] Like BUTTING'S Little Pieces, TIESSEN'S op. 31 was a loose constellation of separate items that did not explicitly constitute a cycle — another criterion for good radio music as defined in the mid-1920s.

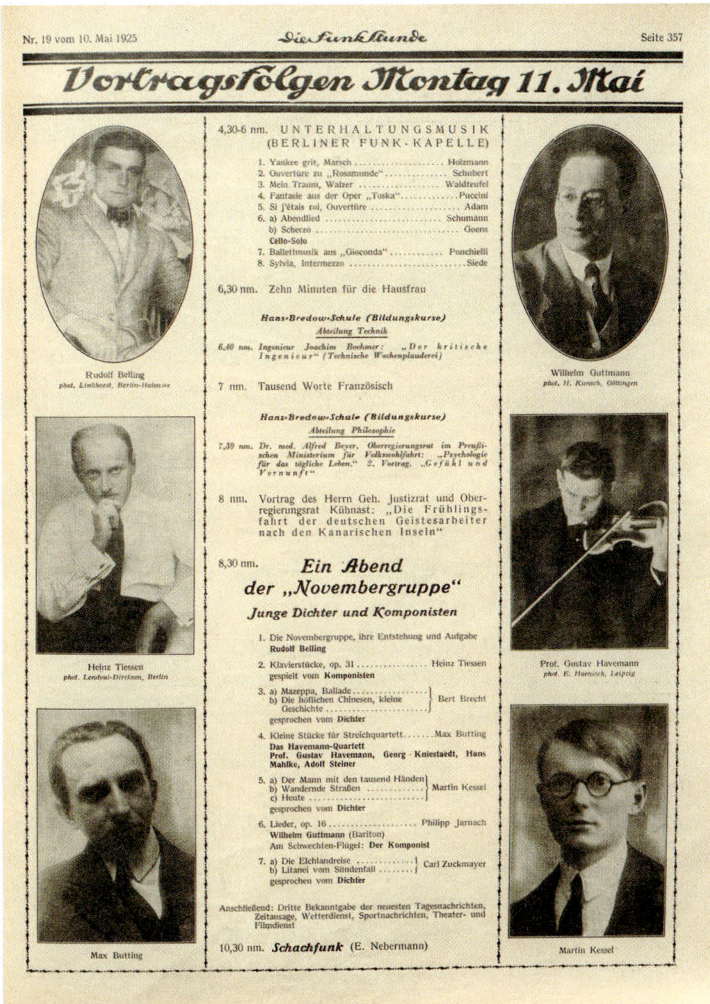

Nr. 19 vom 10. Mai 1925 Die Funk-Stunde Seite 357

Vortragsfolgen Montag 11. Mai

4,30-6 nm. UNTERHALTUNGSMUSIK (BERLINER FUNK-KAPELLE)

1. Yankee grit, Marsch .... Holzmann
2. Ouvertüre zu „Rosamunde" .... Schubert
3. Mein Traum, Walzer .... Waldteufel
4. Fantasie aus der Oper „Toska" .... Puccini
5. Si j'étais roi, Ouvertüre .... Adam
6. a) Abendlied .... Schumann
   b) Scherzo .... Goens
   Cello-Solo
7. Ballettmusik aus „Gioconda" .... Ponchielli
8. Sylvia, Intermezzo .... Siede

6,30 nm. Zehn Minuten für die Hausfrau

Hans-Bredow-Schule (Bildungskurse)
Abteilung Technik

6,40 nm. Ingenieur Joachim Boehmer: „Der kritische Ingenieur" (Technische Wochenplauderei)

7 nm. Tausend Worte Französisch

Hans-Bredow-Schule (Bildungskurse)
Abteilung Philosophie

7,30 nm. Dr. med. Alfred Beyer, Oberregierungsrat im Preußischen Ministerium für Volkswohlfahrt: „Psychologie für das tägliche Leben." 2. Vortrag. „Gefühl und Vernunft"

8 nm. Vortrag des Herrn Geh. Justizrat und Oberregierungsrat Kühnast: „Die Frühlingsfahrt der deutschen Geistesarbeiter nach den Kanarischen Inseln"

8,30 nm. ***Ein Abend der „Novembergruppe"***
Junge Dichter und Komponisten

1. Die Novembergruppe, ihre Entstehung und Aufgabe
   Rudolf Belling
2. Klavierstücke, op. 31 .... Heinz Tiessen
   gespielt vom **Komponisten**
3. a) Mazeppa, Ballade ....
   b) Die höflichen Chinesen, kleine Geschichte .... } Bert Brecht
   gesprochen vom **Dichter**
4. Kleine Stücke für Streichquartett .... Max Butting
   Das Havemann-Quartett
   Prof. Gustav Havemann, Georg Kniestaedt, Hans Mahlke, Adolf Steiner
5. a) Der Mann mit den tausend Händen
   b) Wandernde Straßen ....
   c) Heute .... } Martin Kessel
   gesprochen vom **Dichter**
6. Lieder, op. 16 .... Philipp Jarnach
   Wilhelm Guttmann (Bariton)
   Am Schwechten-Flügel: **Der Komponist**
7. a) Die Elchlandreise ....
   b) Litanei vom Sündenfall .... } Carl Zuckmayer
   gesprochen vom **Dichter**

Anschließend: Dritte Bekanntgabe der neuesten Tagesnachrichten, Zeitansage, Wetterdienst, Sportnachrichten, Theater- und Filmdienst

10,30 nm. ***Schachfunk*** (E. Nebermann)

Rudolf Belling
phot. Linkhorst, Berlin-Halensee

Wilhelm Guttmann
phot. H. Kunsch, Göttingen

Heinz Tiessen
phot. Lendvai-Dircksen, Berlin

Prof. Gustav Havemann
phot. E. Hoenisch, Leipzig

Max Butting

Martin Kessel

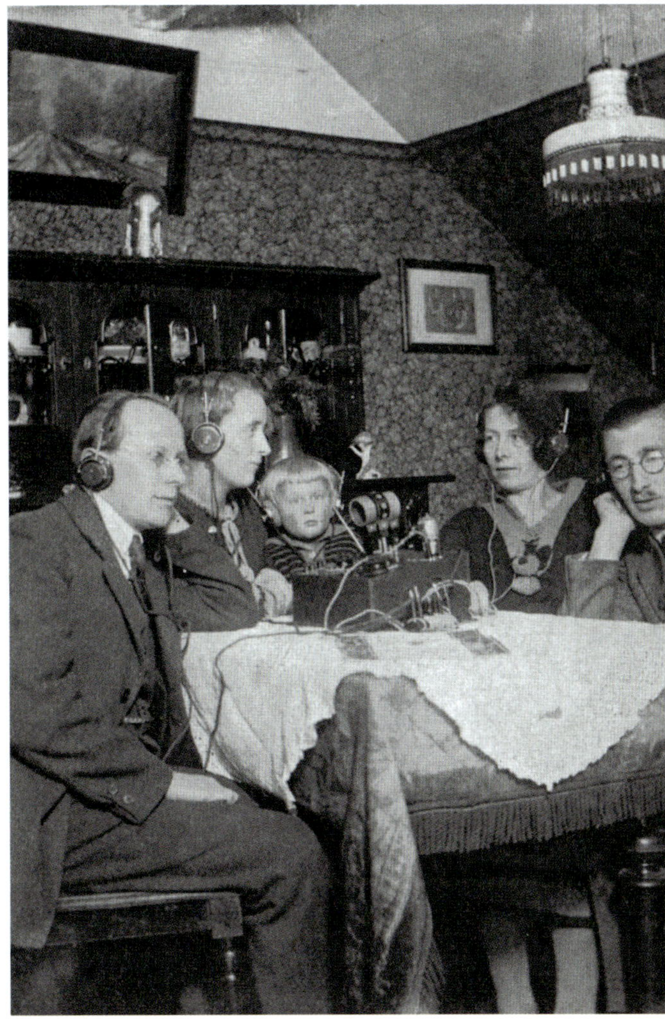

01 The programme for the Novembergruppe Evening on 11 May 1925 is announced in *Funk-Stunde*

02 Early wireless listeners, c. 1926

The third musical contribution was PHILIPP JARNACH'S *Five Songs* [*Fünf Gesänge*] op. 15, performed by the baritone Wilhelm Guttmann and accompanied, just as it had been at the sixth Novembergruppe soirée the previous year, by the composer himself.[32] JARNACH, the composer most frequently featured at musical evenings by the group,[33] was equally positive about radio and called for "the fullest investigations into its acoustic properties" in order to improve the quality of musical transmissions.[34]

In terms of style, JARNACH'S Songs reflect the quest for a new sonic idiom which, like TIESSEN and BUTTING, he did not equate with Schönberg's twelve-tone method but rather with an extension of tonality.[35] The "thoughtful" or "pensive" touch that characterized his work in the minds of his contemporaries[36] is also evident in his Songs. The composer chose lyrics of very different styles — modern poetry by authors like Rainer Maria Rilke and Stefan George, but also romantic verse written by Heinrich Heine or taken from the folk collection *Des Knaben Wunderhorn* — ordering the songs to highlight the contrast between modern and romantic texts.[37] JARNACH blends the words and music into a unity when, in No. 1 ("Song of the Sea"), the advancing waves can be heard in the quavers of the piano accompaniment or when, in No. 5 ("From a Stormy Night"), thunder seems to rumble through the striking chords and the hemidemisemiquavers as they rise and fall.

Like the works by TIESSEN and BUTTING, JARNACH'S Songs — individually composed between 1919 and 1922 — do not constitute a cycle but were first published as five separate scores without a common title.[38] If they were chosen for the radio evening, then probably for their cantabile and instrumentation, as piano and song with their different textures were felt to come across well on the radio. Other factors that made them ideal material for transmission were the absence of outlying pitch and the use of moderate tempi.[39]

If we consider the musical input as a whole, it is clear that the choices had been carefully considered and that a sensitive ear had been given to the music and the fledgling mass medium. What the listeners heard was perhaps not a representative cross-section of New Music, but it was certainly a diverse presentation of contemporary composition: the works on the programme had been written for different musical formations — a string quartet, voice, a piano soloist — and reflected a variety of styles.

Whether the literary contributions that evening were selected to match the music in any way remains a matter for speculation. Bertolt Brecht, MARTIN KESSEL and Carl Zuckmayer were certainly 'young' writers, and yet, as Helga Kliemann pointed out, the Novembergruppe pursued very little independent literary activity.[40] Brecht and Zuckmayer were presumably happy to grasp this opportunity, but we cannot conclude from this that they fostered an intimate relationship with the association. Only MARTIN KESSEL was part of the closer entourage.

All three writers read their works personally. As with the musical items, their contributions were 'miniatures' that would not overtax the listeners' attention. After TIESSEN'S *Pieces*, the ever-enterprising Brecht kicked off with his *Ballade of Mazeppa* [*Ballade von Mazeppa*] and the prose work *The Polite Chinese* [*Die höflichen Chinesen*], both written especially for the occasion. Two days before the Novembergruppe soirée, the *Berliner Börsen-Courier* introduced its readers to the "polite Chinese" whom the poet was about to "speak into the radio".[41] Whether this in any way helped listeners to comprehend Brecht's cryptic exploration of Taoist philosophy is another matter. Later items that evening were readings by MARTIN KESSEL and CARL ZUCKMAYER, including the latter's *Litany of the Fall of Man* [*Litanei vom Sündenfall*], which had recently been printed in Paul Westheim's *Kunstblatt*.[42]

"Evening of Experiment" — the Response in the Press

All in all, compared with what broadcasting had been offering the audience to date, the *Evening with the Novembergruppe* can be described as experimental and novel, but not as revolutionary. There are no sources to tell us whether the items were linked by a presenter, although it is unlikely. In all probability there was no thematic framework to transform this 'pot-pourri' into a serial whole. The way these literary and musical performances were strung together, a format not repeated at any future evening hosted by the Novembergruppe, can be rated as quite conventional, even if the selection was thoughtful.

If the musical contributions were by no means particularly progressive, that was probably a deliberate policy. The literary input likewise shied away from provocative form or content, let alone political positioning. VON HEISTER was no doubt correct to call this a "fairly moderate programme".[43] The circumspection was not solely due to radio's profile as a medium for mainstream consensus. It also reflected the objectives pursued by the Novembergruppe now that artistic rebellion had ebbed away: the aim was not to negate existing culture, but to establish forms of art which would retain their validity over time.

In terms of radio history, the evening broadcast from Berlin might be seen as a catalyst for rapprochement between the avant-garde and the medium. Radio critics responded with enthusiasm. In his review for the professional journal *Funk*, broadcasting journalist Lothar Band put in a fundamental plea for treating the event as a benchmark against which such activities would be measured in coming years: "Surely radio must offer its listeners an opportunity to think about the nature of the latest future-hungry art? The purpose of such an evening is not to propagate such art; but it does provide an opportunity and encourages the thoughtful listener to reflect."[44] VON HEISTER, too, claimed to be championing the cause of listeners by arguing that the medium of radio had now found its true vocation, which was to acquaint people with all the phenomena of the present day, however controversial.[45]

What listeners sitting by their loudspeakers made of all this we do not know. Some idea of the impact is conveyed by a review published by Hans Philipp Weitz in the *Berliner Tageblatt* on 17 May 1925: "Then evening of experiments (also necessary): 'Novembergruppe'. Views of the impartial audience (all classes) would be more interesting here than verdict of initiated critic. This one merely says: the new should be publicized. Must then prove its mettle. Best for new creators (especially writers) to speak for themselves. But take note: as long as they can speak. Sadly, BERT BRECHT and MARTIN KESSEL clearly cannot. Content damaged by delivery. CARL ZUCKMAYER'S self-interpretation by contrast excellent. Composers did not depart too much from familiar line. Havemann Quartet sounded melodious. Popular evening showed orchestra truly well-trained artistically. Vocal tercet clearly rendered, only at times too much tremolo in soprano for microphone."[46]

Apart from this slightly ambivalent praise, the arts pages in the daily newspapers were relatively quiet on the subject. Radio was still seen as a medium that could not seriously compete with the concert hall. But what was the response of the target group, the 'broad mass' of wireless subscribers? In HEISTER'S retrospective assessment their interest was anything but positive: "The impact of the evening among listeners was colossal — but in a negative sense. Radio subscribers were outraged, showered the broadcaster with countless letters about how dare they subject them to such stuff."[47] Lothar Band likewise reported later that the evening had "met with objections from a large section of the audience".[48] Did that mean the attempt to popularize the avant-garde via radio had crashed before it had really taken off? Or was the effort simply marred by conceptual weaknesses?

Band was no doubt right to conclude that more of an introduction would have been appropriate to prepare listeners who may have been awaiting entertainment for the uncustomary experience.[49] It is worth bearing in mind that on the day the Novembergruppe was showcased the radio station had begun the afternoon with a medley of light classical music of quite a different kind. It included things like a march by the American Aby Holzmann (*Yankee Grit*) and a waltz by the Frenchman Émile Waldteufel, as well as various extracts from popular operas. This was the sort of selection usually offered to listeners for pleasure. The corporation's own illustrated magazine had laconically announced the Novembergruppe evening by saying that listeners would be introduced "to modern production",[50] but this was hardly sufficient to generate understanding and acceptance among average listeners. In this respect, the situation in 1925 was not so very different from the conservative taste in music that reigns today among the broader public, as a glance at the concert diaries of major concert halls will confirm. Recitations of contemporary poetry on the radio must also have sounded strange in many ears. The *Funk-Stunde* in Berlin had only recently incorporated such readings into its programme, appointing the writer Hermann Kasack as editor. "Unknown fare which does not attract the public status it deserves, not least because prejudice and indifference pass it by, is supposed be made known as widely as possible," concluded an article in the *Berliner Börsen-Courier* on 2 May 1925 on the matter, although in the same breath it criticized the "dubious nature" of the enterprise, given that the "radio effect" and the glare of publicity tended to undermine the intimate essence of poetry.[51]

As statements like this reveal, in May 1925 both broadcasters and listeners were a long way removed from appraising the education value of the medium or, indeed, from a sophisticated understanding of how radio communication might work. The *Evening with the Novembergruppe* exemplifies above all one thing: that to present and popularize modern art it is not enough simply to distribute it through a 'media channel'. Arousing listeners' interest requires more than radio-oriented performance formats, even though, as this essay has tried to show, the challenge was tackled here with the best of intentions. Nevertheless, this new awareness of radio as a mass medium, epitomized by the *Evening with the Novembergruppe*, prompted many avant-garde musicians to rethink their role and to "break away from the aestheticist, work-based approach of the pre-war period".[52]

The Novembergruppe did not repeat the experiment of 11 May 1925. This was only partly because TIESSEN, BUTTING and JARNACH left the association in 1926 after disputes about the conflicted relationship between mechanical music, commercial music and New Music.[53] The soirée of 1925 was not the last musical and literary evening organized by the Novembergruppe, but it was the last one to be broadcast live on air.[54]

1 Hans Siebert von Heister, "Ein Abend der Novembergruppe", in: *Der Deutsche Rundfunk*, 1925, no. 19, pp. 1197–1199, here 1197.

2 Some of the present essay is based on Zeising 2018, pp. 105–119.

3 For essentials about radio history see Lerg 1980; Leonhard 1997.

4 P.W., "Radio als Erzieher", in: *Vossische Zeitung*, 8 May 1925, no. 216.

5 See Kratz-Kessemeier 2008, esp. pp. 34, 146–165 and 284–301.

6 Martin Thrun, "Neue Musik im Sende-Alltag des Rundfunks der Weimarer Republik", in: *Das Orchester*, year 10, 1996, vol. 44, pp. 2–10, here p. 5.

7 See Wittenbrink 2006.

8 See the detailed list of Novembergruppe concerts in Thrun 1995, pp. 606–608, and in: *Ausstellung Novembergruppe. Malerei, Plastik, Architektur*, Berlin 1925 (= *Archiv der deutschen Kunst*, 1925, no. 3), pp. 15f.

9 See Kliemann 1969, 34. For a detailed assessment of the role the group played from a musicological perspective, see Grosch 1999 and Thrun 1995, 521–526. An acoustic impression is provided by Matthew Rubenstein's rendering *Berlin im Licht. Klaviermusik der Novembergruppe*, Audio-CD, Berlin 2011.

10 Grosch 1999, p. 42.

11 Hans Siebert von Heister, "Fünf Jahre deutscher Funkjournalismus" [1928], in: *Fernseh-Informationen*, Gauting 1985, pp. 326–328, 355f., 383f. and 413f., here 414.

12 See Pabst 1985; also Kliemann 1969, pp. 50f.

13 Individual references to the radio programmes concerned in Zeising 2018.

14 The programme began at 8.30 pm. The schedules do not indicate the exact length. It was followed from 10.30 pm by news and short announcements.

15 This made sense, not only because Belling was so well known, but also because sculptors played a prominent role in the Novembergruppe. See Beloubek-Hammer 1993, pp. 29–48.

16 See *Der Deutsche Rundfunk*, 1925, no. 20, p. 1263. The manuscript appears to have been lost.

17 See Zeising 2018a.

18 Quoted in Leonhard 1997, vol. 1, pp. 251f.

19 See Langner 2016ff., and Grosch 1999, pp. 207.

20 Max Butting, "Radiomusik", in: *Sozialistische Monatshefte*, year 35, 1929, no. 3, p. 261, and, by the same author: "Der Komponist und der Rundfunk", in: *Die Musik*, vol. 20, 1928, no. 8, pp. 592–593.

21 See Butting 1955, p. 144.

22 See Max Butting, "Radiomusik", in: *Sozialistische Monatshefte*, year 33, 1927, no. 5, p. 403.

23 See Stapper 2001, pp. 184–186 and 191.

24 See Grosch 1998, pp. 65–83, here 68.

25 See ibid., p. 67.

26 See Stapper 2001, pp. 204f., and Grosch 1999, pp. 225f.

27 Quoted in Schlösser 1979, p. 155.

28 Tiessen 1953, p. 51.

29 Ibid., p. 101.

30 See ibid., p. 92.

31 See Stapper 2001, pp. 63 and 160.

32 See Weiss 1996, p. 203; Schebera 1990, p. 45.

33 See Weiss 1996, p. 144.

34 Philipp Jarnach, "Das Problem des Musikapparates" [1924], quoted in: Jers 1994, pp. 174–176, here 174.

35 See Hecker 1994, pp. 7–19, here 8.

36 See Weiss 2016ff.

37 Weiss 1996, p. 205.

38 Ibid., p. 202.

39 See Stapper 2001, p. 236.

40 Kliemann 1969, p. 36.

41 Bert[olt] Brecht, "Die höflichen Chinesen", in: *Berliner Börsen-Courier*, 9 May 1925, no. 215.

42 See *Das Kunstblatt*, year 8, 1924, p. 72. On Zuckmayer's work for radio see Wittenbrink 2001, pp. 309–339.

43 Ref. in note 1, p. 1199.

44 Lothar Band, "Moderne Kunst im Rundfunk. Ein Nachwort zum Abend der Novembergruppe", in: *Funk*, 1925, no. 23, pp. 269–270, here 270.

45 Ref. in note 1, p. 1197.

46 Hans Philipp Weitz, "Radio-Kritik", in: *Berliner Tageblatt*, 17 May 1925, no. 232. The programme schedule casts no light on what Weitz meant here by the "vocal tercet". The list in *Ausstellung der Novembergruppe in den Räumen der Berliner Secession in Berlin. Juni 1925. Malerei, Plastik, Architektur* (exhib. cat., June 1925), Berlin 1925 (= Archiv der deutschen Kunst, vol. 5, 1925, no. 3), 16, deviates from the bill announced in the radio listings in that it includes Kurt Weill's *Frauentanz*, op. 10, sung by Lotte Leonard.

47 Ref. in note 11, p. 414.

48 Ref. in note 44, p. 270.

49 Ibid.

50 [No author] "Die neue Funk-Woche", in: *Die Funkstunde*, 1925, no. 19, p. 335.

51 Lg, "Funklyrik", in: *Berliner Börsen-Courier*, 2 May 1925, no. 204.

52 Grosch 1999, p. 5.

53 See Grosch 1998, p. 76.

54 The concert broadcast in 1930 to mark the group's tenth anniversary was inherently retrospective and did not involve other artistic disciplines.

NILS GROSCH

MUSIC FOR A NEW REPUBLIC

The Novembergruppe Evening Experiment

Music played an important role in the Novembergruppe from an early stage, a performative dimension to complement the activities of the visual artists, which usually culminated in exhibitions. There were 21 "Novembergruppe Evenings" altogether, held at irregular intervals and with varying frequency between 19 March 1922 and 8 April 1931. They were associated with a format which did not merely feature "experimental works and works far removed from the usual concert programmes", as the invitation to the last of the evenings in 1931 announced (fig. 01),[1] but which crucially questioned and challenged the concert itself as an established, traditional presentation genre.

Although works of contemporary music, including compositions by members of the group, dominated these evenings, other types of art also played a part.[2] The first six Novembergruppe soirées all included literary items, while the seventh offered a performance of modern dance.

On the first evening, the literary contribution—described in the programme as a "presentation", a term also applied to literary input on subsequent occasions—fell to Fränze Roloff. At the time she was a stage actor with the *Volksbühne* theatre company in Berlin, and from 1923 she was in charge of its acting school. In later years she forged a reputation in radio drama as both an actor and director,[3] but around 1920 she was also performing at other theatres, sometimes with programmes of contemporary German-language literature.[4] A prominent feature of this first evening was music by the composer WOLFGANG ZELLER, born in 1893, who was then a member of the Volksbühne's orchestra—a clue to the connections which may have influenced the choice of programme for this occasion.[5]

The visual artists in the Novembergruppe were likewise involved in the aesthetic conception of these events, not only because they made up a substantial proportion of the audience, but also, like WALTER KAMPMANN, LOTHAR HOMEYER and MORIZ MELZER, by designing artistic invitations and programmes, often Expressionist in style (fig. 02).[6] This latter phenomenon of interart involvement[7] was even maintained when, between 1924 and 1926 and beginning with the eighth Novembergruppe Evening, the growing presence of musicians in the association resulted in a proliferation of purely musical soirées, held once a month at their peak.

The 17th, 18th and 19th Evenings, which took place in the second half of 1926, took on a character all of their own. A disagreement between members of the group had meanwhile caused a number of members to leave, among them the Berlin-based composer MAX BUTTING, who had been in charge of the Novembergruppe Evenings since 1923.[8] By repeating the music and including presentations and discussions, the concert format was now prised open. The result was an early version of the 'lecture performance'. "The work will be played twice during the evening," advised the programme note for the 17th Evening;[9] at the 19th, according to HANS HEINZ STUCKENSCHMIDT, "the concert began at 7.30 and lasted until about 8.45, after which tea and biscuits were served to the audience until about 10 o'clock, and then the entire concert was repeated. It was, indeed, a good idea, apart from the tea and biscuits, which gave the whole proceedings the air of a society salon."[10] The musical offerings for the 18th Evening were provided by a mechanical piano and flanked by a "discussion presentation" given by STUCKENSCHMIDT.[11]

The metaphorical 'fourth wall' of the proscenium, which in a theatre divides the performative situation into a receiving and a producing zone, was perforated here by a "podium at a distance from the listener", an essential element of this particular genre of concert.[12] The "static music" and "mechanical music"—trail-blazing concepts which in a sense supplied a motto and dramaturgical framework for these three concerts—were not merely performed by musicians, but also the subject of deep reflection involving the audience. MAX BUTTING wrote in his memoirs that one principle of musical events by the Novembergruppe had been "to present new works for discussion", in particular those "which had few prospects of performance anywhere else".[13] If the Novembergruppe had made it a deliberate policy to perform anything "whose cultural value has not yet been confirmed", as the radio pioneer and Novembergruppe member HANS SIEBERT VON HEISTER once phrased it,[14] then we can interpret this approach as a considered communication strategy: presenting things for discussion became part and parcel of the performance.

There is nothing trivial about this format if we bear in mind that the concert medium was almost the only performative platform available to contemporary music. 1921 saw the birth of the *Donaueschingen Chamber Music Performances for the Advancement of Contemporary Music* [*Donaueschinger Kammermusikaufführungen zur Förderung zeitgenössischer Tonkunst*] (which later became the Donaueschingen Festival), and 1922 witnessed the foundation of the International Society for Contemporary Music, both of which centred their activities on festivals with a predominance of concerts.[15] However, what distinguished the

01

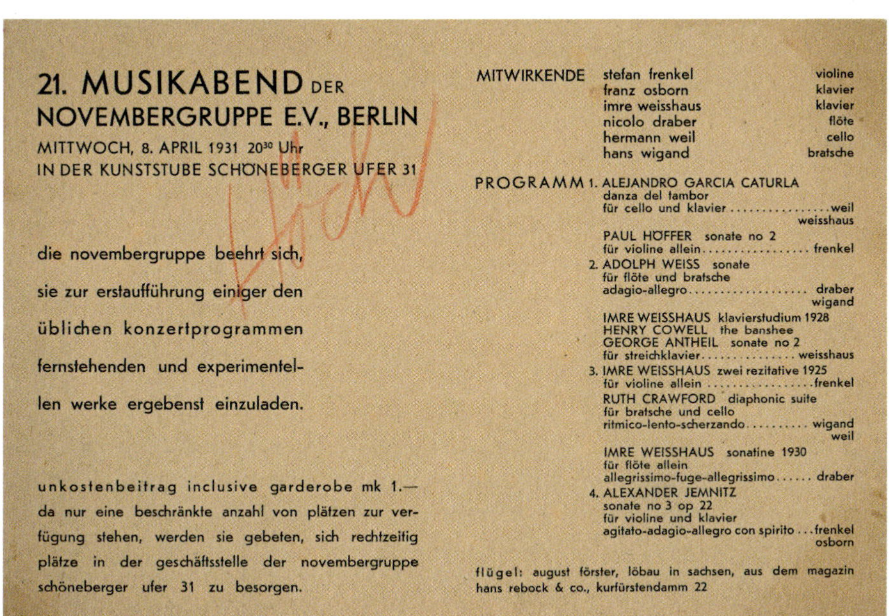

21. MUSIKABEND DER
NOVEMBERGRUPPE E.V., BERLIN
MITTWOCH, 8. APRIL 1931 20³⁰ Uhr
IN DER KUNSTSTUBE SCHÖNEBERGER UFER 31

die novembergruppe beehrt sich,
sie zur erstaufführung einiger den
üblichen konzertprogrammen
fernstehenden und experimentel-
len werke ergebenst einzuladen.

unkostenbeitrag inclusive garderobe mk 1.—
da nur eine beschränkte anzahl von plätzen zur verfügung stehen, werden sie gebeten, sich rechtzeitig plätze in der geschäftsstelle der novembergruppe schöneberger ufer 31 zu besorgen.

MITWIRKENDE
stefan frenkel violine
franz osborn klavier
imre weisshaus klavier
nicolo draber flöte
hermann weil cello
hans wigand bratsche

PROGRAMM
1. ALEJANDRO GARCIA CATURLA
danza del tambor
für cello und klavier .... weil, weisshaus

PAUL HÖFFER sonate no 2
für violine allein .... frenkel

2. ADOLPH WEISS sonate
für flöte und bratsche
adagio-allegro .... draber, wigand

IMRE WEISSHAUS klavierstudium 1928
HENRY COWELL the banshee
GEORGE ANTHEIL sonate no 2
für streichklavier .... weisshaus

3. IMRE WEISSHAUS zwei rezitative 1925
für violine allein .... frenkel

RUTH CRAWFORD diaphonic suite
für bratsche und cello
ritmico-lento-scherzando .... wigand, weil

IMRE WEISSHAUS sonatine 1930
für flöte allein
allegrissimo-fuge-allegrissimo .... draber

4. ALEXANDER JEMNITZ
sonate no 3 op 22
für violine und klavier
agitato-adagio-allegro con spirito ... frenkel, osborn

flügel: august förster, löbau in sachsen, aus dem magazin hans rebock & co., kurfürstendamm 22

02

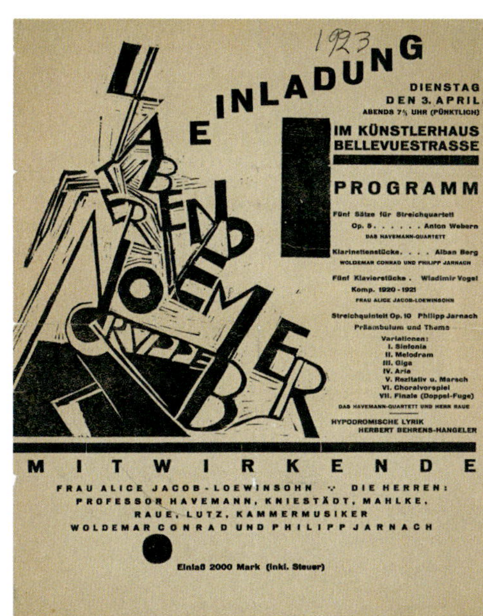

EINLADUNG
DIENSTAG
DEN 3. APRIL
ABENDS 7½ UHR (PÜNKTLICH)
IM KÜNSTLERHAUS BELLEVUESTRASSE

PROGRAMM

Fünf Sätze für Streichquartett Op. 5 ...... Anton Webern
DAS HAVEMANN-QUARTETT

Klarinettenstücke .... Alban Berg
WOLDEMAR CONRAD UND PHILIPP JARNACH

Fünf Klavierstücke . Wladimir Vogel
Komp. 1920 - 1921
FRAU ALICE JACOB-LOEWINSOHN

Streichquintett Op. 10 Philipp Jarnach
Präambulum und Thema
Variationen:
I. Sinfonia
II. Melodram
III. Giga
IV. Aria
V. Rezitativ u. Marsch
VI. Choralvorspiel
VII. Finale (Doppel-Fuge)
DAS HAVEMANN-QUARTETT UND HERR RAUE

HYPODROMISCHE LYRIK
HERBERT BEHRENS-HANGELER

MITWIRKENDE
FRAU ALICE JACOB-LOEWINSOHN · DIE HERREN:
PROFESSOR HAVEMANN, KNIESTÄDT, MAHLKE,
RAUE, LUTZ, KAMMERMUSIKER
WOLDEMAR CONRAD UND PHILIPP JARNACH

Einlaß 2000 Mark (inkl. Steuer)

01 Invitation and programme for the Novembergruppe's 21st Music Evening, 8 April 1931
Berlinische Galerie

02 [MORIZ MELZER]
Invitation and programme for the Novembergruppe's 4th Evening, 3 April 1923
Berlinische Galerie

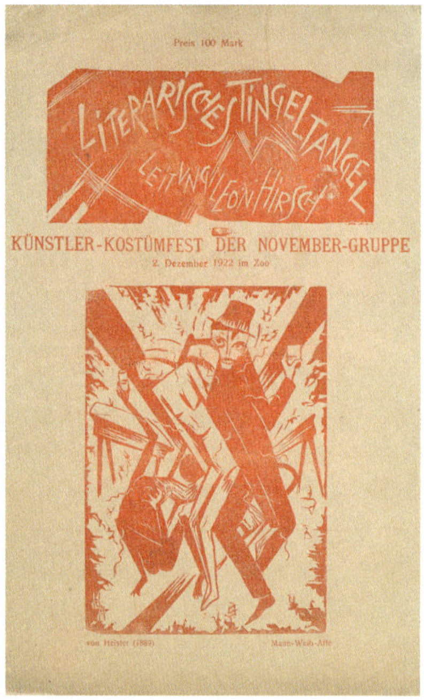

03

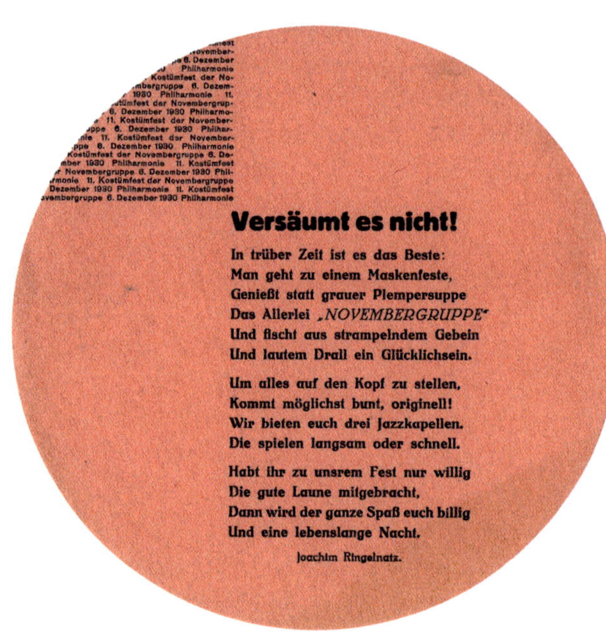

04

03 HANS SIEBERT VON HEISTER
Leaflet for the Artists' Fancy-Dress Ball hosted by the Novembergruppe, 2 December 1922
Berlinische Galerie

04 Invitation to the Novembergruppe's 11th Fancy-Dress Ball on 6 December 1930 with a poem by Joachim Ringelnatz
Staatliche Museen zu Berlin, Zentralarchiv

Novembergruppe here was not so much the choice of works and the aesthetic programme as the fundamental decision to embed the music within a communicative framework, thereby reaching much further beyond the limitations of the traditional concert as a presentation format than other innovations exemplified by the above-mentioned festivals.

Communication Strategies

The communicative arrangements accompanying the dramaturgy for the Novembergruppe Evenings extended to the impact and perceptions which continued to reverberate after the event. It was no accident that the venues chosen for these events were often modest in size, like the small hall in Vox-Haus. "That, too, was deliberate," writes BUTTING, "for the little hall was always full to bursting, and all over the press the point was highlighted that the concerts were exceedingly well attended; had we taken even a medium-sized concert hall, the same number of spectators might have led to reports about half-empty houses."[16] This is not just an anecdote about the limited public interest in New Music. It betrays a carefully considered act of communication, and it was no longer aimed simply at the concert-going public or at the primary medium, a performance in a public space. There were two more, quite different thrusts, as BUTTING explains in the same paragraph: for one thing, communication across the boundaries of the art form was pivotal, especially — as he recounts — because performers received their fee in the form of "drawings, watercolours and small sculptures", while the artists did not "stay away from the concerts when they knew that the musicians were receiving their works. So we always had an audience with a lively interest consisting largely of artists". The performative act, then, derived not so much from a communicative intention targeting a regional audience, but above all from an exchange between representatives of the various arts. Moreover, as BUTTING'S account demonstrates, the Novembergruppe was seeking mediatized visibility beyond the region, and the coverage was precisely calculated and monitored: the influence of the Berlin press would inevitably ensure that information was dispersed far and wide, not only about the works themselves, but also about feedback during the concert from the insiders who were packing the house. This bears all the signs of a deliberate game plan for the media as a reference framework.

The term "mechanical music" caught on during that period as a generic concept for music on gramophone records, on reproducing pianos, in films and on the radio.[17] The young composer HANS HEINZ STUCKENSCHMIDT was a leading light in this field, and in the press he championed the role that mechanical music would one day play in music production and performance. He was an early member of the Novembergruppe and from 1926 the head of its music section, a function he inherited from MAX BUTTING, who presided over the section from 1923 until 1926[18] and had been one of the first people to explore the problems associated with the mass reproduction and transmissibility of music from the various angles of aesthetics, composition, practical orchestration and communication theory. In 1929 he was appointed to the first university chair in radio composition and he is still regarded as a pioneer of original composition for broadcasting purposes.

It was almost inevitable that the Novembergruppe should be given its own radio programme in May 1925.[19] The three pieces of music selected for the evening broadcast were by MAX BUTTING, PHILIPP JARNACH and HEINZ TIESSEN. Readings by three writers were also integrated into the programme. One of them was Bertolt Brecht, and it was in this context that he probably made the personal acquaintance of KURT WEILL. The broadcast sparked vehement disapproval among listeners,[20] and this was naturally noticed and evaluated by the members of the group and by the authors and composers whose works had been featured. Although nothing is known about these discussions, in the ensuing years both BUTTING and Brecht engaged in theoretical reflections about broadcasting, and WEILL — prompted by the Novembergruppe's film matinée — soon began thinking about the "possibilities for absolute radio art", a theme that gave its name to his piece on radio and media theory, which was very influential at the time.[21] WEILL'S essays on the significance of radio attach great importance to its ability to reach a broad, open

05 MORIZ MELZER
Design for a leaflet about a performance organized by the Novembergruppe of Arnold Schönberg's drama *Pierrot Lunaire*, 1922
Berlinische Galerie

06 Invitation and programme for the 12th Evening with the Novembergruppe, 3 April 1925
Berlinische Galerie

07 Programme for the Novembergruppe's 20th Music Evening, 20 November 1930
Berlinische Galerie

05

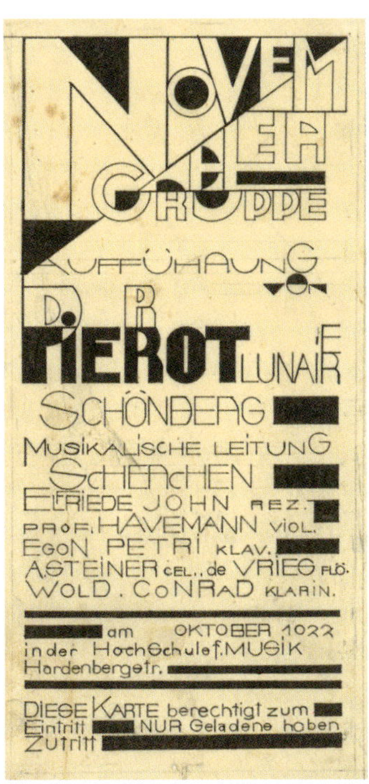

06

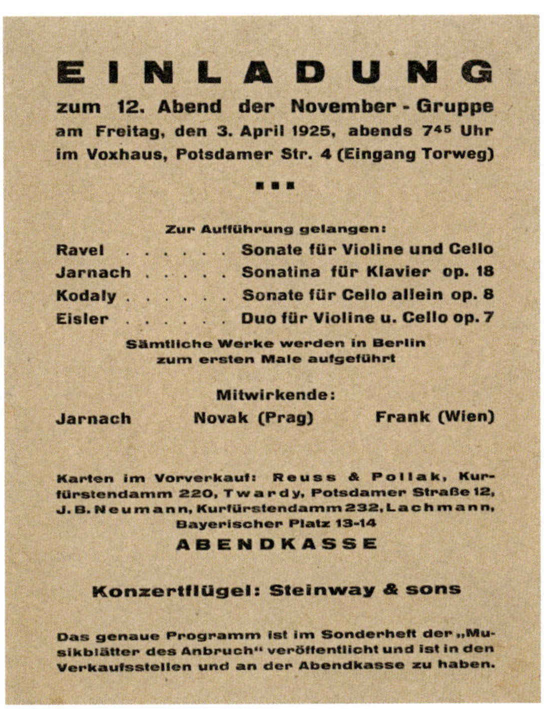

EINLADUNG
zum 12. Abend der November-Gruppe
am Freitag, den 3. April 1925, abends 7[45] Uhr
im Voxhaus, Potsdamer Str. 4 (Eingang Torweg)

Zur Aufführung gelangen:

Ravel . . . . . . Sonate für Violine und Cello
Jarnach . . . . . Sonatina für Klavier op. 18
Kodaly . . . . . . Sonate für Cello allein op. 8
Eisler . . . . . . Duo für Violine u. Cello op. 7

Sämtliche Werke werden in Berlin
zum ersten Male aufgeführt

Mitwirkende:
Jarnach Novak (Prag) Frank (Wien)

Karten im Vorverkauf: Reuss & Pollak, Kurfürstendamm 220, Twardy, Potsdamer Straße 12, J. B. Neumann, Kurfürstendamm 232, Lachmann, Bayerischer Platz 13-14
ABENDKASSE

Konzertflügel: Steinway & sons

Das genaue Programm ist im Sonderheft der „Musikblätter des Anbruch" veröffentlicht und ist in den Verkaufsstellen und an der Abendkasse zu haben.

07

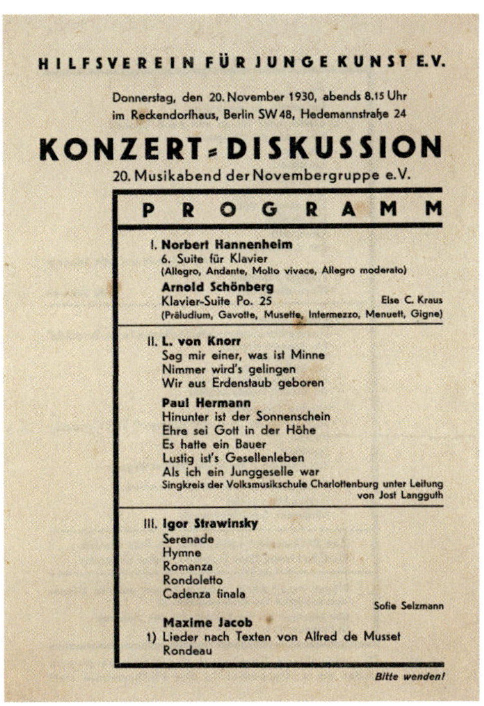

HILFSVEREIN FÜR JUNGE KUNST E.V.

Donnerstag, den 20. November 1930, abends 8.15 Uhr
im Reckendorfhaus, Berlin SW 48, Hedemannstraße 24

KONZERT-DISKUSSION
20. Musikabend der Novembergruppe e.V.

PROGRAMM

I. **Norbert Hannenheim**
6. Suite für Klavier
(Allegro, Andante, Molto vivace, Allegro moderato)
Arnold Schönberg
Klavier-Suite Po. 25 — Else C. Kraus
(Präludium, Gavotte, Musette, Intermezzo, Menuett, Gigne)

II. **L. von Knorr**
Sag mir einer, was ist Minne
Nimmer wird's gelingen
Wir aus Erdenstaub geboren
Paul Hermann
Hinunter ist der Sonnenschein
Ehre sei Gott in der Höhe
Es hatte ein Bauer
Lustig ist's Gesellenleben
Als ich ein Junggeselle war
Singkreis der Volksmusikschule Charlottenburg unter Leitung von Jost Langguth

III. **Igor Strawinsky**
Serenade
Hymne
Romanza
Rondoletto
Cadenza finala
Sofie Selzmann
Maxime Jacob
1) Lieder nach Texten von Alfred de Musset
Rondeau

Bitte wenden!

audience, and this factor merges in his reflections with the role of radio as an "art industry", a positive concept in Weill's thinking.

It was only from 1928, after his works, especially *The Threepenny Opera* [*Die Dreigroschenoper*], had become such a commercial success, that WEILL explicitly contemplated using economic criteria as a positive indicator for the mass appeal of art. It is fair to assume, however, that the scepticism consistently voiced by several members of the Novembergruppe from 1925 onwards about concerts, which they felt were becoming socially and commercially obsolete, was a symptom of discussions taking place within the group.[22] In 1927 BUTTING complained bitterly about a "lack of interest shown by the overwhelming part of the population"[23] in Berlin's concert listings. In fact, in 1925, a few weeks after the radio broadcast, WEILL had already concluded in the Börsencourier that this state of affairs was "untenable": "the concert life of our cities, which owes its origins to a bygone era of bourgeois prosperity, is today pointless, unserviceable and out-of-date. The music business has become unprofitable."[24] STUCKENSCHMIDT (who assured a colleague that he hated concerts) fulminated in the Weltbühne in 1926 that the concert hall would see "the death of this people [...] at the hand of its music".[25] This, it seems, was the downside to the flurry of diagnosis surrounding radio which, not without good reason, concluded that this was a medium which would one day bring art to a mass audience, provide a future commercial framework for musical performance and emerge as a new 'patron'.

The Fancy-Dress Ball as a Symphony of Jazz

Another striking aspect to this is the absence from the discussion of an alternative which might make better sense to us today: a call for state intervention, for broad-based public subsidies for the arts. Radio, which was, after all, owned by the state and monitored and managed by bodies (culture committees) composed partly by political appointments, was seen as a homogenous communication system, largely self-regulating in economic terms — which it certainly was with regard to many of its functional mechanisms.

The Novembergruppe generated its own financial resources for its unquestionably cash-hungry exhibitions and evenings — thanks to a menu of popular, commercially lucrative entertainment: "To ensure its exhibitions and the concerts, the Novembergruppe held two big public fancy-dress balls every year. The reputation of the first of these exuberant, uncensored parties was already such that the revellers of the inflation era could hardly wait for the next and the next, and the Novembergruppe gleefully posted a substantial profit every time. The surplus was quickly converted into dollars, securing the funds to organize the exhibitions and concerts throughout the years of inflation."[26]

These festivities, then, were a pivotal source of income to underpin the association's economic survival.[27] Posters and advertisements for these events testify to a strong element of music and dance (fig. 03). The poster designed by HANNAH HÖCH for the artists' fancy-dress ball thrown by the Novembergruppe on 5 December 1925 with the theme "Sport and Razzmatazz in Wedding" offers a clear indication of the playlist: "And the whole joint jazzing, jazzing" (fig. 08). The whole joint was no less than the Berlin Philharmonia Hall, hired for the occasion. By the mid-1920s modern jazz was playing a decisive role in the ball dramaturgy, as we can tell from a passage of text included in a programme designed by WALTER KAMPMANN in 1926: "Do you know what it's like when the party heads to its climax? Have you any idea how colossal it is when those wonderful whirls of a jazz symphony

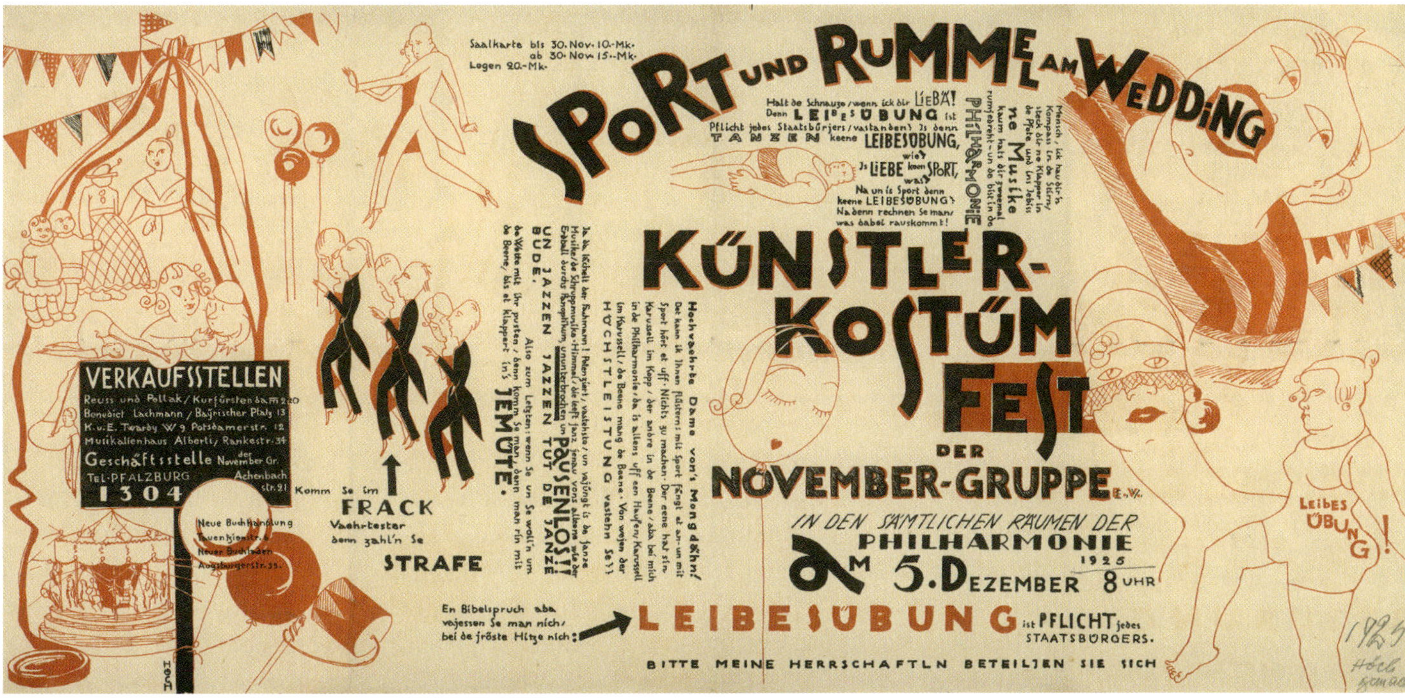

08

08 HANNAH HÖCH
Poster for the Artists' Fancy-Dress Ball *Sport and Razzmatazz in Wedding* hosted by the Novembergruppe, 5 December 1925
Berlinische Galerie

take over? [...] You know, then the Sphinx, then all of you lose your heads, and everything swirls around in a mad maelstrom until the early morning."[28]

This carries overtones of the essay "In Praise of Follies" ["Lob der Revue"] written by STUCKENSCHMIDT, at the time responsible for the musical evenings by the Novembergruppe, where he highlighted "the clash and confluence of sensual effects, the interplay of assorted stimuli".[29] It illustrates how open the avant-garde community was to commercially popular forms of entertainment, and this may seem surprising to later generations. Some aspects of these popular forms certainly rubbed off to great effect on the dramaturgy for the association's fancy dress balls and also on the scale of these events, which attracted "far more than a thousand guests". "Everyone in town was talking about the Novembergruppe ball. You had to have been there," reports Oskar Maria Graf in his memoirs, recalling one of the parties at Zoo and an impressive gig by three musical bands.[30] Music and dance were key components of these memorable events, and JOACHIM RINGELNATZ devoted a poem to them which was printed on the invitation to the fancy dress ball in 1930 (fig. 04). It reads: "When times are glum and you feel stress / Just don a mask and fancy dress. / Don't cry into your cold grey soup, / Come feast with the 'November Group'. / As legs and arms go swinging round / Pluck happiness from roaring sound. / The old world we repudiate: / Wear lots of colours, innovate! / Three jazz bands, you can take your pick, / Play sometimes slowly, sometimes quick. / Come to our party, have no fear, / Bring good spirits and a friend. / It's all good fun and won't be dear / And the night will never end." ["In trüber Zeit ist es das Beste: / Man geht zu einem Maskenfeste, / Genießt statt grauer Plempersuppe / Das Allerlei 'Novembergruppe' / Und fischt aus strampelndem Gebein / Und lautem Drall ein Glücklichsein. / Um alles auf den Kopf zu stellen, / Kommt möglichst bunt, originell! / Wir bieten euch drei Jazzkapellen. / Die spielen langsam oder schnell. / Habt ihr zu unsrem Fest nur willig / Die gute Laune mitgebracht, / Dann wird der ganze Spaß euch billig / Und eine lebenslange Nacht."][31]

The three jazz bands were led, as the programme for the party in the Philharmonie on the Feast of St Nicholas in 1930 reveals, by Ben Berlin (figs. 9-11). Hermann

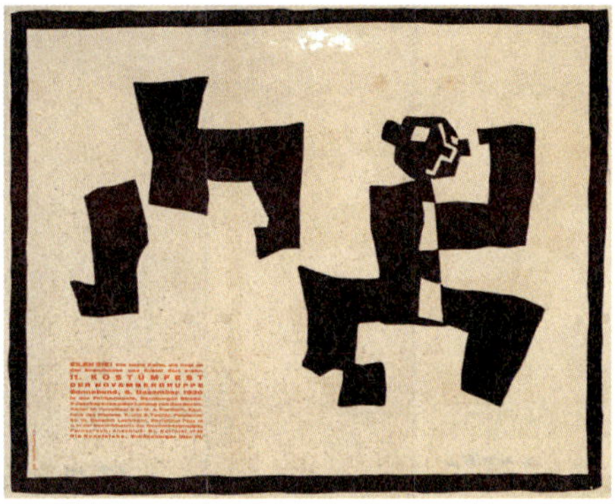

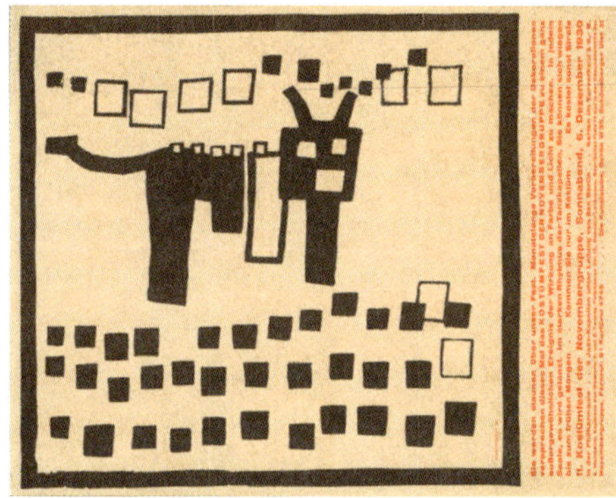

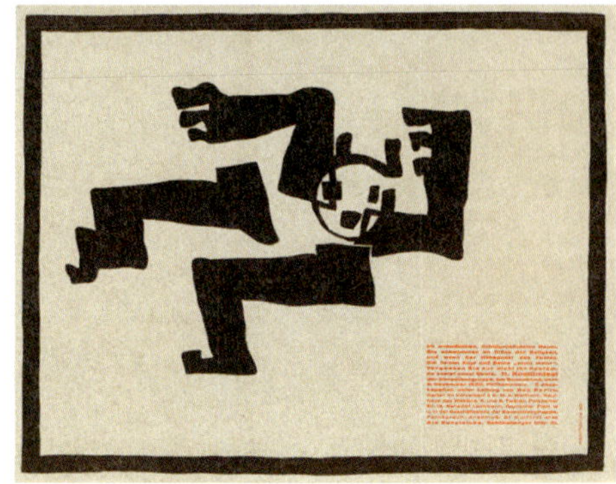

09 — 10 — 11

09 WALTER KAMPMANN
Announcement and programme for the Novembergruppe's 11th Fancy-Dress Ball, 6 December 1930
Berlinische Galerie

10 WALTER KAMPMANN
Announcement and programme for the Novembergruppe's 11th Fancy-Dress Ball, 6 December 1930
Berlinische Galerie

11 WALTER KAMPMANN
Announcement and programme for the Novembergruppe's 11th Fancy-Dress Ball, 6 December 1930
Staatliche Museen zu Berlin, Kunstbibliothek

Biek, who adopted the pseudonym Ben Berlin in 1928, was a concert pianist and jazz musician born in Tallinn in 1896 who had arrived in Berlin in 1925. In 1926 he was already the "artistic director, house pianist and arranger" of *Vox-Schallplatten- und Sprechmaschinen-AG* — the thriving recording company whose hall was used by the Novembergruppe for many of its soirées and lectures. Biek used a studio in the same building on Potsdamer Strasse to record jazz for the albums produced by Vox.[32] By the time of the Novembergruppe concert in winter 1930, he had already been running his own band for over two years and had an exclusive contract to record and tour jazz for *Grammophon-AG*.[33] If we are looking to piece together the jigsaw puzzle of networks and connections driving Novembergruppe activities, we will be struck repeatedly — as in this case — by certain venues and institutions that were at the centre of the dynamic media development in the Weimar Republic. They exercised a pivotal function both in the dissemination of egalitarian proposals about ways to present art and in the lives of the composers in the Novembergruppe. It is equally evident, however, that the fine artists in the association invested commitment and imagination of their own in preparing for the fancy dress balls, especially by decorating the rooms, in a sense generating effective publicity by building a bridge between their art and practices of popular culture.[34] By contrast, the acoustic elements were entrusted entirely to established musicians and genres of popular dance music, rather than involving the musical membership of the group. Nevertheless, in the course of the 1920s these musicians increasingly took on the challenges of modern media and popular culture — albeit not so much by taking up the musical formats devised by the Novembergruppe, but rather by breaking out of these and into musical theatre, radio, cinema and songs for the labour movement.[35]

1 From an invitation card issued by the Novembergruppe on 8 April 1931, estate of Hannah Höch, Berlinische Galerie, Berlin. See Berlinische Galerie 1995, vol. 2, 31.33, p. 424.

2 See the "Chronicle", pp. 226–247 of this catalogue.

3 See Rotthaler 2003, p. 74.

4 See Erich Büttner's poster for Fränze Roloff's "presentation" and Hubert von Meyerinck, www.smb-digital.de/eMuseumPlus?service=ExternalInterface&module=collection&objectId=923824 (accessed on 3 April 2018).

5 Joseph Roth describes Roloff and Zeller performing together in his review of the production *The Dead Day [Der tote Tag]* at the *Volksbühne* on 26 September 1924, see Westermann 1990.

6 Reproduced in Kliemann 1969, pp. 36–41.

7 'Interart' describes the reciprocal influences or interactions between different genres of art, see Rajewsky 2002, pp. 14–16.

8 See Butting 1955, pp. 153f.

9 See Berlinische Galerie 1995, vol. 2, 26.33, p. 269.

10 Stuckenschmidt 1979, p. 95.

11 See "Ankündigung zum 18. Konzert der Novembergruppe", in: *Berliner Börsen-Zeitung*, 19 November 1926, no. 539.

12 Salmen 1988, p. 7.

13 Butting 1955, pp. 120 and 153.

14 Hans S. von Heister, "Ein Abend der Novembergruppe im Berliner Rundfunk", in: *Der deutsche Rundfunk*, year 3, 1925, pp. 1197–1199, here 1197.

15 See Thrun 1995, pp. 592–613.

16 Butting 1955, p. 119.

17 Ibid., p. 118.

18 See Hans Heinz Stuckenschmidt, "Musik und Musiker der Novembergruppe", in: *Zehn Jahre Novembergruppe*, special issue *Kunst der Zeit. Zeitschrift für Kunst und Literatur*, vol. 3, 1928, no. 1–3, pp. 94–101, here 94.

19 See the essay by Zeising and Beimdieke, pp. 176–183 of this catalogue.

20 See Wolfram Wessels, 24.05.1925: *Die „Novembergruppe" im Deutschen Rundfunk*, SWR2 2013, www.swr.de/-/id=11251048/property=download/nid=660694/1e4gaco/swr2-zeitwort-20130524.pdf (accessed on 3 April 2018).

21 Kurt Weill, "Möglichkeiten absoluter Radiokunst", in: Hinton 2000, pp. 264–271.

22 See Grosch 1998, pp. 65–83.

23 Max Butting, "Die Musik und die Menschen", in: *Melos*, year 6, 1927, no. 2, pp. 58–63, here 58.

24 Kurt Weill, "Fort vom Durchschnitt! Zur Krise der musikalischen Interpretation", in: Hinton 2000, pp. 35–39, here 35.

25 Hans Heinz Stuckenschmidt, "Der Deutsche im Konzertsaal", in: *Die Weltbühne*, year 23, 1927, no. 16, pp. 631–633.

26 Butting 1955, p. 119.

27 See Kliemann 1969, p. 33.

28 Cf. the figure in Kliemann 1969, p. 34.

29 Hans Heinz Stuckenschmidt, "Lob der Revue", in: *Anbruch*, vol. 8, March/April 1926, pp. 170–173.

30 Quoted in Graf 2007, p. 339.

31 Joachim Ringelnatz, "Versäumt es nicht! (11. Kostümfest der Novembergruppe, 6. Dezember 1930)", quoted in Pape 1994, vol. 2 Gedichte, p. 347.

32 "Ben Berlin — Hermann Biek Biografie", http://grammophon-platten.de/page.php?152 (accessed on 4 April 2018).

33 Ibid.

34 See Kliemann 1969, p. 33.

35 See Grosch 1999, especially p. 99.

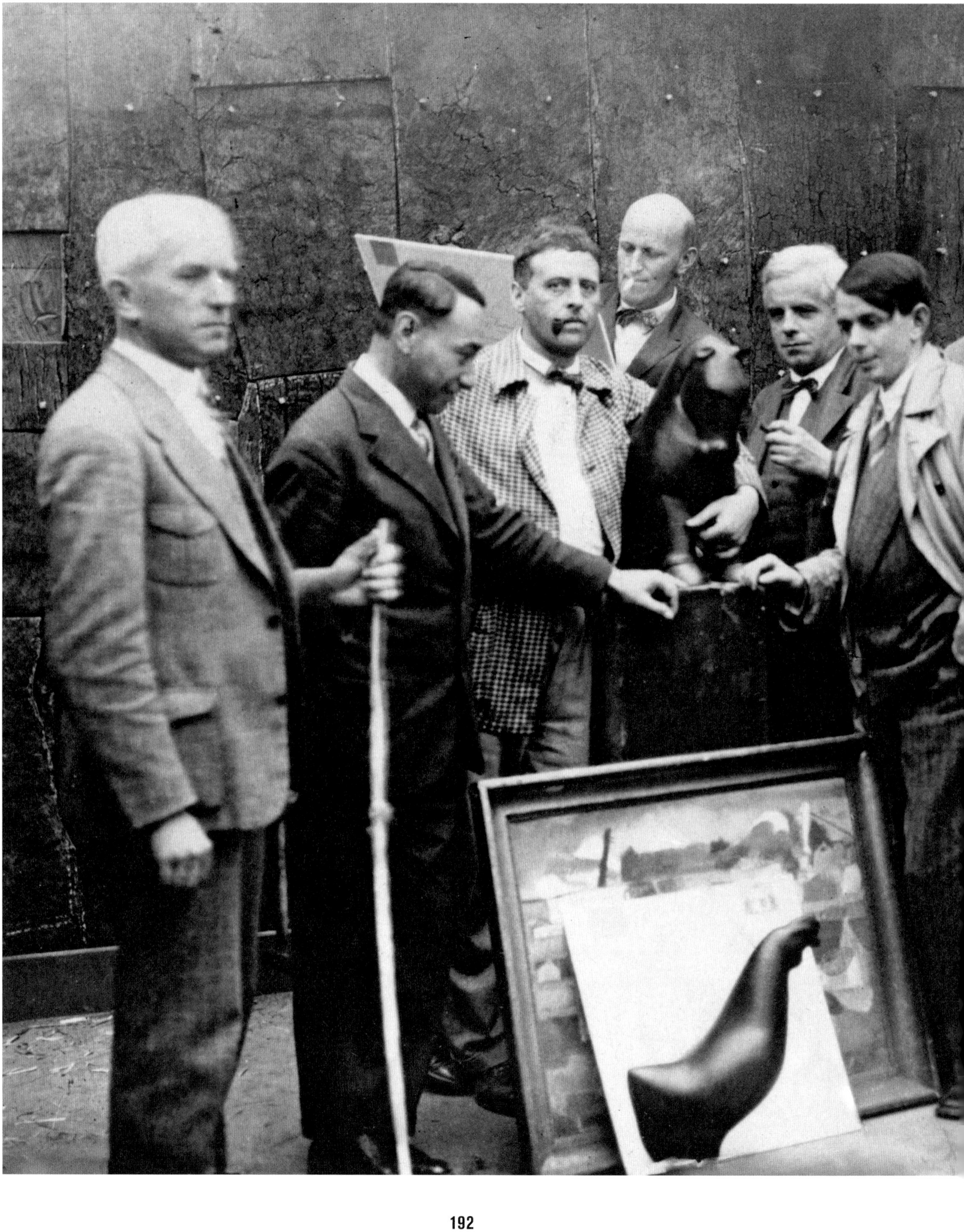

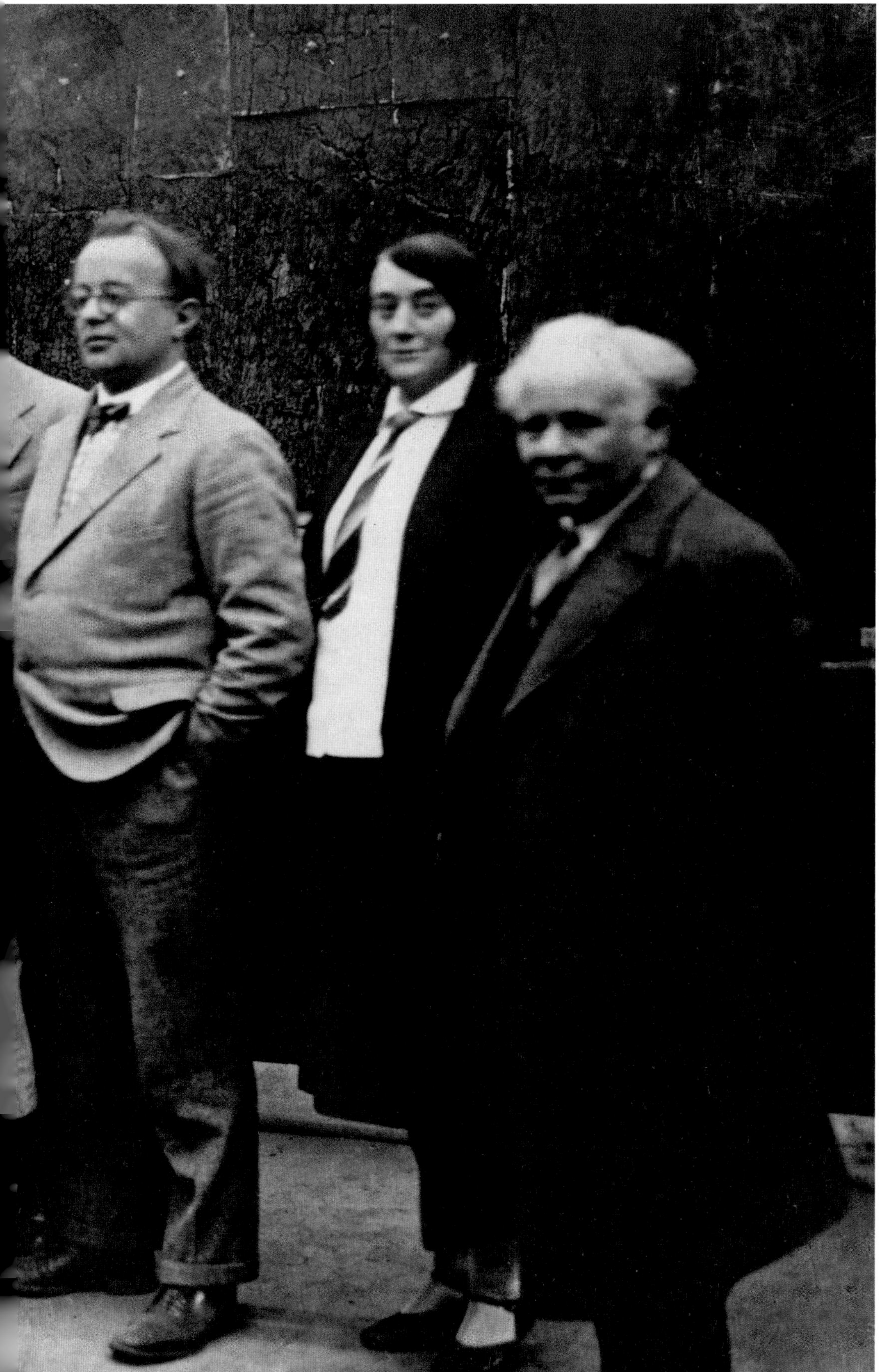

NG
1928 – 1935

Great Berlin Art Exhibition 1928, members of the Novembergruppe's hanging committee
From left to right Moriz Melzer, Hugo Graetz, Ewald Mataré, Otto Möller, Georg Tappert, Max Dungert, Oswald Herzog, Walter Kampmann, Ines Wetzel, Arthur Segal
Berlinische Galerie

JANINA NENTWIG

A BELATED REVOLUTION AND AN ENFORCED ENDING

The Novembergruppe from 1928 to 1937

In the first half of the 1920s the Novembergruppe attracted growing recognition for its versatile exhibition activities at home and abroad. As an open community of artists, the group consistently championed the latest trends in art. In particular, at its annual section of the Great Berlin Art Exhibition [*Grosse Berliner Kunstausstellung*], it presented them to a broad audience consisting not only of connoisseurs and patrons of the avant-garde. The spectrum of exhibiting members and guests, from all over Germany and not just Berlin, ranged from what is known as second-generation Expressionism and Dada via Abstract and Constructivist strands and New Objectivity to the modern architecture of *Neues Bauen*. Colleagues from other countries, notably France, the Netherlands and Eastern Europe, also put in a regular appearance. Painting, sculpture and architecture were complemented by the applied arts. In addition, there were numerous events devoted to modern, mostly atonal music and to experimental film. Without a doubt, the Novembergruppe challenged and sometimes overtaxed viewers and listeners with this abundance of artistic styles, genres and experiments, but this had become its hallmark. Around the middle of the decade, however, the outrage and occasional furore it had provoked with its programme began to wane. In fact, critics observed a fading commitment to the artistic endeavours that they had once so fiercely lampooned. One reviewer at the Novembergruppe exhibition held on the premises of the Berlin Secession in 1925 summed it up as follows: "The 'Novembergruppe' has 'fought through', which means to say that the public has now come over to its side. Partly out of conviction and partly weary of outdated or fashionable zigzagging. Partly out of the sympathy we humans so gladly extend, driven by pity or by vanity, to anything 'daring'. Except — there is no longer much 'daring' about it. Where once the wolf was feared — and who did not enter those exhibitions after the war without a little palpitation? — there now lurks a lamb."[1]

The association was visibly slithering into crisis, and not only because the days of radical artistic innovation and provocation appeared to be over. Disagreements between members about exhibition strategy and financial bottlenecks were causing internal tensions.[2] When all the architects except for ALFRED GELLHORN left in early 1927, the Novembergruppe lost a number of its best-known members, including LUDWIG MIES VAN DER ROHE, who thereby stood down from the chair.[3]

A few musicians and fine artists also left the group, among them the painter PETER FOERSTER, who had worked for the organization with great dedication.[4] In a letter to HANNAH HÖCH, who lived in the Netherlands between 1926 and 1929 and was following affairs from a distance, he questioned whether artists' associations were necessary at all: "It seems to me it's no longer a matter of groups having more or less old baggage. In the Nov. Group it's the drawing instructors with saturated gestures of progress and pedantic hang-ups about honesty (what a mixture eh?)."[5] FOERSTER's jibe at, in his view, backward-leaning "drawing instructors" was aimed both at members who combined their pursuit of the liberal arts with jobs in schools, like RUDOLF AUSLEGER, and at founding fathers such as OTTO MÖLLER and GEORG TAPPERT, who were training future art teachers in the colleges[6] and were now, following the exodus of the architects, once more at the helm — which in the eyes of many Novembrists was detrimental to the group.[7]

Apart from declining membership, the Novembergruppe had been hit by a political decree revamping the Great Berlin Art Exhibition. From 1927 the Prussian art ministry wanted this forum, of such pivotal importance to the association, to be organized by a new confederation, the *Kartell der vereinigten Verbände bildender Künstler Berlins* [*Syndicate of the United Associations of Fine Artists of Berlin*]. This structure brought together ten associations,[8] including a group called *Die Abstrakten*, which at the annual exhibition in 1926 had already threatened to oust the Novembergruppe from its position as 'enfant terrible'.[9] Besides, the official art market had already recognized that there was more to modern art than Impressionism, and this was reflected in exhibitions at the academy and Secession and even at the Nationalgalerie, which in 1924 had granted a one-man show to the Novembergruppe member RUDOLF BELLING and then purchased his sculpture *Triad* (cat. 111, p. 215) for its own collection.[10] But even this successful artist, active on the working committee and exhibition committee of the association ever since its foundation,[11] had since left the Novembergruppe. "Sadly it is now no more than an exhibition club, and that is why I have stopped. It can no longer be an action group, because today everyone has the chance to show their work!"[12] he told HÖCH in the spring of 1928.

The Association Writes Its Own History: a Tenth-Anniversary Publication

The approach of its tenth anniversary provided the Novembergruppe with a welcome opportunity, despite these difficulties, to claim a central role in the artistic life of Berlin. A copious publication was planned for the 'revolutionary month' of November to "offer the public retrospective testimony of its militant artistic activities", as MORIZ MELZER explained on behalf of a specially constituted organizing committee.[13] It would reprint "in lively sequence manifestos, documents, facsimile letters, press clippings, exhibition reviews etc. from the foundation period, above all a large number of the best reproductions of works by Group members from the entire duration of its existence", as long as these works had been shown in exhibitions mounted by the association. "The Group is certain that this publication will make a valuable and indispensable contribution to the history of contemporary art,"[14] MELZER confidently and optimistically added.

The Novembergruppe entrusted the introduction and editing to Will Grohmann, an art historian and critic in Dresden, who had kept up his links with the association ever since its early days through Dresden's Secession Group 1919.[15] The publication with the plain title *Ten Years of the Novembergruppe* [*Zehn Jahre*

Novembergruppe] (fig. 01), which came out in the nick of time in late 1928 as a special edition of the journal *Kunst der Zeit*, contained, as previously announced, a wide range of documents on the history of the association from 1918 until 1928, and it is a genuine gold mine for researchers today, although as a source it does require critical handling. While the Novembergruppe did make an effort, as its own historiographer, to generate a polyphonic record of its existence, selections were nevertheless made to place its past functioning in the right light: the first manifestos and guidelines, declarations by the local groups in other towns which had briefly affiliated in 1919, statements of support and negative replies to circulars canvasing for membership (fig. 02) and scathing newspaper reviews from the early years were included alongside short theoretical and programmatic texts by individual members, most of which had already been published elsewhere. There was also sporadic evidence of internal criticism about group strategy, such as a letter from OTTO FREUNDLICH in 1919 where the artist took the association severely to task for what he saw as its utterly unpolitical attitude.[16] FREUNDLICH's tirade was, however, an exception. Incidents like the censorship of works at the Great Berlin Art Exhibition in 1921 and the subsequent resignation of individual artists close to RAOUL HAUSMANN or the loss of members in 1927 were mentioned marginally and in a roundabout fashion.[17] Moreover, astute pruning of recent newspaper articles resulted in a far more positive picture of the association than its contemporary press image from the mid-1920s onwards,[18] and as no distinctions were made between former and current members when attributing illustrations and contributions, the group's actual composition in 1928 was unclear.

It was patently obvious that the association did not wish to attach too much weight to past and present crises and arguments on the occasion of its anniversary. Instead, the publication deliberately concentrated on its foundation during the revolution of 1918–19 and on the subsequent years until 1922, when it had to fight for recognition of the art it represented — a shift in focus which classically turned the history of the Novembergruppe into a heroic saga about an avant-garde initially misunderstood and unjustly rebuffed. The strategy did not pass unnoticed. In *Die Neue Bücherschau* the reviewer Otto Brattskoven praised the variety of content but saw the citation of these revolutionary beginnings as "playing trump cards which are rather too good to permit insights into the present". Ten years were, of course, a long time, but the Novembergruppe had not exactly evolved for the better, he observed: "What remains today is a painting

01 Cover for the publication *Ten Years of the Novembergruppe*, 1928

02 A page from the publication *Ten Years of the Novembergruppe*, 1928
The facsimiles include a letter from Adolf Hölzel to Georg Tappert and the painting *Forest* by Hans Brass.

03 GEORG PAHL
Jury-Free Art Show Berlin 1929
A room in the exhibition Ten Years of the Novembergruppe with Rudolf Belling' sculpture *Triad*, left of centre in the background Arthur Segal's painting *Airship Over Chicago*

01

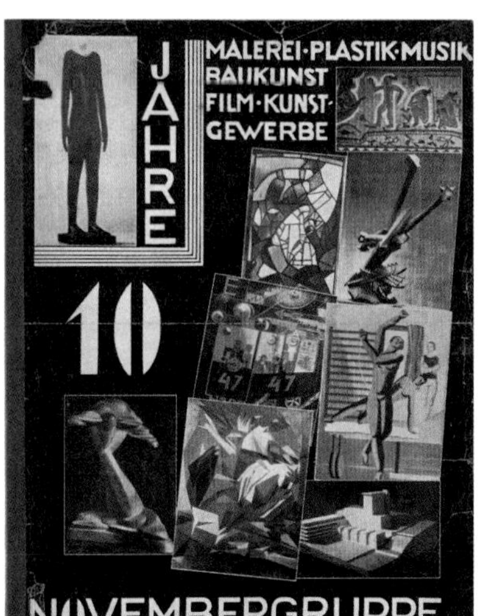

02

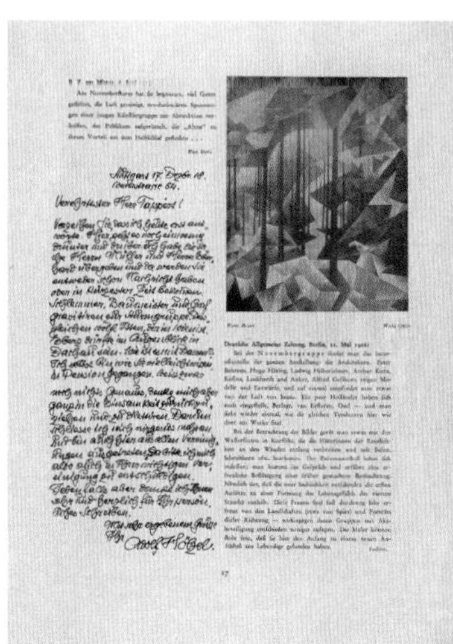

03

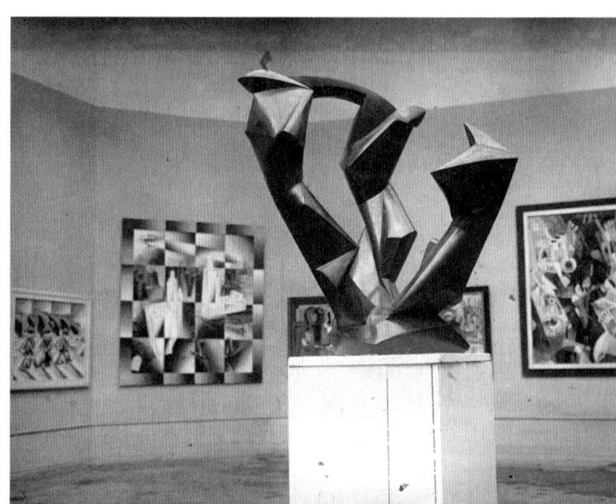

society that behaves in an abstract academic manner. A few 'newly objective' stuffed shirts cannot beef up a thin broth. The architects who most recently added weight have long since gone. Indeed, all the capable figures in the field of design have joined other groupings at some point along the way. Yet the commemorative edition has nothing to say on the subject. With a chirpy aura of freedom and, when it comes to it, business acumen, it drops the names of those who once believed they could team up with the 'Novembergruppe' brand. [...] But the horoscope for the future is a dubious question-mark!"[19]

Not every reviewer reached such a negative verdict on reading the publication. In *Das Kunstblatt*, a leading art magazine, Paul Ferdinand Schmidt paid tribute to the anniversary publication as an effective summary of the Novembergruppe's ten-year record "with no dogmatism or formula, like its origins and bearing, [...] always refreshingly to the point, obsessed not with celebrity but with verve and vitality". Schmidt's assessment was more in tune with the reading intended by the Novembergruppe: "It is a good thing our art life has a sourdough like this: the danger of stagnation is sometimes threateningly close."[20]

Grohmann's introduction to the publication similarly lamented the current stagnation and restoration trends in cultural life, describing the theoretical dilemma now facing the Novembergruppe: in 1918–19, after the political upheaval, it had seemed as though artists would play an important role in the state and in the new course for society: "The boundaries between the arts were trivial, we wanted one thing, to permeate the people and carry them aloft transformed."[21] Today, however, it had to be recognized that these hopes and plans had been dashed "politically, socially and unfortunately also in the intellectual and artistic field".[22] Grohmann was nevertheless upbeat about Novembergruppe efforts to date. If art salons and official events were now far bolder about avant-garde positions, this was partly to the credit of the educational work performed by the Novembergruppe exhibitions, where "outsiders and pioneers"[23] has always been given a chance. The association would persist with its goals, he declared, and wished to help in the construction effort "where an entire people has resolved to shape life anew from the foundations".[24]

In the light of this mission, to which the group remained committed, the emphasis placed on the founding years in the commemorative publication *Ten Years of the Novembergruppe* should not be interpreted merely as an attempt to distract the reader from present difficulties or to attract media publicity during the anni-

04 GEORG PAHL
Jury-Free Art Show Berlin 1929
A room in the exhibition *Ten Years of the Novembergruppe*. In the foreground Oswald Herzog's *Detail from a Fountain*, in the background the paintings *Three Women* (left) and *The Tram* (bottom right) by Otto Dix

05 BRUNO SCHUCH
Jury-Free Art Show Berlin 1929
A room in the exhibition Ten Years of the Novembergruppe. In the background from left to right *Madwoman* by Heinrich Ehmsen, *The Adventurer* by George Grosz, *Funeral of the Anarchist Galli* by Carlo Carrà, *Boys from Wedding* by Otto Nagel, *Barricade* by Otto Dix, an unknown portrait by Nagel, *Execution of Bavarian Revolutionaries* by Ehmsen and *The Funeral, Dedicated to Oskar Panizza* by Grosz

04

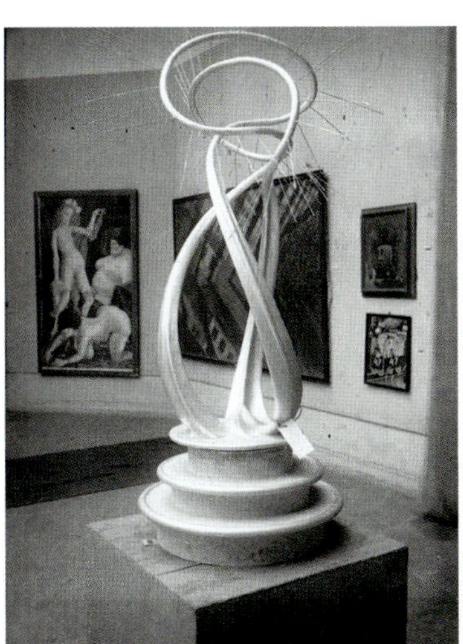

05

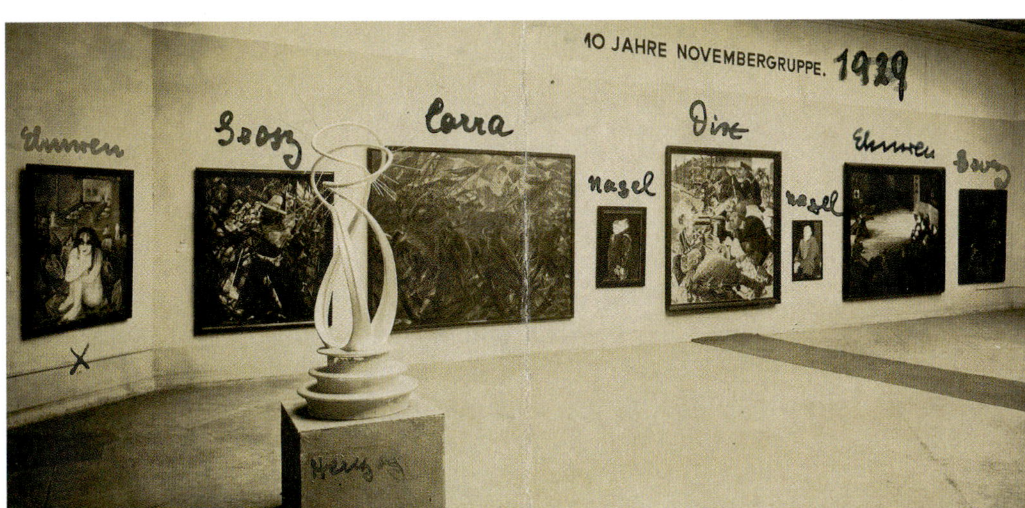

versary year 1928, as Brattskoven suggested. By recalling its genesis in the (art) revolution, the association was also on a quest for identity with a view to redefining its role within an altered art community and within the society of the Weimar Republic — a society which had become less radical than expected.

"Sister of the Revolution": the Exhibition Ten Years of the Novembergruppe

The following year, the Novembergruppe hoped to demonstrate its unbroken potential as a vital factor in the arts landscape by staging a major retrospective.[25] In June 1929 it sent out a call for submissions to the anniversary exhibition:[26] what the organizers had in mind was nothing less than equating the history of the Novembergruppe with the history of modern art. They planned to provide an "insight into the emergence and evolution of the art of the last 10 years" and also to involve artists close to the association "whose impact was fundamental to the development of the new painting, sculpture and architecture even before the Novembergruppe was founded". Interdisciplinary links would be traced by juxtaposing the "formal connections between painting, photography, architecture, technology". Six segments in all were planned, and each would have its own leadership and two advisers. "Abstract and Constructive Design" was entrusted to GEORG MUCHE, who had left the Bauhaus in 1927, WASSILY KANDINSKY, who was still teaching in Dessau, and Willi Baumeister. Founding members GEORG TAPPERT, CÉSAR KLEIN and OTTO MÖLLER took charge of "Expressionism". "Sculpture", too, was in the hands of early activists: OSWALD HERZOG and, returning as a guest, RUDOLF BELLING. "Socially Critical and Figurative Art" were the responsibility of HEINRICH EHMSEN, GEORGE GROSZ and JOHN HEARTFIELD, recent new recruits.[27] The show was to conclude by comparing "official and revolutionary art", managed by Adolf Behne, a companion from the days of the *Arbeitsrat für Kunst*, with EHMSEN and MUCHE again.

The last two proposed segments, in particular, symbolized a reorientation of the Novembergruppe, of which there had already been signs in the anniversary publication. With this retrospective, the association was seeking to pick up on the intellectual and artistic ethos of the revolution in 1918–19, something it had consistently rejected as left-wing politicking. In 1921 RAOUL HAUSMANN'S entourage had left the group precisely because of the "amoral" attitude this reflected,[28] and when referring to this spat in 1925 (not so very long ago), HANS SIEBERT VON HEISTER, an executive committee member from 1920 to 1923,[29] had written: "The Novembergruppe was founded in the year 1918 — during those eventful November days — but to make it clear from the start: these artists have nothing to do with politics. Quite the reverse: 3 years ago [*sic*, four years, J.N.], when a little group demanded a one-sided political stance in an attempt to force a split, the general assembly of the Novembergruppe unanimously and vigorously rejected any amalgamation of art and politics. The total transformation in the field of art occurred long before the political revolution, and so the name derived from the month of foundation should be regarded simply as a symbol."[30]

The fact that figures like GROSZ and HEARTFIELD, who in 1924 had been among the founders of the communist art association *Rote Gruppe* and in 1928 ASSO (the "association of revolutionary artists"), had now joined the Novembergruppe provides further evidence of this U-turn towards an emphatically political course.[31] At the same time, these artists used the anniversary of the Novembergruppe, which they had rejected in its early years as bourgeois and apolitical,[32] to inscribe themselves into its history.[33]

The venue chosen for this tenth-anniversary show also marked a watershed, as it did not take place within the Great Berlin Art Exhibition, but as part of another big annual exhibition, the Jury-Free Art Show [*Juryfreie Kunstschau*]. Presumably the association hoped to acquire greater spatial leeway through this move, now that space for groups at the Great Berlin Art Exhibition had been limited by expanding participation and by switching premises to nearby Schloss Bellevue. The "jury-free" art show had been established in 1911 by Hermann Sandkuhl and gave all artists, whatever their views, an opportunity to take part without having to go before a jury first.[34] This open approach reflected the spirit of the Novembergruppe, even though, unlike the *Juryfreie Kunstschau*, the association strictly drew the line at conservative manifestations and was entirely committed to modern art, beginning with Expressionism.

However, the ambitious proposals of the planning committee for the exhibition *Ten Years of the Novembergruppe* [*Zehn Jahre Novembergruppe*] did not prove feasible here either, at least as far as the available space was concerned. The association was given fewer rooms than it had hoped,[35] as the Italian group *Novecento Italiano* turned up in force in addition to the standard programme. In the end, the Novembergruppe had four rooms at its disposal[36] and had to adapt the plan accordingly. The main hall was given over to the realists and social critics, with one room each for the abstract styles, Expressionism in all its varieties and the architects.[37] Sculpture, as surviving photographs show, was integrated into the other segments (figs. 03 and 04).

The exhibition brought together old and new members as well as numerous guests and former companions from home and abroad. As usual, the Novembergruppe displays made no distinction between the 122 exhibitors. Alongside the 'regulars' from Berlin, they included, for example, PAUL KLEE, WILLI BAUMEISTER and OSKAR SCHLEMMER, MARC CHAGALL, WASSILY KANDINSKY and PETER ALMA. The constellation left out neither departed artists and architects, such as OTTO DIX and MIES VAN DER ROHE, nor prestigious names who were showing with the Novembergruppe for the very first time, like CARLO CARRÀ, MAX ERNST and JOHANNES ITTEN.[38] The presentation appeared 'coherent', even though Paul Westheim drew attention once more in *Das Kunstblatt* to the high churn rate in the Novembergruppe, through which the best artists had "almost all merely passed through": "What remained was the majority made up of those who are there too. It is a shame; a true phalanx might have formed here. It did not. Once again the artists failed to deliver. Those who mattered went their own way".[39]

Most reviewers, however, rated the exhibition as a powerful display and one which fulfilled the very purpose proclaimed by the Novembergruppe in the foreword to the catalogue: "The Novembergruppe, herald and flag-bearer in the fight for spiritual content in art, is seeking once again to declare a great community of attitude that reaches back beyond the foundation years and embraces everyone akin to it in views and objectives."[40] This was a reference to the title of KANDINSKY'S well-known essay *Concerning the Spiritual in Art* [*Über das Geistige in der Kunst*], published in 1912, which laid the theoretical foundations for art to turn its back on imitating nature. The association no longer equated "attitude" with the artistic revolution, which had already found its form in Expressionism, Cubism and Futurism before the First World War. Instead, this exhibition shifted the perspective and confined it to the political revolution of 1918–19. Even the Catholic, conservative newspaper *Germania*, with an influence justifiably claimed to extend beyond the region, was persuaded that the "unfinished work of the revolution" was continuing in the ranks of the Novembergruppe: "The fire of political passion

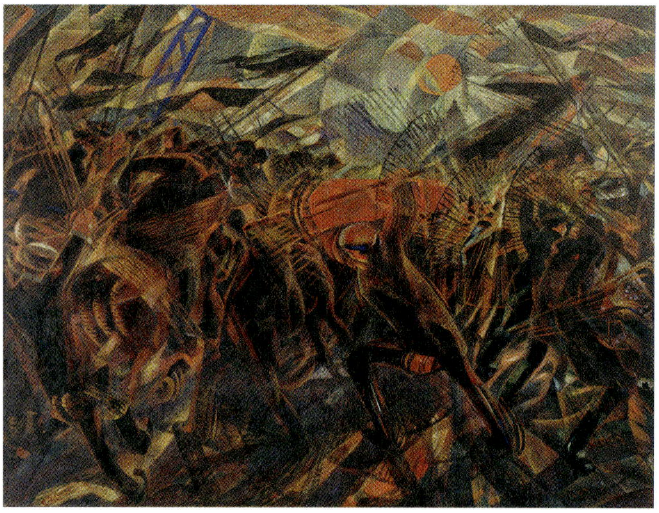

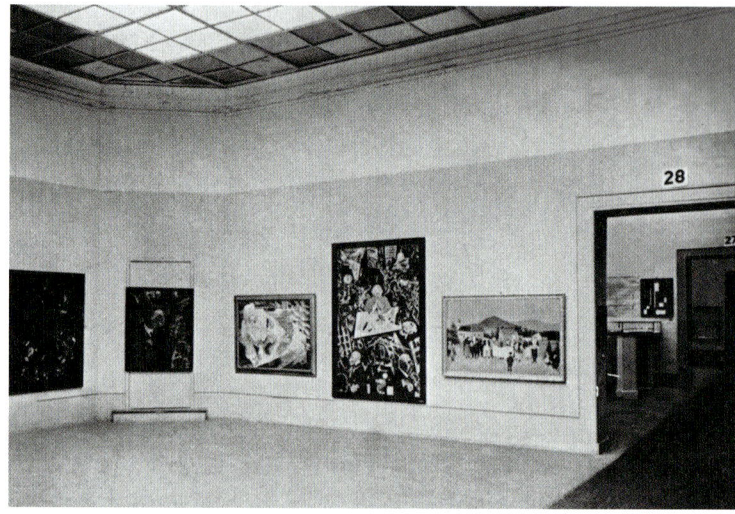

06 / 07

06 CARLO CARRÀ
Funeral of the Anarchist Galli, 1910–11
Museum of Modern Art, New York
Jury-Free Art Show Berlin 1929, exhibition Ten Years of the Novembergruppe, no. 167

07 Jury-Free Art Show Berlin 1929
A room in the exhibition Ten Years of the Novembergruppe. From left to right *The Funeral, Dedicated to Oskar Panizza* by George Grosz, *The Agitator* by Conrad Felixmüller, *The Fisherman* by Heinrich Ehmsen and *Germany, A Winter's Tale* by Grosz

continues burning unextinguished."[41] Max Osborn, the critic for the liberal daily *Vossische Zeitung*, who had covered the association's exhibitions in numerous reviews, expressed a similar standpoint: "The Novembergruppe, which was a sister of the revolution, has every reason to be proud of its work, its stimulating force, its subversive vigour. We know today how much we owe it."[42]

Faced with these concerted memories of the revolutionary period, however, some critics felt "embarrassingly sobered".[43] In the central hall one felt "transplanted into the revolutionary headquarters", recounted the writer and art historian Franz Dülberg,[44] a view endorsed by three surviving photographs (figs. 04, 05 and 07). Taken from three different angles, these images permit an almost total reconstruction of the space. Directly beneath the title of the exhibition, on one of the longer walls, hung *Barricade* [*Barrikade*] by OTTO DIX, since destroyed, where workers and sailors waged a street battle through the distorted lens of Veristic Dada. Flanking this scene were two paintings by OTTO NAGEL, one of them *Boys from Wedding* [*Weddinger Jungen*] (cat. 64, p. 126), and further left was CARLO CARRÀ'S *Funeral of the Anarchist Galli* [*Beerdigung des Anarchisten Galli*] (fig. 06). This icon of both the Italian labour movement and Futurism had been on show in 1912 at the Futurist exhibitions in Paris, London and Berlin.[45] That CARRÀ had exerted a powerful influence on German art — on the young GEORGE GROSZ, for example — was clear from the latter's work *The Adventurer* [*Der Abenteurer*] to its left, but also in his painting *The Funeral, Dedicated to Oskar Panizza* [*Widmung an Oskar Panizza*] (fig. 08). This work had been placed at the other end of the wall between HEINRICH EHMSEN'S painting *Execution of Bavarian Revolutionaries* [*Das Ende bayrischer Revolutionäre*],[46] a reminiscence of the failed soviet republic in Munich, and CONRAD FELIXMÜLLER'S portrayal of the communist politician Otto Rühle entitled *The Agitator* [*Der Agitator*] (cat. 104, p. 208). GROSZ'S funeral scene, a kind of dance of death dedicated to the anti-Wilhelminian physician and journalist Panizza, found itself in the company of revolutionary motifs drawn from the period 1918–19, even though the work had been painted earlier. This interpretative framework was reinforced by a third GROSZ painting, now lost, which hung on the narrow wall of the room: *Germany, A Winter's Tale* [*Deutschland ein Wintermärchen*] (fig. 09) — a panopticon of post-war society, ruled by the old powers of Church, armed forces and industrial bourgeoisie.

Paradoxically, many reviewers in 1929 read these depictions of the revolutionary upheaval as a direct articulation of the early years of the Novembergruppe,[47]

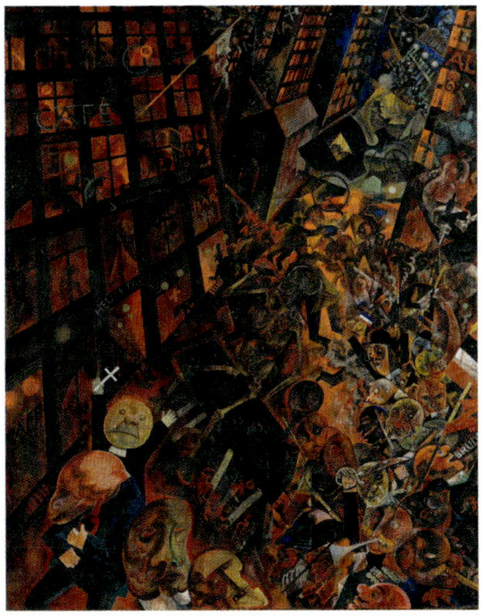
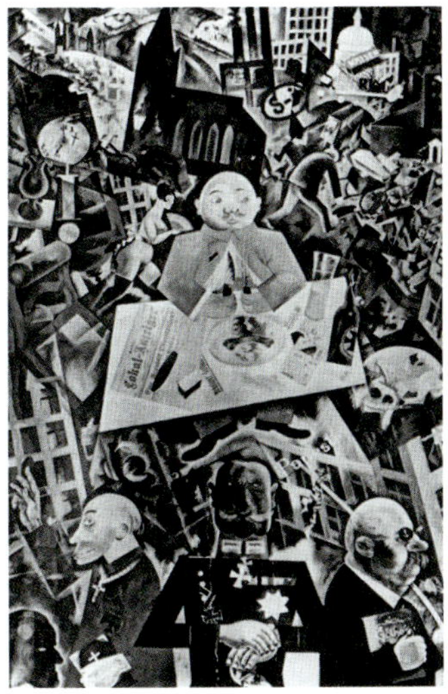
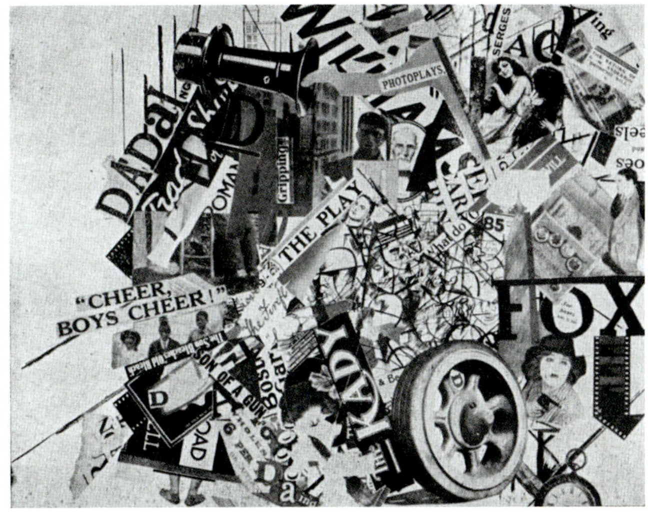

08 09 10

08 GEORGE GROSZ
The Funeral (Dedicated to Oskar Panizza), 1917–1919
Staatsgalerie Stuttgart
Jury-Free Art Show Berlin 1929, exhibition Ten Years of the Novembergruppe, no. 398

09 GEORGE GROSZ
Germany, A Winter's Tale, 1918 whereabouts unknown
Jury-Free Art Show Berlin 1929, exhibition Ten Years of the Novembergruppe, no. 399

10 JOHN HEARTFIELD
Life and Times in Universal City At 5 Past Noon, 1920
whereabouts unknown
Jury-Free Art Show Berlin 1929, exhibition Ten Years of the Novembergruppe, no. 453, repro. in the catalogue

but works like these had precisely *not* been on display it its early exhibitions. These were dominated from 1919 to 1921 by themes of a cosmic and religious nature and by the birth of the New Person in Late Expressionist style.[48] In other words, the Novembergruppe's 'revolutionary' hall effectively manipulated impressions of history and encouraged the idea, in powerful imagery, that the association had always been committed thematically and politically to the ideals of radical left-wing revolution. For most contemporaries, however, the issue had already lost relevance and faded into the mists of time.[49] The *Rote Fahne*, the Communist Party newspaper, naturally took a different view. Its art critic Alfréd Kemény saw through the sudden revolutionary conversion of the Novembergruppe and expressed some scepticism, although welcoming the change of heart: "The ten-year history of the Novembergruppe is the history of a constant ten-year vacillation between the classes, and we do not believe in miracles, as if the Novembergruppe could suddenly turn revolutionary in 1929. Nevertheless, after the stagnation of recent years a decisive step forwards in ideological and artistic terms can be noted this time. The section for socially critical art, which contains some outstanding, characteristic pictorial examples, shows peaks of socially critical — largely still romantic — painting of the recent period."[50]

Kemény perceptively analysed the juxtapositioning of the Novembergruppe and the "fascist" *Novecento Italiano*, which was also taking part in the *Juryfreie Kunstschau* "with picturesque and plastic bigotries under the Mussolini protectorate".[51] CARRÀ had by now also joined this association and was showing a few bucolic and all too classical landscapes. The press response to his presence in both special exhibitions, patently illustrating the shift in his political views, ranged from critical to sarcastic.[52] In Kemény's view, the most blatant antithesis to the works of *Novecento Italiano*, which cultivated the art of the Middle Ages and the Renaissance as a 'ritorno all'ordine' (return to order), were the political photomontage and posters of JOHN HEARTFIELD (fig. 10), presented by the Novembergruppe in a special display[53]: "Those 'artists' who still find today's politics 'nasty' should learn from the spirit of these works."[54]

The urgency of finally adopting a stance in art could not be ignored. The NSDAP, the Nazi party, had been re-founded in 1925 after a ban, and by 1929 it had already entered several regional parliaments, while the *Kampfbund für deutsche Kultur*, set up by Alfred Rosenberg in 1928 to defend "German culture", had declared war on the "cultural bolshevism" of the avant-garde. Although press coverage of the exhibition Ten Years of the Novembergruppe had been predominantly positive and had also proven a success, not least due to several purchases by the Nationalgalerie,[55] the show was targeted by right-wing reviewers. The *Hamburger Nachrichten* berated the art of the Novembergruppe for exuding no "scent of the homeland". It had been affected by too many foreign influences. The reviewer, Fedor von Zobelitz, did not think highly of the international project of the avant-garde: "Painting today lacks a German face. Under alien masks, the physiognomy no longer has any expression."[56]

An Enforced Ending

In October 1929, three weeks after the anniversary show closed, Black Friday on the New York stock exchange triggered the world economic crisis, playing into the hands of ascendant National Socialism. The decline of the Weimar Republic also sealed the fate of the Novembergruppe. The association was plunged into dire financial straits, probably not least because the whole economic climate was catastrophic.[57] The belated commitment to revolution and politics, so powerfully conveyed in 1928–29, was not preserved in the association's section at the Great Berlin Art Exhibition during the following years. The 66 works displayed in 1931 at an additional group show on the premises of the *Verein Berliner Künstler* only reflected the artistic revolution of modernism, so vigorously defended by the association in its earlier period. It is noteworthy that the professional association, an erstwhile antagonist at the Great Berlin Art Exhibition and always seen as a conservative counterweight to the organization with the revolutionary name,[58] made its building available for the Novembergruppe exhibition. Despite this support from the *Verein Berliner Künstler*, the group still needed financial assistance from an allied international association of artists, Porza, which published the catalogue.[59] The foreword was penned by Paul Westheim, who had taken the Novembergruppe to task two years previously but was now an eloquent advocate. Entitled "For the Living!" ["Für die Lebenden!"], his piece warned of a new climate hostile to art, even among intellectuals. The failure to respect progressive artists was responsible, however, for the weakening of the avant-garde. Westheim eloquently urged against stunting the artistic forces who stood both morally and financially for the new, and he ended with a pressing appeal: "[...] we should be mindful: a people that capitulates culturally also capitulates economically and politically."[60]

Only four artists took part in the last known public appearance of the Novembergruppe at the Great Berlin Art Exhibition in 1932: HERBERT BEHRENS-HANGELER, WILHELM SCHMID, WALTER KAMPMANN and KURT SCHWERDTFEGER.[61] The association also stopped organizing its once so popular concerts and parties.[62] Some Novembergruppe members, among them CÉSAR KLEIN, actually founded a new association called *Selection* in mid-1932,[63] but plans for an exhibition[64] were apparently never implemented. Even before the Nazis took power, the Novembergruppe had all but ceased to function.[65] Might it have recovered if Adolf Hitler had not been appointed Chancellor of the Reich in January 1933? It is a futile question. A few months after the Nazi power grab, all artists' associations were brought into line with the regime, which amounted *de facto* to a ban on all avant-garde structures, including the Novembergruppe.[66] All progressive artists' associations were now excluded from the Great Berlin Art Exhibition.[67] Nevertheless, the Novembergruppe continued at first to exist. In 1934 it was still listed in the Berlin directory of addresses. In 1935 it was finally deleted (for a fee) from the register of associations

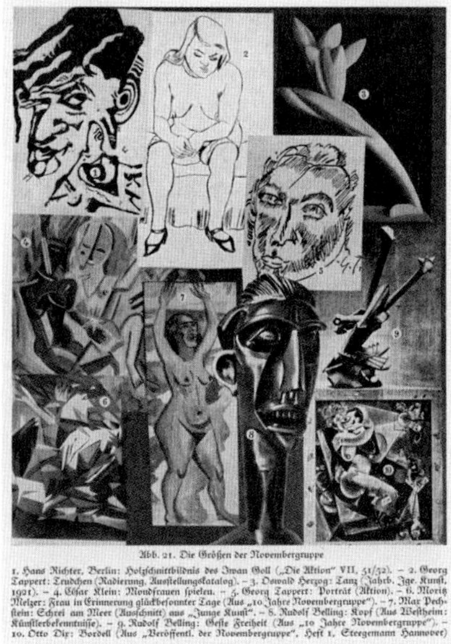

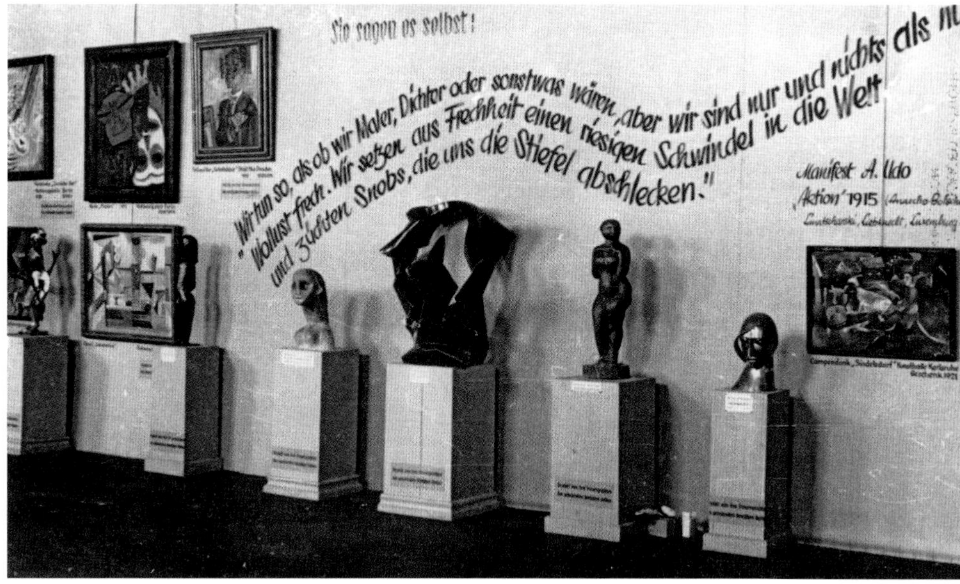

11 Collage of works by Novembergruppe members in Wolfgang Willrich's book *Purging the Temple of Art*, 1937

12 A view of the exhibition *Degenerate Art*, Munich, 1937
In the middle Rudolf Belling's *Triad* and on the far right his *Head in Brass*

(p. 243, cat. 30).[68] The revolutionary beginnings, engraved more firmly on the public consciousness following the commemorative publication and the exhibition to mark its tenth anniversary in 1928–29, now fatally moulded the picture painted of the Novembergruppe by National Socialist propaganda. Nazi periodicals like *Der SA-Mann* and *Der Schulungsbrief*, the principal monthly organ of the NSDAP, repeatedly portrayed the association as a driving force of 'cultural bolshevism' and 'sedition',[69] plunging former members — to the extent that any were still public employees in higher education or other institutions — into serious difficulties.[70] Wolfgang Willrich published an inflammatory tract entitled *Purging the Temple of Art* [*Säuberung des Kunsttempels*], including a list of 174 names identified with the "red Novembergruppe",[71] and drew on illustrative material published by the association itself in order to compile defamatory collages of works exhibited by the group in the course of its existence (fig. 11).[72] Willrich's book laid the ideological foundations for the "Degenerate Art" campaign, which led in the summer of 1937 to the confiscation of modernist works held by public institutions and was an important source for planning the subsequent exhibition, which opened in Munich before travelling on to several other German cities.[73] The exhibits pilloried as "degenerate" included works by former members of the Novembergruppe, among them RUDOLF BELLING.[74] His sculpture *Triad* (cat. 111, p. 215), shown at the vituperative event in Munich (fig. 12) alongside his *Head in Brass* [*Kopf in Messing*] (cat. 108, p. 212), had been exhibited and reproduced on a number of occasions by the Novembergruppe in various different materials. It was a paradigmatic articulation of the desire by the now disbanded association to overcome the boundaries between artistic genres.[75] It speaks volumes for the paradoxical and indifferent nature of art policy at the time that BELLING'S portrait of the boxer *Max Schmeling* was simultaneously being shown at the *Grosse Deutsche Kunstausstellung*, the nationwide exhibition highlight of the year intended by the Nazis as a showpiece in contrast to *Degenerate Art*. All three exhibits had been culled from the Nationalgalerie in Berlin.[76] Other casts of these very same sculptures had been on display at the exhibition Ten Years of the Novembergruppe,[77] but within the space of only eight years the parameters of interpretation had been reversed. Whereas in 1929 these works still epitomized the variety and freedom of avant-garde artistic expression championed by the Novembergruppe, by 1937 *Belling's* works were at one and the same time specimens of the 'ethnic' art of the Third Reich and of the 'degenerate' art of the 'years of decline' when the Novembergruppe had prospered in fertile, liberal soil.

1 "Berliner Frühjahrsausstellungen (Ein Rückblick)", in: *Die Baugilde*, vol. 7, 1925, pp. 800–803, here 801.

2 See *inter alia* the letter from Arthur Segal to Hannah Höch, 25 July 1925, in: Berlinische Galerie 1995, 2. Abt., 25.17, pp. 212f.

3 On the Novembergruppe architects see the essay by Nentwig on pp. 140–151 of this catalogue.

4 In 1923 Peter Foerster was the association's second secretary, in 1923–1925 a member of the exhibition committee and in 1925–26 a member of the working committee, the central body of the Novembergruppe. See the entry "Novembergruppe E.V.", in: Willy Oskar Dressler (ed.), *Dresslers Kunsthandbuch*, Berlin 1923, p. 206; *Handbuch des Kunstmarktes. Kunstadressbuch für das Deutsche Reich, Danzig und Deutsch-Österreich*, Berlin 1926, p. 260; also the catalogues *Grosse Berliner Kunstausstellung 1923 im Landesausstellungsgebäude am Lehrter Bahnhof* (exhib. cat., 19 May – 17 September 1923), Berlin 1923, p. 4; *Grosse Berliner Kunstausstellung 1924 im Landesausstellungsgebäude am Lehrter Bahnhof* (exhib. cat., 31 May – 1 September 1924), Berlin 1924, p. 8; *Ausstellung der Novembergruppe in den Räumen der Berliner Secession in Berlin. Juni 1925. Malerei, Plastik, Architektur*, Berlin 1925 (= Archiv der deutschen Kunst, vol. 5, 1925, no. 3), unpaginated

5 Letter from Peter Foerster to Hannah Höch, 17 July 1927, quoted in: Berlinische Galerie 1995, 2. Abt., 27.3, pp. 288f., here 289.

6 See Kliemann 1969, p. 44, and the contribution by Rocha, p. 68 of this catalogue.

7 See the letter from Ines Wetzel to Otto Freundlich, 5 February 1930, Institut Mémoires de l'édition contemporaine, Saint-Germain la Blanche-Herbe, Fonds Otto Freundlich, 286 FRN, 16.20, Div. 74.

8 See the essay by Kratz-Kessemeier, pp. 35f. of this catalogue.

9 See Wünsche 2015 on the abstract artists who emerged from the *Internationale Vereinigung der Expressionisten, Futuristen, Kubisten und Konstruktivisten*, a close ally of the gallery Der Sturm. At the Great Berlin Art Exhibition in 1926, this group even picked up the Novembergruppe's idea of publishing their own guide, see *Das Wissen um Expressionismus. Führer durch die Ausstellung der Abstrakten. Grosse Berliner Kunstausstellung 1926*, Berlin 1926 (= Veröffentlichungen des Kunstarchivs, vol. 10).

10 See *inter alia* Matelowski 2017, pp. 130–140 and 227–284; Lammert 1996; Scholz 2017. On Belling's *Triad* see also the contribution by von Rüden, p. 214 of this catalogue.

11 See *inter alia* the catalogues to the Great Berlin Art Exhibition 1919–1924; *Ausstellung der Novembergruppe in den Räumen der Berliner Secession in Berlin. Juni 1925. Malerei, Plastik, Architektur*, Berlin 1925 (= Archiv der deutschen Kunst, vol. 5, 1925, no. 3), unpaginated; entry "Novembergruppe E.V.", in: Willy Oskar Dressler (ed.), *Dresslers Kunsthandbuch*, Berlin 1923, p. 206.

12 Letter from Rudolf Belling to Hannah Höch, 24 April 1928, quoted in: Berlinische Galerie 1995, 2. Abt., 28.7, pp. 313f., here 313.

13 Letter from Moriz Melzer on behalf of the Novembergruppe to Otto Freundlich, 4 September 1928, Institut Mémoires de l'édition contemporaine, Saint-Germain la Blanche-Herbe, Fonds Otto Freundlich, 286 FRN, Div. 73; see also Letter from Moriz Melzer on behalf of the Novembergruppe to Fritz Stuckenberg, 1 September 1928, Städtische Galerie Delmenhorst, Fritz Stuckenberg Fonds.

14 Melzer to Freundlich (ref. in note 13).

15 Unlike other artists' associations founded during the revolution of 1918–19, the *Dresdner Sezession Gruppe* never operated officially in 1919 as a so-called local branch of the Novembergruppe, even if it featured along with Conrad Felixmüller on a provisional list of members (p. 252 of this catalogue) and its foundation manifesto was quoted in the publication *Ten Years of the Novembergruppe* (*Zehn Jahre Novembergruppe*, special issue of *Kunst der Zeit. Zeitschrift für Kunst und Literatur*, vol. 3, 1928, nos. 1–3, p. 22). However, many of its members were also organized in the Berlin-based association, among them Felixmüller, Otto Lange and Wilhelm Heckrott. In 1922 *Das Junge Rheinland*, the *Dresdner Sezession* and the Novembergruppe set up the *Kartell fortschrittlicher Künstlergruppen in Deutschland* and jointly published a journal whose title comprised the different group names. On Grohmann see Rudert 2012. Despite the claim in this biography of Grohmann (op. cit., 354), the issue *Zehn Jahre Novembergruppe* was published independently and not on the occasion of the eponymous exhibition which, moreover, was held in 1929 as part of the *Juryfreie Kunstschau* and not as described in 1928 as part of the Great Berlin Art Exhibition.

16 See the Letter from Otto Freundlich to the Novembergruppe, 11 February 1919, in: *Zehn Jahre Novembergruppe*, ref. in note 15, pp. 33f.

17 See Will Grohmann, "Zehn Jahre Novembergruppe", in: *Zehn Jahre Novembergruppe*, ref. in note 15, pp. 1–9, here esp. 3–5. On the crisis in the Novembergruppe in 1921, see the essay by Burmeister, p. 89 of this catalogue.

18 See *inter alia* Max Osborn, "Novembergruppe. Die Ausstellung in der Sezession", in: *Vossische Zeitung*, 24 June 1925, no. 295, and the extract from the article reprinted in the anniversary publication (*Zehn Jahre Novembergruppe*, ref. in note 15, p. 81).

19 Otto Brattskoven, "Kunstchronik: 10 Jahre Novembergruppe—Was ist und treibt 'Porza'—Typographische Besonderheiten", in: *Die Neue Bücherschau*, vol. 7, 1929, pp. 47f., here 47; see also Otto Brattskoven, "Novembergruppe", in: *Sozialistische Monatshefte*, vol. 35, 1929, no. 1, p. 79.

20 Paul F. Schmidt, "10 Jahre Novembergruppe", in: *Das Kunstblatt*, vol. 13, 1929, no. 1, p. 31.

21 Will Grohmann, ref. in note 17, here p. 1.

22 Ibid., p. 2.

23 Ibid., p. 5.

24 Ibid., p. 3.

25 On this exhibition see also Kliemann 1969, pp. 45f.

26 Ausstellungskommission der Novembergruppe, "Ausschreibung zur Ausstellung *Zehn Jahre Novembergruppe*", June 1929, Berlin, Bauhaus-Archiv, Dokumentensammlung, folder "Novembergruppe", first published in Kliemann 1969, p. 83.

27 Documents show that Grosz and Heartfield were already members of the Novembergruppe in 1927. During that year Grosz showed works with the Novembergruppe, such as his painting *The Pillars of Society* [*Stützen der Gesellschaft*] (cat. 106, p. 211), which had initially been rejected by the *Kartell* as an organizer of the Great Berlin Art Exhibition. The Novembergruppe write a protest letter successfully defending the works of "our member George Grosz", and Heartfield was among the members of the Novembergruppe who signed ("Brief von Max Dungert und anderen Mitgliedern der Novembergruppe", 22 April 1927, Berlin, Akademie der Künste, George Grosz Archiv, Grosz 409). Ehmsen also showed at the Great Berlin Art Exhibition in 1927, but as membership of associations was not indicated in that year's catalogue his status with the Novembergruppe is not proven until 1928, see *Grosse Berliner Kunstausstellung 1928. Veranstaltet vom Kartell der vereinigten Verbände bildender Künstler Berlins e. V. im Landesausstellungsgebäude* (exhib. cat., 9 May–end of July 1928), Berlin 1928, nos. 233 and 234. All three artists are mentioned in the membership list for 1930 (see pp. 254–255 of this catalogue). On Grosz's *Pillars of Society* see also the contribution by von Rüden, p. 210 of this catalogue.

28 See the essay by Burmeister, pp. 80–91 of this catalogue.

29 See Hans Siebert von Heister, "Lebenslauf", 30 June 1966, Berlinische Galerie, BG-Ar 13/99, pp. 66f.

30 v. H. [Hans Siebert von Heister], "Ein Abend der Novembergruppe im Berliner Rundfunk", in: *Der deutsche Rundfunk*, vol. 3, 1925, pp. 1197–1199, here 1197.

31 For an introduction to the *Rote Gruppe* and *ASSO* see Wilhelmi 1996, pp. 314–316 and 70–78. The *Rote Gruppe* did not split directly from the Novembergruppe, as often stated in the literature, but was founded independently.

32 Grosz was among the signatories of the open letter in which the opposition around Raoul Hausmann declared their resignation in 1921 (in: *Der Gegner*, vol. 2, 1920–21, nos. 8–9, pp. 297–301).

33 From 1928 to 1930 Grosz and Heartfield's brother Wieland Herzfelde faced court proceedings on a charge of blasphemy over Grosz's folder *Background [Hintergrund]* published by Herzfelde's Malik-Verlag (see *inter alia* Hütt 1990, pp. 60–67). The fact that the Novembergruppe involved Grosz so conspicuously in the organization of the exhibition *10 Jahre Novembergruppe* held in August 1929 and allocated him such prominent hanging slots in the main hall for the three works he had submitted can certainly be interpreted as support for Grosz and his critical views on state and society.

34 For an introduction to the *Juryfreie Kunstschau* see Berlinische Galerie 1979, pp. 34f., although there the date of establishment is erroneously given as 1912.

35 See the letter from Ines Wetzel to Otto Freundlich, 2 September 1929, Institut Mémoires de l'édition contemporaine, Saint-Germain la Blanche-Herbe, Fonds Otto Freundlich, 286 FRN, 16.20, Div. 72.

36 See E. C. [Ernst Collin], "Wie wird die Juryfreie Kunstschau aussehen? In den Ausstellungen", in: *Berliner Volkszeitung*, 15 August 1929, no. 382.

37 See Max Osborn, "Die Juryfreien", in: *Vossische Zeitung*, 31 August 1929, no. 411; see also R. T., "Die Großen Juryfreien in Berlin", in: *München-Augsburger Abendzeitung*, 8 September 1929.

38 The Novembergruppe had also invited Kasimir Malevich (see Vakar and Mikhienko 2015, vol. 1, letter 175, p. 217). Despite expressing an intention to submit works, he does not seem to have done so, as Malevich is not listed in the catalogue to the *Juryfreie Kunstschau* in 1929. It is highly probable that the artist was not, contrary to a widespread assumption (first in Kliemann 1969, p. 24), responding to an initiative from the Novembergruppe when he staged his now legendary solo exhibition at the Great Berlin Art Exhibition in 1927, but that his participation was the result of his contacts with the former member Hugo Häring and the architects' association *Der Ring* (on this see Nentwig, p. 238 of this catalogue).

39 P. W. [Paul Westheim], "Ausstellungen", in: *Das Kunstblatt*, vol. 13, 1929, no. 10, pp. 318f., here 319.

40 Novembergruppe, "Geleitwort zur Ausstellung 10 Jahre Novembergruppe (1918–1928)", in: *Juryfreie Kunstschau Berlin 1929. Malerei, Graphik, Plastik und Architektur. Landes-Ausstellungsgebäude am Lehrter Bahnhof* (exhib. cat., 25 August–5 October 1929), Berlin 1929, unpaginated.

41 Albert Müller, "Juryfreie Kunstschau", in: *Germania*, 3 September 1929 (morning edition).

42 Max Osborn, "Die Juryfreien", in: *Vossische Zeitung*, 31 August 1929, no. 411; for a similarly positive review see Willi Wolfradt, "Berliner Ausstellungen", in: *Cicerone*, vol. 21, 1929, pp. 527–529.

43 Ernst Kállai, "Zehn Jahre Novembergruppe", in: *Der Kunstnarr*, vol. 1, 1929, no. 1, p. 28; see also *inter alia* B. E. Werner, "Die Maler der Juryfreien Kunstschau", in: *Deutsche Allgemeine Zeitung*, 19 September 1929, newspaper cutting, César Klein Fonds.

44 Franz Dülberg, "Die Zehnjahresausstellung der Novembergruppe", in: *Der Türmer*, November issue, 1929, newspaper cutting, Berlinische Galerie, Heinrich Ehmsen Fonds, BG-HE 27.

45 See Weissweiler 2009, pp. 66–68.

46 The painting Ehmsen showed with the Novembergruppe was a version of the same motif found in another painting of the same title (now in the Hermitage in St Petersburg).

47 See *inter alia* Franz Servaes, "J. K. B. 29. Berliner Kunstbrief", in: *Leipziger Neueste Nachrichten*, 27 September 1929; Willi Wolfradt, "Berliner Ausstellungen", in: *Cicerone*, vol. 21, 1929, pp. 527–529; g. [W. K. Gevger], "Juryfreie Kunstausstellung Berlin 1929", in: *Chemnitzer Tageblatt*, 4 October 1929; almost identical text in *Hannoverscher Anzeiger*, 17 September 1929, and *Magdeburger Generalanzeiger*, 8 September 1929, newspaper cuttings, César Klein Fonds.

48 See the essay by Nentwig, pp. 42–55 of this catalogue.

49 See "Juryfreie Kunstschau 1929", in: *Der Tag*, 1 September 1929, newspaper cutting, César Klein Fonds; Curt Glaser, "Juryfreie Kunstschau", in: *Kunst und Künstler* vol. 28, 1929, no. 2, pp. 75f.

50 Dur. [Durus, i.e. Alfréd Kemény], "Juryfreie Kunstschau 1929", in: *Rote Fahne*, 5 September 1929, no. 171 (supplements).

51 Ibid.

52 See Ragazzi 2008, pp. 253f.

53 The Heartfield presentation was arranged by Ines Wetzel (see her letter to Otto Freundlich, 2 September 1929, Institut Mémoires de l'édition contemporaine, Saint-Germain la Blanche-Herbe, Fonds Otto Freundlich, 286 FRN, 16.20, partly reprinted in Heusinger von Waldegg 1978, p. 262). The catalogue to the *Juryfreie Kunstschau* of 1929 contains the general reference "photomontages" under no. 453. The only one illustrated and hence documented is the photomontage *Life and Times in Universal City At 5 Past Noon* [*Leben und Treiben in Universal City 12 Uhr 5 mittags*], now lost, in which he incorporated a drawing by Grosz and which served as the cover illustration for the catalogue to the *Erste Internationale Dada-Messe*.

54 Ref. in note 50.

55 On the purchases for the Nationalgalerie by the culture ministry, including works by Christof Drexel, Willi Baumeister and Jean Metzinger, see the essay by Kratz-Kessemeier, p. 36 of this catalogue. Heinrich Ehmsen was responsible for the invoicing, see *inter alia* the letters from Heinrich Ehmsen (Novembergruppe, working committee) to Ludwig Justi (Nationalgalerie), 5 January 1930, and to Alfred Hentzen (Nationalgalerie), 16 January 1930, Staatliche Museen zu Berlin, Zentralarchiv, NG Gen. 10, col. 14, folio 697 and NG Gen. 10, vol. 15, folio 31.

56 Fedor von Zobelitz, "Aus dem Tagebuch", in: *Hamburger Nachrichten*, 3 September 1929, no. 410.

57 Oskar Schlemmer wrote to Willi Baumeister about the financial Situation without discussing reasons in detail: "Worth knowing that the Novembergruppe burst with a deficit of 3000.–, affidavit, etc." (Letter of 17 November 1932, Kunstarchiv der Staatsgalerie Stuttgart, Oskar Schlemmer Archive, AOS 2015/1688).

58 See the essay by Nentwig, pp. 47–52 of this catalogue.

59 On Porza see Wilhelmi 1996, pp. 226f.; Berlinische Galerie 1979, pp. 47f.; Kliemann 1969, p. 45 and note 72. Porza was founded in 1927 as an aid organization for artists and ran convalescence homes all over Europe. The first centre opened in October 1928 in Lugano in Switzerland. From 1929 the association published its own periodical. Many members of the Novembergruppe, including Oswald Herzog, Max Dungert, Walter Dexel, Walter Kampmann, Issai Kulvianski, Moriz Melzer and Arthur Segal, took part in its exhibitions (see *inter alia* P. Friedrich, "Porza", in: *Berliner Börsen-Zeitung*, 24 April 1928, newspaper cutting, Berlinische Galerie, Issai Kulvianski Fonds, NIK 005).

60 Paul Westheim, "Für die Lebenden!", in: *November-Gruppe. Ausstellung im neuen Hause des Vereins Berliner Künstler, Gemälde, Plastik*, edited by Porza, Berlin 1931 (= Veröffentlichungen des Kunstarchivs, no. 58), pp. 2f., here 3. In his review Westheim describes the show as "one of the most serious exhibitions that we have seen in Berlin for a long time" (Paul Westheim, "Ausstellungen", in: *Das Kunstblatt*, vol. 15, 1931, pp. 251–255).

61 *Grosse Berliner Kunstausstellung 1932 im Schloss Bellevue. Amtlicher Katalog der I. Abteilung. Veranstalter Kartell der vereinigten Verbände bildender Künstler Berlins* (exhib. cat., 8 May – 14 August 1932), Berlin 1932, no. 129–141, 308–313, 445–454, 489f. From 1929 the Great Berlin Art Exhibition took the form of two sections at Schloss Bellevue. Paintings and sculptures were shown in spring and primarily prints and drawings in autumn. No catalogues have been identified for the second sections in the years 1931 and 1932. Reviews indicate that an exhibition of this kind must have taken place from September 1932 (see *inter alia* "Zeitlupe", in: *Das Kunstblatt*, vol. 16, 1932, pp. 71–72). However, the Novembergruppe is not mentioned by name, so its participation is not documented.

62 The last known musical soirée by the Novembergruppe was on 8 April 1931 (see the sheet programme, in: Berlinische Galerie 1995, 2. Abt., 31.33, p. 424). That year the association did not throw any big fancy-dress balls, but evidently there were still some studio parties in a more private setting (see B-y, "Berliner Bälle", in: *Neues Wiener Tagblatt*, 13 February 1931, no. 44). On 23 January 1932 the association was involved once more in a fancy-dress ball to relieve financial distress among fine artists organized by the *Reichsverband bildender Künstler* and other associations of artists (see the poster designed by Ernst Fritsch, Staatliche Museen zu Berlin, Kunstbibliothek, Sammlung Plakat- und Reklamekunst, shelf no. 14004340; fig. 28, p. 242).

63 See Wilhelmi 1996, pp. 326f.; minutes of the foundation meeting and statutes of the group *Selection*, 14 June 1932, César Klein Fonds; also the letters from Oskar Schlemmer to Will Grohmann, 9 August 1932 (Kunstarchiv der Staatsgalerie Stuttgart, Will Grohmann Fonds) and to Willi Baumeister (ref. in note 57).

64 See *inter alia* "Eine neue Künstlervereinigung", in: *Vossische Zeitung*, 19 October 1932, no. 502.

65 See also Kliemann 1969, p. 46.

66 See ibid., p. 48 and note 79.

67 See *inter alia* Kliemann 1969, note 74; Nungesser 1988, pp. 89–91.

68 First in Schulz 1993, p. 21.

69 See *inter alia* "Aber, aber—wie kann man nur!", in: *Der SA-Mann*, 22 May 1937, p. 8; "Oder so?", in: *Der SA-Mann*, 31 July 1937, p. 9; Walter Hansen, [text on page 3 of pictures] in: *Der Schulungsbrief. Das zentrale Monatsblatt der NSDAP und DAF*, March 1937, p. 20.

70 For more detail see Nentwig, p. 243 of this catalogue.

71 Wolfgang Willrich, *Säuberung des deutschen Kunsttempels. Eine kunstpolitische Kampfschrift zur Gesundung deutscher Kunst im Geiste nordischer Art*, Munich 1937, pp. 168f., with an index of 179 names. See especially the section headed "Ursprung und Verlauf der roten Kunstverseuchung" (ibid., pp. 40–90), which uses hate speech in ascribing a pivotal role in the "red contamination of art" to the Novembergruppe.

72 The book is based on a collection of material by Walter Hansen (see Wulf 1966, p. 401), who also attacked the Novembergruppe in the press (ref. in note 69).

73 Even if the Novembergruppe is not explicitly mentioned in the exhibition and accompanying guide, visitors would be familiar with the name from an information panel at the entrance listing artists' associations denigrated as "degenerate" and showing the names of their members (for a description see Hugo Sieker, "Entartete Kunst—Zur Abschreckung ausgestellt", in: *Hamburger Anzeiger*, 20 July 1937, no. 166). The travelling exhibition *Entartete Kunst* was just one of many exhibitions to discredit artists as part of Nazi art policy. For a detailed account see Zuschlag 1995, and on Willrich and his role in the "Degenerate Art" campaign see op. cit., pp. 385f.

74 Other former Novembergruppe members whose works were shown in the Hofgarten Arcades in Munich were Jankel Adler, Willi Baumeister, Herbert Bayer, Heinrich Campendonk, Walter Dexel, Lyonel Feininger, Conrad Felixmüller, Otto Freundlich, George Grosz, Wilhelm Heckrott, Hans Siebert von Heister, Oswald Herzog, Bernhard Hoetger, Alexej von Jawlensky, Wassily Kandinsky, Otto Lange, El Lissitzky, Ewald Mataré, Ludwig Meidner, Johannes Molzahn, Georg Muche, Max Pechstein, Hans Richter, Emy Roeder, Christian Rohlfs, Edwin Scharff, Oskar Schlemmer, Rudolf Schlichter, Kurt Schwitters, Lasar Segall and Karl Völker. The exhibition also included many prominent guests, such as Johannes Itten, Paul Klee and Piet Mondrian, and also members of local "affiliates" like the *Dresdner Sezession*, among them Otto Dix. Many more artists associated with the Novembergruppe had been affected by the preceding seizures of works (see the database recording works confiscated during the "Degenerate Art" campaign, Forschungsstelle "Entartete Kunst", FU Berlin).

75 In 1920 the title of this work was also under consideration as a name for the association's magazine; see the cover design by Moriz Melzer (p. 214, fig. 01).

76 The delivery of the Schmeling figure to the *Grosse Deutsche Kunstausstellung* was explicitly requested by Belling, who was teaching in Istanbul from early 1937 and had been officially requested to take part. After numerous complaints and enquiries about why the artist had been included in the two antithetical events, *Triad* and *Head in Brass* were removed from the exhibition *Degenerate Art* (see Scholz 1997, pp. 66–68).

77 *Juryfreie Kunstschau Berlin 1929. Malerei, Graphik, Plastik und Architektur. Landes-Ausstellungsgebäude am Lehrter Bahnhof* (exhib. cat., 25 August–5 October 1929), Berlin 1929, nos. 78, 80 and 81. Under no. 79 Belling also displayed his *Head in Mahogany [Kopf in Mahagoni]*, now also held by *Staatliche Museen zu Berlin, Nationalgalerie*.

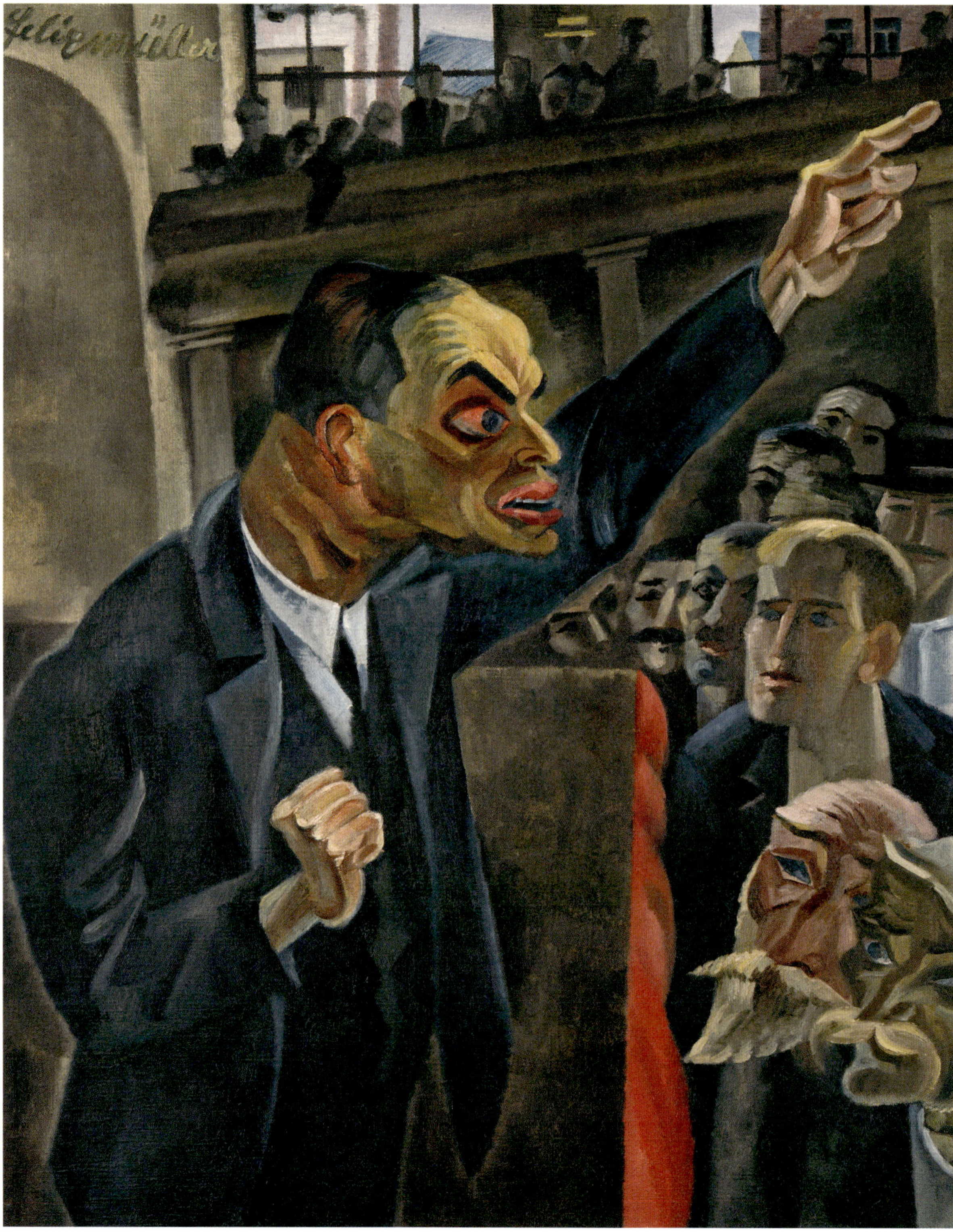

104
CONRAD FELIXMÜLLER
The Agitator, 1946

New version of the destroyed painting of 1920. Oil on canvas, 125 × 93 cm. Staatliche Museen zu Berlin, Nationalgalerie

Jury-Free Art Show Berlin 1929, exhibition Ten Years of the Novembergruppe, no. 270 (original painting)

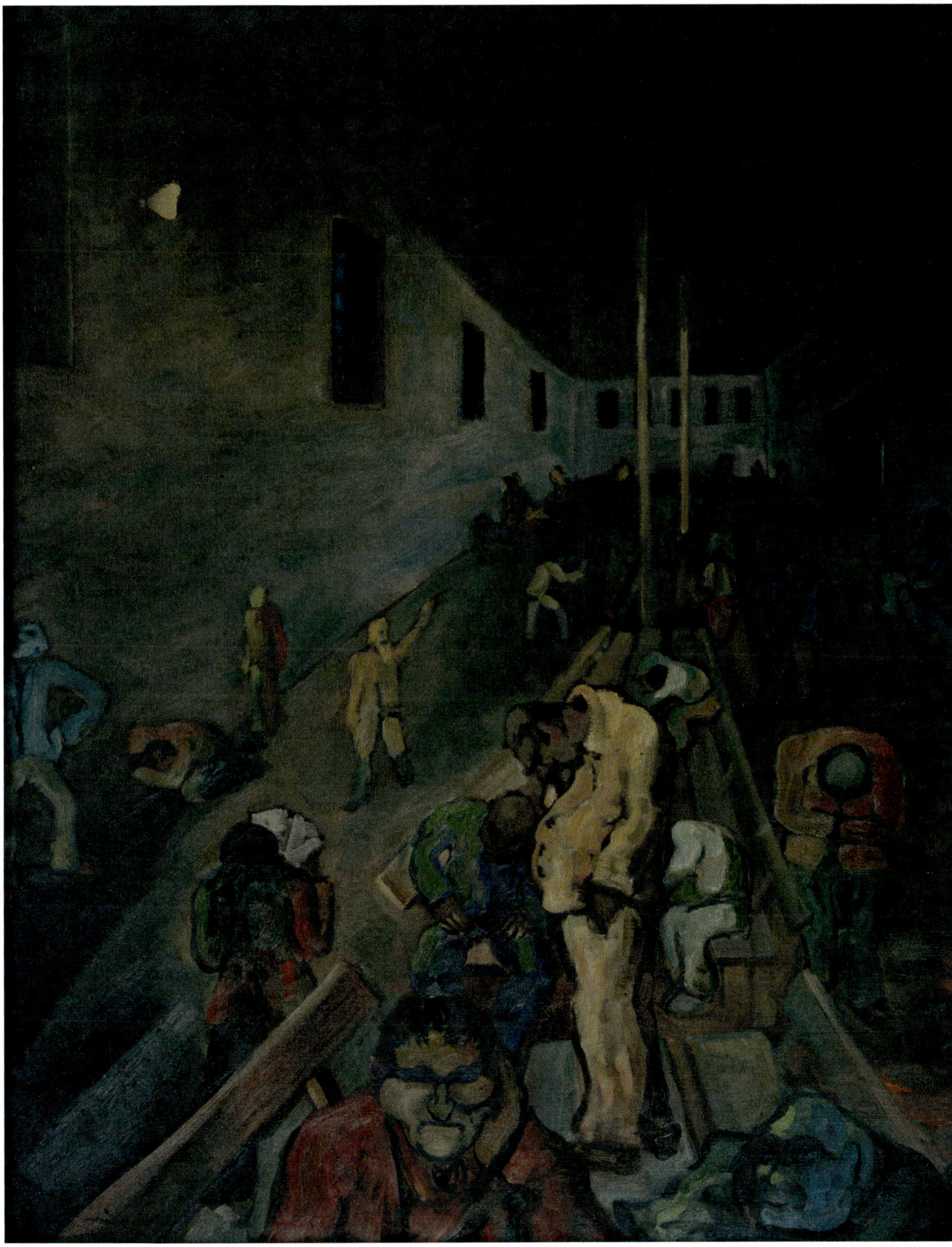

105

HEINRICH EHMSEN

Hall for the Insane, 1925

Oil on canvas, 127 × 100 cm
Kulturstiftung Sachsen-Anhalt, Kunstmuseum Moritzburg Halle (Saale)

Most probably shown as *Hall in a Madhouse* at the
Great Berlin Art Exhibition 1927, Novembergruppe section, no. 103

GEORGE GROSZ
The Pillars of Society, 1926

"At the Great Berlin, GEORGE GROSZ provides a sharp cross-section through the German republic in his *Pillars of Society* [*Stützen der Gesellschaft*],"[1] observed the communist newspaper *Die Rote Fahne*. This was Grosz's entry for the Novembergruppe section in 1927, and it was the first time that the artist had shown at the Great Berlin Art Exhibition.

The "pillars", as the artist ironically called the cast of his painting, occupy the foreground of the vertical format (cat. 106, p. 211): the brutal alumnus of a duelling fraternity, identified by the scars on his face,[2] sits at a table over a beer glaring at the sabre in his right hand. His blue tie sports a swastika; his open skull reveals heroic war fantasies, possibly memories of his younger days in the cavalry. The journalist is armed with a pencil, a blood-drenched palm leaf and a bundle of daily newspapers showing fragments of inflammatory text. Grim-faced, he wears an upside-down chamber pot for a hat. The still-steaming excrement has landed in the fissured head of a portly politician with a resemblance to the country's former president Friedrich Ebert.[3] "Socialism is work" promises the leaflet on his chest, yet in his hand he holds the black, white and red flag of the Reich preferred by anti-republican nationalists and right-wingers. A clergyman, his face warped in frenzied ecstasy, lifts his arms to invoke chaos and violence, a threatening scenario, as the troops marching off in the background and the burning house fronts confirm.

In this painting the communist George Grosz[4] denounced the reactionary forces in the Weimar Republic in response to the unstable constitution of the democratic system, as he describes in his autobiography: "There were speakers on every street corner and songs of hatred everywhere. Everyone was hated: the Jews, the capitalists, the gentry, the communists, the military, the landlords, the workers, the unemployed, the 'Black' *Reichswehr* [German Armed Forces], the [Allied] control commissions, the politicians, the department stores, and again the Jews. It was a real orgy of incitement, and the Republic was so weak that you hardly took notice of it. [...]. Those in power do nothing. Ebert has his beard trimmed and exchanges his democratic worker's cap for a top-hat; he now looks more like a Chairman of the Board, and dresses accordingly."[5] Grosz's reaction was to paint merciless works like *The Pillars of Society*, seeing them as tools to influence society directly and to foster a critical awareness.

Nor did the poignancy of this caricature, an affront to ruling politicians, escape the scrutiny of the exhibition committee at the Great Berlin Art Exhibition. It took a letter from MAX DUNGERT and other members of the Novembergruppe, sent to those responsible on 22 April 1927, to avert the impending censorship: "If the Novembergruppe gives way to the request from the Kartell to exclude the painting by our member George Grosz from the exhibition, the undersigned will withdraw their works."[6] This determination and vehement defence of Grosz, already charged on several occasions for offences including blasphemy and defamation, probably had something to do with the political momentum which had gripped the association in the run-up to its tenth anniversary. The artists deliberately turned to socially critical, left-wing themes[7] — and George Grosz had evidently noticed the trend, motivating him to join an association that had previously appeared to him too bourgeois.

He had been an early champion of greater political commitment from the artistic community: "Come out from your parlours, even if you find it hard, cast aside your individual barriers, be borne along by the ideas of working people and assist them in the struggle against a putrid society."[8]

JUSCHKA MARIE VON RÜDEN

1 "Große Berliner und Juryfreie Kunstschau", in: *Rote Fahne*, 21 May 1927, no. 119.

2 Schuster 1994, p. 348.

3 Kranzfelder 1993, p. 70.

4 He belonged to the Communist Party from 1919 to 1923 and was a key member of the Dada group in Berlin.

5 Grosz 1955, pp. 143f. English version: pp. 149–150.

6 Letter from Max Dungert (and other members of the Novembergruppe), 22 April 1927, ADK, George Grosz Archiv, Grosz 409. I am grateful to Janina Nentwig for drawing my attention to this letter.

7 See the essay by Nentwig, pp. 200f. of this catalogue

8 George Grosz, "Statt einer Biographie", in: *Der Gegner*, vol. 2, 1920, no. 3, pp. 68–70, here 69f.

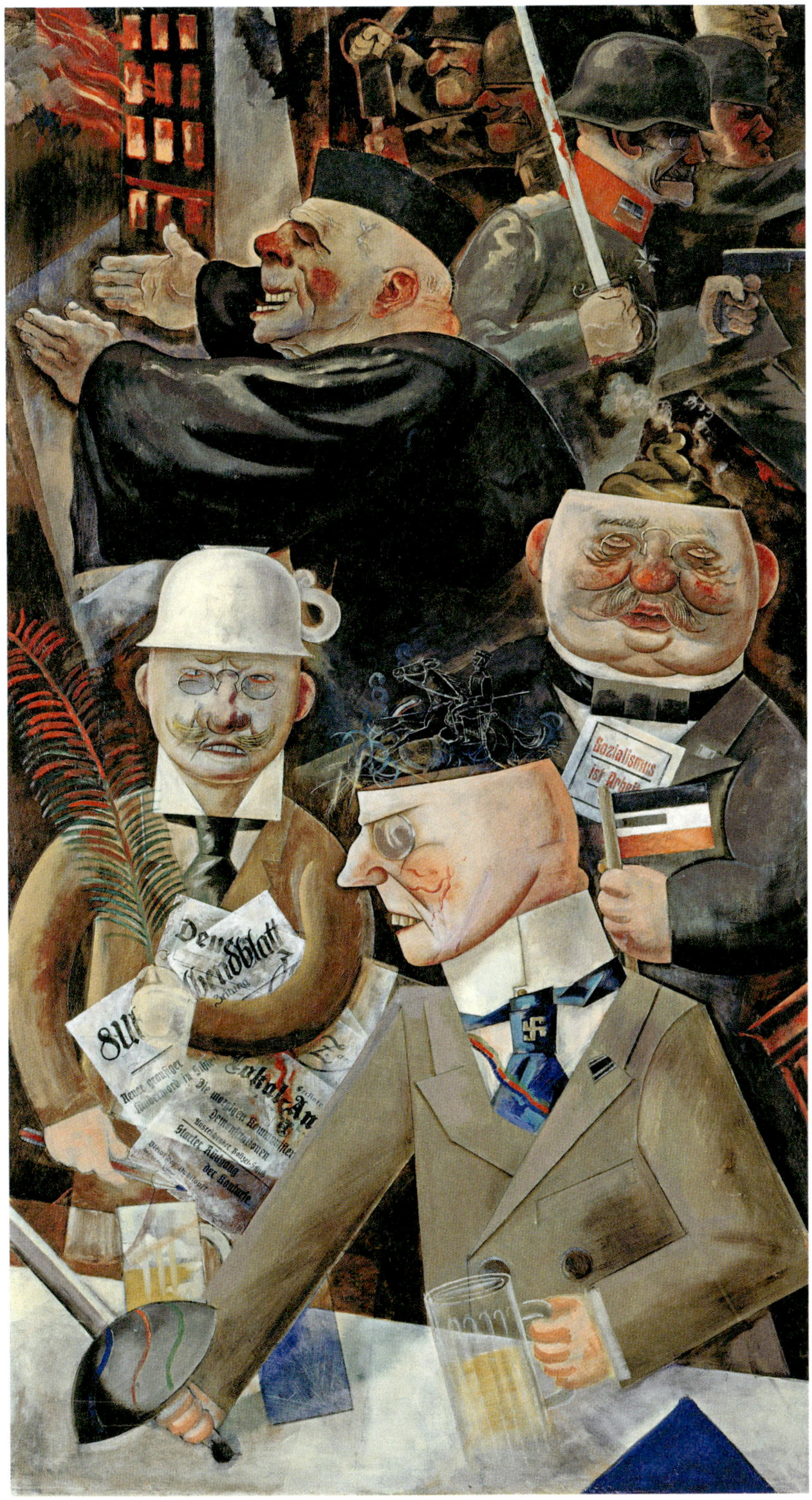

106

GEORGE GROSZ

Pillars of Society, 1926

Oil on canvas, 200 × 108 cm
Staatliche Museen zu Berlin, Nationalgalerie

Great Berlin Art Exhibition 1927,
Novembergruppe section, no. 167a

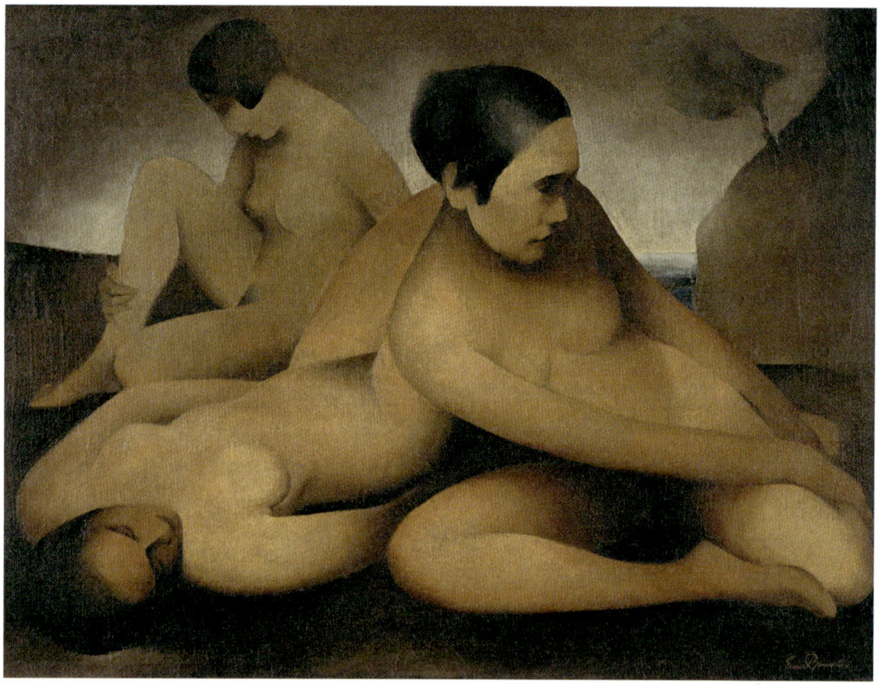

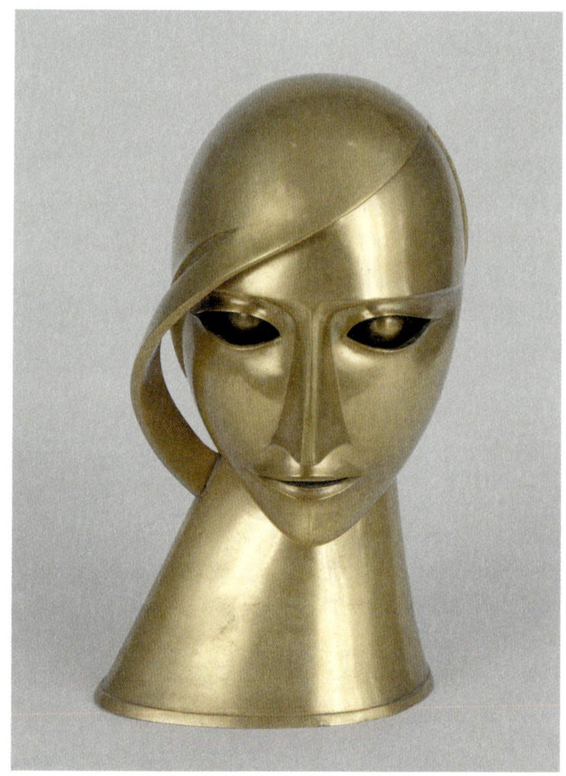

107
ERNST NEUSCHUL
Women Resting, 1926

Oil on canvas, 67 × 87 cm
Berlinische Galerie

Neuschul exhibited with the Novembergruppe several times between 1926 and 1931. None of the works he showed have yet been identified.

108
RUDOLF BELLING
Head in Brass (Toni Freeden), 1925

Brass, 38.3 × 22.5 × 19 cm
Staatliche Museen zu Berlin, Nationalgalerie

Novembergruppe exhibition at the Berlin Secession, 1925, no. 15; Jury-Free Art Show Berlin 1929, exhibition Ten Years of the Novembergruppe, no. 80

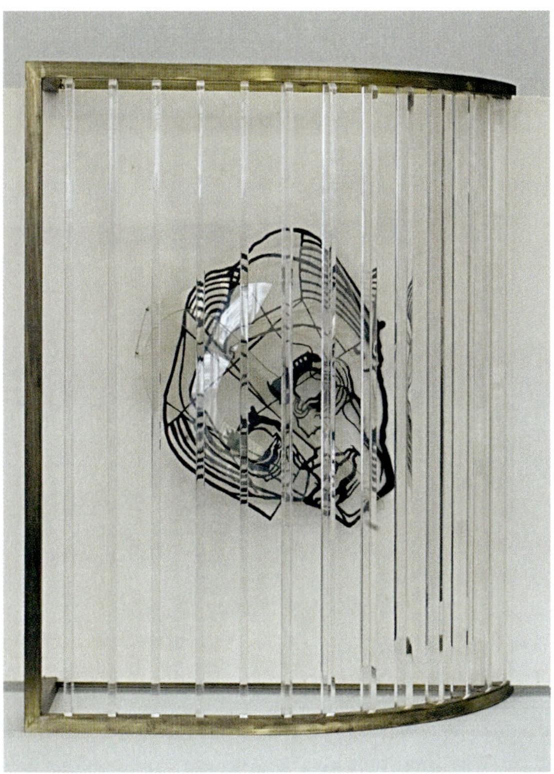

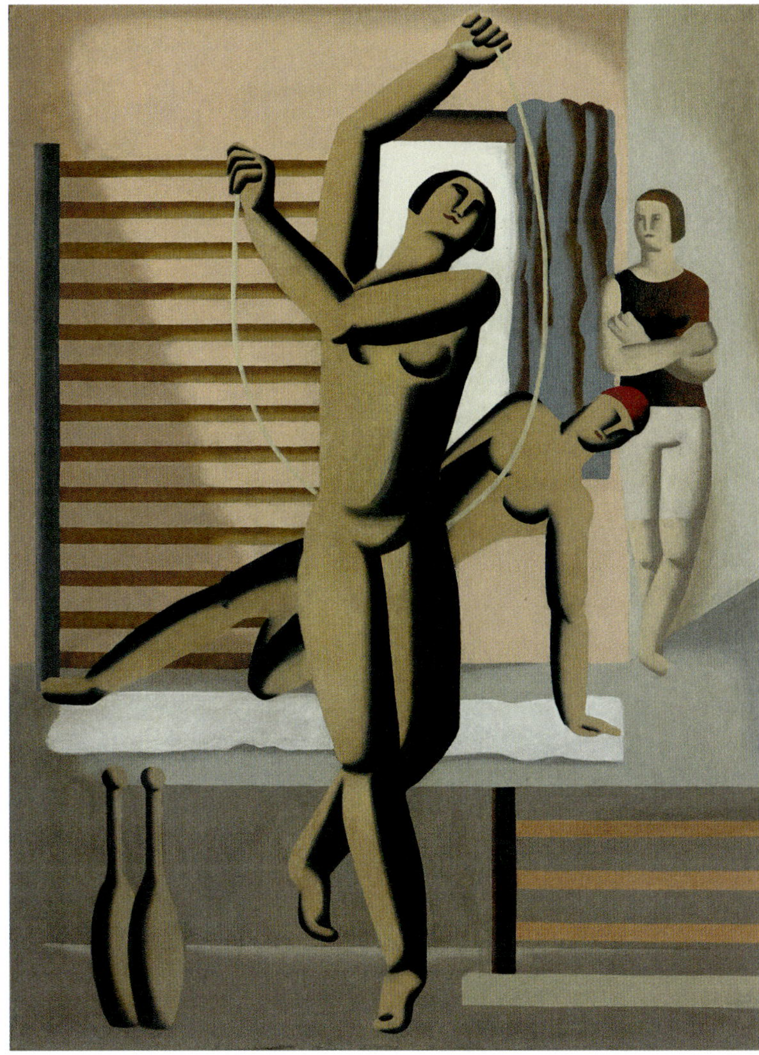

109
WALTER KAMPMANN
Portrait of My Wife, Ether Mask, c. 1930

Zinc plate with plastic on wood, 64 × 62 × 27 cm
Berlinische Galerie

Great Berlin Art Exhibition 1930, Novembergruppe section, no. 188, repro. in the catalogue

110
WILLI BAUMEISTER
Rope Jumper, 1928

Oil on canvas, 111 × 80.5 cm
Staatsgalerie Stuttgart

Repro. in *Zehn Jahre Novembergruppe* 1928, p. 78

RUDOLF BELLING
Triad, 1919–24

Caught in swaying, dynamic movement, three figure-like shapes slant upwards from a shared plinth. Smooth and rounded on the surface, angular elements intricately define the curvaceous space in between. They seem to relate to each other as dancers do, with two figures touching, yet each asserts its position in the roundelay as an autonomous and equal partner. It is not without reason that the sculpture *Triad* [*Dreiklang*] (cat. 111, p. 215) by RUDOLF BELLING is an icon of early twentieth-century modern plastic art, for it adopts a novel approach to the complex relationship between sculpture and space.[1] Belling's work is inherently holistic, integrating the cavity into the genesis of form: "To me sculpture is first and foremost a spatial concept; not, as in the past, illustrations modelled on the two-dimensional impact of the image. I therefore mould the air like solid material and allow the aperture, once called 'dead form', to acquire the same formal value as the processed material that delimits it."[2] The free-standing piece animates and incorporates the space around it: the shape appears to change with every angle of gaze, revealing a new interplay of form and void.

This new concept of sculpture was preceded by Belling's artistic evolution within the Novembergruppe and the *Arbeitsrat für Kunst*, both founded in November 1918. Both associations aspired to a unity between the arts of painting, sculpture and architecture, and the artist lends this principle plastic expression in his work. The three abstract figures symbolize the "triad" of the three arts in "melodious" collaboration. The sculptor is paying homage here to the tradition of the total

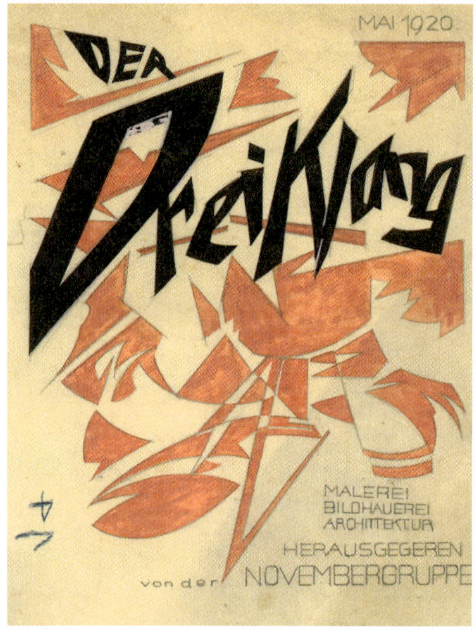

01 MORIZ MELZER, Cover design for the planned Novembergruppe periodical, 1920, Berlinische Galerie

art work, an idea revived in the activities of these revolutionary associations and in the Bauhaus manifesto, reflecting a desire for community among artists and the arts. Belling began collaborating on joint projects with architects in the Novembergruppe in the early 1920s, and this exerted a crucial influence on his sculptural practice in terms of spatial impact and use.[3]

When the sculpture *Triad* was first shown in the Novembergruppe section at the Berlin Art Exhibition, it was just a plaster model for an "original 6m high, built of brick with coloured render".[4] This monumental outdoor sculpture was never made, but the blueprint testified once again to the desire for a fusion of the arts, for it was intended as a stage for performances of modern music.[5]

Triad attracted attention and brought Belling exhibitions in, among other places, Galerie Flechtheim (1920) in Düsseldorf and Galerie Goyert (1921) in Cologne. Even Ludwig Justi, the director of the Nationalgalerie in Berlin, commissioned a wooden version of *Triad* for the collection after putting on a one-man show for the artist in 1924. The sculpture was also much admired within the Novembergruppe. As its title so aptly summarized the association's objectives, "The Triad" was under consideration as a name for the group's first periodical, as evidenced by a cover design by MORIZ MELZER (fig. 01).[6] It was also an important work to the artist himself. After the Second World War, which he spent in exile in Turkey, Belling believed his *Triad* had been lost and dedicated his first postwar sculpture to it as a tribute, a piece he called *Sculpture 49* [*Skulptur 49*] (fig. 02): "I have heard no more of my first Triad and I consider it a victim of the war, a victim of

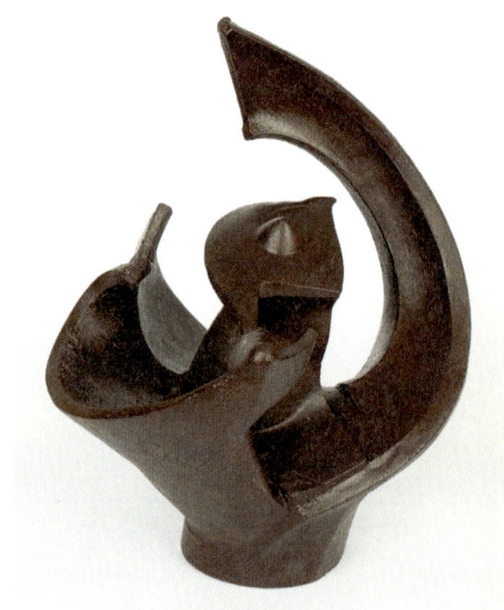

02 RUDOLF BELLING, Sculpture 49 (in Memoriam Triad), 1949 (cast c. 1950), Kunsthandel Wolfgang Werner, Bremen and Berlin

the Third Reich policy of unculture. So I have erected a kind of memorial to it in the form of an Abstract Sculpture. 30 years after its creation."[7]

JUSCHKA MARIE VON RÜDEN

1 See Dogramaci 2009, p. 311.

2 Rudolf Belling, letter to Alfred Flechtheim, in: Marx Burchartz, *Bildwerke von Rudolf Belling* (exhib. cat. Düsseldorf, Galerie Alfred Flechtheim), Düsseldorf 1920, p. 18.

3 See Scholz 2017, p. 34.

4 *Kunstausstellung Berlin. Abteilung der Novembergruppe* (exhib. cat. Berlin, Lehrter Bahnhof), Berlin, 1920, p. 69.

5 See Thomson 2017, p. 103.

6 The name finally chosen for this journal was *Der Kunsttopf*. The first issue came out in July 1920.

7 Rudolf Belling to Hans and Wassili Luckhardt, 2 September 1949, quoted in Scholz 2017, p. 69.

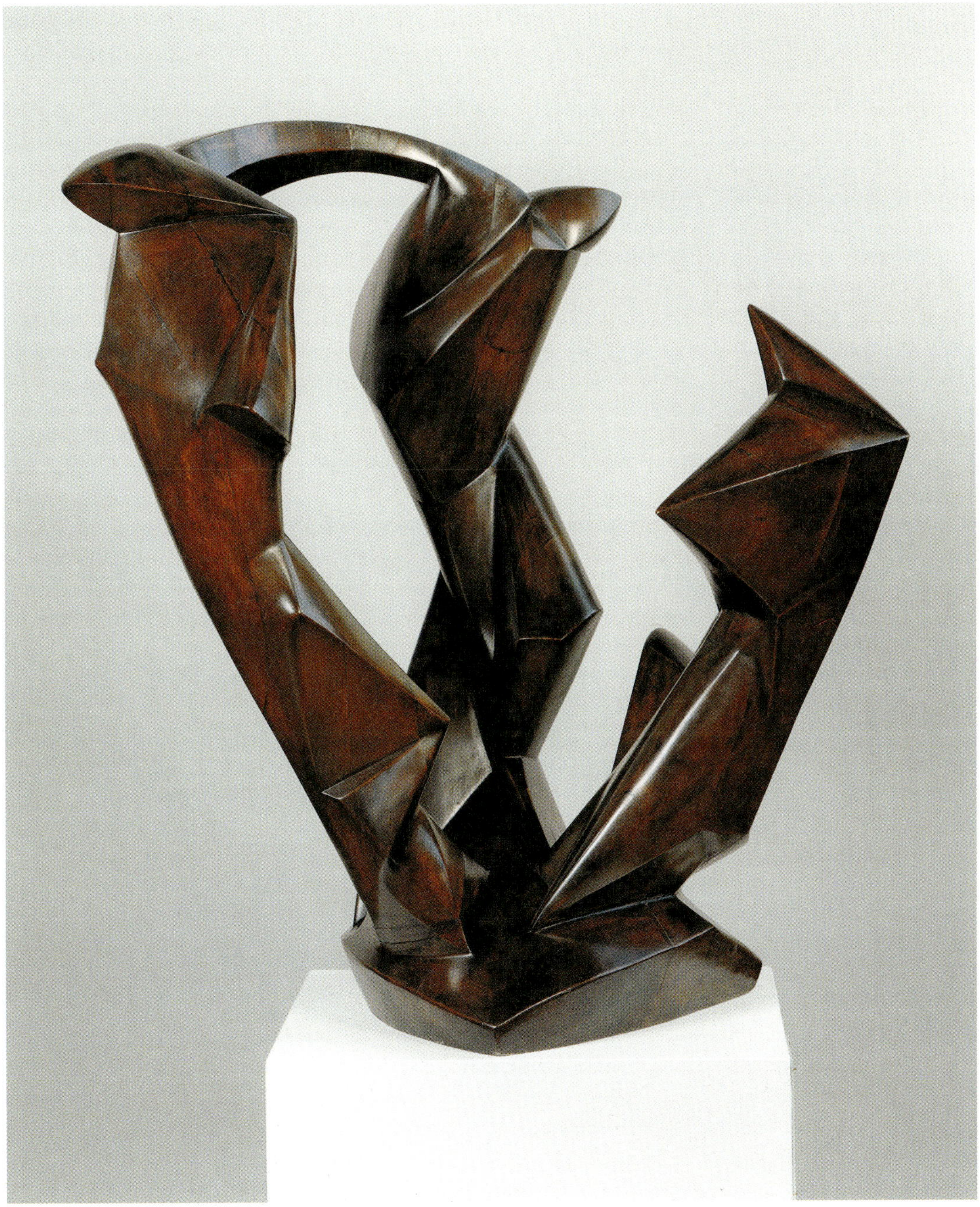

111

RUDOLF BELLING

Triad, 1919–24

Stained birch wood. 91 × 77 × 77 cm
Staatliche Museen zu Berlin, Nationalgalerie

Great Berlin Art Exhibition 1920, Novembergruppe section, no. 1096 (plaster version), Jury-Free Art Show Berlin 1929, exhibition Ten Years of the Novembergruppe, no. 78 (Bronze)

HANNAH HÖCH
Cube, 1926

HANNAH HÖCH was a Dadaist—among other things. Her collage *Dada Review* [*Dada-Rundschau*] of 1919 formulates a creed that was to define both the art and the self-assured lifestyle of the bisexual artist. Above her signature she stuck three decisive words: "for unbridled liberty" (p. 87, fig. 07). Höch's œuvre is a testimony to this declaration of freedom, notably in its great stylistic variation: apart from her outstanding collages, there is an extensive corpus of paintings and drawings revealing an affinity with Surrealism, but also purely abstract works, not to mention specimens of Neue Sachlichkeit and Naturalism. In her determination to resist dogma, Höch appreciated the openness of the Novembergruppe, which aimed to provide a forum for new art of all kinds. The artist herself tells us that she joined the Novembergruppe in 1920.[1] She exhibited regularly with the association and remained loyal—apart from a brief crisis[2]—until 1931. In her biographical accounts, she never failed to mention her membership of this community of creative professionals. In fact, when the municipal art department in the Berlin borough of Charlottenburg decided in 1950 to plan a commemorative exhibition about the Novembergruppe, Höch put the staff in touch with former members and told them she would happily loan items from her collection and works of her own.[3] The show, however, never took place.

Hannah Höch may have been a pluralist in terms of style, but when exhibiting with the Novembergruppe she tended to choose works with fantastical, surreal motifs,[4] whereas she only once showed collages with the group. One example is her painting *Cube* [*Kubus*] (cat. 112, p. 217), displayed in 1926 under the title *From the Human Angle* [*Vom Menschen aus*] at the exhibition grounds of the Great Berlin Art Exhibition at Lehrter Bahnhof. On the left, a mechanical-technical fabrication essentially consisting of turbine blades, a ventilation pipe and a ship's propeller winds upwards, set at the top of the picture against a bird's-eye view of a factory. On the right, Höch placed a formal and thematic counterpart in the shape of braided plant life. Technology and nature, purported opposites rendered with the same palette of paints, are joined by a symbolic rainbow. Dominant at the centre of the work is a reference to humans (endowed with reason), observed here by a cat (symbol of creation). In a cubed crystal, grey in grey, we see the facets of a face: the nose and the lips from below and—the force field for the entire composition, nailing us with their gaze—the eyes of the genius Albert Einstein,[5] whose theory of relativity applied universally to all phenomena.

RALF BURMEISTER

1 See Berlinische Galerie 2001, vol. 2, 63.124, p. 168.

2 See the essay by Burmeister in this catalogue, p. 89.

3 Höch sent the addresses of Heinrich Kosina, J.P.P. Oud, Werner Scholz, Alfred Gellhorn, Hugo Häring and Ludwig Hilberseimer (see Berlinische Galerie 2001, 2. Abt., 50.50, p. 40) and wrote a letter to Gertrud Koref-Stemmler informing her about the proposed retrospective (see Berlinische Galerie 2001, vol. 2, 51.3, p. 44). From her own collection she intended to loan works by Raoul Hausmann, Kurt Schwitters, Otto Freundlich, Arnold Topp, Fritz Stuckenberg, Arthur Segal and Alexej Jawlensky.

4 These include: *He and His Milieu [Er und sein Milieu]*, 1919, watercolour (Great Berlin Art Exhibition 1922, Novembergruppe section, no. 1286); *The Gnat Is Dead [Die Mücke ist tot]*, 1922 (Great Berlin Art Exhibition 1923, Novembergruppe section, no. 1216); *The Stairs [Die Treppe]*, 1926 (Novembergruppe exhibition at the Association of Berlin Artists [*Verein Berliner Künstler*], no. 24); *The Fence* [*Der Zaun*], 1927–28 and *Creatures* [*Geschöpfe*], 1929 (Great Berlin Art Exhibition 1922, Novembergruppe section, no. 172f.); all oil paintings.

5 Ohff 1968, p. 33.

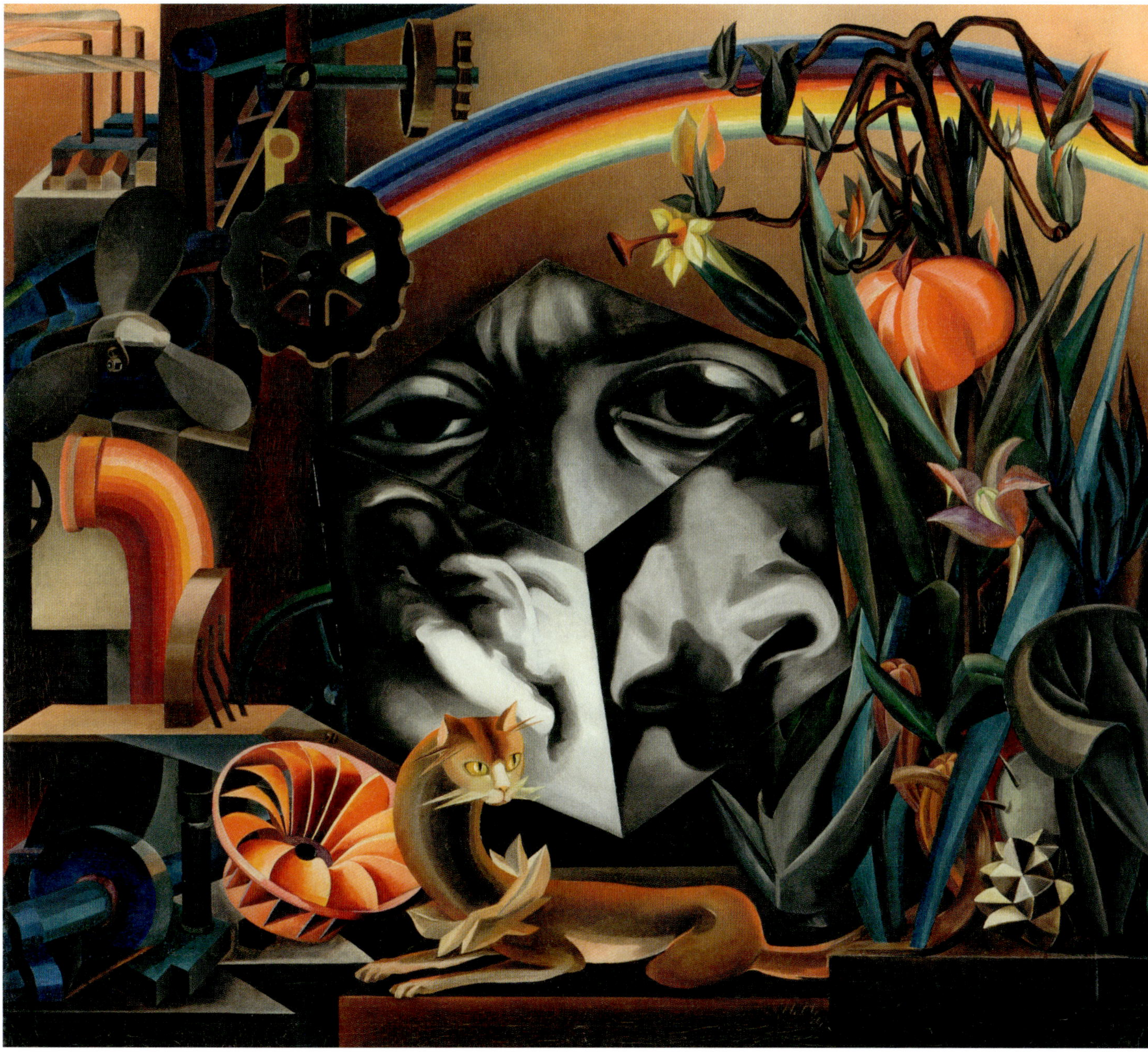

112

HANNAH HÖCH

Cube, 1926

Oil on canvas, 65.5 × 72.5 cm
Berlinische Galerie

Great Berlin Art Exhibition 1926, Novembergruppe section, no. 1555 (with the title *From the Human Angle*)

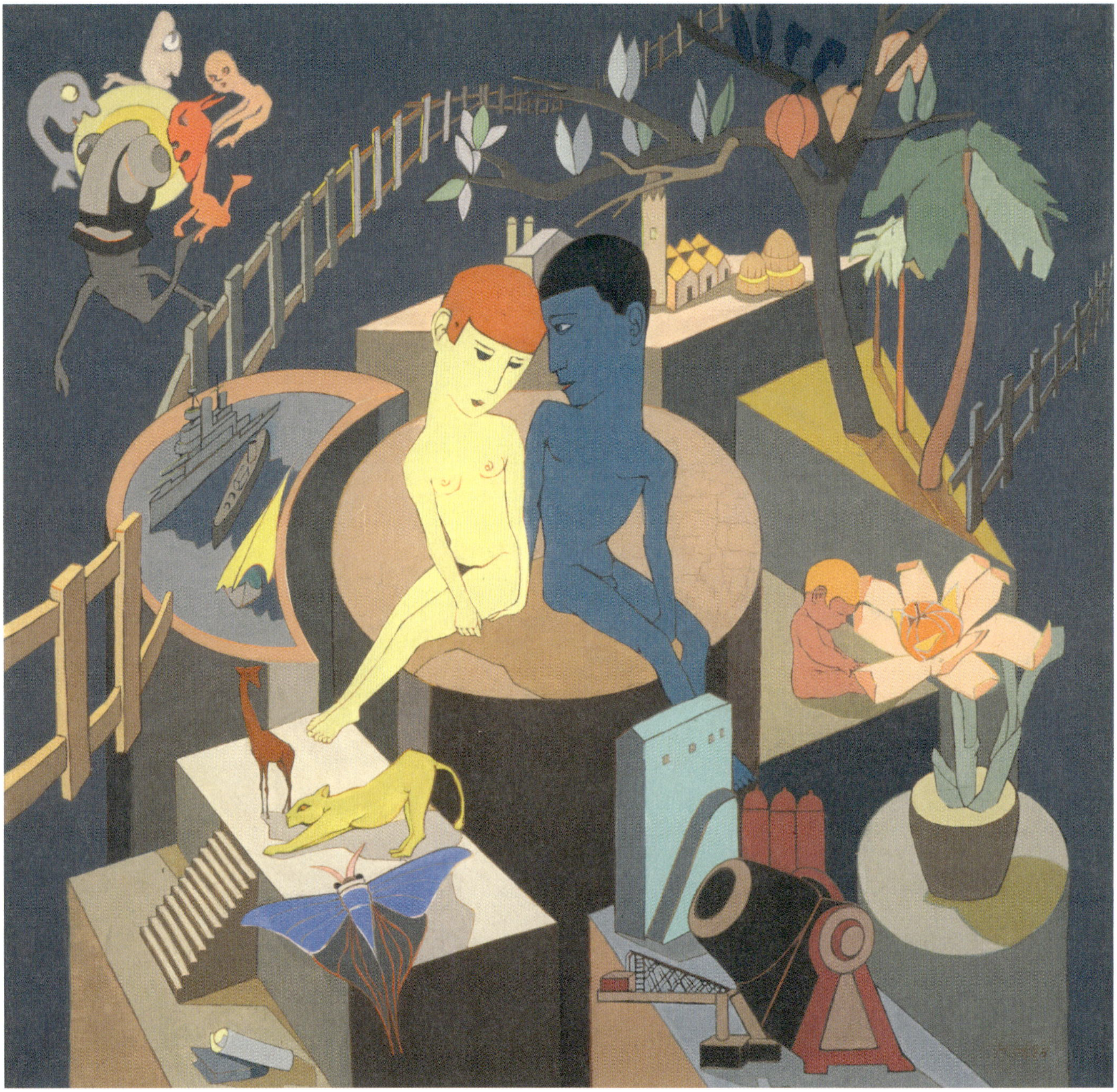

113
HANNAH HÖCH
The Fence, 1928

Oil on canvas, 88.5 × 87 cm
Berlinische Galerie

Great Berlin Art Exhibition 1931, Novembergruppe section, no. 172, repro. in the catalogue

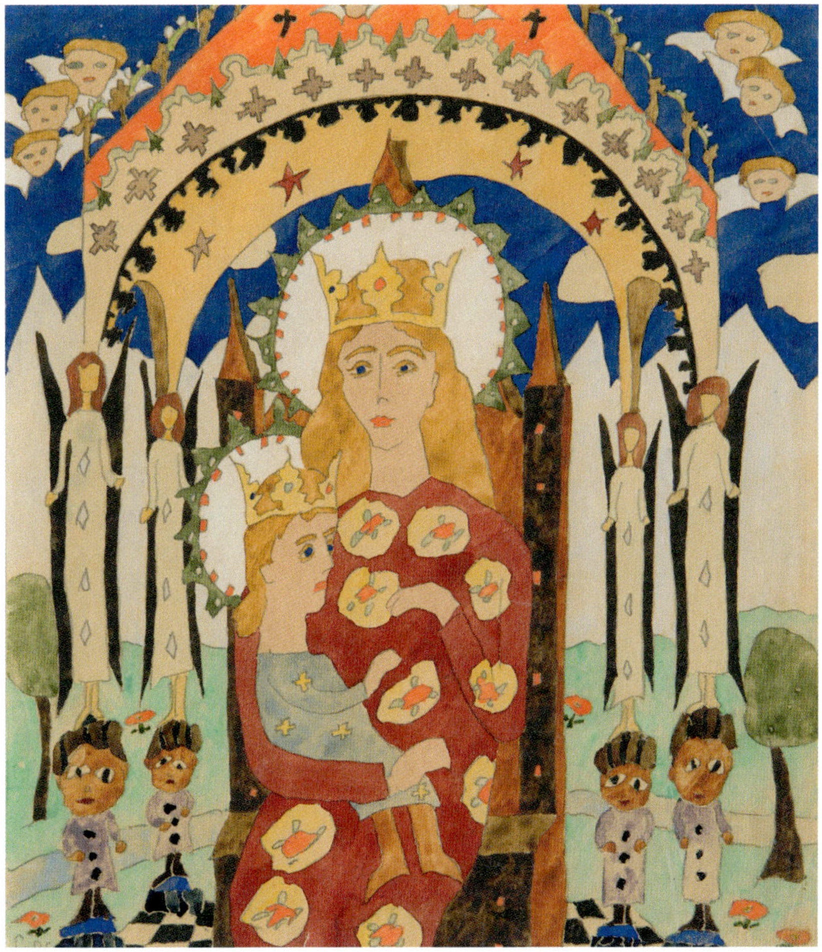

114
PAUL GOESCH
Madonna, 1922

Gouache and opaque white over pencil on paper, 24.9 × 20.6 cm
Berlinische Galerie

Great Berlin Art Exhibition 1923, Novembergruppe section, no. 1186, repro. in *Zehn Jahre Novembergruppe* 1928, p. 48

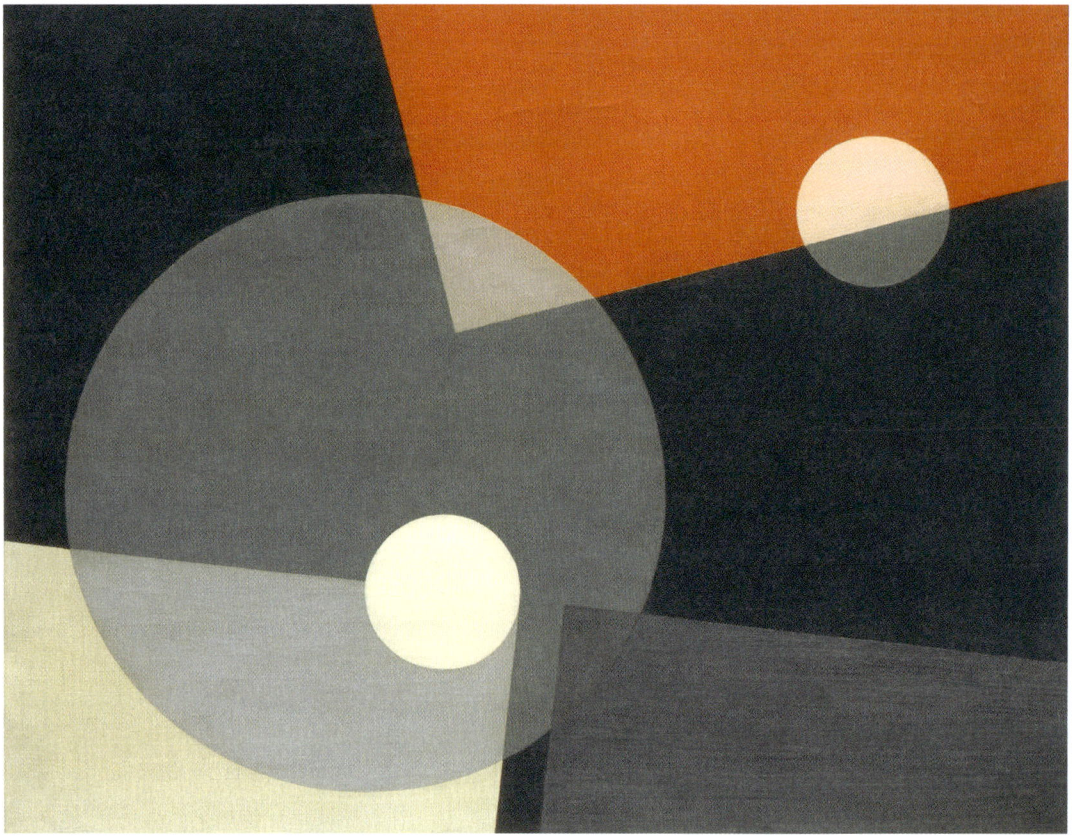

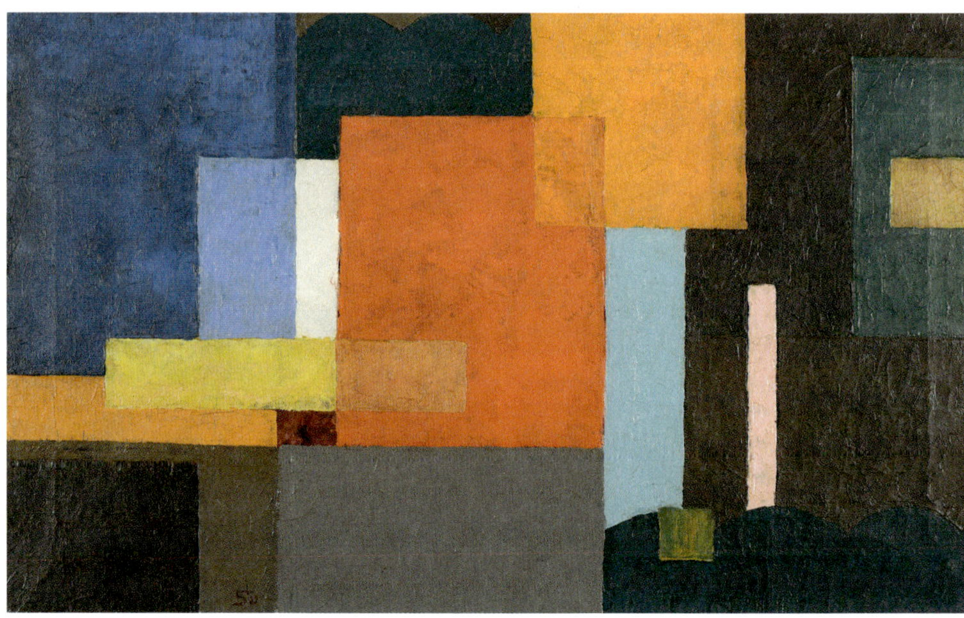

115
LÁSZLÓ MOHOLY-NAGY
Am 7 (26), 1926

Oil on canvas, 75.8 × 96 cm
Kurt und Ernst Schwitters Stiftung, Hannover

Great Berlin Art Exhibition 1931,
Novembergruppe section, no. 273

116
FRITZ STUCKENBERG
Fugue, c. 1924

Oil on canvas, 40.5 × 64.5 cm
Sammlung Städtische Galerie Delmenhorst

Great Berlin Art Exhibition 1930,
Novembergruppe section, no. 417

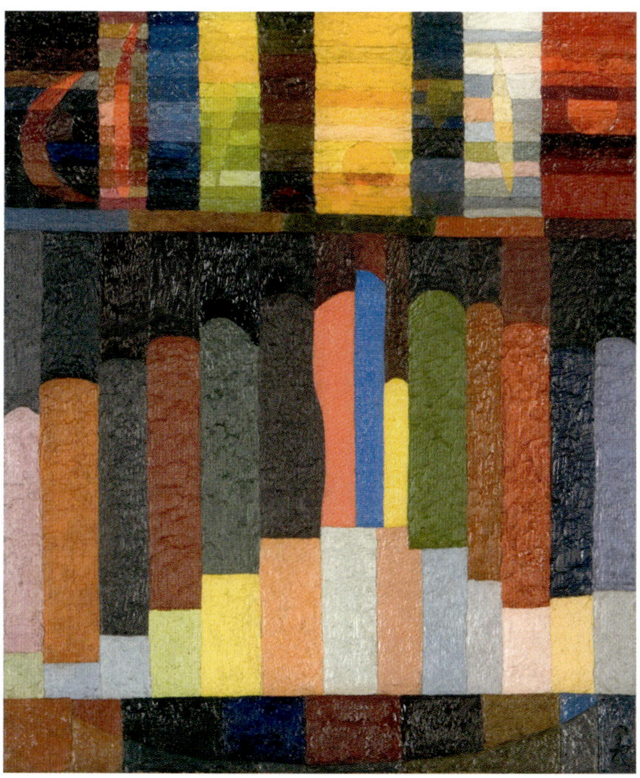

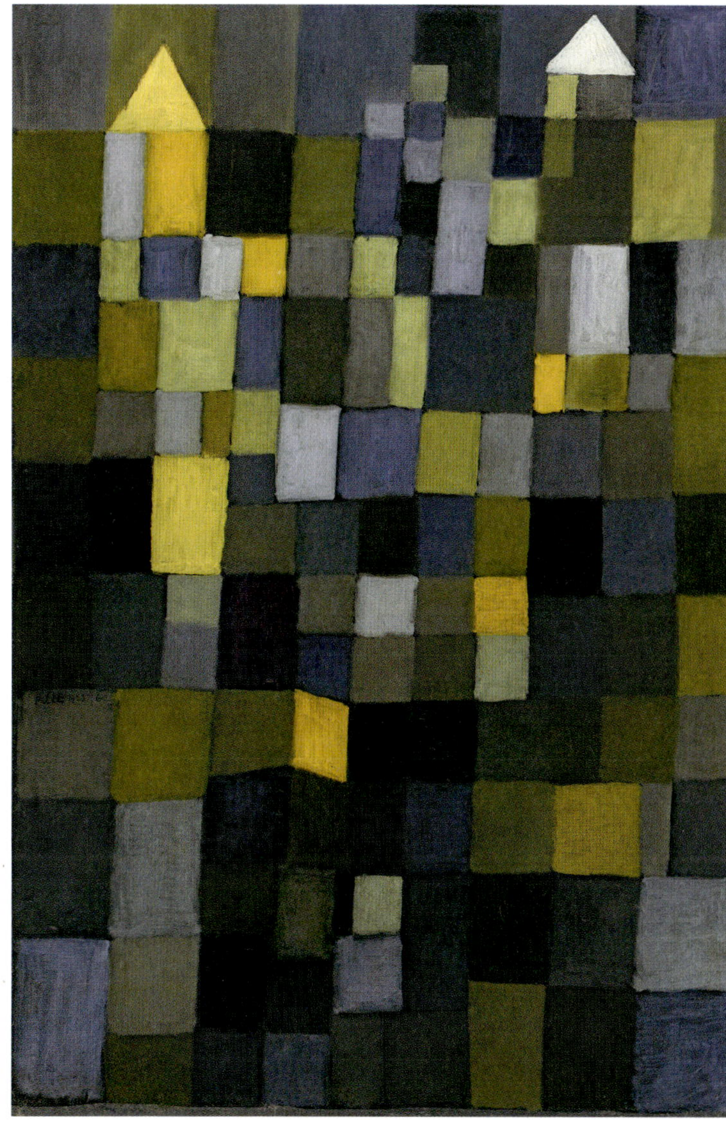

117
OTTO FREUNDLICH
Composition, 1926

Oil on canvas, 46 × 39 cm
Berlinische Galerie

Novembergruppe exhibition at the *Verein Berliner Künstler,* 1931, no. 15

118
PAUL KLEE
Architecture, 1923

Oil on hardboard, 58 × 39 cm
Staatliche Museen zu Berlin, Nationalgalerie

Jury-Free Art Show Berlin 1929, exhibition Ten Years of the Novembergruppe, no. 601

CÉSAR KLEIN
Cross Before Barbarians, 1933

Buildings are ablaze, war dead litter a desolate landscape. Out of the flames rises *The New Phoenix* [*Der Neue Vogel Phönix*] (fig. 01), on its back a human figure reaching for the sun. In this Expressionist drawing CÉSAR KLEIN uses the ancient symbol of the phoenix reborn from the ashes as an allegory for the revolution of 1918–19, when the New Person was to ascend in freedom from the ruins. In 1919 Klein and many other members of the Novembergruppe declared an artistic and also political stance in a brochure socialist in tone addressed *To All Artists!* [*An alle Künstler!*],[1] highlighting the role of the modern, progressive artist in the incipient democracy.

As a founding member of the Novembergruppe, César Klein was one of the few people who remained true to the association from its first hour until its last. His name appears on every surviving list of members (pp. 252-255) and he showed at almost every one of its exhibitions at home and abroad. Exemplifying the group philosophy, César Klein combined free and applied art as he built his reputation as an interior decorator, a stage and cinema set designer and a teacher at the academy. At the same time, membership offered him a platform for encounters with very different styles, from which he drew inspiration.

Man with Pipe [*Mann mit Pfeife*] (cat. 21, p. 61), painted in 1920, reflects his response to the Cubism developed in Paris in the early twentieth century by Pablo Picasso and GEORGES BRAQUE and to the abstract art promoted by the Novembergruppe. Klein dissected the pictorial elements into colourful geometric shapes that rebuff the illusionist principle of perspective, creating instead a two-dimensional, grid-like reality in the image.[2] Although the motif makes no overtly political statement, there is subversive potential in his chosen technique, as Klein was experimenting with the formal repertoire of a "French" avant-garde just two years after the First World War had ended, at a time when conservatives and right-wingers still saw France as Germany's 'arch-enemy'.

From the early 1930s Klein's paintings turned increasingly dark and depressive. He used more and more black paint and his figures gradually became monumental, alienated and isolated in the space.[3] The melancholy feel to these works developed in a context of world economic crisis, the rise of the Nazis and an ever more precarious plight for the artist community. The mood of that period is conveyed symbolically in a work dating from 1933: *Cross Before Barbarians* [*Kreuz vor Barbaren*] (cat. 119, p. 223). In a situation resembling a darkened stage, three abstract and archaic figures with hints of a human physiognomy enter in a kind of ghostly procession. At the front is a small, frail, almost angelic creature bearing a black cross at its breast.[4] It is fol-

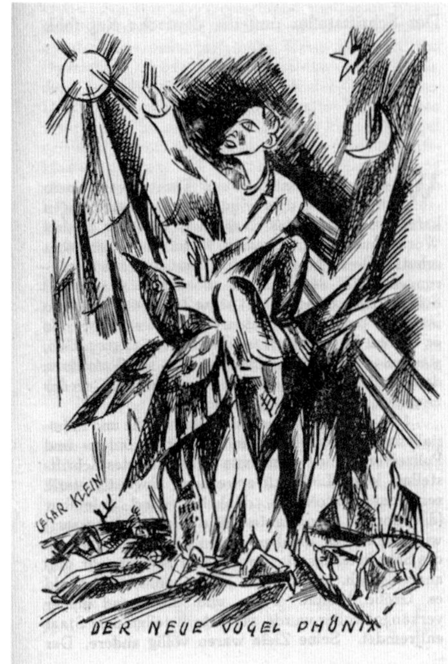

01 CÉSAR KLEIN, The New Phoenix, 1919, Illustration from the brochure To All Artists!, 1919

lowed by two masked warriors armed with lances and bloody spearheads. Was this formation invoked to resist the looming barbarism of the Third Reich?

Once the Nazis took power, the Novembergruppe's fate was sealed, and it was finally struck out from the register of associations in 1935. The bill for this formal act of obliteration was sent to the group's last chairman, César Klein.

JUSCHKA MARIE VON RÜDEN

1 *An alle Künstler!*, Werbedienst der deutschen sozialistischen Republik, no. 68, Berlin 1919, p. 11.

2 See Pfefferkorn 1975, pp. 17f.

3 Pfefferkorn 1962, unpaginated; see also Haupenthal 2004.

4 Berlinische Galerie 1990, p. 216.

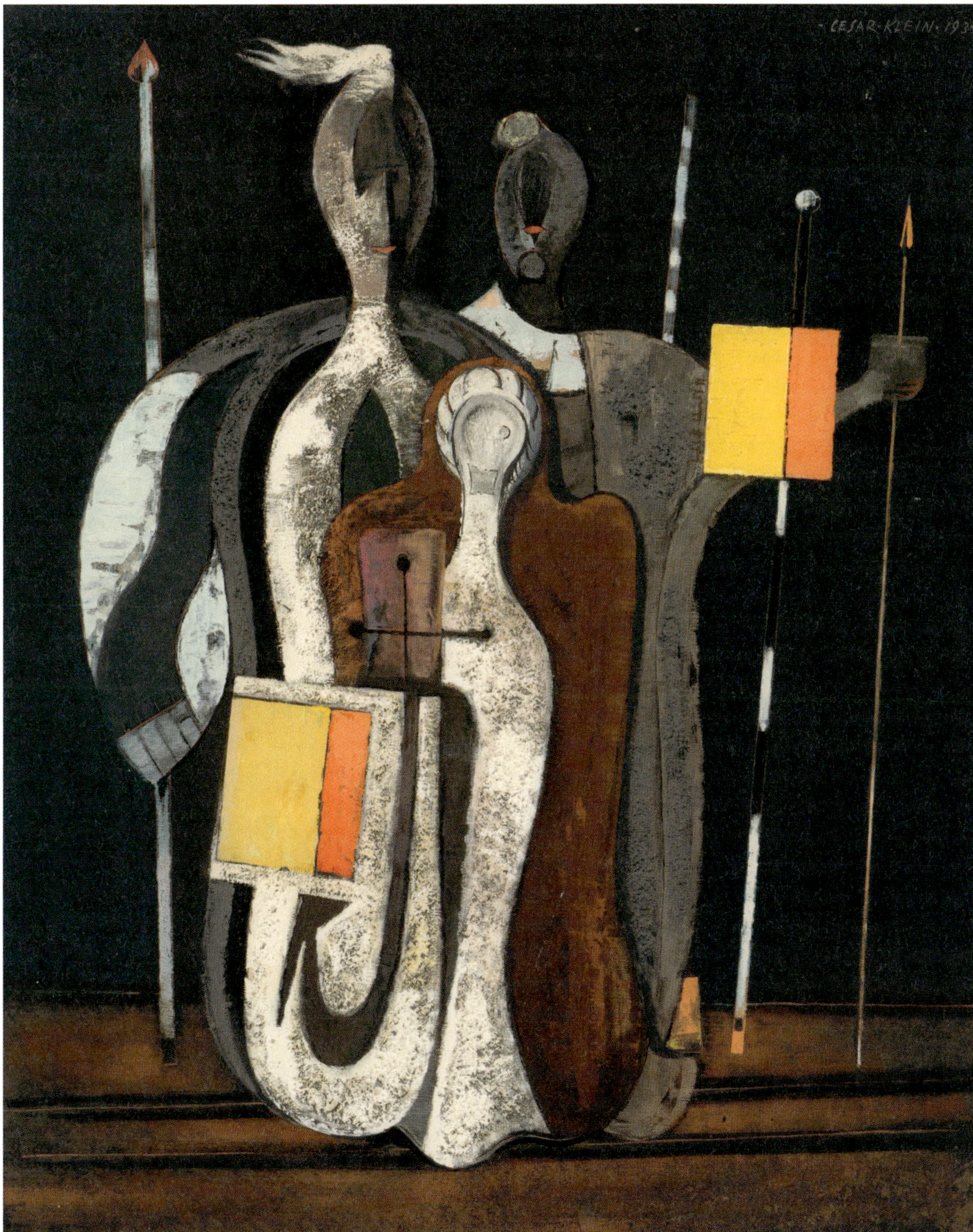

119
CÉSAR KLEIN
Cross Before Barbarians, 1933

Mixed technique on wood, 105 × 80.5 cm
Berlinische Galerie

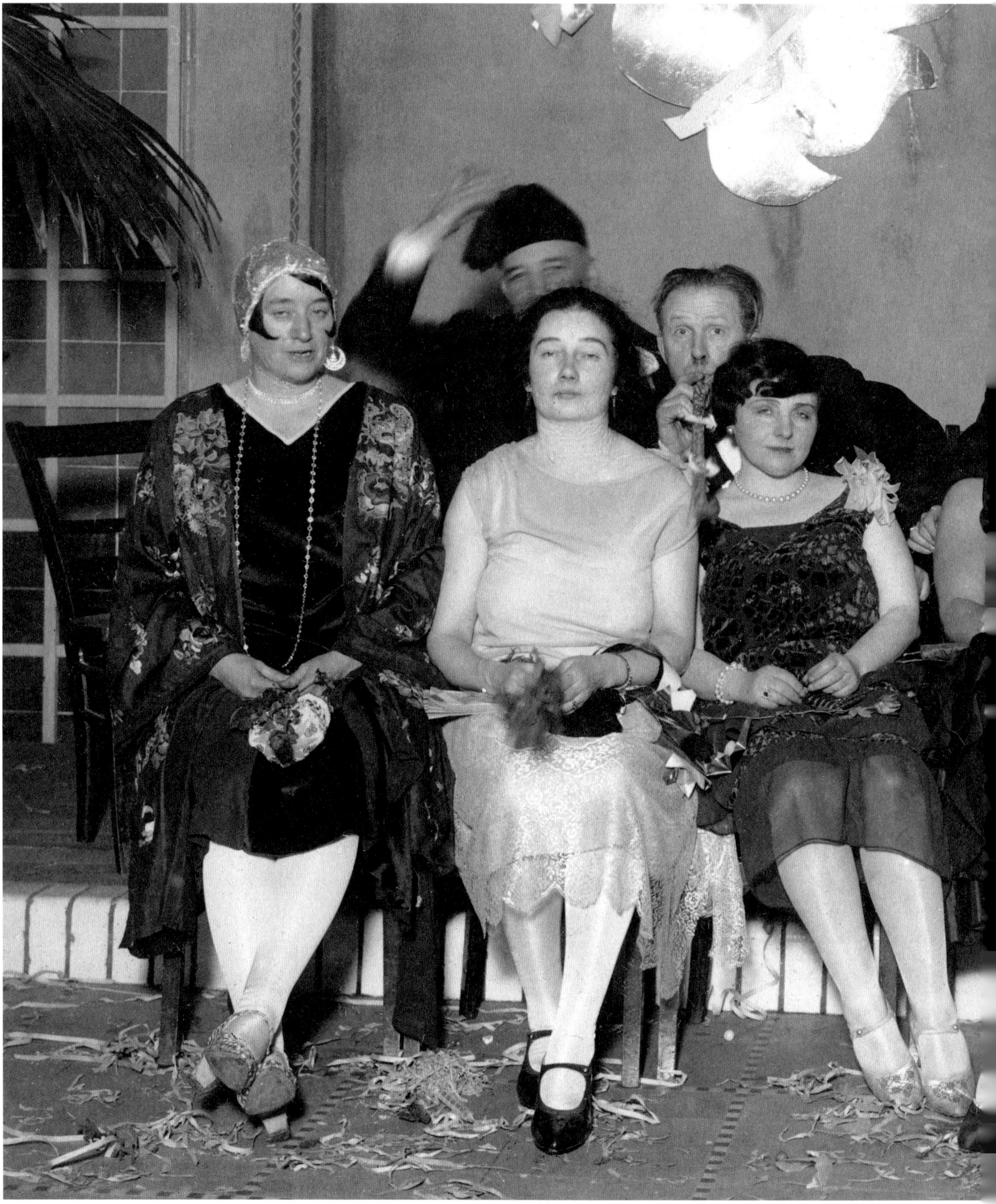

NG
CHRONICLE

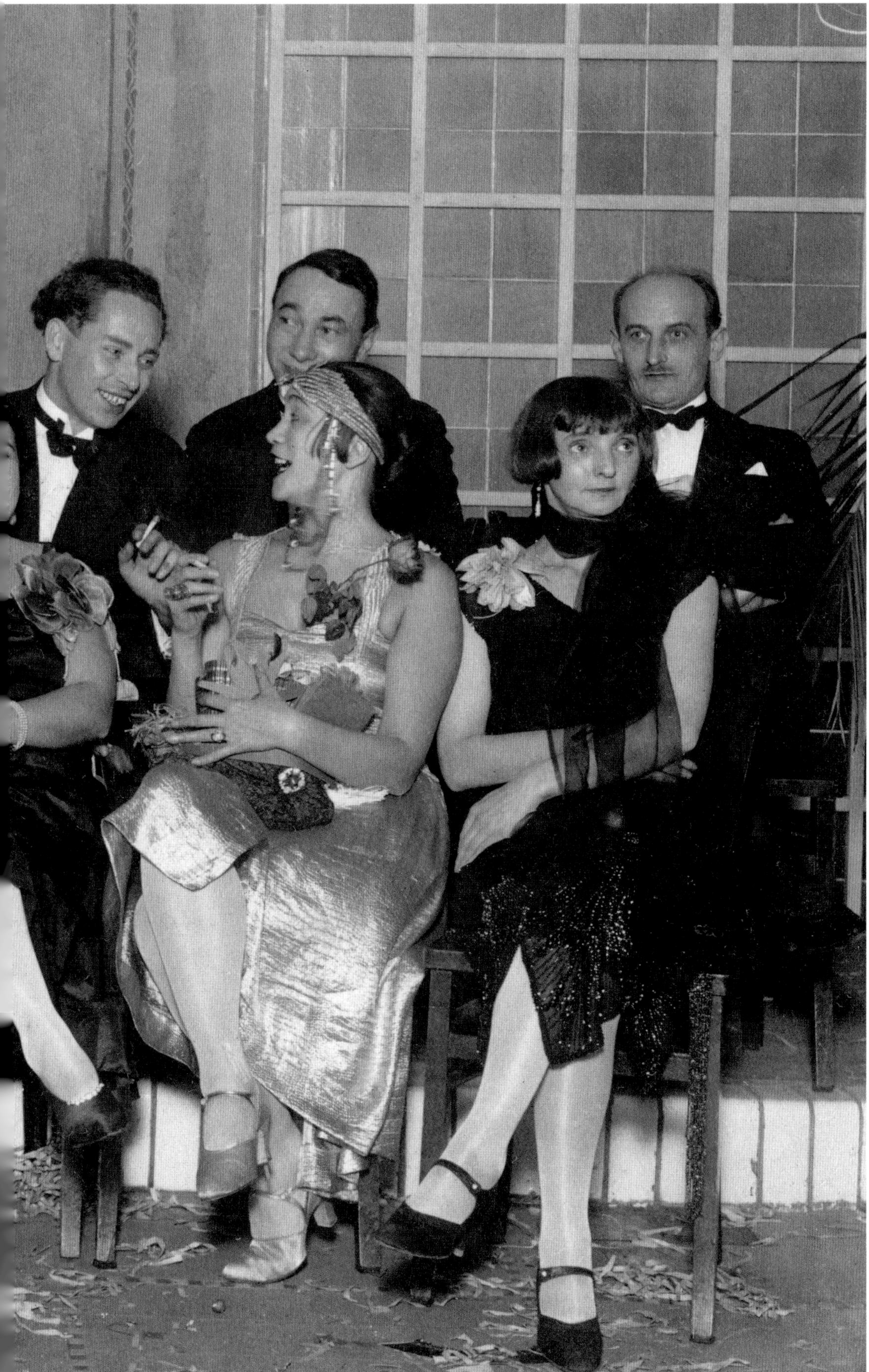

The Novembergruppe's
New Year Ball, 1928
Seated first from left Ines Wetzel, seated second from right Takka-Takka [Lucie Neuschul], back row from left to right N.N., [Oswald Herzog], Ernest Neuschul, Hugo Graetz, Alfred Gellhorn
Khalil and Misha Norland
(private collection)

JANINA NENTWIG

"WE BROOK NEITHER DOGMA NOR DOCTRINE"

A Chronicle of the Novembergruppe

The Novembergruppe's own records have not yet been traced. Founding member GEORG TAPPERT recalled that the documents were seized in 1933 after the Nazis took power.[1] The chronicle below is founded on information in personal papers and printed sources.

1918

In late November 1918 painters, sculptors and architects in Berlin founded the Novembergruppe as an "association of radical fine artists".[2] It was one among many groupings of artists who came together all over Germany during the revolution of 1918–19 seeking to play a role in the new social system after the collapse of the Empire. The first documented meeting was held on 3 December.[3] Many members already knew each other from the Expressionist group *Neue Secession*, which had disbanded during the First World War. Apart from MAX PECHSTEIN, a key figure in setting up the Novembergruppe was GEORG TAPPERT. From 1916 TAPPERT had seen out his war service at the Air Force Inspectorate in Adlershof, where he had brought in other artists, including KARL JAKOB HIRSCH (fig. 01).[4] The troupe were sympathetic to the left-wing political forces that had gathered strength as the war progressed. Just after its foundation the Novembergruppe published an appeal (fig. 02) in the Expressionist magazine *Die schöne Rarität*, and on 13 December 1918 the text was circulated to artists throughout Germany in a membership drive. The prime objectives stated by these "revolutionaries of the mind" were "the closest possible mingling of the people and art" and "renewed exploratory contacts" with the international avant-garde, given that the war had put an end to this communication.[5]

The first Novembergruppe office was in Villa II at Potsdamer Strasse 113, the home of the art dealer and publisher Wolfgang Gurlitt. (The building, on the site of the current no. 81, was destroyed in the Second World War.) CÉSAR KLEIN, RUDOLF BELLING and especially MAX PECHSTEIN had known the gallery owner for some time and had been working since 1917 on the interior decoration for his recently acquired Villa I on the same plot.[6]

The first articles of association and five fundamental "guidelines" for the Novembergruppe (fig. 03) date from 16 December. These called for "decisive influence in the resolution of all artistic questions" and the right to be con-

01

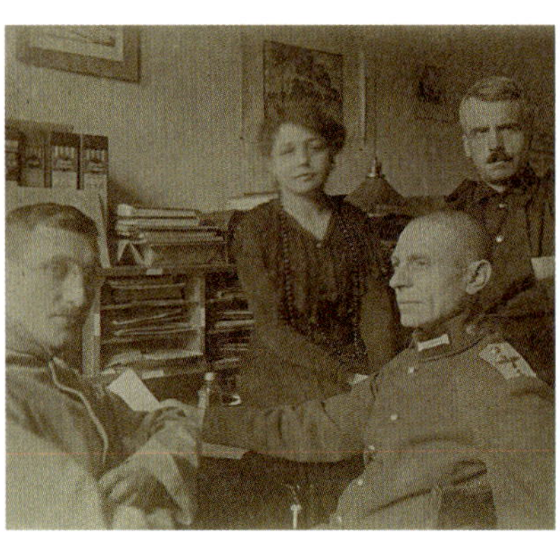

02

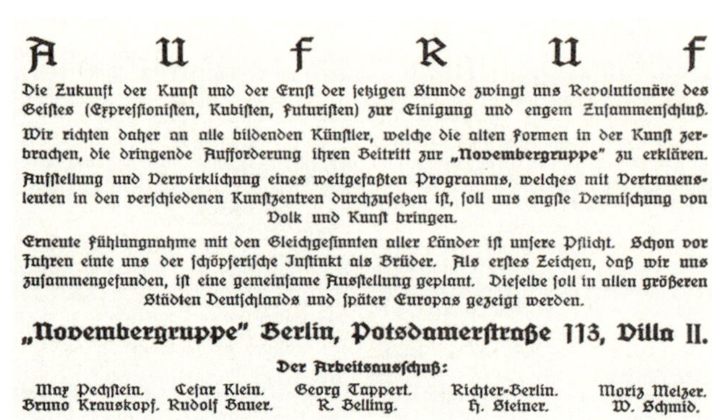

Aufruf

Die Zukunft der Kunst und der Ernst der jetzigen Stunde zwingt uns Revolutionäre des Geistes (Expressionisten, Kubisten, Futuristen) zur Einigung und engem Zusammenschluß.

Wir richten daher an alle bildenden Künstler, welche die alten Formen in der Kunst zerbrachen, die dringende Aufforderung ihren Beitritt zur „Novembergruppe" zu erklären.

Aufstellung und Verwirklichung eines weitgefaßten Programms, welches mit Vertrauensleuten in den verschiedenen Kunstzentren durchzusetzen ist, soll uns engste Vermischung von Volk und Kunst bringen.

Erneute Fühlungnahme mit den Gleichgesinnten aller Länder ist unsere Pflicht. Schon vor Jahren einte uns der schöpferische Instinkt als Brüder. Als erstes Zeichen, daß wir uns zusammengefunden, ist eine gemeinsame Ausstellung geplant. Dieselbe soll in allen größeren Städten Deutschlands und später Europas gezeigt werden.

„Novembergruppe" Berlin, Potsdamerstraße 113, Villa II.

Der Arbeitsausschuß:

Max Pechstein. Cesar Klein. Georg Tappert. Richter-Berlin. Moriz Melzer.
Bruno Krauskopf. Rudolf Bauer. R. Belling. H. Steiner. W. Schmid.

01 Georg Tappert and the flying squad in Adlershof, c. 1917

02 The Novembergruppe appeal in the magazine *Die Schöne Rarität*, December 1918

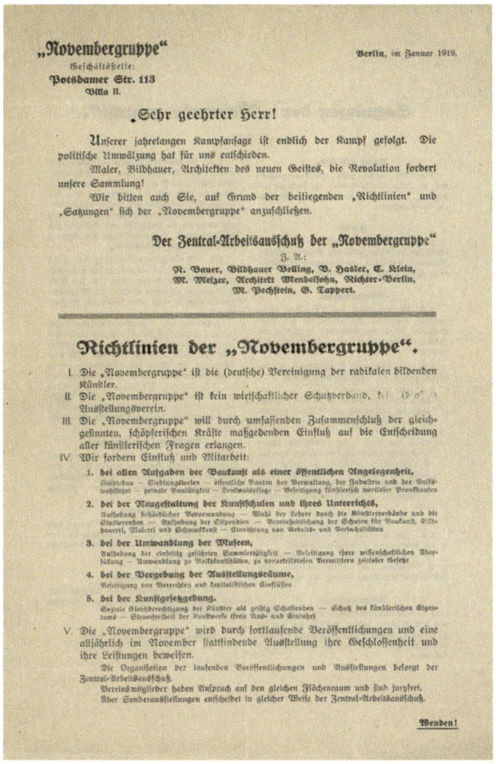

„Novembergruppe"
Geschäftsstelle:
Potsdamer Str. 113
Villa II.

Berlin, im Januar 1919.

Sehr geehrter Herr!

Unserer jahrelangen Kampfansage ist endlich der Kampf gefolgt. Die politische Umwälzung hat für uns entschieden.

Maler, Bildhauer, Architekten des neuen Geistes, die Revolution fordert unsere Sammlung!

Wir bitten auch Sie, auf Grund der beiliegenden „Richtlinien" und „Satzungen" sich der „Novembergruppe" anzuschließen.

Der Zentral-Arbeitsausschuß der „Novembergruppe"
J. A.:
R. Bauer, Bildhauer Belling, B. Hasler, C. Klein, M. Melzer, Architekt Mendelsohn, Richter-Berlin, M. Pechstein, G. Tappert.

Richtlinien der „Novembergruppe".

I. Die „Novembergruppe" ist die (deutsche) Vereinigung der radikalen bildenden Künstler.
II. Die „Novembergruppe" ist kein wirtschaftlicher Schutzverband, [illegible] Ausstellungsverein.
III. Die „Novembergruppe" will durch umfassenden Zusammenschluß der gleichgesinnten, schöpferischen Kräfte maßgebenden Einfluß auf die Entscheidung aller künstlerischen Fragen erlangen.
IV. Wir fordern Einfluß und Mitarbeit:
1. bei allen Aufgaben der Baukunst als einer öffentlichen Angelegenheit,
Städtebau — Siedlungswesen — öffentliche Bauten der Verwaltung, der Industrie und der Volkswohlfahrt — private Bautätigkeit — Denkmalspflege — Beseitigung künstlerisch wertloser Prunkbauten
2. bei der Neugestaltung der Kunstschulen und ihres Unterrichts,
Aufhebung behördlicher Bevormundung — Wahl der Lehrer durch die Künstlerverbände und die Studierenden — Aufhebung der Stipendien — Vereinheitlichung der Schulen für Baukunst, Bildhauerei, Malerei und Schmuckkunst — Einrichtung von Arbeits- und Versuchsstätten
3. bei der Umwandlung der Museen,
Aufhebung der einseitig geführten Sammlertätigkeit — Beseitigung ihrer wissenschaftlichen Überfüllung — Umwandlung zu Volkskunststätten, zu vorurteilslosen Vermittlern zeitloser Gesetze
4. bei der Vergebung der Ausstellungsräume,
Beseitigung von Vorrechten und kapitalistischen Einflüssen
5. bei der Kunstgesetzgebung.
Soziale Gleichberechtigung der Künstler als geistig Schaffenden — Schutz des künstlerischen Eigentums — Steuerfreiheit der Kunstwerke (freie Aus- und Einfuhr)
V. Die „Novembergruppe" wird durch fortlaufende Veröffentlichungen und eine alljährlich im November stattfindende Ausstellung ihre Geschlossenheit und ihre Leistungen beweisen.
Die Organisation der laufenden Veröffentlichungen und Ausstellungen besorgt der Zentral-Arbeitsausschuß.
Vereinsmitglieder haben Anspruch auf den gleichen Flächenraum und sind juryfrei. Über Sonderausstellungen entscheidet in gleicher Weise der Zentral-Arbeitsausschuß.

Wenden!

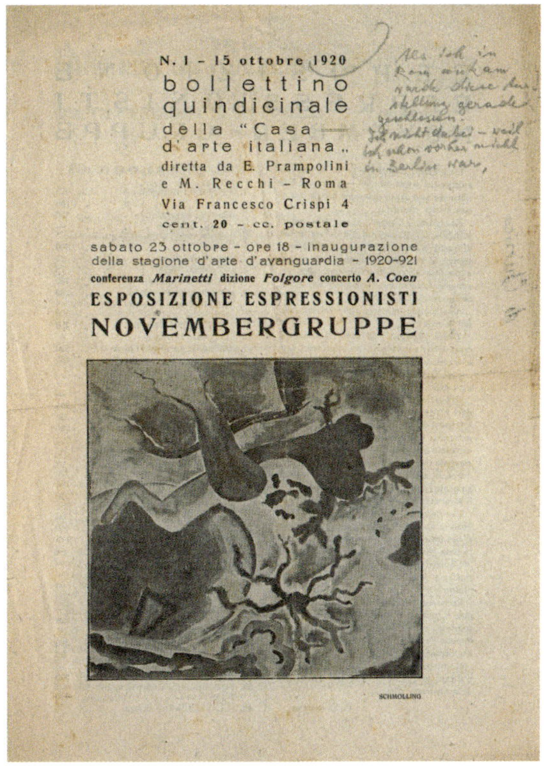

N. 1 - 15 ottobre 1920
bollettino quindicinale della "Casa d'arte italiana„
diretta da E. Prampolini e M. Recchi - Roma
Via Francesco Crispi 4
cent. 20 - cc. postale

sabato 23 ottobre - ore 18 - inaugurazione della stagione d'arte d'avanguardia - 1920-921
conferenza *Marinetti* dizione *Folgore* concerto *A. Coen*
ESPOSIZIONE ESPRESSIONISTI
NOVEMBERGRUPPE

SCHMOLLING

03 Guidelines and articles of association of the Novembergruppe, January 1919
Berlinische Galerie

04 Leaflet on the Novembergruppe exhibition in autumn 1920 at the Casa d'Arte in Rome
Berlinische Galerie

sulted on the award of public building contracts, reform of the art colleges, the reorganization of museums, the allocation of exhibition space and any legislation relevant to the arts. The association assured its members that they would share space equally at a proposed annual exhibition and that they would not be required to submit their works to a jury. The group was to be entered in the register of associations and the purpose defined in its articles of association was the "representation and promotion of [its members'] artistic interests". It chose a structure that would survive the years to come with only minor modifications: the executive board consisted of a chairperson, a secretary and a treasurer;[7] an annual general meeting would elect a working committee, and this would select the executive board from among its number, supervise the board's activities and resolve the admission of new members by a two-thirds majority.[8] Although the association derived its name from the November revolution and the financial year was to commence symbolically on 9 November, these original statutes did not define any supreme revolutionary goals. Instead, the association would campaign solely in the field of arts policy and influence society by artistic means.

1919

A "provisional list of members of the Novembergruppe" (p. 252), kept by GEORG TAPPERT in late 1918 and early 1919, names more than 60 people, including numerous artists and "local branches" outside Berlin who briefly affiliated to the association. Many artists came from the entourage of the gallery Der Sturm, whose founder Herwarth Walden appears to have tolerated membership of the Novembergruppe without explicitly approving of it.[9]

On 6 April groups of artists and "friends of the arts"[10] in Berlin protested at the academy against plans by the victorious powers of the First World War to seize works of art in payment for war reparations. The Novembergruppe did not take part in this event because it felt that the participants, overwhelmingly from conservative circles, shared the blame for the war and for Germany's political isolation. The association therefore adopted its own resolution: "We again reject attempts to involve products of creativity in spheres of political and mercantile power and we feel that in this we are at one with artists all over the world. [...] We believe that we can best serve our people by remaining true to our inner mission and by bridging divisions toward the outside. In memory of our comrades plucked by war from German art we, the living at this assembly, urge: ensure that arts and sciences can blossom in liberty."[11]

Freedom for art became the guiding principle of art policy in the Weimar Republic. In summer 1919 the Novembergruppe took part in the state-funded Berlin Art Exhibition held in the *Landesausstellungsausgebäude*, the exhibition site owned by the State of Prussia near Lehrter Bahnhof (now Berlin's central station). This exhibition was the successor to the traditional Great Berlin Art Exhibition.[12]

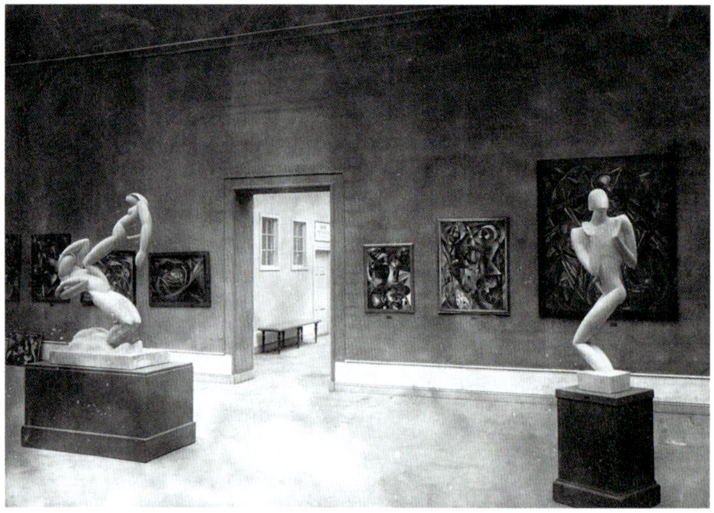

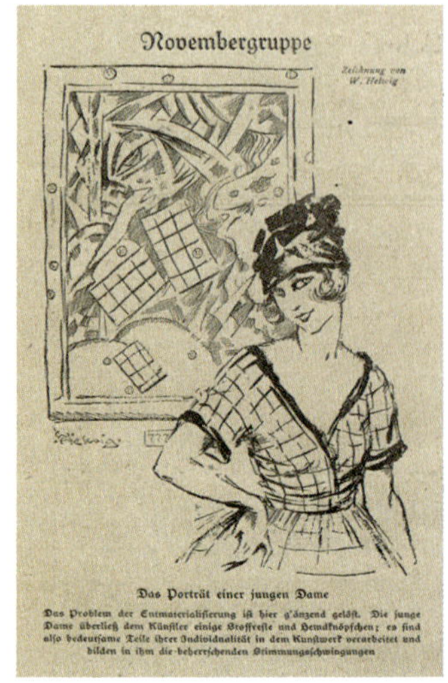

05 Berlin Art Exhibition 1920, a view of the Novembergruppe section, on the left Georg Leschnitzer's sculpture *Birth of Eve*

06 W. HELLWIG
Novembergruppe, caricature in the magazine *Ulk*, 1920

The *Verein Berliner Künstler*, the professional association of Berlin artists henceforth in charge of its organization, also exhibited here, as did the *Berliner Secession* and the *Freie Secession*. The Novembergruppe was, however, the flagship of democratic renewal at this event and was regarded as the protégé of the Prussian Ministry of Culture, the principal public authority, and of Friedrich Ebert as the president of the German Reich. The association had its own independent section, where it showed over 180 works by nearly 80 artists, many of them members of the "local branches" in Magdeburg (*Die Kugel*), Kiel (*Expressionistische Arbeitsgemeinschaft*), Stuttgart (*Üecht*), Karlsruhe (*Rih*) and Hamburg (*Kräfte*) or other guests. The press reviews were scathing, and visitors also expressed bewilderment or contempt. Some exhibits were physically attacked.

In November the *Arbeitsrat für Kunst* and the Novembergruppe decided to work in close partnership, as many artists were active in both associations and the art policy objectives were almost identical.[13]

In December the Dresden-based journal *Menschen* published a special issue on the Novembergruppe in a series devoted to new art, having already published two issues on the Hamburg group *Kräfte*. The foreword to the edition on the Berlin 'parent' was written by Adolf Behne, who was also active in the *Arbeitsrat für Kunst*.[14]

1920

By early 1920 at the latest, the Novembergruppe office had moved to the private apartment of its member WILLY ZIERATH at Spessartstrasse 10a in Berlin-Friedenau.[15] In May it moved again to Bornstrasse 6, also in the district of Friedenau.[16]

The Novembergruppe, entered in the Berlin register of associations on 20 August,[17] stepped up its exhibition activities during this year. In April–May a small-scale group show was held at Galerie Gurlitt.[18] In the spring an exhibition went on tour through southern and eastern Germany.[19] The first stop-over in March was at the *Badischer Kunstverein* in Karlsruhe, where some artists were able to sell works. This led to accusations of "bourgeois dealing".[20] After this the show travelled to the *Kunsthalle Mannheim*,[21] the *Kunstsalon Schaller* in Stuttgart,[22] then probably to the *Kunstverein Jena*[23] and finally, in October, to the *Kunstverein Halle*[24]. For the autumn the association had plans to exhibit in Dresden with the *Dresdner Sezession* at Galerie Arnold and at the gallery of Emil Richter.[25]

The Novembergruppe also showed abroad: the Futurist ENRICO PRAMPOLINI staged an exhibition of drawings and watercolours by the association at the Casa d'Arte in Rome from 23 October until the end of November (fig. 04), calling it the "liveliest unity of an art movement in Germany today". He pointed out that the almost 60 works revealed antithetical personal styles and features of German Expressionism: "People yearning for a new faith see in avant-garde art an answer to social renewal."[26] International artists and high-ranking Italian politicians attended the opening, where Filippo Tommaso Marinetti gave the introductory address, and the show was — at least in the eyes of its organizers — a success with the public.[27]

The main exhibition of the year was once again the independent Novembergruppe section at the Art Exhibition Berlin from 21 May until the end of September. The Novembergruppe showed nearly 450 works by 128 artists. The stylistic spectrum ranged from Expressionism, Cubism and Futurism via Dada to early forms of New Objectivity (figs. 05 and 06). Apart from the Novembergruppe only the *Verein Berliner Künstler* took part, and consequently these opposite poles, with their conservative and avant-garde perspectives on art, collided without the deflecting presence of the Secessions. Fervent criticism was especially aimed at the Dadaist works by YEFIM GOLYSHEV, OTTO DIX and others entered by the Novembergruppe.[28] By contrast, the applied art integrated into the Novembergruppe displays tended to find favour with reviewers.[29]

The Novembergruppe responded to public incomprehension the previous year by producing its own guide. Until 1924 the association published brochures like this to explain its section at the Great Berlin Art Exhibition to a lay audience, consciously seeking to bridge the divide by addressing visitors with no education in art. Moreover, the guide kept the exhibits anonymous, refusing to highlight individual performance in an effort to alter the image of the artist.

From July to December 1920 the Novembergruppe published six issues of its magazine *Der Kunsttopf* (fig. 07). The articles by members and guests reflected the liberal attitude of the Novembergruppe, which offered a forum to rival views on art and art policy. The many illustrations document the stylistic heterogeneity supported by the Novembergruppe. Recurrent themes are social responsibility in art and opening up the disciplines to working together. Stylistic pigeonholing is not on the agenda. ALFRED GELLHORN makes this clear in his programmatic text "The Tendency": "No -ism designates what art is as an expression of its time. As an expression of human life, manifesting the deeper meaning of existence."[30]

From 4 to 30 November there was a much smaller Novembergruppe show in the second-hand book and art shop Fraenkel & Co. at Lützowufer 13, where 19 artists each showed one work[31] (fig. 08). Josef Altmann, who had run the little gallery since 1914, can be seen as the first Novembergruppe art dealer, also acting as an agent for some individual members.[32]

The association held its first fancy-dress ball on 20 March, with the theme "The Cubic Box" (cat. 29, p. 71), at the Gartensaal in the Zoological Gardens.[33] A second ball followed on 1 December in the Scala-Palast (fig. 09) at Lutherstrasse 22–24 (destroyed, now Martin-Luther-Strasse 14–18). A new dance casino had recently opened there with an interior design influenced by Expressionism, to which the architect Walter Würzbach and Novembergruppe members ALFRED GELLHORN, RUDOLF BELLING and HANS BRASS had contributed. Both events featured a "Dada Cabaret" (fig. 08). The second was advertised with additional attractions: "dance performances to make all that has gone before seem provincial. Grand procession through all the palace rooms". There is self-irony in the announcement: "For 10 pfennigs you can buy a work of art!! What would you do with it? If you hang it up at home, you will never want for a topic of conversation; you could infallibly scare off every aged aunt!"[34] The following years saw many more balls and parties, a major source of revenue for the association. During spiralling inflation, profits were converted into dollars to ensure funding for the exhibitions and later also for the musical and literary soirées.[35]

07

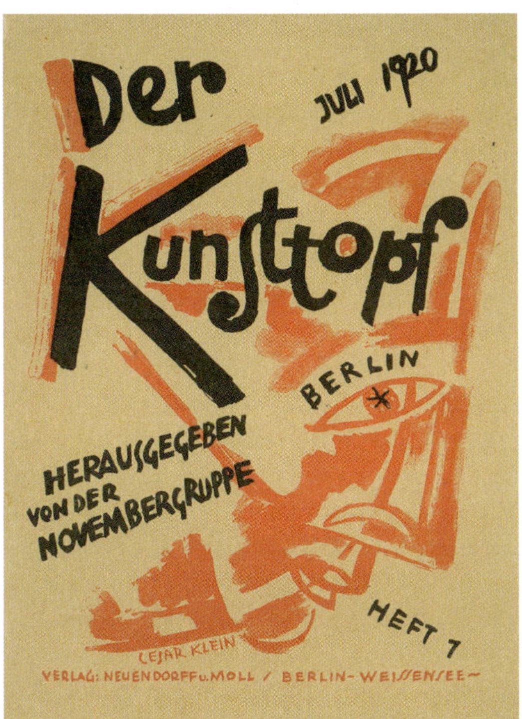

08

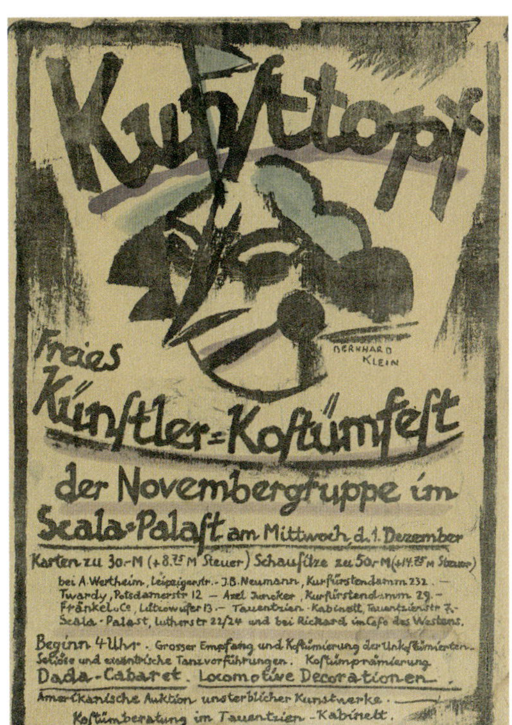

07 *Der Kunsttopf*, the Novembergruppe periodical, July 1920

08 BERNHARD KLEIN
Der Kunsttopf, poster for the Open Artists' Fancy-Dress Ball given by the Novembergruppe, 1 December 1920
Berlinische Galerie

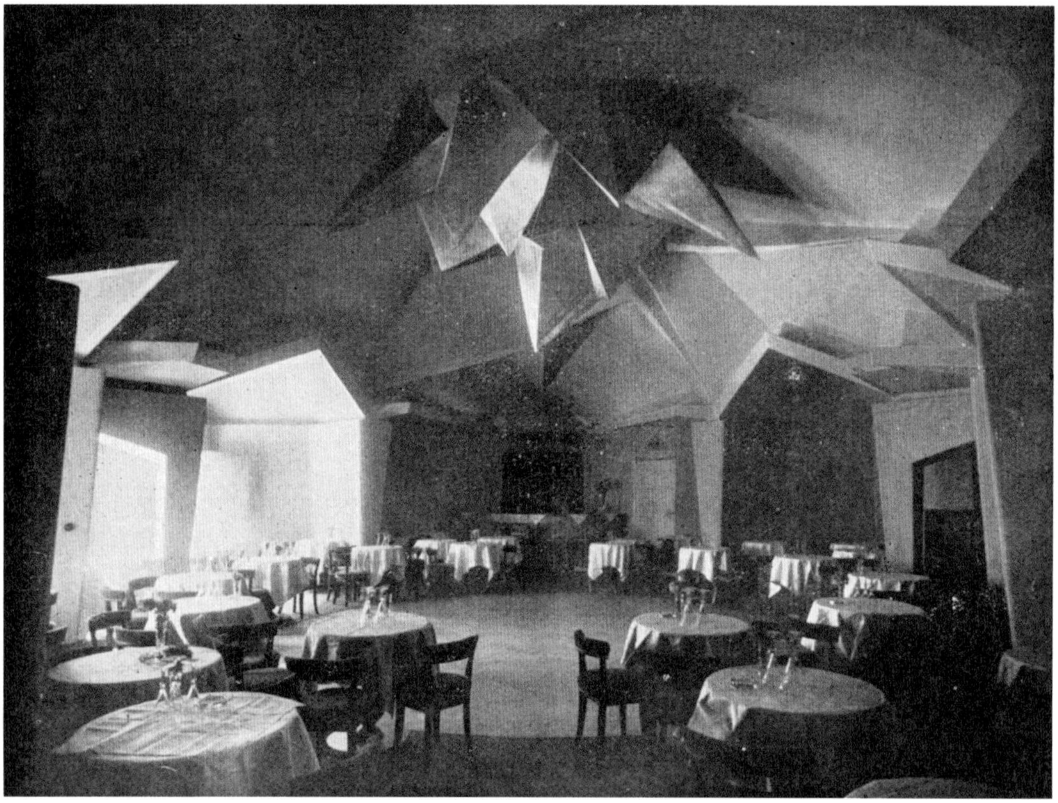

09 The dance casino at the Scala-Palast, Berlin 1920

09

1921

During the early months of the year, RAOUL HAUSMANN sought a leading position in the Novembergruppe, having concluded that Berlin's Club Dada was no longer a suitable forum.[36] In January he outlined a revamp for *Der Kunsttopf*. The aim was not so much to present the current output of members as to provide socially critical art theory on a more universal level.[37] In May he and co-editor HANS SIEBERT VON HEISTER published a new magazine in the name of the group called *NG. Veröffentlichung der Novembergruppe*. The cover was designed by HANNAH HÖCH (fig. 10). Although most of the articles were contributed by friends of HAUSMANN, the Dadaist was not fully able to put his publicized plans into practice. For unknown reasons the project was terminated after a single issue.

From 5 February to 6 March the association took part in the 16th Jury-Free Art Exhibition at the Stedelijk Museum in Amsterdam at the invitation of the artists' association *De Onafhankelijken*. The press was highly critical of the show and a report from the German Legation in the Netherlands to the Foreign Office in Berlin concludes: "The exhibition by the Novembergruppe can therefore hardly qualify as anything but a complete failure which has only damaged the reputation of German culture in Holland."[38]

In spring 1921 the *Arbeitsrat für Kunst* was dissolved. Many architects so far among its members joined the Novembergruppe instead.[39]

In the run-up to the next big exhibition in the *Landesausstellungsgebäude*, which now reverted to its pre-war name, the Great Berlin Art Exhibition, the journalist Otto Koester called the works by Novembergruppe members "dunghill art" and criticized those responsible at the culture ministry in the sharpest tones for using public funds to promote such an "incomparably ridiculous cultural grotesque".[40] Reacting to the accusations, already voiced the previous year in several quarters, the ministry threatened in early May not to open the Novembergruppe section. Under pressure from the management of the Great Berlin Art Exhibition the association's exhibition committee removed two works by OTTO DIX and RUDOLF SCHLICHTER.[41]

The Great Berlin Art Exhibition ran from 14 May until the end of September. The participating organizations were not only the *Verein Berliner Künstler* and the Novembergruppe, but also the *Freie Secession* and the *Bund Deutscher Architekten*. Without SCHLICHTER, who sent no replacement for his disgraced work *Love Life in Berlin W*, the Novembergruppe showed 77 artists (figs. 11 and 12) and accounted for 175 items in the catalogue. Although RAOUL HAUSMANN was already thinking about leaving and setting up a new group of his own,[42] he did show on this occasion and wrote the introduction for the guide to the Novembergruppe section. On 20 June he published an "Open Letter to the Novembergruppe" in the journal *Der Gegner*, making the censorship public. The five-page missive was

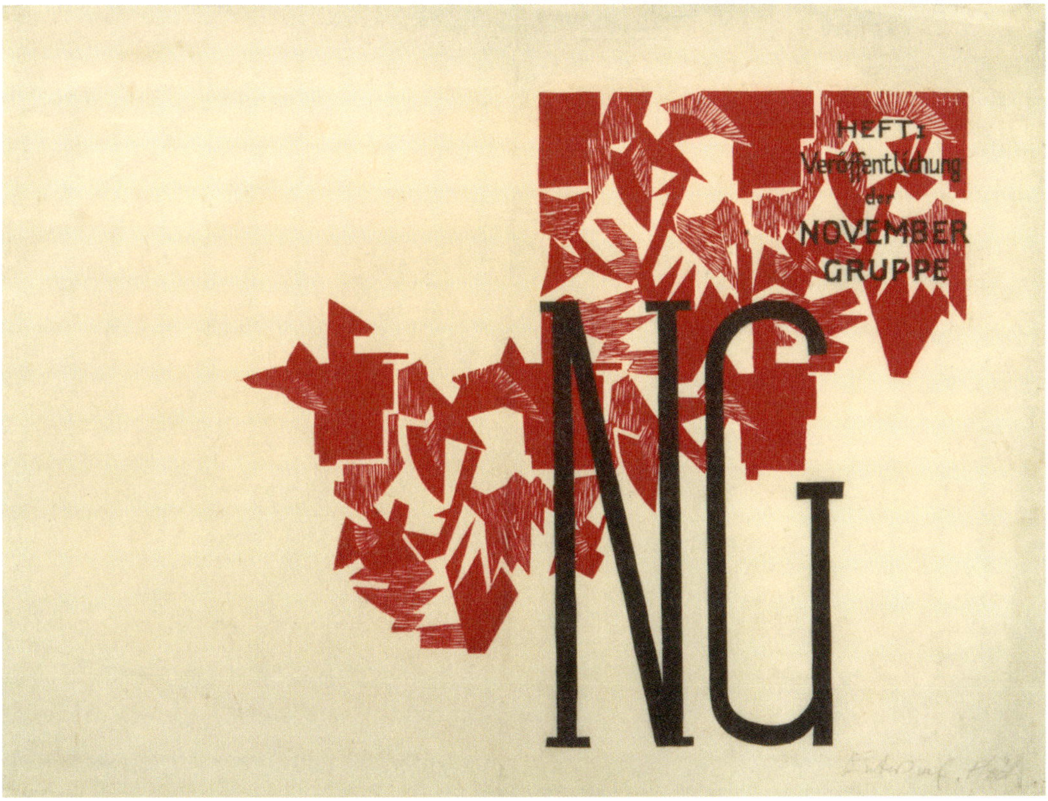

10 HANNAH HÖCH
Cover design for the Novembergruppe magazine *NG*, 1921
Berlinische Galerie

10

signed by the author, the censored artists OTTO DIX and RUDOLF SCHLICHTER and other discontented members of the association.[43]

The Novembergruppe circulated a statement in response: "The news of a split in the Novembergruppe recently reported in the newspapers is not correct. Only a few members have left, most of them admitted only recently, who were demanding, instead of the programme for a revolution in art pursued by this radical group of artists, an exclusively political stance without consideration for quality."[44] An official reply published in *Der Gegner* by the association appeared after a considerable delay and heavily abridged in March 1922.[45]

The closing exhibition of the year was another group show in Josef Altmann's shop from 1 to 30 November (cat. 125, p. 259). "One observes a new perspective emerging here and hastens not to miss out on any potential concessions that might be made to its pressing demands, of which so far nobody knows 'nothing certain'. All in all the outcome is a fantastical concert not lacking in clashes and squawks; although proficiency occasionally butts in to assert its monotony," commented the *Tägliche Rundschau*.[46]

The fancy-dress ball on 3 December was held in the Kaisersaal, a large, neo-classical banqueting hall in the former officers' mess opposite Bahnhof Zoo (now housing the Museum für Fotografie, Staatliche Museen zu Berlin). The collaged invitation by WALTER KAMPMANN promises "intimacy" and warns, promising thrills: "Do not always walk around naked".[47]

1922

From 1922 the office address for the Novembergruppe was given in the Berlin directory as Konstanzer Strasse 9, the private address of painter and writer HANS SIEBERT VON HEISTER, who served on the executive board from 1920 to 1923 and remained active in various functions, including on the exhibition committee, until 1929.[48]

On 20 January the general meeting of the Novembergruppe resolved to admit writers and musicians "who are committed to a radical view of art".[49] The first of altogether 21 Novembergruppe Evenings was held on 19 March in the upper room of the restaurant in the German Opera House.[50] According to the invitation, the compositions played were by Arthur Schnabel, Arnold Schönberg and Wolfgang Zeller,[51] and actor Fränze Roloff recited works by young writers.[52] At least two more events featuring music and literature took place during the year:[53] On 22 May pieces by Eduard Erdmann and Róbert Berény were on the programme for the upper hall in the Schillertheater. The philosopher and writer SALOMO FRIEDLAENDER a.k.a. Mynona read from his *Grotesques* [*Grotesken*].[54] The third Novembergruppe soirée on 16 September included composers Felix Petyrek and MAX BUTTING, while RUDOLF ADRIAN DIETRICH read from his *Gothic Poems* [*Gotische Dichtungen*].[55]

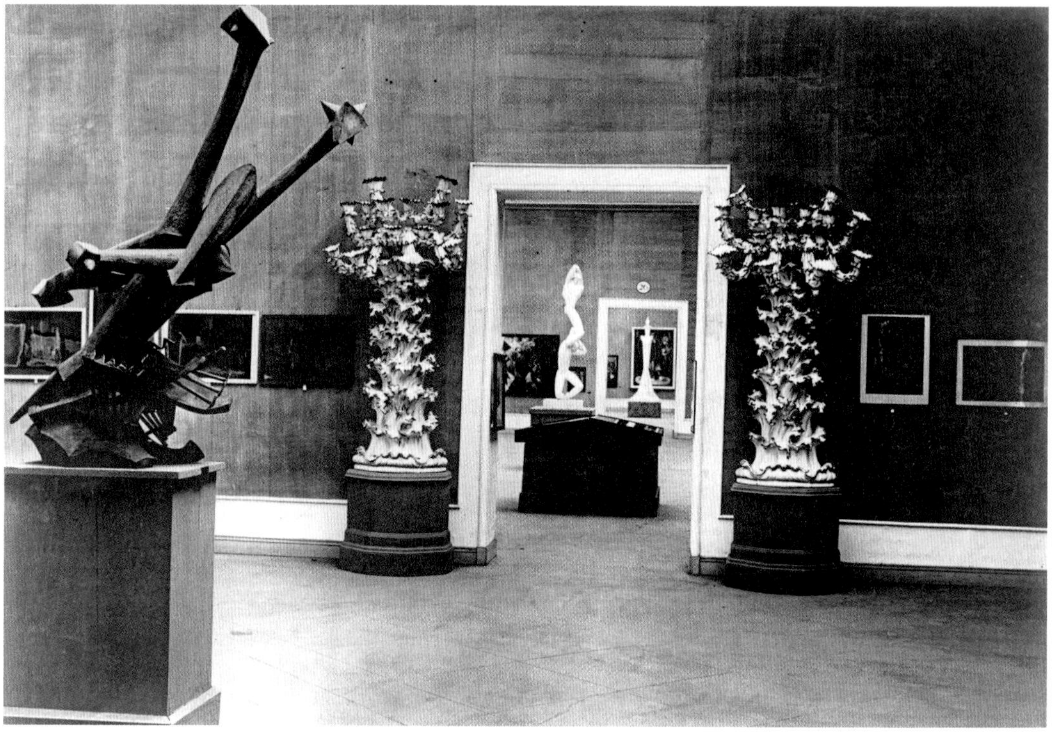

11 Great Berlin Art Exhibition 1921, Novembergruppe section, Room 25
Front left Rudolf Belling's sculpture *Gesture of Freedom*, by the doors candelabras by Hans Poelzig

In March, following an initiative by the Rhenish association *Das Junge Rheinland*, a nationwide alliance of progressive artists' groups was formed called the *Kartell fortschrittlicher Künstlergruppen in Deutschland*,[56] to which the Novembergruppe, the Secessions in Dresden and Darmstadt and a little later the Dresden-based group *Die Schaffenden* affiliated. On 11 and 12 March the new network held its first meeting in Weimar, and MORIZ MELZER attended as chairman of the Novembergruppe.[57] A resolution was passed to join the broader Union of International Progressive Artists [*Union internationaler fortschrittlicher Künstler*]. There was also a decision that the affiliates would jointly publish a new periodical on behalf of the *Kartell* and that this would absorb *Das Junge Rheinland*. In May and July, two issues duly appeared under the title *Das Junge Rheinland, Novembergruppe, Dresdner Sezession* (fig. 13). Each association had its own team of editors and appointed a lead secretary. For the Novembergruppe this task was taken on by the physician and writer EDUARD TRAUTNER.

The association organized three exhibitions in 1922.[58] In the spring, the Novembergruppe took part in an event by the *Bund für Schulkunstausstellungen,* a society founded in 1921 to promote art exhibitions in schools. The event was held at Eckertstrasse 16 in the borough of Friedrichshain, the home of two elementary schools (nos. 258 and 271). The display prompted vehement protests among teachers, leading to a decision by the local school inspector that exhibitions for children should be confined to works of "officially recognized" value. RUDOLF ADRIAN DIETRICH expressed indignation at this outdated approach to art education: "Gradually it is trotting along behind the 'officially recognized' line and teaching not to see things as the child sees them but like that pedagogy that cannot relate to anything new, anything alive, but constructs whatever suits it through the intellect. And with these glasses, adapted to the old, short-sighted eyes of the pedagogue, they wish to teach our young people how to see?"[59]

Following an application from the Novembergruppe to the Prussian Ministry of Culture, *Das Junge Rheinland* took part in the Great Berlin Art Exhibition,[60] held from 20 May until 17 September. The two rooms occupied by this ally formed part of a "Rhenish section" and directly adjoined the rooms of the Novembergruppe. The other participant, apart from the *Verein Berliner Künstler* as organizer, was the *Bund Deutscher Architekten*. The Novembergruppe accounted for almost 270 items in the catalogue. In a German première, its section featured works by EL LISSITZKY, who reaped criticism for his pure abstraction. Just before the show ended, two prints by GEORG SCHOLZ in the Novembergruppe section were seized as "indecent" (e.g. cat. 48, p. 101). Interventions by the Ministry of Culture and the Reich Guardian of the Arts Edwin Redslob, as well as an expert report by Paul F. Schmidt, director of the Dresden Art Collections, had no effect. SCHOLZ was sentenced by a regional court in Berlin (Landgericht I) to pay a fine of 100 million Marks (the inflation currency prior to revaluation).[61]

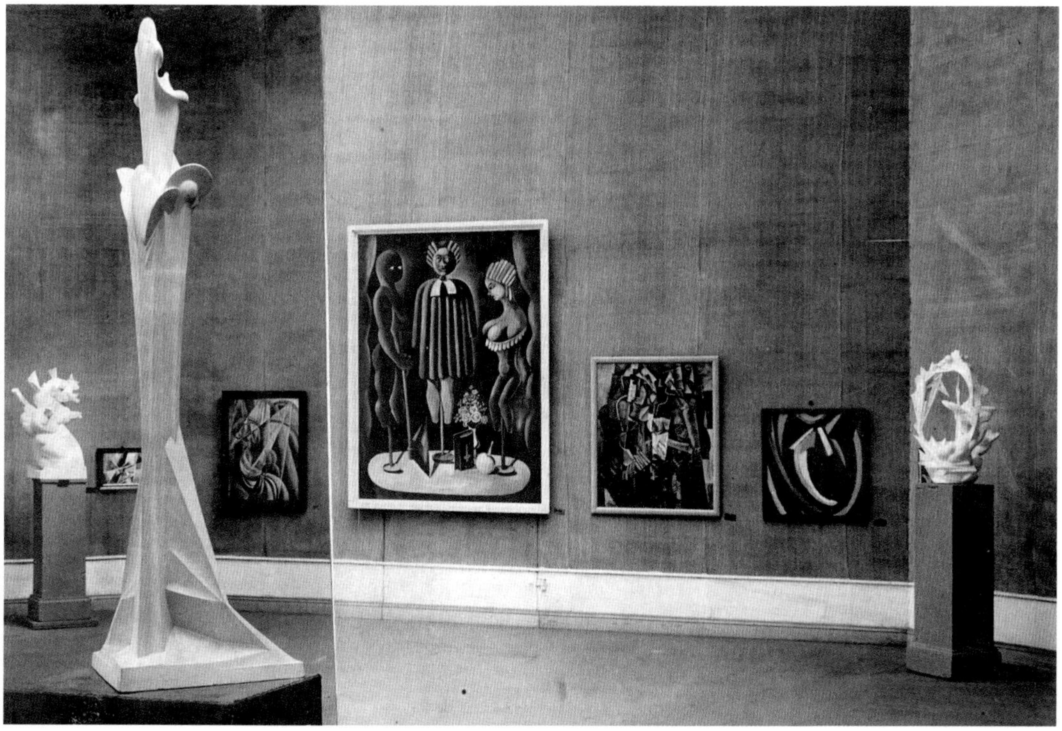

12 Great Berlin Art Exhibition 1921, Novembergruppe section, Room 27
Sculptures by Oswald Herzog (in the foreground *Lament*), in the middle of the wall Wilhelm Schmid's painting *Madame Dubarry*

12

The Novembergruppe sought to recruit more members by placing an advertisement in the guide, for which RUDOLF ADRIAN DIETRICH penned the introduction in 1922. Non-artists were welcome: "Healthy mental aspiration wishing to break out of the constraints of artistic convention seeks involvement. All participants in today's artistic life must create the soil in which a young creative urge can strike root. To permit close exploratory contact between you and us, the Novembergruppe will admit you to its ranks as a passive member."[62] For 500 Marks per annum, passive members could borrow a painting or sculpture for a year, for 250 Marks they were given a print to keep. They were also offered visits to exhibitions and studios and the manuscripts of recital evenings.[63]
From 28 May until 3 July the *Kartell fortschrittlicher Künstlergruppen* participated as one in the First International Art Exhibition in the rooms of the department store Leonhard Tietz in Düsseldorf. The show, organized by *Das Junge Rheinland*, was intended as a supra-regional, avant-garde counterpart to the conservative Great Düsseldorf Art Exhibition. According to the catalogue, almost 150 works were contributed by 52 artists from the Novembergruppe, including RAOUL HAUSMANN, who had actually left the association the previous year[64] and proved one of the show's harshest critics. The forum for protest, especially about close links between the exhibition and the art trade, was the Congress of the Union of International Progressive Artists from 29 to 31 May. The Novembergruppe delegation consisted of visual artists RUDOLF BELLING, HANS SIEBERT VON HEISTER, MORIZ MELZER and WILHELM SCHMID. When HAUSMANN, attending in an individual capacity, was prevented from reading out a declaration, he walked out with like-minded participants.[65]
The artistic fancy-dress ball on 2 December was again held in the Kaisersaal[66] and the theme was "Hot Tip for Investors: Novembergruppe!" The invitation designed by WALTER KAMPMANN (fig. 14) made a tongue-in-cheek pitch for customers stricken by rampant inflation: "The Novembergruppe, least listed of all securities, is on a bull run. Run with us! Dump the mark, invest in the Novembergruppe! Lighten your burden by shedding junk values! The Novembergruppe share is gaining traction. Hedging permitted." Another, alternative invitation announced a "Literary Music Hall" with LEON HIRSCH as master of ceremonies (p. 186, fig. 03).

1923

The fourth Novembergruppe Evening on 3 April at the *Künstlerhaus* on Bellevuestrasse played works by Anton Webern, Alban Berg, WLADIMIR VOGEL and PHILIPP JARNACH. HERBERT BEHRENS-HANGELER recited his *Hypodromic Lyric* [*Hypodromische Lyrik*]. Tickets, due to inflation, cost 2000 Marks including taxes (p. 185, fig. 02). The fifth Evening followed on 5 November in Vox-Haus with string quartets by Alois Hába and Paul Hindemith. Walther von Hollander read from his unpublished manuscript on *Till Eulenspiegel*.[67]
The Great Berlin Art Exhibition ran from 19 May to 17 September with contributions from the *Verein Berliner Künstler*, the applied arts section of the *Bund Deutscher Archi-*

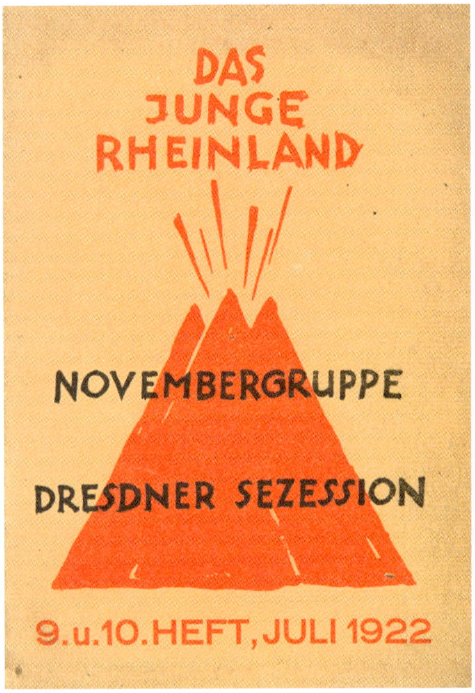

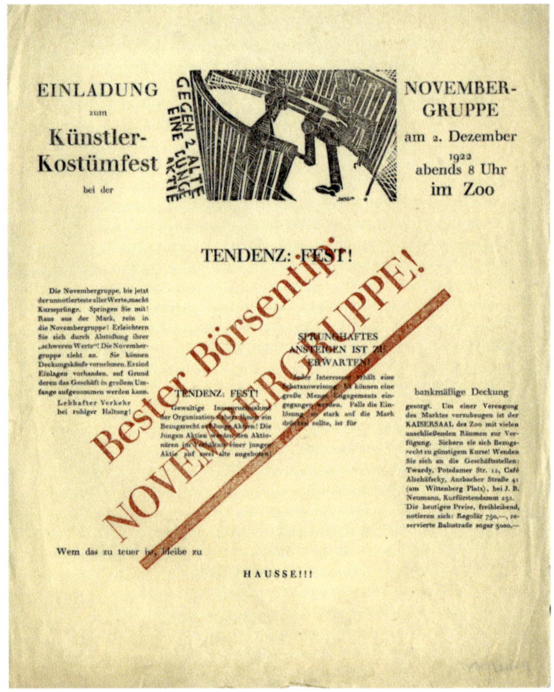

13 The joint publication *Das Junge Rheinland, Novembergruppe, Dresdner Sezession*, July 1922

14 WALTER KAMPMANN
Hot Tip for Investors: Novembergruppe, design for an invitation to the Artists' Fancy-Dress Ball given by the Novembergruppe on 2 December 1922
Staatliche Museen zu Berlin, Zentralarchiv

13 14

tekten and the Novembergruppe. The latter accounted for 348 catalogue items by some 130 artists. The Russian avant-garde turned out in force. Hungarian artists and the Dutch movement *De Stijl* were well represented. The exhibition was particularly praised for its multidisciplinary character, as it was not confined to the visual arts and architecture but extended to films and stage plays.[68] Despite the many positive press reviews, HERBERT BEHRENS-HANGELER appealed in the guide for visitors to be open-minded, an attitude that could still not be taken for granted among the broader public: "The observer requires will and freedom from prejudice to contemplate a work of art. Incomprehensibility means 'getting the picture', and art cannot be comprehended, but must take form in a person to become reality. The force that radiates from the work can lead the soul-body into the intoxicating, ever vibrant land of magic in which humans draw fruit from love, faith and omnipotence."[69]

The ball on 1 December, theme and venue unknown, was broken up by the police for violating the closing hour. The customary raffle was performed on this occasion by a professional agency and the prizes included everyday objects as well as works of art.[70]

1924

In 1924 the association organized five musical and literary events in all. The sixth Novembergruppe Evening was on 22 January at Vox-Haus. On the programme were compositions by STEFAN WOLPE, PHILIPP JARNACH and KURT WEILL. The literary contribution came from MARTIN KESSEL, who read his own poems.[71] The next concert on 26 February in the Schwechten-Saal in Lützowstrasse (fig. 15) witnessed the first performance of a wind quintet by Jan Ingenhoven and a piece for wind instruments by Felix Petyrek. Toni Freeden, the wife of Novembergruppe member RUDOLF BELLING, danced to noise music.[72] After some changes to the programme, the eighth Evening on 18 March, again in the Vox hall, presented music for piano and strings by Béla Bartók, Alban Berg, Heinz Hirschland and Alfredo Casella.[73] The ninth Evening on 23 October featured string quartets and trios by Igor Stravinsky, Anton Webern and Paul Hindemith.[74] At the tenth Evening on 24 November in the Künstlerhaus on Bellevuestrasse Stravinsky featured again, together with compositions for a chamber orchestra by Ernst Toch, Erwin Lendvai, Egon Wellesz and Francesco Malipiero (cat. 160, p. 261).

Prior to the Great Berlin Art Exhibition of 1924 there was a debate about revising the format. The Ministry of Culture called for spatial limitations, which meant a more rigorous selection process, something the Novembergruppe accepted. Initially, therefore, it planned for two rooms.[75] As the *Berliner Secession* and *Freie Secession* pulled out at short notice, the association ultimately had four rooms to itself, almost as much space as the *Verein Berliner Künstler*, which also integrated free submissions within its presentation.[76] Some artists and works were nevertheless rejected, prompting controversy among Novembergruppe members. The exhibition committee was accused of betraying its own principles by subjecting art to jury decisions and cosying up to the government by only selecting art that appealed to official tastes.[77] At this show from 31 May to 1 September the Novembergruppe brought together almost 70 artists and 168 catalogue items. The association attracted particular attention with its hall of architecture, which directly adjoined the special exhibition of the *Bund Deutscher Architekten* and was perceived as the modernist section of this historical display.[78] The painting and sculpture included not only purely and partially abstract trends but also many figurative works using a variety of styles which, one year later at the celebrated exhibition at the Kunsthalle in Mannheim, would enter the canon as "New Objectivity". The introduction to the guide, this time by an anonymous author, declared: "We brook neither dogma nor doctrine and this protects us from the threat of fossilization. That is why our exhibition does not focus on one single trend. [...] Far from considering our task as resolved, we are aware of our ability to show essential work."[79] The influential critic Willi Wolfradt summed up the variety in this section as follows: "There is, in any case, no other association in the art life of Berlin to which so many maverick, unifying forces in the creative movement belong, some known, some as yet hardly noticed."[80]

On 18 October the First Universal German Art Exhibition in Soviet Russia opened in Moscow before travelling on to Leningrad and Saratov. 13 artists' associations participated, the contingent from the Novembergruppe, with 24 artists, being the largest.[81] The show was a great success with the Russian public, hitherto barely acquainted with German art[82] (fig. 16).

At the end of the year LUDWIG MIES VAN DER ROHE took over the chair of the association. From the end of 1924 meetings of members and of the working committee were held in Café Alschäfsky at Ansbacherstrasse 41, including the preparatory meetings for the Novembergruppe's fifth Free Artists' Fancy Dress Ball,[83] celebrated on 6 December at the Philharmonie concert hall in Bernburger Strasse. The theme, absurdly Dada, was "Don't move or you will kill yourself! Mamalla" (fig. 17)—the latter being, according to the invitation, a dreamland to which the guests would be transported. This time the rooms were not decorated by the artists but by a professional studio.[84] The raffle was again run by an agency and the prizes included not only works of art but also a motorbike, canoes and gramophone cabinets.[85] As in 1922, the programme boasted a "Literary Music Hall" with MC LEON HIRSCH, and among the performers were well-known cabaret artists like Rosa Valetti, Lotte Werkmeister, Alexander Granach, Paul Schneider Duncker and Hugo Döblin.[86]

1925

During the first few months of 1925 the working committee of the Novembergruppe met at Uhlandstrasse 175 in the offices of architect ARTHUR KORN, secretary since around 1924.[87] In January 1925 LUDWIG MIES VAN DER ROHE proposed improving the commercial skills of the management in a drive for greater professionalism.[88] The art dealer HUGO GRAETZ was recruited for the purpose. From June, the official domicile of the association was at Achenbachstrasse 21 (where Lietzenburger Strasse 33 now stands).[89] Parallel to this the group continued using the private address of HANS SIEBERT VON HEISTER at Konstanzer Strasse 9 until 1929.

On 12 January the music section of the Novembergruppe hosted a soirée with the influential music critic and conductor PAUL BEKKER, who spoke about "Essential Forms in

15

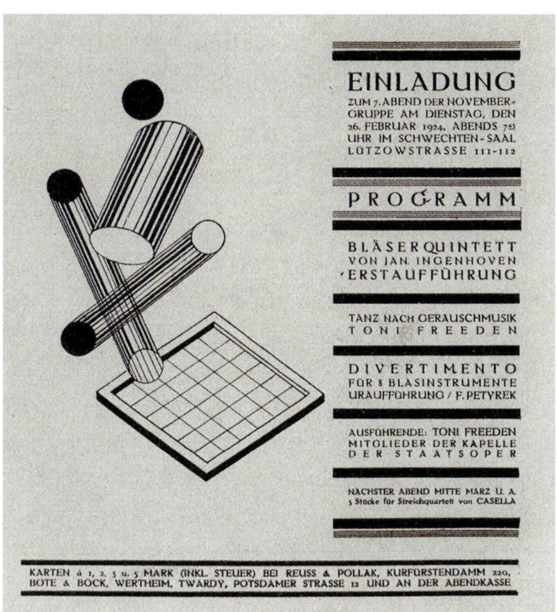

16

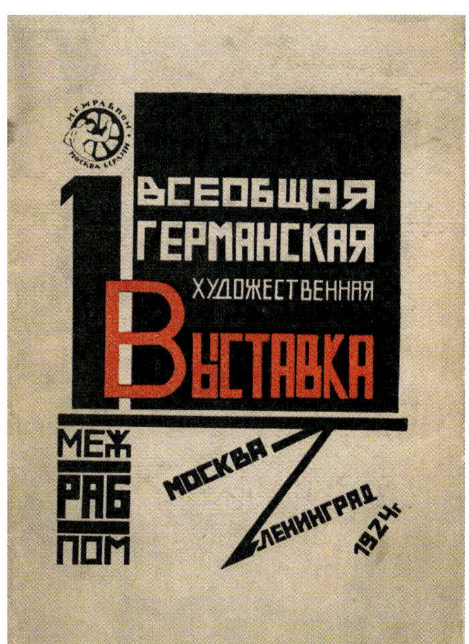

15 Invitation to the 7th Novembergruppe Evening, 23 February 1924, whereabouts unknown

16 Catalogue for the First Universal German Art Exhibition in Moscow and other cities, 1924

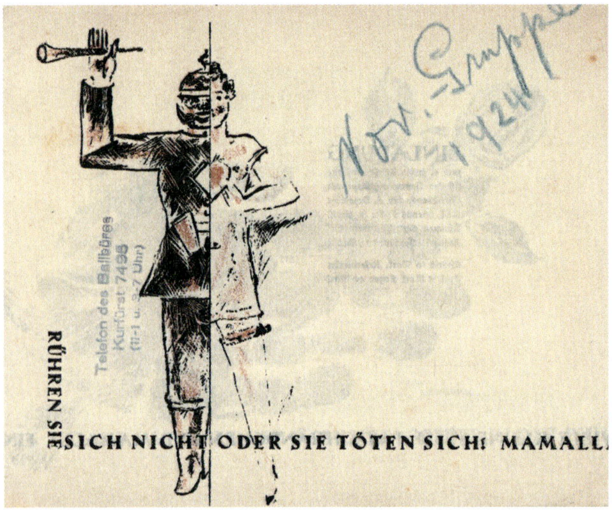

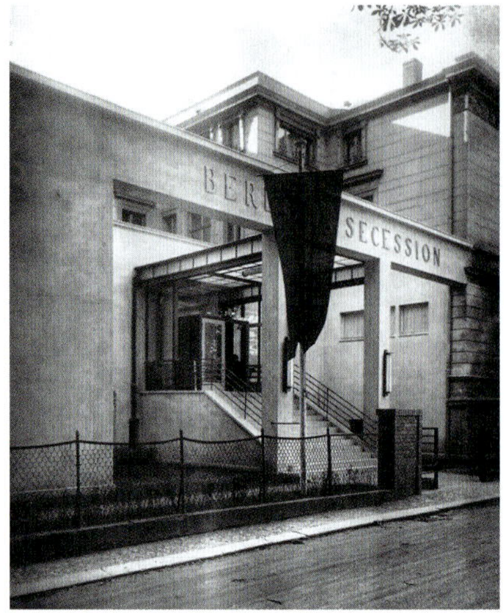

17 WALTER KAMPMANN
An invitation to the 5th Open Artists' Fancy-Dress Ball given by the Novembergruppe, 6 December 1924
Berlinische Galerie

18 The Berlin Secession building, venue for the Novembergruppe exhibition in 1925

Music". BEKKER's reflections were subsequently published by the Novembergruppe under its own imprint.[90]

In 1925 the Novembergruppe also organized three concerts, the first two at Vox-Haus, the third in a newly built venue, the Grotrian-Steinweg-Saal (cat. 160, p. 261).

On 30 January, during the eleventh Novembergruppe Evening, there was music by Alexander Jemnitz, Felix Petyrek, Erich Walter Sternberg and Walter Goehr, some of which was première and some a first in Berlin. The next Evening on 3 April featured works by Maurice Ravel, the Hungarian Zoltán Kodály and the Novembergruppe members PHILIPP JARNACH and HANNS EISLER, all of which were being performed in Berlin for the first time (p. 187, fig. 06). The 13th Evening on 12 November presented the Prague composers Bohuslav Martinů, Emil Axman, Karel Boleslav Jirák and Erwin Schulhoff.

In February, at a meeting of the Prussian Academy of Arts, Karl Hofer suggested inviting the Novembergruppe to take part in the next spring show. This initiative was rejected due to concerns about quality.[91]

In the spring the association played an active role in political debate about setting up a chamber of artists,[92] an idea first mooted in 1919, to succeed the revolutionary councils as a structure representing artists and to establish a counterweight to the academy. The proposal came to nothing.[93]

On 3 and 10 May the Novembergruppe, working with the culture department at the cinema studio UFA, hosted the matinée *Absolute Film*. The venue was the Ufa-Palast on Kurfürstendamm with a seating capacity of 900. Abstract and surreal avant-garde films were screened by Bauhaus artist LUDWIG HIRSCHFELD-MACK, by HANS RICHTER, VIKING EGGELING, WALTER RUTTMANN, by FERNAND LÉGER and DUDLEY MURPHY, by FRANCIS PICABIA and RENÉ CLAIR.[94] Under the heading "Bluff or Revolution?" the reviewer in the *Berliner Volkszeitung* concluded that the French specimens were not far removed from conventional cinematic art, whereas the experimental techniques applied in the German contributions were "the first, exploratory steps of true 'absolute film'", and was intrigued throughout by "the experiments in which movement itself, the melody of line, was born of circles and ellipses, straight and wavy lines, colours and shadows".[95]

On 11 May the Novembergruppe presented a soirée of its own on the radio, thanks to the good offices of its member HANS SIEBERT VON HEISTER, editor-in-chief of *Der Deutsche Rundfunk*:[96] the painter ARTHUR SEGAL introduced the evening by talking about the origins and significance of the Novembergruppe. Listeners were then offered music by Novembergruppe members HEINZ TIESSEN, MAX BUTTING, PHILIPP JARNACH and KURT WEILL, interspersed with literary items. The writer MARTIN KESSEL, another regular member of the Novembergruppe, read from his poems. Bertolt Brecht and Carl Zuckmayer joined in as guests to recite their work live. The programme announcement described events by the Novembergruppe as the "most important artistic gatherings" of the day. "What a pity the original art of the 'Novembergruppe', painting, cannot be transmitted."[97]

In 1925 the Novembergruppe did not participate as usual in the Great Berlin Art Exhibition because of a dispute over management. The *Verein Berliner Künstler* did not wish to renounce its lead function and refused to designate a neutral chair.[98] Under the aegis of its new business manager HUGO GRAETZ, the Novembergruppe mounted its own exhibition from 30 May until the end of June 1925 in the rooms of the *Berliner Secession* (fig. 18), integrating a smaller show to mark the 50th birthday of ARTHUR SEGAL. In the foreword to the catalogue (fig. 19), the association once again took issue with art for art's sake and called for close links between art and life. It endorsed its aspiration to be "not just an exhibition club" but "an organization for creative artistic forces in Germany. [...] One of the most important tasks of the Novembergruppe, therefore, is to clear a path for all that is young and embryonic in the face of superior numbers and conservative bias."[99] The catalogue included an up-to-date list of members with 88 names (see fig. 06, p. 187). The association had to fund the exhibition itself, causing financial strain.[100] The Ministry of Culture made a few purchases[101] and members were expected to pass 50 per cent of the proceeds on to the Novembergruppe to plug the financial gap, but most artists were not prepared to pay such a high levy.[102]

The artists' fancy-dress ball was held on 5 December and filled all the rooms of the Philharmonie on Bernburger Strasse. Works donated by members were once again raffled. Artists received two free tickets in return.[103] The theme for the party was "Sport and Razzmatazz in Wedding". The text of the poster designed by HANNAH HÖCH (p. 189, fig. 08) threatened in broad Berlin dialect: "Turn up in *tails*, guv'nor, and you'll be *fined*".

1926

The first four Novembergruppe concerts in 1926 were staged in the new Grotrian-Steinweg-Saal at Bellevuestrasse 14. The 14th Evening on 15 January witnessed the first performances in Berlin of music by Erik Satie, who had died in 1925, along with works by Maurice Ravel, Arthur Honegger, HEINZ TIESSEN and a premiere for Emil Bohnke. At monthly intervals there followed the 15th Evening on 16 February featuring music by Egon Wellesz, Alban Berg, Karl Horwitz and Ernst Krenek, the 16th Evening on 16 March with pieces by Arthur Schnabel, Luis Gruenberg and once again Krenek, and the 17th Evening on 16 April (cat. 163, p. 261), devoted entirely to WLADIMIR VOGEL.[104] Commenting on the education efforts of the Novembergruppe, the *Berliner Volkszeitung* wrote: "To anyone who has not yet had the natural laws of sound disputed away and who experiences dissonance as tension urging resolution, pure pleasure will hardly be the response on hearing this consistently cacophonous music which an ear can barely grasp. Depending on his disposition and his temperament, he will be obliged to say that he does not understand this music or that the others do not know what music is. And both might be correct!"[105]

The final concert of the year followed on 28 November with works by Ernst Toch, Paul Hindemith and Gerhart Münch.[106] Compositions for the mechanical piano were performed, unplayable by hand. The music was generated instead by 'programming' the roll. The audience was then treated to two pieces for mechanical piano by Claude Debussy and Alexander Nikolayevich Scriabin, and HANS HEINZ STUCKENSCHMIDT, who became head of the Novembergruppe's music section by 1927 at the latest, opened the discussion with a talk.

In March–April 1926 the Novembergruppe architects took part in an exhibition in Gera devoted to residential building.[107] The association returned to the Great Berlin Art Exhibition, which ran from 21 May until the end of August 1926. Participating alongside the *Verein Berliner Künstler* and the Novembergruppe was the group known as *Die Abstrakten*, which had evolved out of the International Association of Expressionists, Futurists, Cubists and Constructivists, closely allied with the gallery Der Sturm. This newcomer challenged the Novembergruppe's reputation as the most progressive association at the event. THEO VAN DOESBURG had tried unsuccessfully in the run-up to put together a small display by *De Stijl* artists for the Novembergruppe section.[108] The latter consisted of nearly 150 catalogue items by 81 artists. The architects were again given special prominence and their hall incorporated a number of Dutch colleagues, among them *De Stijl* architect CORNELIS VAN EESTEREN, attracting much praise from reviewers.[109]

19

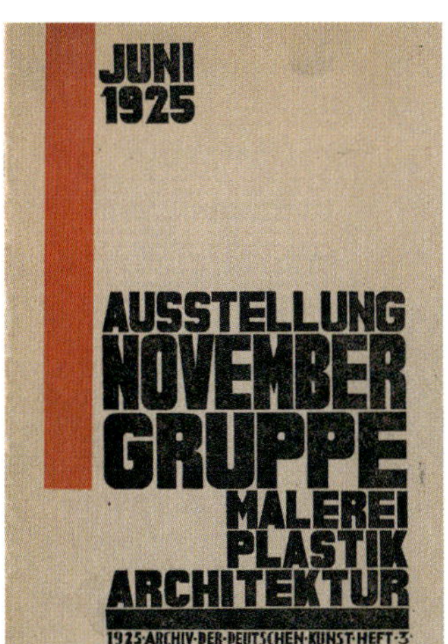

20

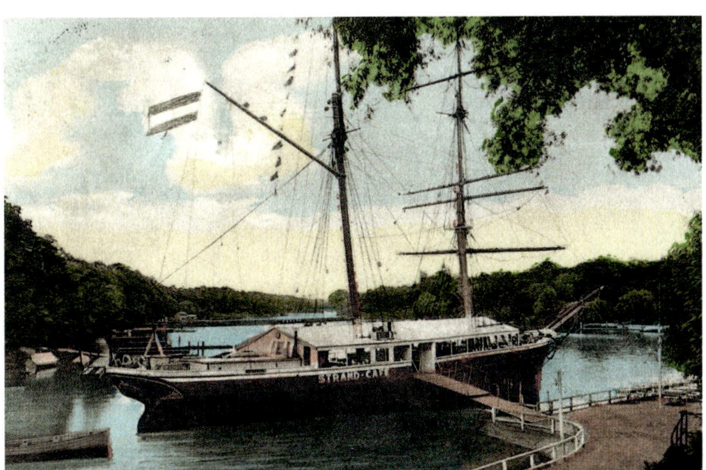

19 Catalogue for the *Novembergruppe Exhibition* at the Berlin Secession, June 1925

20 The brigantine Dorthea, a pleasure boat on Kleiner Wannsee, venue for the summer parties on 19 June 1926 and 25 June 1927
Collection Uwe Gerber, Berlin

For the first time the Novembergruppe threw a summer party. It was on 19 June 1926 aboard a pleasure boat on a lake, Kleiner Wannsee, on the edge of Berlin. The brigantine Dorthea (fig. 21) was sold out. The press reported numerous artists and cinema actors among the guests.[110]

At the general meeting on 13 October in the office on Achenbachstrasse there was an argument about how the association was organized and the use of moneys received from the ministry for purchases at the Great Berlin Art Exhibition.[111] There had already been disagreements, especially between architects and visual artists, in the preceding months.[112] On 27 October the Novembergruppe founded an association, the *Hilfsverein für junge Kunst*, to administer a new charitable fund for young artists.[113] This new body was soon managing its affairs independently[114] and in summer 1927 it staged its first exhibition, entitled *The Problem of Portraiture in Young Art*[115], at the gallery Neumann und Nierendorf, featuring many Novembergruppe members.

On 15 November 1926 an extraordinary plenary assembly of the Novembergruppe met to discuss copious amendments to the articles of association. One demand was that the working committee should also constitute the nominal board and that it should only remain in office for one year. Every member was to have the right to submit one work a year without screening by a jury.[116]

The fancy-dress ball on 4 December was held at the Philharmonie. The theme was "The Feast of the Silver Sphinx: a League of Nations Revue in the Chaos of Infinity", an ironic reference to current events. Germany had just been admitted to the League of Nations, founded in 1920 in response to the First World War but without Germany. The *Berliner Tageblatt* again congratulated the Novembergruppe on a successful party. "The people in the November-Gruppe, one has to say, have a splendid command of staging a ball with all the trimmings."[117]

1927

In early 1927 all the architects except ALFRED GELLHORN left the Novembergruppe, seeking alternative advocacy of their interests in the architects' association *Der Ring*. A few visual artists and musicians also left the Novembergruppe. The loss of so many well-known companions plunged the association, which now had 72 regular members, into a serious crisis.[118]

On 2 May the Vox-Saal hosted the Novembergruppe's 19th musical soirée with compositions by Hansjörg Dammert, STEFAN WOLPE and HANS HEINZ STUCKENSCHMIDT (cat. 165, p. 261). From 1927 to 1933 the composer MAX BUTTING, a Novembergruppe member, served on the cultural advisory board of the broadcaster *Deutsche Funkstunde*.[119]

At the Great Berlin Art Exhibition the reins had passed to the newly formed *Kartell der vereinigten Verbände bildender Künstler Berlins* [*Syndicate of the United Associations of Fine Artists of Berlin*]. Prior to the 1927 exhibition, held from 7 May until 30 September, the works submitted by GEORGE GROSZ, who had recently joined the Novembergruppe, were supposed to be censored,[120] but the association successfully resisted the decision (cat. 106, p. 211). This year the catalogue to the Great Berlin Art Exhibition did not indicate whether the exhibitors were affiliated to any of the ten participating groups of artists. The *Juryfreie Kunstschau* was taking place in the same venue, the *Landesausstellungsgebäude*, at the same time, leading to severe spatial constraints. Moreover, the Great Berlin Art Exhibition ran a series of temporary shows, including in May the legendary display by Kazimir Malevich, the first major presentation of his work outside Russia. This exhibition had nothing to do with the Novembergruppe[121] and was probably initiated by *Der Ring*.[122]

The Prussian Ministry of Culture made numerous purchases at the Great Berlin Art Exhibition, among them works by Novembergruppe artists (see inter alia cat. 78 and 79, pp. 138 and 139).[123]

On 25 June the Novembergruppe threw another summer party on the brigantine Dorthea. The proceeds were given to the *Hilfsverein für junge Kunst*,[124] as was the revenue from the fancy-dress ball at the Philharmonie on 3 December, attended according to the *Vossische Zeitung* by 6000 guests. Highlights were a shooting gallery providing a chance to smash old china and the raffle with prizes ranging from original prints to a doll's house.[125]

1928

The Novembergruppe showed 70 artists and more than 250 works at the Great Berlin Art Exhibition, which was open to the public from 9 May until the end of July (fig. 23). The *Kartell* remained in charge of the organization, but this time the catalogue stated to which participating associations the artists belonged. There were eight of these in addition to the Novembergruppe and the *Verein Berliner Künstler*. The Novembergruppe section devoted special attention to three artists: ADOLF HÖLZEL showed 20 exhibits, and there were 18 works by WILHELM MORGNER, who had died in 1917. The sculptor EWALD MATARÉ had a room of his own with at least 18 works.[126] On 12 July Adolf Hitler visited the Great Berlin Art Exhibition and was able to study Expressionism, Cubism, Futurism, Constructivism and New Objectivity in the sections compiled by the Novembergruppe and *Die Abstrakten*. Recent building trends in *Neues Bauen* could be observed in the section by *Der Ring* and at the Werkbund exhibition on international architecture. Hitler's image of modernism, which he so detested, was influenced by exhibitions such as these.[127]

At the end of the year the association marked its tenth anniversary with the publication *Ten Years of the Novembergruppe*, a special issue of the magazine *Kunst der Zeit*. Will Grohmann was the editor in charge and wrote the introduction. The volume was a colourful mix of documents, press reviews, articles by current and former members, and numerous photographs of works, most of which had been shown at past exhibitions. The focus was deliberately placed on the founding years and the original struggle for recognition, while the current situation remained difficult for the association due to shrinkage and the reform of the Great Berlin Art Exhibition. By taking stock, the Novembergruppe restated its social relevance[128] and expressed its desire to "help construct where an entire people has resolved to shape life anew from the foundations".[129]

On 27 November HANS SIEBERT VON HEISTER summarized the role of the association in his radio lecture for the Berliner Rundfunk on "Ten Years of the Novembergruppe". The talk was repeated on Radio Breslau on 13 December and on Nordischer Rundfunk on 31 January 1929.[130]

Starting at the end of the year the Novembergruppe, the *Hilfsverein für junge Kunst* and the international artists' association Porza met in a pub called *Kunsttopp* on the corner of Meinekestrasse and Kurfürstendamm. The venue was inaugurated as a regular haunt for the member artists with a speech by Eduard Trautner and an "Opening Cantata" by STEFAN WOLPE.[131]

The Novembergruppe fancy-dress ball on 1 December was themed "A Night in Paradise" and again benefitted the *Hilfsverein für junge Kunst*. GEORG TAPPERT's invitation was a collage in several parts offering a prize for a clever text (figs. 21 and 22). The *Berliner Tageblatt* reported the attendance of "several thousand wearers of fig leaves in the banana-adorned Philharmonie", where the principal decoration was a large, luxurious 'paradise bed' suspended above the orchestra.[132] The association also organized its first-ever New Year Ball in the Logenhaus at Kleiststrasse 10.[133]

1929

On 16 February 1929 the Novembergruppe organized an evening of film and dance at the Gloria-Palast. The films were *Emak Bakia* by MAN RAY and *Hands* [*Hände*] by STELLA VON SIMON. The latter was directed by Miklos Blandy and the set designs were by Novembergruppe member MAX DUNGERT. *Hands* was screened in three parts, and between these the dancer Helen Tamiris from the United States (fig. 24) demonstrated experimental studies in movement to music by, among others, George Gershwin and Louis Gruenberg. Other interludes on the programme were the radio reportage by FRED ANTOINE ANGERMAYER and the Charleston and blues arrangements for piano and saxophone by STEFAN WOLPE. The final dance by Tamiris was to GEORGE ANTHEIL's *American Serenades nos.* 1 *and* 2 *(Sonatina for Radio)*. ANTHEIL and ANGERMAYER also belonged to the Novembergruppe, while the overall direction for the evening was undertaken by HEINRICH RICHTER-BERLIN, a long-standing member.[134] The magazine *Die Form* wrote: "An experience, despite hissing opposition, was the appearance of dancer Tamiris. Her dance is free of any hint of either jazz or ballet and is above all free of any hint of romance or motif. With tremendous discipline she dances spatially, not in images. [...] And yet this dance never resembles sport, acrobatics or gymnastics. The artistic method in this dance is absolute."[135]

At the Great Berlin Art Exhibition, henceforth located at Schloss Bellevue as the traditional Prussian exhibition building at Lehrter Bahnhof was about to close down,[136] the Novembergruppe's participation was limited by its

21

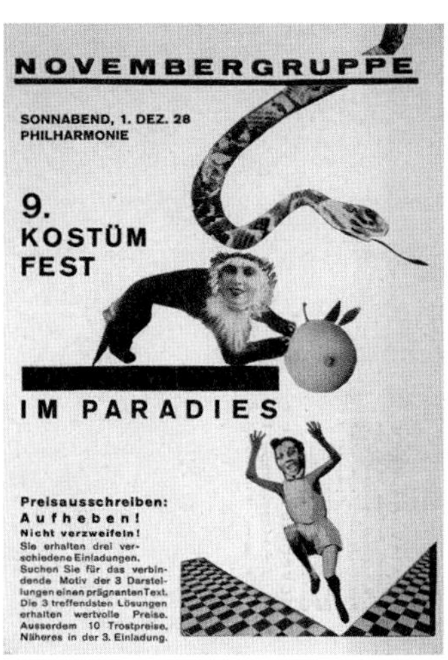

22

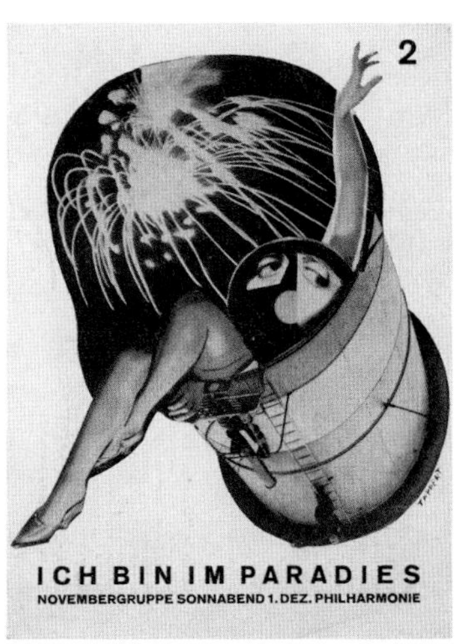

23

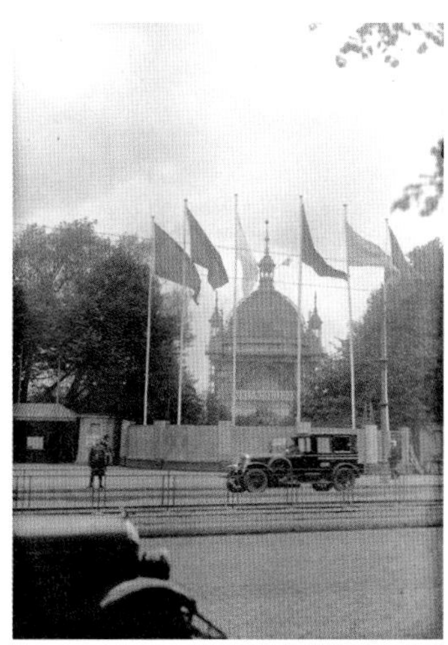

21 [GEORG TAPPERT]
An invitation to the 9th Fancy-Dress Ball given by the Novembergruppe on 1 December 1928
Private collection

22 GEORG TAPPERT
An invitation to the 9th Fancy-Dress Ball given by the Novembergruppe on 1 December 1928
Private collection

23 GEORG PAHL
View of the Landesausstellungsgebäude [State Exhibition Building] at Lehrter Bahnhof, 1928

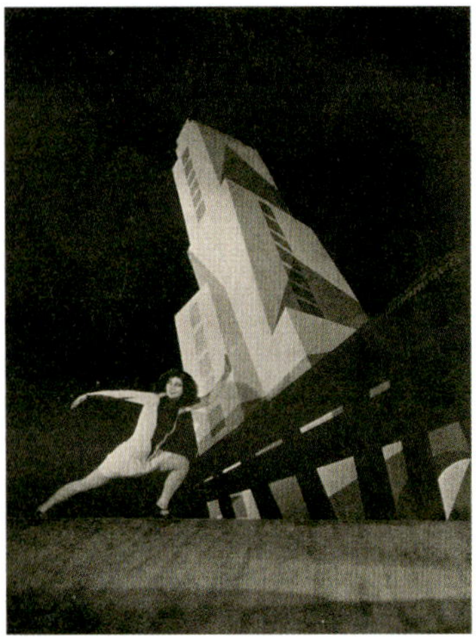

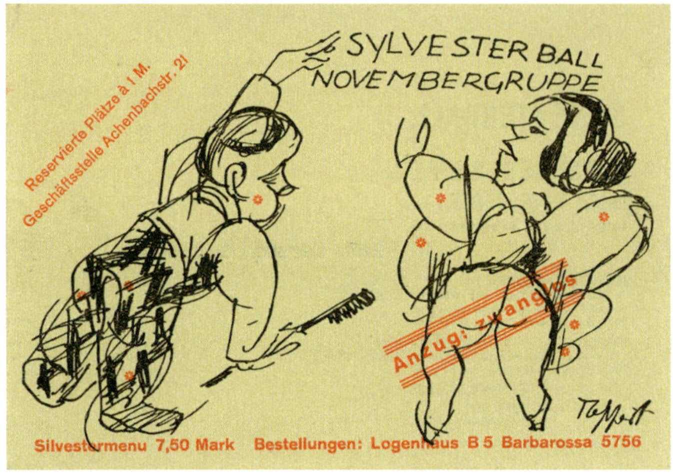

24 Dancer Helen Tamiris in the piece *1927* (performed under the title *1929* at the Novembergruppe's evening of film and dance, 16 February 1929)
Photo: Soichi Sunami

25 GEORG TAPPERT
An invitation to the Novembergruppe's New Year Ball, 1929
Staatliche Museen zu Berlin, Art Library

own exhibition schedule. From 19 May until 15 August it presented eleven works by ten artists.

The anniversary exhibition Ten Years of the Novembergruppe ran from 25 August to 5 October 1929 as part of the *Juryfreie Kunstschau Berlin*, one of the last events permitted in the dilapidated *Landesausstellungsgebäude*. Special shows were put on here not only by the Novembergruppe, but also by the Italian group *Novecento Italiano*. The Novembergruppe exhibited around 240 works by 122 participants, including many guests from abroad:[137] apart from Expressionism, Abstracts, Constructivism and *Neues Bauen* the association devoted an area to socially critical art, mostly Verism, some of which explicitly addressed events during the revolution of 1918–19. This room in particular was picked out by some reviewers as paradigmatic of the Novembergruppe in its totality, even though it had resisted specifically political activities in the past. Purchases by the Ministry of Culture focussed on neutral themes, either moderate versions of New Objectivity or works with abstract tendencies such as *The Boat* by JEAN METZINGER.[138]

Another fancy-dress ball was held, probably on 7 December[139] at the Philharmonie, and the New Year Ball again took place at the Logenhaus on Kleiststrasse (fig. 25).

1930

The association began 1930 with the concert *10 Years of the Novembergruppe 1919–1929* on 24 January in the Meistersaal on Köthener Strasse (fig. 26). On the programme were compositions for piano and strings by PHILIPP JARNACH, MAX BUTTING, HEINZ TIESSEN, STEFAN WOLPE, WLADIMIR VOGEL, HANNS EISLER and KURT WEILL, which were broadcast live on the radio.[140] The *Berliner Börsen-Zeitung* reported: "The Novembergruppe, once thrusting towards the future with so much action and carefree disregard for taste, of which rather little has been heard in recent years, [...] again proudly illuminated those names which now emit a radiance of their own, which once it hauled out of the darkness of the nameless. Looking back, then, history of an assault troop."[141]

In the spring the Novembergruppe parted company with its business manager HUGO GRAETZ and moved its office into the gallery *Die Kunststube* at Königin-Augusta-Strasse 22 (now Reichpietschufer, level with no. 48). Members of the association, including OTTO MÖLLER and ARTHUR SEGAL, had already been offered space here in 1929. The art dealership was managed by Ludwig Hermann Schütze and Charlotte Luke.[142] From 26 May to 26 June *Die Kunststube* hosted a personal show organized by the Novembergruppe for WILHELM SCHMID.[143] In autumn the gallery moved, taking the Novembergruppe office with it, to Schöneberger Ufer 31 (now no. 57 and the current home of the *Verein Berliner Künstler*). The inaugural show at the new address in September–October was devoted to the Novembergruppe.[144] Alongside this, from early October, *Die Kunststube* ran an exhibition with about 30 works by César Klein, eliciting positive press reviews.[145]

The Great Berlin Art Exhibition in Schloss Bellevue was divided into two parts. The first section with paintings and large sculptures, on show from 29 May to 17 August, attracted not only the Novembergruppe but also nine other associations as well as free submissions. The Novembergruppe contributed 44 artists and 64 works. Novembergruppe member MORIZ MELZER served on the overall exhibition management as chief secretary. The second section with prints, drawings and small sculptures followed from 7 September until the end of October. Here the Novembergruppe showed works by 14 artists, including 15 photomontages by HANNAH HÖCH, who represented the association in the themed exhibition *Photography in the Hands of the Artist*. WALTER KAMPMANN was honoured with a small personal show.

On 20 November, aided by the *Hilfsverein für junge Kunst*, the Novembergruppe put on its 20th musical soirée followed by a discussion of the concert at Reckendorfhaus on Hedemannstrasse (p. 187, fig. 07). Apart from works by Norbert von Hannenheim, Arnold Schönberg and Igor Stravinsky the programme included the French composers Maxime Jacob and Francis Poulenc. From Ernst Schoen there was a cantata especially written for radio and from Walter Gronostay excerpts from his experimental music *Train to the Salt Sea* [*Zug zum Salzmeer*] and compilations made for Deutsche Grammophon records, including sound recordings like *Modern Battle Noise* [*Modernes Schlachtgeräusch*]. All these compositions were performed by professional musicians, and the choir of the adult education college in the borough of Charlottenburg sang songs by Ernst Lothar von Knorr, the director of the *Volks- und Jugendmusikschule Süd*, an adult and youth music school in the south of the city, and by the Hungarian composer Pál Hermann.

For the eleventh fancy-dress ball on 6 December 1930 WALTER KAMPMANN designed four different invitations (fig. 27 and p. 190, figs. 09-11). JOACHIM RINGELNATZ and Robert Seitz contributed poems for leaflets.[146]

Despite all this publicity, the familiar flood of party-goers failed to materialize. The *Berliner Volkszeitung* observed: "The economic crisis dispatched the vultures of bankruptcy to hover over the banquet, keeping many guests away from the wine tables. Even so, there was great gaiety right up until the first underground train, as money for cars was short. Thank God the balloons were free and could be plucked from the walls like in the Land of Cockayne."[147]

There are no records of whether attendance was equally low at the fancy-dress ball in the Logenhaus to see out the year 1930.[148] It was the last of the big parties organized solely by the Novembergruppe.

1931

In winter 1931–32 the Novembergruppe threw a number of open parties in studios.[149] This more private format may have had roots in the world economic crisis. Members of the Novembergruppe were not alone in having to fight harder to make ends meet, and any festivity that did not require hall hire was a welcome opportunity to generate additional income.

In February the Novembergruppe dedicated a modest exhibition in *Die Kunststube* to HERBERT BEHRENS-HANGELER.[150] Opinion was divided about the traces of Surrealism in the artist's work and so reviews were mixed.[151] In March–April followed a retrospective to mark the 50th birthday of OSWALD HERZOG.[152]

The 21st and last musical soirée organized by the Novembergruppe (p. 185, fig. 01) was likewise far less ambitious than usual. It took place at *Die Kunststube* with music by Alejandro Garcia Caturla, Paul Höffer, Adolph Weiss, Imre Weisshaus, Henry Cowel and George Antheil, Ruth Crawford and Alexander Jemnitz.

The first section of the Great Berlin Art Exhibition was on show from 3 May until 16 August at Schloss Bellevue.

26

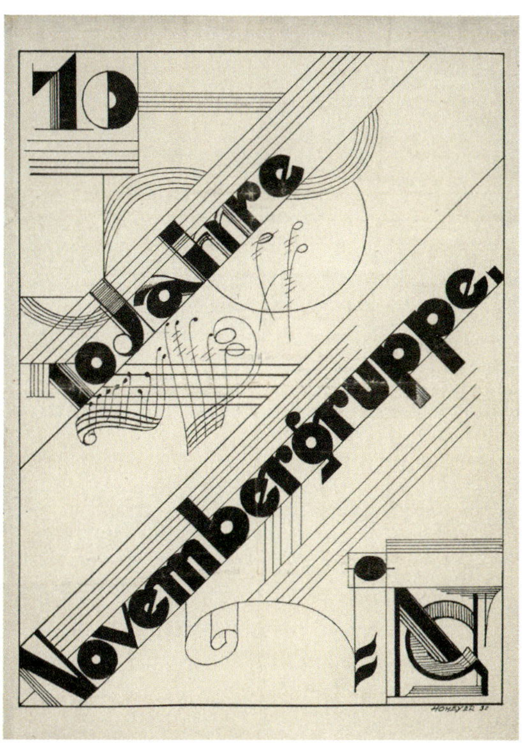

27

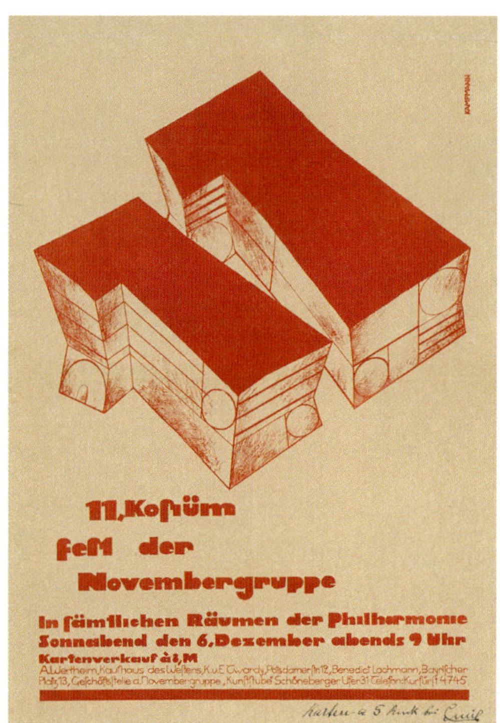

26 LOTHAR HOMEYER
10 Years of the Novembergruppe, programme for the concert on 24 January 1930
Berlinische Galerie

27 WALTER KAMPMANN
An invitation to the 11th Fancy-Dress Ball given by the Novembergruppe on 6 December 1930
Staatliche Museen zu Berlin, Art Library

MORIZ MELZER, again in the function of chief secretary, designed the exhibition poster and the cover for the catalogue.[153] The Novembergruppe participated with 32 artists and showed nearly 60 works. The press paid hardly any attention to the association or to the event. Reviews of the second section from 6 September until the end of October failed to mention the Novembergruppe.[154]

There was a very different response to the exhibition staged by the Novembergruppe from 3 July to 3 August 1931 on the new premises of the *Verein Berliner Künstler* at Tiergartengartenstrasse 2a. Coverage of the collective show was extremely positive. According to one review: "The Novembergruppe [...] mustered the best forces among its membership and friends, chose with care and thus produced an exhibition which, on a modest scale (slightly more than 60 works), offers an intelligently arranged, very substantial overview. Seldom in Berlin have we seen a more significant display of contemporary art in its ramifications, for the emphasis was placed not on the will to achieve new objectives, but above all on skill."[155]

The catalogue, funded by the international art association Porza and with a foreword by Paul Westheim, listed 46 artists.

1932

The Berlin directory of 1932 gives the address of the Novembergruppe office as Laubenheimer Platz 8 (on the square now called Ludwig-Barnay-Platz) in Wilmersdorf. Located at this same address were the home of member MAX DUNGERT and the office of the *Künstlerheim-Kolonie* (also: *Künstlerkolonie Berlin*), the co-operative housing estate for artists which owned the building. Novembergruppe member STEFAN WOLPE and former activist MARTIN KESSEL also lived in this artists' colony.

The fancy-dress ball at the Philharmonie on 23 January 1932 was organized by visual artists in the city to raise funds for colleagues in financial distress. The associations behind it, apart from the Novembergruppe, included among others the nationwide *Reichsverband bildender Künstler*, the Prussian Academy of Arts, the *Berliner Secession*, *Die Juryfreien*, the *Verein Berliner Künstler* and an association for women artists, the *Verein der Künstlerinnen* (fig. 28).

The Novembergruppe was visibly falling apart. Only four members took part in the first section of the Great Berlin Art Exhibition from 8 May to 14 August: HERBERT BEHRENS-HANGELER, WILHELM SCHMID, WALTER KAMPMANN and KURT SCHWERDTFEGER. ARTHUR SEGAL was showing with *Die Abstrakten*. Press reports on the second section from 4 September to 23 October do not mention the Novembergruppe.[156]

On 20 April the Novembergruppe hosted a talk by Paul Westheim at the Staatliche Kunstschule, the state art college in Schöneberg, entitled "'When Experts Err': Notes on the Wacker Affair" (fig. 29). Otto Wacker was an art dealer who placed forgeries of works by Vincent van Gogh on the

28

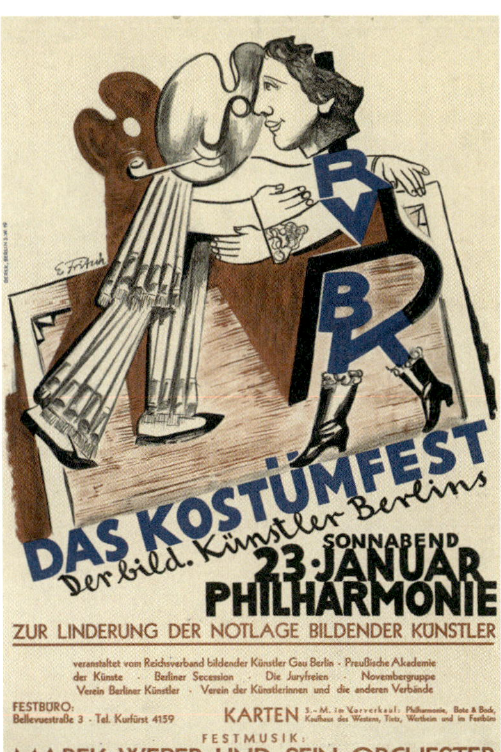

29

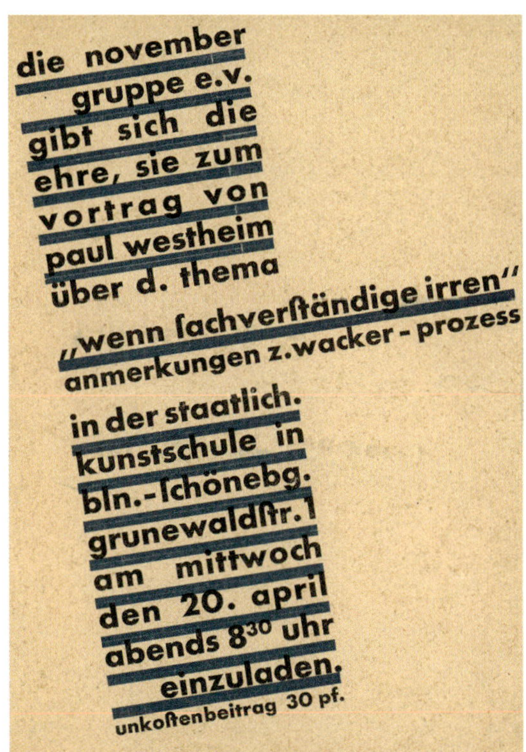

28 ERNST FRITSCH
Poster for the Fancy-Dress Ball given by the visual artists of Berlin, 23 January 1932
Staatliche Museen zu Berlin, Art Library

29 Invitation to Paul Westheim's talk "When Experts Err: Notes on the Wacker Affair" organized by the Novembergruppe, 20 April 1932
Berlinische Galerie

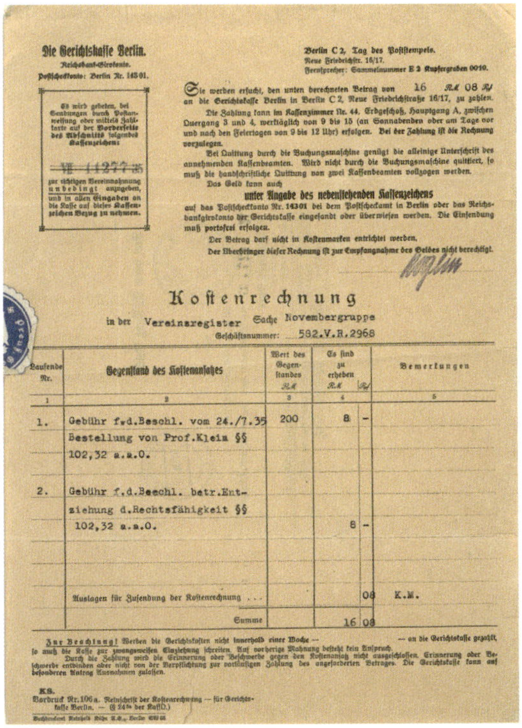
Kostenrechnung

in der Vereinsregister Sache Novembergruppe

Geschäftsnummer: 582.V.R.2968

Laufende Nr.	Gegenstand des Kostenansatzes	Wert des Gegenstandes RM	Es sind zu erheben RM	Rpf	Bemerkungen
1	2	3	4		5
1.	Gebühr f.d.Beschl. vom 24./7.35 Bestellung von Prof.Klein §§ 102,32 a.a.O.	200	8	-	
2.	Gebühr f.d.Beschl. betr.Entziehung d.Rechtsfähigkeit §§ 102,32 a.a.O.		8	-	
	Auslagen für Zusendung der Kostenrechnung ...			08	K.M.
	Summe		16	08	

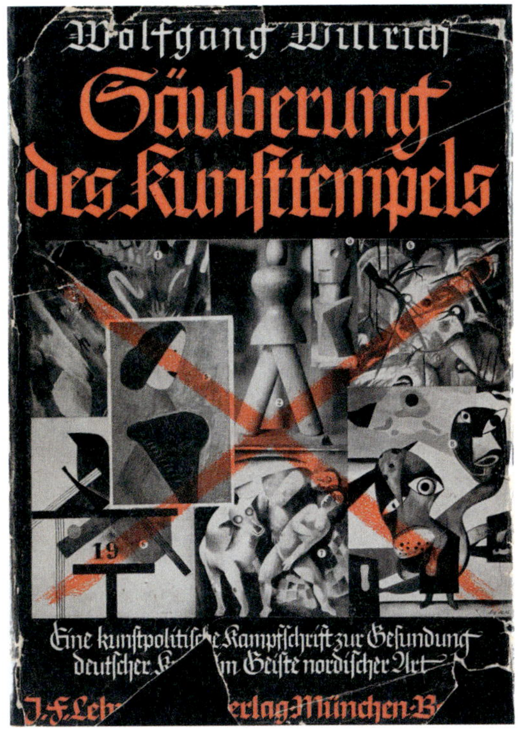

30 Invoice of the Berlin Court Cashier for striking the Novembergruppe from the register of associations, 6 November 1935
Literary estate of César Klein

31 WOLFGANG WILLRICH
Purging the Temple of Art, 1937

art market in the late 1920s, for which experts like Julius Meier-Graefe had mistakenly issued certificates of authenticity.[157]

By autumn at the latest, the Novembergruppe found itself in severe financial difficulties, culminating in a deficit of 3000 Reichsmarks and an oath of disclosure by the board.[158]

1933–1938

In spring 1933, after the Nazis had taken power, all artists' associations and art institutions were brought into line with the regime, and this amounted *de facto* to the prohibition of the Novembergruppe.[159] Like other avant-garde groupings, it was no longer permitted to take part in the Great Berlin Art Exhibition. On 24 July 1935 the association was officially deprived of legal capacity. On 6 November 1936 the Berlin Court Cashier issued the last chairman, CÉSAR KLEIN, with an invoice for 16 Reichmarks and 8 Reichspfennings for striking out the Novembergruppe from the register of associations (fig. 30).[160]

Nazi propaganda defamed the Novembergruppe and its members as the spearhead of "cultural bolshevism" during the "dereliction" wrought by the Weimar Republic.[161] In his diatribe *Purging the Temple of Art* (fig. 31) Wolfgang Willrich named 174 former members and guests of the association, denouncing them publicly as "degenerate". Like many avant-garde artists, former members of the Novembergruppe were dismissed from public office, among them GEORG TAPPERT, removed from his professorship at the Staatliche Kunstschule in Berlin.[162] Jewish members like ARTHUR SEGAL had to flee Germany. OTTO FREUNDLICH was probably murdered in the extermination camp at Sobibór. Others like MORIZ MELZER joined the ruling National Socialist German Workers' Party (NSDAP)[163] and were able to continue teaching despite attacks on them in National Socialist propaganda.[164] Some former members of the Novembergruppe sought to continue practising their art by seeking admission to the *Verein Berliner Künstler*, prompting hefty disagreements and power struggles within this professional association.[165]

After 1945

After 1945 the Novembergruppe initially fell into oblivion. During the 1950s there were attempts to revive it and plans for a retrospective exhibition, but nothing came of it.[166] Not until Helga Kliemann published her book about the association in 1969 did it attract further attention. It was subsequently mentioned from time to time in research by art historians, but it eluded description on account of its stylistic heterogeneity and large membership.

1 Georg Tappert, Curriculum vitae, 11 October 1955, Deutsches Kunstarchiv, Germanisches Nationalmuseum, Nuremberg, Georg Tappert Fonds, I, B-1. This memoir lacking in further detail tallies with press reports about a raid on the artists' colony in Berlin, a housing estate managed as a co-operative where from 1932 the Novembergruppe had its last office at Laubenheimer Platz 8. (On the house searches see *inter alia* "Das Ergebnis der Razzia. Zahlreiche Verhaftungen und Materialfunde in der Künstlerkolonie", in: *Der Westen*, 16 March 1933, no. 75.)

2 Articles of association of the Novembergruppe, 16 December 1918 (p. 46, fig. 01). The precise date of foundation is unknown; see the essay by Nentwig, pp. 42–55 of this catalogue for more about the time frame.

3 See the copy of the minutes by Georg Tappert, in: *Zehn Jahre Novembergruppe*, special issue of *Kunst der Zeit. Zeitschrift für Kunst und Literatur*, vol. 3, 1928, nos. 1–3, p. 10; fig. 01 in the essay by Nentwig, p. 46 of this catalogue.

4 See Nentwig 2015a, pp. 172f.

5 Arbeitsrat der Novembergruppe, "Aufruf", in: *Die schöne Rarität*, vol. 2, 1918, no. 9, ad section, unpaginated; Novembergruppe, circular, 13 December 1918, in: *Zehn Jahre Novembergruppe*, ref. in note 3, p. 12.

6 See the essay by Nentwig, p. 43 of this catalogue.

7 See ref. in note 2. We do not know who took on these functions during the foundation period.

8 The original articles (ref. in note 2) provide additionally for a "central working committee", to be constituted by the working committee. This intermediate structure was eliminated from 1920, as were the "local branches" outside Berlin. See the later articles of association dated 1920 and 1925 (cat. 139–141, p. 260).

9 Recent literature refers to bitter rivalry between the Novembergruppe and Der Sturm (Fitzke 2015). Even if this impression is created by Paul Westheim's caustic comments about Sturm artists leaving for the Novembergruppe (see *inter alia* P.W. [Paul Westheim], "Umschau. November-Gruppe", in: *Kunstblatt*, vol. 4, 1920, 223), other sources do not confirm the escalation. It seems more likely that a group of artists collectively joined the Novembergruppe with Walden's approval. See *inter alia* the letters from Heinrich Campendonk to Walter Dexel, 16 and 18 December 1918, Museum Penzberg, Campendonk Collection, Letters 192 and 193. Only Oskar Fischer reports "trouble" he claims to have had with Walden over his participation in the Novembergruppe section at the Kunstaustellung Berlin in 1919 (see *inter alia* the letter from Oskar Fischer to Adolf Behne, 13 December 1919, Akademie der Künste, Adolf-Behne-Archiv, 84, B. 25-29). On Walden's tolerance see also the letter from Walter Dexel to Helga Kliemann, 22 February 1968, Berlinische Galerie, BG-Ar 13/99,32.

10 K.F., "Gegen die Entführung von Kunstwerken. Kundgebung in der Akademie der Künste", in: *Berliner Tageblatt*, 7. April 1919, no. 153.

11 Resolution by the Novembergruppe, [April 1919], Deutsches Kunstarchiv, Germanisches Nationalmuseum, Nachlass Georg Tappert, I, B-35. Quoted in parts in Andrian-Werburg 2005, pp. 34f.

12 See the essays by Kratz-Kessemeier and Nentwig, pp. 30–39 and 42–55 respectively of this catalogue.

13 See Walter Gropius, Minutes of the Executive Committee and Artistic Working Group of the *Arbeitsrat für Kunst*, 18 November 1919, Berlin, Bauhaus-Archiv, Nachlass Walter Gropius, Arbeitsrat für Kunst, Signatur 123, Mappe 2; letter from Walter Gropius to Adolf Behne, 29 December 1919, Berlin, Akademie der Künste, Adolf-Behne-Archiv, 99, Bl. 10.

14 See the essay by Nentwig, pp. 50f. of this catalogue.

15 The address was used in the following letters among others: Herbert Behrens-Hangeler (Der Wurf) to the Novembergruppe, 2 February 1920, Sächsische Landesbibliothek – Staats- und Universitätsbibliothek, Dresden, Nachlass Herbert Behrens-Hangeler, Mscr. Dresd. App. 2401, 628; Fritz Stuckenberg to Walter Dexel, 10 March 1920, The Getty Research Institute, Research Library, Special Collections, Los Angeles, Walter Dexel letters received, Acc. No. 850835, Box 2, Folder 40.

16 The address is found, for instance, on the cover page for Peter Leu, *Führer durch die Abteilung der* Novembergruppe. *Kunstausstellung Berlin 1920*, Berlin 1920. The reasons for this address are not yet clear. None of the residents listed under Bornstrasse 6 in the Berlin directories of 1919 and 1920 can be linked directly to the association.

17 Date according to Willy Oskar Dressler (ed.), *Dresslers Kunsthandbuch*, Berlin 1923, p. 206; the relevant files of the register are no longer extant (information provided by Landesarchiv Berlin, Gisela Erler, 21 October 2015).

18 No catalogue has been identified. The exhibition is mentioned in: letter from Fritz Stuckenberg to Paul van Ostaijen, 8 February 1920, quoted in Bulhof 1992, p. 60; exhibition diary of Fritz Stuckenberg, undated, Städtische Galerie Delmenhorst, Nachlass Fritz Stuckenberg; Georg Schrimpf to the Novembergruppe, 19 March 1920, private collection.

19 No catalogues have been preserved from the various towns on the itinerary. Some of the planned stop-overs apparently did not happen. Georg Schrimpf, for example, informed the Novembergruppe in a letter on 19 March 1920 (private collection) that he intended to ask the *Neue Secession* in Munich whether they could host the exhibition, but evidently this cooperation did not take place.

20 Letter from Alfred Gellhorn to *Expressionistische Arbeitsgemeinschaft Kiel*, 17 May 1920, Schleswig-Holsteinische Landesbibliothek, Kiel, Richard Blunck Nachlass, Cb 104: 56.06. On the sales see also the letter from the *Badischer Kunstverein* to Otto Möller, 31 March 1920, Berlinische Galerie, Teilnachlass Otto Möller, BG-OM 4.

21 A.M., "Kunstausstellungen. Mannheim", in: *Der Kunstwanderer*, vol. 1, 1919–20, p. 344.

22 See "Ausstellungen", in: *Der Kunsttopf*, vol. 1, 1920, no. 2, 40; P. Faerber, "Die Novembergruppe im Kunstsalon Schaller", in: *Stuttgarter Neues Tageblatt*, 28 August 1920, newspaper cutting, Deutsches Kunstarchiv, Germanisches Nationalmuseum, Nachlass Georg Tappert, I, B 35.

23 See "Ausstellungen", in: *Der Kunsttopf*, vol. 1, 1920, no. 2, p. 40.

24 See *inter alia* ibid.; letter from Alfred Gellhorn to Fritz Stuckenberg, 31 October [1920], Städtische Galerie Delmenhorst, Nachlass Fritz Stuckenberg. Will Gromann noted, when preparing his text for the anniversary publication *Zehn Jahre Novembergruppe,* one last stop-over in Magdeburg, for which no other sources can be found. See Will Grohmann, collection of notes "Nov. Gruppe", [1928], Kunstarchive der Staatsgalerie Stuttgart, Nachlass Will Grohmann, Kasten 85.

25 See announcements and advertisements in: *Der Kunsttopf*, vol. 1, 1920, no. 2, p. 40; no. 4, p. 80 (inside cover); no. 5, p. 99. Whether the exhibitions actually happened is not clear.

26 "Popoli in attesa di uno nuova fede, che giustamente vedono riposta nell'arte d'avanguardia il rinnovamento sociale." Enrico Prampolini, [Introduction], in: *Esposizione Espressionisti Novembergruppe*, Bollettino quindicinale della Casa d'arte italiana, diretta da E. Prampolini e M. Recchi, no. 1 (exhib. leaflet, 23 October to November 1920), Rome 1920, unpaginated (cat. 127, p. 259).

27 For detail see Chytraeus-Auerbach 2018.

28 See the essay by Burmeister, pp. 82–86 of this catalogue.

29 See *inter alia* Fritz Stahl, "Grobeka 1920", in: *Berliner Tageblatt*, 21 May 1920, no. 236; Hans Schmidkunz, "Kunstausstellung Berlin 1920", in: *Die christliche Kunst*, vol. 17, 1920–21, pp. 24–29.

30 Alfred Gellhorn et al., "Die Richtung", in: *Der Kunsttopf*, vol. 1, 1920, no. 3, pp. 47–54, here 47.

31 On the dating to 1920 see Matelowski 2017, pp. 335f.

32 See Werner J. Schweiger, "Fraenkel & Co. (Josef Altmann)" [entry for proposed publication *Lexikon des Kunsthandels der Moderne im deutschsprachigen Raum 1905–1937*], Berlinische Galerie, Kunstarchiv Schweiger, BG-WJS-M-1,10.

33 See the essay by Nentwig, p. 70 of this catalogue.

34 "Achtung!", in: *Der Kunsttopf*, vol. 1, 1920, no. 5, p. 100.

35 See Butting 1955, p. 119.

36 See Nentwig 2015, esp. pp. 49–52.

37 See Raoul Hausmann, "Der Kunsttopf", in: Berlinische Galerie 1995, 2. Abt, 21.54, pp. 42f.

38 German Legation in The Netherlands to the [German] Foreign Office, (signed Rosen), 28 February 1921, Bundesarchiv, Akten des Reichskunstwarts Edwin Redslob, BArch R 32/Bd. 69, pp. 51/52. On this exhibition, to which artists from *Die Brücke* were also invited, see Jong 2009, pp. 22f.

39 See the essay by Nentwig, pp. 141f. of this catalogue.

40 Otto Koester, "Müllgrubenkunst", in: *Die Welt am Montag*, 4 April 1921, no. 14.

41 See the essay by Burmeister, p. 89 of this catalogue.

42 See Berlinische Galerie 1995, 2. Abt., 21.33 and 21.50, pp. 27 and 38f.

43 See the essay by Burmeister, pp. 80–91 of this catalogue.

44 "Die Novembergruppe", in: *Berliner Volkszeitung*, 15 September 1921, no. 434.

45 See Roters 1995, pp. 82f.

46 Reinhold Neubauer, "Kunstausstellungen", in: *Tägliche Rundschau*, 23 November 1921, no. 270.

47 See Kliemann 1969, text ill. 18, p. 33.

48 See *inter alia* Hans Siebert von Heister, Lebenslauf, 30 June 1966, Berlinische Galerie, BG-Ar 13/99,66-67.

49 Ref. in note 17.

50 On music events by the Novembergruppe see the essay by Grosch, pp. 184–191 of this catalogue.

51 See Kliemann 1969, p. 36.

52 "Die Novembergruppe", in: *Berliner Börsen-Zeitung*, 18 March 1922, no. 131.

53 There is no conclusive research on whether the planned performance of Arnold Schönberg's melodrama *Pierrot Lunaire*, announced in a draft invitation (p. 187, fig. 05) for October 1922, really went ahead. The Novembergruppe does not mention this evening in summaries of its music events from 1925 to 1928. See *Ausstellung der Novembergruppe in den Räumen der Berliner Secession in Berlin. Juni 1925. Malerei, Plastik, Architektur* (exhib. cat., June 1925), Berlin 1925 (= Archiv der deutschen Kunst, vol. 5, 1925, no. 3), p. 15; *Zehn Jahre Novembergruppe*, ref. in note 3, p. 28.

54 See Kliemann 1969, p. 37 (an example of the invitation card in the Deutsches Kunstarchiv, Germanisches Nationalmuseum, Nuremberg, Nachlass Georg Tappert, I, B35).

55 See *Zehn Jahre Novembergruppe*, ref. in note 3, p. 28.

56 See *Das Junge Rheinland*, vol. 1, 1921–22, no. 7, p. 9; text of the Appeal ibid., pp. 9–11.

57 See Müller 1992, p. 17 and note 3.

58 Evidence has not been found of the exhibitions in Moscow and Japan in 1922 mentioned in Kliemann (1969, p. 22) without specific details. The information was presumably provided by the painters Issai Kulvianski and Rudolf Ausleger, with whom Kliemann corresponded during her research (see letters to Helga Klimann from Rudolf Ausleger, 10 May 1967, and Issai Kulvianski, 21 September 1967, Berlinische Galerie, BG-Ar 13/99,4 and 10).

59 [Rudolf Adrian] Dietrich, "Schulkunstausstellungen", in: *Das Junge Rheinland. Novembergruppe. Dresdner Sezession*, vol. 1, 1921–22, no. 8, pp. 32f., here 33.

60 *Das Junge Rheinland*, vol. 1, 1921–22, no. 6, p. 19.

61 See Sternfeld 2004, pp. 48f.; Hütt 1990, pp. 51f. and 196–199.

62 *Führer durch die Abteilung der Novembergruppe. Kunstausstellung Berlin 1922* [i.e. *Grosse Berliner Kunstausstellung* 1922], Berlin 1922, p. 15.

63 In subsequent years the loans, for which there are no paper records to demonstrate implementation in practice, were evidently discontinued. Similarly, no list of passive members of the Novembergruppe has been located. The principle of passive membership had already been applied by the artist association *Die Brücke* and by the *Neue Secession* (see Daemgen 2011, pp. 44–46). The painter Arthur Segal was a particular champion of this idea (see Dietze 1987).

64 For details see Finkeldey 1992.

65 For details of the congress see Müller 1992. See also the essay by Burmeister, pp. 104–113 of this catalogue.

66 C., "Das November-Gruppe-Fest" [*sic*], in: *Berliner Börsen-Zeitung*, 5 December 1922, no. 547.

67 See Leopold Schmidt, "Aus den Konzerten", in: *Berliner Tageblatt*, 6 November 1923, no. 522.

68 See *inter alia* Willi Wolfradt, "Große Berliner Kunstausstellung", in: *Cicerone*, vol. 15, 1923, pp. 522f.

69 H.B.H. [Herbert Behrens-Hangeler], "Einleitung", in: *Führer durch die Abteilung der Novembergruppe. Kunstausstellung Berlin 1923*, Berlin 1923, unpaginated

70 This can be deduced from two letters in 1924 recounting the events of the previous year. See [Ludwig Mies van der Rohe], draft letter to the competent police authority, 27 November 1924 and letter from Erich Koch (Ball Entertainments, Advisory Centre for Tax and Police Affairs) to Ludwig Mies van der Rohe, 1 December 1924, Library of Congress, Washington D.C., Ludwig Mies van der Rohe Papers, MSS32847, Correspondence, Box 2.

71 See Kliemann 1969, text ill. 26, p. 40

72 See *Zehn Jahre Novembergruppe*, ref. in note 3, p. 28 and reproduction of the invitation ibid., p. 82.

73 See Siegmund Pisling, "Konzertchronik", in: *Berliner Börsen-Zeitung*, 26 March 1924, no. 146; *Zehn Jahre Novembergruppe*, ref. in note 3, p. 28.

74 See *Zehn Jahre Novembergruppe*, ref. in note 3, p. 38; Max Marschalk, "Konzerte", in: *Vossische Zeitung*, 29 October 1924, no. 514.

75 See letters from Arthur Segal to Walter Dexel, 5 and 22 April 1924, The Getty Research Institute, Research Library, Special Collections, Los Angeles, Walter Dexel, letters received, Acc. No. 850835, Box 2, Folder 38.

76 See *Grosse Berliner Kunstausstellung 1924 im Landesausstellungsgebäude am Lehrter Bahnhof* (exhib. cat., 31 May – 1 September 1924), Berlin 1924, pp. 9f.

77 See *inter alia* ref. in note 75 and letter from Hans Brass to Hans Siebert von Heister, 4 September 1924, private collection.

78 See the essay by Nentwig, p. 145 of this catalogue.

79 *Führer der Novembergruppe* [guide through the Novembergruppe section of the Great Berlin Art Exhibition 1924], Berlin 1924, unpaginated.

80 Willi Wolfradt, "Große Berliner Kunstausstellung 1924", in: *Cicerone*, vol. 16, 1924, pp. 631f., here 632.

81 See *Erste Allgemeine Deutsche Kunstausstellung Moskau–Leningrad* (exhib. cat., 18 October – early 1925, Moscow, Historical Museum, *inter alia*), Moscow 1924.

82 On responses to the exhibition see Berlinische Galerie 1995, 2. Abt., pp. 173f.,

83 See letter from the Novembergruppe (working committee) to members, 29 November 1924, Library of Congress, Washington D.C., Ludwig Mies van der Rohe Papers, MSS32847, Correspondence, Box 2.

84 Erich Minuth & Co., Atelier für Dekorationen, receipt for 1000 Marks, 5 December 1924, Library of Congress,

Washington D.C., Ludwig Mies van der Rohe Papers, MSS32847, Correspondence, Box 2.

85 Letter from Erich Koch to Mies van der Rohe, ref. in note 70.

86 "Das Fest der Novembergruppe", in: *Vossische Zeitung*, 4 December 1924, no. 576.

87 See *inter alia* letter from Arthur Korn to Helga Kliemann, 4 December 1967, Berlinische Galerie, BG-Ar 13/99,87.

88 Letter from Ludwig Mies van der Rohe to the members of the Novembergruppe, 9 January 1925, Library of Congress, Washington D.C., Ludwig Mies van der Rohe Papers, MSS32847, Correspondence, Box 2.

89 This address is first mentioned in *Ausstellung der Novembergruppe in den Räumen der Berliner Secession in Berlin. Juni 1925. Malerei, Plastik, Architektur* (exhib. cat., June 1925), Berlin 1925 (= Archiv der deutschen Kunst, vol. 5, 1925, no. 3), p. 2. On Hugo Graetz see also Werner J. Schweiger, "Kunsthandlung Hugo Graetz" [entry for a proposed publication *Lexikon des Kunsthandels der Moderne im deutschsprachigen Raum 1905–1937*], Berlinische Galerie, Kunstarchiv Schweiger, BG-WJS-M-1,26, although here Graetz's appointment as business manager to the Novembergruppe is wrongly described as occurring in the early 1920s. Current research suggests that Graetz never showed a Novembergruppe exhibition in his own gallery, but merely acted as business manager.

90 See Eichhorn 2018.

91 Minutes of the Prussian Academy of Arts, Exhibition Commission, 13 February 1925, Akademie der Künste, Berlin, PrAdK 1254.

92 See Minutes of the Prussian Academy of Arts, Fine Arts Section, 20 April 1925, Akademie der Künste, Berlin, PrAdK 1223. The Novembergruppe representative was Rudolf Belling.

93 See Kratz-Kessemeier 2008, pp. 97 and 351.

94 See the essay by Wünsche, pp. 168–175 of this catalogue.

95 M.-H., "Bluff oder Revolution? Matinee der 'Absoluten'", in: *Berliner Volkszeitung*, 6 Mai 1925, no. 212.

96 See the essay by Zeising and Beimdieke, pp. 176–183 of this catalogue.

97 *Die Funkstunde*, vol. 2, 1925, no. 19, p. 356.

98 See Matelowski 2017, p. 337, also letter from the Novembergruppe (working committee) to members, 11 February 1925, Library of Congress, Washington D.C., Ludwig Mies van der Rohe Papers, MSS32847, Correspondence, Box 2.

99 Catalogue to the Novembergruppe exhibition in 1925, ref. in note 53, pp. 4f.

100 See *inter alia* letter from Arthur Segal to [Max Dungert], 22 November 1925, Landesarchiv Berlin, F Rep. 241, Acc. 841, no. 10.

101 See the essay by Kratz-Kessemeier, p. 35 of this catalogue.

102 See Berlinische Galerie 1995, 2. Abt., 25.17, pp. 212–214.

103 Letter from the Novembergruppe to Ludwig Mies van der Rohe (circular), 2 December 1925, Library of Congress, Washington D.C., Ludwig Mies van der Rohe Papers, MSS32847, Correspondence, Box 2.

104 See the programmes for the 14th and 16th Novembergruppe Evenings, 15 January and 16 March 1926, Akademie der Künste, Berlin, Heinz-Tiessen-Archiv, Tiessen 2175 and Arthur-Schnabel-Archiv, Schnabel 609; and 17th Evening (cat. 163, p. 261). No official programme has yet been located for the 15th Evening, see the summary of concerts in *Zehn Jahre Novembergruppe*, ref. in note 3, p. 38, with wrong numbering.

105 Heinz Pringsheim, "Neue Musik", in: *Berliner Volkszeitung*, 19 March 1926, no. 132.

106 "18. Konzert der Novembergruppe", in: *Berliner Börsen-Zeitung*, 19 November 1926, no. 539; *Zehn Jahre Novembergruppe*, ref. in note 3, p. 39, here wrongly numbered as the 17th Evening.

107 *Zehn Jahre Novembergruppe*, ref. in note 3, p. 35.

108 See Berlinische Galerie 1995, 2. Abt., 26.6 and 26.7, pp. 254–258.

109 See the essay by Nentwig, p. 146 of this catalogue.

110 See *inter alia* "Ball an Bord", in: *Vossische Zeitung*, 22 June 1926, no. 290.

111 See *inter alia* letter from Hugo Graetz to the members of the Novembergruppe, 28. September 1926, Libary of Congress, Washington D.C., Ludwig Mies van der Rohe Papers, MSS32847, Correspondence, Box 2.

112 See the essay by Nentwig, p. 146 of this catalogue.

113 Letter from Alfred Gellhorn, Oswald Herzog and Moriz Melzer (Novembergruppe committee) to members, 22 October 1926, Library of Congress, Washington D.C., Ludwig Mies van der Rohe Papers, MSS32847, Correspondence, Box 2.

114 See the articles of association of the *Hilfsverein für junge Kunst*, 27 October 1926, Berlinische Galerie, Teilnachlass Otto Möller, BG-OM 300.

115 The catalogue names the former foreign minister Adolf Köster, Reich Guardian of the Arts Edwin Redlob and Nationalgalerie director Ludwig Justi as members of the honorary committee of the *Hilfsverein für junge Kunst*. A membership fee of 20 Reichmarks entitles subscribers to free admission to events by both the *Hilfsverein* and the Novembergruppe. See *Das Problem der Bildnisgestaltung in der jungen Kunst* (exhib. cat. Galerie Neumann und Nierendorf, Berlin, [June–July 1927]), Berlin 1927 (= Veröffentlichungen des Kunstarchivs no. 43), p. 2.

116 See invitation from Hugo Graetz to members of the Novembergruppe to the General Meeting on 15 November 1926, undated, Library of Congress, Washington D.C., Ludwig Mies van der Rohe Papers, MSS32847, Correspondence, Box 2. There is no known record, however, of a resolution on these amendments or of new articles of association.

117 u., "Ball der Novembergruppe", in: *Berliner Tageblatt*, 8 December 1926, no. 578. Reproduction of the invitation in Kliemann 1969, p. 34 and Schulz 1993, p. 13.

118 For details see the essay by Nentwig, pp. 194–207 of this catalogue.

119 www.dra.de/rundfunkgeschichte/radiogeschichte/organisation/pdf/FST_1924-1933.pdf (last accessed on 22 August 2018).

120 Letter from Max Dungert and other members of the Novembergruppe, 22 April 1927, Akademie der Künste, Berlin, George-Grosz-Archiv, Grosz 409. See also the contribution by Von Rüden, p. 210 of this catalogue.

121 The widespread assumption that the Malevich exhibition was initiated by the Novembergruppe can be attributed to Helga Kliemann (1969, p. 24). She bases her account on the memories of Ludwig Hilberseimer, an architect who belonged first to the Novembergruppe, then to Der Ring. However, the Novembergruppe does not mention the Malevich show in the overview of exhibitions compiled in 1928 (see *Zehn Jahre Novembergruppe*, ref. in note 3, p. 35) and reviews at the time made no connection between the Suprematist and the association. Letters Malevich sent from Berlin also make no reference to such a link (see Vakar and Mikhienko 2015, vol. 1, pp. 196–205, letters 155a to 158). If Hilberseimer erroneously attributed the organization of the Malevich exhibition to the Novembergruppe, this was no doubt because the association had done so much important work in the first half of the 1920s to present the Russian avant-garde.

122 Letters sent from Berlin by Malevich in 1927 (as in Vakaar and Mikhienko 2015, ref. in note 121) suggest that the artist arrived in the German capital without a specific invitation and originally intended to organize an exhibition at his own expense. He probably met the former Novembergruppe member Hugo Häring through El Lissitzky. As the representative of Der Ring, Häring was now also treasurer to the Great Berlin Art Exhibition, and it was he who kept the works that remained in Berlin after the exhibition safe during the Second World War. See Boersma 1997, pp. 300–308; Schirren and Claus 2001, p. 61.

123 See the essay by Kratz-Kessemeier, pp. 35f. of this catalogue.

124 "Die Novembergruppe", in: *Vossische Zeitung*, 17 June 1927, no. 283.

125 See f. a., "Kostümfest der Novembergruppe", in: *Vossische Zeitung*, 5 December 1927, no. 574; le, "Ball der Novembergruppe", in: *Berliner Börsen-Zeitung*, 6 December 1927, no. 569.

126 See the essay by Nentwig, p. 132 of this catalogue.

127 See Bruppacher 2014, p. 195.

128 See the essay by Nentwig, pp. 194–207 of this catalogue.

129 Will Grohmann, "Zehn Jahre Novembergruppe", in: ref. in note 3, p. 3.

130 See *inter alia* letter from Fred Antoine Angermayer to Hans Siebert von Heister, 11 November 1928, private collection; "Wochenprogramm des Berliner Rundfunks", in: *Berliner Tageblatt*, 23 November 1928, no. 554.

131 tr., "Kunsttopp", in: *Vossische Zeitung*, 8 December 1928, no. 580. On Porza see the essay by Nentwig, p. 202 of this catalogue, esp. note 59, p. 206.

132 "Bälle, Bälle, Bälle", in: *Berliner Tageblatt*, 3 December 1928, no. 571

133 a. p., "Silversterfeier der Novembergruppe", in: *Vossische Zeitung*, 2 January 1929, no. 3.

134 See "Nachtvorstellung der Novembergruppe im Gloria Palast Kurfürstendamm. Sonnabend, den 16. Februar 1929", Programmzettel, Cologne, Deutsches Tanzarchiv, Nachlass Hertha Feist.

135 L. [Wilhelm Lotz], "Modernes aus Amerika", in: *Die Form*, vol. 4, 1929, no. 5, pp. 127f., here 128.

136 See Kratz-Kessemeier 2008, p. 537.

137 See the essay by Nentwig, pp. 198–202 of this catalogue.

138 On the purchases see the essay by Kratz-Kessemeier, pp. 35f. of this catalogue.

139 See the report f. a., "Kostümfest der Novembergruppe", in: *Vossische Zeitung*, 10 December 1929, no. 581. No date is given. The previous Saturday was 7 December 1929.

140 The concert was broadcast by Deutschlandsender Königs Wusterhausen, see *Die Funkstunde*, vol. 7, no. 3, p. 74.

141 Sthg., "Zehn Jahre Novembergruppe", in: *Berliner Börsen-Zeitung*, 28 January 1930, no. 45.

142 See Werner J. Schweiger, "Kunststube G. m. b. H." [entry for the proposed publication *Lexikon des Kunsthandels der Moderne im deutschsprachigen Raum 1905–1937*], Berlinische Galerie, Kunstarchiv Schweiger, BG-WJS-M-1,39.

143 See *inter alia* g. [Curt Glaser], "Wilhelm Schmid", in: *Berliner Börsen-Courier*, 28 May 1930, no. 245.

144 See *inter alia* R. M., "Neue Kunst in Berlin", in: *Kölnische Volkszeitung und Handelsblatt*, 20 October 1930, newspaper cutting, Nachlass César Klein.

145 See *inter alia* Max Osborn, "César Klein. Ausstellung in der 'Kunststube'", in: *Vossische Zeitung*, 28 October 1930, as well as the numerous press cuttings on this exhibition in Nachlass César Klein.

146 See also the essay by Grosch, p. 189 of this catalogue.

147 Ro., "Kostümfest der Novembergruppe", in: *Berliner Volkszeitung*, 11 December 1930, no. 583.

148 "Silvesterkostümball der Novembergruppe im Logenhaus, Kleiststraße 10", invitation, Zentralarchiv, Staatliche Museen zu Berlin, IV/Nachlass Behrens-Hangeler, 246.

149 B-y, "Berliner Bälle", in: *Neues Wiener Tagblatt*, 13 February 1931, no. 44.

150 See the invitation to the exhibition at, for example, Staatliche Museen zu Berlin, Zentralarchiv, IV/ Nachlass Herbert Behrens-Hangeler, 145.

151 See *inter alia* Curt Glaser, "Wochenschau der Kunst", in: *Berliner Börsen-Courier*, 11 February 1931, no. 69; Max Deri, "Eine Kunstwanderung", in: *BZ am Mittag*, 13 February 1931, no. 37.

152 See *inter alia* g. [Curt Glaser], "Ausstellungen", in: *Kunst und Künstler*, vol. 29, 1931, pp. 297f., here 297.

153 See *Grosse Berliner Kunstausstellung 1931 im Schloß Bellevue. Amtlicher Katalog der I. Abteilung. Gemälde und Plastik. Veranstalter Kartell der Vereinigten Verbände Bildender Künstler Berlins e. V.* (exhib. cat., 3 May – 16 August 1931), Berlin 1931, p. 2.

154 See Curt Glaser, "Zum 2. Mal 'Große Berliner'", in: *Berliner Börsen-Courier*, 9 September 1931, no. 419. To date no catalogue has been located for this exhibition.

155 "Kunst der Gegenwart. Die Novembergruppe im Künstlerverein", unmarked newspaper cutting [1931], Nachlass César Klein.

156 See *inter alia* "Zeitlupe", in: *Kunstblatt*, vol. 16, 1932, pp. 71f. As for the second section of the *Grosse Berliner Kunstausstellung* in 1931 no catalogue has been traced, and so there is no evidence that the Novembergruppe took part.

157 On the court case, which attracted major publicity, see *inter alia* Paul Westheim, "Expertisenglaube. Die Lehre aus dem Wacker-Prozess", in: *Kunstblatt*, vol. 16, 1932, pp. 34–38.

158 Letter from Oskar Schlemmer to Willi Baumeister, 17 November 1932, Kunstarchive der Staatsgalerie Stuttgart, Archiv Oskar Schlemmer, AOS 2015/1688.

159 See Kliemann 1969, p. 48 and note 79.

160 See also Schulz 1993, p. 21. It is uncertain, due to gaps in the records, whether the Novembergruppe itself applied to be dissolved or was disbanded involuntarily.

161 For more detail see the essay by Nentwig, pp. 201–204 of this catalogue.

162 See Bartholomeyczik 2005, pp. 12f.

163 Parteistatistische Erhebung 1939, Fragebogen Moriz Melzer, Bundesarchiv, Berlin, BArch R 9361-IX KARTEI 28250390, here the date of the artist's admission to the NSDAP is given as 1 May 1933.

164 See Leistner 2007, pp. 25f. According to his employment record Melzer was able to teach until 1943 at the former Reimann-Schule, where the director from 1935, following the emigration of its Jewish founder Albert Reimann, was the former Novembergruppe member Hugo Häring.

165 See Matelowski 2017b, pp. 28–30; Matelowski. 2007, pp. 65–69.

166 On this plan see the letter from Rudolf Ausleger to the Kunstamt Berlin-Charlottenburg, 12 May 1950, Landesarchiv, Berlin, Rep. 207, Acc. 207, no. 650, 9 and the correspondence in the Hannah-Höch-Archiv, Berlinische Galerie 2001, vol. III, 2. Abt., 50.16, 50.16.1, 50.22, 50.28, 50.50, 51.3, 51.9, 52.24, pp. 39f., 44, 48.

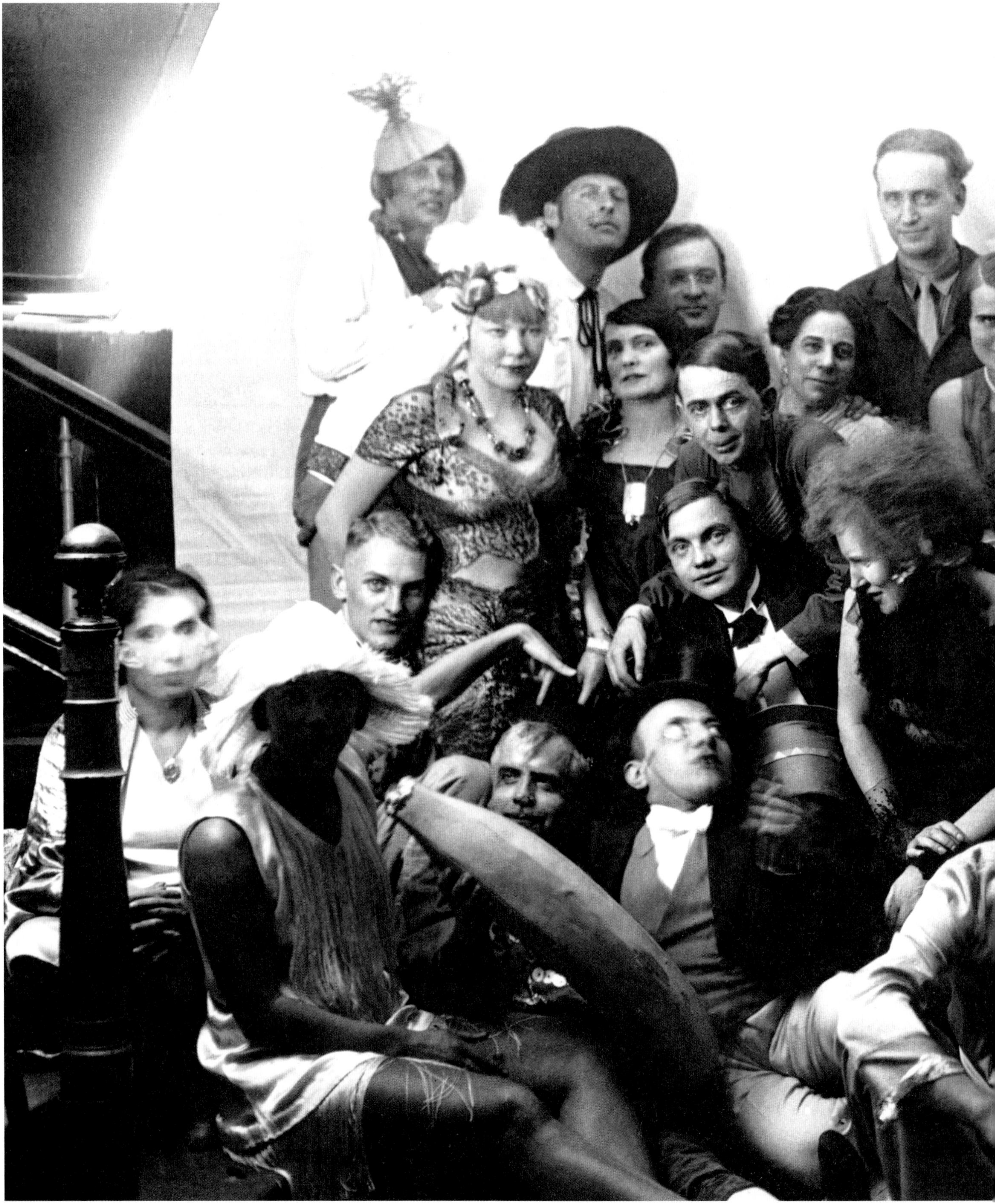

NG
WORKS AND DOCUMENTS

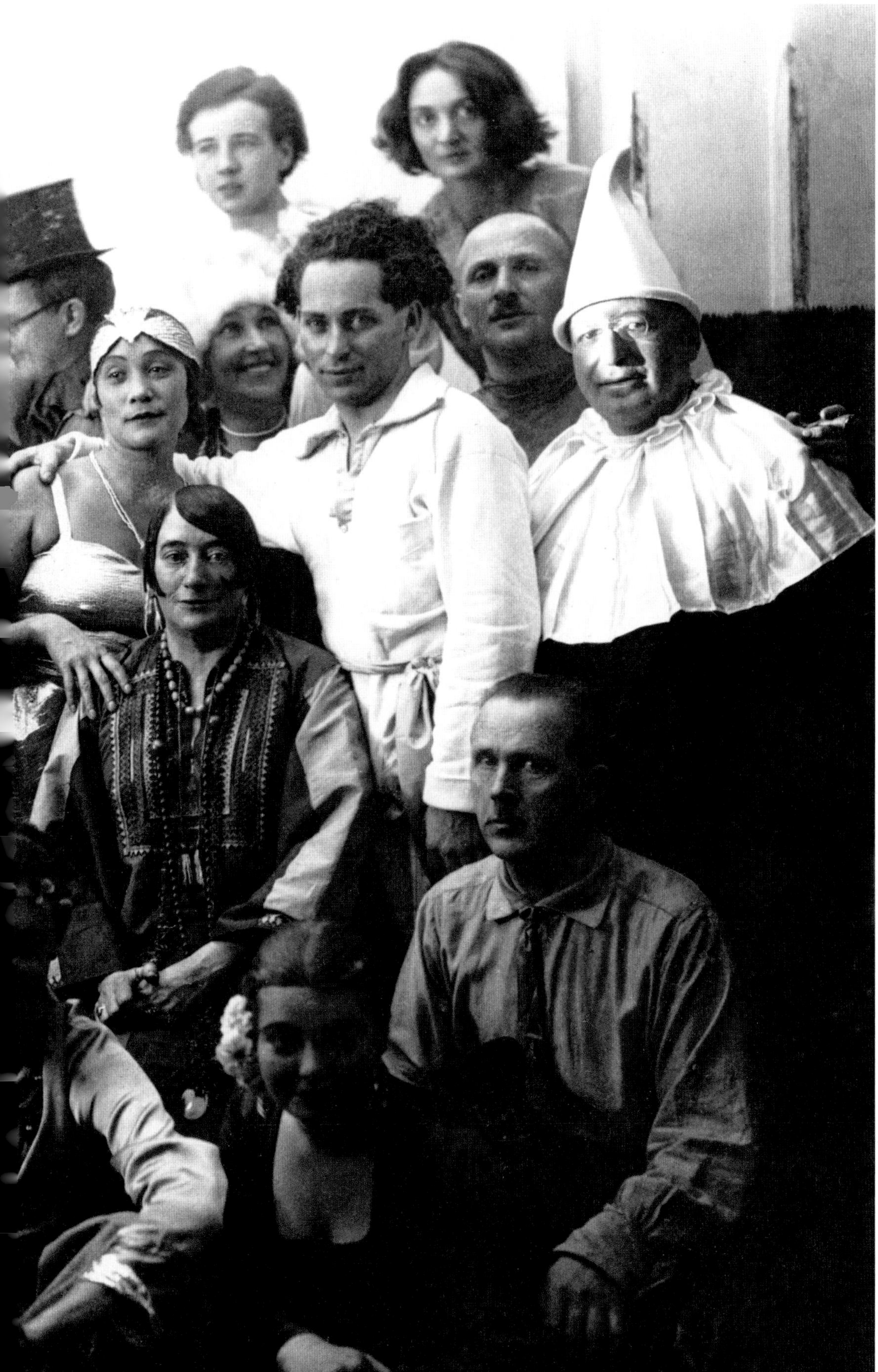

The Novembergruppe's Fancy-Dress Ball, 1 December 1928
Khalil and Misha Norland
(private collection)

JANINA NENTWIG

MEMBERSHIP PROCEDURES IN THE NOVEMBER-GRUPPE

As far as can be deduced from printed catalogues, more than 480 artists exhibited with the Novembergruppe between 1919 and 1932. An overview of all exhibition entries so far identified is being made available on the Berlinische Galerie website (www.berlinischegalerie.de/en/collection/artists-archives/) and will be updated as new findings emerge. Taking part in an exhibition was not the same thing, however, as belonging to the association. From the outset, it was the Novembergruppe's explicit policy to include numerous guests in its shows. Official membership was not required in order to participate, as exhibitions were invitation-based. Although members of the Novembergruppe seem to have enjoyed certain privileges when the hanging committee came to place their works,[1] neither the catalogues nor the exhibition guides distinguished between members and non-members. The external impact of the Novembergruppe consequently always depended on the totality of participating artists.

Nevertheless, this raises a question about which artists were indeed regular members of the association, especially as the composition of the group fluctuated considerably.[2] Apart from isolated correspondence about individual affiliations, three membership lists have survived, dating from the years 1918–19, 1925 and 1930. These sources are particularly valuable as they enable us to make robust statements for those years at least. They have therefore been reprinted in full on the following pages.

How did people join the Novembergruppe? Especially in the initial years, membership procedures ranged from casual to chaotic. The first members were recruited by personal invitation issued by the "central working committee".[3] Sometimes, however, the people invited were listed as members even though the Novembergruppe had never received a concrete answer.[4] Collective admissions were also allowed. In 1919 members of the so-called local branches thus automatically became members of the association, and Rudolf Bauer enlisted a whole troupe of artists from Der Sturm without telling them first.[5] In some cases, members were declared to have left without their knowledge and even against their will.[6]

In its articles of association the Novembergruppe did, however, attempt to impose some order on its membership procedures: the seven-strong working committee elected at each annual general meeting decided by a two-thirds majority whether to admit new members. These individuals could either be proposed by others or apply themselves.[7] The final decision on admission required the approval of the general meeting.[8]

The only figures about the costs of membership date from the early years: in 1920 the fee increased from 20 to 22 Marks.[9] According to the statistical yearbook for the German Reich, a tonne of coal briquettes cost 134.49 Marks at the time.[10]

1 See *inter alia* letter from Arthur Segal to Hannah Höch, 30 October 1931, in: Berlinische Galerie 1995, 2. Abt., 31.18, pp. 415f.

2 See also Kliemann 1969, p. 12.

3 See *inter alia* the circular of 13 December 1918, in: *Zehn Jahre Novembergruppe*, special issue of *Kunst der Zeit. Zeitschrift für Kunst und Literatur*, vol. 3, 1928, nos. 1–3, p. 12.

4 See *inter alia* letter from Conrad Felixmüller to the Novembergruppe, 16 August 1920, private collection; letter from Martin Kessel to Helga Kliemann 14 May 1968, in: Kliemann 1969, pp. 74f., here 75.

5 Letter from Heinrich Campendonk to Walter Dexel, 16 December 1918, Museum Penzberg, Sammlung Campendonk, Brief 192.

6 See letter from Hannah Höch to Hugo Häring, 19 March 1930, in: Berlinische Galerie 1995, 2. Abt., 30.20, pp. 397f.

7 See cat. 139 – 141, p. 260 (Articles of association of 1919, § 3, Articles of association of 1920, § 6, Articles of association of 1925, § 6); letter from Philipp Jarnach to Hans Siebert von Heister, 19 April 1923, private collection; letter from Arthur Segal to Anneliese Braun-Ratkowski and Nikolaus Braun, 26 January 1926, Leo Baeck Institute, New York, Anneliese Wagner-Ratkowski Collection, AR 6326, Box 1, Folder 2, folios 86-89.

8 See *inter alia* the following letters confirming admission: Hans Siebert von Heister (Novembergruppe, Arbeitsausschuss) to Heinz Tiessen, 5 February 1924, Akademie der Künste, Heinz-Tiessen-Archiv, Tiessen 1449; Hugo Graetz (Novembergruppe) to Herbert Behrens-Hangeler, 4 October 1929, Sächsische Landesbibliothek – Staats- und Universitätsbibliothek, Dresden, Nachlass Herbert Behrens-Hangeler, Mscr. Dresd. App. 2401, 424.

9 See letters to the Novembergruppe from Max Burchartz [1920] and Heinrich Campendonk, 4 October 1920, private collection.

10 http://www.digizeitschriften.de/dms/img/?PID=PPN514401303_1921|log18&physid=phys325#navi, last accessed on 26 July 2018.

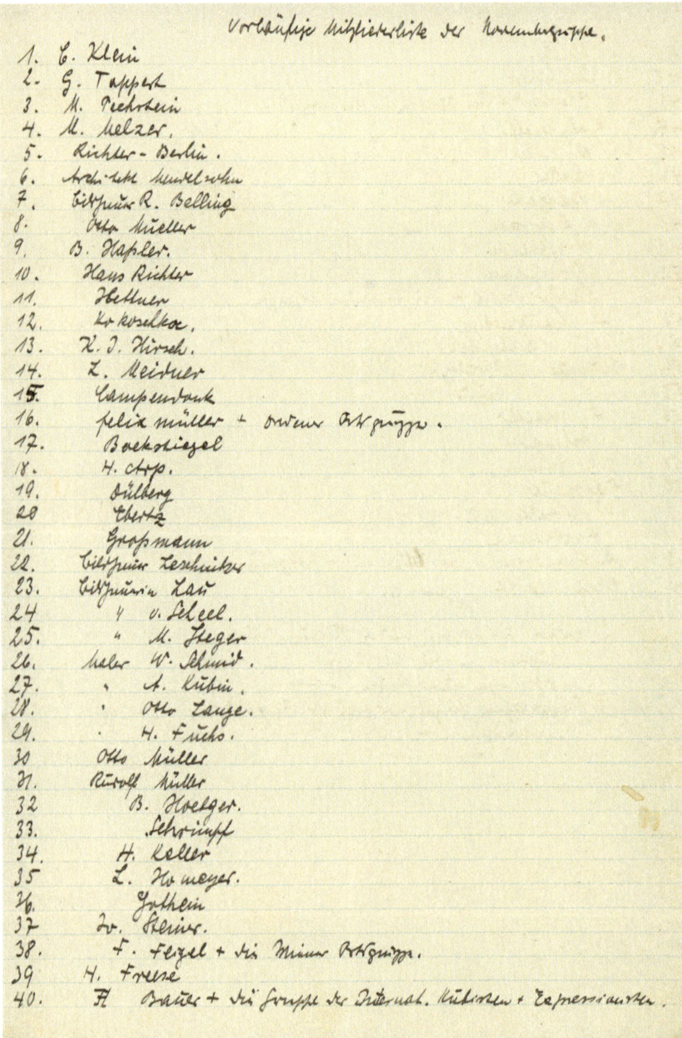

Vorläufige Mitgliederliste der Novembergruppe.

1. C. Klein
2. G. Tappert
3. M. Pechstein
4. M. Melzer.
5. Richter-Berlin.
6. Architekt Mendelsohn
7. Bildhauer R. Belling
8. Otto Müller
9. B. Hasler.
10. Hans Richter
11. [illegible]
12. Kokoschka.
13. K. J. Hirsch.
14. L. Meidner
15. Campendonk
16. Felix Müller + Dresdner Ortsgruppe.
17. Boeckstiegel
18. H. Arp.
19. Dülberg
20. [illegible]
21. Großmann
22. Bildhauer [illegible]
23. Bildhauerin [illegible]
24. " v. Scheel.
25. " M. [illegible]
26. Maler W. Schmidt.
27. " A. Kubin.
28. " Otto Lange.
29. " H. Fuchs.
30. Otto Müller
31. Rudolf Müller
32. B. Hoetger.
33. Schrimpf
34. H. Keller
35. L. [illegible]
36. [illegible]
37. Dr. Steiner.
38. F. [illegible] + die Münchner Ortsgruppe.
39. H. Freese
40. R. Bauer + die Gruppe der Internat. Kubisten + Expressionisten.

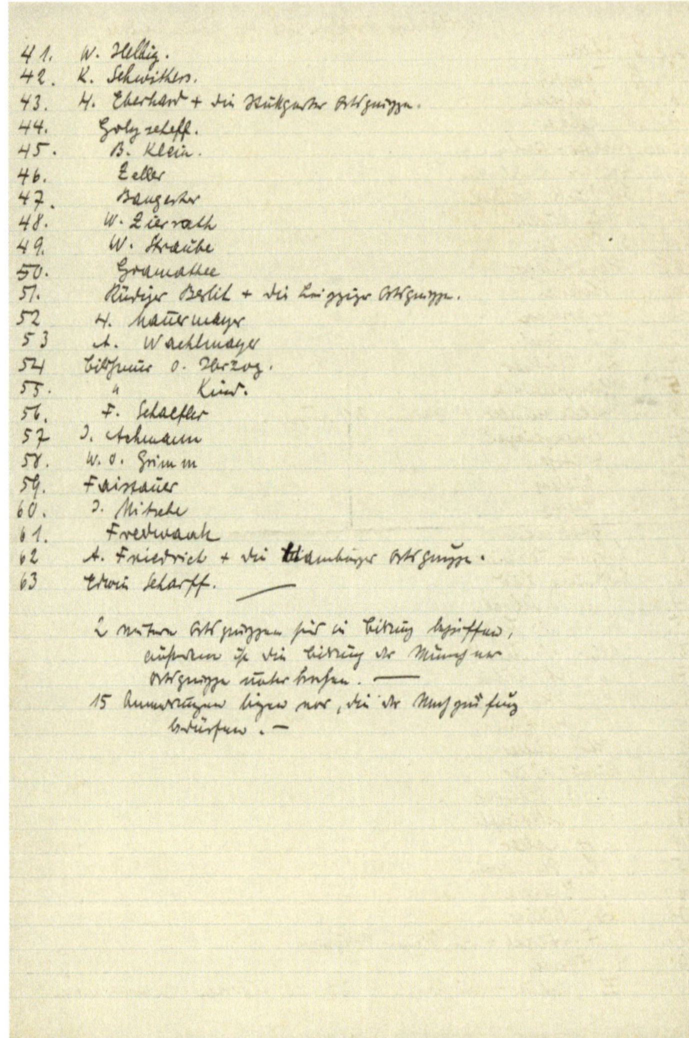

41. W. Helbig.
42. K. Schwitters.
43. H. Eberhard + die Stuttgarter Ortsgruppe.
44. Golyscheff.
45. B. Klein.
46. Eller
47. [illegible]
48. W. [illegible]
49. W. [illegible]
50. [illegible]
51. Rüdiger Berlit + die Leipziger Ortsgruppe.
52. H. [illegible]
53. A. [illegible]
54. Bildhauer O. Herzog.
55. " [illegible]
56. F. Schaefler
57. J. [illegible]
58. W. O. Grimm
59. Faistauer
60. J. [illegible]
61. Freundlich
62. A. Friedrich + die Hamburger Ortsgruppe.
63. Erwin Scharff.

2 weitere Ortsgruppen sind in Bildung begriffen, [illegible] die Bildung der [illegible] Ortsgruppe [illegible].

15 Anmeldungen liegen vor, die der [illegible] bedürfen.

[GEORG TAPPERT]
Provisional list of Novembergruppe members, [1918–1919], Two sheets
Bauhaus-Archiv Berlin

Nr. 3 ARCHIV DER DEUTSCHEN KUNST 13

MITGLIEDERVERZEICHNIS DER NOVEMBERGRUPPE

Fred Antoine Angermayer, Schriftsteller, Charlottenburg, Kaiserdamm 3a.
Hans Arp, Maler, Zürich, Arbenzstr. 10
Rudolf Ausleger, Maler, Friedenau, Wiesbadener Str. 12
Willi Baumeister, Maler, Stuttgart, Gymnasiumstr. 53
Rudolf Belling, Bildhauer, Halensee, Joachim-Friedrichstr. 10
Max Butting, Komponist, Schöneberg, Merseburger Str. 5
Prof. Peter Behrens, Architekt, Neubabelsberg
Kinner v. Dresler, Maler, Hamburg, Hagedornstr. 31
Max Dungert, Maler, Charlottenburg, Hebbelstr. 20
Walter Dexel, Maler, Jena, Fuchsturmweg 15
A. Eberhardt, Maler, Stuttgart, Stafflenbergerstr. 64a
Josef Eberz, Maler, München, Kräuslinstraße 5
Viking Eggeling †, Maler
Ignaz Epper, Maler, Paris
Professor Lyonel Feininger, Maler, Dessau, Bauhaus
Oscar Fischer, Maler, Charlottenbg., Schulstr. 14
Peter Förster, Maler, Lichterfelde, Lortzingstr. 2
Hans Freese, Maler, Südende, Lindenstr. 6
Heinz Fuchs, Maler, Lichterfelde, Moltkestr. 24
Dr. Alfred Gellhorn, Architekt, Schöneberg, Steinacherstr. 2
Paul Goesch, Maler, Berlin
Gottfried Graf, Maler, Stuttgart, Urbanstr. 37
Otto Griebel, Maler, Dresden, Rietschelstr.
Paul Grunwaldt, Maler, Lichterfelde-Ost, Jägerstr. 16a
Prof. Walter Gropius, Architekt, Dessau, Bauhaus
Prof. Gustav Havemann, Musiker, Neubabelsberg, Berliner Str. 145
Willi Heckroth, Maler, Dresden, Pfotenhauerstr. 81
H. S. v. Heister, Maler, Wilmersdorf, Konstanzer Straße 9
Karl Jakob Hirsch, Maler, Worpswede b. Bremen
Leon Hirsch, Schriftsteller, Schöneberg, Bozener Str. 10
Hanna Hoech, Malerin, Friedenau, Büsingstr. 16
Lothar Homeyer, Maler, Halensee, Westfälische Str. 31
Oswald Herzog, Bildhauer, Steglitz, Goebenstr. 16
Hugo Häring, Architekt, Berlin W, Lützowstr. 34
Ludwig Hilberseimer, Architekt, Charlottenburg 9, Wachholderweg 5
Philipp Jarnach, Komponist, Südende, Tempelhofer Str. 12a
Hans Krebs, Architekt, Friedenau, Taunusstr. 31
Wassili Kandinsky, Maler, Dessau, Bauhaus
Dr. Martin Kessel, Schriftsteller, Wilmersdorf, Landauer Str. 16
Walter Kampmann, Maler, Berlin SW, Wartenburgstr. 21

14 ARCHIV DER DEUTSCHEN KUNST Nr. 3

Bernhard Klein, Maler, Wilmersdorf, Saalfeld-Str. 13
Prof. Cesar Klein, Maler, Wilmersdorf, Landauer Str. 1
Fritz Klein, Maler, Stuttgart, Herdweg 44
Arthur Korn, Architekt, Berlin W15, Uhlandstr. 175
H. Kosina, Architekt, Berlin W 30, Neue Winterfeldtstr. 27
Otto Lange, Maler, Dresden, Gerockstraße 47
Hans Luckhardt, Architekt, Charlottenburg, Branitzerplatz
Wassili Luckhardt, Architekt, Charlottenburg, Branitzerplatz
M. H. Maxy, Maler, Bukarest, Passage
Ewald Mataré, Maler, Charlottenburg, Berliner Str. 153
Moriz Melzer, Maler, Schöneberg, Innsbrucker Str. 4
Carlo Mense, Maler, Bonn a. Rh., Coblenzer Str. 88
Otto Möller, Maler, Steglitz, Mittelstraße 1
Rudolf Möller, Maler, Steglitz, Schloßstr. 83
Albert Müller, Maler, Stuttgart, Kernerplatz 5
Mies van der Rohe, Architekt, Berlin W, Am Karlsbad 24
J. J. P. Oud, Architekt, Rotterdam, Schiedamscherweg 110a
Felix Petyrek, Komponist, Charlbg., Hardenbergstraße
Prof. Hans Poelzig, Architekt, Potsdam, Neues Palais
Enrico Prampolini, Maler, Rom, via calometta 4
Carl Puxkandl, Maler, Gmunden, O.-Oesterr., Keimstr. 3
Prof. Walter Reger, Bildhauer, Charlottenburg, Hardenbergstr. 33
Hans Richter, Maler, Friedenau, Eschenstr. 7
Heinrich Richter, Maler, Friedenau, Wiesbadener Str. 1
K. H. Rosenberg, Maler, Wilmersdorf, Barstr. 30
Frau Dr. Rosenberg, Malerin, Magdeburg, Himmelreichstr. 22
Walter Ruttmann, Maler, Friedenau, Wagnerplatz 2
Oscar Schlemmer, Maler, Dessau, Bauhaus
Wilhelm Schmid, Maler, Paris, 36 avenue de Chatillon
Paul Schmolling, Maler, Insterburg, Augustastr. 5
Georg Schrimpf, Maler, München, Barerstraße
Arthur Segal, Maler, Charlottenburg, Dernburgstr. 25
Lasar Segall, Adresse unbek.
Hans Spiegel, Maler, Stuttgart, Akademie
Heinrich Stegemann, Maler, Hamburg, Mundsburgerdamm 31
Mark Stam, Architekt, Basel
Gertrud Stemmler, Malerin, Stuttgart, Herdweg 60
Franz Stock, Maler, Niederschönhausen, Bismarckstr. 27
Prof. Hans Soeder, Acd. Dir., Cassel, Akademie
Stadtbaurat Bruno Taut, Architekt, Berlin W 9, Linkstr. 20
Max Taut, Architekt, Berlin W 9, Linkstr. 20
Prof. Georg Tappert, Maler, Steglitz, Birkbuschstr. 64
Dr. Trautner, Schriftsteller, Berlin W 15, Fasanenstr. 13
Heinz Tiessen, Komponist, Friedenau, Wilhelmshöher Str. 17
Prof. Dr. Heinrich Tessenow, Archit., Dresden, Techn. Hochschule
K. Völker, Maler, Halle, Belforthstr. 9
Kurt Weil, Komponist, Berlin, Winterfeldtstr. 21
Dr. Rudolf Utzinger, Kunstschriftsteller, Stuttgart, Tulpenstr. 5.

Index of Novembergruppe members, 1925
Two pages in the catalogue for the Novembergruppe exhibition at the Berlin Secession, 1925

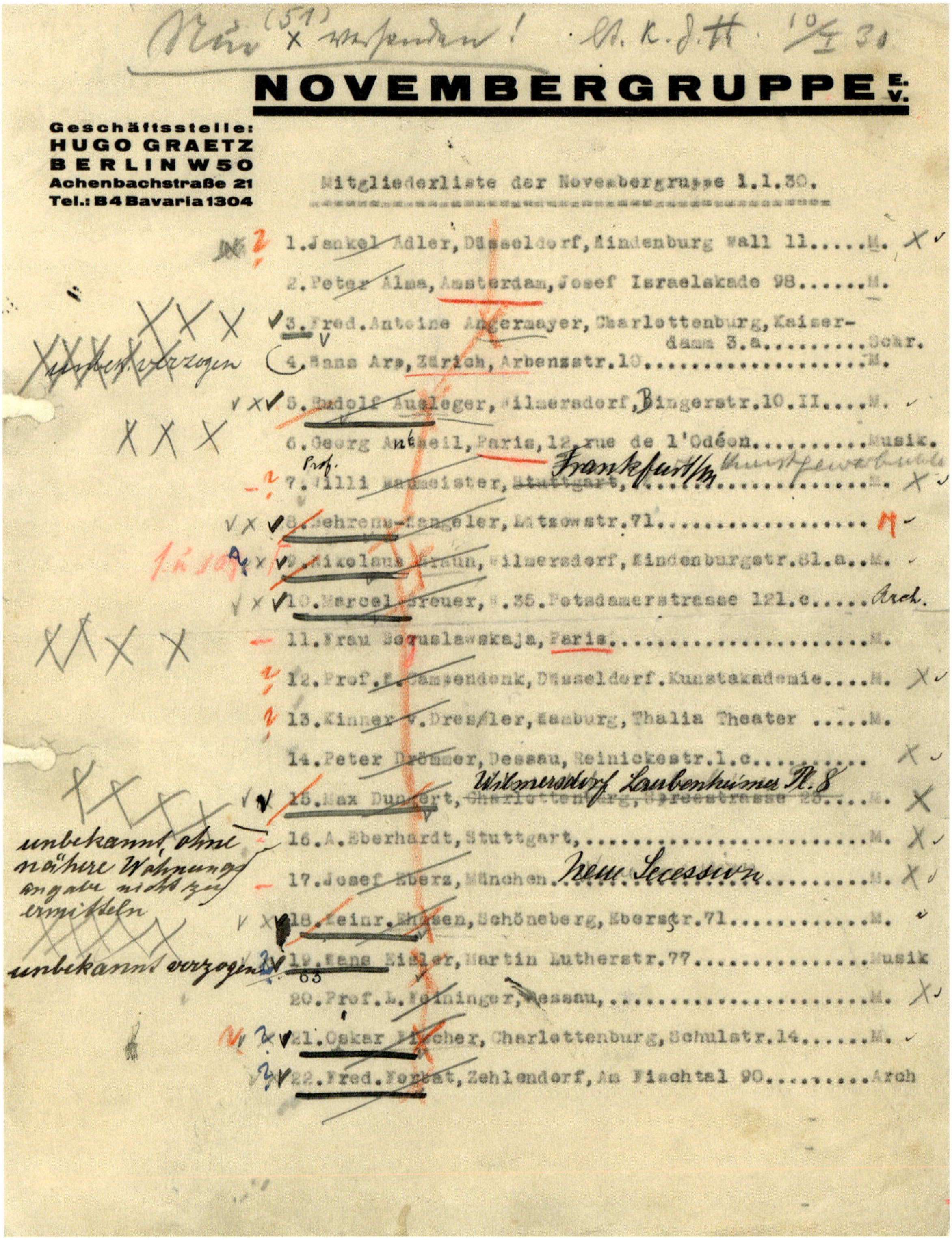

NOVEMBERGRUPPE E.V.

Geschäftsstelle:
HUGO GRAETZ
BERLIN W50
Achenbachstraße 21
Tel.: B4 Bavaria 1304

Mitgliederliste der Novembergruppe 1.1.30.

1. Jankel Adler, Düsseldorf, Hindenburg Wall 11.....M.
2. Peter Alma, Amsterdam, Josef Israelskade 98......M.
3. Fred. Antoine Angermayer, Charlottenburg, Kaiserdamm 3.a.........Schr.
4. Hans Arp, Zürich, Arbenzstr.10...................M.
5. Rudolf Ausleger, Wilmersdorf, Bingerstr.10.II....M.
6. Georg Antheil, Paris, 12 rue de l'Odéon.........Musik.
7. Willi Baumeister, Stuttgart,...................M.
8. Behrens-Hangeler, Lützowstr.71..................
9. Nikolaus Braun, Wilmersdorf, Hindenburgstr.81.a..M.
10. Marcel Breuer, W.35. Potsdamerstrasse 121.c.....Arch.
11. Frau Boguslawskaja, Paris.......................M.
12. Prof. H. Campendonk, Düsseldorf. Kunstakademie....M.
13. Kinner v. Dressler, Hamburg, Thalia Theater .....M.
14. Peter Drömmer, Dessau, Heinickestr.1.c..........
15. Max Dungert, Charlottenburg, Spreestrasse 26....M.
16. A. Eberhardt, Stuttgart,........................M.
17. Josef Eberz, München............................M.
18. Heinr. Ehmsen, Schöneberg, Eberstr.71............M.
19. Hans Eisler, Martin Lutherstr.77...............Musik
20. Prof. L. Feininger, Dessau,......................M.
21. Oskar Fischer, Charlottenburg, Schulstr.14......M.
22. Fred. Forbat, Zehlendorf, Am Fischtal 90.........Arch

[HUGO GRAETZ]
List of Novembergruppe members,
1 January 1930, Five sheets
Akademie der Künste, Berlin

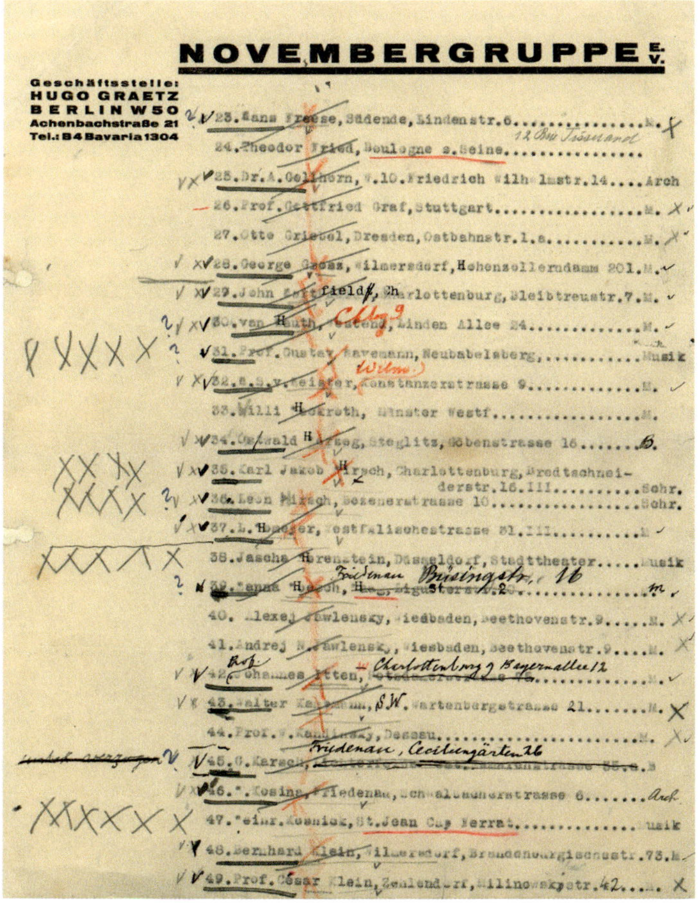

NOVEMBERGRUPPE E.V.

Geschäftsstelle:
HUGO GRAETZ
BERLIN W50
Achenbachstraße 21
Tel.: B4 Bavaria 1304

23. Hans Freese, Südende, Lindenstr.6 .... M.
24. Theodor Fried, Boulogne s. Seine ....
25. Dr. A. Gellhorn, W.10. Friedrich Wilhelmstr.14 .... Arch
26. Prof. Gottfried Graf, Stuttgart .... M.
27. Otto Griebel, Dresden, Ostbahnstr.1.a .... M.
28. George Grosz, Wilmersdorf, Hohenzollerndamm 201. M.
29. John Heartfield, Charlottenburg, Bleibtreustr.7. M.
30. van Heemskerck, Westend, Linden Allee 24 .... M.
31. Prof. Gustav Havemann, Neubabelsberg, ... Musik
32. H. H. v. Meister, Konstanzerstrasse 9 .... M.
33. Willi Heckroth, Münster Westf .... M.
34. Oswald Herzog, Steglitz, Göbenstrasse 16 .... B.
35. Karl Jakob Hirsch, Charlottenburg, Bredtschneiderstr.16.III .... Schr.
36. Leon Hirsch, Bozenerstrasse 10 .... Schr.
37. L. Hoeniger, Westfälischestrasse 51.III .... M.
38. Jascha Horenstein, Düsseldorf, Stadttheater ..... Musik
39. Hanna Höch, Büsingstr. 16 .... M.
40. Alexej Jawlensky, Wiesbaden, Beethovenstr.9 ..... M.
41. Andrej N. Jawlensky, Wiesbaden, Beethovenstr.9 .... M.
42. Johannes Itten, Charlottenburg 9 Bayernallee 12 .... M.
43. Walter Kampmann, SW. Wartenbergstrasse 21 .... M.
44. Prof. W. Kandinsky, Dessau .... M.
45. G. Karsch, Friedenau, Ceciliengärten 26 .... B
46. F. Kosina, Friedenau, Schwalbacherstrasse 6 .... Arch.
47. Heinr. Kosnick, St. Jean Cap Ferrat .... Musik
48. Bernhard Klein, Wilmersdorf, Brandenburgischestr.73. M.
49. Prof. César Klein, Zehlendorf, Milinowskistr.42 .... M.

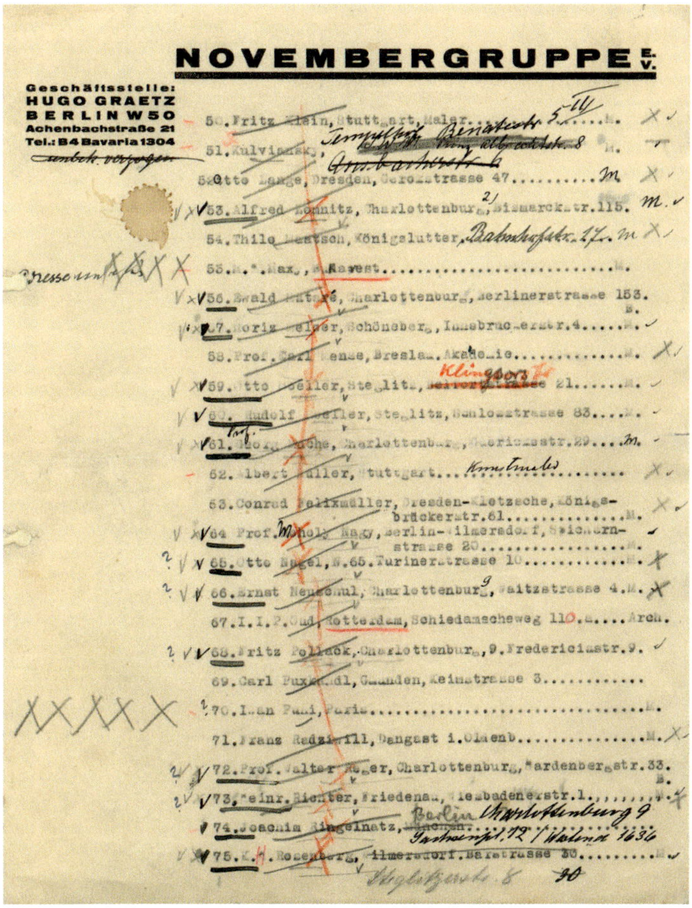

NOVEMBERGRUPPE E.V.

Geschäftsstelle:
HUGO GRAETZ
BERLIN W50
Achenbachstraße 21
Tel.: B4 Bavaria 1304

50. Fritz Klein, Stuttgart, Maler .... M.
51. Kulvianski, ... M.
52. Otto Lange, Dresden, Grossestrasse 47 .... M.
53. Alfred Lörnitz, Charlottenburg, Bismarckstr.115. M.
54. Thilo Maatsch, Königslutter, Bahnhofstr. 17 .. M.
55. M. T. Max, Kasvest .... M.
56. Ewald Mataré, Charlottenburg, Berlinerstrasse 153. B.
57. Moriz Melzer, Schöneberg, Innsbruckerstr.4 ..... M.
58. Prof. Carl Mense, Breslau, Akademie .... M.
59. Otto Möller, Steglitz, Klingsorstr. 21 .... M.
60. Rudolf Möller, Steglitz, Schlossstrasse 83 .... M.
61. Prof. Georg Muche, Charlottenburg, Friedrichstr.29 .... M.
62. Albert Müller, Stuttgart ....
63. Conrad Felixmüller, Dresden-Klotzsche, Königsbrückerstr.61 .... M.
64. Prof. Moholy Nagy, Berlin-Wilmersdorf, Spichernstrasse 20 .... M.
65. Otto Nagel, N.65. Turinerstrasse 10 .... M.
66. Ernst Neuschul, Charlottenburg 9, Waitzstrasse 4. M.
67. I. I. P. Oud, Rotterdam, Schiedamscheweg 110 ..... Arch.
68. Fritz Pollack, Charlottenburg, 9. Fredericiastr.9.
69. Carl Puxbaudl, Gmunden, Keimstrasse 3 ....
70. Ivan Puni, Paris .... M.
71. Franz Radziwill, Dangast i. Oldenb .... M.
72. Prof. Walter Reger, Charlottenburg, Hardenbergstr.33. B.
73. Heinr. Richter, Friedenau, Wiesbadenerstr.1 .... M.
74. Joachim Ringelnatz, Berlin Charlottenburg 9 Sachsenpl. 12 / Walind 1636
75. K. H. Rosenberg, Wilmersdorf. Barstrasse 30 .... M.

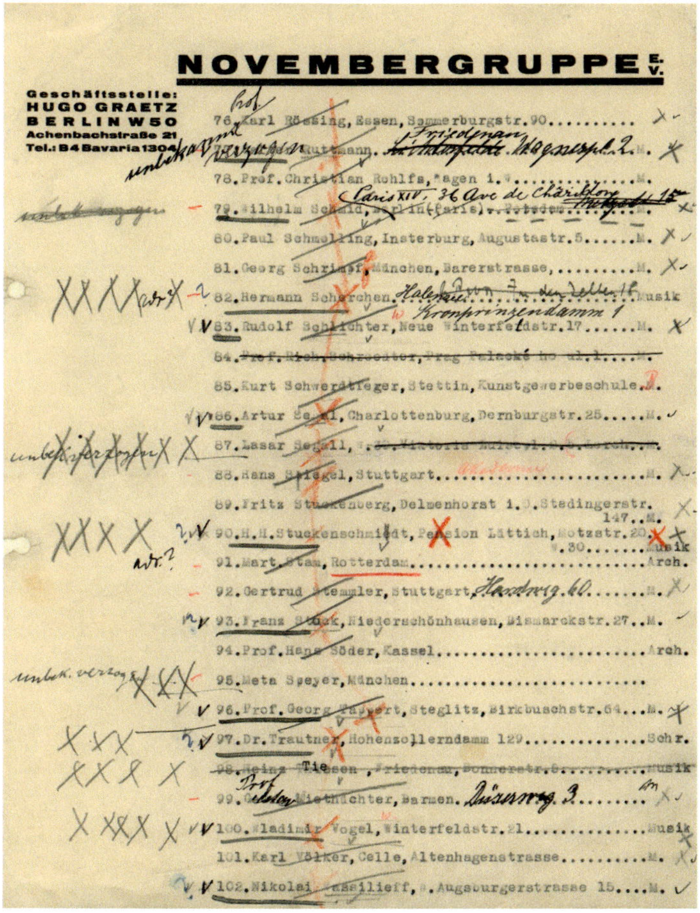

NOVEMBERGRUPPE E.V.

Geschäftsstelle:
HUGO GRAETZ
BERLIN W50
Achenbachstraße 21
Tel.: B4 Bavaria 1304

76. Karl Rössing, Essen, Sommerburgstr.90 ....
77. Ruttmann, Friedenau Wagnerpl. 2 .... M.
78. Prof. Christian Rohlfs, Hagen i. W .... M.
79. Wilhelm Schmid, Berlin (Paris) Paris XIV, 36 Ave de Châtillon ...... M.
80. Paul Schmelling, Insterburg, Augustastr.5 ...... M.
81. Georg Schrimpf, München, Barerstrasse, ... M.
82. Hermann Scherchen, ... Musik
83. Rudolf Schlichter, Neue Winterfeldstr.17 .... M.
84. Prof. Rich. Schroeder, Prag .... M.
85. Kurt Schwerdtfeger, Stettin, Kunstgewerbeschule. B.
86. Artur Segal, Charlottenburg, Dernburgstr.25 ..... M.
87. Lasar Segall, ... M.
88. Hans Spiegel, Stuttgart .... M.
89. Fritz Stuckenberg, Delmenhorst i. O. Stedingerstr. 147 .. M.
90. H. H. Stuckenschmidt, Pension Lüttich, Motzstr.20. W.30 ...... Musik
91. Mart. Stam, Rotterdam .... Arch.
92. Gertrud Stemmler, Stuttgart, Hardweg 60 .... M.
93. Franz Stuck, Niederschönhausen, Bismarckstr.27 .. M.
94. Prof. Hans Söder, Kassel .... Arch.
95. Meta Speyer, München ....
96. Prof. Georg Tappert, Steglitz, Birkbuschstr.64 ... M.
97. Dr. Trautner, Hohenzollerndamm 129 .... Schr.
98. Heinz Tiessen, Friedenau, Sonnerstr.6 .... Musik
99. Prof. Gustav Wietschichter, Barmen. Düsserweg 3 .... M.
100. Wladimir Vogel, Winterfeldstr.21 .... Musik
101. Karl Völker, Celle, Altenhagenstrasse .... M.
102. Nikolai Wassilieff, W. Augsburgerstrasse 15 .... M.

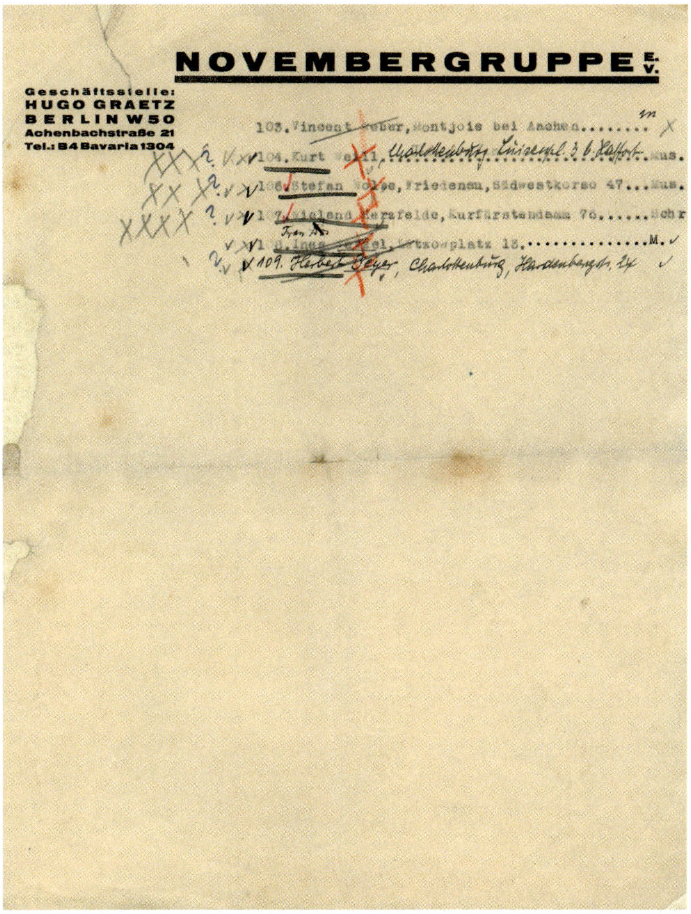

NOVEMBERGRUPPE E.V.

Geschäftsstelle:
HUGO GRAETZ
BERLIN W50
Achenbachstraße 21
Tel.: B4 Bavaria 1304

103. Vincent Weber, Montjoie bei Aachen .... M
104. Kurt Weill, Charlottenburg Luisenpl. 3 b. Hafort .... Mus.
106. Stefan Wolpe, Friedenau, Südwestkorso 47 ... Mus.
107. Wieland Herzfelde, Kurfürstendamm 76 ...... Schr
108. Frau Dr. Ines Wetzel, Lützowplatz 13 .... M.
109. Herbert Beyer, Charlottenburg, Hardenbergstr. 24

Works on Display

A

RUDOLF AUSLEGER (1897–1974)
Untitled, 1924
Collage with pencil and printed, embossed wrapping papers on art paper, 39.2 × 28.7 cm
Berlinische Galerie, bequeathed by Manfred Thamke, Berlin 2017
Cat. 59, p. 124

Still Life with Pipe, 1924
Oil on paperboard, 30 × 38 cm
Berlinische Galerie, acquired with funds from the Senator for Cultural Affairs, Berlin 1984
Cat. 60, p. 124

B

OTTO BARTNING (1883–1959)
Star Church (design), 1921–1922, model after 1944
Plaster, wood, 42.5 × 80 × 79 cm
Berlinische Galerie, gift from the Union Evangelischer Kirchen, Berlin 2000
Cat. 98, p. 163

WILLI BAUMEISTER (1889–1955)
Rope Jumper, 1928
Oil on canvas, 111 × 80.5 cm
Staatsgalerie Stuttgart, transferred from the Baden-Württembergisches Kultusministerium, 1971
Cat. 110, p. 213

RUDOLF BELLING (1886–1972)
Eroticism, 1920
Bronze, 32 × 30 × 24 cm
Berlinische Galerie, acquired with funds from Stiftung DKLB, Berlin 1973
Cat. 33, p. 74

Triad, 1924
Stained birch wood, 91 × 77 × 77 cm
Staatliche Museen zu Berlin, Nationalgalerie
Cat. 111, p. 215

Petrol station in Halle an der Saale (designed with Alfred Gellhorn and Martin Knauthe), 1923/2017
Reconstruction in 2017 by Fach Modell + Design, Technische Universität Berlin
Plaster, 47.8 × 62 × 62 cm
Staatliche Museen zu Berlin, Nationalgalerie, acquired in 2017 by the Verein der Freunde der Nationalgalerie
Cat. 99, p. 163

Head in Brass (Toni Freeden), 1925
Brass, 38.3 × 22.5 × 19 cm
Staatliche Museen zu Berlin, Nationalgalerie
Cat. 108, p. 212

HENRYK BERLEWI (1894–1967)
Woman Seated, 1922
Gouache on art paper, 48.2 × 31.2 cm
Berlinische Galerie, acquired with funds from Stiftung DKLB, Berlin 1980
Cat. 62, p. 125

D

WALTER DEXEL (1890–1973)
Composition 1923 IV, 1923
Oil on canvas, 48 × 39 cm
Private collection
Cat. 57, p. 122

Composition 1927 I, 1927
Oil on canvas, 89 × 67 cm
Von der Heydt-Museum Wuppertal
Cat. 56, p. 121

OTTO DIX (1891–1969)
Suleika, the Tattooed Wonder (Maud Arizona) [from the "Circus" portfolio], 1922
Drypoint, 30 × 20 cm
Staatliche Museen zu Berlin, Kupferstichkabinett
Cat. 45, p. 99

MAX DUNGERT (1896–1945)
Tower, 1922
Oil on canvas
Berlinische Galerie, acquired with funds from Stiftung DKLB, Berlin 1979
Cat. 23, p. 63

E

HEINRICH EHMSEN (1886–1964)
Hall for the Insane, 1925
Oil on canvas, 127 × 100 cm
Kulturstiftung Sachsen-Anhalt, Kunstmuseum Moritzburg Halle (Saale)
Cat. 105, p. 209

CURT EHRHARDT (1895–1972)
The Coffee Grinder, 1920
Mixed technique, collage, 70 × 93 cm
Berlinische Galerie, acquired with funds from the Senator for Cultural Affairs, Berlin 1985
Restored with the kind support of the Ernst von Siemens Kunststiftung
Cat. 40, p. 92

At 12 Midnight, 1921
Oil on paperboard, 112 × 62.5 cm
Private collection Harald Gnade, Berlin
Cat. 41, p. 93

CONRAD FELIXMÜLLER (1897–1977)
The Agitator, 1946
Oil on canvas, 125 × 93 cm
Staatliche Museen zu Berlin, Nationalgalerie
Cat. 104, p. 208

F

PETER FOERSTER (1887–1948)
Italian Landscape II, 1927
Oil on wood, 50 × 61 cm
Staatliche Museen zu Berlin, Nationalgalerie
Cat. 79, p. 139

OTTO FREUNDLICH (1878–1943)
The Marks, Sheet 1, 1920
Zincograph, brush overworking, 6 prints, each 78 × 62 cm
Lindenau-Museum Altenburg, formerly Sammlung Horn
Cat. 36 and 37, pp. 76 and 77

Composition, 1926
Oil on canvas, 46 × 39 cm
Berlinische Galerie, acquired with funds from Stiftung DKLB, Berlin 1979
Cat. 117, p. 221

ERNST FRITSCH (1892–1965)
Tiergarten Bridge, 1923
Oil on canvas, 74 × 89 cm
Berlinische Galerie, acquired with funds from the Senator for Science and Art, Berlin 1962
Cat. 76, p. 136

HEINZ FUCHS (1886–1961)
Call to work on the land and in mining, 1919
Lithograph, 76 × 84 cm
Stiftung Deutsches Historisches Museum, Berlin
Cat. 07, p. 26

Call to work and not strike, 1919
Lithograph, 73.7 × 103.9 cm
Stiftung Deutsches Historisches Museum, Berlin
Cat. 08, p. 27

Picture XV (Houses on a Hill), 1920–21
Oil on canvas, 68 × 87 cm
Berlinische Galerie, acquired with funds from Stiftung DKLB and from the Senator for Science and Art, Berlin 1976
Restored with the kind support of the Ernst von Siemens Kunststiftung
Cat. 22, p. 62

G

HERBERT GARBE (1888–1945)
Lovers (Sleep), 1919
Limewood, 45 × 90 × 36.5 cm
Sprengel Museum Hannover
Cat. 32, p. 74

PAUL GOESCH (1885–1940)
Untitled, c. 1920
Gouache on the reverse of Bernhard Klein's draft invitation for the "Cubic Box" fancy-dress ball hosted by the Novembergruppe in Berlin, 28.5 × 23.8 cm
Berlinische Galerie, gifted from the artist's estate by the heirs, Berlin 1978
Cat. 120

Madonna, 1922
Gouache and opaque white over pencil on paper, 24.9 × 20.6 cm
Berlinische Galerie, gifted from the artist's estate by the heirs, Berlin 1978
Cat. 114, p. 219

WALTER GROPIUS (1883–1969)
ADOLF MEYER (1881–1929)
Tribune Tower, south-west perspective, competition entry for a Chicago Tribune office building, Chicago, 1922
India ink and wash on thin paper, 135 × 71.5 cm
Bauhaus-Archiv Berlin
Cat. 95, p. 161

GEORGE GROSZ (1893–1959)
Pillars of Society, 1926
Oil on canvas, 200 × 108 cm
Staatliche Museen zu Berlin, Nationalgalerie
Restored with the kind support of the Ernst von Siemens Kunststiftung
Cat. 106, p. 211

PAUL GRUNWALDT (1891–1962)
Varieté, 1925
Oil on canvas, 59 × 46.5 cm
Stiftung Stadtmuseum Berlin
Cat. 68, p. 129

H

HUGO HÄRING (1882–1958)
Gut Garkau, Scharbeutz (Ostholstein), August 1924
Blueprint, 89.4 × 76.8 cm
Akademie der Künste, Berlin, Hugo-Häring-Archiv, 1204 LJ 18/7
Cat. 88, p. 157

Gut Garkau, cattle shed, Scharbeutz (Ostholstein), 1922–1926
Photograph, 25.5 × 27.2 cm
Akademie der Künste, Berlin, Hugo-Häring-Archiv, 49. F1
Cat. 90, p. 158

Gut Garkau, cattle shed, Scharbeutz (Ostholstein), 1922–1926
Photograph, 31.7 × 21.5 cm
Akademie der Künste, Berlin, Hugo-Häring-Archiv, 49. F2
Cat. 91, p. 158

Exhibition pavilion for the Berlin Secession, Savignyplatz, Berlin-Charlottenburg (not realized), November 1925
India ink on tracing paper, 47.3 × 55 cm
Akademie der Künste, Berlin, Hugo-Häring-Archiv, 1216 LJ 25/11
Cat. 89, p. 158

HANS SIEBERT VON HEISTER (1888–1967)
The Peak, 1922
Oil on canvas, 53 × 63 cm
Loan from a private collection
Cat. 14, p. 56

ELSE HERTZER (1884–1978)
Kapp-Putsch, c. 1920
Oil on paperboard, 32 × 39.5 cm
Berlinische Galerie, acquired with funds from the Senator for Cultural Affairs, Berlin 1978
Cat. 02, p. 22

OSWALD HERZOG (1881–C. 1941)
Rapture, 1919
Wood, silver stain, 53 × 42 × 33 cm
Kunsthalle Mannheim
Restored with the kind support of the Ernst von Siemens Kunststiftung
Cat. 34, p. 75

Enjoying, c. 1920
Bronze, 20.5 × 38.5 × 7 cm
Berlinische Galerie, acquired with asset protection funds from the Senator for Cultural Affairs, Berlin 1987
Cat. 30, p. 73

Woman Kneeling, c. 1920
Wood, 48.5 × 49.5 × 15.5 cm
Staatliche Museen zu Berlin, Nationalgalerie
Cat. 35, p. 75

HANNAH HÖCH (1889–1978)
NG (design for the magazine cover), 1921
Colour linocut on Japan paper, 37.4 × 50 cm
Berlinische Galerie, acquired with museum funds from the Senator for Cultural Affairs, Berlin 1979
Cat. 178, p. 231, fig. 10

The Journalists, 1925
Oil on canvas, 86 × 101 cm
Berlinische Galerie, acquired with funds from Stiftung DKLB and from the Senator for Science and Art, Berlin 1974
Cat. 65, p. 127

Cube, 1926
Oil on canvas, 65.5 × 72.5 cm
Berlinische Galerie, acquired with funds from Stiftung DKLB, Berlin 1993
Cat. 112, p. 217

The Fence, 1928
Oil on canvas, 88.5 × 87 cm
Berlinische Galerie, acquired with funds from Stiftung DKLB, Berlin 1979
Restored with the kind support of the Ernst von Siemens Kunststiftung
Cat. 113, p. 218

LOTHAR HOMEYER (1883–1969)
Revolution (Youth and Age), 1920
Woodcut, 42 × 26.5 cm
Berlinische Galerie, acquired with funds from the Senator for Science and Art, Berlin 1976
Cat. 19, p. 59

K

WALTER KAMPMANN (1887–1945)
The Commander, 1922
Oil on canvas, 62 × 51 cm
Berlinische Galerie, gift from Winnetou Kampmann, 1997
Cat. 38, p. 78

Portrait of My Wife, Ether Mask, c. 1930
Zinc plate with plastic on wood, 64 × 62 × 27 cm
Berlinische Galerie, gift from Winnetou Kampmann, 1994
Cat. 109, p. 213

PAUL KLEE (1879–1940)
Destruction and Hope (Ruins and Hope; Conquered Fort; Destroyed Fort), 1916
Lithograph, watercolour, 48 × 33 cm
Wolfgang Wittrock, Berlin
Cat. 24, p. 64

Architecture, 1923
Oil on hardboard, 58 × 39 cm
Staatliche Museen zu Berlin, Nationalgalerie
Cat. 118, p. 221

BERNHARD KLEIN (1888–1967)
Elbe Shore (II), 1927
Oil on canvas, 70 × 91 cm
Staatliche Museen zu Berlin, Nationalgalerie
Cat. 78, p. 138

CÉSAR KLEIN (1876–1954)
Call to vote for the National Assembly, 1919
Lithograph, 68 × 99.5 cm
Stiftung Deutsches Historisches Museum, Berlin
Cat. 04, p. 24

Mann with Pipe, 1920
Oil on canvas, 114 × 88 cm
Berlinische Galerie, acquired with funds from Stiftung DKLB, Berlin 1981
Cat. 21, p. 61

Cross Before Barbarians, 1933
Mixed technique on wood, 105 × 80.5 cm
Berlinische Galerie, acquired with funds from Stiftung DKLB, Berlin 1981
Restored with the kind support of the Ernst von Siemens Kunststiftung
Cat. 119, p. 223

ISSAI KULVIANSKI (1892–1970)
My Little Daughter Kiki, 1927
Oil on canvas, 127 × 96 cm
Berlinische Galerie, acquired with funds from Stiftung DKLB and from the Senator for Science and Art, Berlin 1972
Cat. 63, p. 126

L

EL LISSITZKY (1890–1941)
Proun 1 D (Proun portfolio), 1921
Lithograph, 34 × 44.5 cm
Staatliche Museen zu Berlin, Kupferstichkabinett
Cat. 52, p. 116

Proun 2 B (Proun portfolio) 1921
Lithograph, 34.2 × 45.5 cm
Staatliche Museen zu Berlin, Kupferstichkabinett
Cat. 51, p. 116

Proun 2 C (Proun portfolio), 1921
Lithograph, 45.2 × 35.5 cm
Staatliche Museen zu Berlin, Kupferstichkabinett
Cat. 53, p. 116

Proun 5 A (Proun portfolio), 1921
Lithograph, 29 × 26.7 cm
Staatliche Museen zu Berlin, Kupferstichkabinett
Cat. 54, p. 117

Proun Room for the Great Berlin Art Exhibition, 1923 (reconstruction 1965)
Wood, painted, glass, 310 × 365 × 365 cm
Berlinische Galerie, acquired with funds from Stiftung DKLB Berlin on the occasion of the exhibition *Berlin – Moscow/Moscow – Berlin*, 1995
Cat. 55, p. 119

HANS LUCKHARDT (1890–1954)
WASSILI LUCKHARDT (1889–1972)
House of Music and Festivals, 1919
Photograph, 13 × 18.2 cm
Akademie der Künste, Berlin, Luckhardt-und-Anker-Archiv, WV 7 F. 2.1.-2.2.6
Cat. 80, p. 152

House of Music and Festivals, 1919
Photograph, 13 × 18.2 cm
Akademie der Künste, Berlin, Luckhardt-und-Anker-Archiv, WV 7 F. 2.1.-2.2.7.
Cat. 81, p. 152

House of Music and Festivals, 1919
Photograph, 18.3 × 13.2 cm
Akademie der Künste, Berlin, Luckhardt-und-Anker-Archiv, WV 7 F. 2.1.-2.2.10
Cat. 82, p. 152

Supergarage for 1000 motor cars, 1924
Photograph, 69.5 × 113 cm
Akademie der Künste, Berlin, Luckhardt-und-Anker-Archiv, WV 31 F. 11.46.302
Cat. 96, p. 162

WASSILI LUCKHARDT (1889–1972)
People's theatre, before 1921
Watercolour on paper, 43.5 × 76.5 cm
Akademie der Künste, Berlin, Luckhardt-und-Anker-Archiv, WV 20 Pl 11.46.2
Cat. 83, p. 153

M

EWALD MATARÉ (1887–1965)
Female Head (Portrait of Hanna H.), 1922
Birchwood, 24 × 14.3 × 20.9 cm
Museum Kurhaus Kleve – Ewald Mataré-Sammlung, Kleve / Permanent loan from the Ewald Mataré estate
Cat. 72, p. 134

Female torso "Woman Standing", 1924–1925
Walnut wood, originally gilded, 55 × 14.3 × 11.8 cm
Lehmbruck Museum, Duisburg
Cat. 71, p. 134

Hen, 1925
Wood, 48 × 36 × 19 cm
Sammlung Karl H. Knauf, Berlin
Cat. 73, p. 135

Bull Lying, 1927
Cocobolo wood, 27 × 59 × 30.5 cm
Hamburger Kunsthalle
Cat. 75, p. 135

Cat, 1928
Bronze, 20 × 58 × 9.3 cm
Private collection
Cat. 74, p. 135

Historical view of the Mataré Room at the Great Berlin Art Exhibition, 1928
Gelatin silver print (vintage print), 16.5 × 12 cm
Museum Kurhaus Kleve – Ewald Mataré-Sammlung, Kleve / Permanent loan from the Ewald Mataré estate
Cat. 70, p. 133

MORIZ MELZER (1877-1966)
The Frog, c. 1920
Oil on canvas, 130.5 × 99.5 cm
Galerie Berinson, Berlin
Cat. 27, p. 67

Blessing, 1917–1922
Oil on wood, with slats, 136 × 103 cm
Staatliche Museen zu Berlin, Nationalgalerie
Restored with the kind support of the Ernst von Siemens Kunststiftung
Cat. 26, p. 66

Der Dreiklang [design for a Novembergruppe magazine to be named after "Triad"], 1920
Watercolour and pencil, 30 × 21.8 cm
Berlinische Galerie, Helga-Kliemann-Archiv, purchased from budgetary funds, Berlin 1999
Restored with the kind support of the Ernst von Siemens Kunststiftung
Cat. 121, p. 214, fig. 01

Design for a leaflet about a performance of Arnold Schönberg's Pierrot Lunaire, organized by the Novembergruppe, 1922
India ink on paper, 37.5 × 20 cm
Berlinische Galerie, Helga-Kliemann-Archiv, purchased from budgetary funds, Berlin 1999
Cat. 122, p. 186, fig. 03

Novembergruppe (typographic design), c. 1922
India ink on blue high-gloss paper, 35.5 × 21.5 cm
Berlinische Galerie, Helga-Kliemann-Archiv, purchased from budgetary funds, Berlin 1999
Restored with the kind support of the Ernst von Siemens Kunststiftung
Cat. 01, p. 2

ERICH MENDELSOHN (1887-1953)
Einstein Tower on Telegraphenberg, Potsdam (copy from model), after 1950
Plaster, wood
Berlinische Galerie, acquired with funds from Stiftung DKLB, Berlin 1995
Cat. 100, p. 163

LUDWIG MIES VAN DER ROHE (1886-1969)
Model of a glass skyscraper, 1922 (reconstruction 1986)
Wood, lacquered, perspex, metal, 94.2 × 50.2 × 100 cm
Bauhaus-Universität Weimar – Archiv der Moderne
Cat. 102, p. 166

Model of a glass skyscraper, 1921 (photo: Curt Rehbein)
Gelatin silver paper (Reproduction from the Edward A. Duckel Collection, around 1987), 24 × 17.7 cm
Berlinische Galerie, gift from Ingrid Kühne, 2010
Cat. 101, p. 165

OTTO MÖLLER (1883-1964)
Street Noise, 1920
Oil on canvas, 62.5 × 75.5 cm
Berlinische Galerie, acquired with funds from Stiftung DKLB, Berlin 1987
Cat. 28, p. 69

The Speaker, 1920/1950
Woodcut on Japan paper, 21.1 × 15.7 cm
Berlinische Galerie, gift from Christoph Möller, Diessen am Ammersee 1999
Cat. 17, p. 58

Sheet 6 in the portfolio of 10 woodcuts based on the short story "A Gentle Spirit" by F. M. Dostoyevsky, 1921
Woodcut, 16.8 × 13.9 cm
Berlinische Galerie, gift from Christoph Möller, Diessen am Ammersee 1999
Cat. 16, p. 58

Portrait of Walter Kampmann, 1927
Oil on canvas, 94 × 67 cm
Berlinische Galerie, acquired with funds from the Senator for Science and Art, Berlin 1977
Cat. 67, p. 128

LÁSZLÓ MOHOLY-NAGY (1895-1946)
Am 7 (26), 1926
Oil on canvas, 75.8 × 96 cm
Kurt und Ernst Schwitters Stiftung, Hanover
The Kurt and Ernst Schwitters Foundation was founded by the Schwitters family with the support of NORD/LB Norddeutsche Landesbank, the Niedersächsische Sparkassenstiftung (Savings Bank Foundation of Lower Saxony), the Niedersächsische Lottostiftung (The Lottery Foundation of Lower Saxony), the Cultural Foundation of the Federal States, the State Minister at the Federal Chancellery for Media and Cultural Affairs, the Ministry for Science and Culture of the Land of Lower Saxony and the City of Hanover.
Cat. 115, p. 220

JOHANNES MOLZAHN (1892-1965)
Primal Forms, 1921
Oil on canvas, 63 × 48.5 cm
Museum Wiesbaden
Cat. 20, p. 60

PIET MONDRIAN (1872-1944)
Tableau I, 1921
Oil on canvas, 96.5 × 60.5 cm
Museum Ludwig, Cologne, purchased in 1967
Restored with the kind support of the Ernst von Siemens Kunststiftung
Cat. 58, p. 123

FRANZ MUTZENBECHER (1880-1968)
Drawing for a glass window, undated
Gouache on paperboard, 19.5 × 11.3 on 26 × 17.7 cm
Akademie der Künste, Berlin, Franz-Mutzenbecher-Sammlung, no. 98
Cat. 85, p. 154

Display space for the music specialists Heinrichshofen in Magdeburg, glass ceiling by Franz Mutzenbecher, 1921–1922
Photograph, 18 × 24 cm
Akademie der Künste, Berlin, Max-Taut-Fotosammlung, no. 40 F. 3
Cat. 84, p. 154

N

OTTO NAGEL (1894-1967)
Boys from Wedding, 1928
Oil on canvas, 91 × 62 cm
Staatliche Museen zu Berlin, Nationalgalerie
Cat. 64, p. 126

ERNST NEUSCHUL (1895-1968)
Women Resting, 1926
Oil on canvas, 67 × 87 cm
Berlinische Galerie, acquired with funds from Stiftung DKLB, Berlin 1981
Restored with the kind support of the Ernst von Siemens Kunststiftung
Cat. 107, p. 212

P

MAX PECHSTEIN (1881-1955)
A call for law and order, 1919
Lithograph, 100 × 67.3 cm
Stiftung Deutsches Historisches Museum, Berlin
Cat. 05, p. 24

LÁSZLÓ PÉRI (1889-1967)
Wall composition for the Great Berlin Art Exhibition (design), 1923–1924 / c. 1960
Silkscreen print from a linocut, 33.5 × 46.5 cm
Berlinische Galerie, purchased from budgetary funds, Berlin 1992
Cat. 61, p. 125

HANS POELZIG (1869-1936)
Annagrube [ore mine]. Electrical Substation, c. 1914
Gelatin silver print, 28.9 × 38.7 cm
Architekturmuseum TU Berlin
Restored with the kind support of the Ernst von Siemens Kunststiftung
Cat. 97, p. 162

Competition for "Turmhaus AG" high-rise building on Friedrichstrasse, Berlin, perspective view from Point D, Solution B, 1921
Charcoal on tracing paper, 109.9 × 77.5 cm
Architekturmuseum TU Berlin
Cat. 94, p. 160

Competition for "Turmhaus AG" high-rise building on Friedrichstrasse, Berlin, perspective view from Point C, Solution B, 1921
Blueprint on art paper, 58 × 56.9 cm
Architekturmuseum TU Berlin
Cat. 94a

IVAN PUNI (1894-1956)
Composition, Constructivist Still Life, 1920
Oil on canvas and ceramic collage, 54 × 63 cm
Berlinische Galerie, gift from Hermann Berninger, Zürich 1988
Cat. 49, p. 114

Synthetic Musician, 1921
Oil on canvas, 145 × 98 cm
Berlinische Galerie, purchased with donations and funds from the Senate Department of Cultural Affairs, Berlin 1991
Cat. 50, p. 115

R

HANS RICHTER (1888-1976)
Revolution, 1914
Oil on paperboard, 63.5 × 48 cm
Berlinische Galerie, gift from the estate, 1982
Cat. 03, p. 23

EMY ROEDER (1890-1971)
Mare and Foal, 1919
Bronze, 31.5 × 35.5 × 29 cm
Staatliche Museen zu Berlin, Nationalgalerie
Cat. 31, p. 74

WILLY RÖMER (1887-1979)
Untitled (outside Hotel Adlon, People's Navy division enters Berlin), November 1918
Gelatin silver print, 10.6 × 16.3 cm
Berlinische Galerie, purchased from budgetary funds, Berlin 2013
Cat. 10, p. 29

Untitled (troops returning), 10 December 1918
Gelatin silver print, 11.9 × 17 cm
Berlinische Galerie, purchased from budgetary funds, Berlin 2013
Cat. 179, pp. 18–19

Untitled (people wounded in shooting at Brandenburg Gate tended in Hotel Adlon), 1919
Gelatin silver print, 11.7 × 17.2 cm
Berlinische Galerie, purchased from budgetary funds, Berlin 2013
Cat. 11, p. 29

Untitled (Kapp-Putsch, 7 am on Unter den Linden), 13 March 1920
Gelatin silver print, 11.6 × 17.2 cm
Berlinische Galerie, purchased from budgetary funds, Berlin 2013
Cat. 12, p. 29

S

HANS SCHAROUN (1893–1972)
Competition entry entitled "Operation, not representation" showing the station square, street An der Weide and post office, Bremen, 1922
Watercolour on paper, 50 × 66 cm
Akademie der Künste, Berlin, Hans-Scharoun-Archiv, no. 1227 f. 27/1
Cat. 92, p. 159

"Börsenhof" with shops and offices, Königsberg [now Kaliningrad], competition, 1922
Blueprint [probably an iron gall ink copy] on paper with highlights in coloured pencil, 84.6 × 62.2 cm
Akademie der Künste, Berlin, Hans-Scharoun-Archiv, no. 1229 f. 32/12
Cat. 93, p. 159

GEORG SCHOLZ (1890–1945)
Industrial Farmers, 1920
Oil and collage over pencil on plywood, 98 × 70 cm
Von der Heydt-Museum Wuppertal
Cat. 42, p. 95

The Lords of the World, 1922
Lithograph, 29.7 × 40 cm
Sammlung Frank Brabant, Wiesbaden
Cat. 47, p. 100

The Sentimental Sailor, 1922
Lithograph, 15.9 × 22.3 cm
Sammlung Frank Brabant, Wiesbaden
Cat. 48, p. 101

Newspaper Carriers, 1922
Lithograph, 20 × 22 cm
Sammlung Frank Brabant, Wiesbaden
Cat. 46, p. 100

KURT SCHWITTERS (1887–1948)
Watercolour 5: He and She, 1919
Watercolour and pencil on paper, Original passe-partout cut-out 23.1 × 18.6 cm, Original passe-partout 26.5 × 21.9 cm
Kurt und Ernst Schwitters Stiftung, Hanover The Kurt and Ernst Schwitters Foundation was founded by the Schwitters family with the support of NORD/LB Norddeutsche Landesbank, the Niedersächsische Sparkassenstiftung (Savings Bank Foundation of Lower Saxony), the Niedersächsische Lottostiftung (The Lottery Foundation of Lower Saxony), the Cultural Foundation of the Federal States, the State Minister at the Federal Chancellery for Media and Cultural Affairs, the Ministry for Science and Culture of the Land of Lower Saxony and the City of Hanover.
Cat. 43, p. 97

Watercolour 23: Coquetry, 1919
Watercolour and pencil on paper, Original passe-partout cut-out 18.6 × 18.6 cm, Original passe-partout 39.5 × 29.5 cm
Kurt und Ernst Schwitters Stiftung, Hanover The Kurt and Ernst Schwitters Foundation was founded by the Schwitters family with the support of NORD/LB Norddeutsche Landesbank, the Niedersächsische Sparkassenstiftung (Savings Bank Foundation of Lower Saxony), the Niedersächsische Lottostiftung (The Lottery Foundation of Lower Saxony), the Cultural Foundation of the Federal States, the State Minister at the Federal Chancellery for Media and Cultural Affairs, the Ministry for Science and Culture of the Land of Lower Saxony and the City of Hanover.
Cat. 44, p. 98

ARTHUR SEGAL (1875–1944)
Heligoland, 1923
Oil on canvas, 101 × 130 cm
Berlinische Galerie, acquired with funds from Stiftung DKLB, Berlin 1981
Cat. 39, p. 79

LASAR SEGALL (1891–1957)
Untitled (Wandering Women), 1920–1925
Woodcut, 27 × 32.5 cm
Galerie Berinson, Berlin
Cat. 18, p. 59

ROBERT SENNECKE (1885–1940)
Karl Liebknecht speaks in Tiergarten, December 1918
Gelatin silver print, 17 × 23.2 cm
Berlinische Galerie, purchased with budgetary funds, Berlin 1989
Cat. 09, p. 28

SASHA STONE (1895–1940)
Pavilion by Mies van der Rohe to represent the German Reich at the Barcelona International Exposition, different views, 1928–1930
Gelatin silver print, 11.2 × 22.5 cm
Berlinische Galerie, Nachlass Sergius Ruegenberg, 1995
Cat. 103, p. 167

FRITZ STUCKENBERG (1881–1944)
Sticky Air, c. 1919
Oil on canvas, 76 × 72 cm
Sammlung Stuckenberg der Niedersächsischen Sparkassenstiftung at the Städtische Galerie Delmenhorst
Cat. 25, p. 65

Fugue, c. 1924
Oil on canvas, 40.5 × 64.5 cm
Sammlung Städtische Galerie Delmenhorst
Cat. 116, p. 220

T

GEORG TAPPERT (1880–1957)
Composition I, 1919
Oil on canvas, 124.5 × 94 cm
Germanisches Nationalmuseum, Nuremberg
Cat. 15, p. 57

MAX TAUT (1884–1967)
House of Blossoms, 1921
Colour drawing, mixed technique, 36 × 22 cm
Akademie der Künste, Berlin, Max-Taut-Archiv, no. 842
Cat. 86, p. 155

Wissinger family grave, Stahnsdorf near Berlin [with Rudolf Belling], 1921–1922
Photograph, 18 × 24 cm
Akademie der Künste, Berlin, Max-Taut-Fotosammlung, no. 41 f. 3a
Cat. 87, p. 155

V

KARL VÖLKER (1889–1962)
Birth, 1919
Oil on canvas, 77.5 × 129.5 cm
Kulturstiftung Sachsen-Anhalt, Kunstmuseum Moritzburg Halle (Saale)
Cat. 13, p. 56

Concrete, c. 1924
Oil on canvas, 84.5 × 100 cm
Kulturstiftung Sachsen-Anhalt, Kunstmuseum Moritzburg Halle (Saale)
Cat. 69, p. 131

W

VINCENT WEBER (1902–1990)
The Lodger's Breakfast, 1925
Oil on canvas, 64 × 78 cm
Berlinische Galerie, gift from the artist
Cat. 77, p. 137

INES WETZEL (1878–1940)
Self-Portrait, 1930
Watercolour, gouache and pencil on art paper, 47 × 38.4 cm
Berlinische Galerie, acquired with funds from Stiftung DKLB and from the Senator for Science and Art, Berlin 1976
Cat. 66, p. 128

Documents on Display (selected)

Exhibition Catalogues, Invitations and Guides
See page 262 for detailed bibliography

Great Berlin Art Exhibition 1919 to 1932 (named simply Berlin Art Exhibition in 1919 and 1920)
Catalogues
Berlinische Galerie, library and archives Restored with the kind support of the Ernst von Siemens Kunststiftung
Cat. 123

Novembergruppe guides to its section at the Berlin Art Exhibition of 1920 and the Great Berlin Art Exhibitions of 1921 to 1924
Berlinische Galerie, Hannah-Höch-Archiv, acquired with funds from the Senator for Cultural Affairs, Berlin 1979; Teilnachlass Otto Möller, private gift 1999; Helga-Kliemann-Archiv, acquired with budgetary funds 1999; and Staatliche Museen zu Berlin, Zentralarchiv, IV/NL Behrens-Hangeler, 241
Restored with the kind support of the Ernst von Siemens Kunststiftung
Cat. 124

First Novembergruppe exhibition at Fraenkel & Co. (Josef Altmann), Berlin [1920]
Leaflet
Berlinische Galerie, Teilnachlass Otto Möller, private gift 1999
Cat. 125

Novembergruppe Berlin exhibition at Josef Altmann Kunsthandlung und Antiquariat, Berlin 1921
Invitation
Berlinische Galerie, Teilnachlass Otto Möller, private gift 1999
Cat. 126

Esposizione Espressionisti Novembergruppe, Casa d'arte italiana, Rome 1920
Leaflet
Berlinische Galerie, Hannah-Höch-Archiv, acquired with funds from the Senator for Science and Art, Berlin 1979
Cat. 127, p. 227, fig. 04

First Universal German Art Exhibition, Moscow–Leningrad 1924
Catalogue
Berlinische Galerie, Teilnachlass Otto Möller, private gift 1999
Cat. 128, p. 235, fig. 16

Novembergruppe exhibition at the Berlin Secession 1925
Catalogue, several copies, different printed versions
Berlinische Galerie, Hannah-Höch-Archiv, acquired with funds from the Senator for Cultural Affairs, Berlin 1979; Teilnachlass Otto Möller, private gift 1999; Helga-Kliemann-Archiv, acquired with budgetary funds 1999
Cat. 129

Jury-Free Art Show Berlin 1929
Catalogue
Berlinische Galerie, Helga-Kliemann-Archiv, acquired with budgetary funds 1999
Cat. 130

Novembergruppe exhibition at the Verein Berliner Künstler, Berlin 1931
Catalogue
Staatliche Museen zu Berlin, art library and Berlinische Galerie, library
Cat. 131

Magazines and books

Menschen. Buchfolge neuer Kunst, vol. 2, issue XIV (nos. 81/86), 1919
Berlinische Galerie, Teilnachlass Otto Möller, private gift 1999
Cat. 132

To All Artists! [An alle Künstler!], 1919
Brochure published by the Werbedienst der deutschen sozialistischen Republik, Berlin
Berlinische Galerie, acquired with budgetary funds 1983
Cat. 133, p. 25, fig. 06

Der Kunsttopf, published by the Novembergruppe, vol. 1, 1920, nos. 1, 3, 4 and 5
Berlinische Galerie, Hannah-Höch-Archiv, acquired with artist support funds from the Senator for Cultural Affairs, Berlin 1978; Helga-Kliemann-Archiv, acquired with budgetary funds, Berlin 1999
Cat. 134, p. 229, fig. 07 (H. 1)

Der Kunsttopf, vol. 1, 1920, nos. 1–6, bound, cover designed by [Otto Möller]
Berlinische Galerie, Teilnachlass Otto Möller, private gift 1999
Cat. 135, p. 12, fig. 02

NG. Veröffentlichung der Novembergruppe, edited by Hans Siebert von Heister and Raoul Hausmann, H. 1, May 1921
Three copies
Berlinische Galerie, Hannah-Höch-Archiv, acquired with funds from the Senator for Cultural Affairs, Berlin 1979; Teilnachlass Otto Möller, private gift 1999; Helga-Kliemann-Archiv, acquired with budgetary funds 1999
Cat. 136, p. 87, fig. 08 (Höch copy)

Das Junge Rheinland. Novembergruppe. Dresdner Sezession, nos. 8 and 9–10, July 1922
Harald Gnade private collection, Berlin
Cat. 137, p. 234, fig. 13 (nos. 9-10)

Zehn Jahre Novembergruppe, special issue of Kunst der Zeit, vol. 3, 1928, nos. 1–3
Two copies
Staatliche Museen zu Berlin, Kunstbibliothek; Berlinische Galerie, Hannah-Höch-Archiv, acquired with funds from the Senate Department of Cultural Affairs, Berlin 1979
Cat. 138, p. 196, figs. 01, 02 (Höch copy)

Articles of association

Novembergruppe Guidelines and Articles of association, 16 December 1918 and January 1919
Print matter, 1 sheet
Berlinische Galerie, Teilnachlass Otto Möller, private gift 1999
Cat. 139, p. 227, fig. 03

Novembergruppe Articles of association, 1920
Print matter, 5 pages
Berlinische Galerie, Teilnachlass Otto Möller, private gift 1999
Cat. 140

Articles of the registered association Novembergruppe e.V., 1925
Print matter, 4 pages
Berlinische Galerie, Teilnachlass Otto Möller, private gift 1999
Cat. 141

Photographs

BRUNO SCHUCH
Special exhibition Ten Years of the Novembergruppe during the Jury-Free Art Show, Berlin 1929
Gelatin silver print, with handwritten comments
Berlinische Galerie, Nachlass Heinrich Ehmsen, private gift 1995
Restored with the kind support of the Ernst von Siemens Kunststiftung
Cat. 142, p. 197, fig. 05

UNKNOWN PHOTOGRAPHER
Group portrait of the Novembergruppe, [1920]
Gelatin silver print, 16.2 × 21.6 cm
Stiftung Stadtmuseum Berlin
Cat. 143, figs. on pp. 40-41

UNKNOWN PHOTOGRAPHER
Members of the Novembergruppe hanging committee, 1928
Gelatin silver print, reproduction c. 1968, 15.3 × 20 cm
Berlinische Galerie, acquired with funds from the Senate Department of Cultural Affairs, Berlin 1978
Cat. 144, figs. on pp. 192-193

Posters, programmes and invitations

Novembergruppe balls

BERNHARD KLEIN (1888-1967)
The Cubic Box, Fancy-Dress Ball given by the Novembergruppe, 20 March 1920
Poster, 28.2 × 24.2 cm
Berlinische Galerie, Hannah-Höch-Archiv, acquired with funds from the Senate Department of Cultural Affairs, Berlin 1979
Restored with the kind support of the Ernst von Siemens Kunststiftung
Cat. 29, p. 71

Kunsttopf, Open Artists' Fancy-Dress Ball given by the Novembergruppe, 1 December 1920
Poster, partly hand-coloured, 71 × 50 cm
Berlinische Galerie, acquired with budgetary funds, Berlin 2017
Restored with the kind support of the Ernst von Siemens Kunststiftung
Cat. 145, p. 229, fig. 08

HANS SIEBERT VON HEISTER (1888-1967)
Artists' Fancy-Dress Ball given by the Novembergruppe, 2 December 1922
Leaflet, 32 × 20.1 cm
Berlinische Galerie, Helga-Kliemann-Archiv, acquired with budgetary funds, Berlin 1999
Cat. 146, p. 186, fig. 03

WALTER KAMPMANN (1887-1945)
Artists' Fancy-Dress Ball hosted by the Novembergruppe, 2 December 1922
Invitation, 28.1 × 22.1 cm
Staatliche Museen zu Berlin, Zentralarchiv, IV/NL Behrens-Hangeler, 243
Cat. 147, p. 234, fig. 14

5th Open Artists' Fancy-Dress Ball given by the Novembergruppe, 6 December 1924
Invitation
Berlinische Galerie, Hannah-Höch-Archiv, acquired with funds from the Senator for Cultural Affairs, Berlin 1979
Cat. 148, p. 236, fig. 17

HANNAH HÖCH (1889-1978)
Artists' Fancy-Dress Ball given by the Novembergruppe on the theme "Sport and Razzmatazz in Wedding", 5 December 1925
Poster, 33 × 68 cm
Berlinische Galerie, Hannah-Höch-Archiv, acquired with funds from the Senate Department of Cultural Affairs, Berlin 1979
Cat. 149, p. 189, fig. 08

GEORG TAPPERT (1880-1957)
9th Fancy-Dress Ball given by the Novembergruppe, 1 December 1928
Two invitations, each 14.7 × 10.6 cm
Private collection
Cat. 150, p. 239, figs. 21, 22

The Novembergruppe's New Year Ball, 1929
Invitation, 10.5 × 14.8 cm
Staatliche Museen zu Berlin, Kunstbibliothek, Sammlung Grafikdesign
Cat. 151, p. 240, fig. 25

WALTER KAMPMANN (1887-1945)
The Novembergruppe's 11th Fancy-Dress Ball, 6 December 1930
Announcement and programme, 27.3 × 31.1 cm
Berlinische Galerie, Hannah-Höch-Archiv, private gift 1981
Restored with the kind support of the Ernst von Siemens Kunststiftung
Cat. 152, p. 190, fig. 09

The Novembergruppe's 11th Fancy-Dress Ball, 6 December 1930
Announcement and programme, 27.3 × 33.1 cm
Berlinische Galerie, Teilnachlass Otto Möller, private gift 1999
Cat. 153, p. 190, fig. 10

The Novembergruppe's 11th Fancy-Dress Ball, 6 December 1930
Announcement and programme, 25.6 × 32.9 cm
Staatliche Museen zu Berlin, Kunstbibliothek, Sammlung Grafikdesign
Cat. 154, p. 190, fig. 11

The Novembergruppe's 11th Fancy-Dress Ball, 6 December 1930
Poster, 71.8 × 47.5 cm
Staatliche Museen zu Berlin, Kunstbibliothek, Sammlung Grafikdesign
Cat. 155, p. 241, fig. 27

UNKNOWN DESIGNER
The Novembergruppe's 11th Fancy-Dress Ball, 6 December 1930
Invitation (with a poem by Robert Seitz), 19.8 × 10 cm
Staatliche Museen zu Berlin, Zentralarchiv, IV/NL Behrens-Hangeler, 244
Cat. 156

The Novembergruppe's 11th Fancy-Dress Ball, 6 December 1930
Invitation (with a poem by Joachim Ringelnatz), two copies
Diameter: 15.8 cm
Staatliche Museen zu Berlin, Zentralarchiv, IV/NL Behrens-Hangeler, 245
Cat. 157, p. 186, fig. 04

The Novembergruppe's New Year Ball, 1930
Invitation (postcard to Franz Richard Behrens, 24 December 1930), 10.4 × 14.7 cm
Staatliche Museen zu Berlin, Zentralarchiv IV/NL Behrens-Hangeler, 246
Cat. 158

Novembergruppe Evenings and other events

4th Novembergruppe Evening, 3 April 1923
Invitation and programme, designed by [MORIZ MELZER], 28.8 × 22.8 cm
Berlinische Galerie, Hannah-Höch-Archiv, acquired with funds from the Senator for Cultural Affairs, Berlin 1979
Restored with the kind support of the Ernst von Siemens Kunststiftung
Cat. 159, p. 185, fig. 02

10th to 13th Novembergruppe Evenings, 24 November 1924, 30 January, 3 April and 12 November 1925
Invitation and programme for each, various formats
Berlinische Galerie, Hannah-Höch-Archiv, acquired with funds from the Senator for Cultural Affairs, Berlin 1979
Cat. 160, p. 187, fig. 06 (12th Evening)

Absolute Film, a film matinée organized by the Novembergruppe and UFA's Culture Department, 3 May 1925
Invitation and programme, 29.5 × 22.9 cm
Berlinische Galerie, Teilnachlass Otto Möller, private gift 1999
Restored with the kind support of the Ernst von Siemens Kunststiftung
Cat. 161

16th Novembergruppe Evening, 16 March 1926
Programme, 23 × 14.8 cm
Akademie der Künste, Berlin, Arthur Schnabel-Archiv 609
Cat. 162

17th Novembergruppe Evening, 16 April 1926
Programme, 14.8 × 10.6 cm
Berlinische Galerie, Hannah-Höch-Archiv, acquired with funds from the Senator for Cultural Affairs, Berlin 1979
Cat. 163

10 Years of the Novembergruppe, concert, 24 January 1930
Programme, 6 pages, cover page by LOTHAR HOMEYER, 29.7 × 21 cm
Berlinische Galerie, Helga-Kliemann-Archiv, acquired with budgetary funds, Berlin 1999
Cat. 164, p. 241, fig. 26

19th Evening of Music by the Novembergruppe, 21 April 1927 [postponed until 2 May 1927]
Invitation and programme, 22.4 × 14.1 cm
Berlinische Galerie, Teilnachlass Otto Möller, private gift 1999
Cat. 165

20th Evening of Music by the Novembergruppe, organized by the Hilfsverein für Junge Kunst, 20 November 1930
Programme, 20.3 × 14.5 cm
Berlinische Galerie, Hannah-Höch-Archiv, acquired with funds from the Senator for Cultural Affairs, Berlin 1979
Cat. 166, p. 187, fig. 07

21th Evening of Music by the Novembergruppe, 8 April 1931
Invitation and programme
Berlinische Galerie, Hannah-Höch-Archiv, acquired with funds from the Senator for Cultural Affairs, Berlin 1979
Cat. 167, p. 185, fig. 01

Talk by Paul Westheim, organized by the Novembergruppe, 20 April 1932
Invitation, 20.8 × 14.7 cm
Berlinische Galerie, Teilnachlass Otto Möller, private gift 1999
Cat. 168, p. 242, fig. 29

Letters and documents

RAOUL HAUSMANN (1886–1971)
Open letter to the Novembergruppe in collaboration with Otto Dix, Max Dungert, Otto Freundlich, George Grosz, H. [Hannah] Höch, Ernst Krantz, [Franz] Mutzenbecher, Thomas Ring, Rudolf Schlichter, Georg Scholz, Willy Zierath, [1921]
Typed, 6 sheets, carbon copy with handwritten additions
Berlinische Galerie, Teilnachlass Raoul Hausmann, acquired with funds from the Senate Department of Cultural Affairs, Berlin, and donations 1991
Cat. 169

Der Kunsttopf, January 1921
Typed, 3 sheets, carbon copy with handwritten corrections
Berlinische Galerie, Hannah-Höch-Archiv, acquired with funds from the Senator for Cultural Affairs, Berlin 1979
Cat. 170

OTTO DIX to RAOUL HAUSMANN, Dresden, [May 1921]
Letter, 2 sheets, handwritten
Berlinische Galerie, Hannah-Höch-Archiv, acquired with funds from the Senator for Cultural Affairs, Berlin 1979
Cat. 171

OTTO DIX to RAOUL HAUSMANN, Dresden, [May/June 1921]
Letter, 2 sheets, handwritten
Berlinische Galerie, Hannah-Höch-Archiv, acquired with funds from the Senator for Cultural Affairs, Berlin 1979
Cat. 172

THEO VAN DOESBURG to HANNAH HÖCH, Clamart, 17 April 1926
Letter, 2 sheets, typed with handwritten additions
Berlinische Galerie, Hannah-Höch-Archiv, acquired with funds from the Senator for Cultural Affairs, Berlin 1979
Cat. 173, p. 111, fig. 07

HANS SIEBERT VON HEISTER to HANNAH HÖCH, 30 December 1921
Postcard, handwritten
Berlinische Galerie, Hannah-Höch-Archiv, acquired with asset protection funds from the Senator for Cultural Affairs, Berlin 1979
Cat. 174, p. 11, fig. 01

Protest letter from the Novembergruppe to the Berliner Künstlerkartell about the exclusion of a work by George Grosz, 22 April 1927
Manuscript, 1 sheet, 2 pages
Akademie der Künste, Berlin, Georg-Grosz-Archiv 409
Cat. 175

[HUGO GRAETZ]
List of Novembergruppe members, 1 January 1930
Typed, 5 sheets, with handwritten additions
Akademie der Künste, Berlin, Autographen-Sammlung Bildende Kunst, Autographen-Bildende-Kunst 1
Cat. 176, figs. on pp. 254–255

Fee note from the Berlin Court Cashier to CÉSAR KLEIN in re Register of Associations / Novembergruppe, 6 November 1935
Print matter, 1 sheet
Nachlass César Klein
Cat. 177, p. 243, fig. 30

Printed Sources on the Novembergruppe

Catalogues and Flyers for Novembergruppe Exhibitions 1919–1932

Kunstausstellung Berlin 1919 im Landesausstellungsgebäude [*Art Exhibition Berlin 1919 in the State Exhibition Building*] (exhib. cat., 24 July – 30 September 1919), Berlin 1919, Novembergruppe section, nos. 1100–1282

Kunstausstellung Berlin 1920 im Landesausstellungsgebäude, das vom Ministerium für Wissenschaft, Kunst und Volksbildung dem Verein Berliner Künstler und der Novembergruppe zur Verfügung gestellt ist [*Art Exhibition Berlin 1919 in the State Exhibition Building, provided to the Association of Berlin Artists and the Novembergruppe by the Ministry of Science, Culture and Public Education*] (exhib. cat., 21 May – end of September 1920), Berlin 1920, Novembergruppe section, nos. 1077–1512

Esposizione Espressionisti Novembergruppe, Bollettino quindicinale della Casa d'arte italiana, diretta da E. Prampolini e M. Recchi [*Exhibition of the Novembergruppe Expressionists*, Bimonthly Bulletin of the Institue of Italian Art, directed by E. Prampolini and M. Recchi], no. 1 (flyer for the exhibition, 23 October to November 1920), Rome 1920

Erste Ausstellung der Novembergruppe. Gemälde, Plastiken [*First Exhibition of the Novembergruppe. Paintings, Sculptures*] (flyer for the exhibition in Berlin, Fraenkel & Co. (Josef Altmann), 4–30 November [1920]), Berlin 1920

Catalogus voor de 16de jury-vrije tentoonstelling [Catalogue for the 16th Jury-Free Exhibition (exhib. cat. Amstersdam, Stedelijk Museum, 5 February – 6 March 1921), Amsterdam 1921, Novembergruppe section, nos. 212–293

Große Berliner Kunstausstellung 1921 im Landesausstellungsgebäude am Lehrter Bahnhof [*Great Berlin Art Exhibition 1921 in the State Exhibtion Building at Lehrter Train Station*] (exhib. cat., 14 May – end of September 1921), Berlin 1921, Novembergruppe section, nos. 1032–1206

Einladung zur Besichtigung der Ausstellung der Novembergruppe Berlin [Invitation to view the Novembergruppe exhibition in Berlin], Josef Altmann Kunsthandlung und Antiquariat Berlin, 1 November to 30 November 1921 [with an index of the participating artists]

I. Internationale Kunstausstellung Düsseldorf 1922 [*First International Art Exhibition Düsseldorf 1922*] (exhib. cat. Düsseldorf, hosted by Das junge Rheinland in the department store Leonhard Tietz, 28 May – 3 Juli 1922), Düsseldorf 1922 [The participants are listed alphabetically in the catalogue with an indication of their membership in an artists' association.]

Große Berliner Kunstausstellung 1921 im Landesausstellungsgebäude am Lehrter Bahnhof [*Great Berlin Art Exhibition 1921 in the State Exhibtion Building at Lehrter Train Station*] (exhib. cat., 14 May – end of September), Berlin 1921, Novembergruppe section, nos. 1032–1334

Große Berliner Kunstausstellung 1922 im Landesausstellungsgebäude am Lehrter Bahnhof [*Great Berlin Art Exhibition 1922 in the State Exhibtion Building at Lehrter Train Station*] (exhib. cat., 20 May – 17 September 1922), Berlin 1922, Novembergruppe section, nos. 1188–1454

Große Berliner Kunstausstellung 1923 im Landesausstellungsgebäude am Lehrter Bahnhof [*Great Berlin Art Exhibition 1923 in the State Exhibtion Building at Lehrter Train Station*] (exhib. cat., 19 May – 17 September 1923), Berlin 1923, Novembergruppe section, nos. 1061–1408

Große Berliner Kunstausstellung 1924 im Landesausstellungsgebäude am Lehrter Bahnhof [*Great Berlin Art Exhibition 1924 in the State Exhibtion Building at Lehrter Train Station*] (exhib. cat., 31 May – 1 September 1924), Berlin 1924, Novembergruppe section, nos. 842–1009

Erste Allgemeine Deutsche Kunstausstellung (exhib. cat. Moskau, Museum of History and others, 18 October 1924 to January 1925), Moscow 1924 [The participants are listed alphabetically in the catalogue with an indication of their membership in one of the participating artists' associations.]

Ausstellung der Novembergruppe in den Räumen der Berliner Secession in Berlin. Juni 1925. Malerei, Plastik, Architektur [*Novembergruppe Exhibition on the Premises of the Berlin Secession. June 1925. Painting, Sculpture, Architecture*], Berlin 1925 (= Archiv der deutschen Kunst, vol. 5, 1925, no. 3)

Große Berliner Kunstausstellung 1926 im Landesausstellungsgebäude am Lehrter Bahnhof. Farbige Raumkunst [*Great Berlin Art Exhibition 1926 in the State Exhibtion Building at Lehrter Train Station. Colour Interior Art*] (exhib. cat., 21 May – end of August 1926), Berlin 1926, Novembergruppe section, nos. 1507–1653a

Große Berliner Kunstausstellung 1927. Veranstaltet vom Kartell der Vereinigten Verbände Bildender Künstler Berlins e. V. im Landesausstellungsgebäude [*Great Berlin Art Exhibition 1927. Hosted by the Syndicate of the United Associations of Fine Artists of Berlin in the State Exhibtion Building*] (exhib. cat., 7 May – 30 September 1927), Berlin 1927 (= Veröffentlichungen des Kunstarchivs; nos. 41–42) [Because the catalogue does not indicate the participants' membership in associations, it is not possible to list the catalogue numbers for the Novembergruppe.]

Große Berliner Kunstausstellung 1928. Veranstaltet vom Kartell der vereinigten Verbände bildender Künstler Berlins e.V. im Landesausstellungsgebäude am Lehrter Bahnhof [*Great Berlin Art Exhibition 1928. Hosted by the Syndicate of the United Associations of Fine Artists of Berlin in the State Exhibtion Building at Lehrter Tranin Station*] (exhib. cat., 9 May – end of Juli 1928), Berlin 1928 [The participants are listed alphabetically in the catalogue with an indication of their membership in an artists' association.]

Große Berliner Kunstausstellung 1929. Veranstaltet vom Kartell der vereinigten Verbände bildender Künstler Berlins e.V. im Schloss Bellvue [*Great Berlin Art Exhibition 1929. Hosted by the Syndicate of the United Associations of Fine Artists of Berlin in Bellvue Palace*] (exhib. cat., 19 May – 15 August 1929), Berlin 1929 [The participants are listed alphabetically in the catalogue with an indication of their membership in an artists' association.]

Juryfreie Kunstschau Berlin 1929. Malerei, Graphik, Plastik und Architektur. Landes-Ausstellungsgebäude am Lehrter Bahnhof [*Jury-Free Art Show Berlin 1929. Painting, Drawing, Print, Sculpture and Architecture. State Exhibtion Building at Lehrter Tranin Station*] (exhib. cat., 25 August – 5 October 1929), Berlin 1929, special exhibiton *Zehn Jahre Novembergruppe* [The participants are listed alphabetically in the catalogue with an indication of their membership in an artists' association.]

Große Berliner Kunstausstellung 1930 im Schloß Bellevue. Amtlicher Katalog der I. Abteilung. Veranstalter Kartell der Vereinigten Verbände Bildender Künstler Berlins e. V. [*Great Berlin Art Exhibition 1930 in Bellvue Palace. Official Catalogue of the First Section. Hosted by the Syndicate of the United Associations of Fine Artists of Berlin*] (exhib. cat. 29 May – 17 August 1930), Berlin 1930 [The participants are listed alphabetically in the catalogue with an indication of their membership in an artists' association.]

Große Berliner Kunstausstellung 1930 im Schloß Bellevue. Amtlicher Katalog der II. Abteilung. Veranstalter Kartell der Vereinigten Verbände Bildender Künstler Berlins e. V. [*Great Berlin Art Exhibition 1930 in Bellvue Palace. Official Catalogue of the Second Section. Hosted by the Syndicate of the United Associations of Fine Artists of Berlin*] (exhib. cat. 7 September – end of October 1930), Berlin 1930 [The participants are listed alphabetically in the catalogue with an indication of their membership in an artists' association.]

Große Berliner Kunstausstellung 1931 im Schloß Bellevue. Amtlicher Katalog der I. Abteilung. Gemälde und Plastik. Veranstalter Kartell der Vereinigten Verbände Bildender Künstler Berlins e. V. [*Great Berlin Art Exhibition 1931 in Bellvue Palace. Official Catalogue of the First Section. Painting and Sculpture. Hosted by the Syndicate of the United Associations of Fine Artists of Berlin*] (exhib. cat., 3 May – 16 August 1931), Berlin 1931 [The participants are listed alphabetically in the catalogue with an indication of their membership in an artists' association.]

No catalogue has been found for the Second Section of the Great Berlin Art Exhibition with Watercolours, pastels, drawings, prints and small sculptures [2. Abteilung der Großen Berliner Kunstausstellung mit Aquarellen, Pastellen, Graphik und Klein-Plastik], 6 September – end of October 1931.

November-Gruppe. Ausstellung im neuen Hause des Vereins Berliner Künstler, Gemälde, Plastik [*November-Gruppe. Exhibition on the new premises of the Association of Berlin Artists, Painting, Sculpture*], ed. by Porza (exhib. cat., 3 Juli – 3 August 1931), Berlin 1931 (= Veröffentlichungen des Kunstarchivs, no. 58) [with the introductory text "Für die Lebenden!" [For the Living!] by Paul Westheim, pp. 2–3]

Große Berliner Kunstausstellung 1932 im Schloss Bellevue. Amtlicher Katalog der I. Abteilung. Veranstalter Kartell der vereinigten Verbände bildender Künstler Berlins [*Great Berlin Art Exhibition 1932 in Bellvue Palace. Official Catalogue of the First Section. Hosted by the Syndicate of the United Associations of Fine Artists of Berlin*] (exhib. cat., 8 May – 14 August 1932), Berlin 1932 [The participants are listed alphabetically in the catalogue with an indication of their membership in an artists' association.]

No catalogue has been found for the Second Section of the Great Berlin Art Exhibition with watercolours, pastels, drawings, prints and small sculptures [2. Abteilung der Großen Berliner Kunstausstellung mit Aquarellen, Pastellen, Graphik und Klein-Plastik], 4 September – 23 October 1932.

Novembergruppe Exhibition Guides

Peter Leu, *Führer durch die Abteilung der Novembergruppe. Kunstausstellung Berlin* 1920 [*Guide Through the Novembergruppe Section. Art Exhibition Berlin* 1920], Berlin 1920

Führer durch die Abteilung der Novembergruppe. Kunstausstellung Berlin 1921 [scil. *Große Berliner Kunstausstellung* 1921] {*Guide Through the Novembergruppe Section. Great Berlin Art Exhibition 1922*}, Berlin 1921 [with the introductuory text "Die neue Kunst" {New Art} by Raoul Hausmann, pp. 3–11]

Führer durch die Abteilung der Novembergruppe. Kunstausstellung Berlin 1922 [scil. Große Berliner Kunstausstellung 1922] {*Guide Through the Novembergruppe Section. Great Berlin Art Exhibition 1922*}, Berlin 1922 [with an introduction by Rudolf Adrian Dietrich, pp. 3–7]

Führer durch die Abteilung der Novembergruppe. Kunstausstellung Berlin 1923 [scil. Große Berliner Kunstausstellung 1923] {*Guide Through the Novembergruppe Section. Great Berlin Art Exhibition* 1923}, Berlin 1923 [with an introduction by Herbert Behrens-Hangeler, unpag.]

Führer der Novembergruppe [durch die Abteilung auf der Großen Berliner Kunstausstellung 1924] {*Novembergruppe Guide* [through its section of the Great Berlin Art Exhibition]}, Berlin 1924

Periodicals and Other Novembergruppe Publications

Menschen. Buchfolge Neuer Kunst, vol. 2, 1919, issue. 14 (nos. 81/86), *Sonderheft Novembergruppe. Graphik und Plastik von Mitgliedern der Novembergruppe Berlin.* [with a foreword by Adolf Behne, pp. 1f.]

Der Kunsttopf, published by the Novembergruppe, vol. 1, 1920, nos. 1–6

NG. Veröffentlichung der Novembergruppe, ed. by Hans Siebert von Heister and Raoul Hausmann, vol. 1, 1921, no. 1

Das Junge Rheinland 1, 1921–22, nos. 8 and 9–10 under the title *Das junge Rheinland. Novembergruppe. Dresdner Sezession* as the periodical for the Kartell fortschrittlicher Künstlergruppen [Syndicate of Progressive Artists' Groups]

Paul Bekker, *Wesensformen der Musik. Veröffentlichung der Novembergruppe*, Berlin 1925

Zehn Jahre Novembergruppe, special issue of *Kunst der Zeit. Zeitschrift für Kunst und Literatur*, vol. 3, 1928, nos. 1–3 [with the introductory text "Zehn Jahre Novembergruppe" [Ten Years of the Novembergruppe] by Will Grohmann, pp. 1–9].

Bibliography

A

Adkins 1988
Adkins, Helen, "Erste Internationale Dada-Messe, Berlin 1920", in: *Stationen der Moderne. Die bedeutenden Kunstausstellungen des 20. Jahrhunderts in Deutschland* (exhib. cat. Berlin, Berlinische Galerie), Berlin 1988, pp. 156–183

Akademie der Künste 1980
Arbeitsrat für Kunst. Berlin 1918–1921 (exhib. cat. and documentation Berlin, Akademie der Künste), Berlin 1980

Akademie der Künste 1990
Die Brüder Luckhardt und Alfons Anker. Berliner Architekten der Moderne. With a catalogue Raisonné by Francesco Fresa (exhib. cat. Berlin, Akademie der Künste), Berlin 1990

Akademie der Künste 1996
"Die Kunst hat nie ein Mensch allein besessen". Dreihundert Jahre Akademie der Künste und Hochschule der Künste (exhib. cat. Berlin, Akademie der Künste und Hochschule der Künste), Berlin 1996

Albersmeier 2004
Albersmeier, Franz-Josef, "Zwischen den Künsten und Medien (Film, Tanz, Theater). René Clair: Entr'acte", in: Michael Lommel (ed.), *Französische Theaterfilme zwischen Surrealismus und Existentialismus*, Bielefeld 2004, pp. 215–234

Andrian-Werburg 2005
Andrian-Werburg, Irmtraud Freifrau von, "Der Maler und Lehrer Georg Tappert in Dokumenten", in: *Georg Tappert. Deutscher Expressionist* (exhib. cat. Schleswig, Schloss Gottorf, Stiftung Schleswig-Holsteinische Landesmuseen; Nuremberg, Germanisches Nationalmuseum), Nuremberg 2005, pp. 31–41

Arlt 2002
Arlt, Peter, *Des Lebens dunkle Tänze. Der Maler Curt Ehrhardt 1895–1972*, ed. by Georg F. Hesselbach and Michael Hebecker, Weimar 2002

B

Bareither 2012
Bareither, Christoph, *Hans Richters "Rhythmus 21". Schlüsselfilm der Moderne*, Würzburg 2012

Barron 1992
Barron, Stephanie (ed.), *"Entartete Kunst". Das Schicksal der Avantgarde im Nazi-Deutschland* (exhib. cat. Los Angeles, County Museum of Art; Berlin, Deutsches Historisches Museum), Munich 1992 [simultaneously published in English under the title: *"Degenerate art": the Fate of Avant-Garde in Nazi Germany*, New York 1991]

Bartholomeyczik 2005
Bartholomeyczik, Gesa: "Biographie", in: *Georg Tappert. Deutscher Expressionist* (exhib. cat. Schleswig, Schloss Gottorf, Stiftung Schleswig-Holsteinische Landesmuseen; Nuremberg, Germanisches Nationalmuseum) Nuremberg 2005, pp. 10–13

Bartmann 2000
Bartmann, Dominik (ed.), *Max und Erwin Fabian. Berlin — London — Melbourne* (exhib. cat. Berlin, Stiftung Stadtmuseum Berlin), Berlin 2000

Bauhaus-Archiv 1988
Der Schrei nach dem Turmhaus. Der Ideenwettbewerb Hochhaus am Bahnhof Friedrichstraße Berlin 1921/22 (exhib. cat. Berlin, Bauhaus-Archiv, Museum für Gestaltung), Berlin 1988

Baumann 2016
Baumann, Jana, *Museum als Avantgarde. Museen moderner Kunst in Deutschland 1918–1933*, Berlin and Munich 2016

Belling 1955
Belling, Rudolf, "Novembergruppe und Kunstpflege zur Zeit der Weimarer Republik", in: Georg Rohde et al. (ed.), *Edwin Redslob zum 70. Geburtstag. Eine Festgabe*, Berlin 1955, pp. 169–171

Beloubek-Hammer 1993
Beloubek-Hammer, Anita, "Wider die 'Stand- und Spielbein'-Skulptur. Die Bildhauer der Novembergruppe", in: Niemann 1993

Beloubek-Hammer 2007
Beloubek-Hammer, Anita, *Die schönen Gestalten der besseren Zukunft. Die Bildhauerkunst des Expressionismus und ihr geistiges Umfeld*, 2 vols., Cologne 2007

Benson and Shatskikh 2013
Benson, Timothy O., Aleksandra Shatskikh, "Malevich and Richter. An Indeterminate Encounter", in: *October*, no. 143, Cambridge, Massachusetts 2013

Bergius 1989a
Bergius, Hanne, *Das Lachen Dadas. Berliner Dadaisten und ihr Aktionen*, Gießen 1989

Bergius 1989b
Bergius, Hanne, "'Dada Rundschau' – Eine Photomontage", in: *Hannah Höch 1889–1978. Ihr Werk, ihr Leben, ihre Freunde* (exhib. cat. Berlin, Berlinische Galerie), ed. by Berlinische Galerie e. V. and Museumspädagogischer Dienst, Berlin 1989, pp. 101–106

Bergius 2000
Bergius, Hanne, *Montage und Metamechanik. Dada Berlin – Artistik von Polaritäten*, Berlin 2000

Berlinische Galerie 1975
Berlinische Galerie. Sammlungen zur bildenden Kunst und Architektur des 19. Und 20. Jahrhunderts, Berlin [1975]

Berlinische Galerie 1979
Berlinische Galerie 1913–1933. Bestände: Malerei, Skulptur, Graphik. Berlin [1979]

Berlinische Galerie 1989
Berlinische Galerie (ed.), *Hannah Höch. Eine Lebenscollage*, vol. 1 (1889–1920), ed. by Cornelia Thater-Schulz, Berlin 1989

Berlinische Galerie 1990
Berlinische Galerie (ed.), *Berliner Kunststücke. Die Sammlung der Berlinischen Galerie* (exhib. cat. Leipzig, Museum der bildenden Künste; Berlin, Altes Museum), Berlin 1990

Berlinische Galerie 1995
Künstler-Archiv der Berlinischen Galerie (ed.), *Hannah Höch. Eine Lebenscollage*, vol. 2 (1921–1945), ed. by Ralf Burmeister and Eckhard Fürlus, Ostfildern-Ruit 1995; Part 1 (Texts), Part 2 (Documents)

Berlinische Galerie 2001
Künstler-Archive der Berlinischen Galerie (ed.), *Hannah Höch. Eine Lebenscollage*, vol. 3 (1946–1978), ed. by Ralf Burmeister with Eckhard Fürlus and Karin Hoerstel, Berlin 2001; Part 1 (Texts), Part 2 (Inventory List)

Billard 1998
Billard, Pierre, *Le mystère René Clair*, Paris 1998

Boersma 1997
Boersma, Linda Sandra, *Kasimir Malevich. de 0,10-tentoontstelling en de Große Berliner Kunstausstellung. Aspecten van een artistieke carrière*, Diss., Amsterdam 1997

Bruognolo 1988
Bruognolo, Bruno, "Der Wettbewerb der Chicago Tribune. '100 000 Dollar Preise für Architekten'. Die Wettbewerbsausschreibung", in: Bauhaus-Archiv 1988, pp. 284–298

Bruppacher 2014
Bruppacher, Paul, *Adolf Hitler und die Geschichte der NSDAP. Eine Chronik. Teil 1 1889–1937*, Norderstedt 2014

Bürger 1974
Bürger, Peter, *Theorie der Avantgarde*, Frankfurt/Main 1974

Bulhof 1992
Bulhof, Francis (ed.), *Eine Künstlerfreundschaft. Der Briefwechsel zwischen Fritz Stuckenberg und Paul van Ostaijen 1919–1927*, Oldenburg 1992

Bußmann 2004
Bußmann, Annette, *Zu Adaption und Demontage von Architekturgeschichte im 'Neuen Bauen' der Weimarer Republik. Alfred Gellhorn (1885–1972). Bauten, Projekte, Schriften 1920 bis 1933*, Diss., Marburg 2004; http://nbn-resolving.de/urn:nbn:de:hebis:04-z2006-07977 (Accessed: 9 May 2018)

Butting 1955
Butting, Max, *Musikgeschichte, die ich miterlebte*, Berlin 1955

C

Chytraeus-Auerbach 2018
Chytraeus-Auerbach, Irene, "German Expressionism in Italy. Herwarth Walden's Der Sturm, the Berlin Novembergruppe, and the Modernist Circles of Florence, Turin, and Rome", in: Isabel Wünsche (ed.), *The Routledge Companion to Expressionism in a Transnational Context*, London and New York 2018 [Forthcoming]

Columbia University 1963
Architecture 1918–1928. From the Novembergruppe to the C. I. A. M. (Functionalism and Expressionism). Modern Architecture Symposium Columbia University, 4–5 May 1962, New York 1963 (typescript)

Cossart 1985
Cossart, Axel von, *René Clair. Regisseur und Schriftsteller*, Cologne 1985

D

Daemgen 2011
Daemgen, Anke, "Die Neue Secession in Berlin", in: *Liebermanns Gegner. Die Neue Secession in Berlin und der Expressionismus* (exhib. cat. Berlin, Stiftung Brandenburger Tor, Max-Liebermann-Haus; Schleswig, Schloss Gottorf, Stiftung Schleswig-Holsteinische Landesmuseen), Cologne 2011, pp. 13–83

Dietze 1987
Dietze, Horst, "Arthur Segal und der Kunstverleih", in: Herzogenrath and Liska 1987, pp. 169–173

Dogramaci 2009
Dogramaci, Burcu, "Die zwiespältige Rezeption eines Bildhauers. Rudolf Belling und seine Plastik 'Dreiklang'", in: Uwe Fleckner (ed.), *Das verfemte Kunstwerk*, Berlin 2009, pp. 307–333

Düchting 1996
Düchting, Hajo, *Farbe am Bauhaus. Synthese und Synästhesie*, Berlin 1996

E

Eichhorn 2018
Eichhorn, Andreas, "Musik als bildende Kunst. Paul Bekkers Berliner Vortrag 'Wesensformen der Musik' (1925)", in: Grosch 2018, pp. 131–139

Elder, Richter and Eggeling 2007
Elder, R. Bruce, Hans Richter, Viking Eggeling, "The Dream of Universal Language and the Birth of the Absolute Film", in: Alexander Graf, Dietrich Scheunemann (eds.), *Avant-garde Film*, Amsterdam 2007, pp. 3–53

Erlhoff 1982
Erlhoff, Michael (ed.), *Raoul Hausmann. Texte bis 1933*; vol. 1 *Bilanz der Feierlichkeit*, vol. 2 *Sieg, Triumph, Tabak mit Bohnen*, Munich 1982

F

Finkeldey 1992
Finkeldey, Bernd, "Die 'I. Internationale Kunstausstellung' in Düsseldorf 28th May bis 3th July 1922", in: *Konstruktivistische internationale schöpferische Arbeitsgemeinschaft. 1922–1927. Utopien für eine europäische Kultur* (exhib. cat. Düsseldorf, Kunstsammlung Nordrhein-Westfalen; Halle, Staatliche Galerie Moritzburg), Stuttgart 1992, pp. 23–30

Fitzke 2015
Fitzke, Kirsten, "Der ewige Kampf gegen die Konkurrenz. Herwarth Walden und der politische Aufbruch der Avantgarde nach dem Ersten Weltkrieg", in: Henriette Herwig, Andrea von Hülsen-Esch (ed.), *Der Sturm. Literatur, Musik, Graphik und die Vernetzung in der Zeit des Expressionismus*, Berlin 2015, pp. 317–333

Foerster 1996
Foerster, Carolin, "Die Malerin Anne Ratkowski und die Entwicklung des 'Neuen Naturalismus'", in: *Anne Ratkowski. Eine vergessene Künstlerin der Novembergruppe* (exhib. cat. Berlin, Berlinische Galerie), Berlin 1996, pp. 25–66

Forgács 2003
Forgács, Éva, "Definitive Space. The Many Utopias of El Lissitzkys Proun Room", in: Nancy Perloff, Brian Reed (eds.), *Situating El Lissitzky. Vitebsk, Berlin, Moscow*, Los Angeles 2003, pp. 47–75

Freeman 1987
Freeman, Judi, "Léger's Ballet mécanique", in: Rudolf E Kuenzli, *Dada and Surrealist Film*, Cambridge, Massachusetts 1987, pp. 28–45

Friedel 1993
Friedel, Helmut (ed.), *Süddeutsche Freiheit. Kunst der Revolution in München 1919* (exhib. cat. Munich, Lenbachhaus), Munich 1993

Friedrich 2017
Friedrich, Julia (ed.), *Otto Freundlich. Kosmischer Kommunismus*, Munich 2017

G

Galerie Bodo Niemann 1993
Max Dungert 1896–1945. Ein Maler der Novembergruppe, with texts by Helga Kliemann and Adolf Behne (exhib. cat. Berlin, Galerie Bodo Niemann), Berlin 1993

Göckede 2008
Göckede, Regina, "Von 'Ringern' und anderen Beziehungsgeflechten des Neuen Bauens. Perspektiven einer netzwerktheoretisch generierten Analyse der Weimarer Architekturmoderne", in: *Jahrbuch zur Kultur und Literatur der Weimarer Republik*, vol. 12, 2008, pp. 225–258

Goergen 1989
Goergen, Jeanpaul, *Walter Ruttmann. Eine Dokumentation*, Berlin 1989

Goergen 2003
Goergen, Jeanpaul, *Hans Richter. Film ist Rhythmus*, Berlin 2003

Gottdang 2018
Gottdang, Andrea, "Die Schwierigkeit, Volk und Kunst zu vermischen. Die Führer durch die Abteilung der Novembergruppe auf der Großen Berliner Kunstausstellung 1920–1924", in: Grosch 2018, pp. 29–42

Graf 2007
Graf, Oskar Maria, *Gelächter von außen. Aus meinem Leben 1918–1933*, Munich 2007

Gropp 2000
Gropp, Birgit, *Studien zur Kunsthandlung Fritz Gurlitt in Berlin. 1880–1943*, Diss., Berlin 2000 (Microfiche)

Grosch 1998
Grosch, Nils, "Kurt Weill, die 'Novembergruppe' und die Probleme einer musikalischen Avantgarde in der Weimarer Republik", in: Heinz-Klaus Metzger, Reiner Riehn (ed.), *Kurt Weill. Die frühen Werke 1916–1928*, Musik-Konzepte, vol. 101–102, Munich 1998, pp. 65–83

Grosch 1999
Grosch, Nils, *Die Musik der Neuen Sachlichkeit*, Stuttgart and Weimar 1999

Grosch 2018
Grosch, Nils (ed.), *Novembergruppe 1918. Studien zu einer interdisziplinären Kunst für die Weimarer Republik*, Veröffentlichungen der Kurt-Weill-Gesellschaft Dessau, vol. 10, Münster 2018

Grosskopf 2015
Grosskopf, Anna, "Die Neue Secession", in: Hoffmann 2015, pp. 99–121

Grosz 1955
Grosz, George, *Ein kleines Ja, ein großes Nein: sein Leben von ihm selbst erzählt*, Hamburg 1955 [published in English under the title: *A Little Yes, a Big No. The Autobiography of George Grosz*. Illus. by the author. Trans. by Lola Sachs Dorin. New York 1946]

Guenther 1989
Guenther, Peter W., "Die Künstlergruppen. Ziele, Rhetorik, Echo", in: *Expressionismus. Die zweite Generation 1915–1925* (exhib. cat. Los Angeles County Museum of Art; Düsseldorf, Kunstmuseum et al.), Munich 1989, pp. 103–119 [published simultaneously in English under the title: *German Expressionism 1915–1925. The Second Generation*, Munich 1989]

Gülker 2001
Gülker, Bernd A., *Die verzerrte Moderne. Die Karikatur als populäre Kunstkritik in deutschen satirischen Zeitschriften*, Münster et al. 2001

H

Hamann 1997
Hamann, Albert, *Reformpädagogik und Kunsterziehung. Ästhetische Bildung zwischen Romantik, Reaktion und Moderne*, Innsbruck 1997

Hannemann 1993
Hannemann, Horst, [Entry] "Stoermer, Curt", in: Alken Bruns (ed.), *Lübecker Lebensläufe aus neun Jahrhunderten*, Neumünster 1993, pp. 378–382

Haupenthal 2004
Haupenthal, Uwe, "'Phantasien, die von den Dingen erlösen'. Anmerkungen zu Cesar Kleins Spätwerk", in: Uwe Haupenthal (ed.), *Cesar Klein 1876–1954. Metamorphosen*, Dresden 2004

Hecker 1994
Hecker, Wilhelm, "Der Komponist Philipp Jarnach", in: Jers 1994

Hein and Herzogenrath 1978
Hofmann, Justin, "Hans Richter – Filmemacher des Konstruktivismus", in: Herbert Gehr, Marion Hofacker (ed.), *Hans Richter. Malerei und Film* (exhib. cat. Frankfurt/Main, Filmmuseum), Frankfurt/Main 1989, pp. 9–15

Hemken 1990
Hemken, Kai-Uwe, *El Lissitzky. Revolution und Avantgarde*, Cologne 1990

Herzogenrath and Liska 1987
Herzogenrath, Wulf, Pavel Liska (ed.), *Arthur Segal 1875–1944* (exhib. cat. Cologne, Kölnischer Kunstverein Cologne et al.), Berlin 1987

Heusinger von Waldegg 1978
Heusinger von Waldegg, Joachim, *Otto Freundlich (1878–1943). Monographie mit Dokumentation und Werkverzeichnis* (exhib. cat. Cologne, Rheinisches Landesmuseum, et al.), Cologne 1978

Hinton 2000
Hinton, Stephen (ed.), *Kurt Weill. Gesammelte Schriften*, Mainz 2000

Hoek 2000
Hoek, Els (ed.), *Theo van Doesburg. Œuvre catalogue* (on the occasion of the exhib. *Theo van Doesburg. Painter, Poet, Architect*, Utrecht, Centraal Museum, Otterloo, Kröller-Müller Museum), Utrecht 2000

Hoffmann 1982
Hoffmann, Claus W. (ed.), *Hugo Häring in seiner Zeit. Bauen in unserer Zeit*, Biberach/Riss 1982

Hoffmann 2010
Hoffmann, Justin, "Vom Sturm zur Revolution. Politik und Kunst nach dem I. Weltkrieg", in: *Gesamtkunstwerk Expressionismus* (exhib. cat. Darmstadt, Mathildenhöhe), Ostfildern-Ruit 2010, pp. 142–150

Hoffmann 2015
Hoffmann, Tobias (ed.), *Zeitenwende. Von der Berliner Secession zur Novembergruppe* (exhib. cat. Berlin, Bröhan-Museum, Munich 2015

Hoffmann 2015a
Hoffmann, Tobias, "Suche nach Objektivität – Neue Sachlichkeit und Konstruktivismus", in: Hoffmann 2015, pp. 230–241

Hoffmann 2015b
Hoffmann, Tobias, "Die Ausstellung 1919. Die Gleichzeitigkeit des Ungleichzeitigen", in: Hoffmann 2015, pp. 200–228.

Hofmann 1989
Hofmann, Justin, "Hans Richter. Filmemacher des Konstruktivismus", in: Herbert Gehr, Marion Hofacker (eds.), *Hans Richter. Malerei und Film* (exhib. cat. Frankfurt/Main, Filmmuseum), Frankfurt/Main 1989, pp. 9–15

Holsten 1990
Holsten, Siegmar, *Georg Scholz. Gemälde, Zeichnungen, Druckgraphik*, Karlsruhe 1990

Hoormann 2003
Hoormann, Anne, *Lichtspiele. Zur Medienreflexion der Avantgarde in der Weimarer Republik*, Munich 2003

Horak 1995
Horak, Jan-Christopher (ed.), *Lovers of Cinema. The First American Film Avant-garde, 1919–1945*, Madison, Wisconsin 1995

Huse 1985
Huse, Norbert, *'Neues Bauen' 1918–1933. Moderne Architektur in der Weimarer Republik*, second revised and extended edition, Berlin 1985

Hütt 1990
Hütt, Wolfgang (ed.), *Hintergrund. Mit den Unzüchtigkeits- und Gotteslästerungsparagraphen des Strafgesetzbuches gegen Kunst und Künstler. 1900–1933*, Berlin 1990

I

Ilk 2013
Ilk, Michael (ed.), *Erich Buchholz 1891–1972. Catalogue Raisonné.* In collaboration with Ella Schrader-Buchholz und Albert Schrader (on the occasion of the exhib. *Erich Buchholz und die Avantgarde*, Ingolstadt, Museum für konkrete Kunst), Ingolstadt 2013

J

Jers 1994
Jers, Norbert (ed.), *Philipp Jarnach. Schriften zur Musik*, Beiträge zur rheinischen Musikgeschichte, vol. 153, Kassel 1994

Joedicke 1982
Joedicke, Jürgen (ed.), *Das andere Bauen. Gedanken und Zeichnungen*, Stuttgart 1982

Jong 2009
Jong, Karlijn de, *De Onafhankelijken 1919–1929. 'Onbevooroordeeld, belangeloos en Onafhankelijk'*, Master Thesis, Utrecht 2009

Joosten 1998
Joosten, Joop M., *Piet Mondrian. Catalogue raisonée of the work of 1911–1944*, Munich 1998

K

Kerbs 1976
Kerbs, Diethart (ed.), *Kind und Kunst. Eine Ausstellung zur Geschichte des Zeichen- und Kunstunterrichts*, vol. 1, Bund Deutscher Kunsterzieher, Berlin 1976

Kiening and Adolf 2012
Kiening, Christian, Heinrich Adolf (eds.), *Der absolute Film. Dokumente der Medienavantgarde (1912–1936)*, Zürich 2012

Kliemann 1969
Kliemann, Helga, *Die Novembergruppe*, Berlin 1969

Kranzfelder 1993
Kranzfelder, Ivo, *George Grosz 1893–1959*, Cologne 1993

Kratz-Kessemeier 2008
Kratz-Kessemeier, Kristina, *Kunst für die Republik. Die Kunstpolitik des preußischen Kultusministeriums 1918 bis 1932*, Berlin 2008

Kratz-Kessemeier 2010
Kratz-Kessemeier, Kristina, "Wer gestaltete die Kunstpolitik der Weimarer Republik? Zum Verhältnis von preußischem Kultusministerium und Reichskunstwart", in: Christian Welzbacher (ed.), *Der Reichskunstwart. Kulturpolitik und Staatsinszenierung in der Weimarer Republik 1918–1933*, Weimar 2010, pp. 232–252

Kratz-Kessemeier 2011
Kratz-Kessemeier, Kristina, "Justis Nationalgalerie und die republikanische Kunstpolitik", in: Kristina Kratz-Kessemeier, Tanja Moormann-Schulz (eds.), *Ludwig Justi. Kunst und Öffentlichkeit. Beiträge des Symposiums aus Anlaß des 50. Todestages von Ludwig Justi (1876–1957)*, 19th–20th October 2007, Jahrbuch der Berliner Museen, N. F., vol. 52, 2010, Beiheft, Berlin 2011 pp. 33–40

Kratz-Kessemeier 2013
Kratz-Kessemeier, Kristina, "'… um uns zu einer wirklich höheren Kultur emporzuarbeiten'. Kunstvermittlung als republikanisches Bildungskonzept des Weimarer Preußen", in: Joseph Imorde, Andreas Zeising (eds.), *Teilhabe am Schönen. Kunstgeschichte und Volksbildung zwischen Kaiserreich und Diktatur*, Weimar 2013, pp. 29–46

Kratz-Kessemeier 2015
Kratz-Kessemeier, Kristina, "'… um dem Talent Gelegenheiten zu eröffnen, frei nach seinem Gewissen zu schaffen'. Harry Graf Kessler und die preußische Kunstpolitik der Weimarer Republik", in: Julia Drost, Alexandre Kostka (eds.), *Harry Graf Kessler. Porträt eines europäischen Kulturvermittlers*, Passagen/Passages, vol. 52, Berlin and Munich 2015, pp. 221–240

Kremer 1985
Kremer, Sabine, *Hugo Häring (1882–1958). Wohnungsbau, Theorie und Praxis*, Stuttgart 1985

Kunstamt Wedding 1977
Die Novembergruppe. Tendenzen der Zwanziger Jahre. Teil 1. Die Maler [15. Europäische Kunstausstellung Berlin] (exhib. cat. Berlin, Kunstamt Wedding), Berlin 1977

Kunstsammlung Nordrhein-Westfalen 1992
Konstruktivistische internationale schöpferische Arbeitsgemeinschaft. 1922–1927. Utopien für eine europäische Kultur (exhib. cat. Düsseldorf, Kunstsammlung Nordrhein-Westfalen; Halle, Staatliche Galerie Moritzburg), Stuttgart 1992

L

Lach 1981
Lach, Friedhelm (ed.), *Kurt Schwitters. Das literarische Werk*, vol. 5 *Manifeste und kritische Prosa*, Cologne 1981

Lammert 1996
Lammert, Angela, "Max Liebermann und die Ausstellungen. Moderne und Antimoderne in der Akademie", in: *'Die Kunst hat nie ein Mensch allein besessen' 1696–1996. Dreihundert Jahre Akademie der Künste, Hochschule der Künste* (exhib. cat. Berlin, Akademie der Künste und Hochschule der Künste), Berlin 1996, pp. 491–504

Langner 2016ff.
Langner, Thomas-M., "Butting, Max", in: Laurenz Lütteken (ed.), *MGG Online*, Kassel, Stuttgart and New York 2016ff.; www.mgg-online.com/mgg/stable/17329 (Accessed: 11 June 2018)

Leistner 2007
Leistner, Gerhard, "Moriz Melzer. Stationen seines Lebens", in: *Moriz Melzer, Streben nach reiner Kunst. Werke von 1907 bis 1927* (exhib. cat. Regensburg, Kunstforum Ostdeutsche Galerie), Regensburg 2007, pp. 11–29

Leonhard 1997
Leonhard, Joachim-Felix (ed.), *Programmgeschichte des Hörfunks in der Weimarer Republik*, 2 vols., Munich 1997

Lerg 1980
Lerg, Winfried B., *Rundfunkpolitik in der Weimarer Republik*, Munich 1980

Leutloff 2011
Leutloff, Ariane, *Turmhaus, Großhaus, Wolkenschaber. Eine Studie zu Berliner Hochhausentwürfen der 1920er Jahre*, Kiel 2011

Ludwig 1993
Ludwig, Annette, "Provinz oder Metropole? Ein Exkurs über die Ortsgruppen und ihre Programmatik am Beispiel der Karlsruher 'Gruppe Rih'", in: Niemann 1993, pp. 23–27

M

Marx and Weber 2003
Marx, Andreas, Paul Weber, "Konventioneller Kontext der Moderne. Mies van der Rohes Haus Kemper 1921–23. Ausgangspunkt einer Neubewertung des Hochhauses Friedrichstraße", in: *Berlin in Geschichte und Gegenwart. Jahrbuch des Landesarchivs Berlin*, Berlin 2003, pp. 65–107

Mataré and Schilling 1997
Mataré, Sonja, Sabine Maja Schilling (eds.), *Ewald Mataré. Tagebücher 1915 bis 1965*, Cologne 1997

Matelowski 2007
Matelowski, Anke, *Berliner Künstlerleben. Fotografien und*

Dokumente des Vereins Berliner Künstler seit 1841, Berlin 2007

Matelowski 2017a
Matelowski, Anke, *Die Berliner Secession 1899–1937. Chronik, Kontext, Schicksal*, Wädenswil am Zürichsee 2017

Matelowski 2017b
Matelowski, Anke, "Greisenhaftes Gebilde oder Gesamtvertretung der Berliner Kunst? Der Verein Berliner Künstler in der Zeit des Nationalsozialismus", in: Verein Berliner Künstler, *Immer wieder zeitgenössisch. Texte und Materialien zum 175. Bestehen des Vereins Berliner Künstler*, Berlin 2017, pp. 22–37

Meinel 2007
Meinel, Sabine, "Zum Leben und Werk Karl Völkers", in: Klaus Völker, Bärbel Zausch (eds.), *Karl Völker. Utopie und Sachlichkeit*, Halle 2007

Meinel 2008
Meinel, Sabine, *Karl Völker. Leben und Werk*, Diss., Halle-Wittenberg 2008

Menting 2003
Menting, Annette, *Max Taut. Das Gesamtwerk*, Munich 2003

Mertins 2002
Mertins, Detlef, "Architektonik des Werdens. Mies van der Rohe und die Avantgarde", in: Riley and Bergdoll 2002, pp. 107–133

Moholy-Nagy 1972
Moholy-Nagy, Sibyl, *Laszlo Moholy-Nagy, ein Totalexperiment*, mit einem Vorwort von Walter Gropius, Berlin 1972

Moritz 1993
Moritz, William, "Oskar Fischinger", in: *Optische Poesie. Oskar Fischinger. Leben und Werk* (exhib. cat. Frankfurt/Main, Deutsches Filmmuseum), Frankfurt/Main 1993

Mülhaupt 2007
Mülhaupt, Freya, "Allem Jungem und Werdendem die Wege zu bahnen. Die Novembergruppe: Ein expressionistisches Projekt", in: *Moriz Melzer. Streben nach reiner Kunst. Werke von 1907 bis 1927* (exhib. cat. Regensburg, Kunstforum Ostdeutsche Galerie), Regensburg 2007, pp. 157–162

Müller 1992
Müller, Maria, "Der Kongress der 'Union internationaler fortschrittlicher Künstler' in Düsseldorf", in: Kunstsammlung Nordrhein-Westfalen 1992, pp. 17–22

Museum Kurhaus Kleve 2015
Ewald Mataré. Die Berliner Jahre 1907–32 (exhib. cat. Kleve, Museum Kurhaus, Ewald Mataré-Sammlung), Cologne 2015

Museum Villa Stuck 1985
Otto Dix 1891–1969 (exhib. cat. Munich, Museum Villa Stuck), Munich 1985

N

Nationalgalerie 1960
Berlin, Ort der Freiheit für die Kunst (exhib. cat. Berlin, Nationalgalerie der ehemals Staatlichen Museen Berlin; Berlin, Hochschule für bildende Künste), Berlin 1960

Nentwig 2015
Nentwig, Janina, "Art and Anti-Art in Berlin Around 1920. Dada and the Novembergruppe", in: Olaf Peters (ed.), *Berlin Metropolis 1918–1933* (exhib. cat. New York, Neue Galerie), Munich, London and New York 2015, pp. 36–57

Nentwig 2015a
Nentwig, Janina, "Die Novembergruppe", in: Hoffmann 2015, pp. 171–201

Nentwig 2018
Nentwig, Janina, "Revolution?! Dada, Arbeitsrat für Kunst und Novembergruppe", in: *The New Berlin* (exhib. cat. Brussels, Musées royaux des Beaux-Arts de Belgique), Brussels 2018 [Forthcoming]

Nentwig 2018a
Nentwig, Janina, "'Outsider und Bahnbrecher'. Die Ausstellungen der Novembergruppe 1918 bis 1932", in: Grosch 2018, pp. 9–28

Niemann 1993
Novembergruppe (exhib. cat. Berlin, Galerie Bodo Niemann), Berlin 1993

Nierendorf 1974
Heinrich Richter-Berlin (exhib. cat. Berlin, Galerie Nierendorf), Berlin 1974

Nierendorf 1985
Künstler der Novembergruppe (exhib. cat. Berlin, Galerie Nierendorf), Berlin 1985

Noll Brinckmann 1997
Noll Brinckmann, Christine "'Abstraktion' und 'Einfühlung' im deutschen Avantgardefilm der 20er Jahre", in: dies., *Die anthropomorphe Kamera und andere Schriften zur filmischen Narration*, Zürich 1997, pp. 247–275

Nungesser 1988
Nungesser, Michael, *Als die SA in den Saal marschierte ... Das Ende des Reichsverbandes bildender Künstler Deutschlands* (exhib. cat. Berlin, Staatliche Kunsthalle), Berlin (West) 1988

O

O'Konor 1971
O'Konor, Louise, *Viking Eggeling, 1880–1925. Artist and Filmmaker, Life and Work*, Stockholm 1971

Ohff 1968
Ohff, Heinz, *Hannah Höch*, hrsg. von Deutsche Gesellschaft für Bildende Kunst e.V., Berlin 1968

Orchard and Schulz 1998
Orchard, Karin, Isabel Schulz, *Kurt Schwitters. Werke und Dokumente. Verzeichnis der Bestände im Sprengel Museum Hannover*, Hanover 1998

P

Pabst 1985
Hans Siebert von Heister. Ein Maler der "Novembergruppe" (exhib. cat. Munich, Galerie Michael Pabst), Munich 1985

Pape 1994
Pape, Walter (ed.), *Joachim Ringelnatz. Das Gesamtwerk in sieben Bänden*, Zürich 1994

Pehnt 1970
Pehnt, Wolfgang (ed.), *Aus neuen Sachbüchern. Helga Kliemann. Die Novembergruppe*, Deutschlandfunk, Typoskript, Sendung am 14. Februar 1970

Pfefferkorn 1962
Pfefferkorn, Rudolf, *Cesar Klein*, Berlin 1962

Pfefferkorn 1975
Pfefferkorn, Rudolf, *Œuvrekatalog Cesar Klein*, Berlin 1975

Pfefferkorn 1977
Pfefferkorn, Rudolf, "Die Novembergruppe. Programm und Weg", in: Kunstamt Wedding 1977, pp. 5–23

Plüm 2013
Plüm, Kerstin (ed.), *Mies van der Rohe im Diskurs. Innovationen – Haltungen – Werke. Aktuelle Positionen*, Bielefeld 2013

Poppelreuther 2003
Poppelreuther, Tanja, *Das Neue Bauen für den Neuen Menschen. Zur Wandlung und Wirkung des Menschenbildes in der Architektur der 1920er Jahre in Deutschland*, Hildesheim, Zürich and New York 2003

Prange 2000
Prange, Regine, "Architekturphantasie ohne Architektur? Der Arbeitsrat für Kunst und seine Ausstellungen", in: Thorsten Scheer, Josef Kleihues, Paul Kahlfeldt (eds.), *Stadt der Architektur, Architektur der Stadt. Berlin 1900–2000* (exhib. cat. Berlin, Neues Museum), Berlin 2000, pp. 93–103

Prelinger 1977
Prelinger, Elizabeth Anne, *The November Group. The Dilemma of Avantgarde Art and Politics in the Weimar Republic*, Diss., Cambridge/Massachusetts 1977

R

Ragazzi 2008
Ragazzi, Franco, "Giorgio de Chirico and the Exhibitions of the 'Novecento Italiano'", in: *Metafisica* 7–8, 2008, pp. 233–262

Rajewsky 2002
Rajewsky, Irina O., *Intermedialität*, Tübingen 2002

Richter 1973
Richter, Hans, *Begegnungen von Dada bis heute. Briefe, Dokumente, Erinnerungen*, Cologne 1973

Riha and Kämpf 1992
Riha, Karl, Günter Kämpf (eds.), *Raoul Hausmann. Am Anfang war Dada*, 3., completely revised ed., Gießen 1992

Riley and Bergdoll 2002
Riley, Terence, Barry Bergdoll (eds.), *Mies in Berlin. Ludwig Mies van der Rohe. Die Berliner Jahre 1907–1938* (exhib. cat. New York, Museum of Modern Art; Staatliche Museen zu Berlin, Altes Museum;

Barcelona, Fundacion La Caixa), Munich et al. 2002 [published simultaneously in English: *Mies in Berlin*, New York 2001]

Robbers 2013
Robbers, Lutz, "Filmkämpfer Mies", in: Plüm 2013, pp. 63–95

Roters 1989
Roters, Eberhard, "Novembergruppe", in: *Freiheit, Gleichheit, Brüderlichkeit. Künstlergruppen in Deutschland 1918–1923* (exhib. cat. Recklinghausen, Städtische Kunsthalle), Recklinghausen 1989, unpag.

Roters 1995
Roters, Eberhard, "Novembergruppe", in: Berlinische Galerie 1995, 1. Abt., pp. 74–96

Rotthaler 2003
Rotthaler, Viktor (ed.), *Marcellus Schiffer – Heute Nacht oder nie. Tagebücher, Erzählungen, Gedichte, Zeichnungen*, Berlin 2003

Rudert 2012
Rudert, Konstanze (ed.), *Im Netzwerk der Moderne. Kirchner, Braque, Kandinsky, Klee, Richter, Bacon, Altenbourg und ihr Kritiker Will Grohmann* (on the occasion of the exhib., Dresden, Staatliche Kunstsammlungen, Kunsthalle im Lipsiusbau), Munich 2012

Rudert 2012a
Rudert, Konstanze (ed.) für die Staatlichen Kunstsammlungen Dresden, *Will Grohmann. Texte zur Kunst der Moderne*, bearbeitet von Volkmar Billig, Munich 2012

Rüdiger 1999
Rüdiger, Ulrike, "Gera und die Moderne. Streifzüge durch die expressionistische Provinz", in: Cornelia Nowak, Kai Uwe Schierz, Justus H. Ulbricht (eds.), *Expressionismus in Thüringen. Facetten eines kulturellen Aufbruchs* (Ausst.-Kat. Erfurt, Galerie am Fischmarkt), Erfurt 1999, pp. 60–73

S

Saehrendt 2005
Saehrendt, Christian, *"Die Brücke" zwischen Staatskunst und Verfemung. Expressionistische Kunst als Politikum in der Weimarer Republik, im "Dritten Reich" und im Kalten Krieg*, Pallas Athene, vol. 13, Stuttgart 2005

Salmen 1988
Salmen, Walter, *Das Konzert. Eine Kulturgeschichte*, Munich 1988

Schebera 1990
Schebera, Jürgen, *Kurt Weill*, Mainz 1990

Scheugl and Schmidt 1974
Scheugl, Hans, Ernst Schmidt, *Eine Subgeschichte des Films. Lexikon des Avantgarde-, Experimental- und Undergroundfilms*, 2 vols., Frankfurt/Main 1974

Schilling 1987
Schilling, Sabine Maja (ed.), *Ewald Mataré. Das plastische Werk. Werkverzeichnis* (on the occasion of Ewald Mataré's one hundredth birthday and the exhibition of the Archdiocese and the Artists' Union of Cologne at the Kölnischer Kunstverein), Cologne 1987

Schirren and Claus 2001
Schirren, Matthias, Sylvia Claus, *Hugo Häring. Architekt des neuen Bauens 1882–1958* (exhib. cat. Berlin, Akademie der Künste), Ostfildern-Ruit 2001

Schlösser 1979
Schlösser, Manfred (ed.), *Für Heinz Tiessen, 1887–1971. Aufsätze, Analysen, Briefe, Erinnerungen, Dokumente, Werkverzeichnis, Bibliographie*, Schriftenreihe der Akademie der Künste, vol. 13, Berlin 1979

Scholz 2017
Scholz, Dieter, "Sculpturen 1924. Rudolf Belling und die Nationalgalerie", in: Dieter Scholz, Christina Thomson (eds.), *Rudolf Belling. Skulpturen und Architekturen* (exhib. cat. Berlin, Staatliche Museen zu Berlin, Nationalgalerie), Munich 2017, pp. 31–75

Schrader and Schebera 1987
Schrader, Bärbel, Jürgen Schebera, *Kunstmetropole Berlin 1918–1933. Die Kunststadt in der Novemberrevolution, die "goldenen" Zwanziger, die Kunststadt in der Krise*, Berlin and Weimar 1987

Schulz 1993
Schulz, Armin, "Hinein in die Menschheitswogen", in: Niemann 1993, pp. 9–21

Schulz 2011
Schulz, Isabel (ed.), *Anna Blume und ich. Zeichnungen von Kurt Schwitters*, Ostfildern 2011

Schulze 1974
Schulze, Ingrid, "Karl Völker und die 'Hallische Künstlergruppe' in ihrer Zusammenarbeit mit der kommunistischen Presse", in: Staatliche Galerie Moritzburg (ed.), *Karl Völker. Leben und Werk*, Halle 1974, pp. 9–16

Schulze 1974a
Schulze, Ingrid, "Zum Verhältnis zwischen Mensch und Arbeit in der frühen proletarisch-revolutionären Kunst Halles", in: Staatliche Galerie Moritzburg (ed.), *Karl Völker. Leben und Werk*, Halle 1974, pp. 17–21

Schulze 1986
Schulze, Franz, *Mies van der Rohe. Leben und Werk*, Berlin 1986 [also published in English under the title: *Mies van der Rohe. A Critical Biography*, Chicago 1985]

Schuster 1994
Peter-Klaus Schuster (ed.), *George Grosz. Berlin – New York* (exhib. cat. Berlin, Neue Nationalgalerie; Düsseldorf, Kunstsammlung Nordrhein-Westfalen), Berlin 1994

Schwarz 1998
Schwarz, Birgit, "Wie der 'Furor Teutonicus' Dada den Weg bahnte. Corinth, Dix und die Berliner Secession", in: *Marburger Jahrbuch für Kunstwissenschaft*, vol. 25, 1998, pp. 133–147

Shapiro 1976
Shapiro, Theda, *Painters and Politics. The European Avant-Garde and Society 1900–1925*, New York, Oxford and Amsterdam 1976

Söll 2012
Änne Söll, "'Neue Männlichkeit'. Die Matrosenbilder von Otto Dix", in: *Das Auge der Welt. Otto Dix und die Neue Sachlichkeit* (exhib. cat. Stuttgart, Kunstmuseum), Ostfildern 2012, pp. 48–60

Stapper 2001
Stapper, Michael, *Unterhaltungsmusik im Rundfunk der Weimarer Republik*, Würzburger musikhistorische Beiträge, vol. 24, Tutzing 2001

Stasny 2000
Stasny, Peter, "Die Farbenlichtspiele", in: Andreas Hapkemeyer, Peter Stasny (eds.), *Ludwig Hirschfeld-Mack. Bauhäusler und Visionär* (exhib. cat. Bozen, Museion – Museum für Moderne Kunst; Vienna, Jüdisches Museum der Stadt Wien; Frankfurt/Main, Jüdisches Museum der Stadt Frankfurt), Ostfildern 2000, pp. 94–112

Steinkamp 2013
Steinkamp, Maike, "Ludwig Justi und die 'soziale Kunstpflege'", in: Joseph Imorde, Andreas Zeising (eds.), *Teilhabe am Schönen. Kunstgeschichte und Volksbildung zwischen Kaiserreich und Diktatur*, Weimar 2013, pp. 285–298

Steneberg 1987
Steneberg, Eberhard, *Arbeitsrat für Kunst. Berlin 1918–1921*, Düsseldorf 1987

Sternfeld 2004
Sternfeld, Felicia H., *Georg Scholz (1890–1945). Monographie und Werkverzeichnis*, Frankfurt/M. et al. 2004

Straaten 1983
Straaten, Evert van (ed.), *Theo van Doesburg 1883–1931. Een documentaire op basis van materiaal uit de schenking van Moorsel*, 's-Gravenhage 1983

Stuckenschmidt 1979
Stuckenschmidt, Hans Heinz, *Zum Hören geboren. Ein Leben mit der Musik unserer Zeit*, Munich 1979

Sudhalter 2017
Sudhalter, Adrian, "Friedrichstraße. Die Kontexte eines Bildes, 1922–24", in: Andreas Beitin, Wolf Eiermann, Brigitte Franzen (eds.), *Mies van der Rohe. Montage Collage* (on the occasion of the exhib. *Mies van der Rohe. Die Collagen aus dem MoMA*, Aachen, Ludwig Forum; Schweinfurt, Museum Geog Schäfer), London 2017, pp. 68–85

T

Tegethoff 1981
Tegethoff, Wolf, *Mies van der Rohe. Die Villen und Landhausprojekte*, Essen 1981

Thomas 1969
Thomas, Helmut, *Otto Möller*, Kunstblätter der Galerie Nierendorf, Nr. 16, Berlin 1969

Thomson 2017
Thomson, Christina, "Bewegte Form – Umkämpfter Raum. Tanz und Kampf in den Skulpturen von Rudolf Belling", in: Dieter Scholz, Christina Thomson (eds.), *Rudolf Belling. Skulpturen und Architekturen* (exhib. cat. Berlin, National-

galerie, Staatliche Museen zu Berlin), Munich 2017, pp. 90–107

Thrun 1995
Thrun, Martin, *Neue Musik im deutschen Musikleben bis 1933*, 2 vols., Bonn 1995

Tiessen 1953
Tiessen, Heinz, *Musik der Natur*, Freiburg 1953

Tupitsyn 2002
Tupitsyn, Margarita, *Malevich and Film*, New Haven, Connecticut 2002

U

Ullmann 1978
Ullmann, Helga, *Karl Völker*, ed. by Staatlicher Kunsthandel der DDR, Halle c. 1978

V

Vakar and Mikhienko 2015
Vakar, Irina A., Tatiana N. Mikhienko (eds.), *Kazimir Malevich. Letters, Documents, Memoirs, Criticism*, 2 vols., London 2015

Vogel 2008
Vogel, Christian, *Werben für Weimar. Der "Werbedienst der deutschen sozialistischen Republik" in der Novemberrevolution 1918–19*, Berichte aus der Kunstgeschichte, Aachen 2008

W

Wandschneider and Götte 1993
Wandschneider, Andrea, Gisela Götte (eds.), *Fritz Stuckenberg 1881–1944* (exhib. cat. Delmenhorst, Städtische Galerie), Berlin 1993

Weber 2013
Weber, Paul, "Ludwig Mies van der Rohes frühe Architekturentwürfe und Hans Vaihingers Philosophie des Als Ob", in: Plüm 2013, pp. 13–62

Weinstein 1990
Weinstein, Joan, *The End of Expressionism. Art and the November Revolution in Germany 1918–19*, Chicago 1990

Weipert 2015
Weipert, Axel, *Die Zweite Revolution. Rätebewegung in Berlin 1919/1920*, Berlin 2015

Weiss 1996
Weiss, Stefan, *Die Musik Philipp Jarnachs*, Cologne 1996

Weissweiler 2009
Weissweiler, Lilli, *Futuristen auf Europa-Tournee. Zur Vorgeschichte, Konzeption und Rezeption der Ausstellungen futuristischer Malerei (1911–1913)*, Bielefeld 2009

Wendermann 2007
Wendermann, Gerda, *Der Internationale Kongress der Konstruktivisten und Dadaisten in Weimar im September 1922. Versuch einer Chronologie der Ereignisse*; https://sprengel-museum.de/bilderarchiv/sprengel_deutsch/download¬dokumente/pdf/ks2007_wendermann_kongress.pdf (Accessed: 8/2/2018)

Westermann 1990
Westermann, Klaus (ed.), *Joseph Roth, Werke 2. Das journalistische Werk 1924–1928*, Cologne 1990

Whyte 1981
Whyte, Iain Boyd, *Bruno Taut. Baumeister einer neuen Welt. Architektur und Aktivismus 1914–1920*, Stuttgart 1981

Wiese 1989
Wiese, Stephan von, "Sturm durch diese Welt. Die internationale Zielrichtung des Expressionismus", in: Stephanie Barron (ed.), *Expressionismus. Die zweite Generation 1915–1925* (Ausst.-Kat. Los Angeles, Los Angeles County Museum of Art et al.), Munich 1989, pp. 121–127

Wietek 1980
Wietek, Gerhard, *Georg Tappert 1880–1957. Ein Wegbereiter der Deutschen Moderne*, Munich 1980

Wilhelmi 1996
Wilhelmi, Christoph, *Künstlergruppen in Deutschland, Österreich und der Schweiz seit 1900. Ein Handbuch*, Stuttgart 1996

Wilmesmeier 1994
Wilmesmeier, Holger, *Deutsche Avantgarde und Film. Die Filmatinee "Der Absolute Film" 3. und 10. Mai 1925*, Münster 1994

Winkler 2009
Winkler, Klaus-Jürgen, "Das Staatliche Bauhaus und die Negation der klassischen Tradition in der Baukunst. Die Architekturausstellungen in Weimar – 1919, 1922, 1923", in: Hellmuth Th. Seemann, Thorsten Valk (eds.), *Klassik und Avantgarde. Das Bauhaus in Weimar 1919–1925*, Göttingen 2009, pp. 261–284

Wittenbrink 2001
Wittenbrink, Theresa, "Carl Zuckmayer im Rundfunk der Weimarer Republik", in: *Carl Zuckmayer und die Medien. Beiträge zu einem internationalen Symposion*, 2 vols., Zuckmayer Jahrbuch, vol. 4, St. Ingbert 2001

Wittenbrink 2006
Wittenbrink, Theresa, *Schriftsteller vor dem Mikrophon. Autorenauftritte im Rundfunk der Weimarer Republik 1924–1932. Eine Dokumentation*, Berlin 2006

Wolf 1989
Wolf, Eva, "Von der universellen zur poetischen Sprache", in: Herbert Gehr, Marion Hofacker (eds.), *Hans Richter. Malerei und Film* (exhib. cat. Frankfurt/Main, Filmmuseum), Frankfurt/Main 1989, pp. 16–23

Wulf 1966
Wulf, Joseph, *Die Bildenden Künste im Dritten Reich. Eine Dokumentation*, Reinbek 1966 (Original edition: Gütersloh 1963)

Wünsche 2015
Wünsche, Isabel, "Der Sturm und Die Abstrakten. Internationale Vereinigung der Expressionisten, Futuristen, Kubisten und Konstruktivisten e.V.", in: Henriette Herwig, Andrea von Hülsen-Esch (eds.), *Der Sturm. Literatur, Musik, Graphik und die Vernetzung in der Zeit des Expressionismus*, Berlin 2015, pp. 357–375

Z

Zeising 2018
Zeising, Andreas, "Arthur Segal und die Kunst der Vermittlung", in: Grosch 2018, pp. 61–75

Zepter 2012
Zepter, Michael Cornelius, *Maskerade. Künstlerkarneval und Künstlerfeste in der Moderne*, Vienna, Cologne and Weimar 2012

Zglinicki 1956
Zglinicki, Friedrich von, *Der Weg des Films. Die Geschichte der Kinematographie und ihre Vorläufer*, Berlin 1956

Zuschlag 1995
Zuschlag, Christoph, *'Entartete Kunst'. Ausstellungsstrategien im Nazi-Deutschland*, Worms 1995

The Authors

SARA BEIMDIEKE studied school music and English before completing a doctoral thesis in music history on Ernst Krenek's relationship with television and his first television opera *Ausgerechnet und Verspielt* (*Computed and Confounded*, 1961). She is currently a research fellow at the University of Siegen's Chair of Historical Musicology. Her present research centres on musical theatre and mediality and on twentieth-century Austrian composers.

RALF BURMEISTER heads the Artists' Archives at the Berlinische Galerie. The doctor in art history has published the posthumous papers of Hannah Höch, co-edited the bio-bibliographic lexicon on Raoul Hausmann and written numerous essays, in particular on Dada. He curated the retrospective *Hannah Höch: All Beginning is DADA!* (2007), co-curated the exhibitions *Vienna Berlin: The Art of Two Cities* (2013, Belvedere, Vienna, and Berlinische Galerie) and *Dada Africa: Dialogue with the Other* (2016, Museum Rietberg, Zürich, and Berlinische Galerie) and teaches at the Humboldt University in Berlin.

NILS GROSCH studied musicology, history and German in Bochum and Freiburg (Breisgau); he wrote his doctoral thesis on the music of New Objectivity at the University of Freiburg and his post-doctoral treatise on song, the media shift and popular culture during the sixteenth century at the University of Basel. He holds the Chair of Musicology at the University of Salzburg, where he also heads the Department of Art History, Musicology and Dance Studies and the Gluck Research Centre for Musical Theatre. In addition, he chairs the Expert Advisory Board of the Kurt-Weill-Gesellschaft in Dessau. Principal research themes are music and migration, popular musical theatre, and music and media.

THOMAS KÖHLER graduated in art history, classical archaeology and Romance languages in Frankfurt (Main) in 1994, obtaining his doctorate from the University of Darmstadt in 2003. He was a researcher at the Museum für Moderne Kunst in Frankfurt, curator in residence at the Whitney Museum of American Art in New York, programme director at documenta X in Kassel, acting director of the Kunstmuseum Wolfsburg and from 2008 to 2010 deputy director at the Berlinische Galerie, where he was in charge of the collections and the exhibition programme before being appointed on 1 September 2010 as director of Berlin's Museum of Modern Art, Photography and Architecture.

KRISTINA KRATZ-KESSEMEIER works in Berlin as a freelance historian, art historian and editor. She studied history, art history and journalism in Münster and at the Freie Universität in Berlin. Since obtaining her doctorate in Berlin in 2005 for a thesis on the art policy of the Prussian Ministry of Culture between 1918 and 1932 ("Art for the Republic", 2008), she has organized many conferences and publications on cultural and museum history in the nineteenth and twentieth centuries, including on Ludwig Justi, museums under the Nazis, the Berlin art dealer Paul Graupe, the Deutscher Museumsbund (Association of German Museums), education and architecture strategies in museums after 1945 and—a recurrent theme—public art policy in the Weimar Republic.

JANINA NENTWIG is an art historian and writer with a particular focus on classical modernism. She studied art history, European ethnology and communication studies in Münster and Vienna, obtaining her doctorate at the University of Münster with a thesis on the depiction of nudes in New Objectivity (2008). From 2005 to 2007 she was a trainee curator at the Berlinische Galerie, where she was part of the research team for the exhibition *Hannah Höch: All Beginning is DADA!* (2007). From 2015 to 2017 she conducted a research project devoted to the Novembergruppe funded by the Gerda Henkel Stiftung.

NUNO DE BRITO ROCHA studied architecture and urban design at the University of São Paulo and the Technische Universität in Berlin, completing his MA in art and visual history at Berlin's Humboldt University. A DAAD scholarship took him to Stanford University in Palo Alto for his MA dissertation on *The Floating Museum, by Lynn Hershman Leeson*. He worked as an assistant curator at the Museu da Casa Brasileira in São Paulo (including the show on Lina Bo Bardi, 2014) and was part of the team for *Dada Africa: Dialogue with the Other* (2016) at the Berlinische Galerie, where he became a trainee curator in 2017.

JUSCHKA MARIE VON RÜDEN studied art history and curatorial studies at the Université Paris-Sorbonne and museology at the École du Louvre. She was an assistant curator at the Centre Pompidou, Paris (2015–16) and the Palais de Tokyo (2017). She has been working at the Berlinische Galerie as a trainee curator since 2017. Her monograph *Franz West: Du Passstück à la Legitime Skulptur. Invention d'une sculpture interactive* (1973–1990) appeared in *Octopus-notes*, no. 7, in 2016.

ISABEL WÜNSCHE has been a professor of art history at the Jacobs University in Bremen since 2001. She studied art history, classical and Christian archaeology, and received her doctorate in 1997 at the University of Heidelberg for a thesis on the Russian avant-garde. Her research focusses are the art of the classical modern era and European avant-garde movements. Her most recent book publications are *Practices of Abstract Art: Between Anarchism and Appropriation* (Cambridge Scholars 2016) and *The Routledge Companion to Expressionism in a Transnational Context* (Routledge 2018).

ANDREAS ZEISING studied art history, philosophy and German and wrote his doctoral thesis on the art critic Karl Scheffler (1869–1951). After completing a museum traineeship in Düsseldorf, he lectured and took interim academic posts in Düsseldorf, Wuppertal, Dortmund, Siegen, Bremen and Bonn. He is now a lecturing researcher at the Chair of Art History at the University of Siegen. In 2016 he successfully completed his post-doctoral treatise on broadcasting about art in the early years of radio.

Copyrights

Picture credits

© 2018 for the reproduced works of Rudolf Ausleger, Rudolf Belling, Carlo Carrà, Marc Chagall, Otto Dix, Curt Ehrhardt, Conrad Felixmüller, Ernst Fritsch, Peter Ludwig Foerster, Walter Gropius, Hugo Häring, Hannah Höch, César Klein, Ewald Mataré, Ludwig Mies van der Rohe, Otto Nagel, J.J.P. Oud, Francis Picabia, Iwan Puni, Kurt Schwitters, Georg Tappert: VG Bild-Kunst, Bonn

© 2018 for the reproduced works of George Grosz: Estate of George Grosz, Princeton, N.J. and VG Bild-Kunst, Bonn
John Heartfield: The Heartfield Community of Heirs and VG Bild-Kunst, Bonn

© 2018 for the reproduced works of Otto Bartning: legal successors of Otto Bartning; Henryk Berlewi: Henryk Berlewi Archive; Walter Dexel: joint heirs of Walter Dexel; Heinrich Ehmsen: estate of Heinrich Ehmsen; Heinz Fuchs: Fuchs family and Anna-Dorothea Klein; Alfred Gellhorn: Peter Gellhorn; Paul Grunwaldt: legal successors of Paul Grunwaldt, Hans Siebert von Heister: legal successors of Hans Siebert von Heister; Else Hertzer: joint heirs of Else Hertzer; Lothar Homeyer: legal successors of Lothar Homeyer; Bernhard Klein: Karsch–Nierendorf collection; Heinrich Kosina: legal successors of Heinrich Kosina, Issai Kulvianski: estate of Kulvianski; Hans and Wassili Luckhardt: Adelheid Freese; Moriz Melzer: legal successors of Moriz Melzer; Erich Mendelsohn: Daria Joseph; Otto Möller: Christoph Möller, Dießen/Ammersee; Johannes Molzahn: Johannes-Molzahn-Centrum für Dokumentation und Publikation® in D 34131 Kassel; Franz Mutzenbecher: Elisbeth Richter-Mutzenbecher, Mathilde Rienau; Ernst Neuschul: Khalil Norland and Misha Norland; Georg Pahl: Georg Pahl; Max Pechstein: 2018 Pechstein Hamburg/Tökendorf; László Péri: legal successors of László Péri; Hans Richter: Estate Hans Richter; Emy Roeder: Museum im Kulturspeicher Würzburg together with the estate of Emy Roeder; Wilhelm Schmid: Museo Wilhelm Schmid, Brè sopra Lugano; Lasar Segall: Museu Lasar Segall; Soichi Sunami: Sunami Family; Max Taut: Christine and Jenny Schily; Karl Völker: estate of Karl Völker

Photo credits

© Akademie der Künste, Berlin: 152–159, 162 left, 254–255
© akg-images: 112
© Kai-Annett Becker: 22, 37 right, 58, 59 below, 61-63, 69, 71, 73, 74 above right, 78, 79, 92, 93, 114, 115, 124, 125, 127, 128, 135 below, 136, 137, 163 below left, 212 left, 213 left, 217, 219, 221 left, 223, 231, 234 left
© Architekturmuseum TU Berlin, inv. no. F 1569: 162 right
© Architekturmuseum TU Berlin, inv. no. 2809: 160
© Archiv der Moderne, Weimar: 166
© Bauhaus-Archiv Berlin: 252
© Bauhaus-Archiv Berlin, photograph: Felix Jork: 161
© Fotostudio Bartsch, Karen Bartsch, Berlin: 122
© Octavian Beldiman: 134 left
© Berlinische Galerie, Berlin: 2, 12 left, 23, 25, 46 left, 87 right, 118 left, 119, 126 left, 142 right, 147 middle, 147 right, 186 left, 187 left, 189, 190 middle, 196 left, 196 middle, 197 right, 200 right, 214 left, 227 left, 229, 235 left, 237 left, 239 left, 239 middle, 241 left, 242 right, 243 left, 253
© bpk: 83 left, 201 middle
© bpk/CNAC-MNAM/Adam Rzepka: 108 right
© bpk/Dietmar Katz: 242 left
© bpk/Hamburger Kunsthalle/Elke Walford: 135 above right
© bpk/Kupferstichkabinett, SMB/Jörg P. Anders: 116, 117
© bpk/Kupferstichkabinett, SMB/Volker-H. Schneider: 99
© bpk/Nationalgalerie, SMB: 212 right
© bpk/Nationalgalerie, SMB/Jörg P. Anders: 211, 221 right
© bpk/Nationalgalerie, SMB/Klaus Göken: 126 right, 208, 215
© bpk/Nationalgalerie, SMB/Andres Kilger: 74 above left, 138, 163 right
© bpk/Nationalgalerie, SMB/Reinhard Saczewski: 139
© bpk/Nationalgalerie, SMB/Volker-H. Schneider: 66
© bpk/Nationalgalerie, SMB/Jens Ziehe: 75 right
© bpk/Staatsgalerie Stuttgart: 201 left, 213 right
© bpk/Sprengel Museum Hannover/Michael Herling/Aline Gwose: 97, 98
© bpk/Sprengel Museum Hannover/Michael Herling/Benedikt Werner/Aline Gwose: 74 below, 220 left
© bpk/Zentralarchiv, SMB: 36 middle and right, 37 left, 186 right, 203 right, 234 right
© Bundesarchiv: 106 right, 196 right, 197 left, 239 right
© Bundesarchiv/Scherl: 48 right, 102/103, 228 left, 232, 233, 236 right
© Collection Cinémathèque Royale – Royal Film Archive, all rights reserved: 81 left
© Peter Cox: 48 left
© Deutsches Historisches Museum, Berlin: 24 above, 49 middle
© Deutsches Historisches Museum, Berlin/I. Desnica: 26, 27
© Deutsches Historisches Museum, Berlin/S. Ahlers: 24 below
© Deutsches Literaturarchiv Marbach: 171 second from right, 226 right, 240 left
© Anja Elisabeth Witte: 11, 12 right, 28, 32 middle, 35 left and right, 36 left, 49 left and right, 52 second from left, 64, 70, 85, 87 left, 106 left, 108 left, 110, 111, 142 left, 165, 167, 179 right, 185, 187 middle and right, 190 left, 192/193, 201 right, 203 left, 222, 227 right, 230, 235 right, 236 left, 243 right
© Bernd Fickert: 100 left, 101
© Joachim Fliegner: 65
© Fondazione Torino Musei, Studio Fotografico Gonella 2013: 83 right
© Sammlung Uwe Gerber, Berlin: 237 right
© Germanisches Nationalmuseum Nürnberg, Deutsches Kunstarchiv: 226 left
© Photograph: Klaus E. Göltz: 131, 209
© Markus Hawlik: 18–19, 29
© Collection Het Nieuwe Instituut/OUDJ, cu7: 120 above
© Friedhelm Hoffmann, Berlin: 59 above, 67
© Collection Kröller-Müller Museum, Otterlo, the Netherlands, Van Moorsel donation to the Dutch State 1981: 109
© Photograph: Kulturstiftung Sachsen-Anhalt: 130
© Photograph: Kunsthalle Mannheim, Cem Yücetas: 75 left, 144 left
© Kunstmuseum Stuttgart: 88
© Günter Ladwig: 135 above left
© Mediathek des Instituts für Kunst- und Bildgeschichte der Humboldt-Universität zu Berlin: 143 middle
© Museum Kurhaus Kleve – Ewald Mataré-Sammlung, Kleve: 133
© Museum Kurhaus Kleve – Ewald Mataré-Sammlung, Kleve (photography: Annegret Gossens, 2012): 134 right
© 2018 The Museum of Modern Art, New York/Scala, Florenz: 143 left, 143 right, 144 middle, 164, 200 left
© Museum Wiesbaden, photograph: Bernd Fickert: 60
© Photograph: Jürgen Musolf, Germanisches Nationalmuseum: 72 left
© Photograph Jörg Müller: 52 left
© Khalil Norland: 224–225, 248–249
© Osthaus Museum Hagen, photograph: Friedrich Rosenstiel, Köln: 113
© Photo von Oven, Delmenhorst: 220 right
© Photograph: Punctum/Bertram Kober: 56 above
© Rheinisches Bildarchiv Köln, www.museenkoeln.de/rba.de: 123
© Ilona Ripke: 163 above left
© M. Runge: 57
© Scherl/Süddeutsche Zeitung Photo: 169 left
© Corinne Schweizer and Peter Böhm: 169 middle and right
© Bernd Sinterhauf, Berlin: 76, 77, 81 right
© Stadtmuseum Jena: 120 right
© Staatliche Museen zu Berlin, Kunstbibliothek: 190 right, 240 right, 241 right
© Stiftung Deutsche Kinemathek: 171 left, 171 second from left
© Stadtmuseum Berlin: 228 right
© Collection Stedelijk Museum, Amsterdam: 144 right
© Stiftung Stadtmuseum Berlin, reproduction: Christel Lehmann, Berlin: 52 second from right
© Stiftung Stadtmuseum Berlin, reproduction: Michael Setzpfandt, Berlin: 40–41, 46 right, 129
© Technische Universität Berlin: 52 right, 179 left
© ullstein bild – John Graudenz: 72 right
© ullstein bild – Robert Sennecke: 50 left
© ullstein bild – Süddeutsche Zeitung Photo/Scherl: 32 left
© ullstein bild – ullstein bild: 50 right, 147 left
© Von der Heydt-Museum Wuppertal, photograph: Antje Zeis-Loi, Medienzentrum Wuppertal: 95, 121

From published sources

© *Fünfundneunzig Köpfe von Orlik.* With a foreword by Max Osborn, Berlin 1920, p. 13: 32 right
© Max Dungert, *20 Köpfe*, with a foreword by Otto Brattskoven, Berlin 1925, p. 11: 35 middle

Colophon

This catalogue is published to accompany the exhibition

Freedom: The Art of the Novembergruppe 1918–1935
9 November 2018 – 11 March 2019

Berlinische Galerie
Museum of Modern Art, Photography and Architecture
A foundation under public law
Alte Jakobstrasse 124–128
10969 Berlin

www.berlinischegalerie.de

EXHIBITION

Curators
Ralf Burmeister, Janina Nentwig

Assistant curators
Nuno de Brito Rocha, Juschka Marie von Rüden

Trainee
Alice Cazzola

Conservation team
Maria Bortfeldt, Sabina Fernandez, Corinna Nisse, Andreas Piel

Registrar
Annemarie Seyda

Archivist
Philip Gorki

Technical manager
Wolfgang Heigl, Roland Pohl

Exhibition architecture
david saik studio

Exhibition set-up
RT Ausstellungstechnik

Communication and Education
Ulrike Andres, Christine van Haaren, Marie-Claire Krahulec, Ulrike Schuhose

Strategic communication adviser
Uli Mayer-Johanssen

Media relations
SmithBerlin

Media partners

arte, Tagesspiegel, der Freitag, tip Berlin, INFOradio rbb, Wall, ZITTY

CATALOGUE

Responsible editors
Thomas Köhler, Ralf Burmeister, Janina Nentwig on behalf of the Berlinische Galerie, Landesmuseum für Moderne Kunst, Fotografie und Architektur

Idea
Ralf Burmeister, Janina Nentwig

Editorial team
Ralf Burmeister, Janina Nentwig, with Juschka Marie von Rüden

Picture editor
Nuno de Brito Rocha

English translation
Katherine Vanovitch

English copy editor
Donald Goodwin

Layout design
e o t . essays on typography
Lilla Hinrichs + Anna Sartorius

Editorial direction, Prestel
Markus Eisen

Production management
Corinna Pickart

Lithography
Reproline mediateam GmbH & Co. KG, Unterföhring

Printing & binding
PASSAVIA Druckservice GmbH & Co. KG, Passau

Typeface
ITC Usherwood, Akzidenz Grotesk Pro

Paper
Omnibulk 1.3 (IGEPA) 135 g/qm

MIX Paper from responsible sources FSC® C022274

Verlagsgruppe Random House FSC® N001967
Printed in Germany

A member of Verlagsgruppe Random House GmbH
Neumarkter Strasse 28
81673 München

Prestel Publishing Ltd.
14–17 Wells Street
London W1T 3PD

Prestel Publishing
900 Broadway, Suite 603
New York, NY 10003

A CIP catalogue record for this book is available from the British Library.

ISBN 978-3-7913-5781-2 (book trade edition)
ISBN 978-3-7913-6858-0 (museum edition)

www.prestel.de

Cover illustration
Hannah Höch, *Cube*, 1926, oil on canvas
Berlinische Galerie
© VG Bild-Kunst, Bonn 2018

BERLINISCHE GALERIE STAFF

Director
Dr Thomas Köhler

Director of administration
Birgitta Müller-Brandeck

Director's office
Wiebke Hess

Curatorial assistant to the director
Anne Bitterwolf

Assistant to the director of administration
Daniela Siegel

Collections:

Fine Arts
Dr Stefanie Heckmann (Head), Guido Fassbender, Annemarie Seyda, Christian Tagger

Photography
Ulrich Domröse (Head), Kerstin Diether, Tanja Keppler

Prints & Drawings
Dr Annelie Lütgens (Head), Kathrin Aurich, Katharina Hoffmann

Architecture
Ursula Müller (Head), Frank Schütz, Julia Schubert, Anja Elisabeth Witte

Artists' Archives
Dr Ralf Burmeister (Head), Philip Gorki, Christiane Necker, Dr Janina Nentwig, Dr Wolfgang Schöddert

Library
Jan-Tillmann Rierl (Head), Marion Molnos, Christina Strauch, Zoe Spehr (voluntary year)

Conservation
Andreas Piel (Head), Maria Bortfeldt, Sabina Fernandez, Corinna Nisse

Trainee curators
Anna Bauer, Nuno de Brito Rocha, Kati Renner, Juschka Marie von Rüden, Cornelia Siebert

Communication & Education
Ulrike Andres (Head), Christine van Haaren (Head of Education and Outreach), Katrin Kaptain, Marie-Claire Krahulec, Ulrike Schuhose, Andreas Krüger (trainee), Paula Rosenboom (trainee), Kira Welker (voluntary year)

Friends of the Museum
Stephanie Krumbholz, Carolin Wagner, Katharina Faller

Administration:

Organization & IT
Christiane Friedrich (Head), Martin von Piechowski, Jan Salzberger

Finance & controlling
Susanne Teuber (Head), Laila Ayyache, Kerstin Böhme, Dagmar Petzold

Human resources
Christian Monschke (Head), Cornelia Remky

Visitor services
Carola Semm (Manager), Gerald Friedrich (Deputy manager)
Museum shop: Friederike von Born-Fallois, Carsten Fedderke, Dr Eva-Maria Kaufmann, Reinhard Kuh, Merwe Reckenfelderbäumer, Dirk Schäfer
Visitor support: Helmut Andersen, Christiane Boese, Brigitte Heilmann, Nihal Isigan, Gerhard Jende, Daniela Lamprecht, Matthias Linde, Katarina Roters, Olaf Schümann, Nasrin Sheikh Zadeh, Reza Soltani

Technical unit
Roland Pohl (Head), Wolfgang Fleischer, Robert Frank, Ralf Geelhaar, Wolfgang Heigl, Andreas Kamprath, Frank Rohrbeck, Leander Wiesner (voluntary year)